Lecture Notes in Computer Science 15694

Advanced Research in Computing and Software Science
Subline of Lecture Notes in Computer Science

More information about this series at https://link.springer.com/bookseries/558

Viktor Vafeiadis

Editor

Programming Languages and Systems

34th European Symposium on Programming, ESOP 2025
Held as Part of the International Joint Conferences on
Theory and Practice of Software, ETAPS 2025
Hamilton, ON, Canada, May 3–8, 2025, Proceedings, Part I

 Springer

Editor
Viktor Vafeiadis
MPI-SWS
Kaiserslautern, Germany

ISSN 0302-9743   ISSN 1611-3349 (electronic)
Lecture Notes in Computer Science
ISBN 978-3-031-91117-0   ISBN 978-3-031-91118-7 (eBook)
https://doi.org/10.1007/978-3-031-91118-7

This Springer imprint is published by the registered company Springer Nature Switzerland AG
The registered company address is: Gewerbestrasse 11, 6330 Cham, Switzerland

ETAPS Foreword

Welcome to the 28th ETAPS! ETAPS 2025 took place in Hamilton, Canada. It is the first time ETAPS was held outside of Europe.

ETAPS 2025 was the 28th instance of the International Joint Conferences on Theory and Practice of Software. ETAPS is an annual federated conference established in 1998, and consists of four conferences: ESOP, FASE, FoSSaCS, and TACAS. Each conference has its own Program Committee (PC) and its own Steering Committee (SC). The conferences cover various aspects of software systems, ranging from theoretical computer science to foundations of programming languages, analysis tools, and formal approaches to software engineering. Organizing these conferences in a coherent, highly synchronized conference programme enables researchers to participate in an exciting event, having the possibility to meet many colleagues working in different directions in the field, and to easily attend talks of different conferences. On the weekend before the main conference, numerous satellite workshops took place that attracted many researchers from all over the globe.

ETAPS 2025 received 329 submissions in total, 106 of which were accepted, yielding an overall acceptance rate of 32.2%. I thank all the authors for their interest in ETAPS, all the reviewers for their reviewing efforts, the PC members for their contributions, and in particular the PC (co-)chairs for their hard work in running this entire intensive process. Last but not least, my congratulations to all authors of the accepted papers!

ETAPS 2025 featured the unifying invited speakers Ina Schaefer (Karlsruhe Institute of Technology, Germany) and Matthew B. Dwyer (University of Virginia, USA), and the invited speakers Amal Ahmed (Northeastern University, USA) for ESOP and José Meseguer (University of Illinois Urbana-Champaign, USA) for FASE. Invited tutorials were provided by Suguman Bansal (Georgia Institute of Techology, USA) on reinforcement learning from logical specifications and Arun Ross (Michigan State University, USA) on biometrics.

ETAPS 2025 was organized by McMaster University. The Faculty of Engineering at McMaster University has a reputation for innovative programs, cutting-edge research, leading faculty, and aspiring students. It has earned a strong reputation as a center for academic excellence and innovation. The Faculty has approximately 180 faculty members, along with close to 4,500 undergraduate and 1,000 graduate students. The local organization team consisted of Claudio Menghi and Mark Lawford (general chairs), Melissa Alzaeim (event organizer), Alan Wassyng and Angelo Gargantini (workshop chairs), Sébastien Mosser and Matt Luckcuck (publicity chairs), Patrizio Pelliccione (sponsor chair), Silvia Bonfanti and Andrea Bombarda (web chairs), Jacques Carette and Christos Tsigkanos (local proceedings chair), Lena Liberale and Martin von Mohrenschildt (finance chairs), Damiano Torre and Lina Marsso (registration chairs), and Vera Pantelic and Denise Geiskkovitch (student volunteer chairs).

ETAPS 2025 is further supported by the following associations and societies: ETAPS e.V., EATCS (European Association for Theoretical Computer Science), EAPLS (European Association for Programming Languages and Systems), and EASST (European Association of Software Science and Technology).

The ETAPS Steering Committee consists of an Executive Board, and representatives of the individual ETAPS conferences, as well as representatives of EATCS, EAPLS, and EASST. The Executive Board consists of Marieke Huisman (Twente, chair), Andrzej Wąsowski (Copenhagen), Thomas Noll (Aachen), Jan Kofroň (Prague), Barbara König (Duisburg-Essen), Arnd Hartmanns (Twente), Caterina Urban (INRIA), Jan Křetínský (Munich), Elizabeth Polgreen (Edinburgh), and Lenore Zuck (Chicago).

Other members of the steering committee are: Elvira Albert (Madrid), Maurice ter Beek (Pisa), Nathalie Bertrand (Rennes), Dirk Beyer (Munich), Artur Boronat (Leicester), Luís Caires (Lisboa), Ferruccio Damiani (Torino), Gordon Fraser (Passau), Arie Gurfinkel (Waterloo), Reiner Hähnle (Darmstadt), Reiko Heckel (Leicester), Marijn Heule (Pittsburgh), Sebastian Junges (Nijmegen), Joost-Pieter Katoen (Aachen and Twente), Guy Katz (Jerusalem), Delia Kesner (Paris), Fabrice Kordon (Paris), Robbert Krebbers (Nijmegen), Kim Guldstrand Larsen (Aalborg), Mark Lawford (Hamilton), Claudio Menghi (Hamilton and Bergamo), Stefan Milius (Erlangen-Nürnberg), Andrzej Murawski (Oxford), Corina Păsăreanu (Ames), Laure Petrucci (Paris), Peter Y.A. Ryan (Luxembourg), Don Sannella (Edinburgh), Viktor Vafeiadis (Kaiserslautern), and Anton Wijs (Eindhoven).

I would like to take this opportunity to thank all authors, keynote speakers, attendees, organizers of the satellite workshops, and Springer Nature for their support. ETAPS 2025 was also generously supported by Tourism Hamilton and the Tutte Institute for Mathematics and Computing. I hope you all enjoyed ETAPS 2025.

Finally, a big thanks to Claudio, Mark and Melissa and their local organization team for all their enormous efforts to make ETAPS a fantastic event.

May 2025

Marieke Huisman
ETAPS SC Chair
ETAPS e.V. President

Preface

The LNCS volumes 15694 and 15695 contain papers that were presented at the 34th European Symposium on Programming (ESOP 2024), held during May 3–8 in Hamilton, Canada. ESOP is part of the International Joint Conferences on Theory and Practice of Software (ETAPS) and promotes the specification, design, analysis and implementation of programming languages and systems.

In total, these two volumes contain 30 papers and two short artifact reports associated with the corresponding research papers. Following ESOP 2024, ESOP 2025 had three submission categories: research papers, "fresh perspective" papers and experience report. For the first time in its history, ESOP 2025 also instituted two submission and evaluation rounds. The first round had a submission deadline on 30th May 2024, while the second had the usual submission deadline in October. Round 1 submissions could receive one of three outcomes: Accept, Reject, Revise. In the latter case, the PC provided a concrete list of revision requests to be completed by the Round 2 submission deadline. Such revised submissions were then reviewed by the same set of reviewers and were either accepted or rejected. Rejected Round 1 submissions were prevented from being resubmitted to Round 2. Papers submitted directly to Round 2 were either accepted or rejected.

The first round attracted 26 submissions, of which 8 (31%) were accepted, and 13 were rejected completely and another 5 were rejected but allowed to resubmit a revised version to the second submission deadline. The second deadline attracted 67 submissions, 5 of which were revisions of rejected round-1 submissions. Of these submissions, 22 papers (33%) were accepted: 4 of the 5 round-1 resubmissions, and 18 of the 62 fresh submissions. In total, this amounts to 30 accepted papers out of 88 unique submissions, yielding an acceptance rate of 34%. Or, if accounted differently, 30 accepted papers out of 93 total submissions, yielding an acceptance rate of 32%. By submission category, 27 of the 76 research papers were accepted (36%), 2 of the 9 fresh perspective papers were accepted (22%), 1 of the 3 experience reports was accepted (33%).

Papers were reviewed in a double-blind fashion, with author identities only revealed to reviewers on paper acceptance. Each submission typically received three reviews by the members of the ESOP program committee, occasionally supported by external reviewers. In both submission rounds, authors were given a chance to respond to their reviews, before the program was selected through an online, asynchronous PC meeting, facilitated by the HotCRP system.

ESOP 2025 also employed an artifact evaluation process. Fourteen of the accepted papers elected to make their artifacts available on archival websites. The committee awarded the badge "Functional" to seven of these and the badges "Functional and reusable" to the remaining seven. Two accepted papers in this volume are accompanied by artifact reports.

My sincere thanks go to all who worked together to produce this event and its proceedings. Foremost, to the authors, who provided the technical content of the meeting. Also to the program committee, artifact evaluation committee, and external reviewers, who provided their well-reasoned and detailed judgments, sometimes on short notice. Michalis Kokologiannakis, as the representative for ESOP among the artifact evaluation committee co-chairs, deserves particular thanks. I also would like to thank the ETAPS steering committee and its chair Marieke Huisman, the Proceedings coordinator Barbara König, the local proceedings chairs Jacques Carette and Christos Tsigkanos, and the webmaster Jan Kofroň for their assistance in the organization of ESOP as a part of the entire ETAPS meeting. Finally, thanks are due to the members of the ESOP steering committee and, in particular, its chair, Luís Caires, who were a constant source of support, encouragement, information and guidance.

May 2025   Viktor Vafeiadis

Organization

ESOP Steering Committee

Luís Caires	Instituto Superior Técnico, Universidade de Lisboa, Portugal
Robbert Krebbers	Radboud University Nijmegen, Netherlands
Brigitte Pientka	McGill University, Canada
Thomas Wies	New York University, USA
Nobuko Yoshida	Imperial College London, UK
Viktor Vafeiadis	MPI-SWS, Germany
Stephanie Weirich	University of Pennsylvania, USA

ESOP 2025 Program Chair

Viktor Vafeiadis	MPI-SWS, Germany

ESOP Program Committee

Kazuyuki Asada	Tohoku University, Japan
Dariusz Biernacki	University of Wrocław, Poland
Laura Bocchi	University of Kent, UK
James Cheney	University of Edinburgh, UK
Brijesh Dongol	University of Surrey, UK
Jana Dunfield	Queen's University at Kingston, Canada
Javier Esparza	Technical University of Munich, Germany
Simon Fowler	University of Glasgow, UK
Jacques-Henri Jourdan	CNRS, France
Burcu Kulahcioglu Ozkan	Delft University of Technology, Netherlands
Hongjin Liang	Nanjing University, China
Umang Mathur	National University of Singapore, Singapore
Peter Müller	ETH Zürich, Switzerland
David Pichardie	Meta, France
Jean Pichon	Aarhus University, Denmark
Noam Rinetzky	Tel Aviv University, Israel
Amr Sabry	Indiana University, USA
Michael Sammler	ETH Zürich, Switzerland

Sam Staton	University of Oxford, UK
Milijana Surbatovich	University of Maryland, College Park, USA
Niki Vazou	IMDEA Software Institute, Spain
Tobias Wrigstad	Uppsala University, Sweden

ESOP/FASE/FoSSaCS Joint Artifact Evaluation Committee

AEC Co-chairs

Michalis Kokologiannakis	ETH Zürich, Switzerland
Laura Bussi	University of Luxembourg, Luxembourg
Stefan Winter	LMU Munich, Germany
Ondřej Lengál	Brno University of Technology, Czech Republic

AEC Members

Alexandre Moine	NYU, USA
András Kovács	University of Gothenburg, Sweden
Andrea Colledan	University of Bologna, Italy
Bernardo Almeida	LASIGE, University of Lisbon, Portugal
David Chocholatý	Brno University of Technology, Czech Republic
Gennaro Zanfardino	University of L'Aquila, Italy
Giordano d'Aloisio	University of L'Aquila, Italy
Gustavo Carvalho	Universidade Federal de Pernambuco, Brazil
Hongjian Jiang	RPTU, Germany
Julia Sapiña	Universitat Politècnica de València, Spain
Loïc Pujet	Stockholm University, Sweden
Loïc Germerie Guizouarn	Université de Rennes, CNRS, Inria, IRISA, France
Lucas Sakizloglou	Brandenburg University of Technology, Germany
Manolis Pitsikalis	NCSR Demokritos, Greece
Michal Hečko	Brno University of Technology, Czeck Republic
Noa Izsak	Ben-Gurion University of the Negev, Israel
Pablo Gómez-Abajo	Universidad Autónoma de Madrid, Spain
Raúl Gutiérrez	Universitat Politècnica de València, Spain
Raúl López-Rueda	Universitat Politècnica de València, Spain
Sougata Bose	University of Liverpool, UK
Soumodev Mal	Chennai Mathematical Institute, India
Srinidhi Nagendra	IRIF, CNRS, Université Paris Cité, France, and Chennai Mathematical Institute, India

Szumi Xie	Eötvös Loránd University, Hungary
Thomas Holger	Forschungsinstitut CODE, Germany
Vincent Cheval	University of Oxford, UK
Wei-Lun Tsai	Academia Sinica, Taiwan
Zainab Fatmi	University of Oxford, UK
Zsófia Ádám	Budapest University of Technology and Economics, Hungary

Contents – Part I

Contents – Part II

The Vanilla Sequent Calculus is Call-by-Value

Beniamino Accattoli[(✉)] [iD]

Inria & LIX, Ecole Polytechnique, UMR 7161, Palaiseau, France
beniamino.accattoli@inria.fr

Abstract. Existing Curry-Howard interpretations of call-by-value evaluation for the λ-calculus are either based on ad-hoc modifications of intuitionistic proof systems or involve additional logical concepts such as classical logic or linear logic, despite the fact that call-by-value was introduced in an intuitionistic setting without linear features.

This paper shows that the most basic sequent calculus for minimal intuitionistic logic—dubbed here *vanilla*—can naturally be seen as a logical interpretation of call-by-value evaluation. This is obtained by establishing mutual simulations with a well-known formalism for call-by-value evaluation.

Keywords: λ-calculus, proof theory, Curry-Howard.

1 Introduction

The connection between functional languages and proof theory stems from Howard's insight that the system of simple types for the λ-calculus is exactly Gentzen's natural deduction for minimal intuitionistic logic [41]. Additionally, *β-reduction* exactly matches the logical process of *detour elimination*, also called *normalization*. This correspondence concerns the unrestricted, or *call-by-name*, notion of β-reduction.

In practice, the evaluation mechanism at work in functional languages never follows that of call-by-name of the ordinary λ-calculus. Plotkin's call-by-value λ-calculus [52] restricts β-reduction to fire when the argument is a *value*, that is, a variable or an abstraction, and it is often seen as a better fit for applications.

Call-by-Value and Natural Deduction. Natural deduction, unfortunately, does not provide a solid logical foundation for call-by-value (shortened to CbV). On the positive side, values are proofs ending in a logical introduction rule. The restriction to values in the proof normalization process, however, has to be *enforced*; it does not arise naturally from the structure of natural deduction. Moreover, when one considers open terms and/or strong evaluation (that is, under abstraction), the normal forms of Plotkin's CbV calculus have a complex inductive structure not corresponding to any natural concept in natural deduction. The study of strong evaluation is essential for proof assistants based on dependent types. Notably, Leroy and Grégoire use strong CbV for Coq [37]. Strong evaluation is also advocated by Scherer and Rémy [57] as relevant for a solid theory of functional languages. Lastly, in proof theory one speaks of *cut/detour elimination*, and they can be eliminated only if evaluation goes under abstractions.

© The Author(s) 2025
V. Vafeiadis (Ed.): ESOP 2025, LNCS 15694, pp. 1–22, 2025.
https://doi.org/10.1007/978-3-031-91118-7_1

$$\frac{\Gamma \vdash A \qquad \Gamma, A \vdash B}{\Gamma \vdash B} \; \text{cut} \qquad\qquad \frac{}{\Gamma, A \vdash A} \; \text{ax}$$

$$\frac{\Gamma \vdash A \qquad \Gamma, B \vdash C}{\Gamma, A \Rightarrow B \vdash C} \Rightarrow_l \qquad\qquad \frac{\Gamma, A \vdash B}{\Gamma \vdash A \Rightarrow B} \Rightarrow_r$$

Fig. 1. Vanilla sequent calculus for minimal intuitionistic logic (MIL).

The issue with normal forms is delicate. It is well-known that the rewriting rules of Plotkin's calculus are not suited for open terms and strong evaluation, causing *premature normal forms*, as pointed out by Paolini and Ronchi della Rocca [51,50,55]. The literature contains many alternative CbV λ-calculi fixing this defect, as surveyed by Accattoli and Guerrieri [6], often extending the syntax of the λ-calculus with let-expressions or explicit substitutions, as for instance is the case in Moggi's calculus [46,47].

Logically, both let-expressions and explicit substitutions are decorations for the (intuitionistic) cut rule. Even when one considers these alternative CbV λ-calculi not suffering of premature normal forms, natural deduction with cut is not really a solid logical foundation, because CbV *normal* terms correspond to proofs *with cuts*. That is, *not all cuts are eliminable*.

Call-by-Value and Proof Theory. Beyond natural deduction for minimal intuitionistic logic (shortened to MIL), there are two main ways of looking at CbV via proof theory. One of them is as a certain intuitionistic fragment of linear logic, as first done by Girard [35], which can also be seen as a certain embedding into the modal logic S4, as pointed out recently by Espírito Santo et al. [30]. Another way is via the duality between CbV and call-by-name (CbN) in classical logic, usually traced back to Filinski [31]. This duality was then analyzed through linear logic lenses by Danos et al. [21], and crystalized as the computational interpretation of a sequent calculus by Curien and Herbelin [18].

What is not ideal, however, is that these are *additional logical concepts*. In Plotkin's CbV (and in many of the alternative CbV λ-calculi), indeed, there is no trace of linearity nor of classical principles. It is natural to wonder whether there is a neat logical way of modeling CbV using *only* MIL. There are works connecting CbV and MIL, such as Dyckhoff and Lengrand's study of Herbelin's LJQ [40,25,26] or Ohori [49], but they are based on modifications of the deductive system *imposing* the CbV reading. This paper presents a fresh perspective on this question.

The Vanilla Sequent Calculus. Our result is that the most basic presentation of Gentzen's sequent calculus [34] for MIL, here dubbed *vanilla sequent calculus* and shown in Fig. 1 (the proper additive presentation of MIL requires some further details about contractions, see Sect. 3), is a natural Curry-Howard reading of CbV evaluation. The system comes with a natural notion of *values*, which are proofs ending with right deduction rules. Crucially, we exploit a *splitting property* that is specific to sequent proofs of MIL: every proof of $\Gamma \vdash A$ can be uniquely split into a value sub-proof of $\Delta \vdash A$ followed by a sequence of *left* rules turning Δ into Γ without touching A. Thanks to this feature, there is no need to modify the sequent calculus with a so-called *stoup* (i.e. a distinguished formula in a formula context) as in Curien and Herbelin [18], adding restrictions on the shape of proofs as in Herbelin's presentation of LJQ [40] or Ohori [49], or having a separate judgement for values as in Lengrand and Dyckhoff's presentation of LJQ [25,26]. Essentially, values are recovered on-the-fly, with no need to mark them out explicitly.

Beyond the splitting property, our fresh perspective stems from the observation that the ineliminable cuts in the CbV reading of natural deduction correspond exactly to occurrences of the left rule $(\Rightarrow_l)$ for $\Rightarrow$ in the vanilla sequent calculus. In other words, the cut rule in CbV natural deduction is *overloaded*. When one looks at it through the vanilla sequent calculus, it represents *both* the vanilla (cut) and $(\Rightarrow_l)$ rules. Disentangling the two concepts, the vanilla sequent calculus provides a neater logical foundation where *CbV normal terms have no cuts*, as one would expect.

Concretely, we adopt proof terms for the vanilla sequent calculus defined without the application ts construct (which is specific to natural deduction) and with *distinct* explicit substitutions constructs for rules (cut) and $(\Rightarrow_l)$, what we dub here *vanilla λ-terms*.

Cut Elimination at a Distance: the Vanilla λ-Calculus. Once it is clarified that cut-free vanilla proofs are a good formalism for CbV normal forms, one needs to pair them with a natural notion of cut elimination. Quoting Zucker [61]: "we know at the outset what a cut-free derivation is, and the problem is to define the conversions".

For that, we give a very compact definition of cut elimination following the *at a distance* style of rewriting rules promoted by Accattoli and Kesner for natural deduction calculi [10,4,42], and recently shown to be a good fit for the intuitionistic linear logic sequent calculus (without stoup) by Accattoli [1]. To avoid misunderstandings, note that, while rewriting at a distance is also an additional concept, it is fundamentally different from linear or classical logic. Linear and classical logic are *logical* concepts; they change the logic. Rewriting at a distance is a *rewriting* concept, not a logical one; the logic stays the same, what changes is only how proofs/terms are rewritten.

The key point of rewriting at a distance is that it avoids the many rewriting rules propagating explicit substitutions through the term structure, which are found in many extended λ-calculi, via generalizations of the rewriting rules exploiting contexts (that is, terms with a hole). This is particularly useful in the study of sequent calculi, where commuting cut elimination cases are a notorious burden. Essentially, rewriting at a distance allows one to have only *principal* cut elimination cases, avoiding completely the commutative ones. This is similar to what happens with proof nets, except that it is simpler, because the graphical language is avoided altogether by means of—again—contexts.

Rules at a distance rest on *on-the-fly* decompositions of a term into a context and a sub-term. In our setting, this decomposition becomes the splitting property mentioned above. Distance thus allows for a smooth treatment of values at the rewriting level.

Our proof terms plus cut elimination at a distance form what we dub as the *vanilla λ-calculus*.

Results. The central result of the paper is that two standard translations, from natural deduction to sequent calculus, and back, induce termination-preserving simulations between the vanilla λ-calculus and one of the formalisms extending Plotkin's CbV. To make things as smooth as possible, our choice of formalism for CbV is Accattoli and Paolini's *value substitution calculus* [13], a natural deduction λ-calculus with explicit substitutions at a distance, used in various recent studies about CbV [6,5,8,9,12].

For the sake of keeping this *fresh perspective* light and readable, we focus on explaining the inception of the calculus, rewriting rules at a distance, and the simulation results. As a check of good design for the vanilla λ-calculus, we also prove strong normalization for typed terms. This result is more challenging than the simulations, but it is expected and proved via an established technique, namely, the bi-orthogonal reducibility method. Therefore, we only give the statements and refer to the technical report [3] for the details of the proof, which is adapted from Accattoli [1].

How Our Approach Fits in the Literature. Certainly, ours is not the first computational interpretation of a sequent calculus for MIL, whether *vanilla* or not. Essentially, there are three kinds of interpretations in the literature. For the first two, we adopt Mint's local / global terminology [44]:

1. *The local approach*. It decorates sequent proofs using a language of terms *without application* and with let-expressions (or explicit substitutions) for both the cut rule and the left rule for $\Rightarrow$, as we do. In particular, this approach does *not* use ordinary λ-terms to decorate proofs. These alternative terms are then endowed with (usually many) rewriting rules mimicking the *propagation* of cuts (that is, they are not at a distance). This approach is followed e.g. by Gallier [33], Ohori [49], Dyckhoff and Lengrand [25,26], and Cerrito and Kesner [16]. Gallier and Cerrito and Kesner do not notice the connection with CbV, while Ohori and Dyckhoff and Lengrand do embrace it, but use non-standard sequent calculi and complex sets of rewriting rules. Gallier (1993) revisits standard proof theoretical concepts under the influence of linear logic. Cerrito and Kesner (2004) develop a Curry-Howard for pattern matching. Ohori's (1999) aim is to show a connection between proof theory and Sabry and Felleisen's *A-normal forms* [56,32]. This paper can be seen as a re-elaboration of Ohori's work, where the focus is a minimalistic logical foundation rather than A-normal forms. Our aim is also similar to Dyckhoff and Lengrand [26] (2007) but the outcome is considerably simpler: they have three notions of cut and 14 rewriting rules, while we have only one cut and one rewriting rule.

2. *The global approach*. It amounts to decorate sequent proofs with ordinary λ-terms and endowing them with call-by-name rewriting. It is rooted in Prawitz's *many-to-one* translation of sequent calculus to natural deduction [54], it possibly first appears with proof terms in Pottinger [53], and it is nicely presented by Barendregt and Ghilezan using the vanilla sequent calculus [15]. The idea is to decorate rules (cut) and $(\Rightarrow_l)$ using meta-level substitution, as follows:

$$\frac{\Gamma \vdash s : A \qquad \Gamma, x : A \vdash t : B}{\Gamma \vdash \{s \to x\}t : B} \; \text{cut} \qquad \Bigg| \qquad \frac{\Gamma \vdash s : A \qquad \Gamma, x : B \vdash t : C}{\Gamma, y : A \Rightarrow B \vdash \{ys \to x\}t : C} \Rightarrow_l$$

The serious drawback of the global approach is the potential *size mismatch* between a sequent calculus proof π and the λ-term u_π decorating π, stemming from the fact that in the sequent calculus the formula B in $(\Rightarrow_l)$ can be treated non-linearly, that is, it can be weakened or contracted, leading to duplications/erasures of ys. The non-linear use of B is referred to as *the root of all evil* by Danos et al. [21], in their study of representations of System F in linear sequent calculi.

3. *The stoup approach.* A third approach departs from the vanilla sequent calculus, adopting a form of enriched sequent or adding further judgements to the deductive system. Typically, at the logical level it uses *two* judgements $\Gamma; \vdash A$ and $\Gamma; B \vdash A$, where the space between the semicolon and $\vdash$ is called *stoup*—terminology due to Girard [36]—and it is either empty or contains a single, distinguished formula. The non-decorated version of rule $(\Rightarrow_l)$ then becomes:

$$\frac{\Gamma; \vdash A \qquad \Gamma; B \vdash C}{\Gamma; A \Rightarrow B \vdash C} \Rightarrow_l$$

The key point is that the rules of the system (which can be defined in various ways) treat the stoup *linearly*, that is, the stoup formula is never weakened nor contracted. This fact is what circumvents the size mismatch of the global approach, and thus allows for a good match between sequent proofs with stoup and ordinary λ-terms. It is usually associated with CbN evaluation.

The stoup approach is first studied by Danos et al. [21], building on Girard [36]. It then became the basis for Herbelin [39], who studies the intuitionistic CbN case, and then Curien and Herbelin [18], who study the classical case in both CbN and CbV, with three judgements and stoup on both sides of the sequent. From [18], it is easy to extract a CbV intuitionistic fragment (as done for instance by Accattoli and Guerrieri [6]), but one obtains a sequent calculus with stoup, not the *vanilla* one. A different presentation of essentially the same system is the mentioned approach to LJQ by Dyckhoff and Lengrand [25,26], who use two distinct judgements—with one dedicated to values and connected to focalization—rather than the stoup.

Nowadays, a number of works have built over Curien and Herbelin's work, for instance [28,60,29,22,14,48,17,24,23,45], to the point that it became the standard computational interpretation of sequent calculi.

Our work is orthogonal, and somewhat more basic, as it looks at the intuitionistic case without any form of stoup, focalization, or separate judgement.

Non-Canonicity vs *Sharing.* In the proof theoretical literature, the vanilla sequent calculus is often criticized as *non-canonical* because (CbN) normal λ-terms correspond to more than one cut-free proof, when one embraces the global approach—this is another face of Danos et al.'s *root of all evil* mentioned above.

A key point of our fresh perspective is that this is a *feature* rather than a drawback: it is simply the fact that CbV normal terms such as let $x = yz$ in $(wxxx)$ can be seen as *shared* representations of CbN normal forms such as $w(yz)(yz)(yz)$, and that a term can be shared in various ways—another one is let $x = yz$ in $(wxx(yz))$. Therefore, the vanilla sequent calculus gives a first-class status to sub-term sharing for normal forms.

More precisely, let-expressions annotate cuts and give a first-class status to sub-term sharing independently of the proof system. The concept of *value* induces a dynamic / static refinement of sub-term sharing. Dynamically, only values are *unshared* (that is, duplicated or erased). Non-values are never unshared, thus end up being *statically shared* in normal forms, as in let $x = yz$ in $(wxxx)$, making sub-term sharing visible *denotationally*. These two roles are entangled in natural deduction for MIL while they are handled separately in sequent calculus via its two *left rules*, namely cut captures

(Natural) λ-Calculus

Terms	$\Lambda_N \ni t, s ::= x \in \mathcal{V}_N \mid \lambda x.t \mid ts$		Root β	$(\lambda x.t)s \mapsto_\beta \{s{\to}x\}t$
Contexts	$C, C' ::= \langle \cdot \rangle \mid \lambda x.C \mid Cs \mid tC$		Ctx closure	$\dfrac{t \mapsto_\beta t'}{C\langle t \rangle \to_\beta C\langle t' \rangle}$

Decorated (Additive) Natural Deduction

Formulas $A, B, C ::= X \mid A \Rightarrow B$

$$\dfrac{}{\Gamma, x : A \vdash_N x : A}\ \text{ax}$$

$$\dfrac{x : A, \Gamma \vdash_N t : B}{\Gamma \vdash_N \lambda x.t : A \Rightarrow B}\ \Rightarrow_r$$

$$\dfrac{\Gamma \vdash_N t : A \Rightarrow B \qquad \Gamma \vdash_N s : A}{\Gamma \vdash_N ts : B}\ @$$

Detours

$$\dfrac{\dfrac{x : A, \Gamma \vdash_N t : B}{\Gamma \vdash_N \lambda x.t : A \Rightarrow B}\ \Rightarrow_r \qquad \Gamma \vdash_N s : A}{\Gamma \vdash_N (\lambda x.t)s : B}\ @$$

Fig. 2. λ-calculus and natural deduction $\vdash_N$.

dynamic sharing and subtraction captures static sharing. Therefore, the left rules of the sequent calculus for MIL encapsulate the sharing features of values.

For an extensive informal discussion about the deep relationship between sharing and CbV see Accattoli's dissemination paper [2].

Proofs Omitted proofs are in the associated technical report on arXiv [3].

2   Natural Deduction, Call-by-Name, and Rewriting at a Distance

In this section, we give our presentation of Howard's standard correspondence between natural deduction for minimal intuitionistic logic and the simply typed (call-by-name) λ-calculus [41], here also referred to as the *natural λ-calculus*, to distinguish it from the one that shall be associated to the sequent calculus. The correspondence is in Fig. 2. Curiously, in [41] Howard mentions that his work stems from Tait's "discovery of the close correspondence between cut elimination and reduction of λ-terms" [59].

Routine Definitions: Terms and Contexts. We assume given a countable set of variables $\mathcal{V}_N$, where $\mathbb{N}$ stresses that they are for the natural λ-calculus. The meta-level capture-avoiding substitution of s for x in t is denoted with $\{s{\to}x\}t$.

Contexts are terms with exactly one occurrence of the *hole* $\langle \cdot \rangle$, an additional constant, standing for a removed sub-term. We shall use various notions of contexts. For the λ-calculus, the most general ones are *(general) contexts* C, which simply allow the hole to be anywhere. The main operation about contexts is *plugging* $C\langle t \rangle$ where the hole $\langle \cdot \rangle$ in context C is replaced by t. Plugging, as usual with contexts, can capture variables—for instance $(\lambda x.\langle \cdot \rangle t)\langle x \rangle = \lambda x.xt$.

Routine Definitions: Types and Derivations. Types are built out of an unspecified atomic type X and the implication $\cdot \Rightarrow \cdot$ connective. Type contexts Γ are implicitly considered

$$\text{TERMS} \quad \Lambda_N^{\text{ES}} \ni t, s ::= x \mid \lambda x.t \mid ts \mid [s{\to}x]t$$

$$\text{CONTEXTS} \quad C, C' ::= \langle\cdot\rangle \mid \lambda x.C \mid Cs \mid tC \mid [C{\to}x]t \mid [s{\to}x]C$$

$$\text{SUBSTITUTIONS CTXS} \quad L, L' ::= \langle\cdot\rangle \mid [s{\to}x]L$$

ROOT RULES	CONTEXTUAL CLOSURE
β AT A DISTANCE $L\langle\lambda x.t\rangle s \mapsto_{\text{dB}} L\langle[s{\to}x]t\rangle$	$\dfrac{t \mapsto_a t'}{C\langle t\rangle \to_a C\langle t'\rangle} \quad a\in\{\text{dB}, \text{s}\}$
SUBSTITUTION $[s{\to}x]t \mapsto_{\text{s}} \{s{\to}x\}t$	SUBST. CALCULUS REWRITING
	$\to_{\text{SC}} ::= \to_{\text{dB}} \cup \to_{\text{s}}$

CUT RULE DECORATED WITH AN EXPLICIT SUBSTITUTION

$$\dfrac{\Gamma \vdash_N s : A \qquad \Gamma, x : A \vdash_N t : B}{\Gamma \vdash_N [s{\to}x]t : B} \ \text{cut}$$

Fig. 3. Substitution Calculus (SC).

modulo exchange, that is, Γ is a partial function from variables to formulas such that $\text{dom}(\Gamma) := \{x \mid \Gamma(x) \text{ is defined}\}$ is finite, usually written as $x_1 : A_1, \ldots, x_n : A_n$ (with $n \in \mathbb{N}$) if $\text{dom}(\Gamma) = \{x_1, \ldots, x_n\}$ and $\Gamma(x_i) = A_i$ for $1 \le i \le n$. As it is standard, writing $\Gamma, x : A$ implicitly assumes that $x \notin \text{dom}(\Gamma)$.

We write $\pi \triangleright \Gamma \vdash_N t : A$ if π is a *(type) derivation*, that is, a tree constructed using the rules for $\vdash_N$, having axioms as leaves, and of final judgment $\Gamma \vdash_N t : A$.

Left and Right Rules. The typing rule $(\Rightarrow_r)$ for abstraction carries a right r subscript, to later distinguish it from the left rule for implication of the sequent calculus. We shall constantly refer to left and right rules, and yet we shall dodge abstract definitions of these notions. Rules ax, $\Rightarrow_r$, and @ are right rules.

Detours. The logical analogues of β-redexes are *detours*, which are simply given by a $\Rightarrow_r$ rule followed by a @ rule, that is exactly what is required to type a β-redex—see Fig. 2. λ-terms in normal form are exactly those typed by proofs of $\vdash_N$ without detours.

Explicit Substitutions. In Fig. 3, the λ-calculus is extended with an explicit substitution (shortened to ES) constructor $[s{\to}x]t$, which binds x in t. It can be thought as a more compact notation for let $x = s$ in t, with the slight difference that the evaluation order is not fixed in $[s{\to}x]t$. At the logical level, ESs are decorations for cuts, as shown in Fig. 3. Note that in the literature about λ-calculi at a distance, ESs are usually rather written using the mirrored construct $t[x{\leftarrow}s]$. We here prefer to use $[s{\to}x]t$ because it more faithfully reflects the structure of type derivations.

A point of view underlying our study is that ESs are a form of *sub-term sharing*, meaning that $[t{\to}x](xx)$ is a version of tt where t is shared.

In this paper, cut shall be considered as a left rule (for its right premise), according to the view outlined at the end of the introduction that left rules account for sharing.

LANGUAGE	ROOT RULE
TERMS $\Lambda_N \ni t, s, u ::= v \mid ts$ VALUES $\quad v, v' ::= x \mid \lambda x.t$	$(\lambda x.t)v \mapsto_{\beta_v} t\{x \leftarrow v\}$

WEAK EVALUATION	STRONG EVALUATION
WEAK CTXS $E ::= \langle \cdot \rangle \mid Et \mid tE$	STRONG CTXS $C ::= \langle \cdot \rangle \mid Ct \mid tC \mid \lambda x.C$
$\dfrac{t \mapsto_{\beta_v} t'}{E\langle t \rangle \to_{w\beta_v} E\langle t' \rangle}$	$\dfrac{t \mapsto_{\beta_v} t'}{C\langle t \rangle \to_{\beta_v} C\langle t' \rangle}$

Fig. 4. Plotkin's (natural) CbV λ-calculus.

Rewriting Rules. We endow natural λ-terms with ESs with *small-step* rewriting rules, that is, rules based on meta-level substitution, obtaining Accattoli and Kesner's *substitution calculus* (SC) [11], of rewriting relation $\to_{SC}$. It is composed of two rewriting rules, namely the standard substitution rule $\to_s$, and the perhaps less standard β *at a distance* rule $\to_{dB}$. Rule $\to_{dB}$ generalizes β-redexes as to fire even when there are some ESs (i.e. left rules) in between the abstraction and the argument, fact that is formalized in the definition of the rule via the (possibly empty) substitution context L (mnemonic: L stands for *List* of substitutions). For instance,

$$([u \to z][s \to y](\lambda x.t))rp \quad \to_{dB} \quad ([u \to z][s \to y][r \to x]t)p. \tag{1}$$

This kind of rule circumvents the need of having commuting rewriting rules such as $[s \to y](\lambda x.t) \to \lambda x.[s \to y]t$ or $([s \to y]t)u \to [s \to y](tu)$ in order to expose the β-redex in (1). The rewriting theory of ESs at a distance has simpler proofs and stronger properties (e.g. residuals) than for commuting-based ESs, see Accattoli and Kesner [10,11,4].

Note that ESs can always be reduced, thus there are no ESs in $\to_{SC}$-normal forms. In other words, normal forms are sharing-free.

Clearly, the substitution calculus simulates β, since $(\lambda x.t)s \to_{dB} [s \to x]t \to_s \{s \to x\}t$.

3   The Natural λ-Calculus By Value

In this section, we discuss the presentation of CbV in a natural deduction calculus, first in Plotkin's style and then with cuts / ESs. In particular, we shall see the advantages and the limits of ESs for CbV.

Plotkin's Call-by-Value and Open Terms. The definition of CbV *à la Plotkin* following the modern presentation by Dal Lago and Martini [20] is in Fig. 4. Values v are defined as variables and abstraction, and the β_v-rule is obtained by restricting β-redexes to fire only when the argument is a value. Strong evaluation allows one to reduce β_v-redexes everywhere in a term, and weak evaluation instead forbids β_v-redexes under abstraction.

It is well-known that Plotkin's approach works smoothly only in the important and yet limited case of weak evaluation of closed terms. Open terms are an issue, and even more so is strong evaluation, because they cause *stuck β-redexes* such as $(\lambda x.t)(yz)$

TERMS Λ_N^{ES} (as for the SC)

ROOT RULES		CONTEXTUAL CLOSURE
β AT A DISTANCE	$L\langle\lambda x.t\rangle s \mapsto_{dB} L\langle[s{\rightarrow}x]t\rangle$	$a \in \{dB, vs\}$
VALUE SUBSTITUTION	$[L\langle v\rangle{\rightarrow}x]t \mapsto_{vs} L\langle\{v{\rightarrow}x\}t\rangle$	$\dfrac{t \mapsto_a t'}{C\langle t\rangle \rightarrow_a C\langle t'\rangle}$
NOTATION	$\rightarrow_{VSC} ::= \rightarrow_{dB} \cup \rightarrow_{vs}$	

Fig. 5. Value Substitution Calculus (VSC).

where the argument is $\rightarrow_{\beta_v}$-normal and not a value, thus the β_v-rule cannot fire. These stuck configurations are problematic, as first noticed by Paolini and Ronchi della Rocca [51,50,55]. The easiest way of stating the problem is that the paradigmatic looping term $\Omega := \delta\delta$, where $\delta := \lambda x.xx$, and its variant $\Omega_{stuck} := (\lambda x.\delta)(yz)\delta$ are contextual equivalent and yet Ω loops while Ω_{stuck} is normal in Plotkin's approach. Terms such as Ω_{stuck} are sometimes called *premature normal forms*, and break expected properties of Plotkin's calculus with respect to denotational models, see Accattoli and Guerrieri [7].

Logically, the issue is that not all detours can be eliminated using Plotkin's β_v-rule.

Substitutions by Value. The issue with open terms has been studied at length by Accattoli and Guerrieri and co-authors [6,38,7,8,12], who in [6] study and compare various ways of circumventing it. One of the most flexible and studied solutions amounts to add *ESs at a distance*. The framework is Accattoli and Paolini's *value substitution calculus* (VSC) [13], defined in Fig. 5, which is the variant of the substitution calculus (of the previous section) modelled over the CbV translation of λ-calculus in linear logic proof nets. The VSC has the same β at a distance rule $\rightarrow_{dB}$ of the SC, which does *not* require the argument to be a value. It has instead a different substitution rule, which is where the value restriction takes place. Its value substitution rule $\rightarrow_{vs}$ uses distance (i.e. the substitution context L around the value v). For instance, $[[u{\rightarrow}y]v{\rightarrow}x](zxx) \rightarrow_{vs} [u{\rightarrow}y](zvv)$. Distance allows one to avoid commuting rules such as $[[u{\rightarrow}y]s{\rightarrow}x]t \rightarrow [u{\rightarrow}y][s{\rightarrow}x]t$ which are often found in CbV calculi with let-expressions, for instance in Moggi's calculus [46,47], where that rule is called *assoc*.

Advantages of ESs by Value. The VSC handles open terms correctly thanks to distance and having moved the value restrictions from β-redexes to substitution redexes. As evidence of correct behavior, let's have a look at the variant Ω_{stuck} of Ω that is a premature normal form in Plotkin's calculus. It now (correctly) diverges in the VSC:

$$\Omega_{stuck} := (\lambda x.\delta)(yz)\delta \qquad \rightarrow_{dB} ([yz{\rightarrow}x]\delta)\delta$$
$$\rightarrow_{dB} [yz{\rightarrow}x][\delta{\rightarrow}w](ww) \rightarrow_{vs} [yz{\rightarrow}x](\delta\delta) \rightarrow_{dB} \cdots$$

The VSC has a number of operational and denotational good properties, as shown by Accattoli and co-authors in various recent works [5,8,12], essentially providing a CbV calculus that mimics in CbV most of the good properties of the CbN λ-calculus, considerably improving over Plotkin's presentation. At the same time, the VSC and Plotkin's calculus induce the same contextual equivalence on closed terms (see [8]), thus the VSC is a *conservative* refinement of Plotkin's calculus.

VANILLA TERMS $\Lambda_s \ni t, s, u ::= x \in \mathcal{V}_s \mid \lambda x.t \mid [\![s{\to}x]\!]t \mid (y \triangleright s|x)t$

DECORATED (ADDITIVE) VANILLA SEQUENT CALCULUS

$$\frac{\Gamma \vdash_s s : A \qquad \Gamma, x : A \vdash_s t : B}{\Gamma \vdash_s [\![s{\to}x]\!]t : B} \text{ cut} \qquad \frac{}{\Gamma, x : A \vdash_s x : A} \text{ ax}$$

$$\frac{\Gamma \vdash_s s : A \qquad \Gamma, x : B \vdash_s t : C}{\Gamma \cup y : A \Rightarrow B \vdash_s (y \triangleright s|x)t : C} \Rightarrow_l \qquad \frac{x : A, \Gamma \vdash_s t : B}{\Gamma \vdash_s \lambda x.t : A \Rightarrow B} \Rightarrow_r$$

Fig. 6. Vanilla λ-terms and how they decorate the vanilla sequent calculus $\vdash_s$ for MIL.

Limits of ESs by Value in Natural Deduction. The VSC, however, is not free from glitches. In contrast to the CbN case, in the VSC *not all ESs are eliminable*, because of the value constraint. Namely, an ES such as $[yz{\to}x]t$ cannot be eliminated, since yz is normal and not a value. It might seem that this is the same issue that we pointed out for Plotkin's approach, for which some detours are not eliminable. The situation however is different: in Plotkin's case, ineliminable detours break operational and denotational properties, while ineliminable ESs do not cause similar problems in the VSC.

It is important to stress that—in itself—the presence of ineliminable ESs is not a drawback. They actually are a *feature* of CbV and of the VSC. The fact that some ESs are ineliminable, indeed, means that sub-term sharing ends up in normal forms, and thus becomes *denotationally visible*, which is a good thing, since it opens the way to a mathematical understanding of sharing and efficiency. In Ehrhard's CbV relational denotational model [27], for instance, $[yz{\to}x](wxx)$ and $w(yz)(yz)$ have *different* interpretations; they instead have the *same* interpretation in the CbN relational model. An extensive high-level discussion of the relationship between sharing and CbV can be found in Accattoli's dissemination paper [2].

The glitch of the VSC is the fact that its ESs are still typed with cuts, as in the SC. Therefore, if some ESs are ineliminable then some cuts are ineliminable, in the CbV interpretation of natural deduction with cuts. This clearly goes against the expected property of the cut rule, which is *admissibility*, that is, that all cuts are eliminable. What happens in the VSC is that only cuts containing values are eliminable.

Ideally, one would like to have two *separate* constructors, one for eliminable cuts and one for ineliminable cuts. This does not seem to be naturally achievable in natural deduction, where the two are entangled. The aim of this paper is to show that, instead, it is exactly what naturally happens in the sequent calculus.

4   Proof Terms for the Vanilla Sequent Calculus

Here, we present the sequent calculus for minimal intuitionistic logic (MIL). We adopt an additive presentation of the MIL fragment of Gentzen's original one [34] (which was multiplicative), mimicking the nowadays standard use of additive natural deduction for Howard's correspondence with the λ-calculus (see e.g. Sørensen and Urzyczyn [58]), despite the fact that Howard's original presentation was multiplicative [41]. The rules are in Fig. 6, which we refer to as *vanilla*, to stress that we do not considered distinguished formulas (also called *stoup*) on the left of sequent symbol $\vdash_s$, nor any other tweak.

The main difference with natural deduction is that the application rule (@) is replaced by the left rule ($\Rightarrow_l$) for $\Rightarrow$ (see Fig. 6, the notation $\Gamma \cup y : A \Rightarrow B$ is explained below), beyond having the cut rule from the start (while in natural deduction we added it only at a later moment). For the sequent calculus, we shall re-use most basic concepts introduced for natural deduction without re-defining them.

Vanilla λ-Terms and the Left Rule for $\Rightarrow$. We adopt what Mint calls the *local approach* [44], followed also, for instance, by Gallier [33, Section 10], Dyckhoff and Lengrand [25,26], Ohori [49], and Cerrito and Kesner [16], introducing a language Λ_S of *vanilla* λ-terms faithfully coding the structure of sequent proofs. We write the terms of Λ_S using a different font t, s, u (with respect to the one used for natural λ-terms), also for the variables x, y, z, w, whose set is noted $\mathcal{V}_S$. The main point of Λ_S is that there are no applications (which decorate (@) rules). They are replaced by a new constructor $(y \triangleright s | x) t$, dubbed here *subtraction* (following Accattoli [1]), and which binds x in t and adds a free occurrence of y. Intuitively, subtraction can be thought of as let $x = ys$ in t (which is the notation used by Gallier [33]) but we prefer to avoid such a notation, for various reasons. Firstly, writing ys we would still be resting on application, while we want to stress that application is not part of the new language, since there is no (@) rule at the logical level. Secondly, in let $x = ys$ in t the two active premises x and s of the ($\Rightarrow_l$) logical rule are given asymmetric roles, while in $(y \triangleright s | x) t$ their roles are symmetric. Thirdly, let-expressions are verbose, thus we adopt a bracket notation.

Note that the typing rule for subtractions uses a new notation $\Gamma \cup x : A$, defined as:

$$\Gamma \cup x : A \quad := \quad \Gamma, x : A \qquad \text{if } x \notin \text{dom}(\Gamma)$$
$$\Gamma \cup x : A \quad := \quad \Gamma \qquad\qquad \text{if } x \in \Gamma \text{ and } \Gamma(x) = A$$

and it is undefined if $x \in \Gamma$ and $\Gamma(x) \neq A$. The notation is needed because the additive presentation might have to do on-the-fly contractions on the newly introduced formula $A \Rightarrow B$, as for instance in the following case, where the free variable occurrence introduced by rule ($\Rightarrow_l$) is immediately identified with the already existing variable y:

$$\frac{\Gamma \vdash_S s : A \qquad \dfrac{}{\Gamma, x : B, y : A \Rightarrow B \vdash_S y : A \Rightarrow B} \text{ax}}{\Gamma, y : A \Rightarrow B \vdash_S (y \triangleright s | x) y : B} \Rightarrow_l$$

This phenomenon is not present in natural deduction because therein formulas and variables are introduced on the left of $\vdash_N$ only by axioms.

Given that weakenings are freely available (in axioms), rule ($\Rightarrow_l$) can alternatively be formulated without using $\cup$, as follows:

$$\frac{\Gamma, y : A \Rightarrow B \vdash_S s : A \qquad \Gamma, x : B, y : A \Rightarrow B \vdash_S t : C}{\Gamma, y : A \Rightarrow B \vdash_S (y \triangleright s | x) t : C} \Rightarrow_l'$$

This approach is adopted for instance by Herbelin [40] and Dyckhoff and Lengrand [26]. We preferred to avoid rule ($\Rightarrow_l'$), however, as we find it counter-intuitive. Yet another equivalent approach is adopting a mixed multiplicative-additive presentation: having the simpler rule ($\Rightarrow_l$) of Fig. 1 that does not use $\cup$ and adding a stand-alone contraction rule (which is multiplicative) for the left-hand side of $\vdash_S$.

NATURAL λ TO VANILLA λ

$$\overline{x}^{S} := x$$

$$\overline{\lambda x.t}^{S} := \lambda x.\overline{t}^{S}$$

$$\overline{[s \to x]t}^{S} := [\![\overline{s}^{S} \to x]\!]\overline{t}^{S}$$

$$\overline{ts}^{S} := [\![\overline{t}^{S} \to x]\!](x \rhd \overline{s}^{S} | y)\, y \quad x, y \text{ fresh}$$

VANILLA λ TO NATURAL λ

$$\underline{x}_{N} := x$$

$$\underline{\lambda x.t}_{N} := \lambda x.\underline{t}_{N}$$

$$\underline{[\![s \to x]\!]t}_{N} := [\underline{s}_{N} \to x]\underline{t}_{N}$$

$$\underline{(y \rhd s | x)\, t}_{N} := [y\underline{s}_{N} \to x]\underline{t}_{N}$$

$$\frac{\Gamma \vdash_{N} A \Rightarrow B \qquad \Gamma \vdash_{N} A}{\Gamma \vdash_{N} B} \ @$$

is simulated in $\vdash_{S}$ *by*

$$\frac{\Gamma \vdash_{S} A \Rightarrow B \qquad \dfrac{\Gamma \vdash_{S} A \qquad \dfrac{}{\Gamma, B \vdash_{S} B}\ ax}{\Gamma, A \Rightarrow B \vdash_{S} B}\ \Rightarrow_{l}}{\Gamma \vdash_{S} B}\ cut$$

$$\frac{\Gamma \vdash_{S} A \qquad \Gamma, B \vdash_{S} C}{\Gamma, A \Rightarrow B \vdash_{S} C}\ \Rightarrow_{l}$$

is simulated in $\vdash_{N}$ *by*

$$\frac{\dfrac{}{\Gamma, A \Rightarrow B \vdash_{N} A \Rightarrow B}\ ax \qquad \Gamma \vdash_{N} A}{\dfrac{\Gamma, A \Rightarrow B \vdash_{N} B}{\Gamma, A \Rightarrow B \vdash_{N} C}\ @ \qquad \Gamma, B \vdash_{N} C}\ cut$$

Fig. 7. Translations between the natural λ-terms (with ESs) and the vanilla λ-terms.

Different Decoration for Cuts. Another difference between Λ_{N} and Λ_{S} is that, since in Λ_{S} cuts shall play a slightly different role than in the VSC / natural deduction by value, for the sake of clarity we decorate them differently, with $[\![s \to x]\!]t$ rather than with $[s \to x]t$.

Translations. Translations from the natural λ-calculus to the vanilla one and vice-versa are given in Fig. 7. They induce translations of the related logical systems, whose key ingredients are highlighted in Fig. 7, namely the simulation of the (@) rule by $\vdash_{S}$ and the simulation of the ($\Rightarrow_{l}$) rule by $\vdash_{N}$. Both translations are obtained by introducing axioms and cuts, and are standard. For instance, Girard's CbN and CbV translations of natural deduction to linear logic [35] are modal decorations of $\overline{\cdot}^{S}$, and the cuts used in the translation of applications are called *correction cuts* by Danos et al. [21]. Note that the translations preserve (and reflect) values.

Translation of Cut-Free Vanilla Terms. We have not yet introduced rewriting rules for vanilla λ-terms (that is, cut elimination), but there are no doubts about the expected notion of normal vanilla terms: they must be the cut-free ones. The next proposition states the starting observation of this work, that is, the fact that cut-free vanilla terms are mapped to natural terms that are CbV normal, but not necessarily CbN normal.

Proposition 4.1. *Let* $t \in \Lambda_{S}$ *be cut-free. Then* $\underline{t}_{N}$ *is* $\to_{VSC}$-*normal but not necessarily* $\to_{SC}$-*normal.*

Proof. By induction on t. For $\rightarrow_{VSC}$, simply note that, for cut-free vanilla terms, ESs and applications (which form $\rightarrow_{VSC}$ redexes) are only introduced by the translation of subtractions, and they receive as left sub-terms the application of a free variable to a term: thus the introduced application is not a $\rightarrow_{dB}$-redex, nor it is a value (nor can reduce to one) thus the introduced ES is not a $\rightarrow_{vs}$-redex. For $\rightarrow_{SC}$, the translation of subtraction instead introduces $\rightarrow_s$ redexes.   □

In the other direction, $\rightarrow_{VSC}$-normal natural terms are not mapped by $\cdot^S$ to cut-free vanilla terms, because the translation of applications adds cuts. It is possible to optimize the translation as to avoid this mismatch, but the optimized translations would considerably complicate the translation of contexts (introduced and used in the next sections), which is why we refrain from it. At the same time, we shall show that the translation of normal natural terms are *almost* cut-free, in a suitable harmless way.

5   Defining Cut Elimination for the Vanilla λ-Calculus

In this section, we define cut elimination on vanilla λ-terms, obtaining the *vanilla λ-calculus*. Our cut elimination shall be based on meta-level substitution. The notion of value shall emerge naturally, and rules at a distance shall play a role.

Left Variable Occurrences. At first sight, defining small-step cut elimination for vanilla terms is conceptually easy, since one would simply define it as follows:

$$[\![s \rightarrow x]\!]t \quad \rightarrow_{cut} \quad \{\![s \rightarrow x]\!\}t$$

for a notion of meta-level substitution $\{\![s \rightarrow x]\!\}t$ for vanilla λ-terms. The problem however is that the definition of $\{\![s \rightarrow x]\!\}t$ cannot be the same as for natural terms.

In natural deduction, the free occurrences of a variable are introduced by axioms, and axioms can always be replaced by proofs having the same ending sequent. Since we consider axiom as a right rule, let us say that variables have only *right occurrences*, and that on right occurrences one can always define meta-level substitution $\{u \rightarrow x\}t$ simply as the *replacement* of x by u in t.

On vanilla terms, subtractions $(y \rhd s | x)\, t$ introduce *left occurrences* of y. In contrast to right occurrences, the left ones cannot be simply replaced by a vanilla term u, because $(u \rhd s | x)\, t$ does *not* belong to the grammar of vanilla terms. Therefore, the definition of meta-level substitution $\{\![u \rightarrow x]\!\}t$ on vanilla terms is a bit tricky on subtractions.

Easy Cases and Values. To define $\{\![u \rightarrow x]\!\}t$, we have to inspect the shape of u. The simplest case is when u is a variable y, since in that case it is possible to simply replace x by y. A second clear case is when u is an abstraction $\lambda y.s$. Then, we can set:

$$\{\![\lambda y.s \rightarrow x]\!\}(x \rhd r | z)\, t \quad := \quad [\![[\![\{\![\lambda y.s \rightarrow x]\!\}r \rightarrow y]\!]s \rightarrow z]\!]\{\![\lambda y.s \rightarrow x]\!\}t$$

This complex definition amounts to do the expected elimination of the principal cut between the abstraction and the subtraction (roughly, corresponding to the $\rightarrow_{dB}$ step $(\lambda y.s)r \rightarrow_{dB} [\![r \rightarrow y]\!]s$ of the (V)SC) *plus* putting the resulting term in a second created cut on z *and* propagating the substitution $\{\![\lambda y.s \rightarrow x]\!\}$ to the sub-terms r and t of the

$$\text{TERMS} \quad \Lambda_S \ni t, s, u ::= x \in \mathcal{V}_S \mid \lambda x.t \mid [\![s{\to}x]\!]t \mid (y \triangleright s|x)t$$
$$\text{VALUES} \quad v ::= x \mid \lambda x.t$$

$$\text{CONTEXTS} \quad C ::= \langle \cdot \rangle \mid \lambda x.C \mid [\![t{\to}x]\!]C \mid [\![C{\to}x]\!]t \mid (y \triangleright t|x)C \mid (y \triangleright C|x)t$$
$$\text{LEFT CTXS} \quad L ::= \langle \cdot \rangle \mid [\![t{\to}x]\!]L \mid (y \triangleright t|x)L$$

META-LEVEL SUBSTITUTION OF VALUES FOR VANILLA TERMS

$$\{\!\{v{\to}x\}\!\}x := v$$
$$\{\!\{v{\to}x\}\!\}y := y$$
$$\{\!\{v{\to}x\}\!\}\lambda y.t := \lambda y.\{\!\{v{\to}x\}\!\}t$$
$$\{\!\{\lambda y.u{\to}x\}\!\}(x \triangleright s|z)t := [\![[\![\{\!\{\lambda y.u{\to}x\}\!\}s{\to}y]\!]u{\to}z]\!]\{\!\{\lambda y.u{\to}x\}\!\}t$$

$$\{\!\{v{\to}x\}\!\}[\![s{\to}y]\!]t := [\![\{\!\{v{\to}x\}\!\}s{\to}y]\!]\{\!\{v{\to}x\}\!\}t$$
$$\{\!\{v{\to}x\}\!\}(y \triangleright s|z)t := (y \triangleright \{\!\{v{\to}x\}\!\}s|z)\{\!\{v{\to}x\}\!\}t$$
$$\{\!\{y{\to}x\}\!\}(x \triangleright s|z)t := (y \triangleright \{\!\{y{\to}x\}\!\}s|z)\{\!\{y{\to}x\}\!\}t$$

ROOT CUT ELIMINATION

$$[\![L\langle v \rangle {\to} x]\!]t \quad \twoheadrightarrow_{cut} \quad L\langle \{\!\{v{\to}x\}\!\}t \rangle$$

CTX CLOSURE

$$\frac{t \twoheadrightarrow_{cut} t'}{C\langle t \rangle \twoheadrightarrow_{cut} C\langle t' \rangle}$$

Fig. 8. The vanilla λ-calculus.

---

subtraction. Note that the two clear cases $u = y$ and $u = \lambda y.s$ are exactly those for *values*, which correspond to the right rules of $\vdash_S$. The full definition of meta-level substitution $\{\!\{v{\to}x\}\!\}t$ for values is in Fig. 8. The following property is proved by induction on t.

Lemma 5.1. *Let* $x \notin \mathrm{fv}(t)$. *Then* $\{\!\{v{\to}x\}\!\}t = t$.

The Vanilla λ-Calculus. For defining small-step cut elimination for all terms, we rely on the crucial observation that *every* vanilla term t *splits uniquely* as $t = L\langle v \rangle$, where L is a left context—defined in Fig. 8—and v is a value. Note that a similar splitting is also used in the value substitution rule $\to_{vs}$ of the VSC, but there is a key difference: in the VSC applications *cannot* be split as $L\langle v \rangle$ (because application is not a left rule), which is why some ESs cannot be eliminated, while *all* vanilla terms can be split (because application is replaced by subtraction, which is a left rule).

We know how to substitute v, and we are left to define what to do with L. There are two options, namely mimicking the substitution rules by name (namely $\to_s$) and by value ($\to_{vs}$) for natural terms: either we carry L along with v in the propagation of the substitution, possibly duplicating or erasing it, as in the CbN rule $\to_s$ of the SC, or we commute it out, as in the CbV rule $\to_{vs}$ of the VSC. While in principle both are valid choices, the latter seems more natural because—even if we adopt the CbN approach— cut-free vanilla terms map to CbV normal natural terms, as shown by Proposition 4.1, and *not* to the CbN ones. Essentially, to catch a CbN semantics we should also modify something about cut-free proofs, but that goes against the starting point of our work, namely that vanilla cut-free proofs are a good representation of CbV normal forms.

The cut elimination rule $\twoheadrightarrow_{cut}$ is then defined in Fig. 8 by commuting out the left context L, completing the definition of the vanilla λ-calculus. Equivalently, one can also set $\{\!\{L\langle v \rangle {\to} x\}\!\}t := L\langle \{\!\{v{\to}x\}\!\}t \rangle$ and $[\![s{\to}x]\!]t \twoheadrightarrow_{cut} \{\!\{s{\to}x\}\!\}t$.

Subject Reduction. The standard check for the definition of $\twoheadrightarrow_{cut}$ is subject reduction.

Proposition 5.1 (Subject reduction). *Let* $t \in \Lambda_S$ *and* $\pi \triangleright \Gamma \vdash_S t : A$ *be a derivation. If* $t \twoheadrightarrow_{cut} s$ *then there exists a derivation* $\rho \triangleright \Gamma \vdash_S s : A$.

Proof. Let $t = C\langle\llbracket L\langle v\rangle\!\to\!x\rrbracket u\rangle \twoheadrightarrow_{cut} C\langle L\langle\{\!|v\!\to\!x\}\!|u\rangle\rangle = s$. The proof is by induction on u, L, and C. Details are in the Appendix of the technical report [3]. □

6   Simulating the Vanilla λ-calculus in the VSC

To simulate the vanilla λ-calculus in the VSC, we need to look at how the $\cdot^{\mathsf{S}}$ translation relates the respective notions of meta-level substitution. On vanilla terms, substitution on left variable occurrences does also the work that is done by rule $\to_{dB}$ on the VSC. Unsurprisingly, then, the translation commutes with substitution only up to $\to_{dB}$.

Lemma 6.1 (Substitution and $\cdot_N$ commute up to $\to_{dB}$). $\underline{\{v_N\!\to\!x\}t_N} \to^*_{dB} \underline{\{\!|v\!\to\!x\}\!|t}_N$.

To establish the simulation, we need a lemma about the commutation of contexts and of the translation. *Technicality*: the translations are extended to contexts by setting $\underline{\langle\cdot\rangle}_N := \langle\cdot\rangle$ and $\overline{\langle\cdot\rangle}^{\mathsf{S}} := \langle\cdot\rangle$, and defining them as for terms on the other cases.

Lemma 6.2 (Contexts and $\cdot_N$ translation).

1. $\underline{L}_N$ *is a* L *context and* $\underline{L\langle t\rangle}_N = \underline{L}_N\langle\underline{t}_N\rangle$.
2. $\underline{C}_N$ *is a* C *context and* $\underline{C\langle t\rangle}_N = \underline{C}_N\langle\underline{t}_N\rangle$.

Proposition 6.1 (VSC simulates vanilla). *If* $t \twoheadrightarrow_{cut} s$ *then* $\underline{t}_N \to_{vs}\to^*_{dB} \underline{s}_N$.

Proof. For a root step $t = \llbracket L\langle v\rangle\!\to\!x\rrbracket u \twoheadrightarrow_{cut} L\langle\{\!|v\!\to\!x\}\!|u\rangle = s$, we have:

$$\underline{\llbracket L\langle v\rangle\!\to\!x\rrbracket u}_N = \llbracket\underline{L\langle v\rangle}_N\!\to\!x\rrbracket\underline{u}_N =_{L.6.2.1} \llbracket\underline{L}_N\langle\underline{v}_N\rangle\!\to\!x\rrbracket\underline{u}_N \mapsto_{vs} \underline{L}_N\langle\{\underline{v}_N\!\to\!x\}\underline{u}_N\rangle$$
$$(L.6.1) \to^*_{dB} \underline{L}_N\langle\{\!|v\!\to\!x\}\!|u}_N\rangle =_{L.6.2.1} \underline{L\langle\{\!|v\!\to\!x\}\!|u\rangle}_N.$$

For steps in contexts, the simulation follows from the root case and Lemma 6.2.2. □

Putting together the simulation of cut elimination with the translation of cut-free terms, we obtain the following property.

Lemma 6.3 (Preservation of VSC termination). *Let* $t \twoheadrightarrow^*_{cut} s$ *with* s *cut-free. Then* $\underline{t}_N \to^*_{VSC} \underline{s}_N$ *with* $\underline{s}_N$ *is* $\to_{VSC}$-*normal.*

Proof. By Proposition 6.1, we obtain $\underline{t}_N \to^*_{VSC} \underline{s}_N$. By Proposition 4.1, $\underline{s}_N$ is a $\to_{VSC}$-normal form. □

7   Simulating the VSC in the Vanilla λ-Calculus

In the other direction, the translation and meta-level substitution commute neatly.

Lemma 7.1 (Substitution and $\cdot^{\mathsf{S}}$ commute). $\overline{\{\!|\overline{v}^{\mathsf{S}}\!\to\!x\}\!|\overline{t}}^{\mathsf{S}} = \overline{\{v\!\to\!x\}t}^{\mathsf{S}}$.

As before, for the simulation we need a lemma about contexts.

Lemma 7.2 (Contexts and $\cdot^{\mathsf{S}}$ translation).

1. $\overline{L}^S$ is an L context and $\overline{L\langle t\rangle}^S = \overline{L}^S\langle \overline{t}^S\rangle$.
2. $\overline{C}^S$ is a C context and $\overline{C\langle t\rangle}^S = \overline{C}^S\langle \overline{t}^S\rangle$.

Proposition 7.1 (Vanilla simulates VSC).

1. If $t \to_{dB} s$ then $\overline{t}^S \twoheadrightarrow_{cut} \twoheadrightarrow_{cut} \overline{s}^S$.
2. If $t \to_{vs} s$ then $\overline{t}^S \twoheadrightarrow_{cut} \overline{s}^S$.

Proof. For root steps:

1. *β at a distance*, i.e. $t = L\langle\lambda x.u\rangle r \mapsto_{dB} L\langle[r{\to}x]u\rangle = s$. With y and z fresh:

$$
\begin{aligned}
\overline{L\langle\lambda x.u\rangle r}^S &= && [\![\overline{L\langle\lambda x.u\rangle}^S{\to}y]\!]\,(y \triangleright \overline{r}^S|z)\,z \\
&=_{L.6.2.1} && [\![\overline{L}^S\langle\lambda x.\overline{u}^S\rangle{\to}y]\!]\,(y \triangleright \overline{r}^S|z)\,z \\
&\twoheadrightarrow_{cut} && \overline{L}^S\langle[\![\{\lambda x.\overline{u}^S{\to}y\}\overline{r}^S{\to}x]\!]\overline{u}^S{\to}z]\!]\{\lambda x.\overline{u}^S{\to}y\}z\rangle \\
&=_{L.5.1} && \overline{L}^S\langle[\![[\![\overline{r}^S{\to}x]\!]\overline{u}^S{\to}z]\!]z\rangle \\
(\star)\quad &\twoheadrightarrow_{cut} && \overline{L}^S\langle[\![\overline{r}^S{\to}x]\!]\overline{u}^S\rangle \\
&= && \overline{L}^S\langle\overline{[r{\to}x]u}^S\rangle && =_{L.6.2.1} \overline{L\langle[r{\to}x]u\rangle}^S
\end{aligned}
$$

Where step $(\star)$ is given by the general fact that $[\![t{\to}x]\!]x \twoheadrightarrow_{cut} t$, since $t = L\langle v\rangle$ for some L and v, thus $[\![t{\to}x]\!]x = [\![L\langle v\rangle{\to}x]\!]x \twoheadrightarrow_{cut} L\langle v\rangle = t$.

2. *Value substitution*, i.e. $t = [\![L\langle v\rangle{\to}x]\!]u \mapsto_{dB} L\langle\{v{\to}x\}u\rangle = s$. Then:

$$
\begin{aligned}
\overline{[\![L\langle v\rangle{\to}x]\!]u}^S &= && [\![\overline{L\langle v\rangle}^S{\to}x]\!]\overline{u}^S \\
&=_{L.6.2.1} && [\![\overline{L}^S\langle\overline{v}^S\rangle{\to}x]\!]\overline{u}^S \\
&\twoheadrightarrow_{cut} && \overline{L}^S\langle\{\overline{v}^S{\to}x\}\overline{u}^S\rangle \\
&=_{L.7.1} && \overline{L}^S\langle\overline{\{v{\to}x\}u}^S\rangle && =_{L.6.2.1} \overline{L\langle\{v{\to}x\}u\rangle}^S
\end{aligned}
$$

For steps in contexts, the simulation follows from the root case and Lemma 7.2.2.   □

Translation of Normal Natural Terms. As anticipated in Sect. 5, the translation of normal VSC terms does not give cut-free vanilla terms, because the translation of applications introduces cuts. Here we show that nonetheless the obtained terms are *almost* cut-free, since they are cut-free up to some trivial cut elimination steps, dubbed *renaming steps*. In particular, they strictly reduce the size of a vanilla term.

Definition 1 (Renaming Cut Elimination Steps). *A step* $t = C\langle[\![L\langle v\rangle{\to}x]\!]u\rangle \twoheadrightarrow_{cut} C\langle L\langle\{v{\to}x\}u\rangle\rangle = s$ *is a renaming step, noted* $t \twoheadrightarrow_{ren\text{-}cut} s$, *if* v *is a variable.*

Proposition 7.2 (The $\overline{\cdot}^S$ translation of VSC normal forms is almost cut-free). *Let* $t \in \Lambda_N^{ES}$ *be* $\to_{VSC}$-*normal. Then there exists* t *cut-free such that* $\overline{t}^S \twoheadrightarrow_{ren\text{-}cut}^k$ t *with* $k \le |t|$, *where* $|t|$ *is the size (i.e. number of constructors) in t.*

As for the other direction, we can put together the simulation and the translation of normal forms, obtaining the preservation of termination by $\overline{\cdot}^S$.

Lemma 7.3 (Preservation of termination). *Let* $t \to^*_{VSC} s$ *with* $s \to_{VSC}$-*normal. Then there exists a cut-free term* s *such that* $\overline{t}^S \leadsto^*_{cut}$ s.

Proof. By Proposition 7.1, we obtain $\overline{t}^S \leadsto^*_{cut} \overline{s}^S$. By Proposition 7.2, there exists s cut-free such that $\overline{s}^S \leadsto^*_{cut}$ s.   □

8 Strong Normalization

The typical theorem for Curry-Howard correspondences is that the logical system ensures strong normalization of the typed terms. We provide such a result for our new correspondence between the vanilla λ-calculus and the vanilla sequent calculus.

In this section, we give only the statement, since the proof is too technical for a fresh perspective paper. The proof is developed in sections D and E of the Appendix of the technical report [3], and is based on the bi-orthogonal reducibility method, adapting and slightly simplifying its presentation in Accattoli [1].

Definition 2 (Strong normalization). *A vanilla term* t *is strongly normalizing, also noted* $t \in SN_{cut}$, *if* $t \leadsto_{cut}$ s *implies* $s \in SN_{cut}$.

Theorem 1 (Typable terms are SN). *Let* $t \in \Lambda_S$ *and* $\Gamma \vdash_S t : A$. *Then* $t \in SN_{cut}$.

9 Conclusions

We introduced the *vanilla* λ-calculus, a computational interpretation of the simplest sequent calculus, and showed that it simulates and it is simulated by call-by-value evaluation. Technically, the simulations are clean and compact, thanks to the use of rewriting rules at a distance for both the new cut elimination rule for the vanilla λ-calculus and the presentation of call-by-value evaluation that we adopt from the literature.

Our study nicely complements the two famous cornerstones by Curry and Howard about minimal intuitionistic logic resting only on basic logical concepts:

1. *Curry 1958* [19]: Hilbert's system matches combinatory logic;
2. *Howard 1969* (but published only in 1980) [41]: Gentzen's natural deduction mirrors the (call-by-name) λ-calculus;
3. *Here*: Gentzen's sequent calculus matches call-by-value evaluation.

We believe that our work provides a fresh perspective over the sequent calculus. Its modern computational interpretation is usually defined starting from sequent calculi with stoups for classical logic, following Curien and Herbelin [18]. The basic, *vanilla* presentation of the intuitionistic case seems to have fallen into a blind spot of the literature. This work shows that it is far from being unworthy of attention.

Future Work. Maraist et al. [43] propose a Curry-Howard correspondence for *call-by-need* using an affine logic with a duplication modality, tweaking the linear logic one for call-by-value. In ongoing work, we are using the results of this paper as the starting point for a Curry-Howard for call-by-need that is *not* based on linear/affine concepts.

References

1. Accattoli, B.: Exponentials as substitutions and the cost of cut elimination in linear logic. Log. Methods Comput. Sci. **19**(4) (2023). https://doi.org/10.46298/LMCS-19(4:23)2023
2. Accattoli, B.: Sharing a perspective on the λ-calculus. In: van der Storm, T., Hirschfeld, R. (eds.) Proceedings of the 2023 ACM SIGPLAN International Symposium on New Ideas, New Paradigms, and Reflections on Programming and Software, Onward! 2023, Cascais, Portugal, October 25-27, 2023. pp. 179–190. ACM (2023). https://doi.org/10.1145/3622758.3622884
3. Accattoli, B.: The vanilla sequent calculus is call-by-value (2024), https://arxiv.org/abs/2409.19722
4. Accattoli, B., Bonelli, E., Kesner, D., Lombardi, C.: A nonstandard standardization theorem. In: Jagannathan, S., Sewell, P. (eds.) The 41st Annual ACM SIGPLAN-SIGACT Symposium on Principles of Programming Languages, POPL '14, San Diego, CA, USA, January 20-21, 2014. pp. 659–670. ACM (2014). https://doi.org/10.1145/2535838.2535886
5. Accattoli, B., Condoluci, A., Sacerdoti Coen, C.: Strong call-by-value is reasonable, implosively. In: 36th Annual ACM/IEEE Symposium on Logic in Computer Science, LICS 2021, Rome, Italy, June 29 - July 2, 2021. pp. 1–14. IEEE (2021). https://doi.org/10.1109/LICS52264.2021.9470630
6. Accattoli, B., Guerrieri, G.: Open call-by-value. In: Igarashi, A. (ed.) Programming Languages and Systems - 14th Asian Symposium, APLAS 2016, Hanoi, Vietnam, November 21-23, 2016, Proceedings. Lecture Notes in Computer Science, vol. 10017, pp. 206–226 (2016). https://doi.org/10.1007/978-3-319-47958-3_12
7. Accattoli, B., Guerrieri, G.: Types of fireballs. In: Ryu, S. (ed.) Programming Languages and Systems - 16th Asian Symposium, APLAS 2018, Wellington, New Zealand, December 2-6, 2018, Proceedings. Lecture Notes in Computer Science, vol. 11275, pp. 45–66. Springer (2018). https://doi.org/10.1007/978-3-030-02768-1_3
8. Accattoli, B., Guerrieri, G.: The theory of call-by-value solvability. Proc. ACM Program. Lang. **6**(ICFP), 855–885 (2022). https://doi.org/10.1145/3547652
9. Accattoli, B., Guerrieri, G., Leberle, M.: Strong call-by-value and multi types. In: Ábrahám, E., Dubslaff, C., Tarifa, S.L.T. (eds.) Theoretical Aspects of Computing - ICTAC 2023 - 20th International Colloquium, Lima, Peru, December 4-8, 2023, Proceedings. Lecture Notes in Computer Science, vol. 14446, pp. 196–215. Springer (2023). https://doi.org/10.1007/978-3-031-47963-2_13
10. Accattoli, B., Kesner, D.: The structural λ-calculus. In: Dawar, A., Veith, H. (eds.) Computer Science Logic, 24th International Workshop, CSL 2010, 19th Annual Conference of the EACSL, Brno, Czech Republic, August 23-27, 2010. Proceedings. Lecture Notes in Computer Science, vol. 6247, pp. 381–395. Springer (2010). https://doi.org/10.1007/978-3-642-15205-4_30
11. Accattoli, B., Kesner, D.: The permutative λ-calculus. In: Bjørner, N.S., Voronkov, A. (eds.) Logic for Programming, Artificial Intelligence, and Reasoning - 18th International Conference, LPAR-18, Mérida, Venezuela, March 11-15, 2012. Proceedings. Lecture Notes in Computer Science, vol. 7180, pp. 23–36. Springer (2012). https://doi.org/10.1007/978-3-642-28717-6_5
12. Accattoli, B., Lancelot, A.: Light genericity. In: Kobayashi, N., Worrell, J. (eds.) Foundations of Software Science and Computation Structures - 27th International Conference, FoSSaCS 2024, Held as Part of the European Joint Conferences on Theory and Practice of Software, ETAPS 2024, Luxembourg City, Luxembourg, April 6-11, 2024, Proceedings, Part II. Lecture Notes in Computer Science, vol. 14575, pp. 24–46. Springer (2024). https://doi.org/10.1007/978-3-031-57231-9_2

13. Accattoli, B., Paolini, L.: Call-by-value solvability, revisited. In: Schrijvers, T., Thiemann, P. (eds.) Functional and Logic Programming - 11th International Symposium, FLOPS 2012, Kobe, Japan, May 23-25, 2012. Proceedings. Lecture Notes in Computer Science, vol. 7294, pp. 4–16. Springer (2012). https://doi.org/10.1007/978-3-642-29822-6_4

14. Ariola, Z.M., Herbelin, H., Saurin, A.: Classical call-by-need and duality. In: Ong, C.L. (ed.) Typed Lambda Calculi and Applications - 10th International Conference, TLCA 2011, Novi Sad, Serbia, June 1-3, 2011. Proceedings. Lecture Notes in Computer Science, vol. 6690, pp. 27–44. Springer (2011). https://doi.org/10.1007/978-3-642-21691-6_6

15. Barendregt, H., Ghilezan, S.: Lambda terms for natural deduction, sequent calculus and cut elimination. J. Funct. Program. **10**(1), 121–134 (2000). https://doi.org/10.1017/s0956796899003524

16. Cerrito, S., Kesner, D.: Pattern matching as cut elimination. Theor. Comput. Sci. **323**(1-3), 71–127 (2004). https://doi.org/10.1016/J.TCS.2004.03.032

17. Curien, P., Fiore, M.P., Munch-Maccagnoni, G.: A theory of effects and resources: adjunction models and polarised calculi. In: Bodík, R., Majumdar, R. (eds.) Proceedings of the 43rd Annual ACM SIGPLAN-SIGACT Symposium on Principles of Programming Languages, POPL 2016, St. Petersburg, FL, USA, January 20 - 22, 2016. pp. 44–56. ACM (2016). https://doi.org/10.1145/2837614.2837652

18. Curien, P., Herbelin, H.: The duality of computation. In: Odersky, M., Wadler, P. (eds.) Proceedings of the Fifth ACM SIGPLAN International Conference on Functional Programming (ICFP '00), Montreal, Canada, September 18-21, 2000. pp. 233–243. ACM (2000). https://doi.org/10.1145/351240.351262

19. Curry, H., Feys, R.: Combinatory Logic. No. 1 in Studies in logic and the foundations of mathematics, North-Holland Publishing Company (1958)

20. Dal Lago, U., Martini, S.: The weak lambda calculus as a reasonable machine. Theor. Comput. Sci. **398**(1-3), 32–50 (2008). https://doi.org/10.1016/J.TCS.2008.01.044

21. Danos, V., Joinet, J.B., Schellinx, H.: LKT and LKQ: sequent calculi for second order logic based upon dual linear decompositions of classical implication. In: Girard, J.Y., Lafont, Y., Regnier, L. (eds.) Advances in Linear Logic, pp. 211–224. No. 222 in London Mathematical Society Lecture Note Series, Cambridge University Press (1995). https://doi.org/10.1017/CBO9780511629150

22. Dougherty, D.J., Ghilezan, S., Lescanne, P.: Characterizing strong normalization in the curien-herbelin symmetric lambda calculus: Extending the coppo-dezani heritage. Theor. Comput. Sci. **398**(1-3), 114–128 (2008). https://doi.org/10.1016/J.TCS.2008.01.022

23. Downen, P., Ariola, Z.M.: A tutorial on computational classical logic and the sequent calculus. J. Funct. Program. **28**, e3 (2018). https://doi.org/10.1017/S0956796818000023

24. Downen, P., Maurer, L., Ariola, Z.M., Peyton Jones, S.: Sequent calculus as a compiler intermediate language. In: Garrigue, J., Keller, G., Sumii, E. (eds.) Proceedings of the 21st ACM SIGPLAN International Conference on Functional Programming, ICFP 2016, Nara, Japan, September 18-22, 2016. pp. 74–88. ACM (2016). https://doi.org/10.1145/2951913.2951931

25. Dyckhoff, R., Lengrand, S.: LJQ: A strongly focused calculus for intuitionistic logic. In: Beckmann, A., Berger, U., Löwe, B., Tucker, J.V. (eds.) Logical Approaches to Computational Barriers, Second Conference on Computability in Europe, CiE 2006, Swansea, UK, June 30-July 5, 2006, Proceedings. Lecture Notes in Computer Science, vol. 3988, pp. 173–185. Springer (2006). https://doi.org/10.1007/11780342_19

26. Dyckhoff, R., Lengrand, S.: Call-by-value lambda-calculus and LJQ. J. Log. Comput. **17**(6), 1109–1134 (2007). https://doi.org/10.1093/LOGCOM/EXM037

27. Ehrhard, T.: Collapsing non-idempotent intersection types. In: Cégielski, P., Durand, A. (eds.) Computer Science Logic (CSL'12) - 26th International Workshop/21st Annual Conference of the EACSL, CSL 2012, September 3-6, 2012, Fontainebleau, France. LIPIcs, vol. 16, pp. 259–273. Schloss Dagstuhl - Leibniz-Zentrum für Informatik (2012). https://doi.org/10.4230/LIPICS.CSL.2012.259

28. Espírito Santo, J.: Revisiting the correspondence between cut elimination and normalisation. In: Montanari, U., Rolim, J.D.P., Welzl, E. (eds.) Automata, Languages and Programming, 27th International Colloquium, ICALP 2000, Geneva, Switzerland, July 9-15, 2000, Proceedings. Lecture Notes in Computer Science, vol. 1853, pp. 600–611. Springer (2000). https://doi.org/10.1007/3-540-45022-X_51

29. Espírito Santo, J.: Completing Herbelin's programme. In: Rocca, S.R.D. (ed.) Typed Lambda Calculi and Applications, 8th International Conference, TLCA 2007, Paris, France, June 26-28, 2007, Proceedings. Lecture Notes in Computer Science, vol. 4583, pp. 118–132. Springer (2007). https://doi.org/10.1007/978-3-540-73228-0_10

30. Espírito Santo, J., Pinto, L., Uustalu, T.: Plotkin's call-by-value λ-calculus as a modal calculus. J. Log. Algebraic Methods Program. **127**, 100775 (2022). https://doi.org/10.1016/J.JLAMP.2022.100775

31. Filinski, A.: Declarative continuations: an investigation of duality in programming language semantics. In: Pitt, D.H., Rydeheard, D.E., Dybjer, P., Pitts, A.M., Poigné, A. (eds.) Category Theory and Computer Science, Manchester, UK, September 5-8, 1989, Proceedings. Lecture Notes in Computer Science, vol. 389, pp. 224–249. Springer (1989). https://doi.org/10.1007/BFB0018355

32. Flanagan, C., Sabry, A., Duba, B.F., Felleisen, M.: The essence of compiling with continuations. In: Cartwright, R. (ed.) Proceedings of the ACM SIGPLAN'93 Conference on Programming Language Design and Implementation (PLDI), Albuquerque, New Mexico, USA, June 23-25, 1993. pp. 237–247. ACM (1993). https://doi.org/10.1145/155090.155113

33. Gallier, J.H.: Constructive logics part I: A tutorial on proof systems and typed gamma-calculi. Theor. Comput. Sci. **110**(2), 249–339 (1993). https://doi.org/10.1016/0304-3975(93)90011-H

34. Gentzen, G.: Investigations into logical deduction. American Philosophical Quarterly **1**(4), 288–306 (1964), http://www.jstor.org/stable/20009142

35. Girard, J.: Linear logic. Theor. Comput. Sci. **50**, 1–102 (1987). https://doi.org/10.1016/0304-3975(87)90045-4

36. Girard, J.: A new constructive logic: Classical logic. Math. Struct. Comput. Sci. **1**(3), 255–296 (1991). https://doi.org/10.1017/S0960129500001328

37. Grégoire, B., Leroy, X.: A compiled implementation of strong reduction. In: (ICFP '02). pp. 235–246 (2002). https://doi.org/10.1145/581478.581501

38. Guerrieri, G., Paolini, L., Ronchi Della Rocca, S.: Standardization and conservativity of a refined call-by-value lambda-calculus. Logical Methods in Computer Science **13**(4) (2017). https://doi.org/10.23638/LMCS-13(4:29)2017

39. Herbelin, H.: A lambda-calculus structure isomorphic to gentzen-style sequent calculus structure. In: Pacholski, L., Tiuryn, J. (eds.) Computer Science Logic, 8th International Workshop, CSL '94, Kazimierz, Poland, September 25-30, 1994, Selected Papers. Lecture Notes in Computer Science, vol. 933, pp. 61–75. Springer (1994). https://doi.org/10.1007/BFb0022247

40. Herbelin, H.: Séquents qu'on calcule: de l'interprétation du calcul des séquents comme calcul de λ-termes et comme calcul de stratégies gagnantes. Ph.D. thesis, University Paris 7 (Jan 1995)

41. Howard, W.A.: The formulae-as-types notion of construction. In: Curry, H., B., H., Roger, S.J., Jonathan, P. (eds.) To H. B. Curry: Essays on Combinatory Logic, Lambda Calculus, and Formalism. Academic Press (1980), Notes written in 1969 and published only in 1980.

42. Kesner, D.: A fine-grained computational interpretation of girard's intuitionistic proof-nets. Proc. ACM Program. Lang. **6**(POPL), 1–28 (2022). https://doi.org/10.1145/3498669

43. Maraist, J., Odersky, M., Turner, D.N., Wadler, P.: Call-by-name, call-by-value, call-by-need and the linear lambda calculus. Theor. Comput. Sci. **228**(1-2), 175–210 (1999). https://doi.org/10.1016/S0304-3975(98)00358-2

44. Mints, G.: Three faces of natural deduction. In: Galmiche, D. (ed.) Automated Reasoning with Analytic Tableaux and Related Methods, International Conference, TABLEAUX '97, Pont-à-Mousson, France, May 13-16, 1997, Proceedings. Lecture Notes in Computer Science, vol. 1227, pp. 16–30. Springer (1997). https://doi.org/10.1007/BFB0027402

45. Miquey, É.: A classical sequent calculus with dependent types. ACM Trans. Program. Lang. Syst. **41**(2), 8:1–8:47 (2019). https://doi.org/10.1145/3230625

46. Moggi, E.: Computational λ-Calculus and Monads. LFCS report ECS-LFCS-88-66, University of Edinburgh (1988), http://www.lfcs.inf.ed.ac.uk/reports/88/ECS-LFCS-88-66/ECS-LFCS-88-66.pdf

47. Moggi, E.: Computational lambda-calculus and monads. In: Proceedings of the Fourth Annual Symposium on Logic in Computer Science (LICS '89), Pacific Grove, California, USA, June 5-8, 1989. pp. 14–23. IEEE Computer Society (1989). https://doi.org/10.1109/LICS.1989.39155

48. Munch-Maccagnoni, G., Scherer, G.: Polarised intermediate representation of lambda calculus with sums. In: 30th Annual ACM/IEEE Symposium on Logic in Computer Science, LICS 2015, Kyoto, Japan, July 6-10, 2015. pp. 127–140. IEEE Computer Society (2015). https://doi.org/10.1109/LICS.2015.22

49. Ohori, A.: A curry-howard isomorphism for compilation and program execution. In: Girard, J. (ed.) Typed Lambda Calculi and Applications, 4th International Conference, TLCA'99, L'Aquila, Italy, April 7-9, 1999, Proceedings. Lecture Notes in Computer Science, vol. 1581, pp. 280–294. Springer (1999). https://doi.org/10.1007/3-540-48959-2_20

50. Paolini, L.: Call-by-value separability and computability. In: Restivo, A., Ronchi Della Rocca, S., Roversi, L. (eds.) Theoretical Computer Science, 7th Italian Conference, ICTCS 2001, Torino, Italy, October 4-6, 2001, Proceedings. Lecture Notes in Computer Science, vol. 2202, pp. 74–89. Springer (2001). https://doi.org/10.1007/3-540-45446-2_5

51. Paolini, L., Ronchi Della Rocca, S.: Call-by-value solvability. RAIRO Theor. Informatics Appl. **33**(6), 507–534 (1999). https://doi.org/10.1051/ITA:1999130

52. Plotkin, G.D.: Call-by-name, call-by-value and the lambda-calculus. Theor. Comput. Sci. **1**(2), 125–159 (1975). https://doi.org/10.1016/0304-3975(75)90017-1

53. Pottinger, G.: Normalization as a homomorphic image of cut-elimination. Annals of Mathematical Logic **12**(3), 323–357 (1977). https://doi.org/10.1016/S0003-4843(77)80004-1

54. Prawitz, D.: Natural deduction. A proof-theoretical study. Almqvist & Wiksell (1965). https://doi.org/10.2307/2271676

55. Ronchi Della Rocca, S., Paolini, L.: The Parametric Lambda Calculus - A Metamodel for Computation. Texts in Theoretical Computer Science. An EATCS Series, Springer (2004). https://doi.org/10.1007/978-3-662-10394-4

56. Sabry, A., Felleisen, M.: Reasoning about programs in continuation-passing style. In: White, J.L. (ed.) Proceedings of the Conference on Lisp and Functional Programming, LFP 1992, San Francisco, California, USA, 22-24 June 1992. pp. 288–298. ACM (1992). https://doi.org/10.1145/141471.141563

57. Scherer, G., Rémy, D.: Full reduction in the face of absurdity. In: Vitek, J. (ed.) Programming Languages and Systems - 24th European Symposium on Programming, ESOP 2015, Held as Part of the European Joint Conferences on Theory and Practice of Software, ETAPS 2015, London, UK, April 11-18, 2015. Proceedings. Lecture Notes in Computer Science, vol. 9032, pp. 685–709. Springer (2015). https://doi.org/10.1007/978-3-662-46669-8_28

58. Sørensen, M.H., Urzyczyn, P.: Lectures on the Curry-Howard isomorphism. Elsevier (2006). https://doi.org/10.5555/1197021

59. Tait, W.: Infinitely long terms of transfinite type. In: Crossley, J., Dummett, M. (eds.) Formal Systems and Recursive Functions, Studies in Logic and the Foundations of Mathematics, vol. 40, pp. 176–185. Elsevier (1965). https://doi.org/10.1016/S0049-237X(08)71689-6

60. Wadler, P.: Call-by-value is dual to call-by-name. In: Runciman, C., Shivers, O. (eds.) Proceedings of the Eighth ACM SIGPLAN International Conference on Functional Programming, ICFP 2003, Uppsala, Sweden, August 25-29, 2003. pp. 189–201. ACM (2003). https://doi.org/10.1145/944705.944723

61. Zucker, J.: The correspondence between cut-elimination and normalization. Annals of Mathematical Logic 7(1), 1–112 (1974). https://doi.org/10.1016/0003-4843(74)90010-2

Formulas as Processes,
Deadlock-Freedom as Choreographies

Matteo Acclavio[1], Giulia Manara[2,3](✉),
and Fabrizio Montesi[3]

[1] University of Sussex, Brighton, UK
[2] Université Paris Cité, Paris, France
manara@imada.sdu.dk
[3] Universitá Roma Tre, Roma, Italy
[4] University of Southern Denmark, Odense, Denmark

Abstract. We introduce a novel approach to studying properties of processes in the π-calculus based on a processes-as-formulas interpretation, by establishing a correspondence between specific sequent calculus derivations and computation trees in the reduction semantics of the recursion-free π-calculus. Our method provides a simple logical characterisation of deadlock-freedom for the recursion- and race-free fragment of the π-calculus, supporting key features such as cyclic dependencies and an independence of the name restriction and parallel operators. Based on this technique, we establish a strong completeness result for a nontrivial choreographic language: all deadlock-free and race-free finite π-calculus processes composed in parallel at the top level can be faithfully represented by a choreography.

With these results, we show how the computation-as-derivation paradigm extends the reach of logical methods for the study of concurrency, by bridging gaps between logic, the expressiveness of the π-calculus, and the expressiveness of choreographic languages.

1 Introduction

The Curry-Howard isomorphism is a remarkable example of the synergy between logic and programming languages, which establishes a *formulas-as-types* and *proofs-as-programs* (and *computation-as-reduction*) correspondences for functional programs [67,90]. In view of this success, an analogous *proofs-as-processes* correspondence has been included in the agenda of the study of concurrent programming languages [1,17]. The main idea in this research line is that, as types provide a high-level specification of the input/output data types for a function, propositions in linear logic correspond to *session types* [56] that specify the communication actions performed by processes (as in process calculi) [20]. However, while the Curry-Howard correspondence fits functional programming naturally, it does not come without issues when applied to concurrency (we discuss the details in related work, section 5). This is because functional programming deals with the 'sequential' aspect of computation (given an input, return a specific output), while most of the interesting aspects of concurrent computation are

© The Author(s) 2025
V. Vafeiadis (Ed.): ESOP 2025, LNCS 15694, pp. 23–55, 2025.
https://doi.org/10.1007/978-3-031-91118-7_2

about the communication patterns used during the computation itself. Therefore, as suggested in numerous works (e.g., [69,72,11,11,13]), the Curry-Howard correspondence may not be the right lens for the study of concurrent programs.

In this paper we investigate an alternative proof-theoretical approach to the study of processes, which is based on logical operators that faithfully model the fundamental operators of process calculi (like prefixing, parallel, and restriction). Our approach is close to the *computation-as-deduction* paradigm, where program executions are modelled as proof searches in a given sequent calculus; executions are therefore grounded in a logic by construction, as originally proposed by Miller in [69]. Specifically, we interpret formulas as processes, inference rules as rules of an operational semantics, and (possibly partial) derivations as execution trees (snapshots of computations up to a certain point).

The approach we follow is not to be confused with the intent of using logic as an auxiliary language to enunciate statements about computations, that is, viewing *computation-as-model* as done in Hennessy-Milner logic [51,54], modal μ-calculus [65], Hoare logic [52], or dynamic logics [48,10]. We are instead interested in directly reasoning on programs and their execution using the language of the programs itself. This allows for an immediate transfer of properties of proofs to properties of programs, without needing intermediate structures (e.g., models) or languages (e.g., types).

1.1   Contributions of the paper

We consider the recursion-free fragment of the π-calculus – as presented in [22,42] – and embed it in the language of the system PiL from [8]. PiL extends Girard's first order multiplicative and additive linear logic [43] with a non-commutative and non-associative sequentiality connective (◂), and nominal quantifiers (И and its dual Я) for variable scoping.

Using this embedding, we prove the following main results.

1. We show that the operational semantics of the π-calculus is captured by the linear implication ($\multimap$) in PiL: if we denote by $[[P]]$ the formula encoding the process P, then
   - if P is a process reducing to P' by performing a communication or an external choice, then $\vdash_{\mathsf{PiL}} [[P']] \multimap [[P]]$; while
   - if P may reduce to $P_{\ell_1}, \ldots, P_{\ell_n}$ by performing an internal choice, then $\vdash_{\mathsf{PiL}} \&_{i=1}^{n}([[P_{\ell_i}]]) \multimap [[P]]$.

   Crucial to prove this result is our proof that the system PiL supports a substitution principle, which allows us to simulate reductions within a context.
2. We establish a computation-as-deduction correspondence, which we use to characterise two key safety properties studied for race-free processes in terms of derivability in PiL: *deadlock-freedom*, i.e., the property that a process can always keep executing until it eventually terminates [96]; and *progress*, i.e., the property that if a process gets stuck, it is always because of a missing interaction with an action that can be provided by the environment [29].[4]

---

[4] For progress, in this paper we restrict our attention to processes that do not send restricted names.

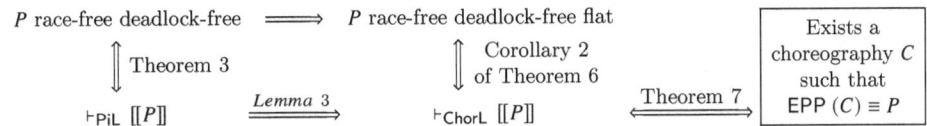

Fig. 1. Road map of the main technical results in this work.

In particular, thanks to the structure of PiL and its operators, we can successfully detect safe processes that were previously problematic in the logical setting due to cyclic dependencies, like the process in Equation (1) below.

$$(\nu x)(\nu y)\,(x!\langle a\rangle.y \triangleleft \{\ell : y!\langle b\rangle.\mathsf{Nil}\} \mid x?(a).y \triangleright \{\ell : y?(b).\mathsf{Nil}, \ell' : z!\langle c\rangle.\mathsf{Nil}\}) \qquad (1)$$

3. We show that our approach provides an adequate logical foundation for choreographic programming, a paradigm where programs are *choreographies* (coordination plans) that express the communications that a network of processes should enact [77].[5] Specifically, we establish a *choreographies-as-proofs* correspondence by using a sequent system, called ChorL, that consists of rules derivable in PiL.

Our choreographies-as-proofs correspondence has an important consequence. An open question in theory of choreographic programming [78] is about how expressive choreographies can be:

$$\textit{What are the processes that can be captured by choreographies?} \qquad (2)$$

To date, there are no answers to this question for the setting of processes with unrestricted name mobility and cyclic dependencies. Our correspondence implies a strong completeness result: in our setting, all and only race- and deadlock-free networks can be expressed as choreographies. This is the first such completeness result in the case of recursion-free networks.

1.2   Structure of the paper

In Section 2 we report PiL and prove the additional technical results required for our development. In Section 3 we recall the syntax and semantics of the π-calculus, introduce an alternative reduction semantics with the same expressiveness with respect to the property of deadlock-freedom, show that the reduction semantics of the π-calculus is captured by linear implication in PiL, and that each step of the reduction semantics of the π-calculus can be seen as blocks of rules in this system. In Section 4 we define our choreographic language and provide our completeness result for choreographies. We discuss related work in Section 5. We conclude in Section 6, where we discuss research directions opened by this work. Due to space constraints, details of certain proofs are provided in the extended version of this paper [9].

---

[5] Networks are parallel compositions of sequential processes assigned to distinct locations.

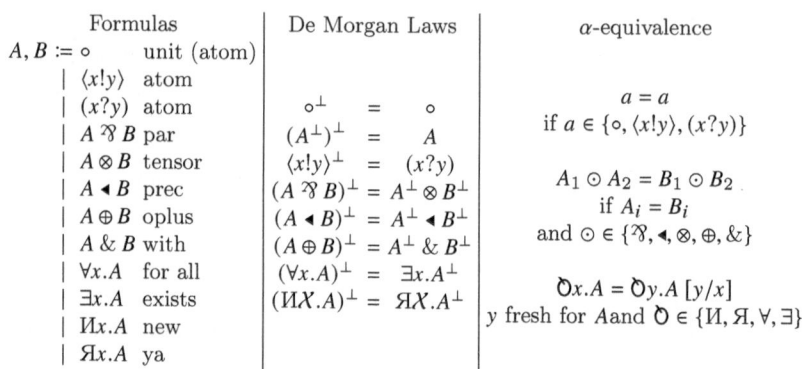

Fig. 2. Formulas (with $x, y \in \mathcal{V}$), and their syntactic equivalences.

2   Non-commutative logic

In this section we recall PiL and some of its established properties [8]. We then prove additional results required for our development.

2.1   The system PiL

The language of PiL is a first-order language containing the following.

- Atoms generated by (i) a countable set of variables $\mathcal{V}$, (ii) a binary predicate on symbols $\langle-!-\rangle$, and (iii) its dual binary predicate $(-?-)$;
- The multiplicative connectives for disjunction ($\invamp$) and conjunction ($\otimes$) and the additive connectives for disjunction ($\oplus$) and conjunction ($\&$) form *multiplicative additive linear logic* [43]. We generalize the standard binary $\oplus$ and $\&$, allowing them to have any positive arity (including 1) in order to avoid dealing with associativity and commutativity when modelling choices;
- A binary non-commutative and non-associative self-dual multiplicative connective **precede** ($\blacktriangleleft$), whose properties reflect the ones of the prefix operator used in standard process calculi (see CCS [74] and π-calculus [75,42]);
- A unit ($\circ$). We observe that its properties reflect the ones of the terminated process Nil. Notably, it is the neutral element of the connectives that we will use to represent parallelism ($\invamp$) and sequentiality ($\blacktriangleleft$), and it is derivable from no assumption (thus also neutral element of $\otimes$);
- The standard first order existential ($\exists$) and universal ($\forall$) quantifiers.
- A *nominal quantifier* **new** (И), and its dual **ya** (Я). We observe that these restrict variable scope in formulas in the same way that the ν constructor in process calculi restricts the scope of names.

More precisely, we consider *formulas* generated by grammar in Figure 2 modulo the standard *α-equivalence* from the same figure. From now on, we assume formulas and sequents to be *clean*, that is, such that each variable $x \in \mathcal{V}$ occurring in them can be bound by at most a unique universal quantifier or at

most a pair of dual nominal quantifiers, and, if bound, it cannot occur free .[6]
The *(linear) implication* $A \multimap B$ (resp. the *logical equivalence* $A \oslash B$) is
defined as $A^\perp \,\mathfrak{R}\, B$ (resp. as $(A \multimap B) \otimes (B \multimap A)$), where the *negation* $(\cdot^\perp)$ is
defined by the *de Morgan duality* in Figure 2.

The set free(A) (resp. free(Γ)) of *free variables* of a formula A (resp. of
a sequent $\Gamma = A_1, \ldots, A_n$) is the set of atoms occurring in A which are not
bound by any quantifier (resp. the set $\bigcap_{i=1}^{n}$ free(A_i)). A *context* is a formula
containing a single occurrence of a propositional variable $\bullet$ (called *hole*). We
denote by $C[A] := C[A/\bullet]$. A $И\mathfrak{R}$-*context* is a context $\mathcal{K}[\bullet]$ of the form
$\mathcal{K}[\bullet] = Иx_1 \ldots Иx_n.([\bullet] \,\mathfrak{R}\, A)$ for a $n \in \mathbb{N}$.

In this work we assume the reader to be familiar with the syntax of sequent
calculus (see, e.g., [93]), but we recall here the main definitions.

Notation 1. *A **sequent** is a set of occurrences of formulas.* [7] *A **sequent rule** r
with **premise** sequents $\Gamma_1, \ldots, \Gamma_n$ and **conclusion** Γ is an expression of the form*

$$r\frac{\Gamma_1 \quad \cdots \quad \Gamma_n}{\Gamma}$$

*. A formula occurring in the conclusion (resp. in a premise) of a
rule but in none of its premises (resp. not in its conclusion) is said **principal**
(resp. **active**). Given a set of rules X, a **derivation** in X is a non-empty tree $\mathcal{D}$
of sequents, whose root is called **conclusion**, such that every sequent occurring
in $\mathcal{D}$ is the conclusion of a rule in X, whose children are (all and only) the
premises of the rule. An **open derivation** is a derivation whose leaves may
be conclusions of no rules, in which case are called **open premises**. We may
denote a derivation (resp. an open derivation with a single open premise Δ) with*

$$\text{conclusion } \Gamma \text{ by } \mathcal{D}\overline{\big\Vert}_{\vdash \Gamma} \left(\text{resp. } \mathcal{D}\Big\Vert\begin{matrix} \vdash \Delta \\ \\ \vdash \Gamma \end{matrix} \right). \text{ Finally we may write } r\frac{\vdash \Gamma_1 \quad \cdots \quad \vdash \Gamma_n}{\vdash \Gamma} \text{ if there}$$

*is an open derivation with premises $\Gamma_1, \ldots, \Gamma_n$ and conclusion Γ made only of
rules r.*

A *nominal variable* is an element of the form x^∇ with $x \in \mathcal{X}$ and $\nabla \in \{И, Я\}$.
If S is a set of nominal variables, we say that x *occurs* in S if $x^И$ or $x^Я$ is an
element of S. A *(nominal) store* S is a set of nominal variables such that
each variable occurs at most once in S. A *judgement* $S \vdash \Gamma$ is a pair consisting
of a clean sequent Γ and a store S. We write judgements $S \vdash \Gamma$ with $S = \varnothing$
(resp. $S = \{x_1^{\nabla_1}, \ldots, x_n^{\nabla_n}\}$) simply as $\vdash \Gamma$ (resp. $x_1^{\nabla_1}, \ldots, x_n^{\nabla_n} \vdash \Gamma$, i.e. omitting
parenthesis). We write S_1, S_2 to denote the union of two stores such that a
same variable does not occur in both S_1 and S_2 – i.e., a disjoint union.

---

[6] This can be considered as a variation of *Barendregt's convention*. It allows us to
avoid variable renaming for universal and nominal quantifier rules in derivations, by
assuming the bound variable to be the eigenvariable of the quantifier or the shared
fresh name in the case of a pair of dual nominal quantifiers.

[7] In a set of occurrences of formulas, it is assumed that each formula has a unique
identifier, differently from a multiset of formulas where each formula has a multiplic-
ity. The former definition simplifies the process of tracing occurrences of formulas in
a derivation, as we need in Section 4.

$$
\mathsf{ax}\,\frac{}{S \vdash \langle x!y \rangle, (x?y)} \qquad
⅋\,\frac{S \vdash \Gamma, A, B}{S \vdash \Gamma, A \,⅋\, B} \qquad
\otimes\,\frac{S_1 \vdash \Gamma, A \quad S_2 \vdash B, \Delta}{S_1, S_2 \vdash \Gamma, A \otimes B, \Delta} \qquad
\circ\,\frac{}{S \vdash \circ} \qquad
\mathsf{mix}\,\frac{S_1 \vdash \Gamma \quad S_2 \vdash \Delta}{S_1, S_2 \vdash \Gamma, \Delta}
$$

$$
\oplus\,\frac{S \vdash \Gamma, A_k}{S \vdash \Gamma, \bigoplus_{i=1}^{n} A_i}\;\text{for a } k \in \{1,\dots,n\} \qquad
\&\,\frac{S \vdash \Gamma, A_1 \;\cdots\; S \vdash \Gamma, A_n}{S \vdash \Gamma, \&_{i=1}^{n} A_i} \qquad
\forall\,\frac{S \vdash \Gamma, A}{S \vdash \Gamma, \forall x.A}\,\dagger \qquad
\exists\,\frac{S \vdash \Gamma, A\,[y/x]}{S \vdash \Gamma, \exists x.A}
$$

$$
◀\,\frac{S_1 \vdash \Gamma, A, C \quad S_2 \vdash \Delta, B, D}{S_1, S_2 \vdash \Gamma, \Delta, A \blacktriangleleft B, C \blacktriangleleft D} \qquad
◀^{\circ}\,\frac{S_1 \vdash \Gamma, A \quad S_2 \vdash \Delta, B}{S_1, S_2 \vdash \Gamma, \Delta, A \blacktriangleleft B} \qquad
\boxed{\;\mathsf{cut}\,\frac{S_1 \vdash \Gamma, A \quad S_2 \vdash A^{\perp}, \Delta}{S_1, S_2 \vdash \Gamma, \Delta}\;}
$$

$$
И_{\circ}\,\frac{S \vdash \Gamma, A}{S \vdash \Gamma, Иx.A}\,\dagger \qquad
И_{\mathsf{load}}\,\frac{S, x^{И} \vdash \Gamma, A}{S \vdash \Gamma, Иx.A}\,\dagger \qquad
И_{\mathsf{pop}}\,\frac{S \vdash \Gamma, A\,[y/x]}{S, y^{И} \vdash \Gamma, Яx.A}
$$

$$
Я_{\circ}\,\frac{S \vdash \Gamma, A}{S \vdash \Gamma, Яx.A}\,\dagger \qquad
Я_{\mathsf{load}}\,\frac{S, x^{Я} \vdash \Gamma, A}{S \vdash \Gamma, Яx.A}\,\dagger \qquad
Я_{\mathsf{pop}}\,\frac{S \vdash \Gamma, A\,[y/x]}{S, y^{Я} \vdash \Gamma, Иx.A}
$$

Fig. 3. Sequent calculus rules, with $\dagger := x \notin \mathsf{free}(\Gamma)$.

The system PiL is defined by the all rules in Figure 3 except the rule cut. We write $\vdash_{\mathsf{PiL}} \Gamma$ to denote that the judgement $\varnothing \vdash \Gamma$ is derivable in PiL.

Remark 1. The system $\mathsf{MLL}^1 = \{\mathsf{ax}, ⅋, \otimes, \exists, \forall\}$ is the standard one for first order multiplicative linear logic [43]. The rules $\oplus$ and $\&$ are generalisations of the standard ones in additive linear logic for the n-ary generalized connectives we consider here; thus, in proof search, the rule $\oplus$ keeps only one A_k among all A_i occurring in $\bigoplus_{i=1}^{n} A_i$, and the rule $\&$ branches the proof search in n premises. The rule mix and $\circ$ are standard for multiplicative linear logic with mix in presence of units[8] [40,28], and the rule $◀^{\circ}$ ensures that the unit $\circ$ is not only the unit for the connectives $⅋$ and $\otimes$, but also for $◀$. The rule $◀$ is required to capture the self-duality of the connective $◀$; it should be read as introducing at the same time the connective $◀$ and its dual (which in this case is $◀$ itself) – as a general underlying pattern for multiplicative connectives, see [2, Remark 5].

The store is used to guarantee that each $И$ is linked to at most a unique $Я$ (or vice versa) in any branch of a derivation. If a rule $И_{\circ}$ (resp. $Я_{\circ}$) is applied, then the nominal quantifier is not linked, reason why the rule reminds the standard universal quantifier rule. Otherwise, either the rule $И_{\mathsf{load}}$ (resp. $Я_{\mathsf{load}}$) loads a nominal variable in the store, or a rule $И_{\mathsf{pop}}$ (resp. $Я_{\mathsf{pop}}$) uses a nominal variable (of dual type) occurring in the store as a witness variable. Note that in a derivation with the conclusion a judgement with empty store any $И_{\mathsf{pop}}$ (resp. $Я_{\mathsf{pop}}$) is uniquely linked to a $И_{\mathsf{load}}$ (resp. $Я_{\mathsf{load}}$) below it.

2.2   Proof Theoretical Properties of PiL

We now recall some basic proof-theoretical properties of the system PiL and then prove additional results (Theorem 2) that will be important for the main technical results in this paper.

---

[8] In presence of mix the two multiplicative units collapse.

In PiL we can prove that atomic axioms are sufficient to prove that the implication $A \multimap A$ holds for any formula A. Moreover, the cut-rule is admissible in these systems, allowing us to conclude the transitivity of the linear implication, as well as the sub-formula property for all the rules of the systems.

Theorem 1 ([8]). *Let Γ be a non-empty sequent in* PiL. *Then*

1. $\vdash_{\mathsf{PiL}} A^{\perp}, A$ *for any formula A;*
2. *if* $\vdash_{\mathsf{PiL} \cup \{\mathsf{cut}\}} \Gamma$, *then* $\vdash_{\mathsf{PiL}} \Gamma$;
3. *if* $\vdash_{\mathsf{PiL}} A \multimap B$ *and* $\vdash_{\mathsf{PiL}} B \multimap C$, *then* $\vdash_{\mathsf{PiL}} A \multimap C$.

Proposition 1 ([8]). *The following logical equivalences are derivable in* PiL *(for any σ permutation over $\{1, \ldots, n\}$).*

$$
\begin{array}{c|c}
\begin{array}{c}
(A \,\invamp\, \circ) \multimapboth A \\
(A \,\blacktriangleleft\, \circ) \multimapboth A \\
(A \,\invamp\, B) \,\invamp\, C \multimapboth A \,\invamp\, (B \,\invamp\, C) \\
A \,\invamp\, B \multimapboth B \,\invamp\, A \\
(\bigoplus_{i=1}^{n} A_i) \multimapboth (\bigoplus_{i=1}^{n} A_{\sigma(i)}) \\
(\binampersand_{i=1}^{n} A_i) \multimapboth (\binampersand_{i=1}^{n} A_{\sigma(i)})
\end{array}
&
\begin{array}{c}
(\textit{И}x.\textit{И}y.A) \multimapboth (\textit{И}y.\textit{И}x.A) \\
(\binampersand_{i=1}^{n} \textit{И}x.A_i) \multimapboth (\textit{И}x. \binampersand_{i=1}^{n} A_i) \\
(\bigoplus_{i=1}^{n} \textit{И}A_{\cdot i}) \multimapboth (\textit{И}x. \bigoplus_{i=1}^{n} A_i) \\
\hline
\textit{И}x.(A \,\invamp\, D) \multimapboth (\textit{И}x.A) \,\invamp\, D \\
\textit{И}x.D \multimapboth D \\
\textit{if } x \notin \mathsf{free}(D)
\end{array}
\end{array}
\tag{3}
$$

Moreover, $\vdash_{\mathsf{PiL}} \left(\binampersand_{i=1}^{n} (A_i \,\invamp\, B) \right) \multimap \left((\binampersand_{i=1}^{n} A_i) \,\invamp\, B \right)$.

In addition to these properties, our development requires some new ones showing that implication is preserved in different contexts. This is necessary because some rules in the operational semantics of the π-calculus enables rewriting of deeply nested subterms. For this reason, we are required to establish properties similar to those for proving *subject reduction* in λ-calculus. That is, we prove that in PiL we can still reproduce the application of inference rules inside contexts preserving soundness and completeness. These necessary properties are collected in the next theorem.

Theorem 2. *For any context $C[\bullet]$ and $\textit{И}\invamp$-context $\mathcal{K}[\bullet]$ we have:*

1. *if* $\vdash_{\mathsf{PiL}} A \multimap B$, *then* $\vdash_{\mathsf{PiL}} C[A] \multimap C[B]$;
2. *if* $\vdash_{\mathsf{PiL}} A_i \multimap B$ *for $i \in \{1, \ldots, n\}$, then* $\vdash_{\mathsf{PiL}} \binampersand_{i=1}^{n} \mathcal{K}[A_i] \multimap \mathcal{K}[B]$;
3. *if* $\vdash_{\mathsf{PiL}} A \multimap A'$ *and* $\vdash_{\mathsf{PiL}} C[A'] \multimap B$, *then* $\vdash_{\mathsf{PiL}} C[A] \multimap B$.

Proof. Item 1 and Item 2 are proven by induction on the structure of the contexts. To prove Item 3 we use Theorem 1.3 since if $\vdash_{\mathsf{PiL}} A \multimap A'$, then by 1 also $\vdash_{\mathsf{PiL}} C[A] \multimap C[A']$. Details of the proof are available in [9].

Remark 2. In the proofs-as-processes interpretation, cut is the linchpin that triggers the rewriting simulating the reduction semantics (cut elimination). In our work, as in general in the study of processes-as-formulas, the cut-rule is freed from being the keystone of the system. Instead, the admissibility of the cut-rule in the computation-as-deduction approach guarantees the existence of canonical models [71,70,53]. In particular, we use this property to tame the syntactic bureaucracy of the reduction semantics due to rules Par, Res, and Struc$^{\Rightarrow}$, as well as to ensure the transitivity of logical implication (required to compose reduction steps).

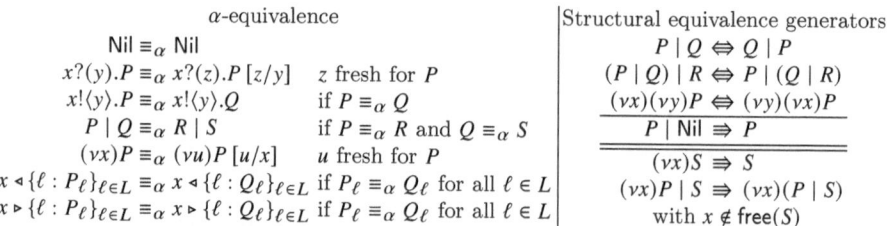

Processes		Free names	bound names
$P, Q, R := \mathsf{Nil}$	nil	$\varnothing$	$\varnothing$
$\mid x!\langle y\rangle.P$	send (y on x)	$\mathcal{F}_P \setminus \{x, y\}$	$\mathcal{B}_P$
$\mid x?(y).P$	receive (y on x)	$\mathcal{F}_P \setminus \{x\}$	$\mathcal{B}_P \cup \{y\}$
$\mid P \mid Q$	parallel	$\mathcal{F}_P \cup \mathcal{F}_Q$	$\mathcal{B}_P \cup \mathcal{B}_Q$
$\mid (vx)P$	nu	$\mathcal{F}_P \setminus \{x\}$	$\mathcal{B}_P \cup \{x\}$
$\mid x \triangleleft \{\ell : P_\ell\}_{\ell \in L}$	label send (on x)	$\bigcup_{\ell \in L} \mathcal{F}_{P_\ell}$	$\bigcup_{\ell \in L} \mathcal{B}_{P_\ell}$
$\mid x \triangleright \{\ell : P_\ell\}_{\ell \in L}$	label receive (on x)	$\bigcup_{\ell \in L} \mathcal{F}_{P_\ell}$	$\bigcup_{\ell \in L} \mathcal{B}_{P_\ell}$

Fig. 4. Syntax for π-calculus processes with $x, y \in \mathcal{N}$ and $L \subset \mathcal{L}$, and their sets of free and bound names.

α-equivalence		Structural equivalence generators
$\mathsf{Nil} \equiv_\alpha \mathsf{Nil}$		$P \mid Q \Leftrightarrow Q \mid P$
$x?(y).P \equiv_\alpha x?(z).P\,[z/y]$	z fresh for P	$(P \mid Q) \mid R \Leftrightarrow P \mid (Q \mid R)$
$x!\langle y\rangle.P \equiv_\alpha x!\langle y\rangle.Q$	if $P \equiv_\alpha Q$	$(vx)(vy)P \Leftrightarrow (vy)(vx)P$
$P \mid Q \equiv_\alpha R \mid S$	if $P \equiv_\alpha R$ and $Q \equiv_\alpha S$	$P \mid \mathsf{Nil} \Rightarrow P$
$(vx)P \equiv_\alpha (vu)P\,[u/x]$	u fresh for P	$(vx)S \Rightarrow S$
$x \triangleleft \{\ell : P_\ell\}_{\ell \in L} \equiv_\alpha x \triangleleft \{\ell : Q_\ell\}_{\ell \in L}$ if $P_\ell \equiv_\alpha Q_\ell$ for all $\ell \in L$		$(vx)P \mid S \Rightarrow (vx)(P \mid S)$
$x \triangleright \{\ell : P_\ell\}_{\ell \in L} \equiv_\alpha x \triangleright \{\ell : Q_\ell\}_{\ell \in L}$ if $P_\ell \equiv_\alpha Q_\ell$ for all $\ell \in L$		with $x \notin \mathsf{free}(S)$

Fig. 5. The standard α-equivalence, and relations generating of the structural equivalence ($\equiv$) π-calculus processes, where $A \Leftrightarrow B$ stands for $A \Rightarrow B$ and $B \Rightarrow A$.

3   Embedding the π-calculus in PiL

In this section we provide an interpretation of π-calculus processes as formulas in PiL, showing also that each successful execution of a process corresponds to a branch in a correct derivation in PiL.

We start by recalling the definition of the π-calculus and its operational semantics. Our presentation has explicit primitives for communicating choices, as usual in the literature of session types [95,96,64]. We then present an alternative semantics in which we use structural precongruence instead of structural equivalence (this is a standard simplification [33,62], which does not affect reasoning about deadlock-freedom, progress, or races). We then provide a translation of processes P into formula $[[P]]$ in PiL and characterise deadlock-freedom for P in terms of provability of $[[P]]$ in PiL.

3.1   The π-calculus and its reduction semantics

The set of π-calculus **processes** is generated by the grammar in Figure 4, which uses a fixed countable set of **(channel) names** $\mathcal{N} = \{x, y, \ldots\}$ and a finite set of **labels** $\mathcal{L}$. We may denote by $(vx_1 \ldots x_k)$ a generic sequence $(vx_1) \cdots (vx_n)$ of v-constructors of length $n > 0$, and we may simply write $x \triangleleft \{\ell : P_\ell\}$ (resp. $x \triangleright \{\ell : P_\ell\}$) as a shortcut for $x \triangleleft \{\ell : P_\ell\}_{\ell \in L}$ (resp. $x \triangleright \{\ell : P_\ell\}_{\ell \in L}$) whenever $L = \{\ell\}$. A process is **sequential** if it contains no parallel ($\mid$) or restrictions (v), it is **flat**[9] if of the form $P = (vx_1 \ldots x_k)(P_1 \mid \cdots \mid P_n)$ for some sequential processes

---

[9] Sometimes referred to as *non hierarchical* in the literature.

Com:	$x!\langle a\rangle.P \mid x?(b).Q \rightarrow P \mid Q\,[a/b]$	Res : $(vx)P \rightarrow (vx)P'$ if $P \rightarrow P'$
Choice:	$x \triangleleft \{\ell : P_\ell\}_{\ell \in L} \rightarrow x \triangleleft \{\ell_k : P_{\ell_k}\}$ if $\ell_k \in L$	Par : $P \mid Q \rightarrow P' \mid Q$ if $P \rightarrow P'$
Label: $x \triangleleft \{\ell_k : P_{\ell_k}\} \mid x \triangleright \{\ell : Q_\ell\}_{\ell \in L} \rightarrow P_{\ell_k} \mid Q_{\ell_k}$	if $\ell_k \in L$	

$$\text{Struc}: \quad P \rightarrow Q \quad \text{if} \quad P \equiv P' \rightarrow Q' \equiv Q$$

Fig. 6. Reduction semantics for the π-calculus.

$P_1, \ldots, P_n$ (also called sequential components of P). We use the common notation $P\,[x/y]$ for substitution (see the Appendix of [9]).

The set $\mathcal{F}_P$ of *free names* and the set $\mathcal{B}_P$ of **bound names** in a process P are defined in Figure 4. The set of **names** in P is denoted $\mathcal{N}_P$ and a name x is **fresh** in P if $x \notin \mathcal{N}_P$. A **context** is a process $\mathcal{P}[\bullet]$ containing a single occurrence of a special free name $\bullet$ called **hole** such that $\mathcal{P}[P] := \mathcal{P}\,[P/\bullet]$ is a process. A **network context** is a context of the form $\mathcal{N}[\bullet] = (vx_1 \ldots x_k)\,([\bullet] \mid P_1 \mid \cdots \mid P_n)$.

The **α-equivalence** ($\equiv_\alpha$) is recalled in Figure 5. To improve the presentation of the technical results, we assume processes written in an **unambiguous** form, that is, in such a way each bound variable $x \in \mathcal{B}_P$ is bound by a unique v-constructor and do not occur free in P. In the same figure we provide the relation $\Rightarrow$, whose reflexive and transitive closure is denoted $\Rrightarrow$, and we define the standard *(structural) equivalence* ($\equiv$) as the equivalence relation generated by the union of $\Rightarrow$ and $\equiv_\alpha$.

The **reduction semantics** for processes is defined by the relation $\rightarrow$ over processes induced by the rules in Figure 6. As standard, we denote by $\twoheadrightarrow$ the reflexive and transitive closure of $\rightarrow$. As in [22], to allow for nondeterminism, the syntax of processes contains a construct $x \triangleleft \{\ell : P_\ell\}_{\ell \in L}$ allowing for different options rather than the typical $x \triangleleft \{P : \ell\}$. Thus, the corresponding rule Choice for choosing among the available options induces a branching in the computation tree of the process. We say that a process P is **stuck** if $P \not\equiv$ Nil and there is no P' such that $P \rightarrow P'$. A process P is called **deadlock-free** if there is no stuck process P' such that $P \twoheadrightarrow P'$. Also, a process P has **progress**[10] if it is deadlock-free or $P \mid Q$ is deadlock-free for a stuck process Q.

Remark 3. Intuitively, deadlock-freedom means that there is always a part of a process that can reduce [62,78]. Progress for processes, instead, was introduced in [29] to characterise processes that get stuck merely because they lack a communicating partner that could be provided by the environment.

For example, the process $P = (vx)(x!\langle a\rangle.\text{Nil} \mid x?(b).\text{Nil} \mid y!\langle c\rangle.\text{Nil})$ is not deadlock-free because it reduces (via Com) to the stuck process $(vx)(\text{Nil} \mid y!\langle c\rangle.\text{Nil}) \equiv y?(d).\text{Nil}$, but this later has progress since $y!\langle d\rangle.\text{Nil} \mid y?(d).\text{Nil}$ is deadlock-free.

A process P has a **race condition** if there is a network context $\mathcal{N}[\bullet]$ such that P is structurally equivalent to a term of the following shape.

$$\mathcal{N}[x!\langle y\rangle.R \mid x!\langle z\rangle.Q] \qquad\qquad \mathcal{N}[x?(y).R \mid x?(z).Q]$$
$$\mathcal{N}[x \triangleleft \{\ell : P_\ell\}_{\ell \in L} \mid x \triangleleft \{\ell : P_\ell\}_{\ell \in L'}] \qquad \mathcal{N}[x \triangleright \{\ell : P_\ell\}_{\ell \in L} \mid x \triangleright \{\ell : P_\ell\}_{\ell \in L'}]$$

---

[10] See Section 1.1 for the precise intended meaning of the term *progress* in this paper.

A process P is **race-free** if there is no P' with a race condition such that $P \twoheadrightarrow P'$.

Remark 4. Race conditions identify in a syntactic way the semantic property of a process *potentially* having nondeterministic executions because of concurrent actions on a same channel. For example, $P = x!\langle a \rangle.\mathsf{Nil} \mid x?(b).\mathsf{Nil} \mid x?(c).\mathsf{Nil}$ has a race condition, and it can reduce either to $P_b = x?(b).\mathsf{Nil}$ or to $P_c = x?(c).\mathsf{Nil}$ according to the way the reduction rule Com is applied. We specify 'potentially' because, for example, the process $Q = (vx)\,(x?(b).\mathsf{Nil} \mid x?(c).\mathsf{Nil})$ has a race but cannot reduce. In fact, in the execution of a race-free process, rules Com and Label are applied deterministically. That is, the same send (resp. selection) is synchronised via a Com (resp. a Label) with the same receive (resp. branching), and vice versa, in any possible (branch of an) execution.

3.2 A Simpler Equivalent Presentation of the Reduction Semantics

To simplify the presentation of the new methodologies we use in our new framework, we replace the structural equivalence $\equiv$ with the *precongruence* $\Rrightarrow$ (as in [62,33]). In particular, such a precongruence orients the direction of scope extrusion (by extending the scope of the binder as much as possible), but also rules out those rewritings that may add superfluous information such as $P \Rrightarrow (P \mid \mathsf{Nil})$ or $P \Rrightarrow ((vx)P)$ for a $x \notin \mathcal{N}_P$. Thus in the reduction semantics we consider in this paper we employ the following rule instead of the standard Struc (see Figure 6):

$$\mathsf{Struc}^{\Rrightarrow} : P \to Q \quad \text{if} \quad \begin{array}{cccc} P \Rrightarrow P' &=& \mathcal{P}[S] \to \mathcal{P}[S'] &= Q \\ \text{with } P \neq P' \text{ and} && S \to S' & \text{not via } \mathsf{Struc}^{\Rrightarrow} \end{array} \qquad (4)$$

Remark 5. The reduction semantics using the rule $\mathsf{Struc}^{\Rrightarrow}$ instead of Struc is weaker because the set of processes reachable via a step of $\mathsf{Struc}^{\Rrightarrow}$ is strictly contained in the set of processes reachable via Struc. By means of example, consider the process $x!\langle y \rangle.\mathsf{Nil} \mid x?(z).\mathsf{Nil}$ which reduces to both $\mathsf{Nil} \mid \mathsf{Nil}$ and Nil using Struc, but can only reduce to $\mathsf{Nil} \mid \mathsf{Nil}$ using $\mathsf{Struc}^{\Rrightarrow}$.

However, it is immediate to show that if $P \to P'$ via Struc, then there is a $Q \equiv P'$ such that $P \to Q$ via $\mathsf{Struc}^{\Rrightarrow}$. Therefore, the standard reduction semantics (containing the rule Struc) is as informative as the one we consider here (where we use the rule $\mathsf{Struc}^{\Rrightarrow}$ instead) for the study of deadlock-freedom and for the definition of the race condition.

In the definition of the rules of the reduction semantics, the rules Com, Choice and Label are, in some sense, performing 'meaningful' transformation on processes, while rules Res, Par and $\mathsf{Struc}^{\Rrightarrow}$ deal with the syntactic bureaucracy of rewriting modulo the structural equivalence. In the proofs in the next sections we need to be able to identify in each reduction step $P \to P'$ the sub-process $\mathsf{rdx}_{(P,P')}$ of P (called *core-redex*) which is irreversibly transformed to the process $\mathsf{rdt}_{(P,P')}$ (called *core-reductum*), as well as to measure the amount of syntactical manipulations we need to 'reach' such a sub-process to apply a reduction step (which we call *entropy*). We make these concepts precise in the next definitions and exemplify them in Figure 7.

S	S'	$\mathrm{rdx}_{(S,S')}$	$\mathrm{rdt}_{(S,S')}$	$\mathrm{Ent}_{(S,S')}$
$(x!\langle a\rangle.P \mid x?(y).Q) \mid R$	$(P \mid Q\,[a/y]) \mid R$	$x!\langle a\rangle.P \mid x?(y).Q$	$P \mid Q\,[a/y]$	2
$(va)\,(b!\langle a\rangle.P)) \mid b?(c).R$	$(va)\,(P \mid R\,[a/c])$	$b!\langle a\rangle.P \mid b?(c).R$	$b!\langle a\rangle.P \mid b?(c).R$	6

Fig. 7. Examples of processes S and S' such that $S \to S'$, and the core-redex, core-reductum, and entropy of the rewriting step.

Definition 1. *Let P and P' processes such that $P \to P'$. The **core** $\mathrm{Core}_{(P,P')} = (\mathrm{rdx}_{(P,P')}, \mathrm{rdt}_{(P,P')})$ and the **entropy** $\mathrm{Ent}_{(P,P')} \in \mathbb{N}$ of $P \to P'$ are defined as:*

- *if $P \to P'$ via Com, Label or Choice, then $\mathrm{Ent}_{(P,P')} = 1$ and $\mathrm{Core}_{(P,P')} = (P,P')$;*
- *if $P \to P'$ via Par (resp. Res), then there are processes Q and Q' such that $Q \to Q'$ and a context $\mathcal{P}[\bullet]$ of the form $\bullet \mid R$ (resp. of the form $(vx)(\bullet)$) such that $P = \mathcal{P}[Q]$ and $P' = [Q']$ by definition of the reduction step. Then $\mathrm{Ent}_{(P,P')} = 2\mathrm{Ent}_{(Q,Q')}$ and $\mathrm{Core}_{(P,P')} = \mathrm{Core}_{(Q,Q')}$;*
- *if $P \to P'$ via $\mathrm{Struc}^{\Rightarrow}$, then there are processes Q and Q' such that $P \Rightarrow Q \to Q' \Rightarrow P'$ with $P \Rightarrow Q$ and $Q' \Rightarrow P'$. Then $\mathrm{Ent}_{(P,P')} = 3\mathrm{Ent}_{(Q,Q')}$ and $\mathrm{Core}_{(P,P')} = \mathrm{Core}_{(Q,Q')}$.*

*The **core-reduction** of $P \to P'$ is the rule used to reduce $\mathrm{rdx}_{(P,P')}$ to $\mathrm{rdt}_{(P,P')}$.*

Definition 2. *A **execution tree** of a process P is a tree of processes $\mathrm{Ctree}(P)$ with root P, such that a process Q' is a child of Q if $Q \to Q'$, and such that:*

- *if the core-reduction of $Q \to Q'$ is a Com or a Label, then Q' is the unique child of Q;*
- *if the core-reduction of $Q \to Q'$ is a Choice, then the set $\{Q_1,\ldots,Q_n\} \ni Q'$ of children of Q is such that the core-reduction of $Q \to Q_i$ is a Choice and $\mathrm{rdx}_{(Q,Q_i)} = \mathrm{rdx}_{(Q,Q')}$ for all $i \in \{1,\ldots,n\}$.*

*It is **maximal** if each leaf of the tree is a process $R \equiv \mathrm{Nil}$ or is stuck.*

We conclude this subsection with this result, which, together with Remark 5, allows us to consider each maximal execution tree as a witness of deadlock-freedom for race-free processes.

Lemma 1. *Let P be a process. If P is deadlock-free, then each execution tree with root P can be extended to a maximal execution tree whose leaves are processes structurally equivalent to Nil.*

3.3   Translating Processes into Formulas

We define a translation of π-calculus processes into PiL formulas.

Definition 3 (Processes as Formulas). *We associate to each π-calculus process P a formula $[[P]]$ inductively defined as follows.*

$$[[\mathrm{Nil}]] = \circ \qquad [[P \mid Q]] = [[P]] \,\mathbin{\mathfrak{N}}\, [[Q]] \qquad [[(vx)(P)]] = \text{И}x.\,[[P]]$$

$$[[\bullet]] = \bullet \qquad [[x!\langle y\rangle.P]] = \langle x!y\rangle \blacktriangleleft [[P]] \qquad [[x?(y).P]] = \exists y.((x?y) \blacktriangleleft [[P]])$$

$$[[x \blacktriangleleft \{\ell : P_\ell\}_{\ell \in L}]] = \underset{\ell \in L}{\&}\,((x!\ell) \blacktriangleleft [[P_\ell]]) \qquad [[x \blacktriangleright \{\ell : P_\ell\}_{\ell \in L}]] = \bigoplus_{\ell \in L}\,((x?\ell) \blacktriangleleft [[P_\ell]]) \qquad (5)$$

Note that assuming P unambiguous, the translation is a clean formula.

Remark 6. The reader familiar with session types could be curious about the choice of representing by a &-formula a process of the form $x \triangleleft \{\ell : P_\ell\}_{\ell \in L}$ (whose session type is a $\oplus$-type) and, dually, by a $\oplus$-formula a process $x \triangleright \{\ell : P_\ell\}_{\ell \in L}$ (whose session type is a &-type). This is only an apparent contradiction because *our formulas are not types*. Rather, they encode processes whose executions are then derivations in the PiL system. Under this new interpretation, during proof search the rule for & gives exactly the expected branching of possible executions of terms like $x \triangleleft \{\ell : P_\ell\}_{\ell \in L}$, corresponding to rule Choice in the reduction semantics. Rule Label can then be applied 'afterwards' (above in the derivation) to select the appropriate branch at the receiver, discarding all the others. Thus, in the formulas-as-processes, receiving a label corresponds to $\oplus$.

For the same reason, parallel composition is represented by $\bindnasrepma$ (as in [71,14]), while in most works using propositions as session types it is represented by cut and $\otimes$. We will come back to this aspect in Section 5.

Proposition 2. *Let P_1 and P_2 processes. If $P_1 \Rightarrow P_2$ then $[[P_2]] \multimap [[P_1]]$.*

Proof. $[[P \mid Q]] \circ\!\!-\!\!\circ [[Q \mid P]]$ and $[[(P \mid Q) \mid R]] \circ\!\!-\!\!\circ [[P \mid (Q \mid R)]]$ derive from commutativity and associativity of $\bindnasrepma$ (see Proposition 1). The logical equivalences $[[P \mid \mathsf{Nil}]] \circ\!\!-\!\!\circ [[P]]$ and $[[(\nu x)\mathsf{Nil}]] \circ\!\!-\!\!\circ [[\mathsf{Nil}]]$ are direct consequence of the ones in Figure 2. The implication $[[(\nu x)(P \mid Q)]] \multimap [[(\nu x)P \mid Q]]$ for $x \notin \mathsf{free}(Q)$ is shown in Proposition 1. Finally, $[[(\nu x)(\nu y)P]] \circ\!\!-\!\!\circ [[(\nu y)(\nu x)P]]$ derives from the quantifier shifts Иx.Иy.$P =$ Иy.Иx.P (Figure 2).

3.4 Deadlock-Freedom as Provability in PiL

We can now establish a correspondence between process reductions and linear implication in PiL, as well as a correspondence between each computation tree with root a process P and a proof search strategy in PiL for the formula $[[P]]$. Combining these two results, we obtain a purely logical characterisation of deadlock-free processes as pre-images via $[[\cdot]]$ of formulas derivable in PiL.

Lemma 2. *Let P and P' processes.*

1. *If $P \Rrightarrow P'$, then $[[P']] \multimap [[P]]$.*
2. *If $P \to P'$, then either*
   (a) *the core-reduction of $P \to P'$ is a Com or a Label, and $\vdash_{\mathsf{PiL}} [[P']] \multimap [[P]]$;*
   (b) *or the core-reduction of $P \to P'$ is a Choice then there is a set $\{P_\ell \mid \ell \in L\} \ni P'$ such that $P \to P_\ell$ for all $\ell \in L$ and $\vdash_{\mathsf{PiL}} (\&_{\ell \in L} [[P_\ell]]) \multimap [[P]]$.*

Proof. Item 1 is proven using Proposition 1 and transitivity of $\multimap$ (see Theorem 1.3). To prove Item 2 we reason by induction on entropy:

– if $\mathsf{Ent}_{(P,P')} = 1$ then $P \to P'$ via Com, Label or Choice and we conclude using the derivations in Figure 8;

$$
\begin{array}{c}
\text{ax}\dfrac{}{\vdash \langle x!y\rangle, (x?y)} \quad
\otimes\dfrac{\vdash [\![P]\!]^{\perp}, [\![P]\!] \quad \vdash [\![Q]\!]^{\perp}[y/z], [\![Q]\!][y/z]}{\vdash [\![P]\!]^{\perp} \otimes ([\![Q]\!]^{\perp}[y/z]), [\![P]\!], [\![Q]\!][y/z]}
\\[4pt]
\blacktriangleleft\dfrac{\vdash ([\![P]\!]^{\perp} \otimes ([\![Q]\!]^{\perp}[y/z])), \langle x!y\rangle \blacktriangleleft [\![P]\!], (x?y) \blacktriangleleft ([\![Q]\!][y/z])}{}
\\[4pt]
\exists\dfrac{\vdash ([\![P]\!]^{\perp} \otimes ([\![Q]\!]^{\perp}[y/z])), \langle x!y\rangle \blacktriangleleft [\![P]\!], \exists z.((x?z) \blacktriangleleft [\![Q]\!])}{}
\\[4pt]
\mathfrak{N}\dfrac{\vdash ([\![P]\!]^{\perp} \otimes [\![Q]\!]^{\perp}[y/z]) \,\mathfrak{N}\, (\langle x!y\rangle \blacktriangleleft [\![P]\!] \,\mathfrak{N}\, \exists z.((x?z) \blacktriangleleft [\![Q]\!]))}{}
\end{array}
$$

$$
\begin{array}{c}
\left\{
\begin{array}{c}
\text{ax}\dfrac{}{\vdash \langle x!\ell\rangle, (x?\ell)} \quad \vdash [\![P_\ell]\!]^{\perp}, [\![P_\ell]\!]
\\[4pt]
\blacktriangleleft\dfrac{\vdash (x?\ell) \blacktriangleleft [\![P_\ell]\!]^{\perp}, \langle x!\ell\rangle \blacktriangleleft [\![P_\ell]\!]}{}
\\[4pt]
\oplus\dfrac{\vdash \bigoplus_{\ell\in L} ((x?\ell) \blacktriangleleft [\![P_\ell]\!]^{\perp}), \langle x!\ell\rangle \blacktriangleleft [\![P_\ell]\!]}{}
\end{array}
\right\}_{\ell\in L}
\\[4pt]
\&\dfrac{\vdash \bigoplus_{\ell\in L} ((x?\ell) \blacktriangleleft [\![P_\ell]\!]^{\perp}), \underset{\ell\in L}{\&} (\langle x!\ell\rangle \blacktriangleleft [\![P_\ell]\!])}{}
\\[4pt]
\mathfrak{N}\dfrac{\vdash \bigoplus_{\ell\in L} ((x?\ell) \blacktriangleleft [\![P_\ell]\!]^{\perp}) \,\mathfrak{N}\, \underset{\ell\in L}{\&} (\langle x!\ell\rangle \blacktriangleleft [\![P_\ell]\!])}{}
\end{array}
$$

$$
\begin{array}{c}
\text{ax}\dfrac{}{\vdash \langle x!\ell_k\rangle, (x?\ell_k)} \quad
\otimes\dfrac{\vdash [\![Q_{\ell_k}]\!]^{\perp}, [\![Q_{\ell_k}]\!] \quad \vdash [\![R_{\ell_k}]\!], [\![R_{\ell_k}]\!]^{\perp}}{\vdash \left([\![Q_{\ell_k}]\!]^{\perp} \otimes [\![R_{\ell_k}]\!]\right), [\![Q_{\ell_k}]\!], [\![R_{\ell_k}]\!]^{\perp}}
\\[4pt]
\blacktriangleleft\dfrac{\vdash \left([\![Q_{\ell_k}]\!]^{\perp} \otimes [\![R_{\ell_k}]\!]^{\perp}\right), \langle x!\ell_k\rangle \blacktriangleleft [\![Q_{\ell_k}]\!], (x?\ell_k) \blacktriangleleft [\![R_{\ell_k}]\!]}{}
\\[4pt]
\oplus\dfrac{\vdash \left([\![Q_{\ell_k}]\!]^{\perp} \otimes [\![R_{\ell_k}]\!]^{\perp}\right), \langle x!\ell_k\rangle \blacktriangleleft [\![Q_{\ell_k}]\!], \bigoplus_{\ell\in L} ((x?\ell) \blacktriangleleft [\![R_\ell]\!])}{}
\\[4pt]
\mathfrak{N}\dfrac{\vdash \left([\![Q_{\ell_k}]\!]^{\perp} \otimes [\![R_{\ell_k}]\!]^{\perp}\right) \,\mathfrak{N}\, \left(\langle x!\ell_k\rangle \blacktriangleleft [\![Q_{\ell_k}]\!] \,\mathfrak{N}\, \bigoplus_{\ell\in L} ((x?\ell) \blacktriangleleft [\![R_\ell]\!])\right)}{}
\end{array}
$$

Fig. 8. Derivations in PiL corresponding to the rules Com, Choice and Label of the reduction semantics of the π-calculus.

- if $P \to P'$ via Par (resp. Res), then there is a context $\mathcal{P}[\bullet] = (\bullet \mid R)$ (resp. $\mathcal{P}[\bullet] = (vx)\bullet$) such that $P = \mathcal{P}[S]$ and $P' = \mathcal{P}[S']$. We conclude using Theorem 2.1 and Theorem 1.3;
- if $P \to P'$ via Struc$^{\Rightarrow}$, then there is S such that $P \Rrightarrow S$ and $S \to P'$ (via a rule different from Struc$^{\Rightarrow}$). We conclude by Theorem 1.3 using Item 1 and Theorem 22.

Using this lemma we can prove the correspondence between deadlock-freedom and derivability in PiL.

Theorem 3. *Let P be a race-free process. Then P is deadlock-free iff $\vdash_{\mathsf{PiL}} [\![P]\!]$. More precisely, $\vdash_{\{\circ,\mathrm{ax},\mathfrak{N},\mathrm{mix},\blacktriangleleft,\&,\oplus,\exists,\mathit{И}^{\circ}\}} [\![P]\!]$.*

Proof. It suffices to establish a correspondence between maximal execution trees and derivations in PiL. Details are provided in the appendix of [9].

($\Rightarrow$) If P is deadlock-free, then, any maximal execution tree Ctree(P) with root P has leaves which are processes structurally equivalent to Nil by Lemma 1. By induction on the structure of Ctree(P), we can define a derivation in PiL∪{cut} composing (using cut) the derivations allowing simulating the transitions of the reduction semantics (Lemma 2); thus we obtain a derivation in PiL by applying cut-elimination (Theorem 1.2). We conclude observing that the subformula property ensures that only rules in such cut-free derivation are in $\{\circ, \mathrm{ax}, \mathfrak{N}, \mathrm{mix}, \blacktriangleleft, \&, \oplus, \exists, \mathit{И}^{\circ}\}$. Note that all judgements in such a derivation are empty.

($\Leftarrow$) To prove the converse, we show that each derivation $\mathcal{D}_P$ of $[\![P]\!]$ can be transformed using the *rule permutations* in Figure 9 into a derivation $\widetilde{\mathcal{D}_P}$ made of blocks of rules consisting of sequences of $\mathit{И}$- and $\mathfrak{N}$-rules only, or blocks as the

$$r_1^1 \frac{r_2^1 \frac{\vdash \Gamma', \Delta'}{\vdash \Gamma', \Delta}}{\vdash \Gamma, \Delta} \sim r_2^1 \frac{r_1^1 \frac{\vdash \Gamma', \Delta'}{\vdash \Gamma, \Delta'}}{\vdash \Gamma, \Delta} \qquad r_2^1 \frac{r_1^1 \frac{\vdash \Gamma', \Sigma'}{\vdash \Gamma', \Sigma} \quad \vdash \Sigma', \Delta}{\vdash \Gamma, \Sigma, \Delta} \sim r^1 \frac{\vdash \Gamma', \Sigma' \quad \vdash \Sigma', \Delta}{\vdash \Gamma, \Sigma, \Delta} \qquad \& \frac{\left\{ r^1 \frac{\vdash \Gamma', A}{\vdash \Gamma, A} \right\}_{i \in I}}{\vdash \Gamma, \&_{i \in I} A_i} \sim r^1 \frac{\& \frac{\{ \vdash \Gamma', A_i \}_{i \in I}}{\vdash \Gamma', \&_{i \in I} A_i}}{\vdash \Gamma, \&_{i \in I} A_i}$$

$$r_1^2 \frac{r_2^2 \frac{\vdash \Gamma', \Sigma' \quad \vdash \Gamma', \Delta}{\vdash \Gamma, \Delta, \Sigma'} \quad \vdash \Sigma'}{\vdash \Gamma, \Delta, \Sigma} \sim r_2^2 \frac{r_1^2 \frac{\vdash \Gamma', \Sigma' \quad \vdash \Sigma'}{\vdash \Gamma', \Sigma} \quad \vdash \Gamma', \Delta}{\vdash \Gamma, \Delta, \Sigma} \qquad r^2 \frac{\& \frac{\{ \vdash \Gamma, \Delta_1, A_i \}_{i \in I}}{\vdash \Gamma, \Delta_1, \&_{i \in I} A_i} \quad \vdash \Delta_2}{\vdash \Gamma, \Delta, \&_{i \in I} A_i} \sim \& \frac{\left\{ r^2 \frac{\vdash \Gamma, \Delta_1, A_i \quad \vdash \Delta_2}{\vdash \Gamma, \Delta, \&_{i \in I} A_i} \right\}_{i \in I}}{\vdash \Gamma, \Delta, \&_{i \in I} A_i}$$

Fig. 9. Rule permutations with $r^1, r_1^1, r_2^1 \in \{ \mathfrak{N}, \exists, \oplus, \mathit{И}_\circ \}$ and $r^2, r_1^2, r_2^2 \in \{ \blacktriangleleft, \otimes, \mathrm{mix} \}$.

ones shown in Equation (6) below.

$$\exists \frac{\blacktriangleleft \frac{\mathrm{ax} \frac{}{\vdash \langle x!y \rangle, (x?y)} \quad \vdash A, B \, [y/z], \Gamma}{\vdash \langle x!y \rangle \blacktriangleleft A, (x?y) \blacktriangleleft B \, [y/z], \Gamma}}{\vdash \langle x!y \rangle \blacktriangleleft A, \exists z. ((x?z) \blacktriangleleft B), \Gamma} \qquad \& \frac{\left\{ \oplus \frac{\blacktriangleleft \frac{\mathrm{ax} \frac{}{\vdash \langle x!\ell \rangle, (x?\ell)} \quad \vdash [\![Q_\ell]\!], [\![R_\ell]\!], \Gamma}{\vdash (x?\ell) \blacktriangleleft [\![Q_\ell]\!], \langle x!\ell \rangle \blacktriangleleft [\![R_\ell]\!], \Gamma}}{\vdash \bigoplus_{\ell \in L_1} ((x?\ell) \blacktriangleleft [\![Q_\ell]\!]), \langle x!\ell \rangle \blacktriangleleft [\![R_\ell]\!], \Gamma} \right\}_{\ell \in L_1}}{\vdash \bigoplus_{\ell \in L_1} ((x?\ell) \blacktriangleleft [\![Q_\ell]\!]), \underset{\ell \in L_2}{\&} (\langle x!\ell \rangle \blacktriangleleft [\![R_\ell]\!]), \Gamma} \tag{6}$$

We conclude by induction on the number of such blocks, since each block in the left (resp. right) of Equation (6) identifies an application of a Com (resp. a Bra followed by a Sel).

Note that since P is race-free, then it suffices to reason on a single execution tree and not to take into account all possible execution trees of P.

Corollary 1. *Let P be a race-free process. Then P has progress iff there is a $\mathit{И}\mathfrak{N}$-context $C[\bullet]$ such that $\vdash_{\mathsf{PiL}} C[P]$.*

We conclude this section by showing that progress for processes which never send 'private' channels can be easily captured in this new setting. Specifically, we say that a process P has **private mobility** if it is of the form $P = \mathcal{P}[a! \langle x \rangle]$ for an a bound by a ν in $\mathcal{P}$. We also denote by $\partial_{x_1, \dots, x_k} [\![P]\!]$ the formula obtained by replacing with a unit ($\circ$) any atom in $[\![P]\!]$ of the form $\langle x!y \rangle$ or $(x?y)$ for any $x \in \{ x_1, \dots, x_k \}$.

Theorem 4. *Let P be a race-free process without private mobility. Then P has progress iff $\vdash_{\mathsf{PiL}} \partial_{\mathcal{F}_P} [\![P]\!]$.*

Proof. We prove a simulation result (as Lemma 2) for $\partial_{\mathcal{F}_P} [\![P]\!]$, and we conclude with the same argument used in the proof of Theorem 3. It P is deadlock-free, then we conclude as in Theorem 3. Otherwise, since P has progress there is Q such that $P \mid Q$ is deadlock-free. By definition, we must have that $N_Q = \mathcal{F}_Q$ (otherwise either Q is not stuck or $P \mid Q$ is not deadlock-free) and that $\mathcal{F}_Q = \mathcal{F}_P = x_1, \dots, x_k$. Thus $\partial_{x_1, \dots, x_k} [\![P \mid Q]\!] \circ\!\!-\!\!\circ \partial_{x_1, \dots, x_k} [\![P]\!]$ by the fact that $\partial_{x_1, \dots, x_k} [\![Q]\!]$ contains no atoms (i.e., only units) and $\circ \blacktriangleleft A \circ\!\!-\!\!\circ A \circ\!\!-\!\!\circ \circ \mathfrak{N} A$ (see Proposition 1).

- If $P \mid Q$ is deadlock-free for Q stuck and $P \mid Q \to R$ via Par then, $R = P' \mid Q$ and $P \to P'$. If the core-reduction of $P \twoheadrightarrow P'$ is a Com or a Label, then

$\vdash_{\mathsf{PiL}} \partial_{x_1,...,x_k} \llbracket P' \rrbracket \multimap \partial_{x_1,...,x_k} \llbracket P \rrbracket$; if the core-reduction is a Choice, there is a set of processes $\{P_\ell\}_{\ell \in L} \ni P'$ such that $\vdash_{\mathsf{PiL}} (\&_{\ell \in L} \partial_{x_1,...,x_k} \llbracket P_\ell \rrbracket) \multimap \partial_{x_1,...,x_k} \llbracket P \rrbracket$. This is proven by induction on the entropy as in Lemma 2.

- If $P' \mid Q \to P'$ not via Par and then the core-reduction is either a Com or a Sel. In this case can prove as that $\vdash_{\mathsf{PiL}} \partial_{x_1,...,x_k} \llbracket P' \rrbracket \multimap \partial_{x_1,...,x_k} \llbracket P' \rrbracket$ because $\partial_{x_1,...,x_k} \llbracket P' \rrbracket \circ\!\!\!-\circ \partial_{x_1,...,x_k} \llbracket P' \mid Q \rrbracket \circ\!\!\!-\circ \partial_{x_1,...,x_k} \llbracket P' \rrbracket$.

Remark 7. To understand the requirement on private mobility in Theorem 4, consider the process $P = (\nu a)(b!\langle a \rangle.a!\langle c \rangle.\mathsf{Nil})$. This process has progress, because

$$(P \mid b?(x).x?(c).\mathsf{Nil}) \equiv (\nu a)(b!\langle a \rangle.a!\langle c \rangle.\mathsf{Nil} \mid b?(x).x?(c).\mathsf{Nil}) \twoheadrightarrow \mathsf{Nil} .$$

However, $\partial_{\{b\}} \llbracket P \rrbracket = \Pi a.(\circ \blacktriangleleft \langle a!c \rangle \blacktriangleleft \circ)$ is not derivable in PiL. This makes our characterisation of progress as powerful as in previous work [22] (where the condition is not made explicit but clearly necessary, see the definition of 'co-process' therein).

4   Completeness of Choreographies

In this section we prove that any deadlock-free flat process can be expressed as a choreography, as intended in the paradigm of choreographic programming [77]. Key to this result is establishing a *proofs-as-choreographies* correspondence, whereby choreographies can be seen as derivations in the PiL system.

To this end, we first introduce the syntax and semantics of *choreographies*, the typical accompanying language for describing their implementations in terms of located processes (the *endpoint calculus*), and a notion of endpoint projection (EPP) from choreographies to processes. We then define the sequent calculus ChorL operating on sequents in which (occurrences of) formulas are labelled by process names, and we conclude by establishing the proofs-as-choreographies correspondence.

4.1   Choreographies

In a choreographic language, terms (called *choreographies*) are coordination plans that express the overall behaviour of a network of processes [78]. The **choreographies** that we consider in this paper are generated by a set of **process names** $\mathcal{P}$, a set of variables $\mathcal{V}$, and a set of **selection labels** $\mathcal{L}$ as shown in Figure 10. A choreography can be either:

- **0**, the terminated choreography;
- $\mathsf{p}.x \to \mathsf{q}.y : k; C$, a communication from a process p to another q with a continuation C (y is bound in C and can appear only under q);
- $\mathsf{p}.L \to \mathsf{q}.L' : k \begin{cases} \ell : C_\ell \mid \ell \in L \\ \ell : S_\ell \mid \ell \in L' \setminus L \end{cases}$, a choice by a process p of a particular branch L offered by another process q[11]; or

---

[11] The set L' of labels the process q can accept contains the set L of labels p can send. For the continuation of labels in $L' \setminus L$ we only allow sequential processes because

Choreographies

$$C, C_\ell ::= \mathbf{0} \mid \underbrace{\mathsf{p}.x \to \mathsf{q}.y : k; C}_{\text{communication}} \mid \underbrace{\mathsf{p}.L \to \mathsf{q}.L' : k \left\{ \begin{matrix} \ell : C_\ell \mid \ell \in L \\ \ell : S_\ell \mid \ell \in L' \setminus L \end{matrix} \right\}}_{\text{choice}} \mid \underbrace{(\nu x) C^x \text{ (with } C^x \text{ containing no } (\nu x))}_{\text{restriction}}$$

$\underbrace{}_{\text{end}}$

Reduction semantics for Choreographies			
Com	:	$\mathsf{p}.x \to \mathsf{q}.y : k; C \xrightarrow{\mathsf{p}\to\mathsf{q}:k} C[x/y]$	
Choice	:	$\mathsf{p}.L \to \mathsf{q}.L' : k \left\{ \begin{matrix} \ell : C_\ell \mid \ell \in L \\ \ell : S_\ell \mid \ell \in L' \setminus L \end{matrix} \right\} \xrightarrow{\mathsf{p}:k} \mathsf{p}.\{\ell_i\} \to \mathsf{q}.L' : k \left\{ \begin{matrix} \ell : C_\ell \mid \ell \in L \\ \ell : S_\ell \mid \ell \in L' \setminus L \end{matrix} \right\}$ for a $\ell_i \in L$
Label	: $\mathsf{p}.\{\ell_i\} \to \mathsf{q}.L' : k \left\{ \begin{matrix} \ell : C_\ell \mid \ell \in L \\ \ell : S_\ell \mid \ell \in L' \setminus L \end{matrix} \right\} \xrightarrow{\mathsf{p}\to\mathsf{q}:k} C_{\ell_i}$	if $\ell_i \in L'$	
Rest	:	$(\nu x) C \xrightarrow{\mu} (\nu x) C'$	if $C \xrightarrow{\mu} C'$
D-Com	:	$\mathsf{p}.x \to \mathsf{q}.y : k; C \xrightarrow{\mu'} \mathsf{p}.x \to \mathsf{q}.y : k; C'$	if $C \xrightarrow{\mu'} C'$
D-Choice	:	$\mathsf{p}.L \to \mathsf{q}.L' : k \left\{ \begin{matrix} \ell : C_\ell \mid \ell \in L \\ \ell : S_\ell \mid \ell \in L' \setminus L \end{matrix} \right\} \xrightarrow{\mu'} \mathsf{p}.L \to \mathsf{q}.L' : k \left\{ \begin{matrix} \ell : C'_\ell \mid \ell \in L \\ \ell : S_\ell \mid \ell \in L' \setminus L \end{matrix} \right\}$	if $C_\ell \xrightarrow{\mu'} C'_\ell$ for all $\ell \in L$

with $\mathsf{pn}(\mu') \cap \{\mathsf{p}, \mathsf{q}, k\} = \varnothing$

Fig. 10. Syntax and semantics for choreographies, where p and q are distinct process names in $\mathcal{P}$, $x, y \in \mathcal{V}$, $L \subseteq L' \subseteq \mathcal{L}$, and S_ℓ are sequential processes (see Remark 8).

- $(\nu x) C^x$, which restricts x in a choreography C^x in which the variable x always occur free (i.e., no (νx) occurs in C^x).[12]

Note that we consider communication of process names or variables only (that is, $k \in \mathcal{P} \cup \mathcal{V}$). We say that a choreography is *flat* if it is of the form $(\nu x_1 \ldots x_k) C^{\mathrm{rf}}$ for a *restriction-free* (i.e., containing no occurrences of ν) choreography C^{rf}. In the same figure we also provide the *reduction semantics* of our choreographic language, where each reduction step is labelled by a *reduction label* μ from the following set.

$$\{\mathsf{p} \to \mathsf{q} : k , \ \mathsf{p} : k \mid \mathsf{p}, \mathsf{q} \in \mathcal{P}, \ k \in \mathcal{V}\} \tag{7}$$

To each reduction label μ we associate the set $\mathsf{pn}(\mu)$ of processes names and variables occurring in it – i.e. $\mathsf{pn}(\mathsf{p} \to \mathsf{q} : k) = \{\mathsf{p}, \mathsf{q}, k\}$ and $\mathsf{pn}(\mathsf{p} : k) = \{\mathsf{p}, k\}$.

In the semantics, Com executes a communication while Choice allows a process p to make an internal choice. Rule Label then communicates a label from p to q, which then continue with the choreography C_ℓ (but never with a sequential process S_ℓ, see Remark 8). Rule Rest lifts reductions under restrictions. Lastly, D-Com (resp. D-Choice) models the standard out-of-order execution of independent communications that can be reduced by rule Com (resp. both rules Choice and Label) – this is the choreographic equivalent of parallel composition in process calculi [78].

---

we do not allow nested parallel in the target language of the projection (see next subsection).

[12] By allowing the construct (νx) only in the case in which x is not bound in C^x, we ensure that choreographies are always written using *Barendregt's convention*. This means that each variable x can be bound by at most one restriction ν, and x cannot appear both free and bound in a choreography C. As a result, we can adopt a lighter labelling discipline for the reduction semantics compared to the one used in [25] – see the rule Rest in Figure 10.

Structural Equivalence

$\mathsf{p} :: \mathsf{Nil} \mid P \equiv P$ and $(\nu x_1) \cdots (\nu x_k) \prod_{i=1}^{n} \mathsf{p}_i :: S_i \equiv (\nu x_{\tau(1)}) \cdot (\nu x_{\tau(k)}) \prod_{i=1}^{n} \mathsf{p}_{\sigma(i)} :: S_{\sigma(i)}$

for any σ permutation over $\{1, \ldots, n\}$ and τ over $\{1, \ldots, k\}$

Reduction Semantics

E-Com : $\mathcal{N}[\mathsf{p} :: k!\langle x \rangle.S \mid \mathsf{q} :: k?(y).S'] \xrightarrow{\mathsf{p} \to \mathsf{q}:k} \mathcal{N}[\mathsf{p} :: S \mid \mathsf{q} :: S'[x/y]]$

E-Choice : $\mathcal{N}\left[\mathsf{p} :: k \triangleleft \{\ell : S_\ell\}_{\ell \in L}\right] \xrightarrow{\mathsf{p}:k} \mathcal{N}\left[\mathsf{p} :: k \triangleleft \{\ell_i : S_{\ell_i}\}\right]$ for each $\ell_i \in L$

E-Label : $\mathcal{N}\left[\mathsf{p} :: k \triangleleft \{\ell_i : S_{\ell_i}\} \mid \mathsf{q} :: k \triangleright \left\{\ell : S'_\ell\right\}_{\ell \in L}\right] \xrightarrow{\mathsf{p} \to \mathsf{q}:k} \mathcal{N}\left[\mathsf{p} :: S_{\ell_i} \mid \mathsf{q} :: S'_{\ell_i}\right]$ if $\ell_i \in L$

Fig. 11. Simplified presentation of the structural equivalence and reduction semantics for the endpoint calculus, where $\mathcal{N}[P] \equiv (\nu x_1 \ldots x_k) \left(P \mid \prod_{i=1}^{n} \mathsf{p}_i :: T_i\right)$.

Example 1. The next choreography expresses the communication behaviour of the processes given in Equation (1).

$$\mathsf{p}.a \to \mathsf{q}.a : x; \mathsf{p}.\{\ell\} \to \mathsf{q}.\{\ell, \ell'\} : y \begin{cases} \ell : \mathsf{p}.b \to \mathsf{q}.b : y; \mathbf{0} \\ \ell' : z!\langle c \rangle.\mathsf{Nil} \end{cases} \tag{8}$$

It can be executed by applying rule Com and then rule Label. Note that we do not need to use rule Choice before applying Label, because the set of labels L in the choice constructor is a singleton.

Remark 8. From the programmer's viewpoint, choice instructions may contain some unnecessary information since no label $\ell' \in L' \setminus L$ will never be selected during the execution of a choreography – and thus no continuation will execute the process $S_{\ell'}$. This 'garbage' code is typical of works on choreographies and logic [26,21], and we share the same motivation: we want to be able to capture the entire flat fragment of the π-calculus, where such garbage code cannot be prohibited. For example, without garbage code, the choreography in Equation (8) would not be a complete representation of the endpoint process in Equation (10) (see also Equation (1)).

4.2 Endpoint Projection

Our choreographies can be mechanically translated into processes via the standard technique of endpoint projection (EPP) [78]. To simplify the presentation of projection, we adopt the standard convention of enriching the language of processes with process names labelling each sequential component of a flat process [50,78]. That is, a flat process of the form $(\nu x_1 \ldots x_k) (S_1 \mid \cdots \mid S_n)$ is represented by an **endpoint process**

$$(\nu x_1 \ldots x_k) (\mathsf{p}_1 :: S_1 \mid \cdots \mid \mathsf{p}_n :: S_n) \quad \text{or} \quad (\nu x_1 \ldots x_k) \left(\prod_{i=1}^{n} \mathsf{p}_i :: S_i\right) \tag{9}$$

where all names $\mathsf{p}_1, \ldots, \mathsf{p}_n$ are distinct.[13] The process calculus over these processes is dubbed **endpoint calculus.**

---

[13] In the literature, a process P with name p is usually written $\mathsf{p}[P]$ [50,78]. We adopt the alternative writing $\mathsf{p} :: P$ to avoid confusion with the notation used for contexts.

The definition of **endpoint projection** is provided by the partial function EPP in Figure 12 (it is defined only for flat choreographies, as in [25]). It is a straightforward adaptation to our syntax of the textbook presentation of projection [78]. In particular, it uses a **merge** operator ⊔ (originally from [23]) to support propagation of knowledge about choices. That is, if a process r needs to behave differently in two branches of a choice communicated from p to q, it can do so by receiving different labels in these two branches. Merge then produces a term for r that behaves as prescribed by the first (respectively the second) branch when it receives the first (respectively the second) label. If EPP (C) is defined for C we say that C is **projectable**.

Example 2. The EPP of the choreography in Equation (8) is

$$(vx)(vy)\,(\mathsf{p} :: x!\langle a \rangle.y \triangleleft \{\ell : y!\langle b \rangle.\mathsf{Nil}\} \mid \mathsf{q} :: x?(a).y \triangleright \{\ell : y?(b).\mathsf{Nil}, \ell' : z!\langle c \rangle.\mathsf{Nil}\}) \quad (10)$$

which is precisely the one in Equation (1) annotated with process names.

Structural equivalence and reduction semantics for the endpoint calculus are obtained by the one of the π-calculus assuming that each structural equivalence ($\equiv$) and reduction step ($\rightarrow$) preserves the process names. Note that, for the purpose of studying deadlock-freedom, structural equivalence and reduction rules can be simplified as shown in Figure 11. Each reduction step is labelled by the same labels used in the reduction semantics of choreographies (see Equation (7)), allowing us to retain the information about which sequential components and channel are involved in each reduction step.

Notation 2. *If P and Q are endpoint processes, we write $P \sqsupseteq Q$ iff $P \sqcup Q = P$.*

Theorem 5. *Let C be a projectable flat choreography.*

- **Completeness:** *if $C \xrightarrow{\mu} C'$, then EPP $(C) \xrightarrow{\mu} P \sqsupseteq$ EPP (C');*
- **Soundness:** *if $P \sqsupseteq$ EPP (C) and $P \xrightarrow{\mu} P'$, then there is a choreography C' such that $C \xrightarrow{\mu} C'$ and $P' \sqsupseteq$ EPP (C').*

Proof. The proof is obtained by adapting the proof provided in, e.g., [77,78,79] to the language we consider in this paper. Details can be found in [4]. ∎

4.3 A Sequent Calculus for the Endpoint Calculus

To establish the correspondence between proofs of (formulas encoding) endpoint processes and choreographies, we enrich the syntax of formulas by adding labels (on sub-formulas) carrying the same information of the process names used in the syntax of the endpoint calculus. More precisely, we consider a translation $[\![\cdot]\!]^N$ from endpoint processes to **annotated formulas** of the form $(A)_\mathsf{p}$.

Definition 4. *For any endpoint process $P = (vx_1 \ldots x_k)\,(\prod_{i=1}^n \mathsf{p}_i :: S_i)$ we define the formula $[\![P]\!]^N = \mathcal{V}x_1.\ldots.\mathcal{V}x_n.([\![S_1]\!])_{\mathsf{p}_1} \,\mathcal{V} \cdots \mathcal{V} ([\![S_n]\!])_{\mathsf{p}_n}$, and the sequent $\lfloor\!\lfloor P \rfloor\!\rfloor = ([\![S_1]\!])_{\mathsf{p}_1}, \ldots, ([\![S_n]\!])_{\mathsf{p}_n}$.*

$$EPP\ (C) = \begin{cases} (vx_1 \ldots x_k)EPP\left(C^{rf}\right) & \text{if } C = (vx_1 \ldots x_k)C^{rf} \text{ with } C^{rf} \text{ restriction-free} \\ p_0 :: Nil & \text{if } C = 0 \text{ (for a given } p_0) \\ EPP_{p_1}(C) \mid \cdots \mid EPP_{p_n}(C) & \text{otherwise, with } p_1, \ldots, p_n \text{ all process names in } C \end{cases}$$

$$EPP_{p_i}(0) = Nil \qquad EPP_{p_i}(S) = \begin{cases} EPP_{p_i}(S) & \text{if } S \text{ is a choreography} \\ EPP_{p_i}(p_i :: S_i) & \text{if } S = \prod_{i=1}^n p_i :: S_i \text{ is a process} \end{cases}$$

$$EPP_{p_i}(p.x \rightarrow q.y : k; C) = \begin{cases} k!\langle x \rangle.EPP_{p_i}(C) & \text{if } p_i = p \\ k?(y).EPP_{p_i}(C) & \text{if } p_i = q \\ EPP_{p_i}(C) & \text{if } p_i \notin \{p, q\} \end{cases}$$

$$EPP_{p_i}\left(p.L \rightarrow q.L' : k \left\{ \begin{matrix} \ell : C_\ell \mid \ell \in L \\ \ell : S_\ell \mid \ell \in L' \setminus L \end{matrix} \right\} \right) = \begin{cases} k \triangleleft \{\ell : EPP_{p_i}(C_\ell)\}_{\ell \in L} & \text{if } p_i = p \\ k \triangleright \left\{ \begin{matrix} \ell : EPP_{p_i}(C_\ell) \mid \ell \in L \\ \ell : S_\ell \mid \ell \in L' \setminus L \end{matrix} \right\} & \text{if } p_i = q \\ \bigsqcup_{\ell \in L} EPP_{p_i}(C_\ell) & \text{if } p_i \notin \{p, q\} \end{cases}$$

$$\left((vx_1 \ldots x_k)\left(\prod_{i=1}^n p_i :: S_i\right)\right) \sqcup \left((vx_1 \ldots x_k)\left(\prod_{i=1}^n p_i :: T_i\right)\right) = (vx_1 \ldots x_k)\left(\prod_{i=1}^n p_i :: S_i \sqcup T_i\right)$$

$$Nil \sqcup Nil = Nil \qquad (x!\langle y \rangle.T) \sqcup (x!\langle y \rangle.S) = x!\langle y \rangle.T \sqcup S \qquad (x?(y).T) \sqcup (x?(y).S) = x?(y).T \sqcup S$$

$$\left(x \triangleright \{\ell : P_\ell\}_{\ell \in L}\right) \sqcup \left(x \triangleright \{\ell : Q_\ell\}_{\ell \in L'}\right) = x \triangleright \left(\{\ell : P_\ell \sqcup Q_\ell\}_{\ell \in L \cap L'} \cup \{\ell : P_\ell\}_{\ell \in L \setminus L'} \cup \{\ell : Q_\ell\}_{\ell \in L' \setminus L}\right)$$

$$\text{only if } L = L' : \left(x \triangleleft \{\ell : P_\ell\}_{\ell \in L}\right) \sqcup \left(x \triangleleft \{\ell : Q_\ell\}_{\ell \in L'}\right) = x \triangleleft \{\ell : P_\ell \sqcup Q_\ell\}_{\ell \in L}$$

Fig. 12. Endpoint Projection for flat choreographies, and the merge operator ($\sqcup$).

Note that because of the subformula property[14] of rules in PiL, such labelling can be propagated in a derivation by labelling each active formula of a rule (which is a sub-formula of one of the principal formulas of the rule) with the same process name of the corresponding active formula.

Example 3. Consider the following derivation in PiL with conclusion the formula $[[p :: x!\langle y \rangle.Nil \mid q :: x?(y).Nil]]^N$:

$$\begin{array}{c} \text{ax} \dfrac{}{\vdash ((\langle x!y \rangle))_p, ((x?y))_q} \quad \text{mix} \dfrac{\overset{\circ}{\vdash (\circ)_p} \quad \overset{\circ}{\vdash (\circ)_q}}{\vdash (\circ)_p, (\circ)_q} \\ \exists \dfrac{\vdash ((\langle x!y \rangle \triangleleft \circ)_p, ((x?y) \triangleleft \circ)_q}{\vdash ((\langle x!y \rangle \triangleleft \circ)_p, (\exists x.((x?y) \triangleleft \circ))_q} \\ \mathrel{\Im} \dfrac{}{\vdash ((\langle x!y \rangle \triangleleft \circ)_p \mathrel{\Im} (\exists x.((x?y) \triangleleft \circ))_q} \end{array} \tag{11}$$

We now introduce a sequent calculus for the endpoint calculus, given in Figure 13, which consists purely of rules that are derivable in PiL. That is, for every rule r in ChorL there is an open derivation in PiL with the same open premises and conclusion as r.

---

[14] Assuming an initial α-renaming on P such that P is unambiguous, and such each variable bound by a receive action is the same as the unique (because of race-freedom) variable sent by the matching send action. For example, we would write $x!\langle a \rangle \mid x?(a)$ instead of $x!\langle a \rangle \mid x?(b)$.

$$\textit{C-flat}\ \frac{\vdash (\llbracket T_1 \rrbracket)_{\mathsf{p}_1}, \ldots, (\llbracket T_n \rrbracket)_{\mathsf{p}_n}}{\vdash \text{И}x_1.\ldots\text{И}x_m.\left((\llbracket T_1 \rrbracket)_{\mathsf{p}_1} \parr \cdots \parr (\llbracket T_n \rrbracket)_{\mathsf{p}_n}\right)}\ m \in \mathbb{N} \qquad \textit{C-Com}\ \frac{\vdash \Gamma, (\llbracket T \rrbracket)_{\mathsf{p}}, (\llbracket T' \rrbracket [y/z])_{\mathsf{q}}}{\vdash \Gamma, (\llbracket x!\langle y\rangle.T \rrbracket)_{\mathsf{p}}, (\llbracket x?(z).T' \rrbracket)_{\mathsf{q}}}$$

$$\textit{C-Init}\ \frac{}{\vdash (\circ)_{\mathsf{p}_1}, \ldots, (\circ)_{\mathsf{p}_n}} \qquad \textit{C-Sel}\ \frac{\left\{\vdash \Gamma, (\llbracket T_\ell \rrbracket)_{\mathsf{p}}, \left(\left\llbracket T'_\ell \right\rrbracket\right)_{\mathsf{q}}\right\}_{\ell \in L}}{\vdash \Gamma, (\llbracket k \triangleleft \{\ell : T_\ell\}_{\ell \in L} \rrbracket)_{\mathsf{p}}, \left(\left\llbracket k \triangleright \{\ell : T'_\ell\}_{\ell \in L'} \right\rrbracket\right)_{\mathsf{q}}}\ L \subseteq L'$$

Fig. 13. Sequent calculus rules for the system ChorL.

C-Init	$\mathcal{D}_n = \mathsf{mix}\dfrac{\dfrac{}{\vdash (\circ)_{\mathsf{p}_1}} \quad \cdots \quad \dfrac{}{\vdash (\circ)_{\mathsf{p}_n}}}{\vdash (\circ)_{\mathsf{p}_1}, \ldots, (\circ)_{\mathsf{p}_n}}$
C-Com	$\mathcal{D}_{\langle \mathsf{p},x,\mathsf{q},y,k\rangle} = \exists\dfrac{\blacktriangleleft\dfrac{\mathsf{ax}\dfrac{}{\vdash (\langle k!x\rangle)_{\mathsf{p}}, ((k?x))_{\mathsf{q}}} \qquad \vdash \Gamma, (\llbracket S \rrbracket)_{\mathsf{p}}, (\llbracket S' \rrbracket [x/y])_{\mathsf{q}}}{\vdash \Gamma, (\langle k!x\rangle \blacktriangleleft \llbracket S \rrbracket)_{\mathsf{p}}, ((k?x) \blacktriangleleft (\llbracket S' \rrbracket [x/y]))_{\mathsf{q}}}}{\vdash \Gamma, (\langle k!x\rangle \blacktriangleleft \llbracket S \rrbracket)_{\mathsf{p}}, (\exists y.((k?y) \blacktriangleleft \llbracket S' \rrbracket))_{\mathsf{q}}}$
C-Sel	$\mathcal{D}_{\langle \mathsf{p},L,\mathsf{q},L',k\rangle} = \&\dfrac{\left\{\blacktriangleleft\dfrac{\mathsf{ax}\dfrac{}{\vdash (\langle k!\ell\rangle)_{\mathsf{p}}, ((k?\ell))_{\mathsf{q}}} \quad \vdash (\llbracket S_\ell \rrbracket)_{\mathsf{p}}, \left(\left\llbracket S'_\ell \right\rrbracket\right)_{\mathsf{q}}}{\vdash \Gamma, (\langle k!\ell\rangle \blacktriangleleft \llbracket S_\ell \rrbracket)_{\mathsf{p}}, \left((k?\ell) \blacktriangleleft \left\llbracket S'_\ell \right\rrbracket\right)_{\mathsf{q}}}\right\}_{\ell \in L}}{\vdash \Gamma, \left(\underset{\ell \in L}{\&} (\langle k!\ell\rangle \blacktriangleleft \llbracket S_\ell \rrbracket)\right)_{\mathsf{p}}, \left(\bigoplus_{\ell \in L'} \left((k?\ell) \blacktriangleleft \left\llbracket S'_\ell \right\rrbracket\right)\right)_{\mathsf{q}}}$
C-flat	$\mathcal{D}_{\varnothing} = \parr\dfrac{\vdash \llbracket S_1 \rrbracket, \ldots, \llbracket S_n \rrbracket}{\vdash \llbracket S_1 \rrbracket \parr \ldots \parr \llbracket S_n \rrbracket}$ or $\mathcal{D}_{\langle x_1,\ldots,x_m\rangle} = \text{И}\dfrac{\parr\dfrac{\vdash \llbracket S_1 \rrbracket, \ldots, \llbracket S_n \rrbracket}{\vdash \llbracket S_1 \rrbracket \parr \ldots \parr \llbracket S_n \rrbracket}}{\vdash \text{И}x_1.\ldots\text{И}x_m.(\llbracket S_1 \rrbracket \parr \ldots \parr \llbracket S_n \rrbracket)}$

Fig. 14. Derivability (in PiL) of the rules in ChorL.

Lemma 3. *Each rule in* ChorL *is derivable in* PiL.
Moreover, if the premise (resp. conclusion) of a rule in ChorL *is of the form* $\llbracket P \rrbracket^{\mathcal{N}}$, *then its conclusion is so (resp. all its premise are so).*

Proof. Derivations with the same premise(s) and conclusion of a rule in ChorL are shown in Figure 14. The second part of the statement follows by rule inspection.

We can refine Theorem 3 for race-free flat processes thanks to the fact that in endpoint processes parallel and restrictions can only occur at the top level. This allows us to consider derivations in PiL made of blocks of rule applications as those in Figure 14, each corresponding to a single instance of a rule in ChorL.

Theorem 6. *A race-free endpoint process* P *is deadlock-free iff* $\vdash_{\mathsf{ChorL}} \llbracket P \rrbracket^{\mathcal{N}}$.

Proof. If $P = (\nu x_1 \ldots x_k)\left(\prod_{i=1}^{n} \mathsf{p}_i :: S_i\right)$ is deadlock-free, then by Theorem 3 there is a derivation $\widetilde{\mathcal{D}}$ in PiL with conclusion $\llbracket P \rrbracket^{\mathcal{N}}$. Using rule permutations, we can transform $\widetilde{\mathcal{D}}$ into a derivation made (bottom-up) of possibly some И-rules followed by $\parr$-rules (i.e., an open derivation of the same shape of $\mathcal{D}_{\langle x_1,\ldots,x_k\rangle}$ or $\mathcal{D}_{\varnothing}$

$$\mathsf{Chor}\left(\textit{C-Init}\,\dfrac{}{\vdash (o)_{p_1},\dots,(o)_{p_n}}\right) = 0 \qquad \mathsf{Chor}\left(\textit{C-flat}\,\dfrac{\mathcal{D}'[\![}{\vdash [\![P]\!]}{\vdash [\![P]\!]^N}\right) = \begin{cases} (\nu x_1\dots x_k)\mathsf{Chor}\!\left(\dfrac{\mathcal{D}'[\![}{\vdash [\![P]\!]}\right) & \text{if } k > 0 \\[2ex] \mathsf{Chor}\!\left(\dfrac{\mathcal{D}'[\![}{\vdash [\![P]\!]}\right) & \text{if } k = 0 \end{cases}$$

$$\mathsf{Chor}\left(\textit{C-Com}\,\dfrac{\mathcal{D}'[\![}{\vdash \Gamma,\big([\![T]\!]^N\big)_p,\big([\![S]\!]^N\,[x/y]\big)_q}{\vdash \Gamma,\big(\langle k!x\rangle\blacktriangleleft[\![T]\!]^N\big)_p,\big(\exists y.\big((k?y)\blacktriangleleft[\![S]\!]^N\big)\big)_q}\right) = p.x \to q.y : k; \mathsf{Chor}\left(\dfrac{\mathcal{D}'[\![}{\vdash \Gamma\big([\![T]\!]^N\big)_p,\big([\![S]\!]^N\,[x/y]\big)_q}\right)$$

$$\mathsf{Chor}\left(\textit{C-Sel}\,\dfrac{\Big\{\vdash \Gamma,\big([\![T_\ell]\!]^N\big)_p,\big([\![T_\ell']\!]^N\big)_q\Big\}_{\ell\in L}}{\vdash \Gamma,\big(\underset{\ell\in L}{\&}\big(\langle k!\ell\rangle\blacktriangleleft[\![T_\ell]\!]^N\big)\big)_p,\big(\underset{\ell\in L'}{\oplus}\big((k?\ell)\blacktriangleleft[\![T_\ell']\!]^N\big)\big)_q}\right) = p.L \to q.L' : k \begin{cases} \ell : \mathsf{Chor}\!\left(\vdash \Gamma,\big([\![T_\ell]\!]^N\big)_p,\big([\![T_\ell']\!]^N\big)_q\right) & \ell \in L \\[1.5ex] \ell : T_\ell' & \ell \in L'\setminus L \end{cases}$$

Fig. 15. Interpretation of a derivation in ChorL as a choreography.

from Figure 14), followed by a derivation $\mathcal{D}$ of the sequent $[\![P_1]\!]^N,\dots,[\![P_n]\!]^N$ which is organized in blocks of rules as open derivations in Figure 14. Note that derivations of the form $\mathcal{D}_{\langle p,x,q,y,k\rangle}$ (resp. $\mathcal{D}_{\langle p,L,q,L',k\rangle}$) correspond to the open derivations in Equation (6). Thus we can replace $\mathcal{D}_{\langle x_1,\dots,x_k\rangle}$ or $\mathcal{D}_\varnothing$ by a C-flat, each $\mathcal{D}_{\langle p,x,q,y,k\rangle}$ (resp. $\mathcal{D}_{\langle p,L,q,L',k\rangle}$) by a C-Com (resp. by a C-Sel), and each $\mathcal{D}_n$ with a C-Init, obtaining the desired derivation in ChorL.

The converse is a consequence of Lemma 3 and Theorem 3.

4.4 Proofs as Choreographies

We can now prove a completeness result of choreographies with respect to the set of deadlock-free flat processes: each deadlock-free flat process is the EPP of a (flat) choreography. To prove this result, we rely on Theorem 6 to establish a direct correspondence between derivations of a sequent encoding a race-free endpoint process in the sequent system ChorL, and execution trees of the same endpoint process. An example the process of choreography extraction from a derivation in ChorL of a deadlock-free endpoint process can be found in the Appendix of [9].

Theorem 7. *Let P be a race-free endpoint process. Then*

$$P \text{ is deadlock-free} \iff \text{there is a choreography } C \text{ such that } \mathsf{EPP}\,(C) = P.$$

Proof. If P is deadlock-free, then by Theorem 6 there is a derivation in ChorL with conclusion $[\![P]\!]^N$. We define the choreography $\mathsf{Chor}(\mathcal{D})$ by case analysis on the bottom-most rule r in $\mathcal{D}$ as shown in Figure 15. We conclude by showing that $\mathsf{EPP}\,(\mathsf{Chor}(\mathcal{D})) = P$ by induction on the structure of $\mathcal{D}$ reasoning on the bottom-most rule r in $\mathcal{D}$. The rigth-to-left implication follows by Theorem 5.

Remark 9. Note that the statement could be made stronger by requiring the choreography C to be flat. In this case, the proof of the right-to-left implication can be proven directly using the inverse of the translation in Figure 15.

	Independent ν and |	Cyclic dependencies	ν-free interaction	Choreography expressivity	Proof System
Caires & Pfenning [20]	✗	✗	✗	N/A	iLL
Wadler [96]	✗	✗	✗	N/A	LL
Dardha & Gay [35]	✓	✓	✗	N/A	LL + mix + ordering
Kokke & Montesi & Peressotti [64]	✓	✗	✓	N/A	LL + hyperenvironments
Carbone & Montesi & Schürmann [26]]	✗	✗	✗	✓	LL
This paper	✓	✓	✓	✓	PiL

Fig. 16. Summary of key results in the literature. We describe each column in order: the term constructors for restriction and parallel are separate (independent) in the syntax of processes; cyclic dependencies are allowed; processes can interact (communicate) on a free name (the name does not need to be restricted in the context); choreographies are proven complete for a class of processes (N/A means that this was not considered).

Since every flat process in the π-calculus can be decorated with process names, we can easily extend the completeness result to the π-calculus. We need to pay attention to the difference that $P \Rrightarrow \mathsf{EPP}\,(C)$ (instead of $P = \mathsf{EPP}\,(C)$) because of the definition of $\mathsf{EPP}\,(\mathbf{0})$. For example, the choreography that captures Nil | Nil is $\mathbf{0}$, and Nil | Nil $\Rrightarrow \mathsf{EPP}\,(\mathbf{0}) = $ Nil.

Corollary 2. *Every race-free and deadlock-free flat process P admits a choreography C such that $P \Rrightarrow \mathsf{EPP}\,(C)$.*

An important consequence of our results is that the processes that can be captured by choreographies can have cyclic dependencies, as we exemplified with Equations (1) and (8). This significantly extends the proven expressivity of choreographic languages with name mobility, which so far have been shown to capture only the acyclic processes typable with linear logic [26,21].

5   Related Work

We now report on relevant related work. A summarising table of the differences between our work and others based on logic is given in Figure 16.

Proofs as Processes: Linear Logic and Session Types. The proofs-as-processes agenda investigates how linear logic [43] can be used to reason about the behaviour of concurrent processes [1,17]. It has inspired a number of works that aim at preventing safety issues, like processes performing incompatible actions in erroneous attempts to interact (e.g., sending a message with the wrong type). Notable examples include *session types* [55,56] and linear types for the π-calculus [63]. The former can actually be encoded into the latter – a formal reminder of their joint source of inspiration [36].

A more recent line of research formally interprets propositions and proofs in linear logic as, respectively, session types and processes [20,96]. This proofs-as-processes correspondence based on linear logic works for race-free processes, as we consider here. However, it also presents some limitations compared to our framework. Parallel composition and restriction are not offered as independent operators, because of a misalignment with the structures given by the standard rules of linear logic. For example, the cut rule in linear logic handles both parallel composition and hiding, yielding a 'fused' restriction-parallel operator $(vx)(- \mid -)$. Also, the $\otimes$ rule for typing output has two premises, yielding another fused output-parallel operator $x!(y).(- \mid -)$ – note that only bound names can be sent, as in the internal π-calculus [87]. In particular, interaction between processes does not arise simply from parallel composition as in the standard π-calculus, but rather requires both parallel composition and restricting all names on which communication can take place (so communication is always an internal action). This syntactic and semantic gap prevents linear logic from typing safe cyclic dependencies among processes, as in this simplification of Equation (1):

$$(vx)(vy) (x!\langle a\rangle.y?(b).\mathsf{Nil} \mid x?(a).y!\langle b\rangle.\mathsf{Nil}) \tag{12}$$

The same gap prevents having communication on unrestricted channels (as in $x!\langle a\rangle.\mathsf{Nil} \mid x?(a).\mathsf{Nil}$) and having a private channel used by more than two processes. Using $\mathfrak{R}$ and $\otimes$ to type input and output is also in tension with the associativity and commutativity isomorphisms that come with these connectives. These isomorphisms yield unexpected equivalences at the process level, like $x?(a).y?(b).\mathsf{Nil} \equiv y?(b).x?(a).\mathsf{Nil}$.

These shortcomings are not present in our approach, thanks to the use of:

1. The connective $\blacktriangleleft$ for prefixing. The latter then has the expected 'rigid' non-commutative and non-associative semantics.
2. The connective $\mathfrak{R}$ for parallelism. The latter then has the expected equivalences supported by the isomorphisms for $\mathfrak{R}$.
3. Nominal quantifiers, which allow for restricting names without imposing artificial constraints on the structure of processes.

While it is not the first time that these limitations are pointed out, our method is the first logical approach that overcomes them without ad-hoc machinery. Previous works have introduced additional structures to linear logic, like hyperenvironments or indexed families of connectives, in order to address some of these issues [35,92,83,64,24,27]. These additional structures are not necessary to our approach.

Choreographic Programming. Choreographic programming was introduced in [77] as a paradigm for simplifying concurrent and distributed programming. Crucial to the success of this paradigm is building choreographic programming languages that are expressive enough to capture as many safe concurrent behaviours as possible [78]. However, most of the work conducted so far on the study of such expressivity is driven by applications, and a systematic understanding of the classes of processes that can be captured in choreographies is still relatively green.

In [31,61] the authors present methods for *choreography extraction* – inferring from a network of processes an equivalent choreography – for an asynchronous process calculus, respectively without and with process spawning. Another purely algorithmic extraction procedure is provided in [66], for simple choreographies without data – global types, which are roughly the choreographic equivalent of session types. In linear logic, extracting global types from session types can be achieved via derivable rules [24].

The only previous completeness result for the expressivity of choreographic programming is given in [26,21], where it is shown that choreographies can capture the behaviours of all well-typed processes in linear logic. Our work extends the completeness of choreographies to processes that, notably, can (i) have cyclic dependencies (like Equation (12)), (ii) perform communication over free channels, (iii) respect the sequentiality of prefixing. Moreover, and similarly to our previous discussion for proofs-as-processes, extraction in [26,21] requires additional structures (hypersequents and modalities to represent connections) that are not necessary in our method.

Non-Commutative Logic and Nominal Quantifiers. Guglielmi proposed in [45,46] an extension of multiplicative linear logic with a non-commutative operator modelling the interaction of parallel and sequential operators. This led to the design of the *calculus of structures* [47], a formalism for proofs where inference rules can be applied at any depth inside a formula rather than at the top-level connective, and the logic BV including the (associative) non-commutative self-dual connective ◁ to model sequentiality. In [19] Bruscoli has established a computation-as-deduction correspondence between specific derivations in BV and executions in a simple fragment of CCS. This correspondence has been extended in the works of Horne, Tiu et al. to include the choice operator (+) of Milner's CCS (modelled via the additive connective ⊕), as well as the restriction to model private channels in the π-calculus [58,59]. In these works, restriction has been modelled via *nominal quantifiers* in the spirit of the ones introduced by Pitts and Gabbay for *nominal logic* [85,41], by considering a pair of dual quantifiers[15], instead of a single self-dual quantifier as in [68,86,73].

The logic PiL we use as logical framework to establish our correspondences in this paper takes inspiration from Bruscoli's work and its extension, but it uses a non-associative non-commutative self-dual connective ◂ instead of the ◁ from BV. This seemingly irrelevant difference (the non-associativity of ◂) guarantees the existence of a cut-free sequent calculus to be used as a framework for our correspondence, while for the logic BV and its extension cut-free sequent calculi cannot exist, as proven in [91]. Note that requiring non-associativity for the connective modelling sequentiality is not a syntactical stretch, because the same restriction naturally occurs in process calculi such as CCS and the π-calculus, where sequentiality is defined by an asymmetric prefix operation only allowing to sequentially compose (on the left) atomic instructions, such as send and receive. The other main difference is that in these works derivations represent a single execution, while our derivations represent execution trees. This allows us to state our Theorem 3 without quantifying on the set of derivations of $[[P]]$.

---

[15] In [57] the authors report the use of a non-self-dual quantifier to model restriction was suggested them by Alessio Guglielmi in a private communication. As explained in detail in [8], the pair of dual nominal quantifiers in [57,59,58] is not the same pair we consider in this paper. This can be observed by looking at the implication $(\text{И}x.(A) \otimes \text{И}x.(B)) \multimap \text{И}x.(A \,\invamp\, B)$, which is valid in these works, but it is not valid in PiL. For this reason we adopted a different symbol for the dual quantifier of И – i.e., our Я instead of their Э.

6   Conclusion and Future Works

We presented a new approach to the study of processes based on logic, which leverages an interpretation of processes in the π-calculus as formulas in the proof system PiL. By seeing derivations as computation trees, we obtained an elegant method to reason about deadlock-freedom that goes beyond the syntactic and semantic limitations of previous work based on logic. This led us to establishing the first completeness result for the expressivity of choreographic programming with respect to mobile processes with cyclic dependencies.

We discuss next some interesting future directions.

Recursion. Recursion could be modelled by extending PiL with fixpoint operators and rules like the ones in [16,15,3,4,10]. We foresee no major challenges in extending the proof of cut-elimination for μMALL to PiL, since the behaviour of the connective ◄ is purely multiplicative (in the sense of [34,44,6]) and the rules for nominal quantifiers do not require the employment of new techniques. In PiL with recursion, properties such as *justness* or *fairness* could be characterised by specific constraints on derivations, corresponding to constraints on threads and paths of the (possibly cyclic) execution trees.

Asynchronous π-calculus. We foresee the possibility of modelling asynchronous communication by including shared buffers, inspired by previous work on concurrent constraint programming [88,82] and its strong ties to logic programming [76,89,60,39,80,81,84]. However, buffers with capacity greater than 2 have non-sequential-parallel structures and therefore cannot be described efficiently using binary connectives [94,30]. We may thus need to consider *graphical connectives* [2,5].

Proof Nets. In [8] we define proof nets for PiL, capturing local rule permutations, and providing canonical representative for execution trees up-to interleaving concurrency. This syntax could be used to refine the correspondence between proofs and choreographies (Theorem 7). We plan to study the extension of the computation-as-deduction paradigm in the case of proof net expansion, following the ideas in [12,13,7], as well as to use a notion of orthogonality for modules of proof nets (in the sense of [34,13,7]) to study testing preorders [37,38,49,18].

Completeness of Choreographies. The literature of choreographic programming languages includes features of practical interest that extend the expressivity of choreographies – like process spawning [32] and nondeterminism [78]. Exploring extensions of PiL to capture these features is interesting future work. For process spawning, a simple solution could be achieved by defining a way to dynamically assign process names to properly define the map $\mathsf{Chor}(\cdot)$.

Acknowledgements. Partially supported by Villum Fonden (grants no. 29518 and 50079). Co-funded by the European Union's Horizon 2020 research and innovation program under the Marie Sklodowska-Curie grant agreement No 945332. Co-funded by the European Union (ERC, CHORDS, 101124225). Views and opinions expressed are however those of the authors only and do not necessarily reflect those of the European Union or the European Research Council. Neither the European Union nor the granting authority can be held responsible for them.

References

1. Abramsky, S.: Proofs as processes. In: Selected Papers of the Conference on Meeting on the Mathematical Foundations of Programming Semantics, Part I: Linear Logic: Linear Logic. pp. 5–9. MFPS '92, Elsevier Science Publishers B. V., NLD (1992)
2. Acclavio, M.: Sequent systems on undirected graphs. In: Benzmüller, C., Heule, M.J., Schmidt, R.A. (eds.) Automated Reasoning. pp. 216–236. Springer Nature Switzerland, Cham (2024)
3. Acclavio, M., Curzi, G., Guerrieri, G.: Infinitary cut-elimination via finite approximations. CoRR **abs/2308.07789** (2023). https://doi.org/10.48550/ARXIV.2308.07789, https://doi.org/10.48550/arXiv.2308.07789
4. Acclavio, M., Curzi, G., Guerrieri, G.: Infinitary cut-elimination via finite approximations (extended version) (2024), `https://arxiv.org/abs/2308.07789`
5. Acclavio, M., Horne, R., Mauw, S., Straßburger, L.: A Graphical Proof Theory of Logical Time. In: Felty, A.P. (ed.) 7th International Conference on Formal Structures for Computation and Deduction (FSCD 2022). Leibniz International Proceedings in Informatics (LIPIcs), vol. 228, pp. 22:1–22:25. Schloss Dagstuhl – Leibniz-Zentrum für Informatik, Dagstuhl, Germany (2022). https://doi.org/10.4230/LIPIcs.FSCD.2022.22, `https://drops.dagstuhl.de/entities/document/10.4230/LIPIcs.FSCD.2022.22`
6. Acclavio, M., Maieli, R.: Generalized Connectives for Multiplicative Linear Logic. In: Fernández, M., Muscholl, A. (eds.) 28th EACSL Annual Conference on Computer Science Logic (CSL 2020). Leibniz International Proceedings in Informatics (LIPIcs), vol. 152, pp. 6:1–6:16. Schloss Dagstuhl – Leibniz-Zentrum für Informatik, Dagstuhl, Germany (2020). https://doi.org/10.4230/LIPIcs.CSL.2020.6, `https://drops.dagstuhl.de/entities/document/10.4230/LIPIcs.CSL.2020.6`
7. Acclavio, M., Maieli, R.: Logic programming with multiplicative structures. CoRR **abs/2403.03032** (2024). https://doi.org/10.48550/ARXIV.2403.03032, `https://doi.org/10.48550/arXiv.2403.03032`
8. Acclavio, M., Manara, G.: Proofs as execution trees for the π-calculus (2024), `https://arxiv.org/abs/2411.08847`
9. Acclavio, M., Manara, G., Montesi, F.: Formulas as processes, deadlock-freedom as choreographies (extended version) (2025), `https://arxiv.org/abs/2501.08928`
10. Acclavio, M., Montesi, F., Peressotti, M.: On propositional dynamic logic and concurrency (2024)
11. Andreoli, J.M.: Focussing and proof construction. Annals of Pure and Applied Logic **107**(1), 131–163 (2001). https://doi.org/https://doi.org/10.1016/S0168-0072(00)00032-4, `https://www.sciencedirect.com/science/article/pii/S0168007200000324`
12. Andreoli, J.M.: Focussing proof-net construction as a middleware paradigm. In: Voronkov, A. (ed.) Automated Deduction—CADE-18. pp. 501–516. Springer Berlin Heidelberg, Berlin, Heidelberg (2002)
13. Andreoli, J.M., Mazaré, L.: Concurrent construction of proof-nets. In: Baaz, M., Makowsky, J.A. (eds.) Computer Science Logic. pp. 29–42. Springer Berlin Heidelberg, Berlin, Heidelberg (2003)
14. Aschieri, F., Genco, F.A.: Par means parallel: multiplicative linear logic proofs as concurrent functional programs. Proc. ACM Program. Lang. 4(POPL) (dec 2019). https://doi.org/10.1145/3371086, `https://doi.org/10.1145/3371086`

15. Baelde, D., Doumane, A., Saurin, A.: Infinitary proof theory: the multiplicative additive case. In: Talbot, J., Regnier, L. (eds.) 25th EACSL Annual Conference on Computer Science Logic, CSL 2016, August 29 - September 1, 2016, Marseille, France. LIPIcs, vol. 62, pp. 42:1–42:17. Schloss Dagstuhl - Leibniz-Zentrum für Informatik (2016). https://doi.org/10.4230/LIPIcs.CSL.2016.42, https://doi.org/10.4230/LIPIcs.CSL.2016.42

16. Baelde, D., Miller, D.: Least and greatest fixed points in linear logic. In: Dershowitz, N., Voronkov, A. (eds.) Logic for Programming, Artificial Intelligence, and Reasoning, 14th International Conference, LPAR 2007, Yerevan, Armenia, October 15-19, 2007, Proceedings. Lecture Notes in Computer Science, vol. 4790, pp. 92–106. Springer (2007). https://doi.org/10.1007/978-3-540-75560-9_9, https://doi.org/10.1007/978-3-540-75560-9_9

17. Bellin, G., Scott, P.: On the π-calculus and linear logic. Theoretical Computer Science **135**(1), 11–65 (1994). https://doi.org/https://doi.org/10.1016/0304-3975(94)00104-9, https://www.sciencedirect.com/science/article/pii/0304397594001049

18. Bernardi, G., Hennessy, M.: Mutually Testing Processes. Logical Methods in Computer Science **Volume 11, Issue 2** (Apr 2015). https://doi.org/10.2168/LMCS-11(2:1)2015, https://lmcs.episciences.org/776

19. Bruscoli, P.: A purely logical account of sequentiality in proof search. In: International Conference on Logic Programming. pp. 302–316. Springer (2002)

20. Caires, L., Pfenning, F.: Session types as intuitionistic linear propositions. In: Gastin, P., Laroussinie, F. (eds.) CONCUR 2010 - Concurrency Theory. pp. 222–236. Springer Berlin Heidelberg, Berlin, Heidelberg (2010)

21. Carbone, M., Cruz-Filipe, L., Montesi, F., Murawska, A.: Multiparty classical choreographies. In: Mesnard, F., Stuckey, P.J. (eds.) Logic-Based Program Synthesis and Transformation - 28th International Symposium, LOPSTR 2018, Frankfurt/Main, Germany, September 4-6, 2018, Revised Selected Papers. Lecture Notes in Computer Science, vol. 11408, pp. 59–76. Springer (2018). https://doi.org/10.1007/978-3-030-13838-7_4, https://doi.org/10.1007/978-3-030-13838-7_4

22. Carbone, M., Dardha, O., Montesi, F.: Progress as compositional lock-freedom. In: Kühn, E., Pugliese, R. (eds.) Coordination Models and Languages. pp. 49–64. Springer Berlin Heidelberg, Berlin, Heidelberg (2014)

23. Carbone, M., Honda, K., Yoshida, N.: Structured communication-centered programming for web services. ACM Trans. Program. Lang. Syst. **34**(2), 8:1–8:78 (2012). https://doi.org/10.1145/2220365.2220367, https://doi.org/10.1145/2220365.2220367

24. Carbone, M., Lindley, S., Montesi, F., Schürmann, C., Wadler, P.: Coherence generalises duality: A logical explanation of multiparty session types. In: Desharnais, J., Jagadeesan, R. (eds.) 27th International Conference on Concurrency Theory, CONCUR 2016, August 23-26, 2016, Québec City, Canada. LIPIcs, vol. 59, pp. 33:1–33:15. Schloss Dagstuhl - Leibniz-Zentrum für Informatik (2016). https://doi.org/10.4230/LIPICS.CONCUR.2016.33, https://doi.org/10.4230/LIPIcs.CONCUR.2016.33

25. Carbone, M., Montesi, F.: Deadlock-freedom-by-design: multiparty asynchronous global programming. In: Giacobazzi, R., Cousot, R. (eds.) The 40th Annual ACM SIGPLAN-SIGACT Symposium on Principles of Programming Languages, POPL '13, Rome, Italy - January 23 - 25, 2013, pp. 263–274. ACM (2013). https://doi.org/10.1145/2429069.2429101, https://doi.org/10.1145/2429069.2429101

26. Carbone, M., Montesi, F., Schürmann, C.: Choreographies, logically. Distributed Comput. **31**(1), 51–67 (2018). https://doi.org/10.1007/S00446-017-0295-1, https://doi.org/10.1007/s00446-017-0295-1

27. Carbone, M., Montesi, F., Schürmann, C., Yoshida, N.: Multiparty session types as coherence proofs. Acta Informatica **54**(3), 243–269 (2017). https://doi.org/10.1007/S00236-016-0285-Y, `https://doi.org/10.1007/s00236-016-0285-y`

28. Cockett, J., Seely, R.: Weakly distributive categories. Journal of Pure and Applied Algebra **114**(2), 133–173 (1997). https://doi.org/https://doi.org/10.1016/0022-4049(95)00160-3, `https://www.sciencedirect.com/science/article/pii/0022404995001603`

29. Coppo, M., Dezani-Ciancaglini, M., Yoshida, N., Padovani, L.: Global progress for dynamically interleaved multiparty sessions. Math. Struct. Comput. Sci. **26**(2), 238–302 (2016). https://doi.org/10.1017/S0960129514000188, `https://doi.org/10.1017/S0960129514000188`

30. Corneil, D., Lerchs, H., Burlingham, L.: Complement reducible graphs. Discrete Applied Mathematics **3**(3), 163–174 (1981). https://doi.org/https://doi.org/10.1016/0166-218X(81)90013-5, https://www.sciencedirect.com/science/article/pii/0166218X81900135

31. Cruz-Filipe, L., Larsen, K.S., Montesi, F.: The paths to choreography extraction. In: Esparza, J., Murawski, A.S. (eds.) Foundations of Software Science and Computation Structures - 20th International Conference, FOSSACS 2017, Held as Part of the European Joint Conferences on Theory and Practice of Software, ETAPS 2017, Uppsala, Sweden, April 22-29, 2017, Proceedings. Lecture Notes in Computer Science, vol. 10203, pp. 424–440 (2017). https://doi.org/10.1007/978-3-662-54458-7_25, `https://doi.org/10.1007/978-3-662-54458-7_25`

32. Cruz-Filipe, L., Montesi, F.: Procedural choreographic programming. In: Bouajjani, A., Silva, A. (eds.) Formal Techniques for Distributed Objects, Components, and Systems - 37th IFIP WG 6.1 International Conference, FORTE 2017, Held as Part of the 12th International Federated Conference on Distributed Computing Techniques, DisCoTec 2017, Neuchâtel, Switzerland, June 19-22, 2017, Proceedings. Lecture Notes in Computer Science, vol. 10321, pp. 92–107. Springer (2017). https://doi.org/10.1007/978-3-319-60225-7_7, `https://doi.org/10.1007/978-3-319-60225-7_7`

33. Cruz-Filipe, L., Montesi, F.: A core model for choreographic programming. Theor. Comput. Sci. **802**, 38–66 (2020). https://doi.org/10.1016/J.TCS.2019.07.005, `https://doi.org/10.1016/j.tcs.2019.07.005`

34. Danos, V., Regnier, L.: The structure of multiplicatives. Archive for Mathematical Logic **28**(3), 181–203 (1989). https://doi.org/10.1007/BF01622878, `https://doi.org/10.1007/BF01622878`

35. Dardha, O., Gay, S.J.: A new linear logic for deadlock-free session-typed processes. In: Baier, C., Dal Lago, U. (eds.) Foundations of Software Science and Computation Structures. pp. 91–109. Springer International Publishing, Cham (2018)

36. Dardha, O., Giachino, E., Sangiorgi, D.: Session types revisited. Inf. Comput. **256**, 253–286 (2017). https://doi.org/10.1016/J.IC.2017.06.002, `https://doi.org/10.1016/j.ic.2017.06.002`

37. De Nicola, R., Hennessy, M.: Testing equivalences for processes. Theoretical Computer Science **34**(1), 83–133 (1984). https://doi.org/https://doi.org/10.1016/0304-3975(84)90113-0, `https://www.sciencedirect.com/science/article/pii/0304397584901130`

38. De Nicola, R., Hennessy, M.: Ccs without τ's. In: Ehrig, H., Kowalski, R., Levi, G., Montanari, U. (eds.) TAPSOFT '87. pp. 138–152. Springer Berlin Heidelberg, Berlin, Heidelberg (1987)

39. Fages, F., Ruet, P., Soliman, S.: Linear concurrent constraint programming: Operational and phase semantics. Information and Computation **165**(1), 14–41 (2001). https://doi.org/https://doi.org/10.1006/inco.2000.3002, `https://www.sciencedirect.com/science/article/pii/S0890540100930025`

40. Fleury, A., Retoré, C.: The mix rule. Mathematical Structures in Computer Science **4**(2), 273–285 (1994). https://doi.org/10.1017/S0960129500000451

41. Gabbay, M.J., Pitts, A.M.: A new approach to abstract syntax with variable binding. Form. Asp. Comput. **13**(3–5), 341–363 (jul 2002). https://doi.org/10.1007/s001650200016, `https://doi.org/10.1007/s001650200016`

42. Gay, S., Hole, M.: Subtyping for session types in the pi calculus. Acta Informatica **42**, 191–225 (2005)

43. Girard, J.Y.: Linear logic. Theoretical Computer Science **50**(1), 1–101 (1987). https://doi.org/10.1016/0304-3975(87)90045-4

44. Girard, J.Y.: On the meaning of logical rules II: multiplicatives and additives. NATO ASI Series F Computer and Systems Sciences **175**, 183–212 (2000)

45. Guglielmi, A.: Concurrency and plan generation in a logic programming language with a sequential operator. In: ICLP. pp. 240–254. Citeseer (1994)

46. Guglielmi, A.: Sequentiality by linear implication and universal quantification. In: Desel, J. (ed.) Structures in Concurrency Theory. pp. 160–174. Springer London, London (1995)

47. Guglielmi, A.: A system of interaction and structure. ACM Trans. Comput. Logic **8**(1), 1–es (Jan 2007). https://doi.org/10.1145/1182613.1182614, `https://doi.org/10.1145/1182613.1182614`

48. Harel, D., Kozen, D., Tiuryn, J.: Dynamic Logic, pp. 99–217. Springer Netherlands, Dordrecht (2002). https://doi.org/10.1007/978-94-017-0456-4_2, `https://doi.org/10.1007/978-94-017-0456-4_2`

49. Hennessy, M.: Algebraic theory of processes. MIT Press, Cambridge, MA, USA (1988)

50. Hennessy, M.: A distributed Pi-calculus. Cambridge University Press (2007)

51. Hennessy, M., Milner, R.: On observing nondeterminism and concurrency. In: de Bakker, J., van Leeuwen, J. (eds.) Automata, Languages and Programming. pp. 299–309. Springer Berlin Heidelberg, Berlin, Heidelberg (1980)

52. Hoare, C.A.R.: An axiomatic basis for computer programming. Commun. ACM **12**(10), 576–580 (oct 1969). https://doi.org/10.1145/363235.363259, `https://doi.org/10.1145/363235.363259`

53. Hodas, J., Miller, D.: Logic programming in a fragment of intuitionistic linear logic. Information and Computation **110**(2), 327–365 (1994). https://doi.org/https://doi.org/10.1006/inco.1994.1036, https://www.sciencedirect.com/science/article/pii/S0890540184710364

54. Holmström, S.: Hennessy-milner logic with recursion as a specification language, and a refinement calculus based on it. In: Rattray, C. (ed.) Specification and Verification of Concurrent Systems. pp. 294–330. Springer London, London (1990)

55. Honda, K.: Types for dyadic interaction. In: Best, E. (ed.) CONCUR'93. pp. 509–523. Springer Berlin Heidelberg, Berlin, Heidelberg (1993)

56. Honda, K., Vasconcelos, V.T., Kubo, M.: Language primitives and type discipline for structured communication-based programming. In: Hankin, C. (ed.) Programming Languages and Systems. pp. 122–138. Springer Berlin Heidelberg, Berlin, Heidelberg (1998)

57. Horne, R., Tiu, A.: Constructing weak simulations from linear implications for processes with private names. Mathematical Structures in Computer Science **29**(8), 1275–1308 (2019). https://doi.org/10.1017/S0960129518000452

58. Horne, R., Tiu, A., Aman, B., Ciobanu, G.: Private Names in Non-Commutative Logic. In: Desharnais, J., Jagadeesan, R. (eds.) 27th International Conference on Concurrency Theory (CONCUR 2016). Leibniz International Proceedings in Informatics (LIPIcs), vol. 59, pp. 31:1–31:16. Schloss Dagstuhl – Leibniz-Zentrum für Informatik, Dagstuhl, Germany (2016). https://doi.org/10.4230/LIPIcs.CONCUR.2016.31, `https://drops.dagstuhl.de/entities/document/10.4230/LIPIcs.CONCUR.2016.31`

59. Horne, R., Tiu, A., Aman, B., Ciobanu, G.: De morgan dual nominal quantifiers modelling private names in non-commutative logic. ACM Trans. Comput. Logic **20**(4) (jul 2019). https://doi.org/10.1145/3325821, `https://doi.org/10.1145/3325821`

60. Jaffar, J., Maher, M.J.: Constraint logic programming: a survey. The Journal of Logic Programming **19-20**, 503–581 (1994). https://doi.org/https://doi.org/10.1016/0743-1066(94)90033-7, https://www.sciencedirect.com/science/article/pii/0743106694900337, special Issue: Ten Years of Logic Programming

61. Kjær, B.A., Cruz-Filipe, L., Montesi, F.: From infinity to choreographies: Extraction for unbounded systems (2022)

62. Kobayashi, N.: A type system for lock-free processes. Information and Computation **177**(2), 122–159 (2002). https://doi.org/https://doi.org/10.1006/inco.2002.3171, `https://www.sciencedirect.com/science/article/pii/S0890540102931718`

63. Kobayashi, N., Pierce, B.C., Turner, D.N.: Linearity and the pi-calculus. ACM Trans. Program. Lang. Syst. **21**(5), 914–947 (1999). https://doi.org/10.1145/330249.330251, `https://doi.org/10.1145/330249.330251`

64. Kokke, W., Montesi, F., Peressotti, M.: Better late than never: a fully-abstract semantics for classical processes. Proc. ACM Program. Lang. **3**(POPL) (jan 2019). https://doi.org/10.1145/3290337, `https://doi.org/10.1145/3290337`

65. Kozen, D.: Results on the propositional μ-calculus. Theoretical Computer Science **27**(3), 333–354 (1983). https://doi.org/https://doi.org/10.1016/0304-3975(82)90125-6, `https://www.sciencedirect.com/science/article/pii/0304397582901256`, special Issue Ninth International Colloquium on Automata, Languages and Programming (ICALP) Aarhus, Summer 1982

66. Lange, J., Tuosto, E., Yoshida, N.: From communicating machines to graphical choreographies. SIGPLAN Not. **50**(1), 221–232 (jan 2015). https://doi.org/10.1145/2775051.2676964, `https://doi.org/10.1145/2775051.2676964`

67. Martin-Löf, P.: Constructive mathematics and computer programming. In: Studies in Logic and the Foundations of Mathematics, vol. 104, pp. 153–175. Elsevier (1982)

68. Menni, M.: About И-quantifiers. Applied categorical structures **11**, 421–445 (2003)

69. Miller, D.: Hereditary harrop formulas and logic programming. In: Proceedings of the VIII International Congress of Logic, Methodology, and Philosophy of Science. pp. 153–156 (1987)

70. Miller, D.: Abstract syntax and logic programming. In: Voronkov, A. (ed.) Logic Programming. pp. 322–337. Springer Berlin Heidelberg, Berlin, Heidelberg (1992)

71. Miller, D.: The π-calculus as a theory in linear logic: Preliminary results. In: Lamma, E., Mello, P. (eds.) Extensions of Logic Programming. pp. 242–264. Springer Berlin Heidelberg, Berlin, Heidelberg (1993)

72. Miller, D., Nadathur, G., Pfenning, F., Scedrov, A.: Uniform proofs as a foundation for logic programming. Annals of Pure and Applied Logic **51**(1), 125–157 (1991). https://doi.org/https://doi.org/10.1016/0168-0072(91)90068-W, `https://www.sciencedirect.com/science/article/pii/016800729190068W`

73. Miller, D., Tiu, A.: A proof theory for generic judgments. ACM Trans. Comput. Logic **6**(4), 749–783 (oct 2005). https://doi.org/10.1145/1094622.1094628, `https://doi.org/10.1145/1094622.1094628`

74. Milner, R.: A Calculus of Communicating Systems, Lecture Notes in Computer Science, vol. 92. Springer (1980). https://doi.org/10.1007/3-540-10235-3, `https://doi.org/10.1007/3-540-10235-3`

75. Milner, R., Parrow, J., Walker, D.: A calculus of mobile processes, i. Information and Computation **100**(1), 1–40 (1992). https://doi.org/https://doi.org/10.1016/0890-5401(92)90008-4, https://www.sciencedirect.com/science/article/pii/0890540192900084

76. Montanari, U.: Networks of constraints: Fundamental properties and applications to picture processing. Information Sciences **7**, 95–132 (1974). https://doi.org/https://doi.org/10.1016/0020-0255(74)90008-5, `https://www.sciencedirect.com/science/article/pii/0020025574900085`

77. Montesi, F.: Choreographic Programming. Ph.D. thesis, IT University of Copenhagen (2013), `https://www.fabriziomontesi.com/files/choreographic-programming.pdf`

78. Montesi, F.: Introduction to Choreographies. Cambridge University Press (2023). https://doi.org/10.1017/9781108981491

79. Montesi, F., Yoshida, N.: Compositional choreographies. In: D'Argenio, P.R., Melgratti, H.C. (eds.) CONCUR 2013 - Concurrency Theory - 24th International Conference, CONCUR 2013, Buenos Aires, Argentina, August 27-30, 2013. Proceedings. Lecture Notes in Computer Science, vol. 8052, pp. 425–439. Springer (2013). https://doi.org/10.1007/978-3-642-40184-8_30, `https://doi.org/10.1007/978-3-642-40184-8_30`

80. Olarte, C., Pimentel, E.: On concurrent behaviors and focusing in linear logic. Theoretical Computer Science **685**, 46–64 (2017). https://doi.org/https://doi.org/10.1016/j.tcs.2016.08.026, `https://www.sciencedirect.com/science/article/pii/S0304397516304832`, logical and Semantic Frameworks with Applications

81. Olarte, C., Pimentel, E., Nigam, V.: Subexponential concurrent constraint programming. Theoretical Computer Science **606**, 98–120 (2015). https://doi.org/https://doi.org/10.1016/j.tcs.2015.06.031, `https://www.sciencedirect.com/science/article/pii/S0304397515005411`, logical and Semantic Frameworks with Applications

82. Olarte, C., Rueda, C., Valencia, F.D.: Models and emerging trends of concurrent constraint programming. Constraints **18**, 535–578 (2013)

83. Padovani, L.: Deadlock and lock freedom in the linear π-calculus. In: Proceedings of the Joint Meeting of the Twenty-Third EACSL Annual Conference on Computer Science Logic (CSL) and the Twenty-Ninth Annual ACM/IEEE Symposium on Logic in Computer Science (LICS). CSL-LICS '14, Association for Computing Machinery, New York, NY, USA (2014). https://doi.org/10.1145/2603088.2603116, `https://doi.org/10.1145/2603088.2603116`

84. Pimentel, E., Olarte, C., Nigam, V.: Process-As-Formula Interpretation: A Substructural Multimodal View. In: Kobayashi, N. (ed.) 6th International Conference on Formal Structures for Computation and Deduction (FSCD 2021).

Leibniz International Proceedings in Informatics (LIPIcs), vol. 195, pp. 3:1–3:21. Schloss Dagstuhl – Leibniz-Zentrum für Informatik, Dagstuhl, Germany (2021). https://doi.org/10.4230/LIPIcs.FSCD.2021.3, https://drops.dagstuhl.de/entities/document/10.4230/LIPIcs.FSCD.2021.3

85. Pitts, A.M.: Nominal logic, a first order theory of names and binding. Information and Computation **186**(2), 165–193 (2003). https://doi.org/https://doi.org/10.1016/S0890-5401(03)00138-X, https://www.sciencedirect.com/science/article/pii/S089054010300138X, theoretical Aspects of Computer Software (TACS 2001)

86. Roversi, L.: A deep inference system with a self-dual binder which is complete for linear lambda calculus. Journal of Logic and Computation **26**(2), 677–698 (2016). https://doi.org/10.1093/logcom/exu033

87. Sangiorgi, D.: Pi-i: A symmetric calculus based on internal mobility. In: Mosses, P.D., Nielsen, M., Schwartzbach, M.I. (eds.) TAPSOFT'95: Theory and Practice of Software Development, 6th International Joint Conference CAAP/FASE, Aarhus, Denmark, May 22-26, 1995, Proceedings. Lecture Notes in Computer Science, vol. 915, pp. 172–186. Springer (1995). https://doi.org/10.1007/3-540-59293-8_194, https://doi.org/10.1007/3-540-59293-8_194

88. Saraswat, V.A., Rinard, M.: Concurrent constraint programming. In: Proceedings of the 17th ACM SIGPLAN-SIGACT Symposium on Principles of Programming Languages. p. 232–245. POPL '90, Association for Computing Machinery, New York, NY, USA (1989). https://doi.org/10.1145/96709.96733, https://doi.org/10.1145/96709.96733

89. Shapiro, E.: The family of concurrent logic programming languages. ACM Comput. Surv. **21**(3), 413–510 (sep 1989). https://doi.org/10.1145/72551.72555, https://doi.org/10.1145/72551.72555

90. Sørensen, M.H., Urzyczyn, P.: Lectures on the Curry-Howard isomorphism. Elsevier (2006)

91. Tiu, A.: A System of Interaction and Structure II: The Need for Deep Inference. Logical Methods in Computer Science **Volume 2, Issue 2** (Apr 2006). https://doi.org/10.2168/LMCS-2(2:4)2006, https://lmcs.episciences.org/2252

92. Torres Vieira, H., Thudichum Vasconcelos, V.: Typing progress in communication-centred systems. In: De Nicola, R., Julien, C. (eds.) Coordination Models and Languages. pp. 236–250. Springer Berlin Heidelberg, Berlin, Heidelberg (2013)

93. Troelstra, A.S., Schwichtenberg, H.: Basic Proof Theory. Cambridge Tracts in Theoretical Computer Science, Cambridge University Press, 2 edn. (2000). https://doi.org/10.1017/CBO9781139168717

94. Valdes, J., Tarjan, R.E., Lawler, E.L.: The recognition of series parallel digraphs. In: Proceedings of the eleventh annual ACM symposium on Theory of computing. pp. 1–12. ACM (1979)

95. Vasconcelos, V.T.: Fundamentals of session types. Information and Computation **217**, 52–70 (2012). https://doi.org/https://doi.org/10.1016/j.ic.2012.05.002, https://www.sciencedirect.com/science/article/pii/S0890540112001022

96. Wadler, P.: Propositions as sessions. In: Proceedings of the 17th ACM SIGPLAN International Conference on Functional Programming. p. 273–286. ICFP '12, Association for Computing Machinery, New York, NY, USA (2012). https://doi.org/10.1145/2364527.2364568, https://doi.org/10.1145/2364527.2364568

Sufficient Conditions for Robustness of RDMA Programs

Guillaume Ambal[1]([✉]) , Ori Lahav[2], and Azalea Raad[1]

[1] Imperial College London, London, UK
{g.ambal,azalea.raad}@imperial.ac.uk
[2] Tel Aviv University, Tel Aviv-Yafo, Israel
orilahav@tau.ac.il

Abstract. Remote Direct Memory Access (RDMA) is a modern technology enabling high-performance inter-node communication. Despite its widespread adoption, theoretical understanding of permissible behaviours remains limited, as RDMA follows a very weak memory model. This paper addresses the challenge of establishing sufficient conditions for RDMA robustness. We introduce a set of straightforward criteria that, when met, guarantee sequential consistency and mitigate potential issues arising from weak memory behaviours in RDMA applications. Notably, when restricted to a tree topology, these conditions become even more relaxed, significantly reducing the need for synchronisation primitives. This work provides developers with practical guidelines to ensure the reliability and correctness of their RDMA-based systems.

Keywords: RDMA · Robustness · Weak Memory Models

1 Introduction

Remote Direct Memory Access (RDMA) is a modern technology that enables a machine to have *direct* read/write access to the memory of another machine over a network, bypassing the operating systems on both ends. This allows such direct memory accesses (reads/writes) to be performed with far fewer CPU cycles, leading to high-throughput, low-latency networking, which is especially useful in massively parallel computer clusters (e.g. data centres). RDMA has achieved widespread adoption as of 2018 [69], thanks to efficient implementations available at comparable cost to traditional infrastructures (e.g. TCP/IP sockets) [32], with several RDMA technologies such as *InfiniBand* and *RDMA over Converged Ethernet* (RoCE) readily available.

RDMA networks directly interact with the hardware through read (get) and write (put) operations on remote memory. As a result, programming RDMA systems is conceptually similar to shared memory systems of existing hardware architectures (e.g. Intel-x86 or ARM). A key difference, however, is that on encountering a remote operation, the CPU forwards it onto the *network interface card* (NIC), which subsequently handles the remote operation without further CPU involvement.

© The Author(s) 2025
V. Vafeiadis (Ed.): ESOP 2025, LNCS 15694, pp. 56–87, 2025.
https://doi.org/10.1007/978-3-031-91118-7_3

The performance gains of RDMA, as well as its wide range of implementations, have led to a surge of RDMA research [4,73,71,27]. RDMA networks exhibit different degrees of concurrency, depending on whether the concurrent threads reside on different nodes (machines) over the network (inter-node concurrency) or on the same node (intra-thread concurrency). To understand the behaviour of RDMA programs and their various notions of concurrency, Ambal et al. [10] recently developed RDMA^{TSO}, a formal semantics of RDMA programs where each node comprises an Intel-x86 CPU and thus intra-node-inter-thread concurrency is governed by the TSO (total store ordering) model [68].

As the real power of RDMA networks is their ability to run parallel programs over different nodes, writing efficient RDMA programs hinges on utilising inter-node concurrency. However, writing such programs *correctly* is far from straightforward. A key challenge is that local operations (accessing the local memory of the executing node) are handled by the CPU, while remote operations (accessing remote memory on other nodes) are handled by the NIC independently and in *parallel* to CPU operations. Hence, operations in the same thread may not be executed in the intended (program) order, leading to surprising outcomes. As Ambal et al. [10] note, this can result in counter-intuitive behaviours even in the case of *sequential* programs comprising a single thread. This is in stark contrast to *all* previously existing concurrency models (be they of CPU architectures or programming languages), where sequential programs do behave sequentially.

The permissive nature of RDMA semantics requires developers to carefully consider potential instruction reorderings. Reasoning about concurrent programs and ensuring proper synchronisation between threads is inherently complex, even without instruction reordering. Accounting for instruction reorderings adds another layer of complexity to this challenge.

As such, we should ideally enable reasoning about RDMA programs under a simpler, more intuitive model such as *sequential consistency* (SC) [43], where no instruction reordering is allowed, and thus instructions in each thread always execute in order. To this end, a common approach to simplify reasoning is to ensure *robustness*. A program P is *robust* under a consistency model CM, if its set of possible behaviours under CM coincide with those of its behaviours under SC; i.e. P is robust under CM if it exhibits no non-SC behaviours. If a program is robust under CM, then we can simply reason about it under SC, without considering the complexities of CM.

Contributions. In this paper, we close this gap and simplify reasoning about RDMA program through robustness. To simplify our presentation and not distract the reader from the RDMA complexities by the *orthogonal* intricacies of CPU concurrency, we first present RDMA^{SC}, a simplification of the RDMA^{TSO} model of Ambal et al. [10], where intra-node concurrency follows the simpler SC model [43], while inter-node concurrency is analogous to that of RDMA^{TSO}. We then identify two sets of sufficient constraints that, if satisfied, ensure the robustness of RDMA^{SC} programs. Our proposed constraints are purely *syntactic*, in that they do not require an understanding of the complex RDMA semantics and can be established by simply checking the syntax of the program. The first set of constraints is restrictive, but can be applied to any RDMA program. The second relaxes the requirements of the first, but requires the RDMA network to follow a tree topology. Our conditions enable a number of useful paradigms for RDMA programs such as the server-client model, which we show can be used for automatically translating existing concurrent algorithms to distributed ones over RDMA, as well as for modelling star network topologies used e.g. in Local Area Networks (LAN). Finally, we adapt our results to the RDMA^{TSO} model and accordingly propose analogous syntactic and topological constraints.

Outline. In §2 we present an intuitive account of the weak RDMA semantics through examples and discuss how we ensure robustness through syntactic constraints. In §3 we present our formal RDMA^{SC} model. In §4 we establish sufficient syntactic conditions that ensure the robustness of RDMA^{SC} programs. In §5 we apply these findings to tree-shaped network topologies, offering a further streamlined set of conditions under RDMA^{SC}. We discuss related work in §6. The proofs of all theorems stated in this paper, as well as the extension of all our results to the RDMA^{TSO} model, are available in the extended version [11].

2   Overview

We present an intuitive account of RDMA semantics through several examples, showing the counter-intuitive and unexpected behaviours they can exhibit due to possible *instruction reorderings* (§2.1). We then discuss how we can tame this complexity by introducing *syntactic constraints* that, if fulfilled, prohibit problematic instruction reorderings, pre-empting unexpected behaviours and thus simplifying the task of reasoning about RDMA programs for developers (§2.2).

2.1   RDMA Semantics at a Glance

Consistency (Concurrency) Models and *Weak* Behaviours. In the literature of shared-memory concurrent (multi-threaded) programming, the set of possible behaviours (i.e. semantics) of a concurrent program is defined via a *consistency model* (a.k.a. memory model or concurrency model), with a number of such models available in different domains such as hardware architectures (e.g. Intel and ARM) and programming languages (e.g. C/C++ and Java). The most well-known and intuitive consistency model is *sequential consistency* (SC, a.k.a. interleaving concurrency) [43], where the instructions are interleaved in program order. That is, under SC the instructions in each thread cannot be *reordered*. While simple, SC is *too strong* in that it precludes many common hardware/compiler optimisations and thus unduly hinders performance. As such, modern hardware architectures and programming languages adhere to *weaker*, more lenient models, admitting more behaviours than SC. In this context a program behaviour (outcome) is referred to as *weak*, if it is not allowed under SC. Such weak behaviours can typically be understood in terms of instruction reorderings within a thread or visibility delays (where the effects of an instruction (e.g. a write) is not observed at the same time by all threads), both of which are disallowed under SC.

Conceptual RDMA Model. We model concurrent RDMA programs running over a network of *nodes* (i.e. computers), where each node hosts zero, one, or more threads, and each thread can *directly* access remote memory of other nodes through its *network interface card* (NIC). As we discuss below, RDMA programs exhibit three sources of weak behaviours: 1. *CPU* weak behaviours, due to the usual interactions (and reordering) of multiple threads on a single node; 2. *intra-thread* weak behaviours, due to RDMA operations being reordered or delayed; and 3. *inter-node* weak behaviours, due to multiple nodes executing concurrently. Here we focus on the latter two sources as they are specific to RDMA programs, and discuss how such weak behaviours may be prevented.

CPU Concurrency. RDMA enacts data transfers between nodes via the NIC subsystems of the constituent nodes, which are independent from the CPU subsystems. Consequently, the RDMA technology can be combined with different CPU architectures governed by different memory models (e.g. TSO or ARM). The first validated formal model of RDMA programs, RDMA^{TSO} [10], assumes that CPU concurrency is governed by the TSO model [68]. To simplify our presentation and not distract the reader from the RDMA complexities by the *orthogonal* intricacies of CPU concurrency, we present the simpler RDMA^{SC} model, where CPU concurrency follow the stronger SC model [43]. We generalise our results to RDMA^{TSO} in the extended version [11].

Almost all weak behaviours introduced by RDMA stem from the NIC and are independent of CPU concurrency (i.e. CPU and RDMA concurrency can often be decoupled). As such, the distinction between RDMA^{TSO} and RDMA^{SC} is often irrelevant, in which case we write RDMA* to encompass both models. In particular, in this overview section we focus on nodes with *at most one thread each*, i.e. with no CPU concurrency, so all behaviours discussed below hold of both RDMA^{SC} and RDMA^{TSO} (i.e. for RDMA*). Note that this is *merely a presentational choice* we have made in this section, and our formal models, theorems, and examples in subsequent sections also account for CPU concurrency.

Litmus Test Outcome Notation. We frequently present small representative examples (known as litmus tests in the literature). In each example, the outcomes annotated with ✓ are allowed by the RDMA model under discussion, while those annotated with ✗ are disallowed.

Remote Direct Memory Access (RDMA). RDMA programs comprise operations that access remote memory, as well as various synchronisation operations. As such, programming RDMA networks is conceptually similar to shared memory systems. To distinguish remote (RDMA) operations from CPU ones, we refer to RDMA reads and writes as *get* and *put* operations, respectively. To distinguish local and remote memory locations, we assume nodes do not reuse location names, we write x^n for a location on a remote node n, and write x for a location on the local node. A put operation is of the form $x^n := y$ and consists of reading from a local location y and writing to a remote location x on n. Similarly, a get operation is of the form $x := y^n$ and consists of reading from a remote location y on n and writing to a local location x. We write $\bar{n}$ to identify

(a)	$x=0$	$z=0$
	$x := 1$ $z^2 := x$

(a) $z=0$✗ $z=1$✓

(b)	$x=0$	$z=0$
	$z^2 := x$ $x := 1$

(b) $z=0$✓ $z=1$✓

(c)	$x=0$	$z=0$
	$z^2 := x$ poll(2) $x := 1$

(c) $z=0$✓ $z=1$✗

(d)	$x=0$	$z=0$
	$z^2 := x$ $z^2 := x$ poll(2) $x := 1$

(d) $z=0$✓ $z=1$✓

(e)	$x=0$	$z=1$	$y=2$
	$x := z^2$ $x := y^3$	

(e) $x=1$✓ $x=2$✓

(f)		$y=0$
	$a := y^2$ $y^2 := 1$

(f) $a=0$✓ $a=1$✓

(g)	$x=1$	$y=z=0$
	$z^2 := x$ $x := y^2$

(g) $z=0$✗ $z=1$✓

(h)	$x=1$	$y=z=0$
	$x := y^2$ $z^2 := x$

(h) $z=0$✓ $z=1$✓

(i)	$x=1$	$y=z=0$
	$x := y^2$ rfence(2) $z^2 := x$

(i) $z=0$✓ $z=1$✗

Fig. 1: Sequential RDMA* litmus tests, where each column (separated by $\|$) denotes a distinct node, the statement on the top line of each column denotes the initial values of locations.

a node other than n. When node n issues a remote operation to be executed on node $\overline{n}$, we state that the operation is *by n towards $\overline{n}$*.

Sequential (Single-Threaded) RDMA* Behaviours. When a thread issues a get or put operation, it is handled by the NIC, in contrast to local reads and writes handled by the CPU. As such, the interaction between CPU and remote operations lead to further behaviours even within a *sequential* (single-threaded) program. We demonstrate this in the examples of Fig. 1, where each column represents a distinct node, numbered from left to right starting from 1. For instance, the example in Fig. 1a comprises a single thread on node 1 (the leftmost column) that writes to the local location x ($x := 1$) and puts x towards the remote location z on node 2 ($z^2 := x$).

Intuitively, when a thread t on n issues remote operations towards node $\overline{n}$, one can view these remote operations as if being executed by a thread running *in parallel* to t. As such, when a remote operation *follows* a CPU one, the order of the two operations is preserved since the parallel thread is spawned only after the CPU operation is executed. This is illustrated in Fig. 1a. By contrast, when a remote operation *precedes* a CPU one, the remote operation is performed by a 'separate thread' run in parallel to the later CPU operation in the main thread, and thus may execute before or after the CPU operation, meaning that in the latter case the execution order is not preserved. This is illustrated in Fig. 1b.

Therefore, before using the result of a get or reusing the memory location of a put, it is desirable to avoid such reorderings and to wait for the remote operation to complete. This can be done through a CPU *poll* operation, poll(n), that blocks until the *earliest* (in program order) remote operation towards node n has completed. This is shown in Fig. 1c, obtained from Fig. 1b by inserting a poll after the remote operation: poll(2) waits for $z^2 := x$ to complete before proceeding with $x := 1$, and thus $z^2 := x$ can no longer be reordered after $x := 1$.

Note that each poll(n) waits for *only one* (the earliest) and *not all* pending remote operations towards n to complete. For instance, in Fig. 1d, poll(2) only blocks until the *first* $z^2 := x$ is complete, and thus $z = 1$ is once again possible.

$y=0$	$x=0$
$x^2 := 1$	$y^1 := 1$
$a := y$	$b := x$

(a) $a=b=0$ ✓

$x=0$	$y=0$
$a := y^2$	$b := x^1$
$x := 1$	$y := 1$

(b) $a=b=1$ ✓

$x=0$	$y=0$
$a := y^2$	$b := x^1$
poll(2)	poll(1)
$x := 1$	$y := 1$

(c) $a=b=1$ ✗

$y=0$	$x=0$
$x^2 := 1$	$y^1 := 1$
poll(2)	poll(1)
$a := y$	$b := x$

(d) $a=b=0$ ✓

$y=w=0$	$x=z=0$
$x^2 := 1$	$y^1 := 1$
$c := z^2$	$d := w^1$
poll(2)	poll(1)
poll(2)	poll(1)
$a := y$	$b := x$

(e) $a=b=0$ ✗

Fig. 2: Concurrent RDMA* litmus tests.

Two remote operations towards *different* nodes are independent and can execute in either order, as illustrated in Fig. 1e. The only way to prevent this reordering is to poll the first operation before running the second.

The ordering guarantees on remote operations towards the *same* node are stronger and only certain reorderings are allowed. Recall that a put operation $x^n := y$ comprises two steps: a local read (on y) and a remote write (on x^n). Similarly, a get operation $x := y^n$ comprises two steps: a remote read (on y^n) and a local write (on x). Intuitively, NIC operations follow the *precedence* order: i) local read; ii) remote write; iii) remote read; iv) local write.

If a step with a higher precedence (e.g. a local read) is in program order before one with a lower precedence (e.g. a local write), then their order is preserved and they cannot be reordered. This is illustrated in Fig. 1g. Otherwise the order is not necessarily preserved and these steps can be reordered, as shown in Fig. 1h where an earlier local write on x can occur after the later local read.

As before, the reordering of the two remote operations in Fig. 1h can be prevented by polling the first operation before the second. However, polling is costly as it blocks the current thread, including the submission of remote operations towards any node. Alternatively, we can use a *remote fence*, rfence(n), that blocks *only* the NIC and *only* towards node n. This in turn ensures that earlier (before the fence) remote operations by the thread towards n are executed before later (after the fence) remote operations towards n. This is illustrated in Fig. 1i, obtained from Fig. 1h by inserting rfence(2) stopping the reordering.

Concurrent (Multi-Threaded) RDMA* Behaviours. The real power of RDMA comes from programs running on *different nodes*, introducing a wide range of weak behaviours. A network can comprise several nodes, each running several concurrent threads. We limit the examples of Fig. 2 to two nodes, each having a single thread.

As shown in Figs. 2a and 2b, well-known weak behaviours such as store buffering (Fig. 2a) and load buffering (Fig. 2b) are possible. This is because earlier RDMA operations can be delayed after later CPU operations.

As one could expect, most weak behaviours can be prevented by polling the remote operations as needed, as shown for load buffering in Fig. 2c. However, this strategy is not enough to prevent the store buffering weak behaviour, as show in Fig. 2d. This is because the specification of polling offers different guarantees for get and put operations. Polling a get operation $a := x^n$ offers the strong intuitive guarantee that the operation completed, i.e. the value of x^n is fetched from node n and written to a. By contrast, polling a put operation $x^n := a$ does not guarantee the write on x^n has completed. When sending the value of a towards node n to be put in x^n, the remote NIC merely *acknowledges* having received the data, but this data may still reside in a *buffer* (i.e. the PCIe fabric) of the remote node, *pending* to be written x^n. Polling a put operation only awaits the acknowledgement of the data receipt. As such, it is possible to poll a put operation successfully before the associated remote write has fully completed. In the case of store buffering in Fig. 2d, it is possible for both poll operations to complete before the values of x and y are updated (to 1) in memory.

We also assume NICs are connected to memory though the *Peripheral Component Interconnect Express* (PCIe) fabric, the *de facto* standard for this category of hardware [10]. This ensures that (PCIe) reads cannot overtake (PCIe) writes. As such, a remote read *flushes* (commits) all pending remote writes to memory, and similarly on local memory. This can be used to prevent weak behaviours such as store buffering, as shown in Fig. 2e, obtained from Fig. 2d by adding additional gets and subsequently polling them. Polling a (seemingly unrelated) later get (e.g. $c := z^2$) ensures previous remote writes (e.g. $x^2 := 1$) have been committed to the remote memory.

2.2 Robustness: Taming Weak RDMA* Behaviours

Given the permissive nature of the RDMA* semantics and the numerous weak behaviours it exhibits (even in the case of single-threaded programs), the task of writing *correct* RDMA programs is laborious. Reasoning about concurrent programs is already challenging even in the absence of weak behaviours. Accounting for potential instruction reorderings (which requires experience with RDMA* semantics) introduces yet another layer of complexity for developers.

As such, we should ideally enable reasoning about RDMA programs under a simpler, more intuitive model such as SC (sequential consistency [43]). Specifically, to simplify program reasoning, a common approach is to ensure *robustness*. A program P is *robust* under a consistency model CM, if its set of possible behaviours under CM coincide with those of its behaviours under SC; i.e. P is robust if it exhibits no weak behaviours. If a program is robust, then we can reason about it *as if* it were executed under SC, without considering the complexities of RDMA*.

To ensure robustness, we must prevent *observable* reorderings, i.e. those leading to weak behaviours. We can achieve this through *syntactic* requirements (e.g. by inserting sufficient remote fences and poll operations). A naive solution is to wait for each remote operation to fully complete before proceeding further, thereby preventing all reorderings. Unfortunately, this *serialises* these operations, and thus defeats the benefits of RDMA, which is designed to parallelise CPU instructions and data transfers by offloading them to the NIC. Instead, we should account for the RDMA* semantics and only add restrictions when necessary, while allowing non-observable reorderings.

Certain reorderings are observable even when considering a single thread in isolation, as in the examples of Figs. 1b, 1e, 1f, and 1h. Specifically, these exam-

		$y = 0$	$z = 0$
$a := y^2$ $z^3 := 1$			

		$y = 0$	$z = 0$
$a := y^2$ $z^3 := 1$	$y := z^3$		

			$y = 0$	$z = 0$
$a := y^2$ $\texttt{poll}(2)$ $z^3 := 1$	$y := z^3$			

(a) $a = 1$ ✗   (b) $a = 1$ ✓   (c) $a = 1$ ✗

Fig. 3: Examples showing that necessary restrictions depend on other threads.

ples contain *data races within a single thread*. Beyond robustness, these patterns should be avoided in any sensible program. However, most weak behaviours arise from the interaction of several threads. For instance, in the single-threaded example of Fig. 3a, although the two remote operations $a := y^2$ and $z^3 := 1$ on node 1 may be reordered, this reordering is *not observable*: it does not lead to additional weak behaviours, and thus no additional constraints are necessary for robustness. By contrast, in the multi-threaded variant of Fig. 3b (with a thread on node 2), nodes 2 and 3 can exchange data and thus we can observe the weak behaviour $a = 1$ due to this reordering. As such, to prohibit this, we must prevent the two operations on node 1 from being reordered, e.g. by polling the first operation, as shown in Fig. 3c.

As seen before, preventing reorderings can be done in different ways. In cases like Fig. 1i, a remote fence is enough. In cases like Fig. 2e, we need dummy get operations. Determining when and how to prevent reorderings is not straightforward. As illustrated in the examples of Fig. 3, it cannot be done *thread-locally*: one must account for the communication between other nodes and thus must take the whole program into account. This raises two questions:

- How do we prevent weak behaviours through simple *purely syntactic* restrictions? Specifically, how can we ensure that a program has enough constraints (e.g. polls) to *prevent weak behaviours*, and how do we make sure that waiting for a specific remote operation (as in Fig. 3a) is unnecessary?
- How do we structure RDMA programs to *minimise* the amount of necessary restrictions in order to maintain efficient implementations?

We set out to answer these questions in the remainder of this paper. Specifically, after defining several formal preliminaries in §3, we present a theorem in §4 stating *sufficient syntactic conditions* guaranteeing robustness (i.e. the absence of weak behaviours). In §5 we then build on this theorem and present a useful RDMA network topology where fewer limitations are necessary to prevent weak behaviours. Notably, following our prescribed network topology ensures that it is *never necessary to poll* a remote operation to prevent multi-threaded weak behaviours.

3   RDMA^{SC}: A Declarative Semantics for RDMA Programs

We present the syntax of RDMA programs (taken from [10]) in §3.1. In §3.2 we then present a formal declarative semantics for our RDMA^{SC} model. As we describe in the extended version [11], we obtain RDMA^{SC} by *strengthening* the RDMA^{TSO} model of Ambal et al. [10] whereby we make a few simple adjustments to ensure that local (CPU) concurrency follows the SC rather than TSO model.

3.1 RDMA^{SC}: Programming Language

Nodes and Threads. We consider a system with N nodes and M threads in total across all nodes. Let $\text{Node} = \{1, \ldots, N\}$ and $\text{Tid} = \{1, \ldots, M\}$ denote the sets of *node* and *thread identifiers*, respectively. We use n and t to range over Node and Tid, respectively. Given a node n, we write $\bar{n}$ to range over $\text{Node} \setminus \{n\}$. Each thread $t \in \text{Tid}$ is associated with a node, written $n(t)$.

Memory Locations. Each node n has a set of *locations*, Loc_n, accessible by all nodes. We define $\text{Loc} \triangleq \biguplus_n \text{Loc}_n$ and $\text{Loc}_{\bar{n}} \triangleq \text{Loc} \setminus \text{Loc}_n$. We use x^n, y^n, z^n, w^n and $x^{\bar{n}}, y^{\bar{n}}, z^{\bar{n}}, w^{\bar{n}}$ to range over Loc_n and $\text{Loc}_{\bar{n}}$, respectively. When the choice of n is clear, we write x for x^n and $\bar{x}$ for $x^{\bar{n}}$. For clarity, we use distinct location names across nodes and write $n(x)$ for the unique $n \in \text{Node}$ where $x \in \text{Loc}_n$. We assume all locations can be accessed by all threads on all nodes. However, for readability, we use a, b, c, and d for (private) locations that are only accessed by a single thread (on a single node).

Values and Expressions. We assume a set of values, Val, with $\mathbb{N} \subseteq \text{Val}$, and use v to range over Val. We assume a language of expressions over Val and Loc, and elide its exact syntax and semantics. We use e to range over expressions, and e^n to range over expressions whose locations are all included in Loc_n.

Sequential Commands and Programs. *Sequential* programs on node n are described by the C^n grammar below and include primitive commands (c^n), sequential composition ($\mathsf{C}_1^n; \mathsf{C}_2^n$), non-deterministic choice ($\mathsf{C}_1^n + \mathsf{C}_2^n$, executing either C_1^n or C_2^n), and non-deterministic loops (C^{n*}, executing C^n any number of times). A (concurrent) *program*, P, is a map from thread identifiers to commands, associating each thread $t \in \text{Tid}$ with a command on node $n(t)$.

$$\text{Comm} \ni \mathsf{C}^n ::= \mathtt{skip} \mid \mathsf{c}^n \mid \mathsf{C}_1^n; \mathsf{C}_2^n \mid \mathsf{C}_1^n + \mathsf{C}_2^n \mid \mathsf{C}^{n*} \qquad \text{PComm} \ni \mathsf{c}^n ::= \mathsf{cc}^n \mid \mathsf{rc}^n$$
$$\text{CComm} \ni \mathsf{cc}^n ::= \quad x := e^n \mid \mathtt{assume}(x = v) \mid \mathtt{assume}(x \neq v)$$
$$\mid x := \mathsf{CAS}(y, e_1, e_2) \mid \mathtt{poll}(\bar{n})$$
$$\text{RComm} \ni \mathsf{rc}^n ::= x := \bar{y} \mid \bar{y} := x \mid \mathtt{rfence}(\bar{n})$$

Primitive commands include *CPU* (cc^n) and *RDMA* (rc^n) operations. A CPU operation on n may be a no-op ($\mathtt{skip}$), an assignment to a local location ($x := e$), an assumption on the value of a local location ($\mathtt{assume}(x = v)$ and $\mathtt{assume}(x \neq v)$), an atomic CAS ('compare-and-set') operation ($x := \mathsf{CAS}(y, e_1, e_2)$), or a 'poll', $\mathtt{poll}(\bar{n})$, that awaits the completion notification of the earliest put/get that is pending (not yet acknowledged). An RDMA operation may be (i) a 'get', $x := \bar{y}$, reading from remote location $\bar{y}$ and writing the result to local location x; (ii) a 'put', $\bar{y} := x$, reading from local location x and writing the result to remote location $\bar{y}$; or (iii) a 'remote fence', $\mathtt{rfence}(\bar{n})$, which ensures that all later (in program order) RDMA operations towards $\overline{n}$ will await the completion of all earlier RDMA operations towards $\overline{n}$. $\texttt{poll}(\overline{n})$ is executed by the CPU and blocks its thread (and prevents the requests of later remote operations), while $\texttt{rfence}(\overline{n})$ blocks the NIC for the execution of remote operations towards $\overline{n}$.

3.2   RDMA^SC: Declarative Semantics

Events and Executions. In the literature of declarative models, the traces of a program are commonly represented as a set of *executions*, where an execution is a graph comprising: i) a set of *events* (graph nodes); and ii) a number of relations on events (graph edges). Each event is associated with the execution of a primitive command (in PComm) and is a tuple (ι, t, l), where ι is the (unique) *event identifier*, $t \in \mathsf{Tid}$ identifies the executing thread, and $l \in \mathsf{ELab}$ is the *event label*, defined below.

Definition 1 (Labels and events). *An event,* $\mathsf{e} \in \mathsf{Event}$, *is a triple* (ι, t, l), *where* $\iota \in \mathbb{N}$, $t \in \mathsf{Tid}$ *and* $l \in \mathsf{ELab}_{n(t)}$. *The set of* event labels *is* $\mathsf{ELab} \triangleq \bigcup_n \mathsf{ELab}_n$ *for all nodes* n. *An* event label *of* n, $l \in \mathsf{ELab}_n$, *is a tuple of one of the following forms:*

- *NIC local read:* $l = \texttt{nlR}(x^n, v_r, \overline{n})$
- *NIC remote write:* $l = \texttt{nrW}(y^{\overline{n}}, v_w)$
- *NIC remote read:* $l = \texttt{nrR}(y^{\overline{n}}, v_r)$
- *NIC local write:* $l = \texttt{nlW}(x^n, v_w, \overline{n})$
- *NIC fence:* $l = \texttt{nF}(\overline{n})$

- *(CPU) local read:* $l = \texttt{lR}(x^n, v_r)$
- *(CPU) local write:* $l = \texttt{lW}(x^n, v_w)$
- *(CPU) CAS:* $l = \texttt{CAS}(x^n, v_r, v_w)$
- *(CPU) poll:* $l = \texttt{P}(\overline{n})$

Each event label denotes whether the associated primitive command is handled by the NIC (left column, prefixed with n), or the CPU (right column). A poll instruction is handled by the CPU. A put operation $x^{\overline{n}} := y^n$ by node n towards node $\overline{n}$ comprises a NIC local read from y^n and a NIC remote write on $x^{\overline{n}}$ and is thus modelled as two events with labels $\texttt{nlR}(y^n, v, \overline{n})$ and $\texttt{nrW}(x^{\overline{n}}, v)$, where v denotes the value read from y^n and written to $x^{\overline{n}}$. Similarly, a get $x^n := y^{\overline{n}}$ is modelled as two events with labels of the form $\texttt{nrR}(y^{\overline{n}}, v)$ and $\texttt{nlW}(x^n, v, \overline{n})$.

CPU operations are modelled by events as expected. A successful operation $x := \texttt{CAS}(y, v_1, v_2)$ is modelled by two events with labels $\texttt{CAS}(y, v_1, v_2)$ and $\texttt{lW}(x, v_1)$. An unsuccessful $x := \texttt{CAS}(y, v_1, v_2)$ operation is modelled by a CPU read instead: $\texttt{lR}(y, v)$ and $\texttt{lW}(x, v)$, with $v \neq v_1$.

We write $\texttt{type}(l)$, $\texttt{loc}(l)$, $v_r(l)$, $v_w(l)$, and $\overline{n}(l)$ for the type (e.g. $\texttt{lR}$), location, read value, write value, and remote node of l, where applicable; e.g. $\texttt{loc}(\texttt{nlR}(x^n, v_r, \overline{n})) = x^n$ and $\overline{n}(\texttt{nlR}(x^n, v_r, \overline{n})) = \overline{n}$. We lift these functions to events as expected. We write $\iota(\mathsf{e})$, $t(\mathsf{e})$, $l(\mathsf{e})$ to project the corresponding components of an event $\mathsf{e} = (\iota, t, l)$, and write $n(\mathsf{e})$ for the node $n(t(\mathsf{e}))$ of an event.

Queue Pairs. As mentioned in §2 (see Fig. 1e), two remote operations by the same thread towards different remote nodes can be reordered. When using RDMA, each thread establishes a communication channel, called a *queue pair*, towards each remote node. The intuition is that operations on different queue pairs are independent and can always be reordered. Different threads, even on the same node, create different queue pairs to connect to the same remote node.

Notation. Given a relation r and a set A, we write r^+ for the transitive closure of r; r^{-1} for the inverse of r; $r|_A$ for $r \cap (A \times A)$; and $[A]$ for the identity relation on A, i.e. $\{(a, a) \mid a \in A\}$. We write $r_1; r_2$ for their relational composition: $\{(a, b) \mid \exists c.\, (a, c) \in r_1 \wedge (c, b) \in r_2\}$. When r is a strict partial order, we write $r|_{imm}$ for the *immediate* edges in r, i.e. $r \setminus (r; r)$. Given a set of events E and a location x, we write E_x for $\{e \in E \mid \mathtt{loc}(e) = x\}$. Given a set of events E and a label type X, we write $E.\mathtt{X}$ for $\{e \in E \mid \mathtt{type}(e) = \mathtt{X}\}$, and define its sets of *reads* as $E.\mathcal{R} \triangleq E.\mathtt{1R} \cup E.\mathtt{CAS} \cup E.\mathtt{n1R} \cup E.\mathtt{nrR}$, *writes* as $E.\mathcal{W} \triangleq E.\mathtt{1W} \cup E.\mathtt{CAS} \cup E.\mathtt{n1W} \cup E.\mathtt{nrW}$, *CPU events* as $E^{\mathrm{cpu}} \triangleq E.\mathtt{1W} \cup E.\mathtt{1R} \cup E.\mathtt{CAS} \cup E.\mathtt{P}$, and *NIC writes* as $E.\mathtt{nW} \triangleq E.\mathtt{n1W} \cup E.\mathtt{nrW}$. We define the '*same-location*' relation as $\mathtt{sloc} \triangleq \{(e, e') \in \mathsf{Event}^2 \mid \mathtt{loc}(e) = \mathtt{loc}(e')\}$; the '*same-thread*' relation as $\mathtt{sthd} \triangleq \{(e, e') \in \mathsf{Event}^2 \mid t(e) = t(e')\}$; and the '*same-queue-pair*' relation as $\mathtt{sqp} \triangleq \{(e, e') \in \mathsf{Event}^2 \mid t(e) = t(e') \wedge \overline{n}(e) = \overline{n}(e')\}$. We use $\mathtt{sqp}$ for events on the same queue pair, i.e. by the same thread and towards the same remote node. Note that $\mathtt{sqp} \subseteq \mathtt{sthd}$ and that $\mathtt{sloc}$, $\mathtt{sthd}$, and $\mathtt{sqp}$ are all symmetric. For a set of events E, we write $E.\mathtt{sloc}$ for $\mathtt{sloc}|_E$; similarly for $E.\mathtt{sthd}$ and $E.\mathtt{sqp}$.

Definition 2 (Pre-executions). *A tuple $\mathcal{G} = \langle E, \mathtt{po}, \mathtt{pf} \rangle$ is a pre-execution of a program if:*

- $E \subseteq \mathsf{Event}$ *is the set of events and includes a set of* initialisation *events, $E^0 \subseteq E$, comprising a single write with label $\mathtt{1W}(x, 0)$ for each $x \in \mathsf{Loc}$.*
- $\mathtt{po} \subseteq E \times E$ *is the 'program order' relation defined as a disjoint union of strict total orders, each ordering the events of one thread, with $E^0 \times (E \setminus E^0) \subseteq \mathtt{po}$, and such that:*
  - *Each put (resp. get) operation corresponds to two events: a read and a write with the read immediately preceding the write in $\mathtt{po}$: 1. if $r \in G.\mathtt{n1R}$ (resp. $r \in G.\mathtt{nrR}$), then $(r, w) \in \mathtt{po}|_{imm}$ for some $w \in G.\mathtt{nrW}$ ($w \in G.\mathtt{n1W}$); and 2. if $w \in G.\mathtt{nrW}$ (resp. $w \in G.\mathtt{n1W}$), then $(r, w) \in \mathtt{po}|_{imm}$ for some $r \in G.\mathtt{n1R}$ ($r \in G.\mathtt{nrR}$).*
  - *Read and write events of a put (resp. get) have matching values: if $(r, w) \in G.\mathtt{po}|_{imm}$, $\mathtt{type}(r) \in \{\mathtt{n1R}, \mathtt{nrR}\}$, and $\mathtt{type}(w) \in \{\mathtt{n1W}, \mathtt{nrW}\}$, then $v_r(r) = v_w(w)$.*
- $\mathtt{pf} \subseteq E.\mathtt{nW} \times E.\mathtt{P}$ *is the 'polls-from' relation, relating earlier (in program-order) NIC writes to later poll operations on the same queue pair; i.e. $\mathtt{pf} \subseteq \mathtt{po} \cap \mathtt{sqp}$. Moreover, $\mathtt{pf}$ is functional on its domain (every NIC write can be be polled at most once), and $\mathtt{pf}$ is total and functional on its range (every poll in $E.\mathtt{P}$ polls from exactly one NIC write). Also, Poll events poll-from the oldest non-polled remote operation on the same queue pair:*
  if $w_1 \in G.\mathtt{nW}$ and $w_1 \xrightarrow{\mathtt{po} \cap \mathtt{sqp}} w_2 \xrightarrow{\mathtt{pf}} p_2$, then there exists p_1 such that $w_1 \xrightarrow{\mathtt{pf}} p_1 \xrightarrow{\mathtt{po}} p_2$.

Pre-executions are constructed syntactically by induction on the structure of the corresponding program. This definition is standard and omitted.

Intuitively, a pre-execution can also be seen as a trace of the execution: for each thread t, $\mathtt{po}$ restricted to t is a total order, and so $\langle E, \mathtt{po} \rangle$ is fundamentally a sequence of events for each thread. In this view, pf should be considered a well-formedness condition: each prefix of the trace needs to have at least as many remote operations as poll operations. So $\langle E, \mathsf{po}, \mathsf{pf} \rangle$ can be seen as providing a well-formed trace for each thread. We later define robustness conditions on pre-executions, and as such they can also be considered conditions on traces.

We next extend the notion of a pre-execution to an *execution* by choosing explicitly how the different events interact.

Definition 3 (Executions). $G = \langle E, \mathsf{po}, \mathsf{pf}, \mathsf{rf}, \mathsf{mo}, \mathsf{nfo} \rangle$ *is an execution if:*

- $\langle E, \mathsf{po}, \mathsf{pf} \rangle$ *is a pre-execution.*
- $\mathsf{rf} \subseteq E.\mathcal{W} \times E.\mathcal{R}$ *is the 'reads-from' relation on events of the same location with matching values; i.e.* $(a, b) \in \mathsf{rf} \Rightarrow (a, b) \in \mathsf{sloc} \wedge v_w(a) = v_r(b)$. *Moreover,* rf *is total and functional on its range: every read in* $E.\mathcal{R}$ *is related to exactly one write in* $E.\mathcal{W}$.
- $\mathsf{mo} \triangleq \bigcup_{x \in \mathsf{Loc}} \mathsf{mo}_x$ *is the 'modification-order', where each* mo_x *is a strict total order on* $E.\mathcal{W}_x$ *with* $E_x^0 \times (E.\mathcal{W}_x \setminus E_x^0) \subseteq \mathsf{mo}_x$ *describing the order in which writes on x reach the memory.*
- $\mathsf{nfo} \subseteq E.\mathsf{sqp}$ *is the 'NIC flush order', such that for all* $(a, b) \in E.\mathsf{sqp}$, *if* $a \in E.\mathtt{nlR}, b \in E.\mathtt{nlW}$, *then* $(a, b) \in \mathsf{nfo} \cup \mathsf{nfo}^{-1}$, *and if* $a \in E.\mathtt{nrR}, b \in E.\mathtt{nrW}$, *then* $(a, b) \in \mathsf{nfo} \cup \mathsf{nfo}^{-1}$.

We define the *reads-before* relation as $\mathsf{rb} \triangleq (\mathsf{rf}^{-1}; \mathsf{mo}) \setminus [E]$, relating each read r to writes that are mo-after the write r reads from. Given a (pre-)execution G (resp. $\mathcal{G}$), we use the '$G.$' prefix to project its various components (e.g. $G.\mathsf{rf}$) and derived relations (e.g. $G.\mathsf{rb}$). When the context is clear, we drop the prefix.

PCIe guarantees that a NIC local read ($\mathtt{nlR}$) propagates all pending NIC local writes ($\mathtt{nlW}$) (processed by the same queue pair) to memory, while a NIC remote read ($\mathtt{nrR}$) propagates all pending NIC remote writes ($\mathtt{nrW}$) (processed by the same queue pair) to memory. We model this total order through the nfo relation, stipulating that all NIC local reads and writes (resp. all NIC remote reads and writes) on the same queue pair be totally ordered.

Issue and Observation Points. In what follows we distinguish between when an instruction is *issued* and when it is *observed*. Intuitively, an instruction is issued when it is processed by the CPU or the NIC, and it is observed when its effect is propagated to memory. As such, since NIC writes can be delayed and have an observable effect on memory, the time points at which they are issued and observed may differ. Since we assume CPUs follow the strong SC memory model, CPU writes are issued and observed at the same time. However, the local (resp. remote) write of a get (resp. put) is issued when it is processed by the NIC and sent to the PCIe fabric, and observed when it is propagated to memory. All other events are *instantaneous* in that *either* they do not have an observable effect on memory (e.g. reads), *or* their effect is written to memory *immediately* (e.g. CAS operations and CPU writes). Given a set of events E, we thus define the set of *instantaneous events in E* as $E.\mathtt{Inst} \triangleq E \setminus (E.\mathtt{nlW} \cup E.\mathtt{nrW})$ Intuitively, the effects of NIC local writes and NIC remote writes (labelled $\mathtt{nlW}$ and $\mathtt{nrW}$) can be delayed in the PCIe fabric and are thus excluded from the set

Later in Program Order

ippo	1 E^{cpu}	2 n1R	3 nrW	4 nrR	5 n1W	6 nF
A E^{cpu}	✓	✓	✓	✓	✓	✓
B n1R	✗	sqp	sqp	sqp	sqp	sqp
C nrW	✗	✗	sqp	sqp	sqp	sqp
D nrR	✗	✗	✗	✗	sqp	sqp
E n1W	✗	✗	✗	✗	sqp	sqp
F nF	✗	sqp	sqp	sqp	sqp	sqp

(Earlier in PO)

Later in Program Order

oppo	1 E^{cpu}	2 n1R	3 nrW	4 nrR	5 n1W	6 nF
A E^{cpu}	✓	✓	✓	✓	✓	✓
B n1R	✗	sqp	sqp	sqp	sqp	sqp
C nrW	✗	✗	sqp	sqp	sqp	✗
D nrR	✗	✗	✗	✗	sqp	sqp
E n1W	✗	✗	✗	✗	sqp	✗
F nF	✗	sqp	sqp	sqp	sqp	sqp

(Earlier in PO)

Fig. 4: The RDMA^{SC} ordering constraints on ippo (left) and oppo (right), where ✓ denotes that instructions are ordered (and cannot be reordered), ✗ denotes they are not ordered (and may be reordered), and sqp denotes they are ordered iff they are on the same queue pair.

of instantaneous events. Note that the observation point either follows the issue point (for NIC writes), or coincides (for instantaneous events).

We next define the '*issue-preserved program order*', ippo, as the subset of po edges (ippo ⊆ po) that must be preserved when issuing instructions. That is, if two events are ippo-related, then they must be issued in program order; otherwise they may be processed in either order. The left table of Fig. 4 describes which po edges are included in ippo, where ✓ denotes that the two instructions are ippo-related (i.e. they must be issued in program order), ✗ denotes that they are not ippo-related (i.e. they may be issued out of order) and sqp denotes that they are ippo-related iff they are on the same queue pair. For instance, when a CPU instruction is followed by anything, they are issued in order (line A); but when a NIC instruction is followed by a CPU one, they may be reordered (cells B1–F1).

Analogously, we define the '*observation-preserved program order*', oppo, as the subset of po edges (oppo ⊆ po) that must be preserved when observing the effects of instructions. I.e., if two events are oppo-related, then they become observable in program order in RDMA^{SC}; otherwise they may become observable in either order. The right table of Fig. 4 describes which po edges are included in oppo. The two tables differ in cells C6 and E6. This is because NIC writes can be delayed, and remote fences do not guarantee propagation to memory.

RDMA^{SC} Consistency. The notion of executions (Def. 3) imposes very few constraints on the po, pf, rf, mo, and nfo relations. Such restrictions and thus the permitted behaviours of a program are determined by defining the set of *consistent* executions, defined below.

Definition 4 (RDMA^{SC}-consistency). *An execution* $\langle E, \text{po}, \text{pf}, \text{rf}, \text{mo}, \text{nfo} \rangle$ *is* RDMA^{SC}-*consistent iff* ib *and* ob *are irreflexive, where:*

$$\text{ib} \triangleq \left(\text{ippo} \cup \text{rf} \cup \text{pf} \cup \text{nfo} \right)^{+} \qquad \text{('issued-before')}$$

$$\text{ob} \triangleq \left(\text{oppo} \cup \text{rf} \cup ([\text{n1W}]; \text{pf}) \cup \text{nfo} \cup \text{rb} \cup \text{mo} \cup ([\text{Inst}]; \text{ib}) \right)^{+} \qquad \text{('observed-before')}$$

The ib (resp. ob) relation is an extension of ippo (resp. oppo), describing the issue (resp. observation) order across the instructions of different threads and nodes. RDMA^{SC}-consistency requires that ib and ob be irreflexive (i.e. yield strict partial orders as they are defined transitively).

The rf (resp. pf) component in ib states that if e reads from (resp. polls from) w, then w must have been issued before e. Recall that nfo totally orders the nlR/nlW and nrR/nrW operations on the same queue pair and is thus in ib. The rf component in ob states that if a read r reads from a write w, then the write has reached memory. This is because reads can only read the main memory and not auxiliary buffers. The [nlW]; pf component states that if p polls from a NIC local write w, then w must have left the PCIe fabric and reached the memory. Note that this is not the case for nrW events: polling an nrW event w might succeeds when w is still in the remote PCIe fabric before reaching the remote memory. The nfo in ob can be justified as in the case of ib. The rb component in ob ensures that a read r on x observes the latest write on x that has reached the memory. As mo describes the order in which the writes on each location reach the memory, it is included in ob. Let (τ_i, τ_o) be the issue and observation points of e and (τ_i', τ_o') be those of e'. The [Inst]; ib in ob ensures that if e $\xrightarrow{\text{ib}}$ e' (i.e. $\tau_i < \tau_i'$) and e is instantaneous $(\tau_i = \tau_o)$, then $\tau_o = \tau_i < \tau_i' \leq \tau_o'$, i.e. e $\xrightarrow{\text{ob}}$ e'.

4   Robustness of RDMA^{SC} Programs

In the traditional setting of CPU concurrency (where all threads execute CPU instructions), the most intuitive consistency model is *sequential consistency* (SC) [43]. While SC is too strong—in that disallowing *all* reorderings does not enable efficient implementations—it provides an intuitive and commonly understood model, making it easier for developers to reason about their programs.

Although none of the existing well-known consistency models follow SC by default, programmers typically address this difficulty by focusing on *robust* implementations of algorithms. Specifically, a program is robust under a weak consistency model CM if every possible behaviour of the program under CM is also an allowed behaviour under SC. In our model, this is defined as follows.

Definition 5 (SC-consistency and RDMA^{SC}-robustness). *Given an execution* $\langle E, \text{po}, \text{pf}, \text{rf}, \text{mo}, \text{nfo} \rangle$, *its associated* sequential-consistency *relation is defined as* sc $\triangleq$ (po $\cup$ rf $\cup$ rb $\cup$ mo). *An execution* G *is SC-consistent iff* G.sc *is acyclic. A pre-execution is robust under* RDMA^{SC} *iff all of its* RDMA^{SC}-*consistent executions (Def. 4) are also SC-consistent.*

Our aim here is to provide guidelines to ensure the robustness of RDMA^{SC} programs. That is, we identify a number of *syntactic* requirements such that if a program fulfils them, then the behaviours of the program under RDMA^{SC} coincide with its behaviours under SC; i.e. the program does not exhibit any weak behaviours brought about by observable reorderings.

There are two complementary approaches to achieve robustness. The first is to structure the program in a way that limits the very existence of problematic

gb (Earlier in po)		Later in po								
		different queue pair					same queue pair			
		1	2	3	4	5	6	7	8	9
		CPU	nlR	nrW	nrR	nlW	nlR	nrW	nrR	nlW
A	CPU	✓	✓	✓	✓	✓	N/A			
B	nlR	P	P	P	P	P	✓	✓	✓	✓
C	nrW	GP	GP	GP	GP	GP	GP	✓	✓	✓
D	nrR	P	P	P	P	P	F	F	F	✓
E	nlW	P	P	P	P	P	F	F	P	✓

Fig. 5: Constraints necessary to guarantee that a pair of po-related events in $\mathcal{R} \cup \mathcal{W}$ will be ob-related for any consistent execution. CPU denotes local events in 1W∪1R∪CAS. The ✓ denotes that no additional constraint is needed and that the events are already in ob. P denotes that the earlier operation must be polled before executing the later one. F denotes that either the earlier operation must be polled (similar to P) or that a remote fence must be inserted between the two operations. GP denotes that a get operation and its associated poll on the first queue pair must be inserted between the two operations.

cases. The second is to extend the program with enough restrictions (e.g. polls and remote fences) to prohibit reorderings. In the next section (§5) we focus on the former and provide a set of explicit guidelines to avoid most problematic cases by design. In this section we focus on the latter, and describe how to identify problematic cases and how to block them. In what follows, we present the general syntactic restrictions required to forbid the reordering opportunities for specific operations (§4.1). We then propose sufficient syntactic conditions that block observable reorderings, and we prove that these conditions imply robustness (§4.2). Finally, we discuss the limitations of this approach (§4.3).

4.1   A Syntactic Approach to Enforce the Program Order

One of our key results relies on enforcing the program order (i.e. blocking instruction reordering) in potentially observable cases. Recall that given an execution, the observed-before order (ob) describes when an event takes effect before another. That is, for $(e_1, e_2) \in$ po, when $e_1 \xrightarrow{ob} e_2$ in an execution G, then they are not reordered in G. Our first aim here is to identify syntactic constraints that ensure that a specific pair of given instructions (of the same thread) are related by ob. However, in order to define syntactic constraints for robustness, we can only rely on the *syntax* of the program and not components such as rf or mo. Our syntactic constraints can only rely on the pre-execution components po and pf, and we cannot directly use the ob relation derived from a specific execution.

To this end, we first define the *guaranteed-before* relation, gb ⊆ po, describing when two instructions in the same thread are guaranteed to remain in order (and their reordering is blocked), as shown in Fig. 5. Specifically, if two instructions are related by oppo, then they are guaranteed to be observed in that order and thus there is no need for additional restrictions; this is denoted by ✓ in cells A1–A5, B6–B9, C7–C9, D9, and E9 (*cf.* oppo in Fig. 4). For most other cases (noted P or F), polling the earlier instruction enforces the ordering. Recall that polling a NIC remote write does not guarantee its completion, and we need to add a 'dummy' get operation and its corresponding poll to ensure ordering (noted GP).

In most cases, when the two operations are on the *same* queue pair, then a remote fence is sufficient to enforce the ordering (noted F in D6–D8, E6–E7), and is a cheaper alternative to a poll. Perhaps surprisingly, a remote fence is not always sufficient: the two outliers are cells C6 and E8. For C6, consider the program $z^2 := x; \mathtt{rfence}(2); w^2 := y$: the local value of y might be read before the value of z is changed. This is because $\mathtt{rfence}$ (2) (as with poll) only awaits the acknowledgement from the remote side which does not necessarily ensure that the first put has completed. For E8, consider $x := z^2; \mathtt{rfence}(2); y := w^2$, where w^2 can be read before x is modified: $\mathtt{rfence}$ (2) only waits for the NIC local write ($x := v_z$) to be sent to the local PCIe fabric and thus the put operation ($y := w^2$) can start earlier than one could expect.

Definition 6 (guaranteed-before). *Given a pre-execution* $\mathcal{G} = \langle E, \mathsf{po}, \mathsf{pf} \rangle$, *its* guaranteed-before *order,* $\mathsf{gb} \subseteq \mathsf{po}$, *is defined as* $\mathsf{gb} \triangleq \mathsf{gb}^+_{\mathsf{base}}$, *with:*

$$
\begin{aligned}
\mathsf{gb}_{\mathsf{base}} \triangleq \quad & \mathsf{oppo} && \text{(A1--A5,B6--B9,C7--C9,D9,E9 in Fig. 5)} \\
& \cup\ [\mathtt{nlR}]; \mathsf{po}|_{imm}; [\mathtt{nrW}]; \mathsf{pf} && \text{(B1--B5 in Fig. 5)} \\
& \cup\ [\mathtt{nrW}]; (\mathsf{po} \cap \mathsf{sqp}); [\mathtt{nlW}]; \mathsf{pf} && \text{(C1--C6 in Fig. 5)} \\
& \cup\ [\mathtt{nrR}]; \mathsf{po}|_{imm}; [\mathtt{nlW}]; \mathsf{pf} && \text{(D1--D8 in Fig. 5)} \\
& \cup\ [\mathtt{nrR}]; (\mathsf{po} \cap \mathsf{sqp}); [\mathtt{nF}]; (\mathsf{po} \cap \mathsf{sqp}) && \text{(D6--D8 in Fig. 5)} \\
& \cup\ [\mathtt{nlW}]; \mathsf{pf} && \text{(E1--E8 in Fig. 5)} \\
& \cup\ [\mathtt{nlW}]; (\mathsf{po} \cap \mathsf{sqp}); [\mathtt{nF}]; (\mathsf{po} \cap \mathsf{sqp}); [\mathtt{nlR} \cup \mathtt{nrW}] && \text{(E6--E7 in Fig. 5)}
\end{aligned}
$$

Given an execution $G = \langle E, \mathsf{po}, \mathsf{pf}, \mathsf{rf}, \mathsf{mo}, \mathsf{rb} \rangle$, we write $G.\mathsf{gb}$ for $\langle E, \mathsf{po}, \mathsf{pf} \rangle.\mathsf{gb}$. Finally, we prove that gb implies ob for any RDMA^{SC}-consistent execution (see the extended version [11] for the proof).

Theorem 1 (gb implies ob). *Given a pre-execution* $\langle E, \mathsf{po}, \mathsf{pf} \rangle$, *for all* RDMA^{SC}-*consistent executions* $G = \langle E, \mathsf{po}, \mathsf{pf}, \mathsf{rf}, \mathsf{mo}, \mathsf{nfo} \rangle$ *and all* $e_1, e_2 \in E$, *if* $(e_1, e_2) \in G.\mathsf{gb}$, *then* $(e_1, e_2) \in G.\mathsf{ob}$.

Given Theorem 1 above, we can use gb as a tool to enforce robustness. Specifically, whenever a program order pair $(e_1, e_2) \in \mathsf{po}$ may be reordered, we can add the prescribed fences to enforce $(e_1, e_2) \in \mathsf{gb}$ and thus block the reordering. The rest of this section describes *when* we should use this tool.

4.2 Conditions for Robustness under RDMA^{SC}

As mentioned before, blocking all instruction reorderings, i.e. by requiring $\mathsf{po} = \mathsf{gb}$, would enforce sequential consistency and thus robustness. However, this is too strict and highly impractical. Instead, we should ideally enforce gb selectively when needed and only prevent observable reorderings.

Two sources of weak behaviours. As presented in §2, RDMA^{sc} programs have two distinct sources of weak behaviours. These come from two different kinds of pairs of events (of the same thread): (1) pairs forming a data race on a certain location, e.g. $a := y^2; y^2 := 1$, as presented in Fig. 1f (copied below-left) and Figs. 1b, 1e, and 1h ; and (2) pairs whose reordering can be observed by other threads, e.g. $a := y^2; z^3 := 1$, as in the examples of Fig. 3b (copied below-right).

	$y=0$
$a := y^2$ $y^2 := 1$	

$a = 1 ✓$

	$y = 0$	$z = 0$
$a := y^2$ $z^3 := 1$	$y := z^3$	

$a = 1 ✓$

As such, stopping these two sources of weak behaviours would be enough to ensure robustness. Data races within a thread are *always* problematic, no matter the context, and we always need to block the reordering of such pairs (i.e. enforce gb to ensure the pair is ob-ordered in any execution). Pairs of the second kind cannot create weak behaviours by themselves, but they might allow weak behaviours depending on the rest of the program of other threads. In the next section (§5), we show conditions making sure that such pairs can never create weak behaviours by design. In this section, we focus on deciding whether such a pair might lead to a weak behaviour and, if so, how to block the reordering.

To formulate this intuition, we write $\text{public}(x)$ to denote that x is a *public* location accessed by multiple threads, and given a set of events E, we define the set of public events in E as $E^{\text{pub}} \triangleq \{e \in E \mid \text{public}(\text{loc}(e))\}$. We further define $E \setminus t \triangleq \{e \in E \mid t(e) \neq t\}$ for the set of events in E that are not by thread t. We can then formulate the two categories of weak behaviours above as two kinds of sc cycles: sc cycles on a single thread (1) and sc cycles on public events across threads (2), as formulated below (see the extended version for the full proof).

Theorem 2 (sc cycle decomposition). *Given a* RDMA^{sc}*-consistent execution* $G = \langle E, \text{po}, \text{pf}, \text{rf}, \text{mo}, \text{nfo} \rangle$*, if* $\exists e \in E.\ e \xrightarrow{G.\text{sc}}^+ e$ *(i.e. a cycle in* $G.\text{sc}$*), then:*

- *either there is a* $G.\text{sc}$ *cycle on a single thread, i.e.* $\exists e \in E.\ e \xrightarrow{G.\text{sc} \cap \text{sthd}}^+ e$;
- *or there exists* $e_1, e_2 \in E^{\text{pub}}$ *such that* $e_1 \xrightarrow{\text{po} \setminus G.\text{ob}} e_2 \xrightarrow{(G.\text{sc};[E^{\text{pub}} \setminus t(e_1)])^+; G.\text{sc}} e_1$. *That is, there is an* sc *cycle on public events, with two* po*-related events on some thread* $t(e_1)$ *not related in* ob*, and where the rest of the cycle does not go through the events of* $t(e_1)$.

The two kinds of problematic reorderings are tackled separately below, and Theorem 5 confirms the two resulting conditions are sufficient for robustness.

Preventing sc cycles from data races. As shown above, when an allowed reordering is part of a data race, it becomes observable independently from the context. Thus, we should always preclude this kind of reordering. Specifically, in Def. 7 below we present a *local data-race freedom* property to block data races within each thread and prevent single-threaded weak behaviours.

Definition 7 (Local DRF). *Given a pre-execution* $\langle E, \mathsf{po}, \mathsf{pf}\rangle$, *two events* $e_1, e_2 \in E$ *are* locally conflicting *iff 1.* $(e_1, e_2) \in \mathsf{sthd}$; *2.* $\mathsf{loc}(e_1) = \mathsf{loc}(e_2)$; *and 3. at least one of* e_1, e_2 *is a write event. A pre-execution* $\mathcal{G}$ *is* locally data-race free *(LDRF), iff for all* $e_1, e_2 \in \mathcal{G}.E$, *if* e_1, e_2 *are locally conflicting, then* $(e_1, e_2) \in \mathcal{G}.\mathsf{gb} \cup \mathcal{G}.\mathsf{gb}^{-1}$. *Put differently, given the definition of* gb *(Fig. 5), a pre-execution* $\langle E, \mathsf{po}, \mathsf{pf}\rangle$ *is* LDRF *iff for all locally conflicting accesses* $e_1, e_2 \in E$, *if* $(e_1, e_2) \in \mathsf{po}$, *then the following four conditions hold:*

1. *If* $e_1 \in \mathsf{nlW}$ *and* $(e_1, e_2) \notin \mathsf{sqp}$, *then there exists* $e_3 \in P$ *such that* $(e_1, e_3) \in \mathsf{pf}$ *and* $(e_3, e_2) \in \mathsf{po}$ *(cells E1, E2, and E5 in Fig. 5).*
2. *If* $e_1 \in \mathsf{nlW}$, $e_2 \in \mathsf{nlR}$, *and* $(e_1, e_2) \in \mathsf{sqp}$, *then either there exists* $e_3 \in P$ *with* $(e_1, e_3) \in \mathsf{pf}$ *and* $(e_3, e_2) \in \mathsf{po}$; *or there exists* $e_3 \in \mathsf{nF}$ *with* $(e_1, e_3) \in \mathsf{po}$ *and* $(e_3, e_2) \in \mathsf{po}$ *(E6).*
3. *If* $e_1 \in \mathsf{nlR}$, $e_2 \in (\mathsf{nlW} \cup \mathsf{lW} \cup \mathsf{CAS})$, *and* $(e_1, e_2) \notin \mathsf{sqp}$, *then there exists* $e_1' \in \mathsf{nrW}$ *and* $e_3 \in P$ *such that* $(e_1, e_1') \in \mathsf{po}|_{imm}$, $(e_1', e_3) \in \mathsf{pf}$, *and* $(e_3, e_2) \in \mathsf{po}$ *(cells B1 and B5).*
4. *If* $e_1 \in \mathsf{nrR}$ *and* $e_2 \in \mathsf{nrW}$, *then either there exists* $e_3 \in \mathsf{nF}$ *such that* $e_1 \xrightarrow{\mathsf{po} \cap \mathsf{sqp}} e_3 \xrightarrow{\mathsf{po} \cap \mathsf{sqp}} e_2$; *or there exists* $e_1' \in \mathsf{nlW}$ *and* $e_3 \in P$ *such that* $e_1 \xrightarrow{\mathsf{po}|_{imm}} e_1' \xrightarrow{\mathsf{pf}} e_3 \xrightarrow{\mathsf{po}} e_2$ *(cell D7 in Fig. 5).*

These cases prohibit all possible races on a location x, i.e. of the form $x := y^n$; $x := -$ (E1,E5), $x := y^n$; $- := x$ (E2), $x := y^n$; $z^n := x$ (E6), $y^n := x$; $x := -$ (B1,B5), or $- := x^n$; $x^n := -$ (D7). Other entries in Fig. 5 cannot create races as either their ordering is already guaranteed (e.g. ✓ in E9); or they are on two read events (e.g. B2,D8); or they cannot be on the same location (e.g. D3,E7).

We argue that the constraints in Def. 7 do not restrict RDMA capabilities in that waiting for remote operations to complete before reusing their locations is already considered standard practice when writing RDMA programs.

We next show that LDRF prevents single-threaded weak behaviours.

Theorem 3. *Given a* RDMA^{SC}*-consistent execution* $G = \langle E, \mathsf{po}, \mathsf{pf}, \mathsf{rf}, \mathsf{mo}, \mathsf{nfo}\rangle$, *if* $\langle E, \mathsf{po}, \mathsf{pf}\rangle$ *is locally data-race free, then there is no* sc *cycle on a single thread; that is,* $(G.\mathsf{sc} \cap \mathsf{sthd})$ *is acyclic and the first case of Theorem 2 does not arise.*

Preventing sc cycles across threads. Unlike data races, pairs of the second kind cannot create weak behaviours by themselves, and their reorderings can only be observed in certain contexts.

The general strategy to prevent observable reorderings is straightforward: for every pair $(e_1, e_2) \in \mathsf{po}$ on public locations, either we know for certain that $e_2 \xrightarrow{\mathsf{sc}}{}^* e_1$ (using other threads) is impossible, or we conservatively block the reordering by enforcing $(e_1, e_2) \in \mathsf{gb}$. The challenge is that the relation sc is heavily dependent on the specific execution. So how can we ascertain *syntactically* that a later event e_2 cannot influence an earlier event e_1?

One easily accessible syntactic property is the communication pattern between nodes (i.e. when one node performs a remote operation towards another).

Thus, to simplify the task, we over-approximate dependency (i.e. sc) with *communication*. Intuitively, if two nodes do not communicate in the network topology, then they cannot causally influence each other.

We write $n_1 \overset{}{\underset{E}{\rightsquigarrow}} n_2$ (defined below) to denote that nodes n_1 and n_2 communicate via some event in E, in that some thread t on n_1 performs a remote operation $e \in E$ towards n_2, written $\mathsf{hasQP}(t, n_2, E)$, or vice versa.

$$n_1 \overset{}{\underset{E}{\rightsquigarrow}} n_2 \triangleq \exists t.\ (n(t) = n_1 \land \mathsf{hasQP}(t, n_2, E)) \lor (n(t) = n_2 \land \mathsf{hasQP}(t, n_1, E))$$

$$\mathsf{hasQP}(t, \overline{n}, E) \triangleq \exists e \in (E.\mathsf{nrW} \cup E.\mathsf{nrR}).\ t(e) = t \land \overline{n}(e) = \overline{n}$$

We next show that if there is an sc-path from one event e_2 to another e_1 using public events in A, then the corresponding nodes (of the locations) of e_2 and e_1 must communicate via A. This is established in Lem. 1 below, with the proof given in the extended version [11].

Lemma 1. *For all $A \subseteq E^{\mathsf{pub}}$, if $e_2 \xrightarrow{\mathsf{sc}|_A}{}^* e_1$ then $n(\mathsf{loc}(e_2)) \overset{}{\underset{A}{\rightsquigarrow}}{}^* n(\mathsf{loc}(e_1))$.*

We are interested in the inverse direction of this lemma: a topological connection between the nodes (of the locations) of e_2 and e_1 is a necessary condition for an sc-path from e_2 to e_1. Put differently, if there is no communication between the nodes of e_2 and e_1, then e_2 cannot influence e_1. As such, we can use this to over-approximate safely whether an event can influence another. We conservatively assume that if the two nodes can communicate (outside of the thread) then e_2 might influence e_1. These communications do not depend on a specific execution and can be ascertained syntactically from the pre-execution.

We can then prevent sc cycles across threads using the *fenced* condition below (Def. 8): for all $e_1 \xrightarrow{\mathsf{po}} e_2$ on public locations, if e_2 might influence e_1, then we block the reordering. We subsequently prove that if a pre-execution is fenced, then it does not admit sc cycles across threads.

Definition 8 (fenced). *A pre-execution $\langle E, \mathsf{po}, \mathsf{pf} \rangle$ is fenced iff for all $e_1, e_2 \in E^{\mathsf{pub}}$, if $e_1 \xrightarrow{\mathsf{po}} e_2$ and $n(\mathsf{loc}(e_1)) \overset{}{\underset{E^{\mathsf{pub}} \backslash t(e_1)}{\rightsquigarrow}}{}^* n(\mathsf{loc}(e_2))$, then $(e_1, e_2) \in \mathsf{gb}$.*

Theorem 4. *Given an $\mathrm{RDMA}^{\mathrm{SC}}$-consistent execution $\langle E, \mathsf{po}, \mathsf{pf}, \mathsf{rf}, \mathsf{mo}, \mathsf{nfo} \rangle$, if its associated pre-execution $\langle E, \mathsf{po}, \mathsf{pf} \rangle$ is fenced, then there is no sc cycle of the shape $e_1 \xrightarrow{\mathsf{po} \backslash \mathsf{ob}} e_2 \xrightarrow{(\mathsf{sc};[E^{\mathsf{pub}} \backslash t(e_1)])^+;\mathsf{sc}} e_1$ with $e_1, e_2 \in E^{\mathsf{pub}}$. That is, the second case of Theorem 2 does not arise.*

Robustness. Lastly, we show that LDRF and fenced imply robustness under $\mathrm{RDMA}^{\mathrm{SC}}$. Thus, this approach can be used to prevent RDMA weak behaviours.

Theorem 5 (Robustness under $\mathrm{RDMA}^{\mathrm{SC}}$). *Given a pre-execution $\mathcal{G} = \langle E, \mathsf{po}, \mathsf{pf} \rangle$, if $\mathcal{G}$ is locally data-race free (Def. 7) and fenced (Def. 8), then $\mathcal{G}$ is also robust under $\mathrm{RDMA}^{\mathrm{SC}}$ (Def. 5).*

	$x = 0$	$y = 0$
$a := x^2$ $y^3 := 1$		

	$x, w = 0$	$y, z = 0$
$a := x^2$ $y^3 := 1$	$b := x$ $z^3 := w$	$c := y$ $d := z$

	$x = 0$	$y = 0$
$a := x^2$ $y^3 := 1$	$x := y^3$	

(a) $a = 0$ ✓ $a = 1$ ✗   (b) $a = 0$ ✓ $a = 1$ ✗   (c) $a = 0$ ✓ $a = 1$ ✓

Fig. 6: Examples illustrating the limitation of Theorem 5, where the programs in (a) and (b) are robust (the weak behaviour $a = 1$ is not allowed in either) while that in (c) is not robust (it admits the weak behaviour $a = 1$); while Theorem 5 rightfully identifies (a) as robust (true positive) and (c) as not robust (true negative), it conservatively deems (b) not robust (false negative).

4.3   Usage and Limitations

Local data-race freedom (Def. 7) and fenced (Def. 8) are intuitive properties that can be checked syntactically. Indeed, given a program, it is straightforward to check mechanically whether these properties hold or to provide an explicit counterexample and a suggested fix using the definition of gb (Def. 6). As a result, sufficient constraints can automatically be added to ensure robustness.

However, this simplicity can occasionally be the limitation of our approach. Specifically, as the main theorem does not account for interactions between threads, it takes a conservative approach, which at times can lead to false negatives (where the program is deemed not robust even though no weak behaviours are possible), recommending unnecessary restrictions.

To see this, consider the example in Fig. 6a, where $a := x^2$ and $y^3 := 1$ can be reordered *without* introducing weak behaviours. In this case, Theorem 5 rightfully confirms that no additional restrictions are necessary. By contrast, consider the variant shown in Fig. 6b: although the two extended threads do not introduce any additional weak behaviours, our approach assumes there might be a causal dependency from $y^3 := 1$ to $a := x^2$, as is the case e.g. in Fig. 6c. As such, Theorem 5 cannot determine Fig. 6b as robust, and our approach would recommend inserting a poll operation in the first thread. Note that removing any of the six operations would enable Theorem 5 to ascertain Fig. 6b as robust.

Understanding that the reordering of the instructions in the first thread of Fig. 6b is not problematic would require a more complex static analysis beyond the scope of this paper.

5   Application: Tree Topology

Theorem 5 outlines the conditions under which we can guarantee that a program is robust under RDMA^{SC}. However, while the LDRF property (Def. 7) is reasonable, the fenced property (Def. 8) can lead to excessive restrictions (e.g. as in Fig. 6). Specifically, for every pair of events (e_1, e_2) in program order, we must either verify that e_2 cannot affect e_1, or ensure that their execution order is preserved. The main issue is that preserving the order of every pair of events can be particularly costly, notably when considering NIC remote write events. In such cases, the only resort is to introduce a 'dummy' get operation and poll it, which is inefficient. Instead, we propose a strategy whereby we stipulate certain conditions on the network *topology* (i.e. the shape of the RDMA network) so that later events are often unable to influence earlier events.

To this end, we propose a *tree topology* that balances generality (supporting a wide range of programs) with efficiency and restrictiveness (requiring minimal additional constraints to respect the fenced property). In §5.1 we present an overview of our new set of restrictions and illustrate their rationale through examples. In §5.2 we formalises these restrictions and prove that they indeed imply robustness under RDMA^{SC}. Finally, in §5.3 we demonstrate specific applications of the tree topology and how RDMA programs can make use of them.

5.1   Overview of the Restrictions

We describe four different conditions that, if satisfied, ensure the robustness of RDMA programs under RDMA^{SC}, and we justify them through examples.

LDRF. As before, we require that programs satisfy LDRF (Def. 7). As discussed, this is considered standard practice when writing RDMA programs and should not be seen as a limitation.

Private Copies. We require the *local locations* of RDMA operations – e.g. location y in $y := x^2$ – to be private (i.e. accessed by only one thread, namely that executing the RDMA operation). Intuitively, to maximise the efficiency of RDMA programs, we should ideally allow arbitrary interleaving of RDMA operations and CPU computations. For instance, let us consider the single-threaded program $C \triangleq y := x^2; c_{\text{cpu}}^y$, where c_{cpu}^y denotes a block of CPU instructions that does not access location y. If y is private, then although c_{cpu}^y and the get $y := x^2$ may be reordered, this reordering will not lead to any observable weak behaviours. That is, when we run C concurrently with *any* RDMA program C' (i.e. as $C||C'$), if y is private, then we do not need to poll $y := x^2$ before proceeding with c_{cpu}^y (even though they may be reordered), as the reordering cannot be observed by C'.

However, if y is accessible by other threads (on the same node or from a remote node), then the reordering becomes visible, allowing additional, potentially unwanted, weak behaviours. This is illustrated in the example below, where $c_{\text{cpu}}^y \triangleq z := 1$ and y is public (accessed by nodes 1 and 3).

$y, z = 0$	$x = 1$	
$y := x^2$ $z := 1$		$a := z^1$ $\texttt{poll}(1)$ $b := y^1$

$(a, b) = (1, 0)$ ✓

More concretely, due to the reordering, the later CPU computation ($z := 1$) can be observed before the earlier get ($y := x^2$), leading to the weak outcome $(a, b) = (1, 0)$.

Therefore, to prevent such weak behaviours, we stipulate that local locations of RDMA operations be private. This is not a costly limitation. Specifically, in the case of put operations, the data can easily be copied beforehand to a one-time-use private location. In the case of get operations, it means the thread running the command needs to acknowledge the data and copy it to make it available to other threads having access to the node.

Get in Order. We stipulate that each get operation be followed by a remote fence. Recall that only certain reorderings are allowed on the operations of the same queue pair. Intuitively, put operations cannot be overtaken, and we do not need to restrict their usage. However, get operations can be overtaken by other get/put operations, as shown in the examples below, where the $a := x^2$ is overtaken by a later remote operation on the same queue pair, leading to weak behaviours.

$a := x^2$ $b := x^2$	$x = 0$ $x := 1$

$(a, b) = (1, 0)$ ✓

$a := x^2$ $y^2 := 1$	$x, y = 0$ $x := y$

$a = 1$ ✓

As such, to prevent non-SC behaviours, we require that each get operation be followed by a remote fence, forcing the queue pair to await the completion of the get before starting the next remote operation. Of course, if the get is polled before another RDMA operation is submitted, the remote fence is not needed. Note that since remote fences do not block CPU computations nor communications with other nodes, they are not very expensive and are a reasonable cost to pay to ensure remote operations towards a specific remote node stay in order.

Tree Topology. Finally, the most important restriction is to constrain the topology of the network over which the program runs. Intuitively, having multiple paths between a set of nodes allows for visible effects to overtake each other (i.e. be reordered) along different paths, leading to weak behaviours. In the extreme case where every thread can communicate directly with every other node, we allow for a large number of visible reorderings, and lose any hope of preventing non-SC behaviours. When such connected topologies are needed to enable more efficient implementations (e.g. consensus algorithms), the developers must carefully account for the possible weak behaviours.

Our proposal is to adhere to a minimal topology where there is (at most) a single communication path between each pair of nodes. In the examples below we show how not adhering to the tree topology can lead to weak behaviours. Note that although we have followed each remote operation with a corresponding (costly) poll, we still cannot prevent the weak behaviours shown.

$y = 0$	$x = 0$
$x^2 := 1$	$y^1 := 1$
$\texttt{poll}(2)$	$\texttt{poll}(1)$
$a := y$	$b := x$

$(a, b) - (0, 0)$ ✓

	$x = 0$	$y, z = 0$
$z^3 := 1$		$a := y$
$\texttt{poll}(3)$	$y^3 := x$	$b := z$
$x^2 := 1$		

$(a, b) - (1, 0)$ ✓

$x = 0$		$y, z = 0$
$z^2 := 1$		$a := y$
$\texttt{poll}(2)$	$y^2 := x$	$b := z$
$x := 1$		

$(a, b) = (1, 0)$ ✓

The first example shows that queue pairs in both directions (between nodes 1 and 2) can lead to weak behaviours as they can observe the reordering of operations on the other node. The second example illustrates two paths between node 1 and 3: a direct path from node 1 to 3 (via $z^3 := 1$) and an indirect path through node 2 (from node 1 to 2 via $x^2 := 1$; from node 2 to 3 via $y^3 := x$). As shown, having multiple paths between two nodes allows threads to observe reorderings: $z^3 := 1$ is submitted first, but the effects of $x^2 := 1$, forwarded via $y^3 := x$, is observed first. The third example is a variant of the second, where the middle node is replaced by an additional thread on the left node. As queue pairs from different threads of the same node towards the same remote are still independent, the weak behaviour shown is permitted.

5.2   Tree Robustness

We next formalise the conditions described in §5.1 in Def. 9 below.

Definition 9 (tree-fenced). *A pre-execution $\langle E, \mathsf{po}, \mathsf{pf} \rangle$ is tree-fenced iff:*

1. *Local locations of RDMA operations are private: $E^{\mathsf{pub}}.\mathsf{nlR} = E^{\mathsf{pub}}.\mathsf{nlW} = \emptyset$*
2. *Each get operation is followed by a remote fence (or is polled) before the next remote operation on the same queue pair.*
   That is, for all e_1, e_2, if $e_1 \in \mathsf{nrR}$, $e_2 \in (\mathsf{nrR} \cup \mathsf{nrW})$, and $(e_1, e_2) \in (\mathsf{po} \cap \mathsf{sqp})$, then: either there exists $f \in \mathsf{nF}$ such that $(e_1, f) \in (\mathsf{po} \cap \mathsf{sqp})$ and $(f, e_2) \in (\mathsf{po} \cap \mathsf{sqp})$; or there exists $e_3 \in \mathsf{nlW}$ and $p \in \mathsf{P}$ such that $(e_1, e_3) \in \mathsf{po}|_{imm}$, $(e_3, p) \in \mathsf{pf}$, and $(p, e_2) \in \mathsf{po}$.
3. *There is (at most) a single communication path between any pair of nodes in that the following three properties hold:*
   (a) *The network does not have cycles, i.e. for all sets of distinct nodes $\{n_1; \ldots; n_k\}$ with $k > 2$: $\neg(n_1 \underset{E}{\leadsto} n_2 \underset{E}{\leadsto} \ldots \underset{E}{\leadsto} n_k \underset{E}{\leadsto} n_1)$*
   (b) *No two nodes have queue pairs towards each other:*
      $\neg \exists t_1, t_2.\ \mathsf{hasQP}(t_1, n(t_2), E) \wedge \mathsf{hasQP}(t_2, n(t_1), E)$
   (c) *Each node has at most one queue pair towards each remote node:*
      $\forall t, t', \overline{n}.\ t \neq t' \wedge \mathsf{hasQP}(t, \overline{n}, E) \wedge \mathsf{hasQP}(t', \overline{n}, E) \implies n(t) \neq n(t')$

Conditions 1 and 2 are purely syntactic and can be straightforwardly checked by examining the RDMA program. Condition 3 pertains to the topology of the RDMA network and can also be checked by examining the RDMA program.

A key advantage of these restrictions is that preventing weak behaviours never requires polling remote operations. This is crucial because the efficiency of RDMA implementations comes from parallelising data transfers and computations. As shown in the overview (§2), polling is very costly as it completely halts local computations and prevents submission of remote operations to any queue pair. With a tree topology, programmers only need to wait for remote operations to use their results (as per LDRF Def. 7), and do not need to sacrifice computation time to prevent reorderings.

We next prove that if a pre-execution is tree-fenced, then it is also fenced. The full proof is given in the extended version [11].

Theorem 6. *If a pre-execution is tree-fenced (Def. 9), then it is fenced (Def. 8).*

Hence, LDRF and tree-fenced properties imply robustness under RDMA^{SC}.

Corollary 1 (Tree robustness under RDMA^{SC}). *If a pre-execution $G = \langle E, \text{po}, \text{pf} \rangle$ satisfies LDRF (Def. 7) and is tree-fenced (Def. 9), then it is also robust under RDMA^{SC} (Def. 5).*

5.3 Specific Applications

The tree-fenced conditions above provide guidelines to ensure programs cannot exhibit weak behaviours. While not all RDMA programs follow the restrictions presented, a tree topology is sufficient for a range of applications. Notably, any setup using RDMA solely for the data transfer capabilities (and not for distributed computations) can easily be configured as a tree.

Star Topology: Single Manager Multiple Workers. The star topology is one of the most typical network configurations, providing simple and reliable communication between nodes, with many common applications such as for implementing local area networks (LAN). The star topology allows a main node to distribute jobs to other nodes and periodically check for progress. As demonstrated in this paper, this setup prevents any network weak behaviour even if communications towards different workers are independent and can be reordered.

Star Topology: Single Server Multiple Clients. The tree-fenced condition (Def. 9) is permissive enough to allow us to translate common concurrent algorithms (comprising loads and stores over shared memory) to distributed ones over RDMA *automatically* as follows. Specifically, consider a concurrent algorithm P_c using k threads $(t_1, ..., t_k)$. We can translate this to a corresponding RDMA program P_r using k nodes $(n_1, ..., n_k)$, where a designated node (say n_1) is the *server* and the others $(n_2, ..., n_k)$ are *clients*, and each node n_i has a single thread simulating t_i. All shared locations and data are located on the server node (n_1 running t_1). For each of the remaining nodes n_i, we replace the loads and stores on shared locations with get and put operations, respectively. Moreover, we insert a remote fence after each get operation (to ensure condition (2) of Def. 9) and poll get operations before using their values (to ensure LDRF).

The resulting RDMA program follows a *star topology*, with n_1 as the central (server) node accessed by multiple clients $(n_2, ..., n_k)$. Client locations are private by definition, ensuring that the tree-fenced condition holds. P_r thus avoids weak behaviours and constitutes a suitable implementation of P_c.

Observe that in this implementation, polling put operations is unnecessary (as long as different local locations are used for copying), and get operations can be optimised by being submitted as early as possible (i.e. after previous RDMA operations and reads on the same location) and before they are needed, allowing them to be interleaved with other computations.

6   Related Work

RDMA Semantics. The first realistic formal model for RDMA programs is RDMA^{TSO} by Ambal et al. [10] (where they assume that CPU concurrency is governed by TSO) formalised both operationally and declaratively, which they show to be equivalent. They also validate RDMA^{TSO} empirically by running an extensive suite of litmus tests on RDMA hardware. While comprehensive in its formal description of the language, this work does not present strategies for mitigating RDMA weaknesses or optimising the use of this technology by using e.g. minimal poll and fence instructions. The only other work on formal RDMA semantics is that by Dan et al. [27], which as demonstrated by Ambal et al. [10] does not follow the RDMA specification.

Weak Memory Models. Existing literature includes multiple examples of weak consistency models. For hardware, several works have formalised the semantics of the x86, ARMv8 and POWER architectures [68,9,2,63,48,5,59,31,67]. However, none of these works covered the consistency semantics of RDMA programs. For software, there has been a number of formal models for C11 [42,40,12,37,44,53,56,25] with verified compilation schemes [58,57,51], Java [49,15], transactional memory [72,61,60], the Linux kernel [8] and the ext4 filesystem [39]. Additionally, there has been several works on formalising the *persistency* semantics of programs in the context of non-volatile memory, describing the behaviour of programs in case of crashes [66,65,64,26,38], as well as program logics for verifying such programs [62,17,70].

Robustness. The concept of robustness against weak memory semantics has been extensively studied across various models as a means to simplify programming, reasoning, and verification. Notably, robustness for Total Store Order (TSO) and its Partial Store Order (PSO) variant [36,55,9] has received significant attention, e.g. [23,24,54,20,35,47,18,1,2,19,45,46]. In addition, robustness has been used as a correctness notion in the context of automatic fence insertion for weak hardware memory models [7,29,28,22,6]. More recent work has developed techniques for checking robustness against concurrency semantics in *programming languages*, particularly the C11 memory model [41,50]. Robustness has also been explored in distributed systems, where Sequential Consistency (SC) is replaced by *serialisability* [30,16,52,21,14,13]. More recently, [34] addressed the problem of checking robustness in the context of weak persistency models for non-volatile memory.

Some of these works provide sound and complete techniques for verifying robustness, along with complexity bounds for specific models. Others, as with our work on RDMA, focus on practical over-approximations, offering programmers guidelines that, when followed, ensure stronger semantics. The well-known Data-Race-Free (DRF) guarantee [3,33] for multicore hardware and programming language models is a prominent criterion of this type.

Acknowledgements. We thank the anonymous reviewers for their valuable feedback and Viktor Vafeiadis for many fruitful discussions. Ambal is supported by the EPSRC grant EP/X037029/1. Lahav is supported by the European Research Council (ERC) under the European Union's Horizon 2020 research and innovation programme (grant agreement no. 851811) and the Israel Science Foundation (grant no. 814/22). Raad is supported by a UKRI fellowship MR/V024299/1, by the EPSRC grant EP/X037029/1 and by VeTSS.

References

1. Abdulla, P.A., Atig, M.F., Lång, M., Ngo, T.P.: Precise and sound automatic fence insertion procedure under PSO. In: NETYS. pp. 32–47. Springer International Publishing, Cham (2015)
2. Abdulla, P.A., Atig, M.F., Ngo, T.P.: The best of both worlds: Trading efficiency and optimality in fence insertion for tso. In: Proceedings of the 24th European Symposium on Programming on Programming Languages and Systems - Volume 9032. pp. 308–332. Springer-Verlag New York, Inc., New York, NY, USA (2015). https://doi.org/10.1007/978-3-662-46669-8_13, http://dx.doi.org/10.1007/978-3-662-46669-8_13
3. Adve, S.V., Hill, M.D.: Weak ordering—a new definition. In: ISCA. pp. 2–14. ACM, New York (1990). https://doi.org/10.1145/325164.325100, http://doi.acm.org/10.1145/325164.325100
4. Aguilera, M.K., Ben-David, N., Guerraoui, R., Marathe, V.J., Zablotchi, I.: The impact of RDMA on agreement. In: Robinson, P., Ellen, F. (eds.) Proceedings of the 2019 ACM Symposium on Principles of Distributed Computing, PODC 2019, Toronto, ON, Canada, July 29 - August 2, 2019. pp. 409–418. ACM (2019). https://doi.org/10.1145/3293611.3331601, https://doi.org/10.1145/3293611.3331601
5. Alglave, J., Deacon, W., Grisenthwaite, R., Hacquard, A., Maranget, L.: Armed cats: Formal concurrency modelling at arm. ACM Trans. Program. Lang. Syst. 43(2), 8:1–8:54 (2021). https://doi.org/10.1145/3458926, https://doi.org/10.1145/3458926
6. Alglave, J., Kroening, D., Nimal, V., Poetzl, D.: Don't sit on the fence: a static analysis approach to automatic fence insertion. ACM Trans. Program. Lang. Syst. 39(2), 6:1–6:38 (May 2017). https://doi.org/10.1145/2994593, http://doi.acm.org/10.1145/2994593
7. Alglave, J., Maranget, L.: Stability in weak memory models. In: CAV. pp. 50–66. Springer-Verlag, Berlin, Heidelberg (2011), http://dl.acm.org/citation.cfm?id=2032305.2032311
8. Alglave, J., Maranget, L., McKenney, P.E., Parri, A., Stern, A.: Frightening small children and disconcerting grown-ups: Concurrency in the linux kernel. SIGPLAN Not. 53(2), 405–418 (Mar 2018). https://doi.org/10.1145/3296957.3177156, https://doi.org/10.1145/3296957.3177156
9. Alglave, J., Maranget, L., Tautschnig, M.: Herding cats: Modelling, simulation, testing, and data mining for weak memory. ACM Trans. Program. Lang. Syst. 36(2) (Jul 2014). https://doi.org/10.1145/2627752, https://doi.org/10.1145/2627752
10. Ambal, G., Dongol, B., Eran, H., Klimis, V., Lahav, O., Raad, A.: Semantics of remote direct memory access: Operational and declarative models of rdma on tso architectures. Proc. ACM Program. Lang. 8(OOPSLA2) (Oct 2024). https://doi.org/10.1145/3689781, https://doi.org/10.1145/3689781
11. Ambal, G., Lahav, O., Raad, A.: Extended version (2025), https://www.soundandcomplete.org/papers/ESOP2025/RDMA/
12. Batty, M., Owens, S., Sarkar, S., Sewell, P., Weber, T.: Mathematizing c++ concurrency. In: Proceedings of the 38th Annual ACM SIGPLAN-SIGACT Symposium on Principles of Programming Languages. pp. 55–66. POPL '11, ACM, New York, NY, USA (2011). https://doi.org/10.1145/1926385.1926394, http://doi.acm.org/10.1145/1926385.1926394

13. Beillahi, S.M., Bouajjani, A., Enea, C.: Checking robustness against snapshot isolation. In: Computer Aided Verification. pp. 286–304. Springer International Publishing, Cham (2019)

14. Beillahi, S.M., Bouajjani, A., Enea, C.: Robustness against transactional causal consistency. In: CONCUR 2019. vol. 140, pp. 30:1–30:18. Schloss Dagstuhl–Leibniz-Zentrum fuer Informatik, Dagstuhl, Germany (2019). https://doi.org/10.4230/LIPIcs.CONCUR.2019.30

15. Bender, J., Palsberg, J.: A formalization of java's concurrent access modes. Proc. ACM Program. Lang. **3**(OOPSLA) (Oct 2019). https://doi.org/10.1145/3360568, https://doi.org/10.1145/3360568

16. Bernardi, G., Gotsman, A.: Robustness against consistency models with atomic visibility. In: CONCUR. pp. 7:1–7:15. Schloss Dagstuhl–Leibniz-Zentrum fuer Informatik, Dagstuhl, Germany (2016). https://doi.org/10.4230/LIPIcs.CONCUR.2016.7, http://drops.dagstuhl.de/opus/volltexte/2016/6165

17. Bila, E.V., Dongol, B., Lahav, O., Raad, A., Wickerson, J.: View-based owicki-gries reasoning for persistent x86-tso. In: Sergey, I. (ed.) Programming Languages and Systems. pp. 234–261. Springer International Publishing, Cham (2022)

18. Bouajjani, A., Derevenetc, E., Meyer, R.: Checking and enforcing robustness against TSO. In: ESOP. pp. 533–553. Springer-Verlag, Berlin, Heidelberg (2013). https://doi.org/10.1007/978-3-642-37036-6_29, http://dx.doi.org/10.1007/978-3-642-37036-6_29

19. Bouajjani, A., Enea, C., Mutluergil, S.O., Tasiran, S.: Reasoning about TSO programs using reduction and abstraction. In: CAV. pp. 336–353. Springer, Cham (2018)

20. Bouajjani, A., Meyer, R., Möhlmann, E.: Deciding robustness against total store ordering. In: ICALP. pp. 428–440. Springer, Berlin, Heidelberg (2011)

21. Brutschy, L., Dimitrov, D., Müller, P., Vechev, M.: Static serializability analysis for causal consistency. In: PLDI. pp. 90–104. ACM, New York (2018). https://doi.org/10.1145/3192366.3192415, http://doi.acm.org/10.1145/3192366.3192415

22. Burckhardt, S., Alur, R., Martin, M.M.K.: CheckFence: Checking consistency of concurrent data types on relaxed memory models. In: PLDI. pp. 12–21. ACM, New York (2007). https://doi.org/10.1145/1250734.1250737, http://doi.acm.org/10.1145/1250734.1250737

23. Burckhardt, S., Musuvathi, M.: Effective program verification for relaxed memory models. In: CAV. pp. 107–120. Springer-Verlag, Berlin, Heidelberg (2008). https://doi.org/10.1007/978-3-540-70545-1_12, http://dx.doi.org/10.1007/978-3-540-70545-1_12

24. Burnim, J., Sen, K., Stergiou, C.: Sound and complete monitoring of sequential consistency for relaxed memory models. In: TACAS. pp. 11–25. Springer, Berlin, Heidelberg (2011)

25. Chakraborty, S., Vafeiadis, V.: Grounding thin-air reads with event structures. Proc. ACM Program. Lang. **3**(POPL) (Jan 2019). https://doi.org/10.1145/3290383, https://doi.org/10.1145/3290383

26. Cho, K., Lee, S.H., Raad, A., Kang, J.: Revamping hardware persistency models: View-based and axiomatic persistency models for intel-x86 and armv8. In: Proceedings of the 42nd ACM SIGPLAN International Conference on Programming Language Design and Implementation. p. 16–31. PLDI 2021, Association for Computing Machinery, New York, NY, USA (2021). https://doi.org/10.1145/3453483.3454027, https://doi.org/10.1145/3453483.3454027

27. Dan, A.M., Lam, P., Hoefler, T., Vechev, M.: Modeling and analysis of remote memory access programming. SIGPLAN Not. **51**(10), 129–144 (oct 2016). https://doi.org/10.1145/3022671.2984033, https://doi.org/10.1145/3022671.2984033

28. Derevenetc, E.: Robustness against relaxed memory models. Ph.D. thesis, University of Kaiserslautern (2015), http://kluedo.ub.uni-kl.de/frontdoor/index/index/docId/4074

29. Derevenetc, E., Meyer, R.: Robustness against Power is PSpace-complete. In: ICALP. pp. 158–170. Springer, Berlin, Heidelberg (2014)

30. Fekete, A., Liarokapis, D., O'Neil, E., O'Neil, P., Shasha, D.: Making snapshot isolation serializable. ACM Trans. Database Syst. **30**(2), 492–528 (Jun 2005). https://doi.org/10.1145/1071610.1071615, http://doi.acm.org/10.1145/1071610.1071615

31. Flur, S., Gray, K.E., Pulte, C., Sarkar, S., Sezgin, A., Maranget, L., Deacon, W., Sewell, P.: Modelling the armv8 architecture, operationally: Concurrency and isa. In: Proceedings of the 43rd Annual ACM SIGPLAN-SIGACT Symposium on Principles of Programming Languages. p. 608–621. POPL '16, Association for Computing Machinery, New York, NY, USA (2016). https://doi.org/10.1145/2837614.2837615, https://doi.org/10.1145/2837614.2837615

32. Gerstenberger, R., Besta, M., Hoefler, T.: Enabling highly scalable remote memory access programming with mpi-3 one sided. Commun. ACM **61**(10), 106–113 (sep 2018). https://doi.org/10.1145/3264413, https://doi.org/10.1145/3264413

33. Gharachorloo, K., Adve, S.V., Gupta, A., Hennessy, J.L., Hill, M.D.: Programming for different memory consistency models. Journal of Parallel and Distributed Computing **15**(4), 399 – 407 (1992). https://doi.org/https://doi.org/10.1016/0743-7315(92)90052-0, http://www.sciencedirect.com/science/article/pii/074373159290052O

34. Gorjiara, H., Luo, W., Lee, A., Xu, G.H., Demsky, B.: Checking robustness to weak persistency models. In: Proceedings of the 43rd ACM SIGPLAN International Conference on Programming Language Design and Implementation. p. 490–505. PLDI 2022, Association for Computing Machinery, New York, NY, USA (2022). https://doi.org/10.1145/3519939.3523723, https://doi.org/10.1145/3519939.3523723

35. Gotsman, A., Musuvathi, M., Yang, H.: Show no weakness: sequentially consistent specifications of TSO libraries. In: DISC. pp. 31–45. Springer-Verlag, Berlin, Heidelberg (2012). https://doi.org/10.1007/978-3-642-33651-5_3, http://dx.doi.org/10.1007/978-3-642-33651-5_3

36. Inc., S.I.: The SPARC architecture manual (version 9). Prentice-Hall, Inc., Upper Saddle River, NJ, USA (1994)

37. Kang, J., Hur, C.K., Lahav, O., Vafeiadis, V., Dreyer, D.: A promising semantics for relaxed-memory concurrency. SIGPLAN Not. **52**(1), 175–189 (Jan 2017). https://doi.org/10.1145/3093333.3009850, https://doi.org/10.1145/3093333.3009850

38. Khyzha, A., Lahav, O.: Taming x86-tso persistency. Proc. ACM Program. Lang. **5**(POPL) (Jan 2021). https://doi.org/10.1145/3434328, https://doi.org/10.1145/3434328

39. Kokologiannakis, M., Kaysın, I., Raad, A., Vafeiadis, V.. Persevere. Persistency semantics for verification under ext4. Proc. ACM Program. Lang. **5**(POPL) (jan 2021). https://doi.org/10.1145/3434324, https://doi.org/10.1145/3434324

40. Lahav, O., Giannarakis, N., Vafeiadis, V.: Taming release-acquire consistency. SIGPLAN Not. **51**(1), 649–662 (Jan 2016). https://doi.org/10.1145/2914770.2837643, https://doi.org/10.1145/2914770.2837643

41. Lahav, O., Margalit, R.: Robustness against release/acquire semantics. In: Proceedings of the 40th ACM SIGPLAN Conference on Programming Language Design and Implementation. p. 126–141. PLDI 2019, Association for Computing Machinery, New York, NY, USA (2019). https://doi.org/10.1145/3314221.3314604, https://doi.org/10.1145/3314221.3314604

42. Lahav, O., Vafeiadis, V., Kang, J., Hur, C.K., Dreyer, D.: Repairing sequential consistency in c/c++11. In: Proceedings of the 38th ACM SIGPLAN Conference on Programming Language Design and Implementation. p. 618–632. PLDI 2017, Association for Computing Machinery, New York, NY, USA (2017). https://doi.org/10.1145/3062341.3062352, https://doi.org/10.1145/3062341.3062352

43. Lamport, L.: How to make a multiprocessor computer that correctly executes multiprocess programs. IEEE Trans. Computers **28**(9), 690–691 (Sep 1979). https://doi.org/10.1109/TC.1979.1675439, http://dx.doi.org/10.1109/TC.1979.1675439

44. Lee, S.H., Cho, M., Podkopaev, A., Chakraborty, S., Hur, C.K., Lahav, O., Vafeiadis, V.: Promising 2.0: Global optimizations in relaxed memory concurrency. In: Proceedings of the 41st ACM SIGPLAN Conference on Programming Language Design and Implementation. p. 362–376. PLDI 2020, Association for Computing Machinery, New York, NY, USA (2020). https://doi.org/10.1145/3385412.3386010, https://doi.org/10.1145/3385412.3386010

45. Linden, A., Wolper, P.: A verification-based approach to memory fence insertion in relaxed memory systems. In: SPIN. pp. 144–160. Springer-Verlag, Berlin, Heidelberg (2011), http://dl.acm.org/citation.cfm?id=2032692.2032707

46. Linden, A., Wolper, P.: A verification-based approach to memory fence insertion in PSO memory systems. In: TACAS. pp. 339–353. Springer-Verlag, Berlin, Heidelberg (2013). https://doi.org/10.1007/978-3-642-36742-7_24, http://dx.doi.org/10.1007/978-3-642-36742-7_24

47. Liu, F., Nedev, N., Prisadnikov, N., Vechev, M., Yahav, E.: Dynamic synthesis for relaxed memory models. In: PLDI. pp. 429–440. ACM, New York (2012). https://doi.org/10.1145/2254064.2254115, http://doi.acm.org/10.1145/2254064.2254115

48. Mador-Haim, S., Maranget, L., Sarkar, S., Memarian, K., Alglave, J., Owens, S., Alur, R., Martin, M.M.K., Sewell, P., Williams, D.: An axiomatic memory model for POWER multiprocessors. In: Madhusudan, P., Seshia, S.A. (eds.) Computer Aided Verification - 24th International Conference, CAV 2012, Berkeley, CA, USA, July 7-13, 2012 Proceedings. Lecture Notes in Computer Science, vol. 7358, pp. 495–512. Springer (2012). https://doi.org/10.1007/978-3-642-31424-7_36

49. Manson, J., Pugh, W., Adve, S.V.: The java memory model. In: Proceedings of the 32nd ACM SIGPLAN-SIGACT Symposium on Principles of Programming Languages. p. 378–391. POPL '05, Association for Computing Machinery, New York, NY, USA (2005). https://doi.org/10.1145/1040305.1040336, https://doi.org/10.1145/1040305.1040336

50. Margalit, R., Lahav, O.: Verifying observational robustness against a c11-style memory model. Proc. ACM Program. Lang. **5**(POPL) (Jan 2021). https://doi.org/10.1145/3434285, https://doi.org/10.1145/3434285

51. Moiseenko, E., Podkopaev, A., Lahav, O., Melkonian, O., Vafeiadis, V.: Reconciling Event Structures with Modern Multiprocessors (Artifact). Dagstuhl Arti-

facts Series **6**(2), 4:1–4:3 (2020). https://doi.org/10.4230/DARTS.6.2.4, https://drops.dagstuhl.de/opus/volltexte/2020/13201

52. Nagar, K., Jagannathan, S.: Automated detection of serializability violations under weak consistency. In: CONCUR 2018. vol. 118, pp. 41:1–41:18. Schloss Dagstuhl–Leibniz-Zentrum fuer Informatik, Dagstuhl, Germany (2018). https://doi.org/10.4230/LIPIcs.CONCUR.2018.41, http://drops.dagstuhl.de/opus/volltexte/2018/9579

53. Nienhuis, K., Memarian, K., Sewell, P.: An operational semantics for c/c++11 concurrency. In: Proceedings of the 2016 ACM SIGPLAN International Conference on Object-Oriented Programming, Systems, Languages, and Applications. p. 111–128. OOPSLA 2016, Association for Computing Machinery, New York, NY, USA (2016). https://doi.org/10.1145/2983990.2983997, https://doi.org/10.1145/2983990.2983997

54. Owens, S.: Reasoning about the implementation of concurrency abstractions on x86-TSO. In: ECOOP. pp. 478–503. Springer-Verlag, Berlin, Heidelberg (2010)

55. Owens, S., Sarkar, S., Sewell, P.: A better x86 memory model: x86-TSO. In: TPHOLs. pp. 391–407. Springer, Heidelberg (2009). https://doi.org/10.1007/978-3-642-03359-9_27

56. Pichon-Pharabod, J., Sewell, P.: A concurrency semantics for relaxed atomics that permits optimisation and avoids thin-air executions. In: Proceedings of the 43rd Annual ACM SIGPLAN-SIGACT Symposium on Principles of Programming Languages. p. 622–633. POPL '16, Association for Computing Machinery, New York, NY, USA (2016). https://doi.org/10.1145/2837614.2837616, https://doi.org/10.1145/2837614.2837616

57. Podkopaev, A., Lahav, O., Vafeiadis, V.: Promising Compilation to ARMv8 POP. In: Müller, P. (ed.) 31st European Conference on Object-Oriented Programming (ECOOP 2017). Leibniz International Proceedings in Informatics (LIPIcs), vol. 74, pp. 22:1–22:28. Schloss Dagstuhl–Leibniz-Zentrum fuer Informatik, Dagstuhl, Germany (2017). https://doi.org/10.4230/LIPIcs.ECOOP.2017.22, http://drops.dagstuhl.de/opus/volltexte/2017/7266

58. Podkopaev, A., Lahav, O., Vafeiadis, V.: Bridging the gap between programming languages and hardware weak memory models. Proc. ACM Program. Lang. **3**(POPL), 69:1–69:31 (Jan 2019). https://doi.org/10.1145/3290382, http://doi.acm.org/10.1145/3290382

59. Pulte, C., Flur, S., Deacon, W., French, J., Sarkar, S., Sewell, P.: Simplifying arm concurrency: Multicopy-atomic axiomatic and operational models for armv8. Proc. ACM Program. Lang. **2**(POPL), 19:1–19:29 (Dec 2018). https://doi.org/10.1145/3158107, http://doi.acm.org/10.1145/3158107

60. Raad, A., Lahav, O., Vafeiadis, V.: On parallel snapshot isolation and release/acquire consistency. In: Ahmed, A. (ed.) Programming Languages and Systems. pp. 940–967. Springer International Publishing, Cham (2018)

61. Raad, A., Lahav, O., Vafeiadis, V.: On the semantics of snapshot isolation. In: Enea, C., Piskac, R. (eds.) Verification, Model Checking, and Abstract Interpretation. pp. 1–23. Springer International Publishing, Cham (2019)

62. Raad, A., Lahav, O., Vafeiadis, V.: Persistent owicki-gries reasoning: A program logic for reasoning about persistent programs on intel-x86. Proc. ACM Program. Lang. **4**(OOPSLA) (nov 2020). https://doi.org/10.1145/3428219, https://doi.org/10.1145/3428219

63. Raad, A., Maranget, L., Vafeiadis, V.: Extending intel-x86 consistency and persistency: Formalising the semantics of intel-x86 memory types and non-temporal

stores. Proc. ACM Program. Lang. **6**(POPL) (jan 2022). https://doi.org/10.1145/3498683, https://doi.org/10.1145/3498683

64. Raad, A., Vafeiadis, V.: Persistence semantics for weak memory: Integrating epoch persistency with the tso memory model. Proc. ACM Program. Lang. **2**(OOPSLA), 137:1–137:27 (Oct 2018). https://doi.org/10.1145/3276507, http://doi.acm.org/10.1145/3276507

65. Raad, A., Wickerson, J., Neiger, G., Vafeiadis, V.: Persistency semantics of the intel-x86 architecture. Proc. ACM Program. Lang. **4**(POPL) (Dec 2020). https://doi.org/10.1145/3371079, https://doi.org/10.1145/3371079

66. Raad, A., Wickerson, J., Vafeiadis, V.: Weak persistency semantics from the ground up: Formalising the persistency semantics of armv8 and transactional models. Proc. ACM Program. Lang. **3**(OOPSLA), 135:1–135:27 (Oct 2019). https://doi.org/10.1145/3360561, http://doi.acm.org/10.1145/3360561

67. Sarkar, S., Sewell, P., Alglave, J., Maranget, L., Williams, D.: Understanding power multiprocessors. In: Proceedings of the 32nd ACM SIGPLAN Conference on Programming Language Design and Implementation. p. 175–186. PLDI '11, Association for Computing Machinery, New York, NY, USA (2011). https://doi.org/10.1145/1993498.1993520, https://doi.org/10.1145/1993498.1993520

68. Sewell, P., Sarkar, S., Owens, S., Nardelli, F.Z., Myreen, M.O.: X86-TSO: A rigorous and usable programmer's model for x86 multiprocessors. Commun. ACM **53**(7), 89–97 (Jul 2010). https://doi.org/10.1145/1785414.1785443, http://doi.acm.org/10.1145/1785414.1785443

69. Shpiner, A., Zahavi, E., Dahley, O., Barnea, A., Damsker, R., Yekelis, G., Zus, M., Kuta, E., Baram, D.: Roce rocks without pfc: Detailed evaluation. In: Proceedings of the Workshop on Kernel-Bypass Networks. p. 25–30. KBNets '17, Association for Computing Machinery, New York, NY, USA (2017). https://doi.org/10.1145/3098583.3098588, https://doi.org/10.1145/3098583.3098588

70. Vindum, S.F., Birkedal, L.: Spirea: A mechanized concurrent separation logic for weak persistent memory. Proc. ACM Program. Lang. **7**(OOPSLA2), 632–657 (2023). https://doi.org/10.1145/3622820, https://doi.org/10.1145/3622820

71. Wei, X., Shi, J., Chen, Y., Chen, R., Chen, H.: Fast in-memory transaction processing using rdma and htm. In: Proceedings of the 25th Symposium on Operating Systems Principles. p. 87–104. SOSP '15, Association for Computing Machinery, New York, NY, USA (2015). https://doi.org/10.1145/2815400.2815419, https://doi.org/10.1145/2815400.2815419

72. Xiong, S., Cerone, A., Raad, A., Gardner, P.: Data Consistency in Transactional Storage Systems: A Centralised Semantics. In: Hirschfeld, R., Pape, T. (eds.) 34th European Conference on Object-Oriented Programming (ECOOP 2020). Leibniz International Proceedings in Informatics (LIPIcs), vol. 166, pp. 21:1–21:31. Schloss Dagstuhl–Leibniz-Zentrum für Informatik, Dagstuhl, Germany (2020). https://doi.org/10.4230/LIPIcs.ECOOP.2020.21, https://drops.dagstuhl.de/opus/volltexte/2020/13178

73. Zhu, Y., Eran, H., Firestone, D., Guo, C., Lipshteyn, M., Liron, Y., Padhye, J., Raindel, S., Yahia, M.H., Zhang, M.: Congestion control for large-scale rdma deployments. In: Proceedings of the 2015 ACM Conference on Special Interest Group on Data Communication. p. 523–536. SIGCOMM '15, Association for Computing Machinery, New York, NY, USA (2015). https://doi.org/10.1145/2785956.2787484, https://doi.org/10.1145/2785956.2787484

Constructive characterisations of the must-preorder for asynchrony

Giovanni Bernardi[1]([⊠])[iD], Ilaria Castellani[2][iD], Paul Laforgue[1,3][iD], and Léo Stefanesco[4][iD]

[1] Université Paris Cité, CNRS, IRIF, 75013 Paris, France
gio@irif.fr
[2] INRIA, Université Côte d'Azur, Nice, France
[3] Nomadic Labs, Paris, France
[4] University of Cambridge, Cambridge, UK

Abstract. De Nicola and Hennessy's MUST-preorder is a liveness preserving refinement which states that a server q refines a server p if all clients satisfied by p are also satisfied by q. Owing to the universal quantification over clients, this definition does not yield a practical proof method, and alternative characterisations are necessary to reason over it. Finding these characterisations for asynchronous semantics, i.e. where outputs are non-blocking, has thus far proven to be a challenge, usually tackled via ad-hoc definitions.

We show that the standard characterisations of the MUST-preorder carry over as they stand to asynchronous communication, if servers are enhanced to act as forwarders, *i.e.* they can input any message as long as they store it back into the shared buffer. Our development is constructive, is completely mechanised in Coq, and is independent of any calculus: our results pertain to Selinger output-buffered agents with feedback. This is a class of Labelled Transition Systems that captures programs that communicate via a shared unordered buffer, as in asynchronous CCS or the asynchronous π-calculus.

We show that the standard coinductive characterisation lets us prove in Coq that concrete programs are related by the MUST-preorder.

Finally, our proofs show that Brouwer's bar induction principle is a useful technique to reason on liveness preserving program transformations.

1   Introduction

Code refactoring is a routine task to develop or update software, and it requires methods to ensure that a program p can be safely replaced by a program q. One way to address this issue is via refinement relations, *i.e.* preorders. For programming languages, the most well-known one is Morris *extensional* preorder [43, pag. 50], defined by letting $p \le q$ if for all contexts C, whenever $C[p]$ reduces to a normal form N, then $C[q]$ also reduces to N.

L. Stefanesco—Work done at MPI-SWS, Germany.

V. Vafeiadis (Ed.): ESOP 2025, LNCS 15694, pp. 88–116, 2025.
https://doi.org/10.1007/978-3-031-91118-7_4

Comparing servers This paper studies a version of Morris preorder for nondeterministic asynchronous client-server systems. In this setting it is natural to reformulate the preorder by replacing reduction to normal forms (*i.e.* termination) with a suitable *liveness* property. Let $p \parallel r$ denote a *client-server system*, that is a parallel composition in which the identities of the server p and the client r are distinguished, and whose computations have the form $p \parallel r = p_0 \parallel r_0 \longrightarrow p_1 \parallel r_1 \longrightarrow p_2 \parallel r_2 \longrightarrow \ldots$, where each step represents either an internal computation of one of the two components, or an interaction between them. Interactions correspond to handshakes, where two components ready to perform matching input/output actions advance together. We express liveness by saying that p MUST pass r, denoted p MUST r, if in every maximal computation of $p \parallel r$ there exists a state $p_i \parallel r_i$ such that GOOD(r_i), where GOOD is a decidable predicate indicating that the client has reached a successful state. Servers are then compared according to their capacity to satisfy clients, *i.e.* via contexts of the form $[-] \parallel r$ and the predicate MUST. Morris preorder then becomes the MUST-preorder by De Nicola and Hennessy [25] : $p \precsim_{\text{MUST}} q$ when $\forall r.\ p$ MUST r implies q MUST r.

Advantages The MUST-preorder is by definition liveness preserving, because p MUST r literally means that "in every execution something good must happen (on the client side)". Results on $\precsim_{\text{MUST}}$ thus shed light on liveness-preserving program transformations.

The MUST-preorder is independent of any particular calculus, as its definition requires simply (1) a reduction semantics for the parallel composition $p \parallel r$, and (2) a predicate GOOD over programs. Hence $\precsim_{\text{MUST}}$ may relate servers written in different languages. For instance, servers written in OCAML may be compared to servers written in JAVA according to clients written in PYTHON, because all these languages use the same basic protocols for communication.

Drawback The definition of the MUST-preorder is *contextual*: proving $p \precsim_{\text{MUST}} q$ requires analysing an *infinite* amount of clients, and so the definition of the preorder does not entail an effective proof method. A solution to this problem is to define an *alternative (semantic) characterisation* of the preorder $\precsim_{\text{MUST}}$, *i.e.* a preorder $\preccurlyeq_{alt}$ that coincides with $\precsim_{\text{MUST}}$ and does away with the universal quantification over clients (*i.e.* contexts). In *synchronous* settings, i.e. when both input and output actions are blocking, such alternative characterisations have been thoroughly investigated, typically via a behavioural approach based on labelled transition systems.

Labelled transition systems A program p is associated with a labelled transition system (LTS) representing its behaviour, which we denote by LTS(p). Figure 1 presents two instances of LTSs, where transitions are labelled by input actions such as str, output actions such as $\overline{\text{str}}$, or the internal action τ (not featured in Figure 1), while dotted nodes represent successful states, *i.e.* those satisfying the predicate GOOD. There, the server p_0 is ready to input either a string or a float. It is the environment that, by offering an output of either type, will make p move to either p_1 or p_2. The client r_0, on the other hand, is ready

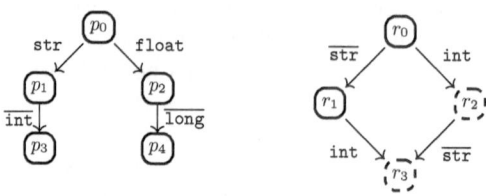

Fig. 1. The behaviours of a server p_0 and of a client r_0.

to either output a string, or input an integer. The input `int` makes the client move to the successful state r_2, while the output $\overline{\mathtt{str}}$ makes the client move to the state r_1, where it can still perform the input `int` to reach the successful state r_3. In an asynchronous setting, output transitions enjoy a commutativity property on which we will return later. Programs p are usually associated with their behaviours LTS(p) via inference rules that we omit in the main body of the paper, as they are standard.

Alternative preorders for synchrony Program behaviours, *i.e.* LTSs, are used to define the alternative preorders for $\lesssim_{\text{MUST}}$ following one of two different approaches: MUST-sets or acceptance sets.

Both approaches were originally proposed for Milner's Calculus of Communicating Systems (CCS) [42], where communication is *synchronous*. The first alternative preorder, which we denote by $\preccurlyeq_{\text{MS}}$, was put forth by De Nicola [25], and it compares server behaviours according to their MUST-sets, *i.e.* the sets of actions that they may perform after doing a given sequence of actions. The second alternative preorder, which we denote by $\preccurlyeq_{\text{AS}}$, was put forth by Hennessy [32], and it compares the acceptance sets of servers, *i.e.* how servers can be moved out of their potentially deadlocked states, namely, states from which the servers cannot evolve autonomously. Both these preorders characterise $\lesssim_{\text{MUST}}$ in the following sense:

$$\forall p, q \in \text{CCS.} \ p \lesssim_{\text{MUST}} q \text{ iff LTS}(p) \preccurlyeq_{\text{MS}} \text{LTS}(q) \tag{1}$$

$$\forall p, q \in \text{CCS.} \ p \lesssim_{\text{MUST}} q \text{ iff LTS}(p) \preccurlyeq_{\text{AS}} \text{LTS}(q) \tag{2}$$

While these alternative preorders do away with the universal quantification over clients, they are not practical to use directly, as they still universally quantify over (finite) traces of actions. A more practical approach [1] is to use a coinductively defined preorder $\preccurlyeq_{\text{co}}$ based on $\preccurlyeq_{\text{AS}}$ [1,41,10]. This preorder has two advantages: first, its definition quantifies universally only on single actions; second, it allows the user to use standard coinductive methods, as found in the literature on bisimulation. In the case where the LTS is image-finite, such as for CCS and most process calculi, the coinductive preorder is sound and complete:

$$\forall p, q \in \text{CCS.} \ p \lesssim_{\text{MUST}} q \text{ iff LTS}(p) \preccurlyeq_{\text{co}} \text{LTS}(q) \tag{3}$$

$$p \xrightarrow{\overline{a}} p' \qquad p \xrightarrow{\overline{a}} p'$$
$$\downarrow \alpha \quad \Rightarrow \quad \downarrow \alpha \qquad \downarrow \alpha$$
$$q \qquad p'' \xrightarrow{\overline{a}} q$$

OUTPUT-COMMUTATIVITY

$$p \xrightarrow{\overline{a}} p' \qquad p \xrightarrow{\overline{a}} p'$$
$$\downarrow a \quad \Rightarrow \quad \searrow^{\tau} \quad \downarrow a$$
$$q \qquad q$$

FEEDBACK

$$p \xrightarrow{\overline{a}} p'$$
$$\downarrow \overline{a} \qquad \Rightarrow p' = p''$$
$$p''$$

OUTPUT-DETERMINACY

$$p \xrightarrow{\overline{a}} p' \qquad p \xrightarrow{\overline{a}} p' \qquad p \xrightarrow{\overline{a}} p'$$
$$\downarrow \tau \quad \Rightarrow \quad \downarrow \tau \qquad \downarrow \tau \quad \text{or} \quad \downarrow \tau \diagdown^{a}$$
$$p'' \qquad p'' \xrightarrow{\overline{a}} q \qquad p''$$

OUTPUT-TAU

$$p \xrightarrow{\overline{a}} p' \qquad p \xrightarrow{\overline{a}} p'$$
$$\downarrow \alpha \quad \Rightarrow \quad \downarrow \alpha \qquad \downarrow \alpha$$
$$p'' \qquad p'' \xrightarrow{\overline{a}} q$$

where $\alpha \neq \overline{a}$ and $\alpha \neq \tau$

OUTPUT-CONFLUENCE

$$p'$$
$$\downarrow \overline{a} \quad \Rightarrow p' = p''$$
$$p'' \xrightarrow{\overline{a}} p$$

BACKWARD-OUTPUT-DETERMINACY

Fig. 2. First-order axioms for output-buffered agents with feedback as given by Selinger [49], extended with the BACKWARD-OUTPUT-DETERMINACY axiom.

Asynchrony In distributed systems, communication is inherently asynchronous. For instance, the standard TCP transmission on the Internet is asynchronous. Actor languages like ELIXIR and ERLANG implement asynchrony via mailboxes, and both PYTHON and JAVASCRIPT offer developers the constructs ASYNC/WAIT, to return promises (of results) or wait for them. In this paper we model asynchrony via *output-buffered agents with feedback*, as introduced by Selinger [49]. These are LTSs obeying the axioms in Figure 2, where a denotes an input action, $\overline{a}$ denotes an output action, τ denotes the internal action, and α ranges over all these actions. For instance, the OUTPUT-COMMUTATIVITY axiom states that an output $\overline{a}$ can always be postponed: if $\overline{a}$ is followed by any action α, it can commute with it. In other words, outputs are non-blocking, as illustrated by the LTS for r_0 in Figure 1. We defer a more detailed discussion of these axioms to Section 2.

Technical difficulties The practical importance of asynchrony motivates a specific study of $\lesssim_{\text{MUST}}$. Efforts in this direction have been made, all of which focussed on process calculi [21,15,52,34], while the axioms in Figure 2 apply to LTSs. Note that these axioms impose conditions only over outputs, and this asymmetric treatment of inputs and outputs substantially complicates the proofs of completeness and soundness of the alternative characterisations of $\lesssim_{\text{MUST}}$. To underline the subtleties due to asynchrony, we note that the completeness result for asynchronous CCS given by Castellani and Hennessy in [21], and subsequently extended to the π-calculus by Hennessy [34], is false (see [8, Appendix I]).

Contributions and paper structure.

Our main contributions may be summarised as follows (where for each of them, we indicate where it is presented in the paper):

- The first behavioural characterisations of the MUST-preorder (Theorem 1, Theorem 3) that are calculus independent, in that both our definitions and our proofs work directly on LTSs. Contrary to all the previous works on the topic, we show that the *standard* alternative preorders characterise the MUST-preorder also in Selinger asynchronous setting. To this end, it suffices to enrich the server semantics with *forwarding*, i.e. ensure that servers are ready to input any message, as long as they store it back in a global shared buffer. This idea, although we use it here in a slightly different form, was pioneered by Honda et al. [38]. In this paper we propose a construction that works on any LTS (Lemma 2) and we show the following counterparts of Equations (1), (2), and (3) where FDB denotes the LTSs of output-buffered agents with feedback, and FW is the function that enhances them with forwarding:

$$\forall p, q \in \text{FDB}. \ p \lesssim_{\text{\tiny MUST}} q \text{ iff } \text{FW}(p) \preccurlyeq_{\text{MS}} \text{FW}(q) \tag{a}$$

$$\forall p, q \in \text{FDB}. \ p \lesssim_{\text{\tiny MUST}} q \text{ iff } \text{FW}(p) \preccurlyeq_{\text{AS}} \text{FW}(q) \tag{b}$$

$$\forall p, q \in \text{FDB}. \ p \lesssim_{\text{\tiny MUST}} q \text{ iff } \text{FW}(p) \preccurlyeq_{\text{co}} \text{FW}(q) \tag{c}$$

  Quite surprisingly, the alternative preorders $\preccurlyeq_{\text{AS}}$, $\preccurlyeq_{\text{MS}}$ and $\preccurlyeq_{\text{co}}$ need not be changed. We present these results in Section 3. We use the coinductive preorder $\preccurlyeq_{\text{co}}$ to prove the correctness of a form of code hoisting (6).
- The first characterisations of the MUST-preorder that fully exploit asynchrony, *i.e.* disregard irrelevant (that is, non-causal) orders of visible actions in traces ([8, Corollary 4]).
- The first constructive account of the MUST-preorder. We show that if the MUST and termination predicates are defined *intensionally* (in the sense of Brede and Herbelin [17]), then $\lesssim_{\text{\tiny MUST}}$ can be characterised constructively. The original definitions of MUST and termination given by De Nicola [25], though, are *extensional*. We show how to use Brouwer bar induction principle to prove that the two approaches are logically equivalent (Corollary 2). Since Rahli et al. [46] have shown bar induction to be compatible with constructive type theory, we argue that our development is entirely constructive.
- The first mechanisation of the theory of MUST-preorder in a fully nondeterministic setting, which consists of around 8000 lines of Coq. In [8, Appendix J] we gather the Coq versions of all the definitions and the results presented in the main body of the paper.

In Section 6, we discuss the impact of the above contributions, as well as related and future work. In Section 2, we recall the necessary background definitions and illustrate them with a few examples.

```
Class Sts (A: Type) := MkSts {
  sts_step: A → A → Prop;
  sts_stable: A → Prop; }.
```

```
Inductive ExtAct (A: Type) :=        Inductive Act (A: Type) :=
| ActIn (a: A) | ActOut (a: A).     | ActExt (ext: ExtAct A) | τ.
```

```
Class Label (L: Type) :=            Class Lts (A L : Type) `{Label L} :=
MkLabel {                            MkLts {
  label_eqdec: EqDecision L;           lts_step: A → Act L → A → Prop;
  label_countable: Countable L; }.    lts_outputs: A → finite_set L;
                                       lts_performs: A → (Act L) → Prop; }.
```

Fig. 3. Highlights of our Sts and Lts typeclasses.

2 Preliminaries

We model individual programs such as servers p and clients r as LTSs obeying Selinger axioms, while client-server systems $p \parallel r$ are modelled as state transition systems with a reduction semantics. We now formally define this two-level semantics.

Labelled transition systems A *labelled transition system* (LTS) is a triple $\mathcal{L} = \langle A, L, \longrightarrow \rangle$ where A is the set of states, L is the set of labels and $\longrightarrow \subseteq A \times L \times A$ is the transition relation. When modelling programs as LTSs, we use transition labels to represent program actions. The set of labels in Selinger LTSs has the same structure as the set of actions in Milner's calculus CCS: one assumes a set of names $\mathcal{N}$, denoting input actions and ranged over by a, b, c, a complementary set of conames $\overline{\mathcal{N}}$, denoting output actions and ranged over by $\overline{a}, \overline{b}, \overline{c}$, and an *invisible* action τ, representing internal computation. The set of all actions, ranged over by α, β, γ, is given by $\mathsf{Act}_\tau \overset{\text{def}}{=} \mathcal{N} \uplus \overline{\mathcal{N}} \uplus \{\tau\}$. We use μ, μ' to range over the set of visible actions $\mathcal{N} \uplus \overline{\mathcal{N}}$, and we extend the complementation function $\overline{\cdot}$ to this set by letting $\overline{\overline{a}} \overset{\text{def}}{=} a$. In the following, we will always assume $L = \mathsf{Act}_\tau$. Once the LTS is fixed, we write $p \overset{\alpha}{\longrightarrow} p'$ to mean that $(p, \alpha, p') \in \longrightarrow$ and $p \overset{\alpha}{\longrightarrow}$ to mean $\exists p'. p \overset{\alpha}{\longrightarrow} p'$.

We use $\mathcal{L}$ to range over LTSs. To reason simultaneously on different LTSs, we will use the symbols $\mathcal{L}_A$ and $\mathcal{L}_B$ to denote respectively the LTSs $\langle A, L, \longrightarrow_A \rangle$ and $\langle B, L, \longrightarrow_B \rangle$.

In our mechanisation LTSs are borne out by the typeclass Lts in Figure 3. The states of the LTS have type A, labels have type L, and lts_step is the characteristic function of the transition relation, which we assume to be decidable. We let $O(p) = \{\overline{a} \in \overline{\mathcal{N}} \mid p \overset{\overline{a}}{\longrightarrow}\}$ and $I(p) = \{a \in \mathcal{N} \mid p \overset{a}{\longrightarrow}\}$ be respectively the set of outputs and the set of inputs of state p. We assume that the set $O(p)$

[S-Srv]
$$\frac{p \xrightarrow{\tau} p'}{p \parallel r \longrightarrow p' \parallel r}$$

[S-Clt]
$$\frac{r \xrightarrow{\tau} r'}{p \parallel r \longrightarrow p \parallel r'}$$

[S-com]
$$\frac{p \xrightarrow{\mu} p' \quad r \xrightarrow{\overline{\mu}} r'}{p \parallel r \longrightarrow p' \parallel r'}$$

Fig. 4. The STS of server-client systems.

is finite for any p. In our mechanisation, the set $O(p)$ is rendered by the function `lts_outputs`, and we shall also use a function `lts_performs` that lets us decide whether a state can perform a transition labelled by a given action.

Client-server systems A *client-server* system (or *system*, for short) is a pair $p \parallel r$ in which p is deemed to be the server of client r. In general, every system $p \parallel r$ is the root of a *state transition system* (STS), $\langle S, \longrightarrow \rangle$, where S is the set of states and $\longrightarrow$ is the reduction relation. For the sake of simplicity[5] we derive the reduction relation from the LTS semantics of servers and clients as specified by the rules in Figure 4. In our mechanisation (Figure 3), `sts_step` is the characteristic function of the reduction relation $\longrightarrow$, and `sts_stable` is the function that states whether a state can reduce or not. Both functions are assumed decidable.

Definition 1 (Computation). *Given an STS $\langle S, \longrightarrow \rangle$ and a state $s_0 \in S$, a computation of s_0 is a finite or infinite reduction sequence starting from s_0. A computation is* maximal *if either it cannot be extended or it is infinite.*

To formally define the MUST-preorder, we assume a decidable predicate GOOD over clients. A computation $p \parallel r = p_0 \parallel r_0 \longrightarrow p_1 \parallel r_1 \longrightarrow p_2 \parallel r_2 \longrightarrow \dots$ is *successful* if there exists a state $p_i \parallel r_i$ such that GOOD(r_i). We assume the predicate GOOD to be *invariant under outputs*:

$$\text{If } r \xrightarrow{\overline{a}} r' \text{ then } \text{GOOD}(r) \Longleftrightarrow \text{GOOD}(r') \tag{4}$$

All the previous works on asynchronous calculi implicitly make this assumption, since they rely on ad-hoc actions such as ω or $\checkmark$ to signal success and they treat them as outputs. In [8, Appendix H] we show that this assumption holds for the language ACCS (the asynchronous variant of CCS) extended with the process 1, which is used as a syntactic means to denote GOOD states. Moreover, when considering an equivalence on programs $\simeq$ that is compatible with transitions, in the sense of Figure 5, we assume the predicate GOOD to be preserved also by this equivalence. These assumptions are met by the frameworks in [21,15,34].

Definition 2 (Client satisfaction). *We write p MUST r if every maximal computation of $p \parallel r$ is successful.*

---

[5] In general the reduction semantics and the LTS of a calculus are defined independently, and connected via the Harmony lemma ([47], Lemma 1.4.15 page 51). We have a mechanised proof of it.

Definition 3 (must-preorder). *We let $p \lesssim_{\text{\tiny MUST}} q$ whenever for every client r we have that p MUST r implies q MUST r.*

Example 1. Consider the system $p_0 \parallel r_0$, where p_0 and r_0 are the server and client given in Figure 1. The unique maximal computation of this system is $p_0 \parallel r_0 \longrightarrow p_1 \parallel r_1 \longrightarrow p_3 \parallel r_3$. This computation is successful since it leads the client to the GOOD state r_3. Hence, client r_0 is satisfied by server p_0. Since OUTPUT-COMMUTATIVITY implies an absence of causality between the output $\overline{\text{str}}$ and the input int in the client, it is the order between the input str and the output $\overline{\text{int}}$ in the server that guides the order of client-server interactions.□

A closer look at Selinger axioms Let us now discuss the axioms in Figure 2. The OUTPUT-COMMUTATIVITY axiom expresses the non-blocking behaviour of outputs: an output cannot be a cause of any subsequent transition, since it can also be executed after it, leading to the same resulting state. Hence, outputs are concurrent with any subsequent transition. The FEEDBACK axiom says that an output followed by a complementary input can also synchronise with it to produce a τ-transition. These first two axioms specify properties of outputs that are followed by another transition. Instead, the following three axioms, OUTPUT-CONFLUENCE, OUTPUT-DETERMINACY and OUTPUT-TAU, specify properties of outputs that are co-initial with another transition[6]. The OUTPUT-DETERMINACY and OUTPUT-TAU axioms apply to the case where the co-initial transition is an identical output or a τ-transition respectively, while the OUTPUT-CONFLUENCE axiom applies to the other cases. When taken in conjunction, these three axioms state that outputs cannot be in conflict with any co-initial transition, except when this is a τ-transition: in this case, the OUTPUT-TAU axiom allows for a confluent nondeterminism between the τ-transition on one side and the output followed by the complementary input on the other side.

We now explain the novel BACKWARD-OUTPUT-DETERMINACY axiom. It is the dual of OUTPUT-DETERMINACY, as it states that also backward transitions with identical outputs lead to the same state. The intuition is that if two programs arrive at the same state by removing the same message from the mailbox, then they must coincide. This axiom need not be assumed in [49] because it can be derived from Selinger axioms when modelling a calculus like ACCS equipped with a parallel composition operator $\parallel$ (see [8, Lemma 53]). We use the BACKWARD-OUTPUT-DETERMINACY axiom only to prove a technical property of clients (see [8, Lemma 25]) that is used to prove our completeness result.

Calculi A number of asynchronous calculi [38,16,21,36,44,48] have an LTS that enjoys the axioms in Figure 2, at least up to some structural equivalence $\equiv$. The reason is that these calculi syntactically enforce outputs to have no continuation, *i.e.* outputs can only be composed in parallel with other processes.[7]. For

---

[6] Two transitions are co-initial if they stem from the same state.

[7] In the calculus TACCS (a variant of ACCS tailored for testing semantics) of [21] there is a construct of asynchronous output prefix, but its behaviour is to spawn the corresponding atom in parallel with the continuation, so it does not act as a prefix.

example, Selinger [49] shows that the axioms of Figure 2 hold for the LTS of the calculus ACCS (the asynchronous variant of CCS[8]) modulo bisimulation, and in (see [8, Lemma 55]) we prove that they hold also for the LTS of ACCS modulo $\equiv$:

Lemma 1. *We have that* $\langle ACCS_\equiv, L, \longrightarrow_\equiv \rangle \in \text{FDB}$.

To streamline reasoning modulo some (structural) equivalence we introduce the typeclass LtsEq, whose instances are LTSs equipped with an equivalence $\simeq$ that satisfies the property in Figure 5. Defining output-buffered agents with feedback using LtsEq does not entail any loss of generality, because the equivalence $\simeq$ can be instantiated using the identity over the states A. Further details can be found in [8, Appendix H.1].

When convenient we denote LTSs using the following minimal syntax for ACCS:

$$p, q, r ::= \overline{a} \mid g \mid p \parallel p \mid \text{rec} x.p \mid x \qquad g ::= 0 \mid a.p \mid \tau.p \mid g + g \quad (5)$$

as well as its standard LTS[9] whose properties we discuss in detail in [8, Appendix H]. This is exactly the syntax used in [49,15], without the operators of restriction and relabelling. Here the syntactic category g defines *guards*, *i.e.* the terms that may be used as arguments for the $+$ operator. As in most process calculi, 0 denotes the terminated process that cannot do any action. Note that, apart from 0, only input-prefixed and τ-prefixed terms are allowed as guards, and that the output prefix operator is replaced by *atoms* $\overline{a}$. In fact, this syntax is completely justified by Selinger axioms, which, as we argued above, specify that outputs cannot cause any other action, nor be in conflict with it.

Fig. 5. Axiom stating that equivalence $\simeq$ is compatible with a transition relation.

Definition 4 (Transition sequence). *Given an LTS* $\langle A, L, \longrightarrow \rangle$ *and a state* $p_0 \in A$, *a transition sequence of* p_0 *is a finite or infinite sequence of the form* $p_0 \alpha_1 p_1 \alpha_2 p_2 \cdots$ *with* $p_i \in A$ *and* $\alpha_i \in L$, *and such that, for every* $n \geq 1$ *such that* p_n *is in the sequence we have* $p_{n-1} \xrightarrow{\alpha_n} p_n$.

---

[8] The syntax of ACCS, which is closely inspired by that of the asynchronous π-calculus with input- and τ-guarded choice [2,3], is given in Equation (5) and discussed later.

[9] Where the recursion rule is replaced by the one usually adopted for testing semantics, which introduces a τ-transition before each unfolding.

If a transition sequence is made only of τ-transitions, it is called a *computation* by abuse of notation, the idea being that usually τ-steps are related to reduction steps via the Harmony lemma (see footnote on page 94).

We give now an example that illustrates the use of the testing machinery in our asynchronous setting. This is also a counter-example to the completeness of the alternative preorder proposed in [21], as discussed in detail in [8, Appendix I].

Example 2. Let $\Omega = \mathsf{rec}x.\tau.x$ and *Pierre* $= b.(\tau.\Omega + c.\bar{d})$. The LTS of *Pierre* is as follows:

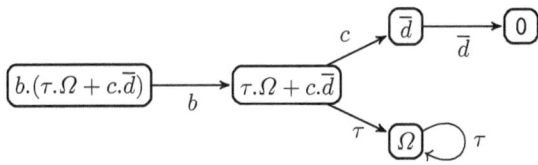

Pierre models a citizen confronted with an unpopular pension reform. To begin with, *Pierre* can only do the input b, which models his getting aware of the brute-force imposition of the reform by the government. After performing the input, *Pierre* reaches the state $\tau.\Omega + c.\bar{d}$, where he behaves in a nondeterministic manner. He can internally choose not to trust the government for any positive change, in which case he will diverge, refusing any further interaction. But this need not happen: in case the government offers the action $\bar{c}$, which models a positive change in political decision, *Pierre* can decide to accept this change, and then he expresses his agreement with the output $\bar{d}$, which stands for "done". □

Example 3. We prove now the inequality *Pierre* $\precsim_{\text{MUST}}$ 0 by leveraging the possibility of divergence of *Pierre* after the input b. Fix an r such that *Pierre* MUST r. Note that, since 0 is the terminated process, the condition for the server 0 to satisfy r is that r reaches by itself a successful state in each of its maximal computations. We distinguish two cases, according to whether $r \xrightarrow{\bar{b}}$ or $r \nrightarrow^{\bar{b}}$.

i) Let $r \xrightarrow{\bar{b}} r'$ for some r'. Consider the maximal computation *Pierre* $\|$ $r \longrightarrow \tau.\Omega + c.\bar{d} \| r' \longrightarrow \Omega \| r' \longrightarrow \ldots$ in which *Pierre* diverges and r does not move after the first output. Since *Pierre* MUST r, either GOOD(r) or GOOD(r'). In case GOOD(r'), by Equation (4) we get also GOOD(r). Hence 0 MUST r.

ii) Let $r \nrightarrow^{\bar{b}}$. Suppose $r = r_0 \xrightarrow{\tau} r_1 \xrightarrow{\tau} r_2 \xrightarrow{\tau} \ldots$ is a maximal computation of r. Then *Pierre* $\|$ r has a maximal computation *Pierre* $\|$ $r_0 \longrightarrow$ *Pierre* $\|$ $r_1 \longrightarrow$ *Pierre* $\|$ $r_2 \longrightarrow \ldots$. As *Pierre* MUST r, there must exist an $i \in \mathbb{N}$ such that GOOD(r_i). Hence 0 MUST r. □

The argument in Example 3 can directly use Definition 3 because it is very simple to reason on the process 0. The issues brought about by the contextuality of Definition 3, though, hinder showing general properties of $\precsim_{\text{MUST}}$. Consider the following form of code hoisting:

$$\tau.(\bar{a} \| \bar{b}) + \tau.(\bar{a} \| \bar{c}) \precsim_{\text{MUST}} \bar{a} \| (\tau.\bar{b} + \tau.\bar{c}) \tag{6}$$

If we see the above nondeterministic sums as representing the two branches of a conditional statement, this refinement corresponds to hoisting the shared action $\bar{a}$ before the conditional statement, a common compiler optimisation. Proving Equation (6) via the contextual definition of $\sqsubseteq_{\text{MUST}}$ is cumbersome. This motivates the study of alternative characterisations for $\sqsubseteq_{\text{MUST}}$, and in the rest of the paper we present several preorders that fit the purpose, in particular the coinductive preorder $\preccurlyeq_{\text{co}}$, which we will use to establish Equation (6) in Section 3.3.

We conclude this section by recalling auxiliary and rather standard notions: given an LTS $\langle A, L, \longrightarrow \rangle$, the weak transition relation $p \xRightarrow{s} p'$, where $s \in \text{Act}^*$, is defined via the rules

[wt-refl] $p \xRightarrow{\varepsilon} p$
[wt-tau] $p \xRightarrow{s} q$ if $p \xrightarrow{\tau} p'$ and $p' \xRightarrow{s} q$
[wt-mu] $p \xRightarrow{\mu.s} q$ if $p \xrightarrow{\mu} p'$ and $p' \xRightarrow{s} q$

We write $p \xRightarrow{s}$ to mean $\exists p'.\ p \xRightarrow{s} p'$.

We write $p \downarrow$ and say that p *converges* if every computation of p is finite, and we lift the convergence predicate to finite traces by letting the relation $\Downarrow \subseteq A \times \text{Act}^*$ be the least one that satisfies the following rules

[cnv-epsilon] $p \Downarrow \varepsilon$ if $p \downarrow$,
[cnv-mu] $p \Downarrow \mu.s$ if $p \downarrow$ and $p \xRightarrow{\mu} p'$ implies $p' \Downarrow s$.

To understand the next section, one should keep in mind that all the predicates defined above have an implicit parameter: the LTS of programs. By changing this parameter, we may change the meaning of the predicates. For instance, letting Ω be the ACCS process $\text{rec}x.\tau.x$, in the standard LTS $\langle \text{ACCS}, \longrightarrow, \text{Act}_\tau \rangle$ we have $\Omega \xrightarrow{\tau} \Omega$ and $\neg(\Omega \downarrow)$, while in the LTS $\langle \text{ACCS}, \emptyset, \text{Act}_\tau \rangle$ we have $\Omega \xnrightarrow{\tau}$ and thus $\Omega \downarrow$. In other words, the *same* predicates can be applied to different LTSs, and since the alternative characterisations of $\sqsubseteq_{\text{MUST}}$ are defined using such predicates, they can relate different LTSs.

3   Preorders based on acceptance sets

We first recall the definition of the standard alternative preorder $\preccurlyeq_{\text{AS}}$, and show how to use it to characterise $\sqsubseteq_{\text{MUST}}$ in our asynchronous setting. We also present a new characterisation that disregards the order of non-causally related actions. We then explain the tools we use to prove these characterisations, and in particular their soundness. This section ends with the coinductive version $\preccurlyeq_{\text{co}}$ of $\preccurlyeq_{\text{AS}}$, which we use to prove the hoisting refinement (6).

3.1   Trace-based characterisations

The *ready set* of a program p is defined as $R(p) = I(p) \cup O(p)$, and it contains all the *visible* actions that p can immediately perform. If a program p is stable, *i.e.* it cannot perform any τ-transition, we say that it is a *potential deadlock*. In general, the ready set of a potential deadlock p shows how to make p move to a different state, possibly one that can perform further computation: if $R(p) = \emptyset$ then there is no way to make p move on, while if $R(p)$ contains some action, then p is a state waiting for the environment to interact with it. Indeed, potential deadlocks are called *waiting states* in [38]. In particular, in an asynchronous setting the outputs of a potential deadlock p show how it can unlock the inputs of a client, which in turn may lead the client to a novel state that can make p move, possibly to a state that can perform further computation. A standard manner to capture all the ways out of the potential deadlocks that a program p encounters after executing a trace s is its *acceptance set*: $\mathcal{A}(p, s, \longrightarrow) = \{R(p') \mid p \overset{s}{\Longrightarrow} p' \overset{\tau}{\nrightarrow}\}$.

In our presentation we indicate explicitly the third parameter of $\mathcal{A}$, *i.e.* the transition relation of the LTS at hand, because when necessary we will manipulate this parameter. For any two LTSs $\mathcal{L}_A, \mathcal{L}_B$ and servers $p \in A, q \in B$, we write $\mathcal{A}(p, s, \longrightarrow_A) \ll \mathcal{A}(q, s, \longrightarrow_B)$ if for every $R \in \mathcal{A}(q, s, \longrightarrow_B)$ there exists $\widehat{R} \in \mathcal{A}(p, s, \longrightarrow_A)$ such that $\widehat{R} \subseteq R$. We can now recall the definition of the behavioural preorder à la Hennessy, $\preccurlyeq_{\mathsf{AS}}$, which is based on acceptance sets [32].

Definition 5. *We write*

- $p \preccurlyeq_{\mathsf{cnv}} q$ *whenever* $\forall s \in \mathsf{Act}^\star. p \Downarrow_A s$ *implies* $q \Downarrow_B s$,
- $p \preccurlyeq_{\mathsf{acc}} q$ *whenever* $\forall s \in \mathsf{Act}^\star. p \Downarrow_A s$ *implies* $\mathcal{A}(p, s, \longrightarrow_A) \ll \mathcal{A}(q, s, \longrightarrow_B)$,
- $p \preccurlyeq_{\mathsf{AS}} q$ *whenever* $p \preccurlyeq_{\mathsf{cnv}} q$ *and* $p \preccurlyeq_{\mathsf{acc}} q$.

In the synchronous setting, the behavioural preorder $\preccurlyeq_{\mathsf{AS}}$ is closely related to the denotational semantics based on Acceptance Trees proposed by Hennessy in [31,32]. There the predicates need not be annotated with the LTS that they are used on, because those works treat a unique LTS. Castellani and Hennessy [21] show in their Example 4 that the condition on acceptance sets, *i.e.* $\preccurlyeq_{\mathsf{acc}}$, is too demanding in an asynchronous setting.

Letting $p = a.0$ and $q = 0$, they show that $p \lesssim_{\mathrm{MUST}} q$ but $p \npreccurlyeq_{\mathsf{AS}} q$, because $\mathcal{A}(p, \epsilon) = \{\{a\}\}$ and $\mathcal{A}(q, \epsilon) = \{\emptyset\}$, and corresponding to the ready set $\emptyset \in \mathcal{A}(q, \epsilon)$ there is no ready set $\widehat{R} \in \mathcal{A}(p, s)$ such that $\widehat{R} \subseteq \emptyset$. Intuitively this is the case because acceptance sets treat inputs and outputs similarly, while in an asynchronous setting only outputs can be tested.

Nevertheless $\preccurlyeq_{\mathsf{AS}}$ characterises $\lesssim_{\mathrm{MUST}}$, if servers are enhanced as with forwarding. We now introduce this concept.

Forwarders We say that an LTS $\mathcal{L}$ is of output-buffered agents *with forwarding*, for short is FWD, if it satisfies all the axioms in Figure 2 except FEEDBACK, and also the two following axioms:

$$p \overset{a}{\underset{\bar{a}}{\rightleftarrows}} p' \qquad\qquad \begin{array}{c} p \overset{\bar{a}}{\longrightarrow} p' \\ \big\downarrow a \\ q \end{array} \Rightarrow p \overset{\tau}{\longrightarrow} q \text{ or } p = q \qquad (7)$$

INPUT-BOOMERANG   FWD-FEEDBACK

The INPUT-BOOMERANG axiom states a kind of input-enabledness property, which is however more specific as it stipulates that the target state of the input should loop back to the source state via a complementary output. This is the essence of the behaviour of a forwarder, whose role is simply to pass on a message and then get back to its original state. The FWD-FEEDBACK axiom is a weak form of Selinger's FEEDBACK axiom, which is better understood in conjunction with the INPUT-BOOMERANG axiom: if the transition sequence $p \xrightarrow{\bar{a}} p' \xrightarrow{a} q$ in the FWD-FEEDBACK axiom is taken to be the transition sequence $p' \xrightarrow{\bar{a}} p \xrightarrow{a} p'$ in the INPUT-BOOMERANG axiom, then we see that it must be $q = p$ in the FWD-FEEDBACK axiom. Moreover, no τ action is issued when moving from p to q, since no synchronisation occurs in this case: the message is just passed on.

To prove that $\preceq_{\mathrm{AS}}$ is sound and complete with respect to $\precsim_{\mathrm{MUST}}$:

1. we define a function $\mathrm{FW} : \mathrm{FDB} \longrightarrow \mathrm{FWD}$ that lifts any LTS $\mathcal{L} \in \mathrm{FDB}$ into a suitable LTS $\mathrm{FW}(\mathcal{L}) \in \mathrm{FWD}$, and
2. we check the predicates $\Downarrow$ and $\mathcal{A}(-, -, -)$ over the LTS $\mathrm{FW}(\mathcal{L})$.

Let MO denote the set of all finite multisets of output actions, for instance we have $\varnothing, \{\![\bar{a}]\!\}, \{\![\bar{a}, \bar{a}]\!\}, \{\![\bar{a}, \bar{b}, \bar{a}, \bar{b}]\!\} \in MO$. We let $M, N, \ldots$ range over MO. The symbol M stands for *mailbox*. We denote with $\uplus$ the multiset union.

Definition 6. *Let* $\mathrm{FW}(\mathcal{L}) = \langle A \times MO, L, \longrightarrow_{\mathrm{fw}} \rangle$ *for every* $\mathcal{L} = \langle A, L, \longrightarrow \rangle$, *where the states in* $\mathrm{FW}(\mathcal{L})$ *are pairs denoted* $p \triangleright M$, *such that* $p \in A$ *and* $M \in MO$, *and the transition relation* $\longrightarrow_{\mathrm{fw}}$ *is defined via the rules in Figure 6.*

$$[\text{L-PROC}] \quad \frac{p \xrightarrow{\alpha} p'}{p \triangleright M \xrightarrow{\alpha}_{\mathrm{fw}} p' \triangleright M} \qquad\qquad [\text{L-COMM}] \quad \frac{p \xrightarrow{a} p'}{p \triangleright (\{\![\bar{a}]\!\} \uplus M) \xrightarrow{\tau}_{\mathrm{fw}} p' \triangleright M}$$

$$[\text{L-MOUT}] \quad \frac{}{p \triangleright (\{\![\bar{a}]\!\} \uplus M) \xrightarrow{\bar{a}}_{\mathrm{fw}} p \triangleright M} \quad [\text{L-MINP}] \quad \frac{}{p \triangleright M \xrightarrow{a}_{\mathrm{fw}} p \triangleright (\{\![\bar{a}]\!\} \uplus M)}$$

Fig. 6. Lifting of an LTS to an LTS with forwarding.

Let us briefly comment on Definition 6 and the rules in Figure 6. The pair $p \triangleright M$ is a kind of asymmetric parallel composition between a process p and a mailbox M. Rule [L-PROC] says that the process can evolve independently of the mailbox. Rule [L-COMM] says that an input in the process can synchronise with a complementary output in the mailbox. Rules [L-MINP] and [L-MOUT] express the essence of the forwarding behaviour: the pair $p \triangleright M$ may input any message from the environment and store it into the mailbox M (Rule [L-MINP]); dually, the pair $p \triangleright M$ may output any message in the mailbox M towards the environment (Rule [L-MOUT]). Note that in both cases, the interaction occurs between the mailbox M and the environment, without any participation of the process p.

Example 4. If a calculus is fixed, then the function FW may have a simpler definition. For instance Castellani and Hennessy [21] define it in their calculus TACCS by letting $\xrightarrow{\alpha}_{\text{fw}}$ be the least relation over TACCS such that (1) for every $\alpha \in \text{Act}_\tau$. $\xrightarrow{\alpha} \subseteq \xrightarrow{\alpha}_{\text{fw}}$, and (2) for every $a \in \mathcal{N}$. $p \xrightarrow{a}_{\text{fw}} p \parallel \bar{a}$. □

The transition relation $\longrightarrow_{\text{fw}}$ is reminiscent of the one introduced in Definition 8 by Honda and Tokoro in [38]. The construction given in our Definition 6, though, does not yield the LTS of Honda and Tokoro, as $\longrightarrow_{\text{fw}}$ adds the forwarding capabilities to the states only at the top-level, instead of descending structurally into terms. As a consequence, in the LTS of [38] $a.0+0 \xrightarrow{b} \bar{b}$, while $a.0+0 \triangleright M \xrightarrow{b}_{\text{fw}} M \uplus \{\!|\bar{b}|\!\}$.

Example 5. As the set $\mathcal{N}$ is countable, every process p that belongs to the LTS $\langle \text{ACCS} \times MO, \text{Act}_\tau, \longrightarrow_{\text{fw}}\rangle$ is infinitely-branching: for every mailbox M we have $p \triangleright M \xrightarrow{a_i}_{\text{fw}} p \triangleright (\{\!|\overline{a_i}|\!\} \uplus M)$ for every $a_i \in \mathcal{N}$. This is illustrated by the following picture, where for simplicity we omit the subscript fw under the arrows.

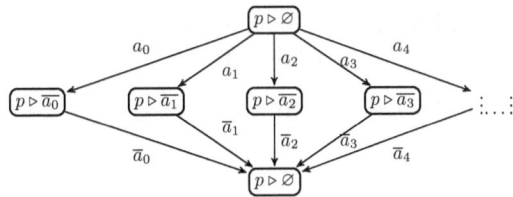

□

The intuition behind Definition 6 is that, when a client interacts with a server asynchronously, the client can send any message it likes, regardless of the inputs that the server can actually perform. In fact, asynchronous clients behave as if the server was saturated with *forwarders*, namely processes of the form $a.\bar{a}$, for any $a \in \mathcal{N}$.

The function FW enjoys two crucial properties: it lifts any LTS of output-buffered agents with feedback to an LTS with forwarding, and the lifting preserves the MUST predicate. We can thus reason on $\lesssim_{\text{MUST}}$ using LTSs in FWD.

Lemma 2. *For every LTS $\mathcal{L} \in$ FDB, $\text{FW}(\mathcal{L}) \in$ FWD.*

Proof. See [8, Appendix C]. □

Lemma 3. *For every $\mathcal{L}_A, \mathcal{L}_B, \mathcal{L}_C \in$ FDB, $p \in A, q \in B, r \in C$,*

1. *p MUST r if and only if $\text{FW}(p)$ MUST r,*
2. *$p \lesssim_{\text{MUST}} q$ if and only if $\text{FW}(p) \lesssim_{\text{MUST}} \text{FW}(q)$.*

We now simplify the definition of acceptance sets to reason on LTSs that are in FWD: for any LTS $\mathcal{L} = \langle A, \text{Act}, \longrightarrow\rangle \subseteq$ FWD and program $p \subseteq A$ we let $\mathcal{A}_{\text{fw}}(p, s, \longrightarrow) = \{O(p') \mid p \xRightarrow{s} p' \xrightarrow{\tau} \!\!\!\!\!/\,\}$. This definition suffices to characterise $\lesssim_{\text{MUST}}$ because in each LTS that is FWD every state performs every input, thus comparing inputs has no impact on the preorder $\preccurlyeq_{\text{acc}}$ of Definition 5. More formally, for every $\mathcal{L}_A, \mathcal{L}_B \in \text{FWD}$ and every $p \in A$ and $q \in B$, we let

$$p \preccurlyeq^{\text{fw}}_{\text{acc}} q \text{ iff } \forall s \in \text{Act}^\star. \, p \Downarrow s \text{ implies } \mathcal{A}_{\text{fw}}(p, s, \longrightarrow_A) \ll \mathcal{A}_{\text{fw}}(q, s, \longrightarrow_B)$$

We have the following logical equivalence.

Lemma 4. *Let* $\mathcal{L}_A, \mathcal{L}_B \in \text{FWD}$. *For every* $p \in A, q \in B, p \preccurlyeq_{\text{acc}} q$ *if and only if* $p \preccurlyeq^{\text{fw}}_{\text{acc}} q$.

Proof. The *only if* implication is trivial, so we discuss the *if* one. Suppose that $p \preccurlyeq^{\text{fw}}_{\text{acc}} q$ and that for some s we have that $R \in \mathcal{A}(q, s, \longrightarrow_B)$. Let X be the possibly empty subset of R that contains only output actions. Since $\mathcal{L}_B$ is FWD we know by definition that $R = X \cup \mathcal{N}$. By definition $X \in \mathcal{A}_{\text{fw}}(q, s, \longrightarrow_B)$, and thus by hypothesis there exists a set of output actions $Y \in \mathcal{A}_{\text{fw}}(p, s, \longrightarrow_A)$ such that $Y \subseteq X$. It follows that the set $Y \cup \mathcal{N} \in \mathcal{A}(p, s, \longrightarrow_A)$, and trivially $Y \cup \mathcal{N} \subseteq X \cup \mathcal{N} = R$. □

In view of the second point of Lemma 3, to prove completeness it suffices to show that $\preccurlyeq_{\text{AS}}$ includes $\precsim_{\text{MUST}}$ over LTSs with forwarding. This is indeed true:

Lemma 5. *For every* $\mathcal{L}_A, \mathcal{L}_B \in \text{FWD}$ *and* $p \in A, q \in B$, *if* $p \precsim_{\text{MUST}} q$ *then we have* $p \preccurlyeq_{\text{AS}} q$.

By a slight abuse of notation, given an LTS $\mathcal{L} = \langle A, L, \longrightarrow \rangle$ and a state $p \in A$, we denote with $\text{FW}(p)$ the LTS rooted at $p \triangleright \varnothing$ in $\text{FW}(\mathcal{L})$.

Theorem 1. *For every* $\mathcal{L}_A, \mathcal{L}_B \in \text{FDB}$ *and* $p \in A, q \in B$,

$$p \precsim_{\text{MUST}} q \quad \text{iff} \quad \text{FW}(p) \preccurlyeq_{\text{AS}} \text{FW}(q).$$

This theorem is the linchpin of this paper, as all other results presented in this paper are corollaries. To begin with, instantiating this theorem to a calculus which can be given an LTS that satisfies the axioms for output-buffered agents with feedback such as ACCS (Lemma 1), the core join-calculus [29] or KLAIM [24], we get a characterisation of the MUST-preorder essentially for free. In our Coq development, we instantiate it with ACCS:

Corollary 1. *For every* $p, q \in \text{ACCS}_\equiv, p \precsim_{\text{MUST}} q$ *iff* $\text{FW}(p) \preccurlyeq_{\text{AS}} \text{FW}(q)$.

Another application of Theorem 1 is a novel behavioural characterisation of the MUST-preorder, which fully exploits asynchrony, *i.e.* disregards irrelevant non-causal orders of visible actions in traces. For space reasons, we defer the discussion of this result to [8, Appendix G].

So far, we have seen the more direct applications of Theorem 1. Before we explain two other applications, namely the coinductive characterisation of the MUST-preorder and the relation of $\precsim_{\text{MUST}}$ with the failure refinement, we outline the proof of Theorem 1, and, in particular, the technical tools we used.

3.2 Proof of Theorem 1

The full proof of Theorem 1, which is given in [8], as well as in the Coq development, comprises two parts: [8, Appendix D] deals with completeness, where the
main aim is to show Lemma 5, and [8, Appendix E] deals with soundness. Here
we outline the main tools we use to prove the soundness of the $\preccurlyeq_{AS}$ preorder:
Bar-induction, which allows us to relate the standard definition of MUST with an
inductive one that is more practical to use, especially in a constructive setting,
and the *LTS of sets*, which is derived from the LTS of the processes.

Bar induction: from extensional to intensional definitions We present
the inductive characterisations of $\downarrow$ and MUST in any state transition system
(STS) $\langle S, \rightarrow \rangle$ that is countably branching. In practice, this condition is satisfied
by most concrete LTS of programming languages, which usually contain count-
ably many terms; this is the case for ACCS and for the asynchronous π-calculus.

Following the terminology of [17] we introduce extensional and intensional
predicates associated to any decidable predicate $Q : S \rightarrow \mathbb{B}$ over an STS $\langle S, \rightarrow \rangle$,
where $\mathbb{B}$ denotes the set of booleans.

Definition 7. *The* extensional predicate $\mathsf{ext}_Q(s)$ *is defined, for $s \in S$, as*

$$\forall \eta \text{ maximal execution of } S. \ \eta_0 = s \text{ implies } \exists n \in \mathbb{N}, \ Q(\eta_n)$$

The intensional predicate int_Q *is the inductive predicate (least fixpoint) defined
by the following rules:*

$$[\text{AXIOM}] \ \frac{Q(s)}{\mathsf{int}_Q(s)} \qquad [\text{IND-RULE}] \ \frac{s \rightarrow \qquad \forall s'. \ s \rightarrow s' \text{ implies } \mathsf{int}_Q(s')}{\mathsf{int}_Q(s)}$$

For instance, by letting

$$Q_1(p) \iff p \nrightarrow \qquad \qquad Q_2(p, r) \iff \text{GOOD}(r)$$

we have by definition that

$$p \downarrow \iff \mathsf{ext}_{Q_1}(p) \qquad p \text{ MUST } r \iff \mathsf{ext}_{Q_2}(p, r) \qquad (\text{ext-preds})$$

that is the standard definitions of $\downarrow$ and MUST are extensional. Our aim now
is to prove that they coincide with their intensional counterparts. The reader
not familiar with this terminology may find in [8, Appendix B] an informal and
hopefully intuitive explanation. Since we will use the intensional predicates in
the rest of the paper a little syntactic sugar is in order, let

$$p \downarrow_i \iff \mathsf{int}_{Q_1}(p) \qquad p \text{ MUST}_i \ r \iff \mathsf{int}_{Q_2}(p, r) \qquad (\text{int-preds})$$

The proofs of soundness, *i.e.* that the inductively defined predicates imply
the extensional ones, are by rule induction:

Lemma 6. *For $p \in S$,*

(a) $p \downarrow_i$ implies $p \downarrow$,
(b) for every r. $p \operatorname{MUST}_i r$ implies $p \operatorname{MUST} r$.

The proofs of completeness are more delicate. To the best of our knowledge, the ones about CCS [22,6] proceed by induction on the greatest number of steps necessary to arrive at termination or at a successful state. Since the STS of $\langle \mathrm{CCS}, \xrightarrow{\tau} \rangle$ is finite branching, Kőnig's lemma guarantees that such a bound exists. This technique does not work on infinite-branching STSs, for example the one of CCS with infinite sums [9]. If we reason in classical logic, we can prove completeness without Kőnig's lemma and also over infinite-branching STSs via a proof *ad absurdum*: suppose $p \downarrow$. If $\neg(p \downarrow_i)$ no finite derivation tree exists to prove $p \downarrow_i$, and then we construct an infinite sequence of τ moves starting with p, thus $\neg(p \downarrow)$. Since we strive to be constructive we replace reasoning *ad absurdum* with a constructive axiom: (decidable) *bar induction*. In the rest of this section we discuss this axiom, and adapt it to our client-server setting. This requires a little terminology.

Bar induction The axiom we want to use is traditionally stated using natural numbers. We use the standard notations $\mathbb{N}^\star$ for finite sequences of natural numbers, $\mathbb{N}^\omega$ for infinite sequences, and $\mathbb{N}^\infty = \mathbb{N}^\star \cup \mathbb{N}^\omega$ for finite or infinite sequences. Remark that, in constructive logics, given $u \in \mathbb{N}^\infty$, we cannot do a case analysis on whether u is finite or infinite. The set $\mathbb{N}^\infty$ equipped with the prefix order can be seen as a *tree*, denoted $T_\mathbb{N}$, in the sense of set theory: a tree is an ordered set $(A, \leq)$ such that, for each $a \in A$, the set $\{b \mid b < a\}$ is well-ordered by $<$. A *path* in a tree A is a maximal element in A. In the tree $\mathbb{N}^\infty$, each node has ω children, and the paths are exactly the infinite sequences $\mathbb{N}^\omega$.

A predicate $P \subseteq \mathbb{N}^\star$ over finite words is a *bar* if every infinite sequence of natural numbers has a finite prefix in P. Note that a bar defines a subtree of $T_\mathbb{N}$ *extensionally*, because it defines each path of the tree, as a path $u \in \mathbb{N}^\omega$ is in the tree if and only if there exists a finite prefix which is in the bar P.

A predicate $Q \subseteq \mathbb{N}^\star$ is *hereditary* if

$$\forall w \in \mathbb{N}^\star, \quad \text{if } \forall n \in \mathbb{N}, w \cdot n \in Q \text{ then } w \in Q.$$

Bar induction states that the extensional predicate associated to a bar implies its *intensional* counterpart: a predicate $P_{int} \subseteq \mathbb{N}^\star$ which contains Q and which is hereditary.

Axiom 8 (Decidable bar induction over $\mathbb{N}$) *Given two predicates P_{int}, Q over $\mathbb{N}^\star$, such that:*

1. for all $\pi \in \mathbb{N}^\omega$, there exists $n \in \mathbb{N}$ such that $(\pi_1, \ldots, \pi_n) \in Q$;
2. for all $w \in \mathbb{N}^\star$, it is decidable whether $Q(w)$ or $\neg Q(w)$;
3. for all $w \in \mathbb{N}^\star$, $Q(w) \Rightarrow P_{int}(w)$;
4. P_{int} is hereditary;

then P_{int} holds over the empty word: $P_{int}(\varepsilon)$.

Bar induction is a generalisation of the fan theorem, i.e. the constructive version of Kőnig's lemma [28, pag. 56], and states that any extensionally well-founded tree T can be turned into an inductively-defined tree t that realises T [17,39].

Our mechanisation of bar induction principle is formulated as a Proposition that is proved using classical reasoning, since it is not provable directly in the type theory of Coq. Unfortunately, while bar induction is a constructive principle, mainstream proof assistants do not support it yet, which is why on the one hand we had to postulate it as a proof principle while on the other hand we proved it in classical logic using the Excluded Middle axiom. This principle though has a computational content, Spector bar recursion[10], which, currently, cannot be used in mainstream proof assistants such as Coq. Developing a type theory with a principle of bar induction is recent and ongoing work [30,46].

Encoding states The version of bar induction we just outlined is not directly suitable for our purposes, as we need to reason about sequences of reductions rather than sequences of natural numbers. The solution is to encode STS states by natural numbers. This leads to the following issue: the nodes of the tree $T_{\mathbb{N}}$ have a fixed arity, namely $\mathbb{N}$, while processes have variably many reducts, including zero if they are stable. To deal with this glitch, it suffices to assume that there exists the following family of surjections:

$$F(p) : \mathbb{N} \to \{q \mid p \to q\} \tag{8}$$

where a surjection is defined as follows.

Definition 9. *A map $f : A \to B$ is a surjection if it has a section $g : B \to A$, that is, $f \circ g = \mathrm{Id}_B$.*

This definition implies the usual one which states the existence of an antecedent $x \in A$ for any $y \in B$, and it is equivalent to it if we assume the Axiom of Choice.

Using this map F as a decoding function, any sequence of natural numbers corresponds to a path in the STS. Its subjectivity means that all paths of the LTS can be represented as such a sequence. This correspondence allows us to transport bar induction from sequences of natural numbers to executions of processes.

Note that such a family of surjections F exists for ACCS processes, and generally to most programming languages, because the set Act_τ is countable, and so are processes. This leads to the following version of bar induction where words and sequences are replaced by finite and infinite executions.

Proposition 1 (Decidable bar induction over an STS). *Let $\langle S, \to \rangle$ be an STS such that a surjection as in (8) exists. Given two predicates Q, P_{int} over finite executions, if*

---

[10] https://en.wikipedia.org/wiki/Bar_recursion

1. *for all infinite execution η, there exists $n \in \mathbb{N}$ such that $(\eta_1, \ldots, \eta_n) \in Q$;*
2. *for all finite execution ζ, $Q(\zeta)$ or $\neg Q(\zeta)$ is decidable;*
3. *for all finite execution ζ, $Q(\zeta) \Rightarrow P_{int}(\zeta)$;*
4. *P_{int} is hereditary, as defined above except that $\zeta \cdot q$ is a partial operation defined when ζ is empty or its last state is p and $p \to q$;*

then P_{int} *holds over the empty execution: that is $P_{int}(\varepsilon)$ holds.*

The last gap towards a useful principle is the requirement that every state in our STS has an outgoing transition. This condition is necessary to ensure the existence of the surjection in Equation (8). To ensure this requirement given any countably-branching STS, we enrich it by adding a *sink* state, which (a) is only reachable from stable states of the original STS, and (b) loops. This is a typical technique, see for instance [40, pag. 17].

Definition 10. *Define $Sink(S, \to) := \langle S \cup \{\top\}, \to^\top \rangle$, where $\to^\top$ is defined inductively as follows:*

$$p \to q \implies p \to^\top q \qquad p \nrightarrow \implies p \to^\top \top \qquad \top \to^\top \top$$

A maximal execution of $Sink(S, \to)$ is always infinite, and it corresponds (in classical logic) to either an infinite execution of S or a maximal execution of S followed by infinitely many $\top$. We finally prove the converse of Lemma 6.

Proposition 2. *Given a countably branching STS $\langle S, \to \rangle$, and a decidable predicate Q on S, we have that, for all $s \in S$, $\mathsf{ext}_Q(s)$ implies $\mathsf{int}_Q(s)$.*

Now we thus obtain completeness of the intensional predicates.

Corollary 2. *For every $p \in A$ we have*

1. *$p \downarrow$ if and only if $p \downarrow_i$, and*
2. *for every r we have that $p \,\mathrm{MUST}\, r$ if and only if $p \,\mathrm{MUST}_i\, r$.*

Proof. Direct consequence of Proposition 2, and Equation (ext-preds) and Equation (int-preds) above.

As we have outlined why Corollary 2 is true, from now on we use $\downarrow_i$ and MUST_i instead of $\downarrow$ and MUST. In [8, Appendix B.2] we prove the properties of these predicates, that we use in the rest of the paper.

The LTS of sets Recall that soundness of $\preccurlyeq_{\mathsf{AS}}$ means that $\preccurlyeq_{\mathsf{AS}} \subseteq \precsim_{\mathrm{MUST}}$. The naïve reasoning does not work. Fix two servers p and q such that $p \preccurlyeq_{\mathsf{AS}} q$. We need to prove that for every client r, if $p \,\mathrm{MUST}_i\, r$ then $p \,\mathrm{MUST}_i\, r$. Rule induction on the predicate $p \,\mathrm{MUST}_i\, r$ fails, as demonstrated by the following example.

Example 6. Consider the two servers $p = \tau.(\bar{a} \parallel \bar{b}) + \tau.(\bar{a} \parallel \bar{c})$ and $q = \bar{a} \parallel (\tau.\bar{b} + \tau.\bar{c})$ of Equation (6). Fix a client r such that $p \,\mathrm{MUST}_i\, r$. Rule induction yields the following inductive hypothesis:

$$\forall p', q'.\ p \parallel r \xrightarrow{\tau} p' \parallel r' \wedge\ p' \preccurlyeq_{\mathsf{AS}} q' \ \Rightarrow\ q' \text{ MUST}_i\, r'.$$

In the proof of q MUST$_i\, r$ we have to consider the case where there is a communication between q and r such that, for instance, $q \xrightarrow{\bar{a}} \tau.\bar{b} + \tau.\bar{c}$ and $r \xrightarrow{a} r'$. In that case, we need to show that $\tau.\bar{b} + \tau.\bar{c}$ MUST$_i\, r'$. Ideally, we would like to use the inductive hypothesis. This requires us to exhibit a p' such that $p \parallel r \xrightarrow{\tau} p' \parallel r'$ and $p' \preccurlyeq_{\mathsf{acc}} \tau.\bar{b} + \tau.\bar{c}$. However, note that there is no way to derive $p \parallel r \xrightarrow{\tau} p' \parallel r'$, because $p \overset{\bar{a}}{\nrightarrow}$. The inductive hypothesis thus cannot be applied, and the naïve proof does not go through. $\qquad\square$

This example suggests that defining an auxiliary predicate MUST$_{\mathsf{aux}}$ in some sense equivalent to MUST$_i$, but that uses explicitly *weak* outputs of servers, should be enough to prove that $\preccurlyeq_{\mathsf{AS}}$ is sound with respect to $\lesssim_{\mathsf{MUST}}$. Unfortunately, though, there is an additional nuisance to tackle: server nondeterminism.

Example 7. Assume that we defined the predicate MUST$_i$ using weak transitions on the server side. Recall the argument put forward in the previous example. The inductive hypothesis now becomes the following:

For every p', q', μ such that $p \overset{\mu}{\Longrightarrow} p'$ and $r \xrightarrow{\mu} r'$, $p' \preccurlyeq_{\mathsf{AS}} q'$ implies q' MUST$_i\, r'$.

To use the inductive hypothesis we have to choose a p' such that $p \overset{\bar{a}}{\Longrightarrow} p'$ and $p' \preccurlyeq_{\mathsf{AS}} \tau.\bar{b} + \tau.\bar{c}$. This is still not enough for the entire proof to go through, because (modulo further τ-moves) the particular p' we pick has to be related also to either $\bar{b}$ or $\bar{c}$. It is not possible to find such a p', because the two possible candidates are either $\bar{b}$ or $\bar{c}$; neither of which can satisfy $p' \preccurlyeq_{\mathsf{AS}} \tau.\bar{b} + \tau.\bar{c}$, as the right-hand side has not committed to a branch yet.

   If instead of a single state p in the novel definition of MUST$_i$ we used a set of states and a suitable transition relation, the choice of either $\bar{b}$ or $\bar{c}$ would be suitably delayed. It suffices for instance to have the following states and transitions: $\{p\} \overset{\bar{a}}{\Longrightarrow} \{\bar{b}, \bar{c}\}$. $\qquad\square$

Now that we have motivated the main intuitions behind the definition of our novel auxiliary predicate MUST$_{\mathsf{aux}}$, we proceed with the formal definitions.

Definition 11 (LTS of sets). *Let $\mathcal{P}^+(Z)$ be the set of non-empty parts of Z. For any LTS $\langle A, L, \longrightarrow \rangle$, $X \in \mathcal{P}^+(A)$ and $\alpha \in L$, we define the sets*

$$D(\alpha, X) = \{p' \mid \exists p \in X.\ p \xrightarrow{\alpha} p'\}, \quad WD(\alpha, X) = \{p' \mid \exists p \in X.\ p \overset{\alpha}{\Longrightarrow} p'\}.$$

We construct the LTS $\langle \mathcal{P}^+(A), \mathsf{Act}_\tau, \longrightarrow \rangle$ by letting $X \xrightarrow{\alpha} D(\alpha, X)$ whenever $D(\alpha, X) \neq \emptyset$. Similarly, we have $X \overset{\alpha}{\Longrightarrow} WD(\alpha, X)$ whenever $WD(\alpha, X) \neq \emptyset$.

Intuitively, this definition lifts the standard notion of state derivative to sets of states. This construction is standard [23,11,12] and goes back to the determinisation of nondeterministic automata.

   Let MUST$_{\mathsf{aux}}$ be defined via the rules in Figure 7. This predicate lets us reason on MUST$_i$ via sets of servers, in the following sense:

[MSET-NOW]   [MSET-STEP]

$$\frac{\text{GOOD}(r)}{X \text{ MUST}_{\text{aux}} r}$$

$$\frac{\neg\text{GOOD}(r) \qquad \forall X'.\ X \xrightarrow{\tau} X' \text{ implies } X' \text{ MUST}_{\text{aux}} r}{\forall p \in X.\ p \,\lVert\, r \xrightarrow{\tau} \qquad \forall r'.\ r \xrightarrow{\tau} r' \text{ implies } X \text{ MUST}_{\text{aux}} r' \qquad \forall X', \mu \in \text{Act}^\star.\ X \overset{\overline{\mu}}{\Longrightarrow} X' \text{ and } r \xrightarrow{\mu} r' \text{ imply } X' \text{ MUST}_{\text{aux}} r'}{X \text{ MUST}_{\text{aux}} r}$$

Fig. 7. Rules to define inductively the predicate MUST$_{\text{aux}}$.

Lemma 7. *For every LTSs $\mathcal{L}_A, \mathcal{L}_B$ and every set of servers $X \in \mathcal{P}^+(A)$, we have that X MUST$_{\text{aux}} r$ if and only if for every $p \in X$. p MUST$_i r$.*

The LTS of sets has two important applications in this paper: first, it is used to define the MUST$_{\text{aux}}$ relation, on which we rely to prove the soundness of the characterisation (see [8, Appendix E]). Additionally, it is used in the definition of the coinductive characterisation, which is the topic of the next section.

3.3 The action-based coinductive characterisation

We conclude this section by introducing a characterisation of the MUST-preorder that is more practical than $\preccurlyeq_{\text{AS}}$, as it allows one to use the usual coinductive techniques. In addition, in the asynchronous case where processes are enhanced with forwarding, being able to use the coinductive proof method allows us to deal easily with the additional transitions due to forwarding. As a demonstration, we use this preorder to prove the code hoisting refinement shown in (6).

First, we recall the definition of this alternative preorder, which, like the other ones, is the same as in the synchronous case [1,41,10].

Definition 12 (Coinductive preorder). *For all image-finite LTSs $\mathcal{L}_A$, $\mathcal{L}_B$ and all $X \in \mathcal{P}^+(A), q \in B$, we let the coinductive preorder $\preccurlyeq_{\text{co}}$ be defined as the greatest relation such that whenever $X \preccurlyeq_{\text{co}} q$, the following requirements hold:*

1. *$X \downarrow$ implies $q \downarrow$,*
2. *For each q' such that $q \xrightarrow{\tau} q'$, we have that $X \preccurlyeq_{\text{co}} q'$,*
3. *$X \downarrow$ and $q \overset{\tau}{\nrightarrow}$ imply that there exist $p \in X$ and $p' \in A$ such that $p \Longrightarrow p' \overset{\tau}{\nrightarrow}$ and $R(p') \subseteq R(q)$,*
4. *For any $\mu \in \text{Act}$, if $X \Downarrow \mu$, then for every X' and q' such that $X \overset{\mu}{\Longrightarrow} X'$ and $q \xrightarrow{\mu} q'$, we have that $X' \preccurlyeq_{\text{co}} q'$.*

This preorder characterises $\precsim_{\text{MUST}}$ when the set X of servers is a singleton.

Theorem 2. *For every image-finite LTS $\mathcal{L}_A$, $\mathcal{L}_B \in \text{FDB}$, every $p \in A$ and $q \in B$, we have that $p \precsim_{\text{MUST}} q$ if and only if $\{\text{FW}(p)\} \preccurlyeq_{\text{co}} \text{FW}(q)$.*

The idea of the proof is to establish that the coinductive preorder characterises a version of the MUST-preorder that also has a set of servers on its LHS, and is defined as follows:

$$X \sqsubseteq^{\text{Set}}_{\text{MUST}} q \iff \forall t.\ (\forall p \in X, p \text{ MUST}_i\ t) \text{ implies } q \text{ MUST}_i\ t.$$

Observe that Definition 12 is based on single actions, instead of traces like $\preccurlyeq_{\text{AS}}$, thus it gives us a practical proof method. To make this point, we now prove the code hoisting refinement (6). According to Theorem 2, it suffices to prove:

$$\{\tau.(\overline{a} \parallel \overline{b}) + \tau.(\overline{a} \parallel \overline{c})\} \preccurlyeq_{\text{co}} \overline{a} \parallel (\tau.\overline{b} + \tau.\overline{c}) \tag{9}$$

As for proofs by induction, when using coinduction it is helpful to prove a more general statement, which yields a useful *coinductive hypothesis*. This vocabulary corresponds to the proof theoretic point of view of coinduction, which matches how Coq implements coinductive proofs using `cofix`. In practice, the prover can use the coinductive hypothesis *after* the predicate defined coinductively has been unfolded at least once. In the set-theoretic setting used in Definition 12, this corresponds to choosing a relation R that is closed under the operations given in the definition. This is borne out by [8, Lemma 47].

4   Preorders based on must-sets and failure refinement

We now establish the second *standard* characterisation of the MUST-preorder, defined using MUST-sets, again thanks to Theorem 1. As an application, we relate the *failure refinement* used by the CSP community to the MUST-preorder.

We begin by defining formally the $\preccurlyeq_{\text{MS}}$ preorder, and we relate it to the MUST-preorder. For every $X \subseteq_{\text{fin}} \text{Act}$, that is for every finite set of visible actions, with a slight abuse of notation we write p MUST X whenever $p \xRightarrow{\varepsilon} p'$ implies that $p' \xRightarrow{\mu}$ for some $\mu \in X$, and we say that X is a MUST-set of p. Let $(p \text{ after } s, \longrightarrow) = \{p' \mid p \xRightarrow{s} p'\}$. For every $\mathcal{L}_A, \mathcal{L}_B$ and $p \in A, q \in B$, let $p \preccurlyeq_{\text{M}} q$ whenever $\forall s \in \text{Act}^*$ we have that $p \Downarrow s$ implies that ($\forall X \subseteq_{\text{fin}} \text{Act}$ if $(p \text{ after } s, \longrightarrow_A)$ MUST X then $(q \text{ after } s, \longrightarrow_B)$ MUST X).

Definition 13. *For all $\mathcal{L}_A, \mathcal{L}_B \in \text{FDB}$ and servers $p \in A$ and $q \in B$, we let $p \preccurlyeq_{\text{MS}} q$ whenever $p \preccurlyeq_{\text{cnv}} q \wedge p \preccurlyeq_{\text{M}} q$.*

Lemma 8. *Let $\mathcal{L}_A, \mathcal{L}_B \in \text{FDB}$. For all $p \in A$ and $q \in B$ such that $\text{FW}(p) \preccurlyeq_{\text{cnv}} \text{FW}(q)$, we have that $\text{FW}(p) \preccurlyeq_{\text{M}} \text{FW}(q)$ if and only if $\text{FW}(p) \preccurlyeq^{\text{fw}}_{\text{acc}} \text{FW}(q)$.*

As a direct consequence, we obtain the following result.

Theorem 3. *Let $\mathcal{L}_A, \mathcal{L}_B \in \text{FDB}$. For all $p \in A$ and $q \in B$, we have that $p \sqsubseteq_{\text{MUST}} q$ if and only if $\text{FW}(p) \preccurlyeq_{\text{MS}} \text{FW}(q)$.*

Failure refinement MUST-sets have been used mainly by De Nicola and collaborators, for instance in [26,15], and are closely related to the failure refinement proposed in [19] by Hoare, Brookes and Roscoe for TCSP (the process algebra based on Hoare's language CSP [37,18]). Following [19], a *failure* of a process p is a pair (s, X) such that $p \overset{s}{\Longrightarrow} p'$ and $p' \overset{\mu}{\nrightarrow}$ for all $\mu \in X$. Then, failure refinement is defined by letting $p \leq_{\mathsf{fail}} q$ whenever the failures of q are also failures of p. This refinement was designed to give a denotational semantics to processes, and mechanisations in Isabelle/HOL have been developed to ensure that the refinement is well defined [50,5]. Both Hennessy [32, pag. 260] and [20] highlight that the failure model can be justified operationally via the MUST testing equivalence: it is folklore dating back to [25, Section 4] that failure equivalence and $\approx_{\mathrm{MUST}}$ coincide. Thanks to Theorem 3 we conclude that in fact $\underset{\mathrm{MUST}}{\sqsubseteq}$ coincides with the *failure divergence refinement* [51], that is, the intersection of $\leq_{\mathsf{fail}}$ and $\preccurlyeq_{\mathsf{cnv}}$.

Corollary 3. *Let* $\mathcal{L}_A, \mathcal{L}_B \in$ FDB. *For every* $p \in A$ *and* $q \in B$, *we have that* $p \underset{\mathrm{MUST}}{\sqsubseteq} q$ *if and only if* $\mathrm{FW}(p) \preccurlyeq_{\mathsf{cnv}} \mathrm{FW}(q)$ *and* $\mathrm{FW}(p) \leq_{\mathsf{fail}} \mathrm{FW}(q)$.

5   Related work

Here we discuss in detail the works more closely related to the results of this paper. Further discussion on related work may be found in [8, Appendix A].

The first investigation on the MUST-preorder in an asynchronous setting was put forth by [21]. While their very clear examples shed light on the preorder, their alternative preorder (Definition 6 in that paper) is more complicated than necessary: it uses the standard LTS of TACCS, its lifting to an LTS with forwarding, and two somewhat ad-hoc notions: a predicate $\overset{I}{\rightsquigarrow}$ and a condition on multisets of inputs. Moreover that preorder is not complete because of a glitch in the treatment of divergence. The details of the counter-example we found to that completeness result are given in [8, Appendix I].

In [34] Hennessy outlines how to adapt the approach of [21] to a typed asynchronous π-calculus. While the LTS with forwarding is replaced by a Context LTS, the predicates to define the alternative preorder are essentially the same as those used in the preceding work with Castellani. Acceptance sets are given in Definition 3.19 there, and the predicate $\rightsquigarrow$ is denoted $\searrow$, while the generalised acceptance sets of [21] are given in Definition 3.20. Owing to the glitch in the completeness of [21], it is not clear that Theorem 3.28 of [34] is correct either.

Also the authors of [15] consider the MUST-preorder in ACCS. There is a major difference between their approach and ours. When studying theories for asynchronous programs, one can either

(1) keep the definitions used for synchronous programs, and enhance the LTS with forwarders; or
(2) adapt the definitions, and keep the standard LTS.

In the first case, the complexity is moved into the LTS, which becomes infinite-branching and infinite-state. In the second case, the complexity is moved into the definitions used to reason on the LTS (i.e. in the meta-language), and in particular in the definition of the alternative preorder, which deviates from the standard one. The authors of [15] follow the second approach. This essentially explains why they employ the standard LTS of CCS and to tackle asynchrony they reason on traces via (1) a preorder $\preceq$ (Table 2 of that paper) that defines on *input* actions the phenomena due to asynchrony; and (2) a rather technical operation on traces, namely $s \ominus s' = (\{\!|s|\!\}_i \setminus \{\!|s'|\!\}_i) \setminus (\overline{\{\!|s|\!\}_o \setminus \{\!|s'|\!\}_o})$. We favour instead the approach in (1), for it helps achieve a modular mechanisation.

The authors of [27] give yet another account of the MUST-preorder. Even though non-blocking outputs can be written in their calculus, they use a left-merge operator that allows writing *blocking* outputs. The contexts that they use to prove the completeness of their alternative preorder use such blocking outputs, consequently their arguments need not tackle the asymmetric treatment of input and output actions. This explains why they can use smoothly a standard LTS, while [21] and [15] have to resort to more complicated structures.

Theorem 5.3 of the PhD thesis by [52] states an alternative characterisation of the MUST-preorder, but it is given with no proof. The alternative preorder given in Definition 5.8 of that thesis turns out to be a mix of the ones by [21] and [15]. In particular, the definition of the alternative preorder relies on the LTS with forwarding, there denoted $\longrightarrow_A$ (Point 1. in Definition 5.1 defines exactly the input transitions that forward messages into the global buffer). The condition that compares convergence of processes is the same as in [21], while server actions are compared using MUST-sets, and not acceptance sets. In fact, Definition 5.7 there is titled "acceptance sets" but it actually defines MUST-sets.

6   Conclusion

In this paper we have shown that the standard characterisations of the MUST-preorder by De Nicola and Hennessy [25,32] are sound and complete also in an asynchronous setting, provided servers are enhanced with the forwarding ability. Lemma 2 shows that this lifting is always possible. We have also shown that the standard coinductive characterisation carries over to the asynchronous setting. Our results are supported by the first mechanisation of the MUST-preorder, and increase proof (i.e. code) factorisation and reusability since the alternative preorders do not need to be changed when shifting between synchronous and asynchronous semantics: it is enough to parameterise the proofs on the set of non-blocking actions. Corollary 3 states that MUST-preorder and failure refinement essentially coincide. This might spur further interest in the mechanisations of failure refinement, carried out so far in Isabelle/HOL [50,5], possibly opening up opportunities of joint efforts for automated checking.

Proof method for MUST-*preorder* Theorems 1, 2 and 3 endow researchers in programming languages for message-passing software with a proof method for $\sqsubseteq_{\text{MUST}}$, namely: to define for their calculi an LTS that enjoys the axioms of output-buffered agents with feedback. An example of this approach is Corollary 1.

Live programs have barred trees We argued that a proof of $p\,\text{MUST}\,r$ is a proof of liveness (of the client). This paper is thus de facto an example that proving liveness amounts to prove that a computational tree has a bar (identified by the predicate GOOD), and hence bar induction is a natural way to reason constructively on liveness-preserving manipulations on programs. While this fact seems to be by and large unexploited by the PL community, we believe that it may be of interest to practitioners reasoning on liveness properties in theorem provers in particular, and to the PL community at large.

Mechanisation Boreale and Gadducci [13] remark that the MUST-preorder lacks a tractable proof method. In constrast, we argue that our contributions, in particular the coinductive characterisation (Theorem 2), being fully mechanised in Coq, let practitioners pursue non-trivial results about testing preorders for real-world programming languages. To make this point, we have proved a form of code-hoisting using this characterisation. Our mechanisation lowers the barrier to entry for researchers versed into theorem provers and wishing to use testing preorders; adds to the toolkit of Coq users an alternative to the well-known (and already mechanised) bisimulation equivalence [45]; and provides a starting point for researchers willing to study testing preorders and analogous refinements within type theory. Researchers working on testing preorders may benefit from it, as there are analogies between reasoning techniques for MAY, MUST, COMPLIANCE, SHOULD, and FAIR testing. For instance Baldan et al. show with pen and paper that a technique similar to forwarding works to characterise the MAY-preorder [4].

Future work Thanks to Theorems 1, 2 and 3 we can now set out to (1) devise an axiomatisation of $\lesssim_{\text{MUST}}$ for asynchronous calculi, as done in [35,14,32,33] for synchronous ones; (2) study for which asynchronous calculi $\lesssim_{\text{MUST}}$ is a precongruence; (3) machine-check semantic models of subtyping for session types [10]; (4) study the decidability of $\lesssim_{\text{MUST}}$.

More in general, given the practical relevance of asynchronous communication, it seems crucial not only to adapt the large body of theory for synchronous communication to the asynchronous setting but also to resort to machine supported reasoning to do it. This paper is meant to be a step in this direction.

Data availability The mechanised proofs have been archived on Zenodo[7].

Acknowledgments. We thank the anonymous reviewers for their helpful comments, and Roberto Amadio for useful remarks. The first author would like to acknowledge his "N+1 honoris causa" Pierre-Evariste Dagand for the systematic and useful feedback, Guillaume Geoffroy for suggesting the use of bar induction, and Hugo Herbelin for discussions on the topic. This work has received funding from the European Research Council (ERC) under the European Union's Horizon 2020 research and innovation programme (grant agreement No. 101003349).

References

1. Aceto, L., Hennessy, M.: Termination, Deadlock, and Divergence. J. ACM **39**(1), 147–187 (1992). `https://doi.org/10.1145/147508.147527`, `https://doi.org/10.1145/147508.147527`

2. Amadio, R.M., Castellani, I., Sangiorgi, D.: On Bisimulations for the Asynchronous pi-calculus. In: Montanari, U., Sassone, V. (eds.) Proceedings CONCUR 96, Pisa. Lecture Notes in Computer Science, vol. 1119, pp. 147–162. Springer Verlag (1996)

3. Amadio, R.M., Castellani, I., Sangiorgi, D.: On Bisimulations for the Asynchronous pi-calculus. Theoretical Computer Science **195**, 291–324 (1998)

4. Baldan, P., Bonchi, F., Gadducci, F., Monreale, G.V.: Asynchronous Traces and Open Petri Nets. In: Bodei, C., Ferrari, G., Priami, C. (eds.) Programming Languages with Applications to Biology and Security - Essays Dedicated to Pierpaolo Degano on the Occasion of His 65th Birthday. Lecture Notes in Computer Science, vol. 9465, pp. 86–102. Springer (2015). `https://doi.org/10.1007/978-3-319-25527-9_8`, `https://doi.org/10.1007/978-3-319-25527-9_8`

5. Baxter, J., Ribeiro, P., Cavalcanti, A.: Sound reasoning in tock-CSP. Acta Informatica **59**(1), 125–162 (2022). `https://doi.org/10.1007/s00236-020-00394-3`, `https://doi.org/10.1007/s00236-020-00394-3`

6. Bernardi, G.: Behavioural equivalences for Web services. Ph.D. thesis, Trinity College Dublin (2013), `http://www.tara.tcd.ie/handle/2262/77595`

7. Bernardi, G., Castellani, I., Laforgue, P., Stefanesco, L.: Artifact for constructive characterisations of the must-preorder for asynchrony (jan 2025). `https://doi.org/10.5281/zenodo.14735088`, `https://doi.org/10.5281/zenodo.14735088`

8. Bernardi, G., Castellani, I., Laforgue, P., Stefanesco, L.: Constructive characterisations of the must-preorder for asynchrony. Tech. rep. (2025), `https://hal.science/hal-04642776`

9. Bernardi, G., Hennessy, M.: Mutually Testing Processes. Log. Methods Comput. Sci. **11**(2) (2015). `https://doi.org/10.2168/LMCS-11(2:1)2015`, `https://doi.org/10.2168/LMCS-11(2:1)2015`

10. Bernardi, G.T., Hennessy, M.: Modelling session types using contracts. Math. Struct. Comput. Sci. **26**(3), 510–560 (2016). `https://doi.org/10.1017/S0960129514000243`, `https://doi.org/10.1017/S0960129514000243`

11. Bonchi, F., Caltais, G., Pous, D., Silva, A.: Brzozowski's and Up-To Algorithms for Must Testing. In: Shan, C. (ed.) Programming Languages and Systems - 11th Asian Symposium, APLAS 2013, Melbourne, VIC, Australia, December 9-11, 2013. Proceedings. Lecture Notes in Computer Science, vol. 8301, pp. 1–16. Springer (2013). `https://doi.org/10.1007/978-3-319-03542-0_1`, `https://doi.org/10.1007/978-3-319-03542-0_1`

12. Bonchi, F., Sokolova, A., Vignudelli, V.: The Theory of Traces for Systems with Nondeterminism, Probability, and Termination. Log. Methods Comput. Sci. **18**(2) (2022). `https://doi.org/10.46298/LMCS-18(2:21)2022`, `https://doi.org/10.46298/lmcs-18(2:21)2022`

13. Boreale, M., Gadducci, F.: Processes as formal power series: A coinductive approach to denotational semantics. Theor. Comput. Sci. (2006). `https://doi.org/10.1016/j.tcs.2006.05.030`, `https://doi.org/10.1016/j.tcs.2006.05.030`

14. Boreale, M., Nicola, R.D.: Testing Equivalence for Mobile Processes. Inf. Comput. **120**(2), 279–303 (1995). `https://doi.org/10.1006/inco.1995.1114`, `https://doi.org/10.1006/inco.1995.1114`

15. Boreale, M., Nicola, R.D., Pugliese, R.: Trace and Testing Equivalence on Asynchronous Processes. Inf. Comput. **172**(2), 139–164 (2002). https://doi.org/10.1006/inco.2001.3080, https://doi.org/10.1006/inco.2001.3080

16. Boudol, G.: Asynchrony and the Pi-calculus. Research Report RR-1702, INRIA (1992), https://hal.inria.fr/inria-00076939

17. Brede, N., Herbelin, H.: On the logical structure of choice and bar induction principles. In: 36th Annual ACM/IEEE Symposium on Logic in Computer Science, LICS 2021, Rome, Italy, June 29 - July 2, 2021. pp. 1–13. IEEE (2021). https://doi.org/10.1109/LICS52264.2021.9470523, https://doi.org/10.1109/LICS52264.2021.9470523

18. Brookes, S.D.: On the Relationship of CCS and CSP. In: Díaz, J. (ed.) Automata, Languages and Programming, 10th Colloquium, Barcelona, Spain, July 18-22, 1983, Proceedings. Lecture Notes in Computer Science, vol. 154, pp. 83–96. Springer (1983). https://doi.org/10.1007/BFb0036899, https://doi.org/10.1007/BFb0036899

19. Brookes, S.D., Hoare, C.A.R., Roscoe, A.W.: A Theory of Communicating Sequential Processes. J. ACM **31**(3), 560–599 (1984). https://doi.org/10.1145/828.833, https://doi.org/10.1145/828.833

20. Castellan, S., Clairambault, P., Winskel, G.: The Mays and Musts of Concurrent Strategies. In: Palmigiano, A., Sadrzadeh, M. (eds.) Samson Abramsky on Logic and Structure in Computer Science and Beyond. pp. 327–361. Springer International Publishing, Cham (2023). https://doi.org/10.1007/978-3-031-24117-8_9, https://doi.org/10.1007/978-3-031-24117-8_9

21. Castellani, I., Hennessy, M.: Testing Theories for Asynchronous Languages. In: Arvind, V., Ramanujam, R. (eds.) Foundations of Software Technology and Theoretical Computer Science, 18th Conference, Chennai, India, December 17-19, 1998, Proceedings. Lecture Notes in Computer Science, vol. 1530, pp. 90–101. Springer (1998). https://doi.org/10.1007/978-3-540-49382-2_9, https://doi.org/10.1007/978-3-540-49382-2_9

22. Cerone, A., Hennessy, M.: Process Behaviour: Formulae vs. Tests. Tech. rep., Trinity College Dublin, School of Computer Science and Statistics (2010)

23. Cleaveland, R., Hennessy, M.: Testing Equivalence as a Bisimulation Equivalence. In: Sifakis, J. (ed.) Automatic Verification Methods for Finite State Systems, International Workshop, Grenoble, France, June 12-14, 1989, Proceedings. Lecture Notes in Computer Science, vol. 407, pp. 11–23. Springer (1989). https://doi.org/10.1007/3-540-52148-8_2, https://doi.org/10.1007/3-540-52148-8_2

24. De Nicola, R., Ferrari, G., Pugliese, R.: Klaim: a kernel language for agents interaction and mobility. IEEE Transactions on Software Engineering **24**(5), 315–330 (1998). https://doi.org/10.1109/32.685256

25. De Nicola, R., Hennessy, M.: Testing Equivalences for Processes. Theor. Comput. Sci. **34**, 83–133 (1984). https://doi.org/10.1016/0304-3975(84)90113-0, https://doi.org/10.1016/0304-3975(84)90113-0

26. De Nicola, R., Melgratti, H.C.: Multiparty testing preorders. Log. Methods Comput. Sci. **19**(1) (2023). https://doi.org/10.46298/lmcs-19(1:1)2023, https://doi.org/10.46298/lmcs-19(1:1)2023

27. De Nicola, R., Pugliese, R.: Linda-based applicative and imperative process algebras. Theor. Comput. Sci. **238**(1-2), 389–437 (2000). https://doi.org/10.1016/S0304-3975(99)00339-4, https://doi.org/10.1016/S0304-3975(99)00339-4

28. Dummett, M.: Elements of Intuitionism. Oxford logic guides, Clarendon Press (2000), https://books.google.fr/books?id=JVFzknbGBVAC

29. Fournet, C., Gonthier, G.: The join calculus: A language for distributed mobile programming. In: Barthe, G., Dybjer, P., Pinto, L., Saraiva, J. (eds.) Applied Semantics. pp. 268–332. Springer Berlin Heidelberg, Berlin, Heidelberg (2002)

30. Fridlender, D.: An Interpretation of the Fan Theorem in Type Theory. In: TYPES (1998), https://doi.org/10.1007/3-540-48167-2_7

31. Hennessy, M.: Acceptance Trees. J. ACM **32**(4), 896–928 (1985). https://doi.org/10.1145/4221.4249, https://doi.org/10.1145/4221.4249

32. Hennessy, M.: Algebraic theory of processes. MIT Press series in the foundations of computing, MIT Press (1988)

33. Hennessy, M.: A fully abstract denotational semantics for the pi-calculus. Theor. Comput. Sci. **278**(1-2), 53–89 (2002). https://doi.org/10.1016/S0304-3975(00)00331-5, https://doi.org/10.1016/S0304-3975(00)00331-5

34. Hennessy, M.: The security pi-calculus and non-interference. J. Log. Algebraic Methods Program. (2005). https://doi.org/10.1016/j.jlap.2004.01.003, https://doi.org/10.1016/j.jlap.2004.01.003

35. Hennessy, M., Ingólfsdóttir, A.: Communicating Processes with Value-passing and Assignments. Formal Aspects Comput. **5**(5), 432–466 (1993). https://doi.org/10.1007/BF01212486, https://doi.org/10.1007/BF01212486

36. Hennessy, M., Riely, J.: Information flow vs. resource access in the asynchronous pi-calculus. ACM Trans. Program. Lang. Syst. **24**(5), 566–591 (2002). https://doi.org/10.1145/570886.570890, https://doi.org/10.1145/570886.570890

37. Hoare, C.A.R.: Communicating Sequential Processes (Reprint). Commun. ACM (1983)

38. Honda, K., Tokoro, M.: An Object Calculus for Asynchronous Communication. In: America, P. (ed.) ECOOP'91 European Conference on Object-Oriented Programming, Geneva, Switzerland, July 15-19, 1991, Proceedings. Lecture Notes in Computer Science, vol. 512, pp. 133–147. Springer (1991). https://doi.org/10.1007/BFb0057019, https://doi.org/10.1007/BFb0057019

39. Kleene, S.C., Vesley, R.E.: The Foundations of Intuitionistic Mathematics: Especially in Relation to Recursive Functions. Studies in logic and the foundations of mathematics, North-Holland Publishing Company (1965), https://books.google.fr/books?id=2EHVxQEACAAJ

40. Lamport, L.: Specifying Systems, The TLA+ Language and Tools for Hardware and Software Engineers. Addison-Wesley (2002), http://research.microsoft.com/users/lamport/tla/book.html

41. Laneve, C., Padovani, L.: The *Must* Preorder Revisited. In: Caires, L., Vasconcelos, V.T. (eds.) CONCUR 2007 - Concurrency Theory, 18th International Conference, CONCUR 2007, Lisbon, Portugal, September 3-8, 2007, Proceedings. Lecture Notes in Computer Science, vol. 4703, pp. 212–225. Springer (2007). https://doi.org/10.1007/978-3-540-74407-8_15, https://doi.org/10.1007/978-3-540-74407-8_15

42. Milner, R.: Communicating and Mobile Systems - the Pi-Calculus. Cambridge University Press (1999)

43. Morris, J.H.: Lambda-calculus models of programming languages. Ph.D. thesis, Massachusetts Institute of Technology (1969), https://dspace.mit.edu/handle/1721.1/64850

44. Palamidessi, C.: Comparing the Expressive Power of the Synchronous and Asynchronous pi-calculi. Mathematical Structures in Computer Science **13**(5), 685–719 (2003). https://doi.org/10.1017/S0960129503004043

45. Pous, D.: Coinduction All the Way Up. In: Grohe, M., Koskinen, E., Shankar, N. (eds.) Proceedings of the 31st Annual ACM/IEEE Symposium on Logic in Computer Science, LICS '16, New York, NY, USA, July 5-8, 2016. pp. 307–316. ACM (2016). https://doi.org/10.1145/2933575.2934564, https://doi.org/10.1145/2933575.2934564

46. Rahli, V., Bickford, M., Cohen, L., Constable, R.L.: Bar Induction is Compatible with Constructive Type Theory. J. ACM **66**(2), 13:1–13:35 (2019). https://doi.org/10.1145/3305261, https://doi.org/10.1145/3305261

47. Sangiorgi, D., Walker, D.: The Pi-Calculus - a Theory of Mobile Processes. Cambridge University Press (2001). https://dblp.org/rec/books/daglib/004377.bib

48. Sangiorgi, D.: Asynchronous pi-calculus at Work: The Call-by-Need Strategy. In: Alvim, M.S., Chatzikokolakis, K., Olarte, C., Valencia, F. (eds.) The Art of Modelling Computational Systems: A Journey from Logic and Concurrency to Security and Privacy - Essays Dedicated to Catuscia Palamidessi on the Occasion of Her 60th Birthday. Lecture Notes in Computer Science, vol. 11760, pp. 33–49. Springer (2019). https://doi.org/10.1007/978-3-030-31175-9_3, https://doi.org/10.1007/978-3-030-31175-9_3

49. Selinger, P.: First-Order Axioms for Asynchrony. In: Mazurkiewicz, A.W., Winkowski, J. (eds.) CONCUR '97: Concurrency Theory, 8th International Conference, Warsaw, Poland, July 1-4, 1997, Proceedings. Lecture Notes in Computer Science, vol. 1243, pp. 376–390. Springer (1997). https://doi.org/10.1007/3-540-63141-0_26, https://doi.org/10.1007/3-540-63141-0_26

50. Taha, S., Ye, L., Wolff, B.: HOL-CSP Version 2.0. Archive of Formal Proofs (April 2019)

51. Taha, S., Wolff, B., Ye, L.: The hol-csp refinement toolkit. Archive of Formal Proofs (November 2020), https://isa-afp.org/entries/CSP_RefTK.html, Formal proof development

52. Thati, P.: A Theory of Testing for Asynchronous Concurrent Systems. Ph.D. thesis, University of Illinois Urbana-Champaign, USA (2003), https://hdl.handle.net/2142/81630

Abstraction of memory block manipulations by symbolic loop folding

Jérôme Boillot[(✉)] [iD] and Jérôme Feret[(✉)] [iD]

DIENS, École Normale Supérieure, PSL University, CNRS, Inria, Paris, France
{jerome.boillot,jerome.feret}@ens.fr

Abstract. We introduce a new abstract domain for analyzing memory block manipulations, focusing on programs with dynamically allocated arrays. This domain computes properties universally quantified over the value of the loop counters, both for assignments and tests. These properties consist of equalities and comparison predicates involving abstract expressions, represented as affine forms in the loop counters and symbolic dereferences. All these methods have been incorporated within the Astrée© static analyzer that checks for the absence of run-time errors in embedded critical software. We also give insights on how to implement this abstract domain within any other C static analyzer.

Keywords: Array analysis · Loop folding · Symbolic methods · Abstract interpretation

1 Introduction

As increasingly complex programs, such as operating systems, are successfully formally verified, the memory properties we aim to prove become progressively more subtle. The framework of abstract interpretation has been prolific at providing techniques to prove memory properties. However, the state-of-the-art approaches still lack precision when manipulating pointers, in particular when the memory regions are unbounded. As an example, during the bootstrap of the expanded memory, linking the physical memory to the virtual memory requires proving relations between those addresses, which requires extending the expressivity of symbolic reasoning.

In particular, as in the Gauge domain [19], our abstraction introduces the values of loop counters to express more properties. This improves accuracy while scaling to the analysis of large programs. The analysis of memory block manipulations requires aggregating the effect of the assignments and tests of the previous loop iterations. For this, we go beyond by quantifying universally abstract properties over the precedent values of each loop counters.

We present in this paper a symbolic approach that keeps track of the history of the memory manipulations that are done in the loops.

© The Author(s) 2025
V. Vafeiadis (Ed.): ESOP 2025, LNCS 15694, pp. 117–143, 2025.
https://doi.org/10.1007/978-3-031-91118-7_5

Related Work. Analyzing the content of arrays has been done by using several methods with different degrees of precision, scalability, and automation. A first one consists in *smashing* all the cells of the array into a single abstract value [3]. Then, the pointed value can represent more than one element and the updates are weak. To improve the precision, new techniques have been introduced such as dimension summarization [7], and dynamically partitioning arrays [8,10,6] to express relational properties about segments of arrays. More recently, the analysis of matrix manipulations considered in [11] was one of the first considering multidimensional arrays. However, those techniques do not allow expressing relationships among values and offsets.

The idea of the creation of this new abstract domain comes from two ideas. First, from the Gauge domain [19] that computes, for each variable, bounds that are affine forms in the loop counters. Then, by combining such reasoning with symbolic methods [16,4], it becomes possible to express properties about parts of the memory unknown at analysis time.

Shape analysis is broadly used to reason about memory manipulation [13]. However, it heavily relies on inductive type definitions specified in separation logics [18]. Whereas our abstraction provides several grains of precision for describing memory states, shape analysis tends to lose too much information when the inductive types are not satisfied or cannot be proved.

Outline. We sketch as follows the outline of the paper. In Sect. 2, we give the syntax and the semantics of the toy imperative and untyped language that we will use all along this paper. Symbolic manipulations of expressions often require additional syntactic constructors to abstract parts of the expressions and to account for the information computed by the other parts of the analysis. In Sect. 3, we introduce the syntax and the semantics of the abstract expressions that are handled by our abstract domain. In Sect. 4, we define the abstraction of sets of memory states, while in Sect. 5, we describe the abstract transformers which lift the computation of the concrete semantics in the abstract. In Sect. 6, we describe the result of our analysis on three case-studies (namely, a matrix transposition, the bootstrap of the paging in an x86 operating system, and an array look-up procedure). In Sect. 7, we discuss the implementation details and the current limitations of our framework. We conclude in Sect. 8.

2   Syntax & Semantics

2.1   Syntax of a toy imperative and untyped language

In this section we present a toy imperative and untyped language.

As presented in Fig. 1, an expression is either a constant in $\mathbb{Z}$, the address of a variable that belongs to the finite set of variables $\mathcal{V}$, the value located at the address pointed by another expression, or a sum/difference/product of two expressions.

The statements are labelled by program labels $\ell \in \mathcal{L}$ that are distinct and follow a total order $\leq_{\mathcal{L}}$ that corresponds to their order of appearance in the program. Statements can be either a no-op, a sequence of statements, an assignment, or a conditional branching/loop with the condition that corresponds to the comparison of two expressions. In the case of the assignment, the left-value is the dereference of the address whose content will be modified by the assignment, and the right-value is either an expression or the dynamic allocation of a memory block of size of the expression given as a parameter.

In addition, we introduce the same syntactic sugar as in the C language to ease the understanding of programs: the value of a variable is the value located at its address, and accessing the $e_2{}^{\text{th}}$ element of e_1 corresponds to dereferencing the address $e_1 + e_2$.

$$V \overset{\text{def}}{=} *[\&V]$$
$$e_1[e_2] \overset{\text{def}}{=} *[e_1 + e_2]$$

$prog$	::=	$^\ell stmt^{\ell'}$	$(program)$
$^\ell stmt^{\ell'}$	::=	$^\ell\textbf{skip}^{\ell'}$	$(no\text{-}op)$
	|	$^\ell stmt\,;^{\ell_1} stmt^{\ell'}$	$(sequence)$
	|	$^\ell lval := rval^{\ell'}$	$(assignment)$
	|	$^\ell\textbf{if } expr \bowtie expr \textbf{ then } ^{\ell_t} stmt^{\ell'_t} \textbf{ else } ^{\ell_f} stmt^{\ell'_f} \textbf{ endif}^{\ell'}$	$(conditional)$
	|	$^\ell\textbf{while } expr \bowtie expr \textbf{ do } ^{\ell_b} stmt^{\ell'_b} \textbf{ done}^{\ell'}$	$(loop)$
$expr$	::=	$c \mid \&V \mid *[expr] \mid expr \diamond expr$	$(arithmetic\ expression)$
$lval$	::=	$*[expr]$	$(left\text{-}value)$
$rval$	::=	$expr \mid \textbf{malloc}(expr)$	$(right\text{-}value)$
$\bowtie$	::=	$= \mid \neq \mid < \mid \leq \mid > \mid \geq$	$(arithmetic\ comparison\ operator)$
$\diamond$	::=	$+ \mid - \mid \times$	$(binary\ arithmetic\ operator)$
c	$\in$	$\mathbb{Z}$	$(constant)$
V	$\in$	$\mathcal{V}$	$(variable)$
ℓ	$\in$	$\mathcal{L}$	$(program\ label)$

Fig. 1. Syntax of an untyped imperative language

```
1 int n;
2 int *arr =
3 malloc(n * sizeof(int));
4 for (int i=0; i<n; i++) {
5   arr[i] = i;
6 }
```

$\ell_1\ *[\&arr] := \textbf{malloc}(*[\&n]);$
$\ell_2\ *[\&i] := 0;$
$\ell_3\ \textbf{while } *[\&i] < *[\&n] \textbf{ do}$
$\ell_4\ \quad *[*[\&arr] + *[\&i]] := *[\&i];$
$\ell_5\ \quad *[\&i] := *[\&i] + 1$
$\ell_6\ \textbf{done}^{\ell_7}$

$\ell_1\ arr := \textbf{malloc}(n);$
$\ell_2\ i := 0;$
$\ell_3\ \textbf{while } i < n \textbf{ do}$
$\ell_4\ \quad arr[i] := i;$
$\ell_5\ \quad i := i + 1$
$\ell_6\ \textbf{done}^{\ell_7}$

Fig. 2. Representation of a simple C function's body in the language of the analyzer

To present the language in more details we depict on the left of Fig. 2 a simple C function's body that fills an array of size **n** such that each cell contains its own index. In the middle of the figure, we wrote an equivalent program in the language that we consider. Note that **malloc(n)** allocates an array of **n** elements in $\mathbb{Z}$. Because of this idealization, we do not have to multiply **n** by the number of bytes on which each element is represented. Then, on the right part of the figure we wrote the same program but with the syntactic sugar described previously.

2.2   Concrete semantics of the language

We now describe the *concrete semantics* of our language, that is a mathematical description of its behaviors.

This semantics is non-standard, because we use loop counters as ghost variables (*i.e.*, variables that do not appear in the program) to track how many times each loop body has been evaluated since the most recent evaluation of the loop's entry point. While these counters are not used in the concrete semantics, they play a crucial role in the abstract semantics, where they allow expressing properties universally quantified over loop counter values. In particular, loop counters are useful to express inductive invariants and prove the soundness of the analysis.

A *memory state* is a triple of functions $(\rho, \sigma, \phi) \in \mathcal{R} \stackrel{\text{def}}{=} S_\rho \times S_\sigma \times S_\phi$.

- The first component ρ is a map from addresses in $\mathbb{N}$ to the corresponding value in $\mathbb{Z}$. It corresponds to considering that the memory is an infinite array with naturals as addresses, and integers as values. Then, $S_\rho \stackrel{\text{def}}{=} \mathbb{N} \to \mathbb{Z}$. Let us skip the second element for now.
- The third component ϕ associates each loop counter $\lambda_\ell \in \Lambda$ to its value, that is the number of times the corresponding loop labelled by λ_ℓ has been executed. Then $S_\phi : \Lambda \rightharpoonup \mathbb{N}$. Notice that the function is partial, because before entering a loop and after leaving it the corresponding loop counter does not exist in the domain of ϕ.
- Finally, the second component σ maps each variable, and each dynamically allocated block, to its corresponding address in ρ and its size that represents the number of cells that are reserved to it starting from this address. As dynamically allocated blocks are identified by the program label of the associated **malloc($\cdot$)** statement and the value of the loop counters at that time, we get $S_\sigma \stackrel{\text{def}}{=} (\mathcal{V} \cup (\mathcal{L} \times S_\phi)) \rightharpoonup (\mathbb{N} \times \mathbb{N})$.

Definition 1 (Initial set of memory states). *The initial set of memory states is:*

$$R_0 \stackrel{\text{def}}{=} \left\{ (\rho_0, \sigma_0, \phi_0) \in \mathcal{R} \;\middle|\; \begin{array}{l} \text{dom}(\sigma_0) = \mathcal{V}, \;\; \text{dom}(\phi_0) = \varnothing, \;\; \forall v_1, v_2 \in \text{dom}(\sigma_0), \\ (a_1, s_1) \stackrel{\text{def}}{=} \sigma_0(v_1), \;\; (a_2, s_2) \stackrel{\text{def}}{=} \sigma_0(v_2), \\ s_1 = 1 \;\wedge\; (v_1 \neq v_2 \implies a_1 \neq a_2) \end{array} \right\}$$

The definition of the initial set of memory states R_0 in Def. 1 that is made of:

- ρ_0 that is any function from $\mathbb{N}$ to $\mathbb{Z}$,
- σ_0 that maps only the variables to their corresponding memory blocks that consist in a non-deterministic address in $\mathbb{N}$ and a constant size of 1, but such that the same address is not given to two different variables,
- ϕ_0 that is the partial function with empty domain. Such functions will be denoted $\varnothing$ in the rest of the article.

$$\llbracket c \rrbracket(\rho, \sigma) \overset{\text{def}}{=} c$$

$$\llbracket \&V \rrbracket(\rho, \sigma) \overset{\text{def}}{=} a \ \text{with} \ (a, s) \overset{\text{def}}{=} \sigma(V)$$

$$\llbracket *[e] \rrbracket(\rho, \sigma) \overset{\text{def}}{=} \rho(\llbracket e \rrbracket(\rho, \sigma))$$

$$\llbracket e_1 \diamond e_2 \rrbracket(\rho, \sigma) \overset{\text{def}}{=} \llbracket e_1 \rrbracket(\rho, \sigma) \diamond \llbracket e_2 \rrbracket(\rho, \sigma)$$

$$\{^{\ell}\mathbf{skip}^{\ell'}\}R \overset{\text{def}}{=} R$$

$$\{^{\ell}s_1 \, ; {}^{\ell_1} s_2 {}^{\ell'}\}R \overset{\text{def}}{=} (\{^{\ell_1}s_2{}^{\ell'}\} \circ \{^{\ell}s_1{}^{\ell_1}\})R$$

$$\{^{\ell}\mathbf{if} \ e_1 \bowtie e_2 \ \mathbf{then} \ {}^{\ell_t}s_t{}^{\ell'_t} \ \mathbf{else} \ {}^{\ell_f}s_f{}^{\ell'_f} \ \mathbf{endif}^{\ell'}\}R \overset{\text{def}}{=}$$
$$(\{^{\ell_t}s_t{}^{\ell'_t}\} \circ filter_{\ell,t}(e_1 \bowtie e_2))R \ \cup \ (\{^{\ell_f}s_f{}^{\ell'_f}\} \circ filter_{\ell,f}(e_1 \not\bowtie e_2))R$$

$$\{^{\ell}\mathbf{while} \ e_1 \bowtie e_2 \ \mathbf{do} \ {}^{\ell_b}s{}^{\ell'_b} \ \mathbf{done}^{\ell'}\}R \overset{\text{def}}{=} (forget_\ell \circ filter_{\ell,f}(e_1 \not\bowtie e_2))$$
$$\left(\bigcup_{n \in \mathbb{N}} (inc_\ell \circ \{^{\ell_b}s{}^{\ell'_b}\} \circ filter_{\ell,t}(e_1 \bowtie e_2))^n \, new_\ell(R) \right)$$

$$\{^{\ell}*[e_1] := e_2{}^{\ell'}\}R \overset{\text{def}}{=} \{ (\rho[a := v], \sigma, \phi) \mid (\rho, \sigma, \phi) \in R, \ a \overset{\text{def}}{=} \llbracket e_1 \rrbracket(\rho, \sigma), \ v \overset{\text{def}}{=} \llbracket e_2 \rrbracket(\rho, \sigma) \}$$

$$\{^{\ell}*[e_1] := \mathbf{malloc}(e_2){}^{\ell'}\}R \overset{\text{def}}{=}$$
$$\left\{ (\rho[a_l := a_r], \sigma[(\ell, \phi) := (a_r, s_r)], \phi) \ \middle| \ \begin{array}{l} (\rho, \sigma, \phi) \in R, \\ a_l \in \mathbb{N} : a_l = \llbracket e_1 \rrbracket(\rho, \sigma), \\ s_r \in \mathbb{N} : s_r = \llbracket e_2 \rrbracket(\rho, \sigma), \\ a_r \in \mathbb{N} : \forall (a_o, s_o) \in \text{im}(\sigma), \\ \quad [a_r, a_r{+}s_r) \cap [a_o, a_o{+}s_o) = \varnothing \end{array} \right\}$$

$$filter_{\ell,v}(e_1 \bowtie e_2)R \overset{\text{def}}{=} \{ (\rho, \sigma, \phi) \in R \mid \llbracket e_1 \rrbracket(\rho, \sigma) \bowtie \llbracket e_2 \rrbracket(\rho, \sigma) \}$$

$$new_\ell(R) \overset{\text{def}}{=} \{ (\rho, \sigma, \phi[\lambda_\ell := 0]) \mid (\rho, \sigma, \phi) \in R \}$$

$$inc_\ell(R) \overset{\text{def}}{=} \{ (\rho, \sigma, \phi[\lambda_\ell := \phi(\lambda_\ell) + 1]) \mid (\rho, \sigma, \phi) \in R \}$$

$$forget_\ell(R) \overset{\text{def}}{=} \{ (\rho, \sigma, \phi \restriction_{\text{dom}(\phi) \setminus \{\lambda_\ell\}}) \mid (\rho, \sigma, \phi) \in R \}$$

Fig. 3. Semantics of the language as a denotational semantics

We now introduce the concrete semantics in Fig. 3. We first define the concrete semantics of expressions $\llbracket expr \rrbracket : \mathcal{R} \rightharpoonup \mathbb{Z}$. It maps a memory state to the evaluation of the expression in that memory state, that is an element of $\mathbb{Z}$, if the dereferences are legal. The evaluation of a constant just returns the constant, the evaluation of the address of a variable V returns the address that was stored as the first element of $\sigma(V)$, dereferencing an expression corresponds to evaluating the address corresponding to the expression in parameter and retrieving the value at this address in the memory map ρ. Then, evaluating binary arithmetic operators consists in evaluating both operands and applying the operator on the evaluations.

Then, we define the concrete semantics of statements $\{\!\!\{\,stmt\,\}\!\!\} : \wp(\mathcal{R}) \to \wp(\mathcal{R})$, that maps each set of memory states to another one on which the transformations corresponding to the statements have been performed.

2.3   Consistency of the semantics

The consistency of the semantics relies on the preservation of two properties. The first one, established by Theorem 1, concerns the absence of aliases between the different allocated regions. The second one, established by Theorem 2, ensures that each allocation identifier is introduced at most once, along a given trace.

Firstly, we introduce few auxiliary definitions to specify the scope of loop counters, to state the absence of aliasing in allocated memory regions, and to state that the allocation identifiers are consistent with the current execution.

Definition 2 (Alive loop counters at each program label). *For every* $\ell \in \mathcal{L}$, *let* Λ_ℓ *be the subset of* Λ *that represents all the loop counters alive at the program point* ℓ,

$$\Lambda_\ell \overset{\text{def}}{=} \{\, \lambda_{\ell_1} \in \Lambda \mid \ell_1 <_{\mathcal{L}} \ell <_{\mathcal{L}} \overline{\ell_1} \,\}$$

with $\forall \lambda_{\ell_1} \in \Lambda, \overline{\ell_1}$ *the program label just after the end of the loop statement labelled by* ℓ_1. *We also define a total order* $\leq_\Lambda$ *on loop counters that mirrors the order of their corresponding program points, i.e.,* $\lambda_\ell \leq_\Lambda \lambda_{\ell'} \Leftrightarrow \ell \leq_{\mathcal{L}} \ell'$.

Definition 3 (Non-aliasing memory state property). *A set of memory states* $R \in \wp(\mathcal{R})$ *is said to be* non-aliasing(R) *when none of its allocated memory regions (described by* σ *in each memory set in* R*) aliases with another one.*

$$\text{non-aliasing}(R) \overset{\text{def}}{=} \forall(\rho, \sigma, \phi) \in R, \ \forall k_1, k_2 \in \text{dom}(\sigma),$$
$$(k_1 \in V \implies s_1 = 1) \ \wedge \ (k_1 \neq k_2 \implies [a_1, a_1{+}s_1) \cap [a_2, a_2{+}s_2) = \varnothing)$$
$$\text{with } (a_1, s_1) \overset{\text{def}}{=} \sigma(k_1), \text{ and } (a_2, s_2) \overset{\text{def}}{=} \sigma(k_2).$$

In particular, non-aliasing(R_0).

Definition 4 (Program label and loop counters identify memory allocations).

$$\text{alloc-consistent}(\ell, R) \overset{\text{def}}{=} \forall(\rho, \sigma, \phi) \in R, \forall \ell_1 \in \mathcal{L}, \forall \phi' : \text{dom}(\phi) \to \mathbb{N},$$
$$(\ell \leq_{\mathcal{L}} \ell_1 \ \wedge \ \phi \preccurlyeq \phi') \implies (\ell_1, \phi') \notin \text{dom}(\sigma)$$

with $\preccurlyeq$ *the lexicographic order of the loop counter values scanned in the order described by* $\leq_\Lambda$ *(defined in Def. 2). That is to say, two functions* ϕ *and* ϕ' *are considered as equal if they map the same value for each loop counter, otherwise they are ordered as the values of the minimal loop counter (with respect to the total order* $\leq_\Lambda$*) that maps to different values. Intuitively,* $\phi \preccurlyeq \phi'$ *when* ϕ' *is reachable only after* ϕ.

In particular, $\forall \ell \in \mathcal{L}$, alloc-consistent$(\ell, R_0)$.

This also implies that, before executing a statement ${}^{\ell}e_1 := \mathbf{malloc}(e_2)^{\ell'}$, $(\ell, \phi) \notin \mathrm{dom}(\sigma)$: the identifier of the newly allocated memory block is used for the first time.

Theorem 1 (Concrete semantics does not introduce aliasing). *Let $R \in \wp(\mathcal{R})$ be a set of memory states and ${}^{\ell}s^{\ell'}$ be a statement, then*

$$\text{non-aliasing}(R) \implies \text{non-aliasing}(\{\!\!\{{}^{\ell}s^{\ell'}\}\!\!\}R)$$

This directly implies that, if p is a program, then non-aliasing$(\{\!\!\{p\}\!\!\}R_0)$.

Theorem 2 (Consistency of the identification of memory allocations). *Let $R \in \wp(\mathcal{R})$ be a set of memory states and ${}^{\ell}s^{\ell'}$ be a statement, then*

$$\text{alloc-consistent}(\ell, R) \implies \text{alloc-consistent}(\ell', \{\!\!\{{}^{\ell}s^{\ell'}\}\!\!\}R)$$

This directly implies that if $p \stackrel{\text{def}}{=} {}^{\ell}s^{\ell'}$ is a program then alloc-consistent$(\ell, \{\!\!\{p\}\!\!\}R_0)$.

Theorems 1 and 2 state that the properties non-aliasing and alloc-consistent are preserved by the concrete semantics of statement, which means that, if the property holds initially, it will continue to hold at each program label.

3   Abstract expressions

In the following section, we introduce abstract expressions. They stand both for left and right values, and they allow expressing and propagating intermediary reasoning about them.

3.1   Syntax of abstract expressions

We present their grammar in Fig. 4.

The goal of the abstract domain is to output properties that are universally quantified over the loop counter values. Then, we introduce $\Pi \stackrel{\text{def}}{=} \{\pi_\ell \mid \lambda_\ell \in \Lambda\}$, with $\pi_\ell \in \Pi$ that corresponds to a universally quantified value of λ_ℓ. Typically, we will infer properties like $\forall \pi_\ell \in [0, \lambda_\ell), p(\pi_\ell)$, with p a predicate over the memory.

We introduce the elements of $base^{\sharp}$ that are either:

- NULL which is used to represent expressions that do not depend on the address of a memory block, with $NULL + 0$ that refers to the value 0. It is used to represent integers,
- $\&V$ which corresponds to the address where the value of the variable V is stored,
- $malloc_\ell(\phi)$ which corresponds to the first address of the memory block dynamically allocated by the statement at label ℓ when the loop counters had the values ϕ. This identifies uniquely the memory block because each statement can be evaluated only once for fixed loop counters values (as a consequence of Theorem. 2).

$$
\begin{aligned}
rval^\sharp &::= (base^\sharp + offset^\sharp) \\
offset^\sharp &::= affine_{deref}[affine_{ctr}[\mathbb{Z}]] \\
lval^\sharp &::= *[base^\sharp + affine_{ctr}[affine_{deref}[\mathbb{Z}]]] \\
base^\sharp &::= \text{NULL} \mid \&V \mid malloc_\ell(malloc_{id}) \\
malloc_{id} &::= \bot \mid \lambda_\ell \mapsto offset^\sharp, \; malloc_{id} \\
affine_{deref}[K] &::= K \mid K \times *[base^\sharp + affine_{deref}[K]] + affine_{deref}[K] \\
affine_{ctr}[K] &::= K \mid K \times \tau_\ell + affine_{ctr}[K] \\
V &\in \mathcal{V} \\
\lambda_\ell &\in \Lambda \\
\tau_\ell &\in \Lambda \cup \Pi
\end{aligned}
$$

Fig. 4. Syntax of abstract expressions

As the goal is to represent expressions as affine forms of loop counters and dereferences, we introduce $affine_{ctr}[K]$ and $affine_{deref}[K]$ that are parametric non-terminals, with K a non-terminal that can be interpreted as an integer.

$affine_{ctr}[K]$ encodes an affine expression with coefficients in K and variables that are the number of times the corresponding loop has been evaluated. As an example, if $^\ell \mathbf{while}$ ... appears in a program, then $(2 \times \lambda_\ell + 1) \in affine_{ctr}[\mathbb{Z}]$ represents the integer value: "twice the number of times the loop's body has been evaluated until now, plus one".

$affine_{deref}[K]$ encodes an affine expression with coefficients in K and variables that are dereferences in the memory block starting from a $base^\sharp$ and an offset that itself is in $affine_{deref}[K]$. As an example, the expression $2 * \mathtt{arr[i+1]}$ can be represented by $2 \times *[\&\mathtt{arr} + 1 \times *[\&\mathtt{i} + 0] + 1] + 0$ that is in $affine_{deref}[\mathbb{Z}]$.

From those bricks, we construct the key elements of $rval^\sharp$ and $lval^\sharp$ that are $affine_{deref}[affine_{ctr}[\mathbb{Z}]]$ and $affine_{ctr}[affine_{deref}[\mathbb{Z}]]$. They differ in that only the first one allows loop counters (elements of Λ or Π depending on whether they are generalized) to appear in the dereferences. This difference will be discussed in Sect. 5.

In particular, elements of $offset^\sharp$ represent integers/addresses that are affine forms in symbolic dereferences, with coefficients that are affine forms in loop counters (generalized or not), with coefficients that are in $\mathbb{Z}$. Then, an abstract right-value in $rval^\sharp$ is just an abstract base plus an abstract offset starting from this base. In Example. 1 we show an element of $rval^\sharp$.

Example 1. The translation of the right-value $\mathtt{n} - \lambda_\ell + 2$, with $\mathtt{n}$ a variable and λ_ℓ the value of a loop counter, can be:

$$
\underbrace{(\underbrace{\text{NULL}}_{base^\sharp} + \underbrace{\underbrace{1}_{affine_{ctr}[\mathbb{Z}]} \times *[\underbrace{\&\mathtt{n}}_{base^\sharp} + \underbrace{0}_{affine_{deref}[affine_{ctr}[\mathbb{Z}]]}] + \underbrace{(-1) \times \lambda_\ell + 2}_{affine_{ctr}[\mathbb{Z}]})}_{affine_{deref}[affine_{ctr}[\mathbb{Z}]]}}_{rval^\sharp}
$$

We now introduce the evaluation of abstract expressions into $\mathbb{Z}$, provided the concrete memory state. This is important to prove the soundness of the translation into abstract expressions in Theorem. 3. The definitions in Fig. 5 really follow the intuition, except for $S_\varphi \stackrel{\text{def}}{=} (\Lambda \cup \Pi) \rightharpoonup \mathbb{N}$ that is a valuation of the (possibly generalized) loop counters. It will be used in the following section while defining the concretization of universally quantified properties: they have to hold for every φ that is a possible valuation of the generalized loop counters.

$$[\![\cdot]\!]^\sharp_{rval^\sharp} : rval^\sharp \to S_\rho \times S_\sigma \times S_\varphi \rightharpoonup \mathbb{Z}$$
$$[\![b + off]\!]^\sharp_{rval^\sharp}(\rho, \sigma, \varphi) \stackrel{\text{def}}{=} [\![b]\!]^\sharp_{base^\sharp}(\sigma) + [\![off]\!]^\sharp_{offset^\sharp}(\rho, \sigma, \varphi)$$

$$[\![\cdot]\!]^\sharp_{offset^\sharp} : offset^\sharp \to S_\rho \times S_\sigma \times S_\varphi \rightharpoonup \mathbb{Z}$$
$$[\![a]\!]^\sharp_{offset^\sharp}(\rho, \sigma, \varphi) \stackrel{\text{def}}{=} [\![a]\!]^\sharp_{affine_{deref}[affine_{ctr}[\mathbb{Z}]]}([\![\cdot]\!]^\sharp_{affine_{ctr}[\mathbb{Z}]}([\![\cdot]\!]^\sharp_{\mathbb{Z}}, \varphi), \rho, \sigma)$$

$$[\![\cdot]\!]^\sharp_{lval^\sharp} : lval^\sharp \to S_\rho \times S_\sigma \times S_\varphi \rightharpoonup \mathbb{Z}$$
$$[\![*[b + a]]\!]^\sharp_{lval^\sharp}(\rho, \sigma, \varphi) \stackrel{\text{def}}{=} [\![b]\!]^\sharp_{base^\sharp}(\sigma) + [\![a]\!]^\sharp_{affine_{ctr}[affine_{deref}[\mathbb{Z}]]}([\![\cdot]\!]^\sharp_{affine_{deref}[\mathbb{Z}]}([\![\cdot]\!]^\sharp_{\mathbb{Z}}, \rho, \sigma), \varphi)$$

$$[\![\cdot]\!]^\sharp_{base^\sharp} : base^\sharp \to S_\sigma \rightharpoonup \mathbb{N}$$
$$[\![\text{NULL}]\!]^\sharp_{base^\sharp}(\sigma) \stackrel{\text{def}}{=} 0$$
$$[\![\&V]\!]^\sharp_{base^\sharp}(\sigma) \stackrel{\text{def}}{=} a \text{ with } (a, s) \stackrel{\text{def}}{=} \sigma(V)$$
$$[\![malloc_\ell(\phi)]\!]^\sharp_{base^\sharp}(\sigma) \stackrel{\text{def}}{=} a \text{ with } (a, s) \stackrel{\text{def}}{=} \sigma(\ell, [\![\phi]\!]^\sharp_{malloc_{id}})$$

$$[\![\cdot]\!]^\sharp_{malloc_{id}} : malloc_{id} \to S_\phi$$
$$[\![\bot]\!]^\sharp_{malloc_{id}} \stackrel{\text{def}}{=} \varnothing$$
$$[\![\lambda_\ell \mapsto off, m]\!]^\sharp_{malloc_{id}} \stackrel{\text{def}}{=} \phi \text{ with } \phi(\lambda_{\ell_1}) \stackrel{\text{def}}{=} \begin{cases} [\![off]\!]^\sharp_{offset^\sharp} & \text{if } \ell = \ell_1, \\ [\![m]\!]^\sharp_{malloc_{id}}(\lambda_{\ell_1}) & \text{otherwise.} \end{cases}$$

$$[\![\cdot]\!]^\sharp_{affine_{ctr}[K]} : affine_{ctr}[K] \to (K \rightharpoonup \mathbb{Z}) \times S_\varphi \rightharpoonup \mathbb{Z}$$
$$[\![k]\!]^\sharp_{affine_{ctr}[K]}([\![\cdot]\!]^\sharp_K, \varphi) \stackrel{\text{def}}{=} [\![k]\!]^\sharp_K$$
$$[\![k \times \tau_\ell + a]\!]^\sharp_{affine_{ctr}[K]}([\![\cdot]\!]^\sharp_K, \varphi) \stackrel{\text{def}}{=} [\![k]\!]^\sharp_K \times \varphi(\tau_\ell) + [\![a]\!]^\sharp_{affine_{ctr}[K]}([\![\cdot]\!]^\sharp_K, \varphi)$$

$$[\![\cdot]\!]^\sharp_{affine_{deref}[K]} : affine_{deref}[K] \to (K \rightharpoonup \mathbb{Z}) \times S_\rho \times S_\sigma \rightharpoonup \mathbb{Z}$$
$$[\![k]\!]^\sharp_{affine_{deref}[K]}([\![\cdot]\!]^\sharp_K, \rho, \sigma) \stackrel{\text{def}}{=} [\![k]\!]^\sharp_K$$
$$[\![k \times *[b + a_1] + a_2]\!]^\sharp_{affine_{deref}[K]}([\![\cdot]\!]^\sharp_K, \rho, \sigma) \stackrel{\text{def}}{=}$$
$$[\![k]\!]^\sharp_K \times \rho\Big([\![b]\!]^\sharp_{base^\sharp}(\sigma) + [\![a_1]\!]^\sharp_{affine_{deref}[K]}([\![\cdot]\!]^\sharp_K, \rho, \sigma) \Big) + [\![a_2]\!]^\sharp_{affine_{deref}[K]}([\![\cdot]\!]^\sharp_K, \rho, \sigma)$$

$$[\![\cdot]\!]^\sharp_{\mathbb{Z}} : \mathbb{Z} \to \mathbb{Z}$$
$$[\![k]\!]^\sharp_{\mathbb{Z}} \stackrel{\text{def}}{=} k$$

Fig. 5. Evaluation of abstract expressions as integers

3.2   Translation from expressions to abstract right-values

We now define the translation of expressions into abstract right-values. At this point, the translation is purely syntactic and does not depend on the memory state. We denote it $(\!(\cdot)\!) : expr \rightharpoonup rval^\sharp$, and we provide a simple definition in Fig. 6. To that extent, we use the helper functions $add_{offset^\sharp}$ (resp. $sub_{offset^\sharp}$) which adds (resp. returns the difference between) two abstract offsets. Those functions only accumulate the dereferences that appear in the operands and merge the remaining constants. In the case of a difference, we take the opposite of the coefficients in head of the dereferences of the second operand.

$$(\!(c)\!) \stackrel{\text{def}}{=} (\text{NULL} + c)$$

$$(\!(\&V)\!) \stackrel{\text{def}}{=} (\&V + 0)$$

$$(\!(*[e])\!) \stackrel{\text{def}}{=} \begin{cases} (\text{NULL} + *[b + off] + 0) \text{ if } (b + off) \stackrel{\text{def}}{=} (\!(e)\!), \\ undefined \text{ otherwise.} \end{cases}$$

$$(\!(e_1 + e_2)\!) \stackrel{\text{def}}{=} \begin{cases} (b + add_{offset^\sharp}(off_1, off_2)) \text{ if } (b + off_1) \stackrel{\text{def}}{=} (\!(e_1)\!), (\text{NULL} + off_2) \stackrel{\text{def}}{=} (\!(e_2)\!), \\ (b + add_{offset^\sharp}(off_1, off_2)) \text{ if } (\text{NULL} + off_1) \stackrel{\text{def}}{=} (\!(e_1)\!), (b + off_2) \stackrel{\text{def}}{=} (\!(e_2)\!), \\ undefined \text{ otherwise.} \end{cases}$$

$$(\!(e_1 - e_2)\!) \stackrel{\text{def}}{=} \begin{cases} (b + sub_{offset^\sharp}(off_1, off_2)) \text{ if } (b + off_1) \stackrel{\text{def}}{=} (\!(e_1)\!), (\text{NULL} + off_2) \stackrel{\text{def}}{=} (\!(e_2)\!), \\ (\text{NULL} + sub_{offset^\sharp}(off_1, off_2)) \text{ if } (b + off_1) \stackrel{\text{def}}{=} (\!(e_1)\!), (b + off_2) \stackrel{\text{def}}{=} (\!(e_2)\!), \\ undefined \text{ otherwise.} \end{cases}$$

$$(\!(e_1 \times e_2)\!) \stackrel{\text{def}}{=} undefined$$

Fig. 6. Simple translation from expressions to abstract right-values

The soundness of the translations is expressed by Theorem 3.

Theorem 3 (Soundness of expression translation). *For every expression* $e \in expr$ *and every memory state* $(\rho, \sigma, \phi) \in \mathcal{R}$,

$$(b + off) \stackrel{\text{def}}{=} (\!(e)\!) \implies [\![e]\!](\rho, \sigma) = [\![b + off]\!]^\sharp_{rval^\sharp}(\rho, \sigma, \phi)$$

Note that, neither this definition of the translation of dereferences is precise, because the abstract base cannot be different from NULL, nor the translation of multiplications is precise. Indeed, such translations are purely syntactic. They could gain precision by relying on semantic properties provided by abstract domains.

We provide some hints about how to improve the translation of multiplications of elements of $offset^\sharp$. There are two cases:

- if one operand is a constant in $\mathbb{Z}$, then we distribute the multiplication by the constant to the coefficients of the other operand (for example, 5 multiplied by $5 \times \lambda_\ell + 0$ would give $25 \times \lambda_\ell + 0$),

– otherwise, if one operand is an affine form in the loop counters while the other one has no loop counters that appear in head, then we can distribute the multiplication by the affine form to the coefficients of the other operand (for example, $5 \times \lambda_\ell + 0$ multiplied by $1 \times *[\&\mathbf{arr} + 1 \times \lambda_\ell + 0] + 0$ would give $(5 \times \lambda_\ell + 0) \times *[\&\mathbf{arr} + 1 \times \lambda_\ell + 0] + 0)$.

4   Description of the abstract memory states

An abstract memory state is represented by an element of $\mathcal{R}^\sharp$ that is a tuple of 5 elements that describe constraints over the memory state. The first component is the program point in which the memory state is observed. The second one expresses properties about the loop counters values. The third and fourth components express properties about the assignments and conditions that were previously evaluated but still effective. The last component describes information about the size of dynamically allocated memory blocks in case they were allocated. In the following section, we provide a detailed explanation of how these constraints are stored. Throughout this depiction, we describe the components of a possible abstract memory state of the program presented in Fig. 8, focusing on the program state at label ℓ_9. This program is given both with C syntax (on the left), and in the language presented in this article (on the right). It makes use of dynamic memory allocation, loops and conditional assignments to cover most of the properties described by the abstract memory state.

To ensure the coherence of abstract elements, the loop counters that appear in an abstract state are constrained by some side conditions about the order of appearance in the program (the order $\leq_\Lambda$). These side-conditions are provided in the explanations of each component of the tuple $R^\sharp \in \mathcal{R}^\sharp$.

$$\mathcal{R}^\sharp \stackrel{\text{def}}{=} \mathcal{L} \times sections^\sharp \times assigns^\sharp \times guards^\sharp \times mallocs^\sharp$$

$$sections^\sharp \stackrel{\text{def}}{=} \Lambda \rightharpoonup (offset^\sharp \times (offset^\sharp \cup \{+\infty\}))$$

$$assigns^\sharp \stackrel{\text{def}}{=} \mathcal{L} \rightharpoonup (\wp(gen\text{-}sections^\sharp) \times (branch\text{-}key \rightharpoonup comp^\sharp) \times lval^\sharp \times rval^\sharp)$$

$$guards^\sharp \stackrel{\text{def}}{=} branch\text{-}key \rightharpoonup (\wp(gen\text{-}sections^\sharp) \times comp^\sharp)$$

$$mallocs^\sharp \stackrel{\text{def}}{=} \mathcal{L} \rightharpoonup (offset^\sharp \cup \{\top\})$$

$$gen\text{-}sections^\sharp \stackrel{\text{def}}{=} \Pi \rightharpoonup (offset^\sharp \cup (offset^\sharp \times offset^\sharp))$$

$$branch\text{-}key \stackrel{\text{def}}{=} \mathcal{L} \times \{\mathbf{t}, \mathbf{f}\}$$

$$comp^\sharp \stackrel{\text{def}}{=} rval^\sharp \times \{=, \neq, <, \leq, >, \geq\} \times rval^\sharp$$

Fig. 7. Definition of the abstract memory states

```
1 int n, m;
2 int *arr = malloc(n * sizeof(int));
3 int i = 0;
4 while (i < n) {
5   if (i != m) {
6       arr[i] = i;
7   }
8   i++;
9 }
```

```
ℓ1 arr := malloc(n);
ℓ2 i := 0;
ℓ3 while i < n do
ℓ4   if i ≠ m then
ℓ5     arr[i] := i
ℓ6   else
ℓ7     skip
ℓ8   endif;
ℓ9   i := i + 1
ℓ10 done ℓ11
```

Fig. 8. Program with a dynamic allocation, a loop, and a conditional assignment

4.1 Abstraction of loop counter sections

The second component of an abstract memory state $s^\sharp$: $sections^\sharp$ represents an over-approximation of the loop counters values. It is a partial map that associates each loop counter that is alive with its possible values. We recall that a loop counter is alive if it occurs in a loop whose body is being evaluated, that is to say, if ℓ stands for the program label, that this loop counter belongs to Λ_ℓ. The possible values are over-approximated by intervals with $offset^\sharp$ as bounds, with possibly no upper-bound. Additionally, the abstraction of sections is constrained by the following side-condition: the image of a loop counter shall only depend on the values of the loop counters that are defined before (that is to say: for every $\lambda_{\ell'} \in \Lambda$ occurring in the image of λ_ℓ, $\lambda_{\ell'} <_\Lambda \lambda_\ell$). Only the functions satisfying this side-condition will be considered in the paper.

For example, in the program presented in Fig. 8, at label ℓ_9, the abstract memory state's sections could be $\{\lambda_{\ell_3} \mapsto (0, 1 \times *[\&n + 0] + 0)\}$. This means that λ_{ℓ_3} has its value within 0 and n (excluded).

We now introduce the concretization function of the corresponding part of the abstract memory state. We denote it $\gamma_{sections^\sharp}$: $sections^\sharp \to \wp(\mathcal{R})$, and it is defined for each element $\phi^\sharp \in sections^\sharp$ as:

$$
\gamma_{sections^\sharp}(\phi^\sharp) \stackrel{\text{def}}{=}
$$

$$
\left\{ (\rho, \sigma, \phi) \in \mathcal{R} \;\middle|\;
\begin{array}{l}
\text{dom}(\phi) = \text{dom}(\phi^\sharp), \; \forall \lambda_\ell \in \text{dom}(\phi^\sharp), \\
\begin{cases}
\phi(\lambda_\ell) \in \mathbb{N} \cap [o_1, o_2) & \text{if } (off_1, off_2) \stackrel{\text{def}}{=} \phi^\sharp(\lambda_\ell), \\
\phi(\lambda_\ell) \in \mathbb{N} \cap [o_1, +\infty) & \text{if } (off_1, +\infty) \stackrel{\text{def}}{=} \phi^\sharp(\lambda_\ell), \\
\end{cases} \\
\text{with } \forall i, o_i \stackrel{\text{def}}{=} [\![off_i]\!]^\sharp_{offset^\sharp}(\rho, \sigma, \phi \!\upharpoonright_{\Lambda_{<\lambda_\ell}})
\end{array}
\right\}
$$

We notice that the side condition of $\phi^\sharp$ is necessary to ensure the well-formedness of the definition, when evaluating the abstraction of offset expressions.

4.2 Abstraction of assignments and tests

We now define the abstraction of constraints coming from previous assignments and tests. This abstraction relies on the description of regions for the potential value of generalized loop counters (described by elements of $gen\text{-}sections^\sharp$), and a tracking of the syntactic comparisons that had to hold to reach a program state (described using $branch\text{-}key$ and $comp^\sharp$ elements).

Elements of $gen\text{-}sections^\sharp$. They are used to express properties that apply to multiple values of loop counters. The image of $\pi_\ell \in \Pi$ represents the values π_ℓ can take, with π_ℓ the generalized version of the loop counter value $\lambda_\ell \in \Lambda$. It can be either:

- an abstract offset $off_1 \in offset^\sharp$: it is used to express that a property holds "$\forall \pi_\ell \in \mathbb{N} \cap [off_1, \lambda_\ell)$", with as a side condition off_1 which depends only on the live loop counters (not-generalized) defined before λ_ℓ (that are in $\{ \lambda_{\ell'} \in \Lambda \mid \lambda_{\ell'} \leq_\Lambda \lambda_\ell \}$),
- a couple of abstract offsets $off_1, off_2 \in offset^\sharp$: it is used to express that a property holds "$\forall \pi_\ell \in \mathbb{N} \cap [off_1, off_2)$", with as a side condition off_1 and off_2 which depend only on the live loop counters (not-generalized) defined strictly before λ_ℓ (that are in $\{ \lambda_{\ell'} \in \Lambda \mid \lambda_{\ell'} <_\Lambda \lambda_\ell \}$).

If a live loop counter λ_ℓ does not appear in the domain of the element of $gen\text{-}sections^\sharp$, it means that the loop counter is not generalized, thus $\pi_\ell = \lambda_\ell$.

We now introduce a helper function that, given the set of live loop counters, an element of $gen\text{-}sections^\sharp$ and a memory state, returns all the valuation functions of the generalized loop counters. We denote it $\gamma_{gen\text{-}sections^\sharp}$: $\wp(\Lambda) \times \wp(gen\text{-}sections^\sharp) \times S_\rho \times S_\sigma \times S_\phi \to \wp(\Pi \rightharpoonup \mathbb{N})$, and it is defined for each set of live loop counters $\Lambda_{\ell_0} \subseteq \Lambda$, each element $\Phi_g^\sharp \in \wp(gen\text{-}sections^\sharp)$ and each memory state $(\rho, \sigma, \phi) \in (S_\rho \times S_\sigma \times S_\phi)$ as:

$$\gamma_{gen\text{-}sections^\sharp}(\Lambda_{\ell_0}, \Phi_g^\sharp, \rho, \sigma, \phi) \stackrel{\text{def}}{=}$$

$$\left\{ \varphi : \Pi_{\ell_0} \to \mathbb{N} \;\middle|\; \begin{array}{l} \exists \phi_g^\sharp \in \Phi_g^\sharp, \; \forall \lambda_\ell \in \Lambda_{\ell_0}, \\[4pt] \varphi(\pi_\ell) \in \begin{cases} \{ \phi(\lambda_\ell) \} & \text{if } \pi_\ell \notin \text{dom}(\phi_g^\sharp), \\[4pt] \mathbb{N} \cap [l, \phi(\lambda_\ell)) & \text{if } off_1 \stackrel{\text{def}}{=} \phi_g^\sharp(\pi_\ell) \\ \quad \text{with } l \stackrel{\text{def}}{=} [\![\, off_1 \,]\!]^\sharp_{offset^\sharp}(\rho, \sigma, \phi \restriction_{\Lambda_{\leq \lambda_\ell}}), \\[4pt] \mathbb{N} \cap [o_1, o_2) & \text{if } (off_1, off_2) \stackrel{\text{def}}{=} \phi_g^\sharp(\pi_\ell) \\ \quad \text{with } o_i \stackrel{\text{def}}{=} [\![\, off_i \,]\!]^\sharp_{offset^\sharp}(\rho, \sigma, \phi \restriction_{\Lambda_{< \lambda_\ell}}). \end{cases} \end{array} \right\}$$

Elements of $branch\text{-}key$ and $comp^\sharp$. They are used together to represent the validity of comparisons. First, $branch\text{-}key$ is used to determine where the comparison comes from, that is from which conditional branching (through its program label in $\mathcal{L}$) and with which outcome (t if the condition was fulfilled, and f otherwise). Then, the comparison is represented by the comparison operator and the two compared abstract right-values.

Elements of $assigns^\sharp$. They describe for each program point ℓ corresponding to an assignment statement that, for each possible value of the generalized loop counters (described by elements of $gen\text{-}sections^\sharp$), if the proof obligations (described

by an element of *branch-key* $\rightharpoonup$ *comp*[#]) hold, then the addresses represented by
a given abstract left-value point to the values represented by a given abstract
right-value. As side conditions, the only loop counters allowed to appear in the
abstract left/right-values are the generalized versions of the live loop counters,
that are the elements of Π_ℓ.

For example, in the program presented in Fig. 8, at label ℓ_9, the abstract
memory state's assignments could be the following:

$$
\begin{aligned}
\{\, \ell_1 &\mapsto (\,\{\varnothing\}, \varnothing, *[\&\mathtt{arr}+0], (malloc_{\ell_1}(\bot)+0)), \\
\ell_2 &\mapsto (\,\{\varnothing\}, \varnothing, *[\&\mathtt{i}+0], (\mathtt{NULL}+0)), \\
\ell_9 &\mapsto (\,\{\{\pi_{\ell_3}\mapsto 0\}\}, \varnothing, *[\&\mathtt{i}+0], (\mathtt{NULL}+1\times\pi_{\ell_3}+0)), \\
\ell_5 &\mapsto (\,\{\varnothing, \{\pi_{\ell_3}\mapsto 0\}\}, \\
&\quad \{(\ell_4,\mathtt{t})\mapsto(\mathtt{NULL}+1\times\pi_{\ell_3}+0,\ \neq,\ \mathtt{NULL}+1\times*[\&\mathtt{m}+0]+0)\,\}, \\
&\quad *[malloc_{\ell_1}(\bot)+1\times\pi_{\ell_3}+0], \\
&\quad (\mathtt{NULL}+1\times\pi_{\ell_3}+0))\,\}
\end{aligned}
$$

Let us describe in details this element of *assigns*[#]:

- The first line describes the assignment at program label ℓ_1. At this point, no
  loop counters are defined, so none of them can be generalized. This is what
  the first occurrence of the symbol $\varnothing$ indicates. Moreover, this assignment is
  evaluated unconditionally. This is what is embedded in the second occurrence
  of the symbol $\varnothing$. The two other elements of the tuple are respectively the left
  and right values after their translations into abstract forms. The left-value
  corresponds to the variable $\mathtt{arr}$ and the right-value to the memory block
  allocated in the statement labelled by ℓ_1.
- The second line is really similar to the first, except that the left-value is $\mathtt{i}$
  and the right-value is the integer 0.
- The third line differs in the presence of a non-$\varnothing$ *gen-sections*[#] element. It
  indicates that the corresponding property holds for all π_{ℓ_3} between 0 and λ_{ℓ_3}
  (excluded, because the considered abstract memory state is in ℓ_9). Indeed, $\mathtt{i}$
  is equal to the number of times the loop's body has been entirely executed.
- The rest is a bit more complex because the assignment is conditional, and
  because it might have already been executed for the current value of the
  loop counter λ_{ℓ_3}. It states that, both for $\pi_{\ell_3}=\lambda_{\ell_3}$ (indicated by the symbol
  $\varnothing$), but also for all π_{ℓ_3} within 0 and λ_{ℓ_3} (indicated by $\{\pi_{\ell_3}\mapsto 0\}$), if the
  condition evaluated at program label ℓ_4 was true (that is $\mathtt{i}\neq\mathtt{m}$), then the
  $\pi_{\ell_3}{}^{\text{th}}$ cell of the memory block allocated at program label ℓ_1 points to the
  value π_{ℓ_3}.

We now introduce the concretization function of the corresponding part of
the abstract memory state. We denote it $\gamma_{assigns^\sharp} : assigns^\sharp \to \wp(\mathcal{R})$, and it is

defined for each element $a^\sharp \in assigns^\sharp$ as

$$\gamma_{assigns^\sharp}(a^\sharp) \overset{\text{def}}{=}$$

$$\left\{ (\rho, \sigma, \phi) \in \mathcal{R} \;\middle|\; \begin{array}{l} \forall \ell \in \mathrm{dom}(a^\sharp),\ (\Phi_g^\sharp, c^\sharp, l^\sharp, r^\sharp) \overset{\text{def}}{=} a^\sharp(\ell), \\ \forall \varphi \in \gamma_{gen\text{-}sections^\sharp}(\Lambda_\ell, \Phi_g^\sharp, \rho, \sigma, \phi), \\ (\rho, \sigma, \varphi) \vdash c^\sharp \;\Longrightarrow\; \rho(\llbracket l^\sharp \rrbracket_{lval^\sharp}^\sharp(\rho,\sigma,\varphi)) = \llbracket r^\sharp \rrbracket_{rval^\sharp}^\sharp(\rho,\sigma,\varphi) \end{array} \right\}$$

with $(\rho, \sigma, \varphi) \vdash c^\sharp$ that represents that all the proof obligations embodied by $c^\sharp$ are satisfied in the memory state (ρ, σ, φ). More formally:

$$(\rho, \sigma, \varphi) \vdash c^\sharp \iff \forall (e_1^\sharp, \bowtie, e_2^\sharp) \in \mathrm{im}(c^\sharp),\ \llbracket e_1^\sharp \rrbracket_{rval^\sharp}^\sharp(\rho,\sigma,\varphi) \bowtie \llbracket e_2^\sharp \rrbracket_{rval^\sharp}^\sharp(\rho,\sigma,\varphi)$$

Elements of guards$^\sharp$. They are used to indicate that a conditional branching statement produced the same result across multiple iterations when evaluated within loops. It is represented by, for each comparison and output (represented by an element of *branch-key*), and for each range of values the loop counters can take (described by an element of *gen-sections$^\sharp$*), the comparison that holds (described by an element of *comp$^\sharp$*).

For example, in the program presented in Fig. 8, at label ℓ_9, the abstract memory state's guards could be the following.

$$\{ (\ell_3, \mathrm{t}) \mapsto (\ \{\varnothing,\ \{\pi_{\ell_3} \mapsto 0\}\},$$
$$(\mathrm{NULL} + 1 \times \pi_{\ell_3} + 0,\ <,\ 1 \times *[\&n + 0] + 0)) \}$$

The domain of this function is the singleton (ℓ_3, t) which indicates that the condition labelled by ℓ_3 (that is i < n) holds for the current value of the loop counter (denoted by the element $\varnothing$), but also for every π_{ℓ_3} between 0 and the current value of the loop counter (denoted by the element $\{\pi_{\ell_3} \mapsto 0\}$).

We now introduce the concretization function of the corresponding part of the abstract memory state. We denote it $\gamma_{guards^\sharp} : guards^\sharp \to \wp(\mathcal{R})$, and it is defined for each element $g^\sharp \in guards^\sharp$ as

$$\gamma_{guards^\sharp}(g^\sharp) \overset{\text{def}}{=} \left\{ (\rho, \sigma, \phi) \in \mathcal{R} \;\middle|\; \begin{array}{l} \forall (\Phi_g^\sharp, (e_1^\sharp, \bowtie, e_2^\sharp)) \in \mathrm{im}(g^\sharp), \\ \forall \varphi \in \gamma_{gen\text{-}sections^\sharp}(\Phi_g^\sharp, \rho, \sigma, \phi), \\ \llbracket e_1^\sharp \rrbracket_{rval^\sharp}^\sharp(\rho,\sigma,\varphi) \bowtie \llbracket e_2^\sharp \rrbracket_{rval^\sharp}^\sharp(\rho,\sigma,\varphi) \end{array} \right\}$$

4.3 Abstraction of memory blocks dynamically allocated

The elements of *mallocs$^\sharp$* describe, for each program point ℓ that is associated to a **malloc** statement, that if for a given valuation of the loop counters at that time the memory allocation was performed, then the size of the corresponding memory block is described by a given *offset$^\sharp$*. If the size cannot be expressed precisely, then $\top$ is used. As side conditions, the only loop counters allowed to appear in the representation are the ones of Λ_ℓ. This is because, as explained in the concrete semantics, the memory allocation is identified uniquely by the program label and the value of the loop counters at that time.

For example, in the program presented in Fig. 8, at label ℓ_9, the corresponding abstract memory state's element could be $\{\ell_1 \mapsto (1 \times *[\&n + 0] + 0)\}$. This represents that, if it has been allocated, the memory block allocated at program label ℓ_1 and identified by the loop counters' values at that time, is of size n.

We now introduce the concretization function of the corresponding part of the abstract memory state. We denote it $\gamma_{mallocs^\sharp} : mallocs^\sharp \to \wp(\mathcal{R})$, and it is defined for each element $m^\sharp \in mallocs^\sharp$ as

$$\gamma_{mallocs^\sharp}(m^\sharp) \overset{\text{def}}{=}$$

$$\left\{ (\rho, \sigma, \phi) \in \mathcal{R} \;\middle|\; \begin{array}{l} \forall \ell' \notin \mathrm{dom}(m^\sharp),\ \forall \varphi' : \Lambda_{\ell'} \to \mathbb{N},\ (\ell', \varphi') \notin \mathrm{dom}(\sigma)\ \wedge \\ \forall \ell \in \mathrm{dom}(m^\sharp),\ s^\sharp \overset{\text{def}}{=} m^\sharp(\ell),\ s^\sharp \neq \top,\ \forall \varphi : \Lambda_\ell \to \mathbb{N}, \\ (\ell, \varphi) \in \mathrm{dom}(\sigma) \implies s = [\![s^\sharp]\!]^\sharp_{offset^\sharp}(\rho, \sigma, \varphi) \\ \text{with } (a, s) \overset{\text{def}}{=} \sigma(\ell, \varphi) \end{array} \right\}$$

4.4 Combining all the constraints described by abstract memory states

We finally introduce the concretization function of abstract memory states. It is denoted $\gamma : \mathcal{R}^\sharp \to \wp(\mathcal{R})$, and it is defined for each abstract memory state $(\ell, \phi^\sharp, a^\sharp, g^\sharp, m^\sharp) \in \wp(\mathcal{R}^\sharp)$ as

$$\gamma(\ell, \phi^\sharp, a^\sharp, g^\sharp, m^\sharp) \overset{\text{def}}{=} \gamma_{sections^\sharp}(\phi^\sharp) \cap \gamma_{assigns^\sharp}(a^\sharp) \cap \gamma_{guards^\sharp}(g^\sharp) \cap$$

$$\gamma_{mallocs^\sharp}(m^\sharp) \cap \{ R \in \mathcal{R} \mid \text{non-aliasing}(\{ R \}) \wedge \text{alloc-consistent}(\ell, R) \}$$

The initial abstract memory state is $R_0^\sharp \overset{\text{def}}{=} (\ell_0, \varnothing, \varnothing, \varnothing, \varnothing)$ with ℓ_0 the first program label. It is a sound abstraction of R_0, that is $R_0 \subseteq \gamma(R_0^\sharp)$, because the only property enforced by $\gamma(R_0^\sharp)$ is to be a non-aliasing memory state, which is verified for R_0.

5   Operations on abstract memory states

In this section we describe the main abstract transfer functions that compute a sound approximation of their concrete counterparts. The abstract semantics is described by $\{\!| stmt |\!\}^\sharp : \mathcal{R}^\sharp \to \mathcal{R}^\sharp$ that is the abstract counterpart of the concrete semantics introduced in Fig. 3. The soundness of the abstract transfer functions is expressed by Theorem 4 and elements of proof are given along their definitions.

Theorem 4 (Soundness of the abstract transfer functions). *For every statement $^\ell s^{\ell'} \in stmt$ and every abstract memory state $R^\sharp \in \mathcal{R}^\sharp$,*

$$\{\!| \,^\ell s \,^{\ell'} |\!\} \circ \gamma(R^\sharp) \subseteq \gamma \circ \{\!| \,^\ell s \,^{\ell'} |\!\}^\sharp(R^\sharp)$$

Definition 5. *We introduce merge : $(\mathcal{R}^\sharp \times \wp(gen\text{-}sections^\sharp) \times rval^\sharp \times \mathcal{R}^\sharp \times \wp(gen\text{-}sections^\sharp) \times rval^\sharp) \rightharpoonup rval^\sharp$ that, given two abstract memory states, sets of universally quantified loop counters, and abstract expressions in $rval^\sharp$, returns* *an abstract expression that matches the semantics of the two original ones when evaluated on their respective domains. We provide an overview of the process that is guided by heuristics:*

- *we identify parts of the expressions that trivially match in order to reduce the size of expressions to be merged,*
- *for each loop counter that both maps to a constant value and that is not generalized in only one abstract memory state, we replace the occurrences of that loop counter by the constant,*
- *then, if both expressions are evaluated in the context of abstract memory states in which a loop counter is not generalized and maps to two different constant values, we linearly interpolate the remaining parts of the expression. As an example, if we try to merge the expressions 0 (with $\lambda_\ell = 0$) and i (with $\lambda_\ell = 1$), then we output the expression $\lambda_\ell \times i$ that is indeed semantically equal to both expressions on their respective abstract memory states.*

Abstract join We describe the abstract transfer function corresponding to the union after a branching at the condition at program point ℓ_0. Given two abstract memory states $(\ell_1, \phi_1^\sharp, a_1^\sharp, g_1^\sharp, m_1^\sharp)$ and $(\ell_2, \phi_2^\sharp, a_2^\sharp, g_2^\sharp, m_2^\sharp)$, it is defined as the following:

- the new section of each loop counter λ_ℓ, if $\forall i, (l_i, u_i) \stackrel{\text{def}}{=} \phi_i^\sharp(\lambda_\ell)$, is (l, u) defined as follows. First the lower-bound l is the minimum between l_1 and l_2 if it exists, otherwise 0 (that is a lower-bound over the values of the loop-counters). Symmetrically, we define u as the maximum value between u_1 and u_2 if it exists, or $+\infty$,
- the universally quantified predicates expressed by the elements of *assigns$^\sharp$* and *guards$^\sharp$* are joined. For all the elements of the domain that appear in the domain of both operands, the expressions involved (either the left/right-values, or the compared right-values) are merged using the *merge* operator described above. In case there are proof obligations in the property, the compared expressions are also merged. In the case where the assignment/test only appears in one operand, if the test located at label ℓ_0 still exists in the corresponding element of *guards$^\sharp$*, it means we can keep the property if we add the proof obligation corresponding to the element of *guards$^\sharp$*,
- lastly, the new element of *mallocs$^\sharp$* is just the result of the *merge* operator with no loop counters generalized, or $\top$ if they could not get merged.

Widening Applying consecutive abstract joins to compute the abstract transfer function corresponding to loops could loop forever. To mitigate this problem, after computing the abstract join, if the lower-bound (resp. upper-bound) of a loop counter's section keeps decreasing (resp. increasing), we widen it to 0 (resp. $+\infty$). However, to limit the loss of precision, we use *widening thresholds*. To that matter, during the first loop iterations we record the array lookups, and in particular the abstract expressions the loop counters would have to take so the offset exceeds the bounds of the memory block. Then, we first try to widen the loop counter bounds to those values. In order to ensure that the suite of abstract memory states is ultimately stationary, we limit the number of such widenings to a fixed number.

Abstract assignments When performing an assignment in the abstract, we first translate the left and right values, then we remove (or replace by its previous value if it can be expressed) all the occurrences of the possibly assigned cell both in the abstract memory state and in the translated left and right values.

To avoid losing the properties about the previous assignments at the same program point but from past iterations, it is necessary to prove that the assigned cell does not alias with the previously assigned cells. To that matter, allowing loop counters to appear only in head of $lval^{\sharp}$ is helpful: if we can order the loop counters such that each coefficient is bigger than the part of the expression with the smaller loop counters, then the wanted property is proven.

Once the possibly affected cells' contents forgotten/rewritten, we can add the assignment (with no generalized counters) to the element of $assigns^{\sharp}$ and (if existing) merge the previous and new abstract left/right values while keeping the previous proof obligations. Finally, if the assignment also corresponds to a memory allocation, the size of the memory block has to be merged with the previously existing one. Note that, for the soundness proof, we use that the memory states in the concretization have to be alloc-consistent. This gives us that the memory block being allocated has never been allocated before, so the expression can indeed be merged.

Abstract filter When filtering the abstract memory state by a comparison, we apply the same strategy as in the assignment case: we translate the expressions, and merge them with the existing abstract comparison (if it was already existing) with no loop counters generalized (that is, adding the element $\{\varnothing\}$ to $\Phi_g^{\sharp}$).

Loop counter handling To define the abstract transfer function for the loop statements, we still need to define the abstract counterparts of new_{ℓ}, $forget_{\ell}$, inc_{ℓ}. The first one only adds the loop counter λ_{ℓ} to the living counters, with default value 0. The second one tries to determine an abstract expression for the value of λ_{ℓ}. If it can find one, it is used to replace the loop counter everywhere it was defined, otherwise all the properties that involve it are forgotten. Finally, the section corresponding to the loop counter is removed from the abstract memory state. The third one is a bit more complicated: when the loop counter λ_{ℓ} is incremented, all its occurrences in the abstract memory state have to be replaced by $\lambda_{\ell} - 1$. Then, the predicates quantified by π_{ℓ} that ranges over an interval with λ_{ℓ} as the upper-bound remain only if the predicate still held for the current value of λ_{ℓ}. The predicates that weren't quantified by π_{ℓ} that ranges over an interval with λ_{ℓ} as the upper-bound but that hold for the current value of λ_{ℓ} that is a constant expression are generalized with π_{ℓ} that ranges over the interval with the current expression of λ_ℓ as the lower bound, and λ_ℓ as the upper-bound. If the current value of λ_ℓ couldn't be proven a constant expression, the predicate is generalized with π_ℓ that ranges over the interval with $\lambda_\ell - 1$ as the lower-bound and λ_ℓ as the upper-bound.

6   Case studies and analysis

In the following section, we describe the properties inferred by the abstract domain presented in the paper on some simple, but still realistic, programs. We first demonstrate the capability of the abstract domain to prove relational properties about multidimensional arrays (here matrices). In a second time, we consider a program that is used to set up the expanded memory of an x86 operating system. In particular, this setting takes into account the memory needed by the BIOS, the bootloader, and the code of the operating system. We are particularly interested in this example that was the initial motivation for this abstract domain. Then, we present a program that computes the index of the first element greater than a given value in a sorted array.

6.1   Relational properties about multidimensional arrays

```
1 int n, i, j;
2 int **mat1 = malloc(n * sizeof(int*));
3 int **mat2 = malloc(n * sizeof(int*));
4 i = 0;
5 while (i < n) {
6    mat1[i] = malloc(n * sizeof(int));
7    mat2[i] = malloc(n * sizeof(int));
8    i++;
9 }
10 i = 0;
11 while (i < n) {
12    j = 0;
13    while (j < n) {
14        mat2[i][j] = mat1[j][i];
15        j++;
16    }
17    i++;
18 }
```

ℓ_1 mat1 := **malloc**(n);
ℓ_2 mat2 := **malloc**(n);
ℓ_3 i := 0;
ℓ_4 **while** i < n **do**
ℓ_5 mat1[i] := **malloc**(n);
ℓ_6 mat2[i] := **malloc**(n);
ℓ_7 i := i + 1
ℓ_8 **done**;
ℓ_9 i := 0;
ℓ_{10} **while** i < n **do**
ℓ_{11} j := 0;
ℓ_{12} **while** j < n **do**
ℓ_{13} mat2[i][j] := mat1[j][i];
ℓ_{14} j := j + 1
ℓ_{15} **done**;
ℓ_{16} i := i + 1
ℓ_{17} **done** ℓ_{18}

Fig. 9. Transposition of a square matrix

The program depicted in Fig. 9 computes the transposition a square matrix mat1 into another one mat2. The abstract domain presented in this paper is able to prove that, at the end of the program, the following properties about the assignments hold:

$$
\begin{cases}
\texttt{mat1} = malloc_{\ell_1}(\bot) \wedge \\
\texttt{mat2} = malloc_{\ell_2}(\bot) \wedge \\
\forall \pi_{\ell_4} \in [0,n), \underbrace{*[malloc_{\ell_1}(\bot) + \pi_{\ell_4}]}_{\texttt{mat1}[\pi_{\ell_4}]} = malloc_{\ell_5}(\lambda_{\ell_4} \mapsto \pi_{\ell_4}, \bot) \wedge \\
\forall \pi_{\ell_4} \in [0,n), \underbrace{*[malloc_{\ell_2}(\bot) + \pi_{\ell_4}]}_{\texttt{mat2}[\pi_{\ell_4}]} = malloc_{\ell_6}(\lambda_{\ell_4} \mapsto \pi_{\ell_4}, \bot) \wedge \\
\forall \pi_{\ell_{10}} \in [0,n), \forall \pi_{\ell_{12}} \in [0,n), \\
\qquad \underbrace{*[malloc_{\ell_6}(\lambda_{\ell_4} \mapsto \pi_{\ell_{10}}, \bot) + \pi_{\ell_{12}}]}_{\texttt{mat2}[\pi_{\ell_{10}}][\pi_{\ell_{12}}]} = \texttt{mat1}[\pi_{\ell_{12}}][\pi_{\ell_{10}}]
\end{cases}
$$

To detail the property, we have :

- both `mat1` and `mat2` are arrays (of size `n`, which is given by a different component of the abstract memory state),
- they both contain, in each of their cells pointers to fresh arrays (again of size `n`) with $*[malloc_{\ell_1}(\bot) + \pi_{\ell_4}]$ that is just $\texttt{mat1}[\pi_{\ell_4}]$ when we unfold the definition of `mat1`,
- then each cell of the matrix `mat2` contains the value of the corresponding cell in the matrix `mat1` that has been transposed, with $*[malloc_{\ell_6}(\lambda_{\ell_4} \mapsto \pi_{\ell_{10}}, \bot) + \pi_{\ell_{12}}]$ that corresponds to $\texttt{mat2}[\pi_{\ell_{10}}][\pi_{\ell_{12}}]$ after unfolding the definition of `mat2` and the one of $*[malloc_{\ell_2}(\bot) + \pi_{\ell_{10}}]$,
- the values of `i` and `j` are not described in the property above because, at the end of the loop, if `n` < 0 their values would be 0 and not `n`.

6.2   Bootstrap of the paging in an x86 operating system

The program introduced in Fig. 10 is an excerpt of an x86 operating system, in particular the bootstrap of the expanded memory. In this context, we consider an array `page_directory` of size 1024, where the entry at index `virtual_page` holds the value `physical_page` × 4096 + `flags`. Each entry of this array, as a first approximation, is used to map the 4 KiB memory region starting at virtual address 4096 × `page_virtual` to the corresponding 4 KiB region beginning at physical address `physical_page`, with some extra parameters defined by `flags` ∈ [0, 4096). Then, setting up `page_directory` allows to describe the first 4 MiB of the virtual memory (each page being 4 KiB long). In Fig. 10, all the pages of the first 4 MiB are mapped such that each virtual address matches its physical address. However, the flags of the memory regions differ. The first 8 pages (32 KiB) are reserved to the BIOS and the bootloader with flag 1 (superviser-only, read-only). The code of the operating system is then placed (by the bootloader) just after. It is of size `os_code_pages` that is only known at link-time, and the flag for this region is 5 (user-accessible, read-only). Then, all the remaining virtual addresses of the first 4 MiB are given as free space to the

```
1 int os_code_pages;
2 uint32_t page_directory[1024];
3 int page = 0;
4 while (page < 8) {
5   page_directory[page] = page * 0x1000 +
    ↪ 0b001;
6   current_page++;
7 }
8 int i = 0;
9 while (i < os_code_pages) {
10  page_directory[page] = page * 0x1000 +
    ↪ 0b101;
11  page++;
12  i++;
13 }
14 while(page < 1024) {
15  page_directory[page] = page * 0x1000 +
    ↪ 0b111;
16  page++;
17 }
```

$$\ell_1 \; \textbf{page\_directory} := \textbf{malloc}(1024);$$
$$\ell_2 \; \textbf{page} := 0;$$
$$\ell_3 \; \textbf{while } \textbf{page} < 8 \textbf{ do}$$
$$\ell_4 \quad \textbf{page\_directory}[\textbf{page}] := \textbf{page} * 4096 + 1;$$
$$\ell_5 \quad \textbf{page} := \textbf{page} + 1$$
$$\ell_6 \; \textbf{done};$$
$$\ell_7 \; \textbf{i} := 0;$$
$$\ell_8 \; \textbf{while } \textbf{i} < \textbf{os\_code\_pages} \textbf{ do}$$
$$\ell_9 \quad \textbf{page\_directory}[\textbf{page}] := \textbf{page} * 4096 + 5;$$
$$\ell_{10} \quad \textbf{page} := \textbf{page} + 1;$$
$$\ell_{11} \quad \textbf{i} := \textbf{i} + 1$$
$$\ell_{12} \textbf{done};$$
$$\ell_{13} \textbf{while } \textbf{page} < 1024 \textbf{ do}$$
$$\ell_{14} \quad \textbf{page\_directory}[\textbf{page}] := \textbf{page} * 4096 + 7;$$
$$\ell_{15} \quad \textbf{page} := \textbf{page} + 1$$
$$\ell_{16} \textbf{done} \; \ell_{17}$$

Fig. 10. Paging bootstrap in an x86 operating system

operating system with flag **7** (user-accessible, read/write). In reality, the memory layout would be more complex (in particular, we need to deal with more range of addresses that are reserved), but this example is representative of what one would find in an operating system.

Analyzing such programs requires to be precise about the content of the paging structures in order to prove that memory accesses are legitimate. In particular, techniques like array smashing [3], or dynamic partitioning of arrays [8,10,6] do not provide enough relations between the indexes of arrays and their contents.

The abstract domain presented in this paper is able to prove that, at the end of the program execution, and if we assume that `os_code_pages` < 1024, the following properties about the assignments hold:

$$
\left\{
\begin{aligned}
&\textbf{page\_directory} = malloc_{\ell_1}(\bot) \; \wedge \\
&\forall \pi_{\ell_3} \in [0, 8), \underbrace{*[malloc_{\ell_1}(\bot) + \pi_{\ell_3}]}_{\textbf{page\_directory}[\pi_{\ell_3}]} = 4096 \times \pi_{\ell_3} + 1 \; \wedge \\
&\forall \pi_{\ell_8} \in [0, \textbf{os\_code\_pages}), \underbrace{*[malloc_{\ell_1}(\bot) + \pi_{\ell_8} + 8]}_{\textbf{page\_directory}[8 + \pi_{\ell_8}]} = 4096 \times \pi_{\ell_8} + 32773 \; \wedge \\
&\forall \pi_{\ell_{13}} \in [0, 1016 - \textbf{os\_code\_pages}), \\
&\qquad \underbrace{*[malloc_{\ell_1}(\bot) + \pi_{\ell_{13}} + \textbf{os\_code\_pages} + 8]}_{\textbf{page\_directory}[8 + \textbf{os\_code\_pages} + \pi_{\ell_{13}}]} = \\
&\qquad\qquad 4096 \times \textbf{os\_code\_pages} + 4096 \times \pi_{\ell_{13}} + 32775 \; \wedge \\
&\textbf{i} = \textbf{os\_code\_pages} \; \wedge \\
&\textbf{page} = 1024
\end{aligned}
\right.
$$

These properties can be understood as follows:

- `page_directory` is an array (of size 1024, which is given by a different component of the abstract memory state),
- the cell at offset $i \in [0, 8)$ contains the value $4096 \times i + 1$,
- the cell at offset $i \in [8, \mathsf{os\_code\_pages} + 8)$ contains the value $4096 \times i + 5$, which is translated into: the cell at offset $j \in [0, \mathsf{os\_code\_pages})$ contains the value $4096 \times j + 8 \times 4096 + 5$,
- the cell at offset $i \in [\mathsf{os\_code\_pages} + 8, 1024)$ contains the value $4096 \times i + 7$, which is translated into: the cell at offset $j \in [0, 1024 - \mathsf{os\_code\_pages} - 8)$ contains the value $4096 \times j + 4096 \times \mathsf{os\_code\_pages} + 8 \times 4096 + 7$,
- the value of i is `os_code_pages` and the one of **page** is 1024.

6.3   Index of the first element greater than a given value

```
 1 int n, x;
 2 int *arr = malloc(n * sizeof(int));
 3 int result;
 4 if (arr[n-1] <= x) {
 5    result = n-1;
 6 } else {
 7    result = 0;
 8    while (arr[result] <= x) {
 9       result++;
10    }
11 }
```

ℓ_1 **arr** := $\mathrm{malloc}(\mathrm{n})$;
ℓ_2 **if** $\mathrm{arr}[\mathrm{n}-1] \leq \mathrm{x}$ **then**
ℓ_3 result := $\mathrm{n} - 1$
ℓ_4 **else**
ℓ_5 result := 0;
ℓ_6 **while** $\mathrm{arr}[\mathrm{result}] \leq \mathrm{x}$ **do**
ℓ_7 result := $\mathrm{result} + 1$
ℓ_8 **done**
ℓ_9 **endif** ℓ_{10}

Fig. 11. Index of the first element greater than a given value in a (sorted) array

We consider the program introduced in Fig. 11 that, given an integer x and a sorted array `arr` of size n (supposed greater than 0), returns the index of the first element of `arr` which is greater than x, or n−1 in case no element is greater. Note that, even if `arr` is not sorted, no out-of-bound accesses are performed. The properties that are computed by the domain and presented below are also useful to analyze linear interpolations of tabulated functions. Indeed, it is required to prove that the point in which a function is interpolated (here x) is between the indexes of two consecutive tabulated keys in order to prove that the result of the interpolation is between the corresponding tabulated values.

The abstract domain is able to express the following loop invariant at program label ℓ_6:

$$\begin{cases} \mathrm{arr} = malloc_{\ell_1}(\bot) \wedge \\ \mathrm{arr}[\mathrm{n} - 1] > \mathrm{x} \wedge \\ \forall \pi_{\ell_6} \in [0, \lambda_{\ell_6}), \mathrm{arr}[\pi_{\ell_6}] \leq \mathrm{x} \wedge \\ \forall \pi_{\ell_6} \in \{ \lambda_{\ell_6} \}, \mathrm{result} = \pi_{\ell_6} \end{cases}$$

with $\lambda_{\ell_6} \in [0, \mathtt{n})$, thanks to the widening threshold (described in Sect. 5) that is used because of $\mathtt{arr}$ is of size $\mathtt{n}$. The reason why λ_{ℓ_6} cannot take the value of $\mathtt{n}$ is because the second line of the invariant contradicts the fourth line. This contradiction is found by using a heuristic that, when applying $filter^{\sharp}_{\ell_6, \mathtt{t}}$, checks whether the negation appears in the still-effective comparison predicates represented by the $guards^{\sharp}$ element of the abstract memory state.

Then, after exiting the loop at program label ℓ_9 we get the following property:

$$
\begin{cases}
\mathtt{arr} = malloc_{\ell_1}(\bot) \land \\
\mathtt{arr}[\mathtt{n} - 1] > \mathtt{x} \land \\
\forall \pi_{\ell_6} \in [0, \mathtt{result}), \mathtt{arr}[\pi_{\ell_6}] \leq \mathtt{x} \land \\
\forall \pi_{\ell_6} \in \{\, \mathtt{result}\,\}, \mathtt{arr}[\pi_{\ell_6}] > \mathtt{x}
\end{cases}
$$

The two last lines of the property indicate that $\mathtt{result}$ is the index of the first element that is greater than $\mathtt{x}$.

7   Implementation details and limits

As mentioned in the introduction, the abstract domain presented in the article has been implemented in the **Astrée©** static analyzer. This section provides some implementation details and discusses the main limitations of the abstract domain.

Representation of partial functions. Partial functions are widely used in the abstract memory state. In the implementation, those functions are represented by functional maps implemented as balanced binary search trees. This allows to access or update elements in logarithmic time in the number of elements (that is always bounded by the number of program labels times the number of nested loops).

Interprocedural analysis. As **Astrée©** performs a polyvariant analysis of procedures (equivalent to a call by copy), like the one described in [2], the abstract domain has been quickly adapted to support multiple procedures' analysis. The solution was to associate to each program label a *path* described as a stack of *tokens*, described in [14]. This method corresponds to applying a partitioning over the traces, and the *tokens* characterize an element of the partition of the traces at specified control points. Thus, it is possible to use the manual directives provided by the partitioning abstract domain to fine-tune the analysis.

Forward goto. Such instructions are supported in the implementation by using a conservative approach: we apply the abstract transfer functions that correspond to the loops exited and entered between the source and destination of the **goto** statement within the AST.

Complex types C programs may include complex elements like casts and struct or union types. Because the abstract domain presented in this paper requires handling pointers as left-values, it was not possible to fully leverage the abstraction layer provided by the *struct* domain described in [15]. At this time, retrieving the value of a previously assigned left-value is possible only when the types trivially match. In particular, it is currently not possible to recompose an expression from multiple assignments. It would be an interesting addition in the future.

Memoization. When an abstract expression has to be dereferenced and a matching assignment is found, the identifier of the assignment is stored in a mutable field of the abstract expression so that, if it is later dereferenced again, the memoized assignment will be checked before going through the usual process.

Types that cannot be represented Some expressions, as floats, cannot be represented by abstract expressions. Still, in the implementation, $rval^\sharp$ can either represent an integer/pointer (as in this paper), but also the dereference of a pointer in a specified type. It is then possible, for example, to copy an array of floats and keep the property that the two arrays contain the same values.

Using information of other domains. In order to enhance the expressiveness of the abstract domain, we use properties inferred by the other domains to refine the abstract memory state. In particular, for each dereference that appears in an abstract expression that is in the abstract state, we add to it its abstract value by using only the non-relational value domains. The properties computed by the interval domain [5], the congruence domain [9] and the bitfield domain [17] are particularly useful to search efficiently which assignments and guards could be affected by a new assignment. The properties inferred by the Andersen's pointer analysis [1] are also used to reduce the loss of information when assigning a left-value which cannot be translated into an abstract left-value, or which cannot be proved within the bounds of its base.

Sharing information to other domains. In order to be beneficial to the analysis, sharing discovered properties to other domains is essential. When a right-value associated to an assignment or a guard is computed thanks to universal eliminations, or when the value of a loop counter is fixed when exiting a loop, then the information is propagated to the other domains. In addition, when an alarm (division by 0, integer overflow, out-of-bound access, ...) was raised by another domain and is proved false in this domain, then it is removed.

8   Conclusion

In this paper, we proposed new abstractions for proving programs that manipulate memory blocks by folding loops — that is — by universally quantifying assignments and comparison predicates. In the case of assignments, quantification is used both for the left and the right values. This typically allows the right-value to be expressed in terms of the left-value. This technique has proven effective for analyzing expanded memory bootstrap in operating systems when it relies on parameters unknown at analysis time. The abstract expressions used in the abstract memory state are affine forms in the loop counter values and in symbolic dereferences. The latest are unfolded lazily, allowing affine forms in loop counter values to be inferred. In the case where no precise information can be inferred by the abstract domain about the left-value of an assignment, other abstract domains can limit the loss of precision. The abstract domain has been implemented the Astrée© static analyzer, and we provided insights on how to move from the idealized abstract domain presented in the paper to an implementation in a real-word C static analyzer.

Future Work. In the short term, we plan to integrate this work into MOPSA [12], a modular open platform for static analysis. Looking ahead, as Astrée© targets mostly critical embedded code, it does not need to support recursive functions and backward goto that are generally prohibited. However, it would be interesting to test the effectiveness of the abstract domain when adding recursion counters that count the number of recursive calls. Another challenge would be to merge this work with the one presented in [4] to rewrite expressions that contain both pointer dereferences and implicit/explicit type conversions. Lastly, we are interested in potential applications of the techniques described in the paper to prove properties about the content of intrusive linked-lists.

Acknowledgements We deeply thank the anonymous referees for the precise reviews. We also thank Marco Campion and Guannan Wei for the insightful conversations.

References

1. Andersen, L., Institut, K.U.D.: Program Analysis and Specialization for the C Programming Language. DIKU rapport, Datalogisk Institut, Københavns Universitet (1994)
2. Blanchet, B., Cousot, P., Cousot, R., Feret, J., Mauborgne, L., Miné, A., Monniaux, D., Rival, X.: Design and implementation of a special-purpose static program analyzer for safety-critical real-time embedded software. In: The Essence of Computation, Complexity, Analysis, Transformation. Springer (2002). https://doi.org/10.1007/3-540-36377-7_5
3. Blanchet, B., Cousot, P., Cousot, R., Feret, J., Mauborgne, L., Miné, A., Monniaux, D., Rival, X.: A static analyzer for large safety-critical software. In: Programming Language Design and Implementation. ACM (2003). https://doi.org/10.1145/781131.781153
4. Boillot, J., Feret, J.: Symbolic transformation of expressions in modular arithmetic. In: Hermenegildo, M.V., Morales, J.F. (eds.) Static Analysis. Springer Nature Switzerland (2023). https://doi.org/10.1007/978-3-031-44245-2_6
5. Cousot, P., Cousot, R.: Static determination of dynamic properties of programs. In: International Symposium on Programming. Dunod (1976). https://doi.org/10.1145/390019.808314

6. Cousot, P., Cousot, R., Logozzo, F.: A parametric segmentation functor for fully automatic and scalable array content analysis. In: Proceedings of the 38th Annual ACM SIGPLAN-SIGACT Symposium on Principles of Programming Languages. POPL '11, Association for Computing Machinery, New York, NY, USA (2011). https://doi.org/10.1145/1926385.1926399

7. Gopan, D., DiMaio, F., Dor, N., Reps, T., Sagiv, M.: Numeric domains with summarized dimensions. In: Tools and Algorithms for the Construction and Analysis of Systems. Springer Berlin Heidelberg, Berlin, Heidelberg (2004). https://doi.org/10.1007/978-3-540-24730-2_38

8. Gopan, D., Reps, T., Sagiv, M.: A framework for numeric analysis of array operations. In: Proceedings of the 32nd ACM SIGPLAN-SIGACT Symposium on Principles of Programming Languages. POPL '05, Association for Computing Machinery, New York, NY, USA (2005). https://doi.org/10.1145/1040305.1040333

9. Granger, P.: Static analysis of arithmetical congruences. International Journal of Computer Mathematics (1989). https://doi.org/10.1080/00207168908803778

10. Halbwachs, N., Péron, M.: Discovering properties about arrays in simple programs. In: Programming Language Design and Implementation. ACM (2008). https://doi.org/10.1145/1375581.1375623

11. Journault, M., Miné, A.: Static analysis by abstract interpretation of the functional correctness of matrix manipulating programs. In: Rival, X. (ed.) Static Analysis. Springer Berlin Heidelberg, Berlin, Heidelberg (2016). https://doi.org/10.1007/978-3-662-53413-7_13

12. Journault, M., Miné, A., Monat, R., Ouadjaout, A.: Combinations of reusable abstract domains for a multilingual static analyzer. In: Verified Software. Theories, Tools, and Experiments. Springer (2020). https://doi.org/10.1007/978-3-030-41600-3_1

13. Liu, J., Rival, X.: An array content static analysis based on non-contiguous partitions. Computer Languages, Systems & Structures **47** (2017). https://doi.org/10.1016/j.cl.2016.01.005, special issue on the 16th International Conference on Verification, Model Checking, and Abstract Interpretation (VMCAI 2015)

14. Mauborgne, L., Rival, X.: Trace partitioning in abstract interpretation based static analyzers. In: Proceedings of the 14th European Conference on Programming Languages and Systems. ESOP'05, Springer-Verlag, Berlin, Heidelberg (2005). https://doi.org/10.1007/978-3-540-31987-0_2

15. Miné, A.: Field-sensitive value analysis of embedded c programs with union types and pointer arithmetics. SIGPLAN Not. **41**(7) (Jun 2006). https://doi.org/10.1145/1159974.1134659

16. Miné, A.: Symbolic methods to enhance the precision of numerical abstract domains. In: Verification, Model Checking, and Abstract Interpretation. Springer (2006). https://doi.org/10.1007/11609773_23

17. Miné, A.: Abstract domains for bit-level machine integer and floating-point operations. In: Fleuriot, J., Höfner, P., McIver, A., Smaill, A. (eds.) ATx'12/WInG'12: Joint Proceedings of the Workshops on Automated Theory eXploration and on Invariant Generation. EPiC Series in Computing, vol. 17. EasyChair (2013). https://doi.org/10.29007/b63g

18. Reynolds, J.C.: Separation logic: A logic for shared mutable data structures. In: 17th IEEE Symposium on Logic in Computer Science (LICS 2002), 22-25 July 2002, Copenhagen, Denmark, Proceedings. IEEE Computer Society (2002). https://doi.org/10.1109/LICS.2002.1029817
19. Venet, A.: The gauge domain: Scalable analysis of linear inequality invariants. In: Computer Aided Verification. Springer (2012). https://doi.org/10.1007/978-3-642-31424-7_15

Cognacy Queries over Dependence Graphs for Transparent Visualisations

Joe Bond[1], Cristina David[1], Minh Nguyen[1], Dominic Orchard[2,3],
and Roly Perera[1,3]

[1] University of Bristol, Bristol, UK
{j.bond,cristina.david,min.nguyen}@bristol.ac.uk
[2] University of Kent, Canterbury, UK
d.a.orchard@kent.ac.uk
[3] University of Cambridge, Cambridge, UK
roly.perera@cl.cam.ac.uk

Abstract. Charts, figures, and text derived from data play an important role in decision making. But making sense of or fact-checking outputs means understanding how they relate to the underlying data. Even for experts with access to the source code and data sets, this poses a significant challenge. We introduce a new program analysis framework (A supporting artifact is available at https://zenodo.org/records/14637654 [5].) which supports interactive exploration of fine-grained IO relationships directly through computed outputs, using dynamic dependence graphs. This framework enables a novel notion in data provenance which we call *linked inputs*, a relation of mutual relevance or cognacy which arises between inputs that contribute to common features of the output. We give a procedure for computing linked inputs over a dependence graph, and show how the presented in this paper is faster on most examples than an implementation based on execution traces.

1 Introduction: Towards Transparent Research Outputs

Whether formulating national policy or making day-to-day decisions about our own lives, we increasingly rely on the charts, figures and text created by scientists and journalists. Interpreting these visual and textual summaries is essential to making informed decisions. However, most of the artifacts we encounter are *opaque*, inasmuch as they are unable to reveal anything about how they relate to the data they were derived from. Whilst one could in principle try to use the source code and data to reverse engineer some of these relationships, this requires substantial expertise, as well as valuable time spent away from the "comprehension context" in which the output in question was encountered. These difficulties are compounded when the information presented uses multiple data sources, such as medical meta-analyses [13], ensemble models in climate science [25], or queries that span multiple database tables [36]. Perhaps more often than we would like, we end up taking things on trust.

Supplementary Information The online version contains supplementary material available at https://doi.org/10.1007/978-3-031-91118-7_6

With traditional print media, a "disconnect" between outputs and underlying data is unavoidable. For digital media, other options are open to us. One way to improve things is to engineer visual artifacts to be more "self-explanatory", revealing the relationship to the underlying data to an interested user. Consider the histogram in Figure 1 showing urban population growth in Asia over a decade [6]. A reader might have many questions about what this chart represents – in other words, how visual elements map to underlying data. Do the points represent individual cities? What does the colour scheme indicate? Which of the points represent large cities or small cities? Legends and other accompanying text can help, but some ambiguities inevitably remain. The purpose of a visual summary after all is to present the big picture at the expense of certain detail.

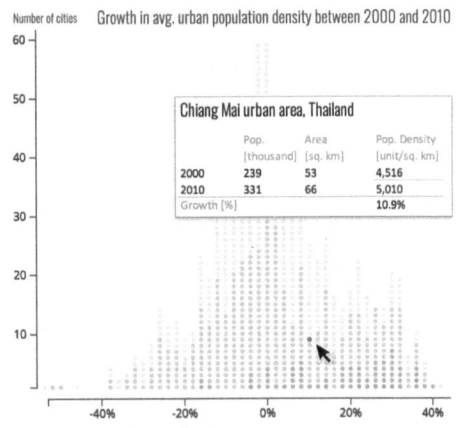

Fig. 1: A hand-crafted transparent visualisation due to Bremer and Ranzijn [6]

Bremer and Ranzijn's [6] approach to this problem is an interactive feature that allows a user to explore some of these provenance-related questions *in situ*, i.e. directly from the chart. Selecting an individual point shows the user a view of the data the point was calculated from. In the figure the highlighted point represents Chiang Mai, and shows that the plotted value of 10.9% was derived from an increase in population density from 4,416 to 5,010 people per sq. km. Features like these are valuable as comprehension aids, but are laborious to implement by hand and require the author to anticipate the queries a user might have. For these reasons they also tend not to generalise: for example Bremer and Ranzijn's [6] visualisation only allows the user to select one point at a time.

1.1 Data transparency as PL infrastructure

Hand-crafted efforts like Bremer and Ranzijn's [6] are labour-intensive because they involve manually embedding metadata about the relationship between outputs and inputs into the same program. When the visualisation or analysis logic changes, the relationship between inputs and outputs also change, and the metadata must be manually updated. A less costly and more robust approach is to treat data provenance as a language infrastructure problem, baking lineage or provenance metadata directly into outputs so that provenance queries can be supported automatically. For example, for an in-memory database engine, Psallidas and Wu [32] describe how to "backward trace" from output selections to input selections, and then "forward trace" to find related output selections in other views, to support a popular feature from data visualisation called *linked brushing*.

Perera et al. [30] implemented a similar system for a general-purpose functional programming language, using execution traces for bidirectional queries.

The advantage of shifting the burden of implementing transparency features onto the language runtime is that the author of the content can concentrate purely on data visualisation, and as the infrastructure improves, the benefits are inherited automatically by end users, at no additional cost to the author. For example if formal guarantees (perhaps that data selections are in some sense minimal and sufficient) are provided, then those can be proved once for the infrastructure rather than for each bespoke implementation.

In this paper, we propose a new bidirectional analysis framework for a general-purpose programming language, which supports fine-grained *in situ* provenance queries, an end-user feature we call *data transparency*. In contrast to prior work, we use *dynamic dependence graphs* [17,2] to implement the analyses, which enables our approach to be fast enough for interactive use and also language-independent, by separating queries over the graph from the problem of deriving the dependence graph for a particular program.

1.2   Contributions and Roadmap

Our specific contributions are as follows:

- § 3 defines a core calculus for data-transparent outputs, where parts of inputs and computed values are assigned unique labels called *addresses*, and programs have an operational semantics that pairs every result with a dynamic dependence graph capturing fine-grained IO relationships between input addresses and output addresses.
- § 4 presents a new formal framework for bidirectional provenance queries over dependence graphs, formalising two operators over such graphs, ∇ (*demands*) and $\triangle$ (*demanded by*). We show these to be *conjugate* in the sense of Jonsson and Tarski [22], and give procedures to compute ∇ and $\triangle$. We show how a novel cognacy operator $\nabla\triangle$ called *linked inputs*, relating inputs when they contribute to common parts of the output, can be obtained by composing ∇ and $\triangle$, and how a dual *linked outputs* operator $\triangle\nabla$, supporting the "linked visualisations" of prior work [32,30], is obtained by transposing the two operators.
- § 5 shows that our implementation performs better than one based on traces and bidirectional interpreters, the primary alternative implementation technique. Using usability metrics from Nielsen [26], we find that 81% of the queries we tested execute at a speed that appears instantaneous to a user, compared to 25% using an implementation based on traces. We also compare overhead of building a trace vs. building a dependence graph for a given program.

Although Psallidas and Wu [32] support fast queries for linked visualisations in a database setting, and Perera et al. [30] support linked outputs in a general-purpose languages, ours is (to the best of our knowledge) the first implementation for a general-purpose language which is fast enough for interactive use. § 6

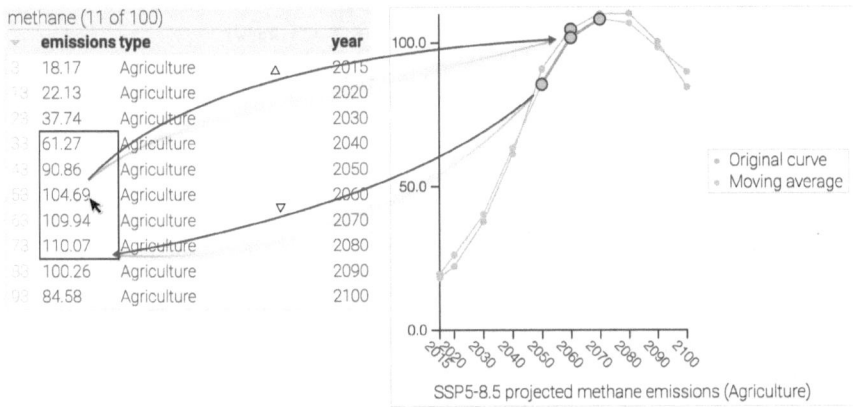

Fig. 2: Data transparency: *demanded by* (△) and *demands* (▽) operators link inputs that share common output dependencies.

discusses other related work in database provenance, program slicing and data visualisation.

§ 7 wraps up with a discussion of some limitations. In particular, the sort of transparency considered in this paper is purely extensional, and falls short of providing full explanations of how output parts are related to input parts. We discuss more intensional forms of transparency in § 7 and propose some other ways in which the present system could be improved.

We implement our approach in a pure functional programming language called Fluid. The author of a visualisation expresses their chart as a pure function of the inputs, using a set of built-in data types for common visualisations; a d3.js front end automatically enriches the rendered outputs with support for interactive selection and the data transparency queries introduced in the next section. Our implementation is available at https://github.com/explorable-viz/fluid.

2   Overview: Fine-Grained Interactive Provenance

In this section, we introduce the main interactive data provenance features that wish to support, using two Fluid examples to illustrate. The line chart in Figure 2 shows projected methane emissions from agricultural sources under a global warming scenario called RCP8.5, with source code in Figure 3; the scatter plot and stacked bar chart in Figure 4 show changing non-renewable energy outputs and capacities for various countries, with source code in Figure 5.

The key idea of a transparent visualisation is that the original data sources are kept around and can be viewed (when a user so requests) alongside the visualisation, and the user is then able to interact with both the data and the view to

```
1    let nthPad n xs = nth (min (max n 0) (length xs — 1)) xs;
2    let movingAvg ys window =
3          [ sum [ nthPad n ys | n ← is ] / (1 + 2 * window)
4          | i ← [ 0 .. length ys — 1 ],
5            let is = [ i — window .. i + window ] ];
6    let movingAvg' rs window =
7          zipWith (fun x y → {x: x, y: y})
8            (map (fun r → r.x) rs)
9            (movingAvg (map (fun r → r.y) rs) window);
10   let points =
11         [ { x: r.year, y: r.emissions } | r ← methane, r.type == "Agriculture" ]
12   in LineChart {
13       tickLabels: { x: Rotated, y: Default },
14       size: { width: 330, height: 285 },
15       caption: "SSP5—8.5 projected methane emissions (Agriculture)",
16       plots: [
17         LinePlot { name: "Original curve", points: points },
18         LinePlot { name: "Moving average", points: movingAvg' points 1 }
19       ] }
```

Fig. 3: Moving average source code

explore how they are related. Crucially the author of the visualisation does not to have to implement any of these interactions themselves; they need only write the visualisation code and the language runtime and rendering infrastructure provides the interactions.

1. Fine-grained linking of the data to the view. In Figure 2, the user has chosen to reveal the underlying data set, which is shown on the left; only rows relevant to the chart are visible, with the other rows hidden automatically. This clarifies that only agricultural data is relevant, confirming the (informal) claim in the caption. The emissions values shown do contribute to the chart in some way, and the user can investigate this by interacting with individual entries. For example, moving their mouse over the number 104.69 highlights *one* point in the projected emissions curve, and *three* points in the other curve, which plots the moving average (see Figure 3) of the projected emissions. The provenance analysis which underpins this we write as $\triangle$ ("demanded by"), and here this tells us that 104.69 was needed to compute either the x or y coordinate (in this case just the y coordinate) of the four highlighted points.

2. Linked inputs. We want to support fine-grained IO queries that run in the other direction too, via another provenance analysis written $\triangledown$ ("demands"). In Figure 2 the $\triangledown$ analysis is initiated automatically on the output of $\triangle$; this reveals that calculating the y coordinates of the points highlighted on the right required not only the 104.69 we started with, but 4 additional emissions values (blue border on the left). These additional inputs we refer to as the *related inputs* of the original input selection; they are the other inputs demanded by any output that demands our starting input, and are computed using the composite operator $\triangledown\triangle$. Given that the initial input selection here contributes to 3 points of the moving average, the "window" of related inputs in this case is 5 wide, comprising all the data points needed to account for the selection on the right. Related inputs is

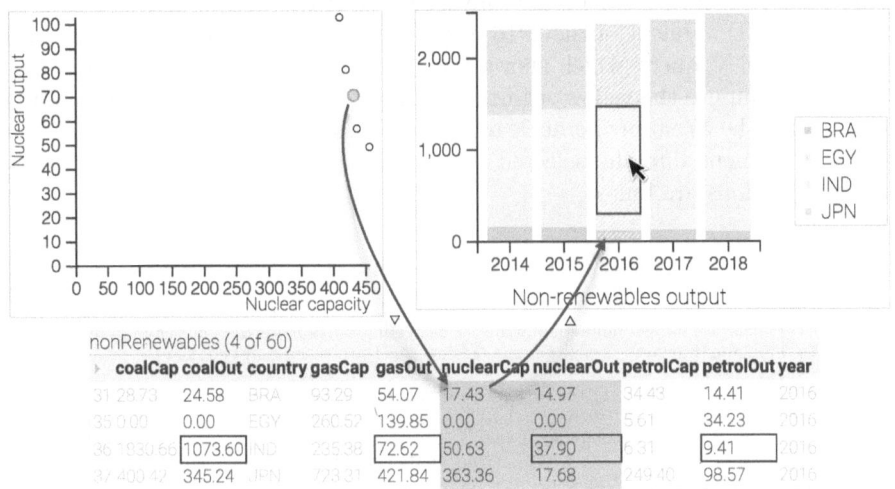

Fig. 4: Data transparency: *demands* (∇) and *demanded by* ($\triangle$) operators link outputs that share common input dependencies.

a *cognacy* relation: two inputs are related if they have a common ancestor in a *dependence graph* that captures how inputs are demanded by outputs.

3. Fine-grained linking of the view to the data. We would also like to support cognacy queries that start from the output rather than the input; this is the basis of a feature called *linked brushing* (or *brushing and linking*) in data visualisation [4,7]. Here we would like to provide linked brushing in a way that is transparent to the user. In Figure 4, the user has again revealed the underlying data set, this time opting to see only rows with active data selections, rather than only rows with data that are used by any part of the output. They then express interest in one of the points in the scatter plot. By clicking on it, rather than just mousing over it, they create what we call a *persistent* selection (shown in green). The demands analysis ∇ reveals (also in green) the inputs needed to compute both the x and y coordinates of the selected point; this shows that the 2016 data for 4 countries was used, although it does not reveal how.

4. Linked outputs. Now that the inputs demanded by the output selection are determined, the $\triangle$ analysis runs automatically on the output of ∇; this reveals that those inputs were also needed for 4 of the bar segments (highlighted with cross-hatching) in the bar chart, namely those for 2016. This is standard linked brushing, and is implemented using the composite operator $\triangle\nabla$, which we call *related outputs*. Related outputs is a "co-cognacy" relation, relating two outputs whenever they have a common descendant, rather than common ancestor, in the dependence graph. Here the user can take advantage of the fact that a persistent selection remains active even when the mouse moves off the original

item of interest; this allows them to investigate further. Moving their mouse over
the yellow IND segment of the 2016 bar (highlighted with blue border) initiates
an orthogonal ∇ query which shows (also with various blue borders) the data
needed to compute the yellow segment. Overlaid on the persistent selection, this
reveals that the 37.90 in the nuclearOut column is needed to compute *both* the
IND bar segment *and* the selected scatter plot point, explaining why the two
output selections are linked.

```
 1   let countries = ["BRA", "EGY", "IND", "JPN"];
 2   let totalFor year country =
 3       let [ row ] =
 4           [ row | row ← nonRenewables, row.year == year, row.country == country ]
 5       in row.nuclearOut + row.gasOut + row.coalOut + row.petrolOut;
 6   let stack year =
 7           [ { y: country, z: totalFor year country } | country ← countries ];
 8   let yearData year =
 9           [ row | row ← nonRenewables,
10                   row.year == year, row.country 'elem' countries ]
11   in MultiView {
12       barChart: BarChart {
13           caption: "Non—renewables output",
14           size: { width: 275, height: 185 },
15           stackedBars:
16               [ { x: numToStr year, bars: stack year } | year ← [2014..2018] ]
17       },
18       scatterPlot: ScatterPlot {
19           caption: "",
20           points:
21               [ { x: sum [ row.nuclearCap | row ← rows ],
22                   y: sum [ row.nuclearOut | row ← rows ] }
23               | year ← [2014..2018], let rows = yearData year ],
24           xlabel: "Nuclear capacity",
25           ylabel: "Nuclear output"
26       }
27   }
```

Fig. 5: Non-renewable energy source code

3   A Core Calculus for Transparent Outputs

We start by introducing a calculus for transparent outputs, which is the core of
Fluid. The core language supports deep pattern-matching and mutual recursion.
Fluid also provides a surface syntax that desugars into the core, providing piecewise function definitions, list comprehensions and other conveniences, as shown
in Figures 3 and 5, which would otherwise complicate the core.

The term syntax of the core language (§ 3.1) is uncontroversial: it is pure
and untyped, and provides datatypes, records and matrices (although we omit a
presentation of matrices here). The syntax of values is less standard: each part
of a value has a unique *address* α which serves to identify that part of the value
in a dependence graph. We give a big-step operational semantics that evaluates
a term to both a value and a *dynamic dependence graph* for that value (§ 3.2),
capturing how parts of the value depend on parts of the input.

Expression		*Eliminator*	
$e ::= x$	variable	$\sigma ::= x \mapsto \kappa$	variable
n	integer	$\{\vec{x}\} \mapsto \kappa$	record
let $x = e$ in e'	let	$\{\overline{c \mapsto \vec{\kappa}}\}$	constructor
$\{\overline{x : \vec{e}}\}$	record	*Value*	
$e.x$	record projection	$v ::= \boldsymbol{v}_\alpha$	
$c(\vec{e})$	constructor	$\boldsymbol{v} ::= n$	integer
$e\,e'$	application	$\{\overline{x : \vec{v}}\}$	record
$f(\vec{e})$	foreign application	$c(\vec{v})$	constructor
$\lambda\sigma$	function	$\mathrm{cl}(\gamma, \rho, \sigma)$	closure
let ρ in e	recursive let	*Environment*	
Continuation		$\gamma ::= \{\overline{x : \vec{v}}\}$	
$\kappa ::= e$	expression	*Recursive definitions*	
σ	eliminator	$\rho ::= \{\overline{x : \vec{\sigma}}\}$	

Fig. 6: Syntax of the core language, including values labeled with addresses

Some notation. We write to $\vec{x}$ denote a finite sequence of elements $x_1, .., x_n$, with ϵ as the empty sequence. Concatenation of sequences is written $\vec{x} \mathbin{++} \vec{x}'$; we also write $x \cdot \vec{x}$ for cons (prepend) and $\vec{x} \cdot x$ for snoc (append). We write $\{\overline{k : \vec{x}}\}$ to denote a finite map, i.e. a set of pairs $k_1 : x_1, .., k_n : x_n$ where keys k_i are pairwise unique. If X and Y are sets, we write $X \uplus Y$ to mean $X \cup Y$ where X and Y are disjoint, and also $x \cdot X$ or $X \cdot x$ to mean $X \uplus \{x\}$.

3.1   Syntax

Terms Figure 6 defines expressions e of the language, which include variables x, integer constants n, let-bindings let $x = e$ in e', record construction $\{\overline{x : \vec{e}}\}$, record projection $e.x$ and (saturated) constructor expressions $c(\vec{e})$, where c ranges over data constructors. The language is parameterised by a finite map Σ from constructors c to arities $\Sigma(c) \in \mathbb{N}$. Function application has two forms: the usual $e\,e'$ and (saturated) *foreign function* application $f(\vec{e})$ (described below). Lastly, expressions include anonymous functions $\lambda\sigma$, where σ is a pattern-matching construct called an *eliminator* (§ 3.1), and sets of mutually recursive functions let ρ in e, where ρ is a finite map $\overline{x : \vec{\sigma}}$ from names to eliminators.

The language is also parameterised by a finite map Φ from variables f to arities $\Phi(f) \in \mathbb{N}$ of the foreign function they denote. For the graph semantics in § 3.2 below, every foreign function name f is required to provide an interpretation $\hat{f}$ that, for a sequence of arguments $\vec{v}$ and dependence graph G, returns the result of applying the foreign function f to $\vec{v}$ plus a dependence graph G' which extends G with information about how the result depends on $\vec{v}$.

Continuations and eliminators A *continuation* κ is a term e or an eliminator σ, describing how an execution proceeds after a value is matched. *Eliminators* are a deep pattern-matching construct based on tries [21,31]; for a language with rich structured values like records and data types, they make for a cleaner presentation than single shallow elimination forms for each type. Piecewise function definitions in the surface language desugar into eliminators.

An eliminator specifies how values of a particular shape are matched, and for a given value, determines how any pattern variables get bound and the continuation κ which will be executed under those bindings. A variable eliminator $x \mapsto \kappa$ says how to match any value (as variable x) and continue as κ. A record eliminator $\{\vec{x}\} \mapsto \kappa$ says how to match a record with fields $\vec{x}$, and provides a continuation κ for sequentially matching the values of those fields. Lastly, a constructor eliminator $\{\overline{c \mapsto \kappa}\}$ provides a branch $c \mapsto \kappa$ for each constructor c in $\vec{c}$, where each κ specifies how any arguments to c will be matched. (We assume that any constructors matched by an eliminator all belong to the same data type, but this is not enforced in the core language.)

Addresses, values and environments We define addressed *values* v mutually inductively with *raw values*. A raw value is simply a value without an associated address; a value decorates a raw value with an address α. Addresses are allocated during evaluation so that new partial values have fresh addresses, which can then be used as vertices in a dependence graph.

Raw values $\boldsymbol{v}$ include integers n, m; records $\{\overline{x \mapsto v}\}$; and constructor values $c(\vec{v})$. Raw values also include closures $\mathrm{cl}(\gamma, \rho, \sigma)$ where σ is the function body, γ the captured environment, and to support mutual recursion, ρ is the (possibly empty) set of named functions with which σ was mutually defined. *Environments* are finite maps from variables to values. Because foreign functions in the core language are not first-class and calls $f(\vec{e})$ are saturated, i.e. $|\vec{e}| = \varPhi(f)$, the surface language provides a top-level environment which maps every foreign function name f of arity n to the closure $\mathrm{cl}(\varnothing, \varnothing, x_1 \mapsto .. \mapsto x_n \mapsto f(\vec{x}))_\alpha$, with α fresh, emulating first-class foreign functions.

3.2   Operational Semantics

We now give a big-step operational semantics for the core language, which evaluates a term to a value paired with a *dynamic dependence graph* for that value.

Dynamic Dependence Graphs A *dynamic dependence graph* [2] (hereafter *dependence graph*) is a directed acyclic graph $G = (V, E)$ with a set V of *vertices* and a set $E \subseteq V \times V$ of edges. When convenient we write $\mathsf{V}(G)$ for V and $\mathsf{E}(G)$ for E. In the dependence graph for a particular program, vertices $\alpha, \beta \in V$ are addresses associated to values (either supplied to the program as inputs or produced during evaluation) and edges $(\alpha, \beta) \in E$ indicate that, in the evaluation of that program, the value associated to β *depends on* (is *demanded by*, in the terminology of § 2) the value associated to α. Such values may be sub-terms of a larger value. This diverges somewhat from traditional approaches to dynamic dependence graphs in only considering one type of edge (data dependency) rather than separate data and control dependencies; moreover our edges point in the direction of dependent vertices, whereas in the literature the other direction is somewhat more common.

During evaluation, when a fresh vertex α is allocated for a constructed value, the dependence graph G is extended by a graph fragment specifying that α depends on a set V of preexisting vertices, given by the following notation:

Definition 1 (In-star notation). *Write* $\{V \mapsto \alpha\}$ *as shorthand for the star graph* $(\{\alpha\} \uplus V, V \times \{\alpha\})$.

Pattern matching Evaluation relies on pattern matching, which is defined by a separate judgement form, computing a vertex set. Figure 7 defines the pattern-matching judgement $\vec{v}, \kappa \rightsquigarrow \gamma, e, V$. Rather than matching a single value v, the judgement matches a "stack" of values $\vec{v}$ against a continuation κ, returning the selected branch e, an environment γ providing bindings for the free variables of e, and the set V of addresses found in the matched portions of $\vec{v}$.

A continuation which is just an expression e matches only the empty stack of values ($\rightsquigarrow$-done), in which case pattern-matching is complete and e is the selected branch. Other rules require an *eliminator* σ as the continuation and a non-empty stack $v \cdot \vec{v}$; any relevant subvalues of v are unpacked and pushed onto the tail $\vec{v}$ and then recursively matched using the continuation κ selected from σ. A variable eliminator $x \mapsto \kappa$ pops v off the stack, using κ to recurse ($\rightsquigarrow$-var); no part of v is consumed so the addresses V consumed by the recursive match are returned unmodified. A record eliminator $\{\vec{y}\} \mapsto \kappa$ matches a record of the form $\{\overline{x : v}\}_\alpha$ as long as the variables in $\vec{y}$ are also fields in $\vec{x}$, augmenting V with the address α associated with the record ($\rightsquigarrow$-record); the premise $\{\overline{y : u}\} \subseteq \{\overline{x : v}\}$ projects out the corresponding values of $\vec{u}$ from $\vec{v}$. Lastly, a constructor eliminator $(c \mapsto \kappa)$ matches any constructor value of the form $c(\vec{v})_\alpha$, augmenting V with the address α associated with the constructor ($\rightsquigarrow$-constr).

$$\boxed{\vec{v}, \kappa \rightsquigarrow \gamma, e, V}$$

$\rightsquigarrow$-done
$$\frac{}{\epsilon, e \rightsquigarrow \varnothing, e, \varnothing}$$

$\rightsquigarrow$-constr
$$\frac{\vec{v} ++ \vec{v}', \kappa \rightsquigarrow \gamma, e, V \qquad \Sigma(c) = |\vec{v}|}{c(\vec{v})_\alpha \cdot \vec{v}', (c \mapsto \kappa) \cdot \{\overline{c \mapsto \kappa}\} \rightsquigarrow \gamma, e, \alpha \cdot V}$$

$\rightsquigarrow$-var
$$\frac{\vec{v}, \kappa \rightsquigarrow \gamma, e, V}{v \cdot \vec{v}, x \mapsto \kappa \rightsquigarrow \gamma \cdot (x : v), e, V}$$

$\rightsquigarrow$-record
$$\frac{\{\overline{y : u}\} \subseteq \{\overline{x : v}\} \qquad \vec{u} ++ \vec{v}', \kappa \rightsquigarrow \gamma, e, V}{\{\overline{x : v}\}_\alpha \cdot \vec{v}', \{\vec{y}\} \mapsto \kappa \rightsquigarrow \gamma, e, \alpha \cdot V}$$

Fig. 7: Pattern matching

$$\boxed{\gamma, e, V, G \Rightarrow v, G'}$$

$\Rightarrow$-var

$$\frac{}{\gamma \cdot (x : v), x, V, G \Rightarrow v, G}$$

$\Rightarrow$-int

$$\frac{\alpha \notin \mathsf{V}(G)}{\gamma, n, V, G \Rightarrow n_\alpha, G \cup \{V \mapsto \alpha\}}$$

$\Rightarrow$-function

$$\frac{\alpha \notin \mathsf{V}(G)}{\gamma, \lambda\sigma, V, G \Rightarrow \mathrm{cl}(\gamma, \varnothing, \sigma)_\alpha, G \cup \{V \mapsto \alpha\}}$$

$\Rightarrow$-record

$$\frac{\gamma, \vec{e}, V, G \Rightarrow \vec{v}, G' \qquad \alpha \notin \mathsf{V}(G')}{\gamma, \{\overline{x : e}\}, V, G \Rightarrow \{\overline{x : v}\}_\alpha, G' \cup \{V \mapsto \alpha\}}$$

$\Rightarrow$-project

$$\frac{\gamma, e, V, G \Rightarrow \{\overline{x : v} \cdot (y : u)\}_\alpha, G'}{\gamma, e.y, V, G \Rightarrow u, G'}$$

$\Rightarrow$-constr

$$\frac{\gamma, \vec{e}, V, G \Rightarrow \vec{v}, G' \qquad \alpha \notin \mathsf{V}(G')}{\gamma, c(\vec{e}), V, G \Rightarrow c(\vec{v})_\alpha, G' \cup \{V \mapsto \alpha\}} \; \Sigma(c) = |\vec{e}|$$

$\Rightarrow$-foreign-app

$$\frac{\gamma, \vec{e}, V, G_1 \Rightarrow \vec{v}, G_2 \qquad \hat{f}(\vec{v}, G_2) = (u, G_3)}{\gamma, f(\vec{e}), V, G_1 \Rightarrow u, G_3} \; \Phi(f) = |\vec{e}|$$

$\Rightarrow$-let

$$\frac{\gamma, e, V, G_1 \Rightarrow v, G_2 \qquad \gamma \cdot (x : v), e', V, G_2 \Rightarrow v', G_3}{\gamma, \mathrm{let}\; x = e \;\mathrm{in}\; e', V, G_1 \Rightarrow v', G_3}$$

$\Rightarrow$-let-rec

$$\frac{\gamma, \rho, V, G_1 \rightarrowtail \gamma', G_2 \qquad \gamma ++ \gamma', e, V, G_2 \Rightarrow v, G_3}{\gamma, \mathrm{let}\; \rho \;\mathrm{in}\; e, V, G_1 \Rightarrow v, G_3}$$

$\Rightarrow$-app

$$\frac{\begin{array}{cc} \gamma, e, V, G_1 \Rightarrow \mathrm{cl}(\gamma_1, \rho, \sigma)_\alpha, G_2 \quad \gamma_1, \rho, \{\alpha\}, G_2 \rightarrowtail \gamma_2, G_3 \quad \gamma, e', V, G_3 \Rightarrow v', G_4 \\ v', \sigma \rightsquigarrow \gamma_3, e'', V' \quad \gamma_1 ++ \gamma_2 ++ \gamma_3, e'', V' \cup \{\alpha\}, G_4 \Rightarrow u, G_5 \end{array}}{\gamma, e\, e', V, G_1 \Rightarrow u, G_5}$$

$$\boxed{\gamma, \vec{e}, V, G \Rightarrow \vec{v}, G'}$$

$$\frac{\gamma, e_i, V, G_i \Rightarrow v_i, G_{i+1} \qquad (\forall i \leq n)}{\gamma, \vec{e}, V, G_1 \Rightarrow \vec{v}, G_{n+1}} \; n = |\vec{e}|$$

$$\boxed{\gamma, \rho, V, G \rightarrowtail \gamma', G'}$$

$$\frac{\begin{array}{c} \gamma'(x_i) = \mathrm{cl}(\gamma, \rho, \rho(x_i))_{\alpha_i} \\ \alpha_i \notin \mathsf{dom}(G_i) \qquad G_{i+1} = G_i \cup \{V \mapsto \alpha_i\} \quad (\forall i \leq n) \end{array}}{\gamma, \rho, V, G_1 \rightarrowtail \gamma', G_{n+1}} \; n = |\vec{x}|$$

Fig. 8: Operational semantics with dependence graph

Evaluation Figure 8 defines a big-step evaluation relation $\gamma, e, V, G \Rightarrow v, G'$ stating that term e, under an environment γ, vertex set V and dependence graph G, evaluates to a value v and extended dependence graph G'. The vertex set V records the (partial) input values consumed by the current active function call providing the dynamic context in which e is being evaluated; V is initially empty and changes whenever a function application is evaluated.

The evaluation rule for variables is fairly standard; the dependence graph is returned unmodified, because no new addresses are allocated as a result of simply looking up a variable. The rule for record projections $e.y$ is similar: if e evaluates to a record of the form $\{\overline{x : \vec{v}} \cdot (y : u)\}_\alpha$, then $e.y$ evaluates to the value u of field y, discarding the address α of the record.

Introduction rules, such as for integers, functions, records and constructors, follow the pattern of assigning a fresh address for the (partial) value being constructed, and then extending G with a set of dependency edges from the vertices in V to α. For example, the integer rule evaluates an expression n to its value form n_α; the $\alpha \notin V(G)$ constraint ensures that α is fresh. The dependence graph is then extended with $\{V \mapsto \alpha\}$, indicating that n_α depended on all matched partial inputs in V. Likewise, the rule for an anonymous function $\lambda\sigma$ constructs the closure $\mathsf{cl}(\gamma, \varnothing, \sigma)_\alpha$ with fresh address α, capturing the current environment γ and using $\varnothing$ as the set of mutually recursive definitions associated with the function, and again establishing dependency edges from V to α_i.

Rules which involve recursively evaluating subterms thread the graph under construction through the evaluation of the subterms. For example, the auxiliary evaluation relation $\gamma, \vec{e}, V \Rightarrow \vec{v}, G$ (bottom of Figure 8), evaluates each e_i in a sequence of terms $\vec{e}$ to a value v_i and dependence graph G_{i+1}, which is used as the input graph for evaluating e_{i+1}. We make use of this judgement in the rules for records $\{\overline{x : \vec{e}}\}$, constructors $c(\vec{e})$, and foreign applications $f(\vec{e})$; in the last rule, $\hat{f}$ is the foreign implementation that evaluates an application of f to a sequence of values $\vec{v}$ and dependence graph G to a result v and extended dependence graph G' (§ 3.1).

The rules for let $x = e$ in e' and application $e\,e'$ may involve mutual recursion, and rely on the auxiliary relation $\gamma, \rho, V, G \rightarrowtail \gamma', G'$ defined at the bottom of Figure 8. This judgement takes a set ρ of recursive definitions, vertex set V and dependence graph G, and returns an environment γ' of closures derived from ρ and extended dependence graph G'. Each function definition $\rho(x_i) \in \rho$ generates a new closure $(\gamma, \rho, \rho(x_i))_{\alpha_i}$ capturing γ and ρ, with fresh address α_i, and extends the dependence graph with a set of edges from V to α_i.

The evaluation rule for let ρ in e is similar to the rule for regular let-bindings, except for using $\rightarrowtail$ to build a set of closures γ' which extends γ. Finally, the rule for $e\,e'$ is notable because this is where the active function context changes and the ambient V is discarded. We compute the closure $\mathsf{cl}(\gamma_1, \rho, \sigma)_\alpha$ from e and the argument v' from e', and then use σ to match v'. If pattern-matching returns selected branch e'', with vertex set V' representing the consumed part of v', then e'' is evaluated and becomes the result of the application, with $V' \cup \{\alpha\}$ serving as set of (partial) inputs associated with the new active function context.

Example Figure 9 shows part of the dependence graph for the moving average example in Figures 2 and 3. The graph shows the calculation of the first 3 points in the moving average plot from entries in the *emissions* table. This is a simplified version of the graph, since in practice they get very large; for example, we omit closures, list cells and the calculation of the divisors. Also note that the node labels here are merely illustrative: the graph only stores value dependencies, and in particular the in-neighbours of a vertex are unordered.

4   Cognacy Queries Over Dependence Graphs

We now turn to cognacy and "co-cognacy" queries over dependence graphs, expressed in terms of the $\triangledown$ and $\triangle$ operators introduced informally in § 2. Boolean algebras (Definition 2) are used to represent selections; we then define $\triangledown$ and $\triangle$ and their De Morgan duals, first for an arbitrary relation (§ 4.1) and then for the *IO relation* of a dependence graph (§ 4.2). Then we give procedures for computing $\triangledown$ and $\triangle$ and their duals over a given dependence graph, via an intermediate graph slice (§ 4.3).

Definition 2 (Boolean algebra). *A* Boolean algebra *(or* Boolean lattice*) A is a 6-tuple* $(A, \wedge, \vee, \bot, \top, \neg)$ *with carrier A, distinguished elements* $\bot$ *(bottom) and* $\top$ *(top), commutative operations* $\wedge$ *(meet) and* $\vee$ *(join) with* $\top$ *and* $\bot$ *as respective units, and unary operation* $\neg$ *(negate) satisfying* $x \vee \neg x = \top$ *and* $x \wedge \neg x = \bot$. *The operations* $\wedge$ *and* $\vee$ *distribute over each other and induce a partial order* $\leq$ *over X.*

An input (or output) selection, where X is the set of all addresses that occur in the input (or output) of the program, is represented by the *powerset* Boolean algebra $\mathbb{P}(X)$ whose carrier is the set of subsets $X' \subseteq X$ ordered by inclusion $\subseteq$. In this case bottom is the empty set $\varnothing$, top is the whole set X, meet and join are given by $\cap$ and $\cup$, and negation by relative complement $\setminus$, so that $\neg X' = X \setminus X'$.

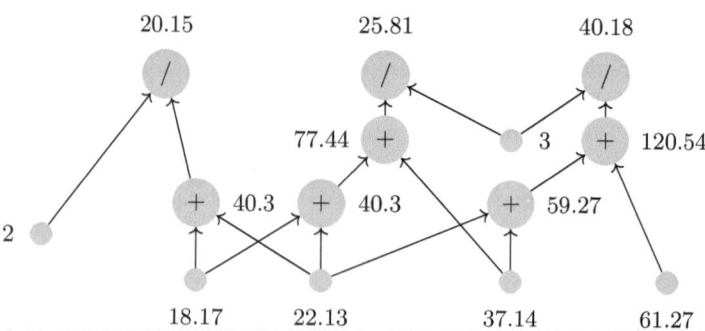

Fig. 9: Portion of dependence graph computed for moving averages example

4.1 $\triangledown$ and $\triangle$ and their duals

The $\triangledown$ and $\triangle$ operators sketched earlier are simply the image and preimage functions for a particular dependency relation R. A mnemonic device may help with reading the symbols; if R is a dependency relation oriented with outputs at the top and inputs at the bottom, then *demanded by* $\triangle$ can be read as an arrow pointing from inputs to outputs, and *demands* $\triangledown$ as an arrow pointing from outputs to inputs.

Definition 3 (Image and Preimage Functions for a Relation). *For a relation $R \subseteq X \times Y$, define $\triangle_R : \mathbb{P}(X) \to \mathbb{P}(Y)$ and $\triangledown_R : \mathbb{P}(Y) \to \mathbb{P}(X)$ as:*

1. $\triangle_R(X') := \{y \in Y \mid \exists x \in X'.(x, y) \in R\}$ *(image)*
2. $\triangledown_R(Y') := \{x \in X \mid \exists y \in Y'.(x, y) \in R\}$ *(preimage)*

Trivially $\triangle_R = \triangledown_{R^{-1}}$. The image and preimage functions form a *conjugate pair*, in the sense of Jonsson and Tarski [22]:

Definition 4 (Conjugate Functions). *For Boolean algebras A, B, functions $f : A \to B$ and $g : B \to A$ form a conjugate pair iff:*

$$f(x) \wedge y = \bot \iff x \wedge g(y) = \bot$$

(Jonsson and Tarski [22] consider only endofunctions; here we extend the idea of conjugacy to maps between Boolean algebras.)

Lemma 1. $\triangle_R$ and $\triangledown_R$ are conjugate.

This should be intuitive enough: for any subsets $X' \subseteq X$ and $Y' \subseteq Y$, if the elements "on the right" to which X' is related are disjoint from Y', then there are no edges in R from X' to Y'; and in virtue of that, the elements "on the left" to which Y' is related must also be disjoint from X'.

Conjugate functions are related to another class of near-reciprocals between Boolean algebras, namely *Galois connections*; in fact every conjugate pair induces a Galois connection [24]. This relates the present setting to previous work on program slicing with Galois connections [28,29,33].

Definition 5 (Galois connection). *Suppose A, B are partial orders, then monotone functions $f : A \to B$ and $g : B \to A$ form a Galois connection iff*

$$f(x) \leq y \iff x \leq g(y)$$

Proposition 1. *Suppose functions $f : A \to B$ and $g : B \to A$ between Boolean algebras. The following statements are equivalent:*

1. *f and g form a conjugate pair*
2. *f and g° form a Galois connection*

It is also useful (both for performance reasons and as a user feature) to consider the *De Morgan duals* of $\triangledown$ and $\triangle$, which we write as $\blacktriangle$ and $\blacktriangledown$; these also form a conjugate pair.

Definition 6 (De Morgan Dual). *Suppose a function $f : A \to B$ between Boolean algebras with $\neg_A$ and $\neg_B$ the negation operators of A and B. Define the De Morgan Dual $f^\circ : A \to B$ of f as:*

$$f^\circ := \neg_B \circ f \circ \neg_A$$

Definition 7 (Dual Image and Preimage Functions for a Relation). *For relations $R \subseteq X \times Y$, define $\blacktriangle_R : \mathbb{P}(X) \to \mathbb{P}(Y)$ and $\blacktriangledown_R : \mathbb{P}(Y) \to \mathbb{P}(X)$ as:*

1. $\blacktriangle_R(X') := \{y \in Y \mid \nexists x \in X \setminus X'.(x,y) \in R\}$ *(dual image)*
2. $\blacktriangledown_R(Y') := \{x \in X \mid \nexists y \in Y \setminus Y'.(x,y) \in R\}$ *(dual preimage)*

Bearing in mind that $\neg$ for $\mathbb{P}(X)$ is just relative complement $X \setminus \cdot$, it is easy to show that these are indeed the intended De Morgan duals.

Lemma 2 (Duality of image and preimage functions).
1. $\triangle_R^\circ = \blacktriangle_R$
2. $\nabla_R^\circ = \blacktriangledown_R$

If $\triangle_R(X')$ picks out the outputs that the elements of X' are *necessary* for, $\blacktriangle_R(X')$ picks out the outputs that the elements of X are *sufficient* for. $\blacktriangledown_R(Y')$ picks out the inputs that are needed *only* by elements of Y'.

4.2 ∇_G and $\triangle_G$ for Dependence Graphs

Reachability in G induces a relation just between *sources* and *sinks*, which we call the *IO* relation of G. We now extend ∇_R and $\triangle_R$ and their duals to a dependence graph G, via its IO relation.

Definition 8 (Sources and sinks). *For a graph $G = (V, E)$, write $\mathsf{S}(G)$ for the sources of G (i.e. those vertices with no in-edges) and $\mathsf{T}(G)$ for the sinks of G (those with no out-edges).*

Definition 9 (Reachability relation). *Define the reachability relation for a graph $G = (V, E)$ to be the reflexive transitive closure of E.*

Definition 10 (IO relation). *For any dependence graph G with reachability relation R, define the IO relation of G to be $R \cap (\mathsf{S}(G) \times \mathsf{T}(G))$.*

The IO relation specifies how specific inputs (sources) are demanded by specific outputs (sinks); thus we interpret $(x, y) \in R$ as "x is *demanded by* y". Clearly the IO relation of G is the converse of the IO relation of G^{-1}. The set of inputs that some outputs Y *demand*, $\nabla_G(Y)$, is simply the subset of the inputs of G reachable from Y (by traversing the graph in its opposite direction). Conversely, the set of outputs *demanded by* some inputs X, $\triangle_G(X)$, is simply the subset of the outputs of G reachable from X.

Definition 11 (∇_G and $\triangle_G$ for a dependence graph). *For a graph G with IO relation R, define:*

1. $\nabla_G := \nabla_R : \mathbb{P}(\mathsf{T}(G)) \to \mathbb{P}(\mathsf{S}(G))$ *(demands)*
2. $\triangle_G := \triangle_R : \mathbb{P}(\mathsf{S}(G)) \to \mathbb{P}(\mathsf{T}(G))$ *(demanded by)*

4.3   Computing $\triangledown_G$, $\triangle_G$, $\blacktriangle_G$ and $\blacktriangledown_G$ for Dependence Graphs

We now show how to compute e$\triangledown_G$, $\triangle_G$, $\blacktriangle_G$ and $\blacktriangledown_G$ for a dependence graph G, via an intermediate graph slice which we then restrict to its IO relation. First some graph notation:

Definition 12 (In-edges and out-edges). *For a graph $G = (V, E)$ and vertex $\alpha \in V$, write* $\mathsf{inE}_G(\alpha)$ *for the in-edges of α in G and* $\mathsf{outE}_G(\alpha)$ *for its out-edges.*

Definition 13 (Opposite graph). *For a graph G define the* opposite *graph* $G^{-1} := (V, E^{-1})$ *where* $\cdot^{-1}$ *denotes relational converse.*

With the trace-based approaches mentioned in § 1, one can use a given algorithm to implement its De Morgan dual; for example, given a procedure for $\triangle_G$ we can compute $\blacktriangle_G$ by pre- and post-composing with negation [30]. In the dependence graph setting, we can also use a given algorithm to compute its conjugate, e.g., given a procedure for $\triangle_G$, we can compute $\triangledown_G$ simply as $\triangle_{G^{-1}}$.

For efficiency, however, we give direct procedures both for $\triangle_G$ (§ 4.3) and $\blacktriangle_G$ (§ 4.3), which can then be used to derive implementations of the other operators, as shown at the end of this section. Each procedure factors through an auxiliary operation that computes a "slice" of the original graph, i.e. a contiguous subgraph. While it is technically possible to compute the desired image/preimage of the IO relation without creating this intermediate graph, we anticipate use cases which will make use of the graph slice; these are discussed in more detail in § 7. Our implementation makes it easy to flip between G and G^{-1} so we freely make use of both in the algorithms to access out-neighbours and in-neighbours.

Direct algorithm for $\triangle_G$ (*demanded by*)

Definition 14 (demBy_G). *Figure 10a defines the family of relations* demBy_G *for dependence graph G.*

For a dependence graph G and inputs $X \subseteq \mathsf{S}(G)$, the judgement $X \mathrel{\mathsf{demBy}_G} Y$ says that X is demanded by $Y \subseteq \mathsf{T}(G)$. The algorithm defers to an auxiliary operation demByV, which takes a (partial) graph slice $H \subseteq G$, initially containing only the original input vertices X and no edges, and which proceeds as follows. If there is a sink of H that still has outgoing edges in G, then the targets of those edges are reachable from the vertices of H, and so we must add them to H and recurse (extend). If $\mathsf{T}(H) \subseteq \mathsf{T}(G)$, then there are no unexplored nodes in G that are reachable from H, and so we terminate with the current state of H (done). We note that it is enough to consider the sinks of H, since we move every outgoing edge of a vertex from G to H all at once. When demByV is done, demBy_G returns the sinks $T(H)$ from the final graph slice H, representing the outputs that the original inputs are demanded by.

Proposition 2 (demBy_G Computes $\triangle_G$). *For any dependence graph G, any $X \subseteq \mathsf{S}(G)$ and any $Y \subseteq \mathsf{T}(G)$ we have*

$$X \mathrel{\mathsf{demBy}_G} Y \iff \triangle_G(X) = Y$$

Proof. See the supplementary material.

$\boxed{X \text{ demBy}_G Y}$

$$\frac{(X, \varnothing), G \text{ demByV } H}{X \text{ demBy}_G \text{ T}(H)} \; X \subseteq \text{S}(G)$$

$\boxed{H, G \text{ demByV } H'}$

done
$$\frac{}{H, G \text{ demByV } H} \; \text{T}(H) \subseteq \text{T}(G)$$

extend
$$\frac{H \cup E, G \setminus_E E \text{ demByV } H'}{H, G \text{ demByV } H'} \; \alpha \in \text{T}(H) \wedge E = \text{outE}_G(\alpha) \neq \varnothing$$

(a) demBy_G algorithm

$\boxed{X \text{ suff}_G U}$

$$\frac{(X, \varnothing), (\varnothing, \varnothing), G \text{ suffE } H}{X \text{ suff}_G \text{ V}(H) \cap \text{T}(G)} \; X \subseteq \text{S}(G)$$

$\boxed{H, P, G \text{ suffE } H'}$

done
$$\frac{}{H, P, G \text{ suffE } H} \; \text{S}(G) \cap \text{V}(P) \subseteq \text{S}(P) \wedge \text{V}(H) \subseteq \text{T}(G)$$

pending
$$\frac{H, P \cup E, G \setminus_E E \text{ suffE } H'}{H, P, G \text{ suffE } H'} \; \alpha \in \text{V}(H) \wedge E = \text{outE}_G(\alpha) \neq \varnothing$$

extend
$$\frac{H \cup E, P \setminus_E E, G \text{ suffE } H'}{H, P, G \text{ suffE } H'} \; \alpha \in \text{S}(G) \wedge E = \text{inE}_P(\alpha) \neq \varnothing$$

(b) suff_G algorithm

Fig. 10: Dual analyses over a dependence graph G

Direct algorithm for $\blacktriangle_G$ (*suffices*)

Definition 15 (suff$_G$). *Figure 10b defines the family of relations* suff$_G$ *for dependence graph G.*

Like demands$_G$, the algorithm suff$_G$ also delegates to an auxiliary operation suffE which builds a slice of G. The operation suffE takes the graph slice H under construction, a "pending" subgraph P of nodes for which we have discovered partial information, and the remaining unexplored graph G, and returns the final graph slice H'. Whenever we have a vertex in H which still has outgoing edges in G, we add those edges and their endpoints to the pending graph P (pending). If a vertex α has no more incoming edges in G, we can then move α and its incoming edges from P to H (extend), as this only happens when we have already moved every ancestor of α into H. If neither scenario is the case, then we terminate with the (potentially incomplete) graph H (done). Once suffE has terminated with H, suff$_G$ returns just the vertices in H that are also sinks in G. If there are no such vertices, it simply means that the input data X was insufficient to compute any of the original program's outputs.

We provide an example of a run of the algorithm in Figure 11. Here, the green vertices and thick edges are in H, the orange vertices and dashed arrows are in P, and the blue vertices and normal arrows are in G. In the figure, steps 2, 3, 5 and 6 correspond to applications of the rule pending, and steps 4 and 7 correspond to applications of the rule extend. After step 7, the run is complete.

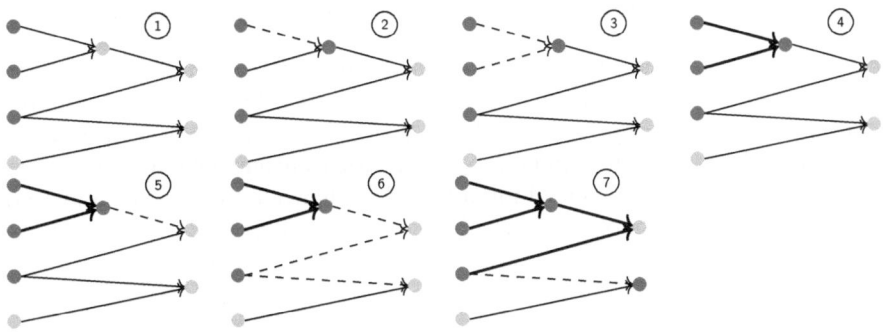

Fig. 11: Run of suff with G and H superimposed on G_0

Proposition 3 (suff$_G$ Computes $\blacktriangle_G$). *For any dependence graph G, any $X \subseteq$ S(G) and any $Y \subseteq$ T(G) we have:*

$$X \text{ suff}_G Y \iff \blacktriangle_g(X) = Y$$

Proof. See the supplementary material.

Derived algorithms Propositions 2 and 3 justify treating demBy_G and suff_G as functions. Using Lemma 2 we can define a direct algorithm for $\triangledown_G$ from demBy_G by simply flipping the graph, and the same can be done to acquire an algorithm for $\blacktriangledown_G$ from suff_G. Using Lemma 2 and Definition 6 we can also define alternative algorithms for all 4 operators using the De Morgan dual construction. These are summarised in the table below.

Abstract operator	Direct algorithm	Alternative algorithm
$\triangle_G$	demBy_G	$\mathsf{suff}_G{}^{\circ}$
$\triangledown_G$	$\mathsf{demBy}_{G^{-1}}$	$\mathsf{suff}_{G^{-1}}{}^{\circ}$
$\blacktriangle_G$	suff_G	$\mathsf{demBy}_G{}^{\circ}$
$\blacktriangledown_G$	$\mathsf{suff}_{G^{-1}}$	$\mathsf{demBy}_{G^{-1}}{}^{\circ}$

In § 5 we contrast the performance of the direct and De Morgan dual implementations of $\triangle_G$, used to implement linked inputs/outputs as shown in § 1.

4.4 $\triangledown\!\triangle_G$ and $\triangle\!\triangledown_G$ for Dependence Graphs

Now we can provide a formal account of the notions of linked inputs and outputs.

Definition 16 (Linked inputs and outputs). *For a dependence graph G let:*

1. $\triangledown\!\triangle_G := \triangledown_G \circ \triangle_G$ *(linked inputs)*
2. $\triangle\!\triangledown_G := \triangle_G \circ \triangledown_G$ *(linked outputs)*

Intuitively, linked outputs and linked inputs are relations of *cognacy* (common ancestry) in G and G^{-1} respectively. For a set of inputs $X \subseteq S(G)$, linked inputs asks "what other inputs are demanded by the outputs which demand X?"; it first finds all outputs $\triangle_G(X)$ that our inputs are demanded by, and then computes the inputs that those outputs demand, i.e. $\triangledown_G(\triangle_G(X'))$. Conversely for a set of outputs $Y \subseteq T(G)$, linked outputs asks "what other outputs demand the inputs that Y demands"; it first finds all inputs $\triangledown_G(Y')$ that our outputs demand, and then computes the outputs that those inputs $\triangledown_G(Y)$ demand, i.e. $\triangle_G(\triangledown_G(Y))$.

5   Evaluation

We now compare two implementations of the dependency-tracking runtime of Fluid, one based on the dependence graph design described in Sections 3 and 4 and one based on the main alternative style of implementation, namely a bidirectional interpreter with two components: a forward evaluator which performs a forwards analysis and produces an execution trace, and a backward evaluator which consumes the execution trace and performs a backwards analysis [33,32,30]. Other Fluid system components were shared by the two implementations, including the parser, desugaring and visualisation layers, and libraries.

For a language implementor, the main benefit of our graph approach is that it removes the need to implement a bidirectional interpreter. Otherwise, changing the language requires modifying each direction of the interpreter in a manner that maintains bidirectionality — a considerable effort. In our approach the graph algorithms for computing ∇_G and $\triangle_G$ (Figure 10) are language-agnostic and only have to be defined once.

For a user, our hypothesis is that our approach has better performance than trace-based techniques; to test this, we evaluated a number of benchmark programs taking examples from data analysis and data visualisation (§ 5 below). Because interactive performance plays a critical role for the user, we measured the following:

- Q1: Overhead of building a dependence graph versus building a trace;
- Q2: Performance of computing *demands* over a graph vs. a trace;
- Q3: Performance of various implementations of *demanded by*: trace-based, graph-based using demands, and graph-based using the dual of suff.

We assessed performance according to the guidelines proposed by Nielsen [26]:

- 100ms: limit for an interaction feeling *instantaneous*;
- 1000ms: limit for a user's train of thought to remain uninterrupted, although they may perceive a delay;
- 10000ms: limit to keep a user's attention on the system.

Ideally, interactive queries (Q2 and Q3) would stay as close as possible to the *instantaneous* category, and the time taken to evaluate programs (Q1) would stay within the limit for keeping a user's attention. Experiments were timed on an Intel Core i7-10850H 2.70GHz with 16Gb of RAM, using Chrome 121.0.6261.69 and JavaScript runtime V8 12.2.281.16. We used PureScript as the host language.

Choice of examples We collected some canonical examples from data visualization and analytics. First, we considered matrix convolution. Given that different kernels give rise to subtly different dependency structures, we implemented three different kernels (**edge-detect, emboss, gaussian**, 31 lines of code (LOC) each). Second, we developed a full-featured graphics library based on SVG that demonstrates the performance on bespoke visualisation code (**grouped-bar-chart**, 140 LOC, **line-chart**, 143 LOC, **stacked-bar-chart**, 136 LOC). Finally, we tested two examples that use a D3.js front end for visualisation (**stacked-bar-scatter-plot**, 26 LOC, and **bar-chart-line-chart**, 38 LOC), the same front end used in Figures 2 and 4. The code for our benchmarks is given in the supplementary material.

In the experiments, each benchmark is run 10 times, and we report the mean runtime and standard deviation (in parentheses, coloured grey). Runtimes are reported in milliseconds, to 1 decimal place. When we refer to *speedup* or *slowdown* in reference to a pair of implementations, we mean the ratio of average runtimes for that benchmark.

Q1: Overhead of graph construction vs. trace construction Table 1 compares the average time taken to evaluate a program in the graph approach

(**G-Eval**) with the time taken in the trace-based approach (**T-Eval**). The ratio of graph-based to trace-based time is shown in the third column (**Eval-Slowdown**). Since building the graph involves maintaining a heap of allocated vertices, and we also build the inverse graph at the same time, we expect a larger overhead for the graph approach. As expected, we do see a higher overhead, being from 2.5x to 15x slower than their trace-based counterparts. For both approaches, program evaluation always stays within the limit to keep a user's attention on the system (10000ms).

Table 1: Average Evaluation Time for Traces vs. Graphs (ms, 1 decimal place)

	T-Eval	G-Eval	Eval-Slowdown
edge-detect	732.4 ($\pm$44.7)	2150.1 ($\pm$109.9)	2.94
emboss	633.4 ($\pm$42.3)	1718.5 ($\pm$30.9)	2.71
gaussian	619.9 ($\pm$48.7)	1714.3 ($\pm$42.5)	2.77
bar-chart-line-chart	2336.9 ($\pm$51.9)	5775.7 ($\pm$131.6)	2.47
stacked-bar-scatter-plot	1212.9 ($\pm$46.2)	7548.9 ($\pm$476.4)	6.22
grouped-bar-chart	89.3 ($\pm$8.4)	1341.6 ($\pm$132.4)	15.03
line-chart	130.0 ($\pm$10.5)	1131.0 ($\pm$14.4)	8.70
stacked-bar-chart	55.9 ($\pm$5.6)	783.0 ($\pm$15.4)	14.00

Q2: Graph-based demands vs. trace-based demands In Table 2, columns **T-Demands** and **G-Demands** show the average times taken to compute *demands* with the trace and graph approaches, respectively. The ratio of graph-based to trace-based performance is in the last column, **Bwd-Speedup**. We compute *demands* over the graph by running the algorithm for *demBy* from Figure 10a over the opposite graph. In these examples, we keep our query selections small, generally only selecting one or two output nodes.

Overall, we observe a significant speedup in the performance of *demands* using the graph approach, from 33x speedup for the **stacked-bar-chart**, to more than 80x for **gaussian**. In particular, every graph-based *demands* query is within the "instantaneous" category, whilst all but two of the examples using the trace approach are in the "noticable delay" category. We attribute this speedup to a couple of factors. First, in the trace approach, each backwards query involves rewinding the entire execution, regardless of whether all of the trace is relevant; graph queries only traverse the relevant parts of the graph. Second, in the trace approach, backwards evaluation makes frequent use of lattice join ($\vee$) to combine slicing information from different branches of the computation; joining closure slices in particular has the potential to be expensive because closures contain environments (which in turn contain closures, and so on). The graph approach lends itself to a more imperative implementation style, where demand information accrues against vertices as the backwards analysis proceeds, with no separate join steps.

Table 2: Trace-Based vs. Graph-Based Implementations of Demands (ms, 1 d.p.)

	T-Demands		G-Demands		Bwd-Speedup
edge-detect	61.0	(± 7.9)	11.9	(± 0.8)	50.84
emboss	504.3	(± 9.1)	8.0	(± 0.7)	63.28
gaussian	511.1	(± 8.3)	6.3	(± 0.8)	81.38
bar-chart-line-chart	1274.0	(± 24.8)	18.5	(± 0.6)	68.86
stacked-bar-scatter-plot	616.6	(± 35.4)	14.0	(± 1.7)	44.14
grouped-bar-chart	74.4	(± 6.2)	1.3	(± 0.3)	55.96
line-chart	114.1	(± 4.8)	1.8	(± 0.2)	65.22
stacked-bar-chart	45.1	(± 5.4)	1.3	(± 0.4)	33.62

Q3: Demanded By Table 3 contrasts average times for the trace implementation of *demanded by* (**T-DemBy**) with the graph-based algorithm from Figure 10a (**G-DemBy**) and the graph-based approach using using the De Morgan dual of the suff algorithm from Figure 10b (**G-DemBy-Suff**). **S** is the speedup of **G-DemBy** compared to **T-DemBy**, and **S'** is the speedup of **G-DemBy-Suff** compared to **T-DemBy**. Again, because our selections are small, the dual of suff, which traverses a "complement" subgraph, potentially explores a much larger subgraph than demBy. For all benchmarks, the graph demBy algorithm in Figure 10a performs better than the other two approaches, with five benchmarks running instantaneously, as opposed to only two for the trace-based approach.

Table 3: Trace-Based vs. Graph-Based Implementations of Demanded By (ms, 1 d.p.) where $S = T\text{-}DemBy/G\text{-}DemBy$ and $S' = T\text{-}DemBy/G\text{-}DemBy\text{-}Suff$

	T-DemBy	G-DemBy	S	G-DemBy-Suff	S'
edge-detect	696.9 (± 14.9)	265.8 (± 19.1)	2.62	664.3 (± 36.3)	1.05
emboss	603.0 (± 18.0)	244.9 (± 16.3)	2.46	481.5 (± 16.4)	1.25
gaussian	596.8 (± 11.6)	224.3 (± 17.4)	2.66	474.0 (± 12.0)	1.26
bar-chart-line-chart	2079.0 (± 97.2)	19.1 (± 1.2)	108.73	2360.2 (± 48.0)	0.88
stacked-bar-scatter-plot	1004.1 (± 72.7)	31.3 (± 1.3)	32.07	11598.9 (± 778.8)	0.09
grouped-bar-chart	82.4 (± 9.4)	5.0 (± 0.6)	16.47	2146.5 (± 158.0)	0.04
line-chart	113.4 (± 4.9)	2.3 (± 0.5)	50.41	900.3 (± 15.3)	0.13
stacked-bar-chart	42.6 (± 1.9)	3.2 (± 1.0)	13.18	1271.1 (± 131.7)	0.03

Discussion When comparing the graph and trace approaches, the main shortcoming of the graph approach is the increased cost of evaluating a program to a graph versus a trace (*Q1*). We propose that this overhead is worth paying; the graph is only constructed once, and evaluation time still remains within the limit for keeping the user's attention. More importantly, the fast response times for *demands* and *demanded by* compared to the trace approach (Q2 and Q3) are good enough for instantaneous queries. Also notable (for Q3), is the performance of **G-DemBy-Suff**, which uses the dual of the suff algorithm, and which tends to perform significantly worse than **G-DemBy**. This can perhaps be explained by the fact that our selections are small: since the selection is complemented, and the portion of the graph that the algorithm traverses is in general much larger. It is also plausible that some of this disparity can be explained by suff requiring more bookkeeping than demBy.

6   Related work

6.1   Data Provenance

Provenance research has a long history, ranging from scientific workflow provenance [9,12] to more fine-grained database techniques like *where* provenance [8], with comparatively less emphasis on general-purpose languages. Dietrich et al. [14] track both value and control dependencies in recursive database queries and user-defined functions by rewriting SQL queries to provenance-tracking counterparts; Fehrenbach and Cheney [16] explore provenance for language-integrated query, extending the SQL fragment of the multi-tier language Links [11] with provenance tracking. For structured outputs like visualisations, the most closely related lines of work are Psallidas and Wu [32] for relational languages, and Perera et al. [30] for general-purpose languages. These authors all emphasise the importance of *cognacy*, i.e. common ancestry, albeit not in the context of dependence graphs, showing how to "link" outputs by tracing back from an output selection to a data selection and then forward to another output selection. This seems to be largely unstudied in the provenance literature, despite its importance in data visualisation.

6.2   Dynamic Dependence Graphs

Dynamic dependence graphs have been used extensively for program slicing [18,19], optimisation [17], incremental computation [1] and fault localisation [37]. Most of these applications are for imperative languages, where it is useful distinguish between control and data edges; because Fluid is pure, we use somewhat simpler dependence graphs with a single kind of edge. However different kinds of edge are likely to be needed for future applications (§ 7). The main contribution of our work to the dependence graph paradigm are cognacy operators which allow the identification of minimally related sets of inputs ($\nabla\triangle$) and minimally related sets of outputs ($\triangle\nabla$), in a formal setting where we show these operators to be self-conjugate and related to Galois connections.

6.3   Galois Slicing

Although we do not consider program slices here, our formal setting is closely related to bidirectional program slicing techniques based on Galois connections [28,29,33]. In these works, the forward and backward directions of the interpreter correspond to our *sufficiency* (▲) and *demands* (▽) queries. Perera et al. [30] extended this approach to a setting where slices have complements, and showed how composing the backward analysis with the De Morgan dual of the forwards analysis can be used to implement linked brushing. As well as requiring a bidirectional interpreter, the main difficulty with this approach has been achieving interactive performance. Implementations have relied on a sequential execution trace, used in the forwards direction to "replay" the computation, propagating sufficiency information from inputs to outputs, and in the backwards direction to "rewind" the computation, propagating demand from outputs to inputs. As discussed in § 5, and in contrast to the graph approach presented here, this approach is overly sequential and unable to exploit the independence of some subcomputations that makes slicing useful in the first place.

6.4   Linked Visualisations

The connection between visual selection (such as clicking or lassoing) and data "selection" has been explored in the visualisation literature, leading to various techniques for inverting selections in visual space to obtain selections in the underlying data [27,20]. There is also a literature on linked brushing [4,23] as a way of connecting output selections via mediating data selections. Although this has long been recognised as an important visual tool, with Roberts and Wright [34] arguing it should be ubiquitous, there is relatively little work on general-purpose infrastructure to support it. For example, Reactive Vega [35] provides a rich set of interactivity features to support linked brushing, but no mechanism for automatically propagating selections through arbitrary intervening queries; Glue [3] is a powerful Python library for building linked visualisations for scientific applications, but the developer is responsible for specifying the relationships between data sets that unpin the linking. More infrastructural approaches to linked brushing [27,23,32], similar in spirit to our work, have been developed mainly for relational languages. Relational languages are a promising direction in data visualisation, but general-purpose languages continue to be widely used too, so it is important to support linked brushing in this context as well.

6.5   Transparent Research Outputs

Dragicevic et al. [15] also develop techniques for transparent research outputs, via explorable multiverse analysis, exposing *analysis parameters*, the methodological choices made in designing a data analysis. Since different methodological choices will impact the conclusions of the analysis, they expose these choices to users and allow them to switch between different choices and observe the impact on the results. Our work is potentially complementary: we are concerned with surfacing the dependencies that arise within a specific choice of analysis parameters, whereas multiverse analyses are about exploring how things change under different choices. It might be useful to package our dependency analysis as part of such a multiverse analysis, allowing the user to observe the different dependency structures that arise from different methodological decisions.

7   Conclusion and Future Work

Visualisations are an essential tool for communicating science and other data-driven claims, but can be hard to make sense of and trust. Visualisations and other outputs that are "transparent" – that can reveal to an interested reader how they are related to data – are more informative and trustworthy but are also more difficult to produce. In this paper, we introduced a novel bidirectional program analysis framework for a general-purpose programming language that makes it easier to create transparent visualisations by shifting much of the burden to the language runtime. Relative to prior work based on execution traces and bidirectional interpreters, our approach also makes life easier for the language implementor, by decomposing the system into a single evaluator that builds a dependence graph, and a pair of language-agnostic bidirectional graph algorithms. We also showed an overall performance improvement for provenance queries, at the cost of some overhead in building the dependence graph.

We identify two important directions for future work. First, the dependency relation captured by the dependence graph semantics in § 3 omits certain intuitively plausible edges, such as the *projection* edge that one might expect to exist between a record and the value of a contained field as a consequence of evaluating a field access expression $e.x$. On the other hand, recording *all* structural dependencies of this nature would significantly bloat the dependence graph with information that is only relevant in certain contexts (for example, when one is specifically concerned with where a value came from, rather than how it was computed). We would like to develop a more semantically justified dependence graph, along with a proof that the graph is "complete" in some formal sense (cf. the *dependency correctness* notion of Cheney et al. [10]), but anticipate that making this richer graph practical will require distinguishing different kinds of query (e.g. "how" vs. "where from") for use in different contexts.

Second, although the algorithms presented in § 4 compute graph slices as an interim structure, the internal nodes of the graph slices are discarded. This is adequate for the use cases in § 2, which only concern "extensional" (IO) transparency. However, intensional information would be useful too: for example, highlighting a point in the moving average in Figure 2 could show not only that 3 emissions inputs were relevant, but that those values were summed and divided by 3. This would connect to work on *executable program slicing* [18]. One challenge here is managing the size and complexity of intensional explanations; again Cheney et al. [10] offer inspiration. Their idea of *expression provenance* may be a way of presenting pared-back but still informative explanations (for example, showing the tree of primitive arithmetic operations that computed a value but omitting user-defined function calls and branches). And the user may only want intensional information for certain subcomputations, in which case graph transformations which elide internal nodes but preserve IO connectivity, such as the Y-Δ transform [38], may also have a role to play.

Acknowledgments This research received support through Schmidt Sciences, LLC via the Institute of Computing for Climate Science (Perera and Orchard).

References

1. Acar, U.A., Blelloch, G.E., Harper, R.: Adaptive functional programming. In: POPL '02: Proceedings of the 29th ACM SIGPLAN-SIGACT Symposium on Principles of Programming Languages. pp. 247–259. ACM Press, New York, NY, USA (2002). https://doi.org/10.1145/503272.503296
2. Agrawal, H., Horgan, J.R.: Dynamic program slicing. In: PLDI '90: Proceedings of the ACM SIGPLAN 1990 Conference on Programming Language Design and Implementation. pp. 246–256. ACM, New York, NY, USA (1990). https://doi.org/10.1145/93542.93576
3. Beaumont, C., Robitaille, T., Goodman, A., Borkin, M.: Multidimensional data exploration with glue. In: van der Walt, S., Millman, J., Huff, K. (eds.) Proceedings of the 12th Python in Science Conference. pp. 8 – 12 (2013). https://doi.org/10.25080/Majora-8b375195-002
4. Becker, R.A., Cleveland, W.S.: Brushing scatterplots. Technometrics **29**(2), 127–142 (May 1987). https://doi.org/10.1080/00401706.1987.10488204
5. Bond, J., David, C., Nguyen, M., Orchard, M., Perera, R.: Fluid. https://zenodo.org/records/14637654 (2025)
6. Bremer, N., Ranzijn, M.: Urbanization in east asia between 2000 and 2010. http://nbremer.github.io/urbanization/ (2015)
7. Buja, A., McDonald, J.A., Michalak, J., Stuetzle, W.: Interactive data visualization using focusing and linking. In: Proceedings of Visualization '91. pp. 156–163 (Oct 1991). https://doi.org/10.1109/VISUAL.1991.175794
8. Buneman, P., Khanna, S., Tan, W.C.: Why and where: A characterization of data provenance. In: Proceedings of the 8th International Conference on Database Theory. pp. 316–330. ICDT '01, Springer-Verlag, London, UK (2001)
9. Callahan, S.P., Freire, J., Santos, E., Scheidegger, C.E., Silva, C.T., Vo, H.T.: VisTrails: Visualization meets data management. In: Proceedings of the ACM SIGMOD International Conference on Management of Data. pp. 745–747 (2006). https://doi.org/10.1145/1142473.1142574
10. Cheney, J., Ahmed, A., Acar, U.A.: Provenance as dependency analysis. Mathematical Structures in Computer Science **21**(6), 1301–1337 (2011)
11. Cooper, E., Lindley, S., Wadler, P., Yallop, J.: Links: web programming without tiers. In: Proceedings of the 5th International Conference on Formal methods for Components and Objects. pp. 266–296. FMCO'06, Springer-Verlag, Berlin, Heidelberg (2007)
12. Davidson, S.B., Freire, J.: Provenance and scientific workflows: challenges and opportunities. In: Proceedings of the 2008 ACM SIGMOD International Conference on Management of Data. pp. 1345–1350. SIGMOD '08, ACM, New York, NY, USA (2008). https://doi.org/10.1145/1376616.1376772
13. DerSimonian, R., Laird, N.: Meta-analysis in clinical trials. Control Clin Trials **7**(3), 177–88 (Sep 1986). https://doi.org/10.1016/0197-2456(86)90046-2
14. Dietrich, B., Müller, T., Grust, T.: Data provenance for recursive sql queries. In: Proceedings of the 14th International Workshop on the Theory and Practice of Provenance. TaPP '22, Association for Computing Machinery, New York, NY, USA (2022). https://doi.org/10.1145/3530800.3534536, https://doi.org/10.1145/3530800.3534536
15. Dragicevic, P., Jansen, Y., Sarma, A., Kay, M., Chevalier, F.: Increasing the transparency of research papers with explorable multiverse analyses. In: CHI 2019 - The ACM CHI Conference on Human Factors in Computing Systems. Glasgow, United Kingdom (May 2019). https://doi.org/10.1145/3290605.3300295

16. Fehrenbach, S., Cheney, J.: Language-integrated provenance by trace analysis. In: Proceedings of the 17th ACM SIGPLAN International Symposium on Database Programming Languages. p. 74–84. DBPL 2019, Association for Computing Machinery, New York, NY, USA (2019). https://doi.org/10.1145/3315507.3330198, https://doi.org/10.1145/3315507.3330198

17. Ferrante, J., Ottenstein, K.J., Warren, J.D.: The program dependence graph and its use in optimization. ACM Trans. Program. Lang. Syst. **9**(3), 319–349 (jul 1987). https://doi.org/10.1145/24039.24041

18. Field, J., Tip, F.: Dynamic dependence in term rewriting systems and its application to program slicing. Information and Software Technology **40**(11–12), 609–636 (November/December 1998)

19. Hammer, C., Grimme, M., Krinke, J.: Dynamic path conditions in dependence graphs. pp. 58–67 (01 2006). https://doi.org/10.1145/1111542.1111552

20. Heer, J., Agrawala, M., Willett, W.: Generalized selection via interactive query relaxation. In: ACM Human Factors in Computing Systems (CHI). pp. 959–968 (2008)

21. Hinze, R.: Generalizing generalized tries. Journal of Functional Programming **10**(4), 327–351 (2000). https://doi.org/10.1017/S0956796800003713

22. Jonsson, B., Tarski, A.: Boolean algebras with operators. part i. American Journal of Mathematics **73**(4), 891–939 (1951), http://www.jstor.org/stable/2372123

23. Livny, M., Ramakrishnan, R., Beyer, K., Chen, G., Donjerkovic, D., Lawande, S., Myllymaki, J., Wenger, K.: Devise: integrated querying and visual exploration of large datasets. SIGMOD Rec. **26**(2), 301–312 (jun 1997). https://doi.org/10.1145/253262.253335, https://doi.org/10.1145/253262.253335

24. Menni, M., Smith, C.: Modes of adjointness. Journal of Philosophical Logic **43**(2/3), 365–391 (2014), http://www.jstor.org/stable/24564097

25. Murphy, J., Sexton, D., Barnett, D., Jones, G., Webb, M., Collins, M., Stainforth, D.: Quantification of modelling uncertainties in a large ensemble of climate change simulations. Nature **430**, 768–72 (09 2004). https://doi.org/10.1038/nature02771

26. Nielsen, J.: Usability Engineering. Morgan Kaufmann Publishers Inc., San Francisco, CA, USA (1994)

27. North, C., Shneiderman, B.: Snap-together visualization: a user interface for coordinating visualizations via relational schemata. In: Proceedings of the Working Conference on Advanced Visual Interfaces. p. 128–135. AVI '00, Association for Computing Machinery, New York, NY, USA (2000). https://doi.org/10.1145/345513.345282

28. Perera, R., Acar, U.A., Cheney, J., Levy, P.B.: Functional programs that explain their work. In: Proceedings of the 17th ACM SIGPLAN International Conference on Functional Programming. pp. 365–376. ICFP '12, ACM, New York, NY, USA (2012). https://doi.org/10.1145/2364527.2364579

29. Perera, R., Garg, D., Cheney, J.: Causally consistent dynamic slicing. In: Desharnais, J., Jagadeesan, R. (eds.) Concurrency Theory, 27th International Conference, CONCUR '16. Leibniz International Proceedings in Informatics (LIPIcs), Schloss Dagstuhl–Leibniz-Zentrum für Informatik, Dagstuhl, Germany (2016). https://doi.org/10.4230/LIPIcs.CONCUR.2016.18

30. Perera, R., Nguyen, M., Petricek, T., Wang, M.: Linked visualisations via galois dependencies. Proc. ACM Program. Lang. **6**(POPL) (2022). https://doi.org/10.1145/3498668

31. Peyton Jones, S., Eisenberg, R., Graf, S.: Triemaps that match. Tech. rep. (July 2022), https://simon.peytonjones.org/triemaps-that-match/

32. Psallidas, F., Wu, E.: Smoke: fine-grained lineage at interactive speed. Proc. VLDB Endow. **11**(6), 719–732 (feb 2018). https://doi.org/10.14778/3199517.3199522, https://doi.org/10.14778/3199517.3199522

33. Ricciotti, W., Stolarek, J., Perera, R., Cheney, J.: Imperative functional programs that explain their work. Proceedings of the ACM on Programming Languages **1**(ICFP), 14:1–14:28 (2017). https://doi.org/10.1145/3110258

34. Roberts, J.C., Wright, M.A.E.: Towards ubiquitous brushing for information visualization. In: Tenth International Conference on Information Visualisation (IV'06). pp. 151–156 (July 2006). https://doi.org/10.1109/IV.2006.113

35. Satyanarayan, A., Moritz, D., Wongsuphasawat, K., Heer, J.: Vega-Lite: A grammar of interactive graphics. IEEE Trans. Visualization & Comp. Graphics (Proc. InfoVis) (2017)

36. Selinger, P.G., Astrahan, M.M., Chamberlin, D.D., Lorie, R.A., Price, T.G.: Access path selection in a relational database management system. In: Proceedings of the 1979 ACM SIGMOD International Conference on Management of Data. p. 23–34. SIGMOD '79, Association for Computing Machinery, New York, NY, USA (1979). https://doi.org/10.1145/582095.582099, https://doi.org/10.1145/582095.582099

37. Soremekun, E., Kirschner, L., Böhme, M., Zeller, A.: Locating faults with program slicing: an empirical analysis. Empirical Software Engineering **26**(3), 51 (Apr 2021). https://doi.org/10.1007/s10664-020-09931-7

38. Truemper, K.: On the delta-wye reduction for planar graphs. Journal of Graph Theory **13**(2), 141–148 (1989). https://doi.org/https://doi.org/10.1002/jgt.3190130202

An abstract, certified account of operational game semantics

Peio Borthelle[1]([✉])([iD]), Tom Hirschowitz[1], Guilhem Jaber[2]([iD]),
and Yannick Zakowski[3]

[1] Université Savoie Mont Blanc, CNRS, LAMA, 73000 Chambéry, France
{peio.borthelle,tom.hirschowitz}@univ-smb.fr
[2] Nantes Université, LS2N, Nantes, France
guilhem.jaber@inria.fr
[3] ENS de Lyon, INRIA, CNRS, Lyon 1, LIP, Lyon, France
yannick.zakowski@inria.fr

Abstract. Operational game semantics (OGS) is a method for interpreting programs as strategies in suitable games, or more precisely as
labelled transition systems over suitable games, in the sense of Levy
and Staton. Such an interpretation is called sound when, for any two
given programs, weak bisimilarity of associated strategies entails contextual equivalence. OGS has been applied to a variety of languages, with
rather tedious soundness proofs.
In this paper, we contribute to the unification and mechanisation of
OGS. Indeed, we propose an abstract notion of language with evaluator,
for which we construct a generic OGS interpretation, which we prove
sound. Our framework covers a variety of simply-typed and untyped
lambda-calculi with various evaluation strategies. These calculi notably
feature recursive definitions, first-class continuations, and a wide variety
of datatypes. All constructions and proofs are entirely mechanised in the
Coq proof assistant.

1 Introduction

Normal form bisimulation is a technique for proving contextual equivalence of
programs in various λ-calculi. Although it is generally finer than contextual
equivalence, its practical value resides in the fact that it is often easier to establish on concrete examples than other such techniques, such as applicative or
environmental bisimulation.

Let us briefly explain why. All three techniques proceed by defining a notion
of label, an interpretation of programs as labelled transition systems (LTSs), and
then comparing the interpretations of programs w.r.t. weak bisimilarity. However, the involved labels are very different. Indeed, applicative or environmental
labels may contain arbitrary values, while normal form labels are restricted to
so-called *ultimate patterns*. This means that they may be, e.g., tuples or elements of sum types, but cannot contain λ-abstractions. In a typed setting, in
particular, all terms of functional type contained in any ultimate pattern must
be variables. Normal form labels thus contain a very limited class of terms.

V. Vafeiadis (Ed.): ESOP 2025, LNCS 15694, pp. 172–199, 2025.
https://doi.org/10.1007/978-3-031-91118-7_7

In order for it to be useful, normal form bisimulation should be *sound*, i.e., at least as fine as contextual equivalence. One standard method for proving soundness goes through an intermediate LTS model, with labels similar to the normal form ones, but a different interpretation, called *operational game semantics* [20, 22] (OGS). This induces a different equivalence, say *operational game bisimulation*. One then proves that normal form bisimulation is at least as fine as operational game bisimulation, which is in turn at least as fine as contextual equivalence. Although the first step is mostly straightforward, the second one is difficult, notably because it involves

- extending the OGS interpretation to suitable contexts, and
- soundly reflecting the syntactic operation of context application at the level of LTSs.

Because such soundness proofs are highly non-trivial, it seems useful to design an abstract version, covering as many existing cases as possible, and hopefully also future ones.

A few authors have started to explore this direction. Notably, Levy and Staton [23] offer a high-level categorical framework. More recently, Laird [21] proposes a unifying framework for OGS, in which he proves that operational game bisimilarity is a congruence w.r.t. composition, a standard lemma towards soundness.

Contribution In this work, we go further, and prove a generic soundness result for OGS, mechanised in Coq. We thus contribute to both unification and mechanisation of normal form bisimulation. Our contributions to unification are as follows.

- We introduce an abstract notion of language with evaluator, called a *language machine*, which notably covers several variants of $\overline{\lambda}\mu\tilde{\mu}$-calculus [5,6].
- For any language machine, we construct an OGS model.
- We prove that this model is sound w.r.t. some abstract analogue of contextual equivalence called *substitution equivalence*, under suitable hypotheses.

We furthermore provide a complete Coq mechanisation of our results [2], to emphasise their computational aspects and firmly ground our model in a constructive meta-theory. We favour a traditional, code-less exposition along the paper for clarity. For the interested reader, we however systematically use hyperlinks represented by (🔗) to link definitions and theorems to their mechanised counterpart. The Coq development is inspired by Levy and Staton's transition systems over games [23], and includes notably the following main contributions.

- We present OGS using the well-scoped approach (🔗), in the sense that everything is indexed by typing contexts, and variables are accessed as de Bruijn indices. This contrasts with previous work, which uses nominal style.
- We instantiate our abstract notion of language on several concrete examples: a simply-typed call-by-value λ-calculus with recursion (🔗), a pure untyped call-by-value λ-calculus (🔗), the $\overline{\lambda}\mu\tilde{\mu}_Q$-calculus [5] (🔗) and the polarised System D (🔗) from Downen and Ariola [6].

- We implement (🐭) an indexed variant of the *interaction trees* library [29], which we use to define LTSs coinductively — as opposed to the more traditional, relational definition. However, in this extended abstract, we focus more on the math than on the Coq implementation, so interaction trees do not appear (see Remark 9).
- We introduce (🐭) a new fixed-point combinator over a system of so-called *eventually guarded* equations, whose solution is unique w.r.t. strong bisimilarity. We use this combinator to define composition of OGS LTSs, which is a crucial ingredient to the soundness proof.

Plan Before diving into the details, let us provide a high-level overview of the technical development in §2. In §3, we explain substitution equivalence, our abstract approach to contextual equivalence, on a concrete example language. In §4, we then introduce abstract language machines, construct the OGS model of any language machine, and state our soundness result. Finally, we provide a comparison with the existing literature in §5, and conclude and give some perspectives in §6.

2   Overview

2.1   Axiomatising contextual equivalence as substitution equivalence

Soundness proofs for normal form bisimulation can be established by the following chain of inclusions

$$\text{normal form bisimulation} \subseteq \text{OGS bisimulation}$$
$$\subseteq \text{CIU equivalence}$$
$$= \text{contextual equivalence.}$$

Compared to contextual equivalence, CIU (*Closed Instantiation of Use*) equivalence restricts the shape of contexts that are considered. This idea of restricting contexts while keeping the same discriminating power was first explored by Milner [27]. This idea was then systematized by Mason and Talcott, who introduced CIU equivalence and proved that it coincides with contextual equivalence [24].

In this work, we focus on the middle inclusion:

$$\text{OGS bisimulation} \subseteq \text{CIU equivalence.}$$

In order to propose an abstract version of it, we start by streamlining the usual concrete presentation of languages and CIU equivalence.

Standard CIU equivalence checks that two programs, say p and q, behave the same under any closed instantiation σ of their free variables, in any closed evaluation context E of some fixed, basic type like the booleans[4]:

$$E[p[\sigma]] \cong E[q[\sigma]],$$

---

[4] It is a bit unfortunate that substitution $p[\sigma]$ and context application $E[p]$ have the same notation. It is, however, so common, that we stick to the usual notation.

for some sensible notion $\cong$ of observation of closed boolean programs, usually cotermination on the same boolean.

This involves both substitution and context application, which is a bit clumsy. In order to avoid having two distinct operations in the abstract setting, we switch to a presentation that unifies them. This presentation is based on abstract machines: one evaluates *configurations* rather than programs, where a configuration consists of a pair $\langle p \mid E \rangle$ of a program p and an evaluation context E. In particular, instead of comparing programs p and q as before, we now compare configurations $\langle p \mid \alpha \rangle$ and $\langle q \mid \alpha \rangle$, where α denotes a fresh *context variable*. And now CIU equivalence is merely a matter of substitution: combining any substitution σ with $\alpha \mapsto E$, we get

$$\langle p \mid \alpha \rangle [\sigma, \alpha \mapsto E] = \langle p[\sigma] \mid E \rangle,$$

and similarly for q.

This is presented in detail in §3, but, briefly, it involves a change of typing paradigm: evaluation contexts are typed like continuations, with "negated" types. E.g., if p has type A, then α has type $\neg A$. And in a configuration $\langle p \mid E \rangle$, p and E have opposite types, e.g., $p : A$ and $E : \neg A$. We tend to use $A, B, \ldots$ to range over simple types, and τ to range over the disjoint union of simple types and formally negated simple types.

In this presentation style, evaluation contexts are written inside-out in a stack-like manner, and reduction rules "push" the evaluation context from p to E, and "pop" it when needed, e.g.,

$$\langle e_1 e_2 \mid E \rangle \rightarrow \langle e_1 \mid (\bullet e_2); E \rangle \tag{1}$$

$$\langle \lambda x.e \mid (\bullet a); E \rangle \rightarrow \langle e[x \mapsto a] \mid E \rangle \tag{2}$$

$$\ldots,$$

Here, $(\bullet e_2); E$ is the inside-out analogue of the evaluation context $E[\square\, e_2]$. Thus:

- the first rule is "searching" for the next redex in the function part of the application $e_1 e_2$, storing the argument part in the evaluation context, while
- in the second rule, the configuration $\langle \lambda x.e \mid (\bullet a); E \rangle$ represents $E[(\lambda x.e)\, a]$, so the rule is like a β-reduction in context E.

In conclusion: in the presentation based on abstract machines, CIU equivalence becomes *substitution equivalence*, which equates configurations c and d when $c[\sigma] \cong d[\sigma]$ for all closed substitutions σ, where $\cong$ denotes some suitable, yet straightforward notion of equivalence on closed configurations.

2.2 Axiomatising evaluation, a.k.a. normal forms as triples

Our next step is to analyse how OGS exploits evaluation, and then abstract over it.

To start with, let us consider a configuration c that gets stuck on a function call $f\,v$, where f is a variable and v is some value, say of the form $\lambda x.p$. In the abstract machine presentation, this means c reduces to

$$\langle f \mid (\bullet v); E\rangle, \tag{3}$$

for some evaluation context E. The compound evaluation context $(\bullet v); E$ means that, once f is evaluated, it should be applied to v, the result of which should be fed to E.

In such a situation, OGS splits the stuck configuration (3) into

- a *head variable*, here f,
- a first-order approximation of the evaluation context, which we will call the *observation*[5], and
- a substitution called a *filling*.

In this case, assuming v has some functional type $A_1 \to A_2$, the observation, say o, is $\langle \square \mid (\bullet x); \beta\rangle$, for fresh variables x and β, and the filling, say γ, is the assignment

$$[x \mapsto v, \beta \mapsto E].$$

In particular, the stuck configuration $\langle f \mid (\bullet v); E\rangle$ may be recovered as $(f.o)[\gamma]$, where

- $f.o$ denotes the result of filling the hole in o with f, i.e., $\langle f \mid (\bullet x); \beta\rangle$, and
- $X[\gamma]$ denotes capture-avoiding substitution of γ in X.

Terminology 1. *For clarity, we will now explicitly distinguish between the two meanings of "substitution": we continue calling the operation* substitution, *while we call the sequence of values passed as arguments to the operation* assignments.

To fix intuition, here is a table displaying a few examples of normal forms, including the one presented previously. They are given both using standard syntax and in the abstract machine presentation. We also present how they may be split into head variable, observation, and filling:

Standard presentation	Abstract machine	Head	Observation	Filling
v	$\langle v \mid \alpha\rangle$	α	$\langle x \mid \square\rangle$	$x \mapsto v$
$E[f\,v]$	$\langle f \mid (\bullet v); E\rangle$	f	$\langle \square \mid (\bullet x); \alpha\rangle$	$x \mapsto v, \alpha \mapsto E$
$E[\mathbf{proj}_i\,x]$	$\langle x \mid \mathbf{proj}_i; E\rangle$	x	$\langle \square \mid \mathbf{proj}_i; \alpha\rangle$	$\alpha \mapsto E$
$E[\mathbf{if}\,x\,\mathbf{then}\,e_1\,\mathbf{else}\,e_2]$	$\langle x \mid (e_1, e_2); E\rangle$	x	$\langle \square \mid (x_1, x_2); \alpha\rangle$	$x_i \mapsto e_i, \alpha \mapsto E$

- A particular case of a normal form is indeed any value v. In the abstract machine presentation, v must be fed to some context variable α, which we view as the head variable. The observation, here denoted by $\langle x \mid \square\rangle$, means that the observed variable α is fed with some value x, while the filling associates v to x.

---

[5] This is sometimes called an *ultimate pattern*.

- The second row is the previous example.
- In the third row, $\mathbf{proj}_i; E$ is an evaluation context that takes the ith component of the running program and continues with E. The corresponding reduction rule is $\langle (e_1, e_2) \mid \mathbf{proj}_i; E \rangle \to \langle e_i \mid E \rangle$.
- In the fourth example, $(e_1, e_2); E$ is an evaluation context that executes e_1 or e_2 according to whether the running (boolean) program evaluates to true or false. The reduction rules are

$$\langle \mathbf{tt} \mid (e_1, e_2); E \rangle \to \langle e_1 \mid E \rangle \qquad \langle \mathbf{ff} \mid (e_1, e_2); E \rangle \to \langle e_2 \mid E \rangle. \qquad (4)$$

Since our axiomatisation of evaluation is devoted to OGS, it inlines this splitting process. It goes in two steps:

- A *language* on a given, fixed set of types consists of suitably indexed sets of *values, configurations*, and *observations. Fillings* are then defined as suitable assignments from variables to values, and they are assumed to act on values, configurations, and observations – this axiomatises substitution.
- An *evaluator* consists of a suitably indexed family of partial maps from configurations to triples of a (head) variable, an observation, and a filling. Intuitively, any configuration either diverges (which is modelled by partiality), or converges to some triple (f, o, γ). In other words, we model normal forms as triples (f, o, γ).
- Conversely, a *refolding* is a map sending such normal forms back to configurations. Intuitively, this merely maps (f, o, γ) to $f.o[\gamma]$.

A *language machine* is a language equipped with an evaluator and a refolding, satisfying a few coherence axioms (Definition 13). Notably, in order to ensure soundness of OGS, we need to require that evaluation respect substitution, which roughly means that evaluating a substituted configuration $c[\gamma]$ amounts to evaluating c, and, if this converges to some normal form (f, o, δ), evaluating the substituted refolding of $(f.o[\delta])[\gamma]$.

Remark 1. Of course, this definition is informal, notably w.r.t. substitution. In particular, Definition 13 relies on the well-known machinery of substitution monoids and modules over them [9–11, 14, 15].

Remark 2. Indexing here refers to the fact that our axiomatisation is intrinsically typed and scoped. Thus, e.g., configurations are indexed over lists of types, values are indexed over *sequents*, i.e., pairs of a list of types and a type, and so on.

2.3   Substitution equivalence

The notion of language machine lets us define substitution equivalence, abstractly. In the usual presentation of λ-calculus, we were observing closed programs of some fixed, basic type like the booleans $\mathbb{B}$. Transposed to the abstract machine presentation, this amounts to observing configurations with a single free variable of type $\neg \mathbb{B}$, which models the final continuation to which the closed context returns. There are only two observations at that type, namely $\langle \mathbf{tt} \mid \square \rangle$ and $\langle \mathbf{ff} \mid \square \rangle$, for true and false, which correspond to the two expected observations.

In the abstract setting, i.e., in any given language machine, we postulate a fixed, "final" typing context Ω, and think of configurations with free variables in Ω as closed programs. The obvious way to observe them is to check whether they diverge, and otherwise record which observation they perform on which free variable of Ω.

Thus, two configurations c and d with free variables in Γ are *substitution equivalent* iff, for all assignments $\gamma \colon \Gamma \to \Omega$ from variables in Γ to values of the same type over Ω, $c[\gamma]$ and $d[\gamma]$ coterminate, and, if they do terminate, perform the same observation on the same variable of Ω.

2.4   Games and strategies

We now would like to construct the OGS of any language machine, but before that we need to define what we mean by games and strategies. For this, we follow Levy and Staton [23], up to slight reformulation.

We first introduce *half-games* from I to J, for any sets I and J of *Player* and *Opponent* positions, respectively. Intuitively, a half-game describes the moves available in each Player position, and the Opponent positions they lead to.

A *game* over I and J then consists of a *Player* half-game from I to J, and an *Opponent* half-game from J to I.

A *strategy* then consists of

- an I-indexed family of *active* states, where Player is to play,
- a J-indexed family of *waiting* states, where Opponent is to play,
- an *action* partial map, which, to any active state over a position $i \colon I$, either diverges, or picks a move from i and a "next" waiting state, and
- a *reaction* map, which, to any waiting state and Opponent move over a position $j \colon J$, associates a "next" active state.

2.5   Constructing the game

We saw that evaluators are viewed as either diverging, or splitting configurations into a head variable x, an observation o, and a filling γ. This splitting is used to interpret the considered configuration c as a strategy in a two-player game, where the program plays as Player and the context plays as Opponent. Let us briefly describe this game, which we call the OGS *game*.

As a first approximation, the game in question has the same Player and Opponent positions, which consist of pairs (Γ, Δ) of typing contexts:

(i) variables in Γ are thought of as defined by the currently waiting player, say W, hence unknown to the currently active player, say A,

(ii) conversely, variables in Δ are defined by A, hence unknown to W.

Accordingly, a move (by A) consists of an observation on some variable in Γ. Such an observation may introduce some fresh variables, which are modelled as a typing context Θ that we call the *context increment*. Intuitively, A holds the definitions of variables in Θ, and the next position is

$$(\Gamma', \Delta') := (\Delta + \Theta, \quad \Gamma).$$

This is consistent with *(i)–(ii)* above:

- the definition of variables in Γ' are held by the now waiting player A, while
- those of variables in Δ' are held by the now active player W.

Example 1. If $f \colon A_1 \to A_2 \in \Gamma$, then a possible move is $(f, \langle \square \mid ((\bullet x); \beta) \rangle)$, with context increment $\Theta = (x : A_1, \beta : \neg A_2)$.

Weak bisimilarity $S \approx T$ of strategies is then defined straightforwardly: either both diverge, or they both converge, play the same move, and reach weakly bisimilar strategies, coinductively.

2.6   Constructing the OGS

The crux of OGS is then to interpret the language machine as a strategy in the OGS game. This strategy, which we call the *machine strategy*, is essentially straightforward:

- an active state over (Γ, Δ) consists of a configuration c with free variables in Γ, and, for each $x \colon \tau \in \Delta$, a value of type τ with free variables in Γ, which we (continue to) call an *assignment* $\Delta \to \Gamma$;
- waiting states over (Γ, Δ) are assignments $\Gamma \to \Delta$;
- the action of any configuration c and assignment $\delta \colon \Delta \to \Gamma$ consists in evaluating c, and diverging if it does; otherwise, it evaluates to some normal form (f, o, φ), for some filling $\varphi \colon \Theta \to \Gamma$ of the context increment Θ of o; the machine strategy then
  - plays the move (f, o), and
  - picks as its next waiting state the compound assignment $[\delta, \varphi] \colon \Delta + \Theta \to \Gamma$, over the position $(\Delta + \Theta, \Gamma)$;
- the reaction of an assignment $\gamma \colon \Gamma \to \Delta$ to any move (f, o) with context increment Θ is the configuration obtained by refolding (f, o, γ), up to some technicalities that we hide under the rug for the moment. In particular, variables in the context increment Θ remain fresh for this player.

At this point, we may state the soundness property: any two configurations which give weakly bisimilar strategies are substitution equivalent.

In order to prove it, it remains to work around a few technical glitches, which we briefly describe in the coming subsections. The first amounts to taking the final typing context Ω into account at the level of games: this is easy. The second is well known to the experts: it is the "infinite chattering" problem. We deal with it in a novel way, by building acyclicity into the model. The final difficulty is new and surprising. It has to do with the fact that, in all sensible languages, repeated, non-trivial instantiation of the head variable eventually leads to some redex. In the abstract setting, we need an additional hypothesis to ensure this is indeed the case.

2.7   Final moves

It might be tempting to treat the "final" typing context Ω normally, i.e., to make it part of positions (Γ, Δ). But it would not work. Indeed, once a player makes a final move, the game must stop, in order to reflect the notion of observation that was fixed for substitution equivalence.

We thus tweak the naive definitions of games and strategies given above to incorporate this idea:

(1) A game comes with a set of *final* moves.
(2) The action map of a strategy may either play a proper move as before, or play a final move.
(3) The final moves of the OGS game are observations on variables in the final typing context Ω.
(4) States of the machine strategy are modified similarly: active states over (Γ, Δ) comprise a configuration with free variables in $\Omega + \Gamma$ and an assignment $\Delta \to \Omega + \Gamma$, while waiting states are assignments $\Gamma \to \Omega + \Delta$.
(5) The action map of the machine strategy discriminates against the head variable: if it is in Γ, then a proper move is played; if it is in Ω, a final move is played.
(6) Finally, we adjust weak bisimilarity accordingly: if one strategy plays a final move, then the other should play the same, and conversely.

At the cost of some moderate additional verbosity, this builds the protocol of substitution equivalence into weak bisimilarity of OGS strategies.

2.8   Infinite chattering

Let us now deal with the second announced technical glitch: the infinite chattering problem. A symptom of it is already visible in our description of OGS. Indeed, from a pair of an active and a passive states on a given position (Γ, Δ), we would like to be able to recover a corresponding configuration with free variables in the final typing context Ω. Such a pair of states amounts to a configuration with free variables in Γ, and assignments

$$\Gamma \xrightarrow{\gamma} \Omega + \Delta \qquad\qquad \Delta \xrightarrow{\delta} \Omega + \Gamma,$$

so one might hope that substituting c with γ and δ in turn would converge to some configuration with free variables in Ω. This in fact holds for pairs of states arising from the game, but not for all pairs.

Example 2. For a silly example, consider a case where some free variable x of c is mapped by γ to some variable y in Δ, which is in turn mapped to x in Γ by δ.

Such cyclic configurations do not arise during the game, though. Crucially, in the above description, when we form the new waiting state $[\delta, \varphi]: \Delta + \Theta \to \Omega + \Gamma$, we know that the other assignment $\gamma: \Gamma \to \Omega + \Delta$ does not depend on the new variables in Θ.

This leads us to introduce a refined version of the game, in which positions record the sequence of context increments, and states of the machine strategy take them into account to build acyclicity into the model. Positions are thus sequences $\Theta_1, \ldots, \Theta_n$ of typing contexts.

The idea is that, if the current position is a sequence $\Theta_1, \ldots, \Theta_n$ of context increments, then Θ_n was introduced by the previously active, now waiting player W. Accordingly:

- A (non-final) move consists of a variable introduced by W, i.e., one in $\ldots +$ $\Theta_{n-2} + \Theta_n$, together with an observation o on it – the first index in the sequence depending on the parity of n. The next position is of course $\Theta_1, \ldots, \Theta_n, \Theta$, where Θ denotes the context increment of o.
- An active state of the machine strategy is a configuration with free variables in $\Omega + \ldots + \Theta_{n-2} + \Theta_n$, equipped with assignments $(\ldots, \delta_{n-3}, \delta_{n-1})$ as on the left below.

$$
\begin{array}{ll}
\text{Active assignments} & \text{Passive assignments} \\[4pt]
\Theta_{n-1} \xrightarrow{\delta_{n-1}} \Omega + \ldots + \Theta_{n-4} + \Theta_{n-2}, & \Theta_n \xrightarrow{\gamma_n} \Omega + \ldots + \Theta_{n-3} + \Theta_{n-1}, \\[6pt]
\Theta_{n-3} \xrightarrow{\delta_{n-3}} \Omega + \ldots + \Theta_{n-6} + \Theta_{n-4}, & \Theta_{n-2} \xrightarrow{\gamma_{n-2}} \Omega + \ldots + \Theta_{n-5} + \Theta_{n-3}, \\[6pt]
\quad \vdots & \quad \vdots
\end{array}
\tag{5}
$$

- A passive state consists of complementary assignments $(\ldots, \gamma_{n-2}, \gamma_n)$ as on the right above.

This time, it is easy to recover a well-defined configuration with free variables in Ω from an active-passive pair of states, as

$$
\bar{c} := c[\gamma_n][\delta_{n-1}][\gamma_{n-2}][\delta_{n-3}] \ldots
\tag{6}
$$

2.9   Focused redexes and eventual guardedness

Let us now come to the last technical glitch that we had to face. It surprised us, as it is rather theoretical: we know of no concrete, sensible language machine in which it arises. It may be viewed as a form of infinite chattering. Let us briefly explain it. A key lemma in virtually any OGS soundness proof roughly states the following: given any compatible pair of an active state (c, δ) and a waiting state γ, the configuration (6), obtained by iterated substitution, behaves the same as letting the strategies associated to (c, δ) and γ play against one another. This lemma is simply wrong in general, so we need an additional hypothesis.

A bit more formally, one defines a *composition* operation. The result of composition may either diverge or play a final move in Ω. And the key lemma states that the refolded configuration (6) diverges iff the composition does, and, if not, both play the same final move in Ω.

The difficulty lies in the definition of composition. In principle, it should work as follows. An invariant is that one of the two given strategies is active while the other is waiting. The composition, say $(c, \delta) \parallel \gamma$, is then computed like so:

- If the active strategy diverges or performs a final move, then so does the composition.
- If the active strategy performs a non-final move, then the waiting strategy reacts to it, the roles are switched, and we start over.

As a first step towards making this precise, we must give a bit more detail on how we handle partiality. For us, a partial map $A \to B$ is a map $A \to \mathcal{D}B$, where $\mathcal{D}$ is Capretta's *delay* monad [3], which we briefly recall in §4.2. This is a rather intensional description of partiality, in the sense that an element of $\mathcal{D}B$ consists of a sequence of "silent computation steps", denoted by τ, which is either infinite or followed by some "result" in B.

This suggests interpreting the above description as a Coq `cofixpoint` definition. However, the second clause does not satisfy Coq's guardedness criterion! Let us illustrate this:

Example 3. Consider $c = \langle x \mid (\bullet v); \alpha \rangle$ and $\gamma = [x \mapsto \lambda z.p, \alpha \mapsto E]$, for some program p and evaluation context E. Since c is a normal form, $(c, \emptyset)$ plays without any computation step the non-final move $(\bullet v); \alpha$ on x, and the second recursive clause above says that the composition $(c, \emptyset) \parallel \gamma$ *equals* the composition

$$(\quad \langle \lambda z.p \mid (\bullet y); E \rangle \quad , \quad \gamma \quad) \quad \parallel \quad [y \mapsto v],$$

thus making an unguarded corecursive call.

Remark 3. At this point, it is tempting to insert a dummy computation step to make the definition guarded. This does give the expected definition *up to weak bisimilarity*, but makes the proof break later on, as explained in §4.7.

To justify further, in the above example, semantically, the unguarded call seems right, because it matches the behaviour of $c[\gamma]$ as a whole, our stated goal for composition. Indeed, the second clause models communication between $(c, \emptyset)$ and γ, which is invisible in the behaviour of $c[\gamma]$.

In order to solve the issue, we need to make sure that no two strategies get stuck in a loop involving only the second clause. This is really subtle: if both players keep on exchanging non-final moves, interleaved with computation steps, then composition is well defined (and diverges); so the only problematic case is when both players exchange non-final moves indefinitely *without performing any computation step*.

How could this happen? In the machine strategy, when both players exchange a non-final move, the head variable gets instantiated. So the question becomes: in concrete cases, how could repeated instantiation of the head variable not lead to a redex? A first possibility is if the head variable always gets replaced by another variable. But this is ruled out by the refinement introduced in the previous subsection to deal with infinite chattering. Indeed, if some non-final move leads to a head variable x being instantiated by another variable y, then acyclicity tells us that y must have been introduced before x. Since this is a well-founded ordering, we are safe on this front.

However, this does not suffice in all languages!

Example 4. Consider a language involving λ-abstraction, with an exotic redex of the form

$$\langle \lambda x.p \mid \lambda y.q \rangle \rightarrow \ldots$$

Then, starting from a situation with

- active state given by the configuration $\langle x_1 \mid \lambda y.q \rangle$ and empty assignment,
- and passive state given by $x_1 \mapsto \lambda x.p$,

the first move consists of the observation $\langle \square \mid y_1 \rangle$ on x_1, leading to

- as active state $(\langle \lambda x.p \mid y_1 \rangle, [x_1 \mapsto \lambda x.p])$ and
- as passive state $[y_1 \mapsto \lambda y.q]$.

We are then stuck in a loop between situations of the following forms

$$(\langle x_m \mid \lambda y.q \rangle, [y_j \mapsto \lambda y.q]_{j=1,\ldots,n}) \quad \| \quad [x_i \mapsto \lambda x.p]_{i=1,\ldots,m}$$

$$x_m.\langle \square | y_{n+1} \rangle \left(\quad \right) y_n.\langle x_{m+1} | \square \rangle$$

$$(\langle \lambda x.p \mid y_n \rangle, [x_i \mapsto \lambda x.p]_{i=1,\ldots,m}) \quad \| \quad [y_j \mapsto \lambda y.q]_{j=1,\ldots,n},$$

where we ignore the fine layering of assignments for readability.

In order to rule out languages in which this issue arises, we state our main result under the hypothesis that a suitable binary relation $>$ on observations should be well-founded. Explicitly, we have $o > o'$ iff there exist x, o, γ, and a non-variable v such that substituting v for x in the refolding $x.o[\gamma]$ yields some normal form (without evaluating!) of the shape (x', o', γ'), i.e.,

$$(x.o[\gamma])[x \mapsto v] = x'.o'[\gamma'].$$

When $>$ is well-founded, we say that the considered language machine has *focused redexes*.

Assuming that the considered language machine has focused redexes, we should be able to define composition. However, Coq does not readily accept the definition sketched above, because it does not know that it is productive. In order to proceed cleanly, we introduce a relaxed fixed point operator which contents with a proof that, even though the given equations are not directly guarded in the usual sense, unfolding the definition of each unknown will reach a guard eventually. This enables us to define composition, and at last prove our main result (Theorem 8), which states that any language machine with focused redexes has a sound OGS.

3   CIU equivalence through substitution equivalence

In this section, we explain the idea of substitution equivalence, and the necessary pre-processing step that comes with it, on a simple example, namely simply-typed, call-by-value λ-calculus with a boolean type and recursive functions. Terms are generated by the following grammar

$$\text{values} \ni v, w ::= x \mid \mathbf{tt} \mid \mathbf{ff} \mid \lambda^{\text{rec}} f, x. p$$

$$\text{programs} \ni p, q ::= v \mid p\,q \mid \mathbf{if}(p, q_1, q_2)$$

where λ^{rec} binds f and x in p, as usual. The language is typed. Types and typing contexts are generated by the following grammar,

$$A, B ::= \mathbb{B} \mid A \to B \qquad\qquad \Gamma ::= \varepsilon \mid \Gamma, x: A$$

with the following, standard typing rules.

$$\frac{x: A \in \Gamma}{\Gamma \vdash x: A} \qquad \frac{}{\Gamma \vdash \mathbf{tt}: \mathbb{B}} \qquad \frac{}{\Gamma \vdash \mathbf{ff}: \mathbb{B}} \qquad \frac{\Gamma, f: A \to B, x: A \vdash p: B}{\Gamma \vdash \lambda^{\text{rec}} f, x. p: A \to B}$$

$$\frac{\Gamma \vdash p: A \to B \qquad \Gamma \vdash q: A}{\Gamma \vdash p\,q: B}$$

From now on, all terms are implicitly considered as coming with a typing derivation. Capture-avoiding substitution is defined as usual, and evaluation contexts are defined by the following grammar, with straightforward typing rules.

$$\text{eval. contexts} \ni E ::= \square \mid p\,E \mid E\,v \mid \mathbf{if}(E, p, q)$$

Context application is defined accordingly. Finally, evaluation is defined by the following inference rules.

$$\frac{}{(\lambda^{\text{rec}} f, x. p)\,v \to p[f \mapsto (\lambda^{\text{rec}} f, x. p), x \mapsto v]} \qquad \frac{p \to q}{E[p] \to E[q]}$$

$$\frac{}{\mathbf{if}(\mathbf{tt}, p, q) \to p} \qquad\qquad \frac{}{\mathbf{if}(\mathbf{ff}, p, q) \to q}$$

As explained in the introduction, CIU equivalence of p and q is defined to mean $E[p[\sigma]] \cong E[q[\sigma]]$, for all closing substitutions σ and boolean contexts E, for some fixed equivalence relation $\cong$ between boolean closed programs. More precisely,

Notation 2. *We write $\Gamma \vdash \sigma: \Delta$ for assignments to each variable $x: A \in \Delta$ of a value of type A in typing context Γ.*

Definition 1. *Two programs $\varepsilon \vdash p, q$ of type $\mathbb{B}$ are deemed observably equivalent whenever we have $p \to^* \mathbf{tt}$ iff $q \to^* \mathbf{tt}$, and similarly with $\mathbf{ff}$.*

Definition 2. *For any context Γ and type A, two programs $\Gamma \vdash p, q : A$ are* CIU-*equivalent, which we denote by $p \approx_{\text{CIU}} q$, iff for all assignments $\varepsilon \vdash \sigma : \Gamma$, and closed evaluation contexts E of type $\mathbb{B}$ with a hole of type A, $E[p[\sigma]]$ and $E[q[\sigma]]$ are observably equivalent.*

With the main purpose of unifying notions, and hence simplifying the abstract framework, we want to put context application $E[-]$ and substitution $(-)[\sigma]$ on an equal footing in this definition. The overall idea is to compile our simply-typed, call-by-value λ-calculus down to a slightly lower-level language, as explained in §2.1.

Let us now introduce the low-level language. Low-level types τ are either simple types A, or negated simple types $\neg A$. Programs have simple types A, while evaluation contexts have negated types $\neg A$. We have syntactic categories for programs and evaluation contexts, and a configuration is a pair of a program of some type A and of an evaluation context of type $\neg A$. Values and programs are defined and typed exactly as before. Evaluation contexts and configurations are specified by the following grammar.

$$\text{values} \ni v, w ::= x \mid \mathbf{tt} \mid \mathbf{ff} \mid \lambda^{\text{rec}} f, x. \, p$$
$$\text{programs} \ni p, q ::= v \mid p \, q \mid \mathbf{if}(p, q_1, q_2)$$
$$\text{eval. contexts} \ni \pi, \kappa ::= x \mid \bullet v; \pi \mid p \bullet; \pi \mid (p, q); \pi$$
$$\text{configurations} \ni c, d ::= \langle \, p \mid \pi \, \rangle$$

The typing rules for values and programs are again exactly as before (except that typing contexts may now comprise evaluation context variables). Furthermore, the variable typing rule now covers the fact that any evaluation context variable $\alpha : \neg A$ is an evaluation context of type $\neg A$. Additional typing rules, for evaluation contexts and configurations, are shown in the first part of Figure 1. Capture-avoiding substitution is defined straightforwardly, and evaluation rules are displayed in the second part of Figure 1. We may now introduce substitution equivalence.

Definition 3. *For any typing context Γ, two configurations $\Gamma \vdash c, d$ are substitution equivalent, which we denote by $c \approx_{\text{SUB}} d$, iff for all assignments $(\alpha : \neg \mathbb{B}) \vdash \sigma : \Gamma$, $c[\sigma]$ and $d[\sigma]$ are observably equivalent, in the sense that we have $c \rightarrow^* \langle \, \mathbf{tt} \mid \alpha \, \rangle$ iff $d \rightarrow^* \langle \, \mathbf{tt} \mid \alpha \, \rangle$, and similarly with $\mathbf{ff}$.*

The main point of this section is:

Proposition 1. *For any typing context Γ and type A of the source language, two programs $\Gamma \vdash p, q : A$ are* CIU-*equivalent iff, in the typing context $(\Gamma, \beta : \neg A)$ (with β fresh w.r.t. Γ), $\langle \, p \mid \beta \, \rangle$ and $\langle \, q \mid \beta \, \rangle$ are substitution equivalent.*

Proof. There is a bijection between assignments $(\alpha : \neg \mathbb{B}) \vdash \sigma : (\Gamma, \beta : \neg A)$ in the lower-level language and pairs of an assignment $\varepsilon \vdash \gamma : \Gamma$ and an evaluation context E of type $\mathbb{B}$ with a hole of type A in the source language. Furthermore, for such assignments and evaluation contexts, $\langle \, p \mid \beta \, \rangle[\sigma]$ and $E[p[\gamma]]$ are observably equivalent in the obvious sense, hence the result follows.

$$\frac{\Gamma \vdash v : A \qquad \Gamma \vdash \pi : \neg B}{\Gamma \vdash \bullet v; \pi : \neg(A \to B)} \qquad\qquad \frac{\Gamma \vdash p : A \to B \qquad \Gamma \vdash \pi : \neg B}{\Gamma \vdash p\bullet; \pi : \neg A}$$

$$\frac{\Gamma \vdash p : A \qquad \Gamma \vdash q : A \qquad \Gamma \vdash \pi : \neg A}{\Gamma \vdash (p, q); \pi : \neg \mathbb{B}} \qquad\qquad \frac{\Gamma \vdash p : A \qquad \Gamma \vdash \pi : \neg A}{\Gamma \vdash \langle p \,|\, \pi \rangle}$$

$$\langle p\, q \,|\, \pi \rangle \to \langle q \,|\, p\bullet; \pi \rangle \qquad \langle \mathbf{if}(p, q_1, q_2) \,|\, \pi \rangle \to \langle p \,|\, (q_1, q_2); \pi \rangle$$

$$\langle v \,|\, p\bullet; \pi \rangle \to \langle p \,|\, \bullet v; \pi \rangle \qquad \langle \lambda^{\mathrm{rec}} f, x.\, p \,|\, \bullet v; \pi \rangle \to \langle p[f \mapsto (\lambda^{\mathrm{rec}} f, x.\, p), x \mapsto v] \,|\, \pi \rangle$$

$$\langle \mathbf{tt} \,|\, (q_1, q_2); \pi \rangle \to \langle q_1 \,|\, \pi \rangle \qquad \langle \mathbf{ff} \,|\, (q_1, q_2); \pi \rangle \to \langle q_2 \,|\, \pi \rangle$$

Fig. 1. Typing and evaluation rules for the lower-level variant of call-by-value λ-calculus

4   Abstract OGS

In this section, we fill the gaps left by the informal overview of §2.

4.1   An abstract account of substitution

Let us first recall (one presentation of) a standard way of abstracting over capture-avoiding substitution.

Notation 3. *We fix a set T of* types *for the whole section, and let T^* denote the set of sequences of types.*

The ambient setting for axiomatising substitution is that of families:

Definition 4. *For any sequence $X_1, \ldots, X_n$ of sets, we extend the set*

$$\widetilde{X_1, \ldots, X_n} = (X_1 \to \ldots \to X_n \to \mathbf{Set})$$

to a category, by taking

$$\forall x_1 : X_1, \ldots, x_n : X_n, \mathcal{X}\, x_1 \ldots x_n \to \mathcal{Y}\, x_1 \ldots x_n$$

as hom-set $\widetilde{X_1, \ldots, X_n}(\mathcal{X}, \mathcal{Y})$, for any $\mathcal{X}, \mathcal{Y}$. In particular, we call the objects of $\widetilde{T^*}$ and $\widetilde{T, T^*}$, unsorted *and* sorted *families, respectively.*

Example 5. A sorted family of particular interest is the one of variables ($\circledast$), given by the proof-relevant $\in$ predicate: $(\tau \in \Gamma)$ denotes the set of indices at which τ occurs in Γ.

Let us now explain what it means for sorted and unsorted families to be equipped with substitution. As is standard in the well-scoped approach, we mean substitution in the parallel sense. The basic ingredient for this is the following standard notion, which we call *assignment*.

Definition 5 (⬛). *For any typing contexts* $\Gamma, \Delta \colon T^*$ *and sorted family* X, *an* X-*assignment* $\sigma \colon \Gamma \to_X \Delta$, *or assignment when* X *is clear from context, consists of an element of* $X \tau \Delta$, *for all* $x \colon \tau \in \Gamma$. *In other words, we have*

$$- \to_- - \colon T^* \to \widehat{T, T^*} \to T^* \to \mathbf{Set}$$
$$\Gamma \to_X \Delta := \forall \tau \colon T, \ \tau \in \Gamma \to X \tau \Delta.$$

In order to axiomatise substitution for both kinds of families, we introduce the following notion of *power* families:

Definition 6. *Fixing a sorted family* M, *for any sorted family* S *and unsorted family* U, *we define the power objects*

$$[\![M, S]\!]_s \colon \widehat{T, T^*} \qquad\qquad [\![M, U]\!] \colon \widehat{T^*}$$

by

$$[\![M, S]\!]_s \tau \Gamma := \forall \Delta \colon T^*, (\Gamma \to_M \Delta) \to S \tau \Delta$$
$$[\![M, U]\!] \Gamma := \forall \Delta \colon T^*, (\Gamma \to_M \Delta) \to U \Delta.$$

We may now axiomatise substitution, for both kinds of families:

Definition 7 (⬛). *A substitution monoid is a sorted family* M, *equipped with morphisms*

$$\mathtt{var} \colon -\in- \to M \qquad\qquad \mathtt{sub} \colon M \to [\![M, M]\!]_s,$$

subject to associativity and unitality laws.

Definition 8 (⬛). *A substitution module over a substitution monoid* $(M, \mathtt{var}, \mathtt{sub})$, *or substitution* M-*module for short, is an unsorted family* U, *equipped with a morphism*

$$\mathtt{sub} \colon U \to [\![M, U]\!],$$

subject to associativity and unitality laws.

In both cases, the substitution morphism takes elements over any context Γ (and type τ, if relevant) and assignments $\Gamma \to_M \Delta$, to elements over Δ: this is indeed the expected type for substitution.

4.2 Modelling divergence: the delay monad

Now that we have recalled the standard axiomatisation of substitution, let us explain more precisely how we handle divergence in Coq, which is very simple and standard: we use Capretta's *delay* monad [3].

Definition 9 (⬛). *The* delay *endomap on* **Set** *is defined coinductively by the following inference rules.*

$$\frac{x \colon X}{\eta\, x \colon \mathcal{D} X} \qquad\qquad \frac{a \colon \mathcal{D} X}{\tau; a \colon \mathcal{D} X}.$$

We also denote by $\mathcal{D}$ *the pointwise liftings of delay to categories of families* $\widehat{X_1, \dots, X_n}$, *e.g.,* $\widehat{T, T^*}$ *and* $\widehat{T^*}$.

Remark 4. The notation $\tau; a$ is meant to suggest a silent computation step. Such τs should not be confused with types, which hopefully will be easy from context.

Elements of $\mathcal{D} X$ are thought of as potentially diverging computations of type X: divergence is modelled by the infinite chain of τs; converging computations have the shape $\tau; \ldots; \tau; \eta x$.

Depending on context, we will consider elements of $\mathcal{D} X$ equivalent up to strong or weak bisimilarity, which we now recall.

Definition 10. *For any relation $R \subseteq X \times Y$ between sets (or families) X and Y, we let $\mathcal{D} R \subseteq \mathcal{D} X \times \mathcal{D} Y$ be such that $(c, d): \mathcal{D} R$ iff c and d either both diverge, or evaluate to some x and y with $(x, y) \in R$. We write $\approx_{\mathcal{D}}$ for weak bisimilarity (●), which we define as $\mathcal{D} (=)$.*

We write $\cong_{\mathcal{D}}$ for strong bisimilarity (●), the canonical lifting of R to the delay coinductive type: either both sides loop or both converge to the same element in the same number of τ steps.

Notation 4. *We write interchangeably $(x \leftarrow u; v\,x)$ and $u \ggg v$ for the bind (●) operator of $\mathcal{D}$—evaluate u, and if it returns some x, then evaluate $v\,x$.*

4.3   Language machines and substitution equivalence

Let us now introduce our axiomatisation of evaluation and observation more formally than in the overview. We will then wrap this all up into the definition of language machines, and define substitution equivalence.

Definition 11 (●). *An evaluation structure on any unsorted families $C, N: \widehat{T^*}$ consists of maps: $\mathbf{eval}: C \to \mathcal{D} N$ and $\mathbf{refold}: N \to C$ such that $\mathbf{eval} \circ \mathbf{refold} \cong_{\mathcal{D}} \eta$.*

Remark 5. By Definition 10, the equation says that evaluating the embedding $\mathbf{refold}\,n$ of some normal form n yields n in zero computation steps.

Definition 12 (●). *An observation structure O is a type-indexed set $O: T \to \mathbf{Set}$ together with a map $\mathrm{dom}: \forall \tau: T, \ O\,\tau \to T^*$.*

For any observation structure O, we define the unsorted family $O^{\bullet}$ of pointed observations by $O^{\bullet}\,\Gamma := \exists \tau : T, (\tau \in \Gamma) \times O\,\tau$. We extend the map dom to $O^{\bullet}$, defining $\mathrm{dom}^{\bullet}: \forall \Gamma, O^{\bullet}\,\Gamma \to T^*$ by $\mathrm{dom}^{\bullet}\,\tau\,(i, o) := \mathrm{dom}\,o$.

Thus, a pointed observation over Γ consists of a variable, together with an observation at its type.

Remark 6. In the literature, observations are sometimes called *ultimate patterns* [22], *continuation patterns* [30], *atomic values* [20], or *abstract values* [18].

Definition 13. *A language machine consists of*

- *a substitution monoid $\mathcal{V}$ of values,*
- *a substitution $\mathcal{V}$-module C of configurations,*
- *an observation structure O,*

- *an evaluation structure on C and $N_{O,V}$,*

where $N_{O,V}\,\Gamma := \exists o : O^{\bullet}\,\Gamma, (\mathrm{dom}^{\bullet}\,o \to_V \Gamma)$.

   Evaluation and refolding are furthermore required to respect substitution *(✿), in the sense that, for all $u : C\,\Gamma$, $\gamma : \Gamma \to_V \Delta$, $(x, o, \theta) : O^{\bullet}\,\Gamma$, with $x : \tau \in \Gamma$ and $\gamma(x) = y : \tau \in \Delta$, the following hold*

$$\mathbf{eval}\,(u[\gamma]) \quad \approx_{\mathcal{D}} \quad n \leftarrow \mathbf{eval}\,u \;;\; \mathbf{eval}\,((\mathbf{refold}\,n)[\gamma])$$
$$x.o(\theta)[\gamma] \quad = \quad y.o(\theta[\gamma]),$$

where we denote

- *both substitution maps and pointwise substitution by $X[\gamma]$, and*
- *the refolding $\mathbf{refold}\,(x, o, \theta)$ of any normal form $(x, o, \theta) : N_{O,V}\,\Gamma$ by $x.o(\theta)$.*

Remark 7. By pointwise substitution, we mean that $\theta[\gamma](z) := \theta(z)[\gamma]$.

Notation 5. *In the sequel, we often treat refolding $\mathbf{refold} : N_{O,V} \to C$ as an implicit coercion. We also extend the notation $x.o(\gamma)$ to arbitrary values, writing $v.o(\gamma)$ for $\mathbf{refold}(x, o, \gamma)[x \mapsto v]$, for fresh x.*

Example 6. The lower-level language of §3 forms a language machine. We take T to consist of types A and negated types $\neg A$ (i.e., it is the disjoint union of two copies of simple types); $C\,\Gamma$ consists of configurations $\Gamma \vdash \langle p \mid \pi \rangle$; $V\,A\,\Gamma$ consists of values $\Gamma \vdash v : A$, and $V\,\neg A\,\Gamma$ consists of all contexts $\Gamma \vdash \pi : \neg A$. Before defining O, we introduce the family $\mathcal{U} : \widehat{T, T^{*}}$ of *ultimate values*, which is the subfamily $\mathcal{U}\,\tau \subseteq \exists \Gamma, V\,\tau\,\Gamma$ defined inductively by the following linear type system,

$$\frac{}{x : A \to B \vdash_{\mathcal{U}} x : A \to B} \qquad \frac{}{\vdash_{\mathcal{U}} \mathbf{tt} : \mathbb{B}} \qquad \frac{}{\vdash_{\mathcal{U}} \mathbf{ff} : \mathbb{B}}$$

$$\frac{\Gamma \vdash_{\mathcal{U}} v : A}{\Gamma, x : \neg B \vdash_{\mathcal{U}} (\bullet v); x : \neg(A \to B)} \qquad \frac{}{x : \neg \mathbb{B} \vdash_{\mathcal{U}} x : \neg \mathbb{B}}$$

where we write $\Gamma \vdash_{\mathcal{U}} v : \tau$ for $(\Gamma, v) : \mathcal{U}\,\tau$. In words, at each τ (a simple or negated simple type), $x : \tau \vdash x : \tau$ is an ultimate value; we have $(\vdash \mathbf{tt}), (\vdash \mathbf{ff}) : \mathcal{U}\,\mathbb{B}$, and so on. We then define O with similar notation:

$$\frac{\Gamma \vdash_{\mathcal{U}} \pi : \neg A}{\Gamma \vdash_{O} \langle \square \mid \pi \rangle : A} \qquad \frac{\Gamma \vdash_{\mathcal{U}} v : A}{\Gamma \vdash_{O} \langle v \mid \square \rangle : \neg A}.$$

   Let us now define substitution equivalence, for any language machine $\mathcal{M} = (V, C, O, \mathbf{eval}, \mathbf{refold})$.

Definition 14 (✿). *We define $\mathbf{eval}^{\circ}_{\mathcal{M}} : C \to O^{\bullet}$ at any Γ to be the composite*

$$C\,\Gamma \xrightarrow{\;\mathbf{eval}\;} \mathcal{D}(N_{O,V}\,\Gamma) \xrightarrow{\;\mathcal{D}\,\pi_1\;} \mathcal{D}(O^{\bullet}\,\Gamma).$$

Definition 15 (✿). *For any fixed* final *typing context $\Omega : T^{*}$, two configurations $u, v : C\,\Gamma$ are* substitution equivalent *at Ω, written $u \approx_{\mathrm{SUB}} w$, iff:*

$$\forall \gamma : \Gamma \to_V \Omega, \; \mathbf{eval}^{\circ}\,(u[\gamma]) \approx_{\mathcal{D}} \mathbf{eval}^{\circ}\,(w[\gamma]).$$

4.4 Games and strategies

We now turn to making precise the contents of §2.4. Levy and Staton's notion of game is parameterised by sets I and J of *client* and *server positions*, respectively. The definition then proceeds to postulate families of client moves from I to J, and server moves from J to I. As this is symmetric, we start by introducing a notion of "half-game", and then define games as pairs thereof.

Definition 16. *A* half-game *(⬤) over sets I and J consists of an I-indexed family of moves* move: $I \rightarrow$ **Set**, *and a* next *map in* $\forall i\colon I,$ move $i \rightarrow J$. *We denote by* HGame $I\,J$ *the set of half-games over I and J.*

A game *(⬤) over sets I and J consists of a* client *half-game in* HGame $I\,J$, *a* server *half-game in* HGame $J\,I$, *and a set of* final *moves. We denote by* Game $I\,J$ *the set of games over I and J.*

Notation 6. *We denote by* move$_{\mathcal{H}}$ *and* next$_{\mathcal{H}}$ *the components of any half-game $\mathcal{H}$, and by* client$_{\mathcal{G}}$, server$_{\mathcal{G}}$, *and* final$_{\mathcal{G}}$ *the components of any game $\mathcal{G}$.*

We will need the following notion of dual game.

Definition 17. *The dual $\mathcal{G}^{\perp}\colon$ Game $J\,I$ of a game $\mathcal{G}\colon$ Game $I\,J$ is defined by swapping the client and server:* client$_{\mathcal{G}^{\perp}}$:= server$_{\mathcal{G}}$, server$_{\mathcal{G}^{\perp}}$:= client$_{\mathcal{G}}$ *and* final$_{\mathcal{G}^{\perp}}$:= final$_{\mathcal{G}}$.

Now that games are defined, we turn to defining strategies in a game. We proceed coalgebraically, for which we need the following "derived" functors.

Definition 18 (⬤). *Given any half-game $\mathcal{H}$: HGame $I\,J$, we define two functors $\widehat{J} \rightarrow \widehat{I}$, the* action functor $[\![\mathcal{H}]\!]^{+}$ *and the* reaction functor $[\![\mathcal{H}]\!]^{-}$:

$$[\![\mathcal{H}]\!]^{+} X\,i := \exists m\colon \text{move}_{\mathcal{H}}\,i,\ X\,(\text{next}_{\mathcal{H}}\,i\,m)$$
$$[\![\mathcal{H}]\!]^{-} X\,i := \forall m\colon \text{move}_{\mathcal{H}}\,i,\ X\,(\text{next}_{\mathcal{H}}\,i\,m).$$

We may now define strategies.

Definition 19. *Given a game $\mathcal{G}\colon$ Game $I\,J$, a* strategy *for $\mathcal{G}$ consists of families $S^{+}\colon \widehat{I}$ and $S^{-}\colon \widehat{J}$ of* active *and* waiting *states, respectively, together with*

$$S^{+} \rightarrow \mathcal{D}\,(\text{final}_{\mathcal{G}} + [\![\text{client}_{\mathcal{G}}]\!]^{+}\,S^{-}) \qquad S^{-} \rightarrow [\![\text{server}_{\mathcal{G}}]\!]^{-}\,S^{+},$$

which we respectively call the action *and* reaction *morphisms.*
We denote by Strat$_{\mathcal{G}}$ *the set of strategies for $\mathcal{G}$.*

Notation 7. *We denote by* play$_{S}$ *and* coplay$_{S}$ *the action and reaction morphisms of any strategy S.*

Remark 8. The occurrence of the (family lifting of the) delay monad in the action morphism means that we allow Proponent to "think forever" and never actually play. This is crucial for interpreting languages with general recursion.

Remark 9. In the code, this is where indexed interaction trees come in. We define strategies ($\spadesuit$) not as coalgebras, as here, but as interaction trees, i.e., elements of the final coalgebra $\nu A.(\mathtt{final}_G + A + [\![\mathtt{client}_G]\!]^+([\![\mathtt{server}_G]\!]^- A))$.

The main point of OGS consists in interpreting configurations as strategies in some game, in the hope that weak bisimilarity between induced strategies entails substitution equivalence. Let us define weak bisimilarity.

Definition 20. *Given two strategies* $\mathcal{S}, \mathcal{T} \colon \mathtt{Strat}_G$, *a weak bisimulation* $\alpha \colon \mathcal{S} \approx_G \mathcal{T}$ *is a pair of an I-indexed relation* $\alpha^+ \subseteq \mathcal{S}^+ \times \mathcal{T}^+$ *between active states and a J-indexed relation* $\alpha^- \subseteq \mathcal{S}^- \times \mathcal{T}^-$ *between waiting states, such that*

$$\mathrm{play}_\mathcal{S} \, {\not\approx} \{\alpha^+ \to \mathcal{D}(\mathrm{Eq}_{\mathtt{final}_G} + [\![\mathtt{client}_G]\!]^+ \, \alpha^-) \} {\approx} \mathrm{play}_\mathcal{T} \; and$$
$$\mathrm{coplay}_\mathcal{S} \, {\not\approx} \{\alpha^- \to [\![\mathtt{server}_G]\!]^- \, \alpha^+ \} {\approx} \mathrm{coplay}_\mathcal{T},$$

where $u \, {\not\approx} \{R \to S \} {\approx} v$ *is shorthand for* $\forall i \, x \, y, \; R \, i \, x \, y \to S \, i \, (u \, x) \, (v \, y)$, *and we lift functors to relations in the straightforward way. Let* weak bisimilarity, *denoted by* $\approx_G$, *be the largest weak bisimulation.*

4.5   The OGS game

Let us now define the OGS game corresponding to any language machine. For §4.5–4.7, we fix a set T of types, a language machine $\mathcal{M} = (\mathcal{V}, \mathcal{C}, \mathcal{O}, \mathbf{eval}, \mathbf{refold})$, and a typing context $\Omega \colon T^*$.

Definition 21 ($\spadesuit$). *An* interleaved context *is a list of contexts. We denote by* $T^{**} = (T^*)^*$ *the set of interleaved contexts.*

Of course, we may extract from any interleaved context the variables introduced by the currently active, resp. waiting player:

Definition 22 ($\spadesuit$). *We define two* collapsing *functions* $\downarrow^+, \downarrow^- \colon T^{**} \to T^*$ *as follows:*

$$\downarrow^+ \emptyset \quad := \emptyset \qquad\qquad \downarrow^- \emptyset \quad := \emptyset$$
$$\downarrow^+(\Phi, \Gamma) := \downarrow^- \Phi + \Gamma \qquad\qquad \downarrow^-(\Phi, \Gamma) := \downarrow^+ \Phi.$$

Remark 10. Intuitively, $\downarrow^+$ retains from an interleaved context the variables that are unknown to the currently active player, starting with the last introduced context. Symmetrically, $\downarrow^-$ retains those that are unknown to the waiting player, which does not include the last introduced context.

Let us now define the OGS game, as expected. This only depends on the fixed context Ω and the observation structure of the considered language machine.

Definition 23 ($\spadesuit$). *We define the* OGS half-game $\mathtt{HOGS} \colon \mathtt{HGame}\, T^{**}\, T^{**}$ *by:*

$$\mathrm{move}_{\mathtt{HOGS}}\, \Phi := \mathcal{O}^\bullet \downarrow^+ \Phi \qquad and \qquad \mathrm{next}_{\mathtt{HOGS}}\, \Phi\, m := (\Phi, \mathrm{dom}^\bullet m).$$

Furthermore, the OGS game $\mathtt{OGS}$ *is defined by*

$$\mathrm{client}_{\mathtt{OGS}} := \mathtt{HOGS} \qquad \mathrm{server}_{\mathtt{OGS}} := \mathtt{HOGS} \qquad \mathrm{final}_{\mathtt{OGS}} := \mathcal{O}^\bullet \Omega.$$

4.6 The machine strategy

Let us now define the machine strategy for the given language machine $\mathcal{M}$ and final typing context Ω, fixed at the beginning of §4.5.

Definition 24 (⚙). *Let* Env^+ *and* Env^- *denote the* T^{**}-*indexed families of active, resp. waiting, interleaved assignments defined inductively as follows.*

$$\frac{}{\varepsilon\colon \text{Env}^+\,\emptyset} \qquad \frac{}{\varepsilon\colon \text{Env}^-\,\emptyset} \qquad \frac{e\colon \text{Env}^-\,\Phi}{e,\cdot\colon \text{Env}^+\,(\Phi,\Gamma)} \qquad \frac{e\colon \text{Env}^+\,\Phi \qquad \gamma\colon \Gamma \to_{\mathcal{V}} (\Omega + \downarrow^+\!\Phi)}{e,\gamma\colon \text{Env}^-\,(\Phi,\Gamma)}$$

Remark 11. This is merely a formal version of (5). Beware, though, that the active player in an even interleaved context is Proponent, while the active player in an odd interleaved context is Opponent.

Like the interleaved contexts by which they are indexed, interleaved assignments can be collapsed into basic assignments.

Definition 25 (⚙). *The* collapsing *functions for interleaved assignments are defined by mutual induction as follows, for all* $\Phi\colon T^{**}$,

$$\downarrow^+\colon \text{Env}^+\,\Phi \to \downarrow^-\!\Phi \to_{\mathcal{V}} (\Omega + \downarrow^+\!\Phi) \qquad\qquad \downarrow^-\colon \text{Env}^-\,\Phi \to \downarrow^+\!\Phi \to_{\mathcal{V}} (\Omega + \downarrow^-\!\Phi)$$

$$\downarrow^+ \varepsilon := \text{elim}_\emptyset \qquad\qquad\qquad\qquad \downarrow^- \varepsilon := \text{elim}_\emptyset$$

$$\downarrow^+ (e,\cdot) := (\downarrow^- e)[\text{wkn}] \qquad\qquad\qquad \downarrow^- (e,\gamma) := [\downarrow^+ e,\ \gamma],$$

where wkn *denotes the obvious weakening: we have* $\Phi = (\Phi',\Gamma)$ *for some* Φ' *and* Γ, *and the result is* $\downarrow^+\!\Phi' \xrightarrow{\downarrow^- e}_{\mathcal{V}} \Omega + \downarrow^-\!\Phi' \xrightarrow{\text{wkn}}_{\mathcal{V}} \Omega + \downarrow^-\!\Phi' + \Gamma$.

We now have everything in place to define the machine strategy.

Definition 26 (⚙). *The machine strategy* $\widetilde{\mathcal{M}}\colon \text{Strat}_{\text{OGS}}$ *is defined as follows:*

- *the family of active states is* $\widetilde{\mathcal{M}}^+\Phi := C\,(\Omega + \downarrow^+\!\Phi) \times \text{Env}^+\,\Phi$;
- *the family of waiting states is* $\widetilde{\mathcal{M}}^-\Phi := \text{Env}^-\,\Phi$;
- *the action morphism is defined by*

$$\text{play}_{\widetilde{\mathcal{M}}}\colon \widetilde{\mathcal{M}}^+ \to \mathcal{D}\,(O^\bullet\,\Omega + [\![\,\text{OGS}\,]\!]^+\,\widetilde{\mathcal{M}}^-)$$

$$\text{play}_{\widetilde{\mathcal{M}}}\,\Phi\,(c,e) := \left(x.o(\gamma) \leftarrow \text{eval}\,c\,;\ \begin{cases} \eta\,(\text{inl}\,(x,o)) & \text{if } x \in \Omega \\ \eta\,(\text{inr}\,((x,o),(e,\gamma))) & \text{if } x \in \downarrow^+\!\Phi \end{cases} \right) ;$$

- *the reaction morphism is defined by*

$$\text{coplay}_{\widetilde{\mathcal{M}}}\colon \widetilde{\mathcal{M}}^- \to [\![\,\text{OGS}\,]\!]^-\,\widetilde{\mathcal{M}}^+$$

$$\text{coplay}_{\widetilde{\mathcal{M}}}\,\Phi\,e\,(x,o) := (x[\downarrow^- e].o(\delta_o),(e,\cdot)),$$

where δ_o *denotes the obvious assignment* $\text{dom}\,o \to_{\mathcal{V}} \Omega + \downarrow^-\!\Phi + \text{dom}\,o$.

To finish up, we define two functions injecting configurations (resp. assignments) into active (resp. waiting) machine strategy states (⚙),

$$[\![-]\!]^+\colon C\,\Gamma \to \widetilde{\mathcal{M}}^+\,(\Gamma,) \qquad\qquad [\![-]\!]^-\colon (\Gamma \to_{\mathcal{V}} \Omega) \to \widetilde{\mathcal{M}}^-\,(\Gamma,)$$

$$[\![u]\!]^+ := (u[w],\varepsilon) \qquad\qquad\qquad [\![\gamma]\!]^- := (\varepsilon,\gamma)$$

where w is the obvious weakening $\Gamma \to_{\mathcal{V}} \Omega+\Gamma$, and $(\Gamma,)$ is the singleton sequence.

4.7 Soundness

We may now state the main result, recalling Notation 5. We introduce the following technical, yet mild conditions on the considered language machine:

Definition 27. *A substitution monoid $\mathcal{V}$ is* clear-cut *iff its unit $(-\in-) \to \mathcal{V}$ is injective (where $\in$ denotes the variables family of Example 5), and has decidable image whose complement is furthermore stable under renaming. For a clear-cut $\mathcal{V}$, we let $\mathcal{V}^{\backslash \in}$ denote the subfamily of non-variable elements.*

Definition 28. *Assuming $\mathcal{V}$ is clear-cut, we define the binary relation $>$ on $\exists \tau : T, O\tau$ by*

$$(\tau, o) > (\tau', o') \qquad iff \qquad \exists v : \mathcal{V}^{\backslash \in}, \gamma, x, \delta, \mathbf{eval}\,(v.o(\gamma)) = \eta\,(x.o'(\delta)).$$

A language machine has focused redexes *iff $>$ is well-founded.*

Theorem 8 (💡). *For any language machine with focused redexes and clear-cut values, weak bisimilarity of induced OGS strategies is sound w.r.t. substitution equivalence, i.e., for any pair of configurations u and w, weak bisimilarity of induced strategies entails substitution equivalence:*

$$\forall c, d, \quad [\![c]\!]^+ \approx^+_{\mathrm{OGS}} [\![d]\!]^+ \to c \approx_{\mathrm{SUB}} d.$$

Remark 12. Let us unfold notations a bit: $\approx^+_{\mathrm{OGS}}$ denotes the positive component of weak bisimilarity between strategies (Definition 20) in the OGS game (Definition 23), and $\approx_{\mathrm{SUB}}$ denotes substitution equivalence (Definition 15).

The rest of this section is devoted to sketching the proof. We first describe the overall structure, and then focus on the main difficulty.

We start by defining a composition operation

$$- \| - : \quad \forall \Phi, \quad C\,(\Omega + \downarrow^+\Phi) \times \mathrm{Env}^+\,\Phi \quad \to \quad \mathrm{Env}^-\,\Phi \quad \to \quad \mathcal{D}\,(O^\bullet\,\Omega).$$

We expect this operation to satisfy the following properties.

Definition 29.

1. *Composition is* adequate *(💡) iff, for all $c : C\,\Gamma$ and $\gamma : \Gamma \to_M \Omega$, we have $\mathbf{eval}^o_M\,(c[\gamma]) \approx_{\mathcal{D}} [\![c]\!]^+ \| [\![\gamma]\!]^-$.*
2. *Weak bisimilarity is a* congruence *(💡) for composition iff, for any $s_1 \approx^+_{\mathrm{OGS}} s_2$ and $t_1 \approx^-_{\mathrm{OGS}} t_2$, we have $s_1 \| t_1 \approx_{\mathcal{D}} s_2 \| t_2$.*

Remark 13. The adequacy equation lives in $\mathcal{D}\,(O^\bullet\,\Omega)$ (recalling Definition 14).

Let us readily show that soundness follows from congruence and adequacy.

Proposition 2. *If any adequate composition for which weak bisimilarity is a congruence exists, then OGS is sound.*

Proof. For any configurations $c_1, c_2 \colon C\Gamma$ with weakly bisimilar interpretations $[\![c_1]\!]^+$ and $[\![c_2]\!]^+$, and any assignment $\gamma \colon \Gamma \to_V \Omega$, we have

$$
\begin{aligned}
\mathsf{eval}^o_{\mathcal{M}}(c_1[\gamma]) &\approx_{\mathcal{D}} [\![c_1]\!]^+ \parallel [\![\gamma]\!]^- && \text{(by adequacy)} \\
&\approx_{\mathcal{D}} [\![c_2]\!]^+ \parallel [\![\gamma]\!]^- && \text{(by congruence of weak bisimilarity)} \\
&\approx_{\mathcal{D}} \mathsf{eval}^o_{\mathcal{M}}(c_2[\gamma]) && \text{(by adequacy again)},
\end{aligned}
$$

hence $c_1 \approx_{\mathrm{SUB}} c_2$, as desired.

It thus remains to define a congruent and adequate composition. The plan for this is to take the fixed point of an equation, in the following sense.

Definition 30 (⚫). *An* equation *consists of a set X of* variables, *a set Y of* constants, *and a* definition *function $X \to \mathcal{D}(Y + X)$.*

Since we are interested in weak bisimilarity, it seems easier to try and construct *weak fixed points* of equations $f \colon X \to \mathcal{D}(Y + X)$, that is, maps $p \colon X \to \mathcal{D}(Y)$ such that $p\, x \approx_{\mathcal{D}} f\, x \gg\!\!=[\eta, p]$ for all $x \colon X$. This may be done by safely guarding all occurrences of "variables" in X by a τ:

Definition 31 (⚫). *Given an equation $f \colon X \to \mathcal{D}(Y + X)$, the* iteration *of f is a map $f^\dagger \colon X \to \mathcal{D}Y$ given coinductively by:*

$$
f^\dagger x := f\, x \gg\!\!= \begin{cases} \mathrm{inl}\, y \mapsto \eta\, y \\ \mathrm{inr}\, x' \mapsto \tau; (f^\dagger x'). \end{cases}
$$

Proposition 3. *The iteration of any equation is a weak fixed point.*

Using this technique, we may define a composition operation for which weak bisimilarity is a congruence. We will see that adequacy is more problematic.

Definition 32 (⚫). *The* composition equation *is:*

$$
\mathsf{comp\text{-}eqn} \colon \exists \Phi, \widetilde{M}^+ \Phi \times \widetilde{M}^- \Phi \to \mathcal{D}(O^\bullet \Omega + \exists \Phi, \widetilde{M}^+ \Phi \times \widetilde{M}^- \Phi)
$$

$$
\mathsf{comp\text{-}eqn}(u, w) := \left(\mathsf{play}_{\widetilde{M}}\, u \gg\!\!= \begin{cases} \mathrm{inl}\, r \mapsto \eta\,(\mathrm{inl}\, r) \\ \mathrm{inr}\,(m, u') \mapsto \eta\,(\mathrm{inr}\,((\mathsf{coplay}_{\widetilde{M}}\, w\, m), u')) \end{cases} \right).
$$

Let naive composition *be the iteration of* comp-eqn.

Proposition 4. *Weak bisimilarity is a congruence for naive composition.*

Proof. By coinduction: the binary relation on $\mathcal{D}(O^\bullet \Omega)$ given by all pairs $(s_1 \parallel t_1, s_2 \parallel t_2)$ such that $s_1 \approx^+_{\mathrm{OGS}} s_2$ and $t_1 \approx^-_{\mathrm{OGS}} t_2$, is a weak bisimulation.

In order to prove adequacy, we have to give a weak bisimulation between $\mathsf{eval}^o_{\mathcal{M}}(c[\gamma])$ and $[\![c]\!]^+ \parallel [\![\gamma]\!]^-$. When facing such an equational proof, where one of the members is defined as a fixed point (here composition), the prime reasoning scheme is uniqueness of fixed points. Indeed, assuming the composition equation has a unique fixed point, and that substituting-then-evaluating-then-observing is one, then both must agree. However, general equations do not have unique *weak* fixed points, so we have to apply uniqueness of *strong* fixed points, i.e., fixed points w.r.t. strong bisimilarity. But there is a further complication: while all equations admit weak fixed points, given by iteration as we saw, this is not the case for strong fixed points. Coq's basic cofixpoint feature enables the construction of strong fixed points for *guarded* equations, in the following sense.

Definition 33 (✿). *An element* $u: \mathcal{D}(Y + X)$ *is guarded if it is not of the form* $\eta(\text{inr}\,x)$. *An equation* $e: X \to \mathcal{D}(Y + X)$ *is guarded if for all* x, $e\,x$ *is guarded.*

However, comp-eqn is *not* guarded in general, as explained in Example 3, which may lead the definition to be ill-founded in some languages, as sketched in Example 4. This is where the focused redexes hypothesis comes in: it allows us to show that comp-eqn is *eventually guarded*, in the following sense.

Definition 34. *An equation* $e: X \to \mathcal{D}(Y + X)$ *is eventually guarded if for all* x, *there exists an* $n: \mathbb{N}$ *such that* $e^n x$ *is guarded, where by definition*

$$e^0 x := \eta(\text{inr}\,x) \qquad\qquad e^{n+1} x := e\,x \ggg \begin{cases} \text{inl}\,y \mapsto \eta(\text{inl}\,y) \\ \text{inr}\,x' \mapsto e^n x'. \end{cases}$$

Proposition 5 (✿,✿). *All eventually guarded equations admit a unique strong fixed point, which is pointwise weakly bisimilar to any weak fixed point.*

Proof (sketch). Since, for all x, an eventually guarded equation e can be pointwise unrolled a finite number n_x of times into a guarded element, $e^{n_x} x$, we construct the fixed point of e as the guarded fixed point of $e' x := e^{n_x} x$.

Proposition 6 (✿). *If M has focused redexes and clear-cut values, then comp-eqn is eventually guarded, and thus admits a strong fixed point, say* $-\|_g-$.

We may now conclude our soundness proof.

Proposition 7 (✿). *If the language machine M has focused redexes, then composition is adequate.*

Proof (sketch). The idea is to show that the map $(c, \gamma) \mapsto \text{eval}^\circ(c[\gamma])$ is something like a strong fixed point of comp-eqn. This does not quite type check, however, so we need to generalize the two arguments (c, γ) to pairs of active and passive machine strategy states. Following (6), we define z-e-obs by:

$$\exists \Phi, \widetilde{M^+} \Phi \times \widetilde{M^-} \Phi \qquad\qquad \to \mathcal{D}(O^\bullet \Omega)$$
$$(\ (c, (\ldots, \delta_{n-3}, \delta_{n-1}))\ ,\ (\ldots, \gamma_{n-2}, \gamma_n)\ ) \mapsto \text{eval}^\circ(c[\gamma_n][\delta_{n-1}][\gamma_{n-2}][\delta_{n-3}]\ldots).$$

We have z-e-obs $[\![c]\!]^+ [\![\gamma]\!]^- = \text{eval}^\circ(c[\gamma])$, and, as desired, z-e-obs is a strong fixed point of comp-eqn (✿). At last, we have, for any $c: C\,\Gamma$ and $\gamma: \Gamma \to \Delta$:

$$
\begin{array}{rll}
[\![c]\!]^+ \| [\![\gamma]\!]^- & \approx_{\mathscr{D}}\ [\![c]\!]^+ \|_g [\![\gamma]\!]^- & \text{by Proposition 5} \\
& \cong_{\mathscr{D}}\ \text{z-e-obs}\, [\![c]\!]^+ [\![\gamma]\!]^- & \text{by Proposition 5 again} \\
& =\ \text{eval}^\circ(c[\gamma]) & \text{as we just saw.}
\end{array}
$$

5   Related work

Beyond the already discussed, closely related work [21, 23, 29], let us mention recent work on the structure needed to collapse the composition of an active and a waiting state into a language machine configuration [19,21]. Unlike in our work is that acyclicity is not built into the OGS game, but proved after the fact.

The issue of infinite chattering was also studied in game semantics [1, 4, 17] for showing that total strategies are closed under composition. This notion of infinite chattering thus differs from the one studied here, which allows programs to have infinite reduction paths. In our setting, an infinite chattering would be an artifact of the composition looping without even creating a reduction step.

Finally, there is a lot of work on unique solutions of (co)recursive equations. Deducing bisimilarity of two LTSs from the fact that they satisfy the same recursive equation, and that this equation admits a unique solution (up-to bisimilarity), is a standard technique in process calculi, introduced by Hoare [16] and Milner [28], which is still explored today [7]. Let us also mention the category-theoretic work on monads with iteration operators [8, 12, 25, 26], which recently culminated in a widely unifying approach [13], that features an abstract notion of guardedness. Links with the interaction trees library [29] have been established, showing that the `itree` datatype, considered up to weak bisimilarity, forms a coinductive resumption monad, i.e., it computes cofree coalgebras for a functor of the form $A \mapsto T(X + \Sigma(A))$. The resulting monad is furthermore complete Elgot (i.e., it admits potentially non-unique solutions of all equations), and iterative (i.e., it admits unique solutions of "guarded" equations).

6   Conclusion and perspectives

We have proposed an abstract notion of language with evaluator, for which we have constructed a generic OGS interpretation, which we have proved sound, in Coq [2]. We have demonstrated the expressiveness of our framework by instantiating it on a variety of simply-typed λ-calculi with control effects – although only one is treated here for lack of space.

An important direction for future work is to incorporate more language features into the framework. Notably, we plan to cover effectful evaluators by generalising from the delay monad to richer, well-behaved monads. It would also be useful to handle more sophisticated type systems, including, e.g., polymorphism or subtyping.

Another direction consists in investigating completeness in the abstract framework, be it by restricting attention to sufficiently effectful languages, or by refining the OGS model to make it fully abstract, i.e., by enforcing conditions like well-bracketing or visibility.

Finally, it might be fruitful to investigate the link between OGS and other models in the abstract framework, including denotational game semantics and Lassen's normal form bisimilarity.

References

1. Abramsky, S., et al.: Semantics of interaction: an introduction to game semantics. Semantics and Logics of Computation **14**(1) (1997)
2. Borthelle, P., Hirschowitz, T., Jaber, G., Zakowski, Y.: Coq proof artifact for an abstract, certified account of operational game semantics (Jan 2025). https://doi.org/10.5281/zenodo.14627318
3. Capretta, V.: General recursion via coinductive types. Log. Methods Comput. Sci. **1**(2) (2005). https://doi.org/10.2168/LMCS-1(2:1)2005
4. Clairambault, P., Harmer, R.: Totality in arena games. Ann. Pure Appl. Log. **161**(5), 673–689 (2010). https://doi.org/10.1016/J.APAL.2009.07.016, `https://doi.org/10.1016/j.apal.2009.07.016`
5. Curien, P., Herbelin, H.: The duality of computation. In: Odersky, M., Wadler, P. (eds.) Proc. 5th International Conference on Functional Programming. pp. 233–243. ACM (2000). https://doi.org/10.1145/351240.351262, `https://doi.org/10.1145/351240.351262`
6. Downen, P., Ariola, Z.M.: Compiling with classical connectives. Log. Methods Comput. Sci. **16**(3) (2020), `https://lmcs.episciences.org/6740`
7. Durier, A., Hirschkoff, D., Sangiorgi, D.: Divergence and unique solution of equations. Log. Methods Comput. Sci. **15**(3) (2019). https://doi.org/10.23638/LMCS-15(3:12)2019, `https://doi.org/10.23638/LMCS-15(3:12)2019`
8. Elgot, C.C.: Monadic computation and iterative algebraic theories. In: Rose, H., Shepherdson, J. (eds.) Logic Colloquium '73, Studies in Logic and the Foundations of Mathematics, vol. 80, pp. 175–230. Elsevier (1975). https://doi.org/https://doi.org/10.1016/S0049-237X(08)71949-9
9. Fiore, M., Plotkin, G., Turi, D.: Abstract syntax and variable binding. In: Proc. 14th Symposium on Logic in Computer Science. IEEE (1999). https://doi.org/10.1109/LICS.1999.782615
10. Fiore, M., Szamozvancev, D.: Formal metatheory of second-order abstract syntax. Proc. ACM Program. Lang. **6**(POPL), 1–29 (2022). https://doi.org/10.1145/3498715, `https://doi.org/10.1145/3498715`
11. Fiore, M.P.: Second-order and dependently-sorted abstract syntax. In: Proc. 23rd Symposium on Logic in Computer Science. pp. 57–68. IEEE (2008). https://doi.org/10.1109/LICS.2008.38
12. Goncharov, S., Schröder, L., Rauch, C., Jakob, J.: Unguarded recursion on coinductive resumptions. Log. Methods Comput. Sci. **14**(3) (2018). https://doi.org/10.23638/LMCS-14(3:10)2018, `https://doi.org/10.23638/LMCS-14(3:10)2018`
13. Goncharov, S., Schröder, L., Rauch, C., Piróg, M.: Unifying guarded and unguarded iteration. In: Esparza, J., Murawski, A.S. (eds.) Proc. 20th International Conference on Foundations of Software Science and Computation Structures. Lecture Notes in Computer Science, vol. 10203, pp. 517–533 (2017). https://doi.org/10.1007/978-3-662-54458-7_30, `https://doi.org/10.1007/978-3-662-54458-7_30`
14. Hirschowitz, A., Maggesi, M.: Modules over monads and linearity. In: Proc. 14th International Workshop on Logic, Language, Information and Computation Lecture Notes in Computer Science, vol. 4576, pp. 218–237. Springer (2007). https://doi.org/10.1007/978-3-540-73445-1_16
15. Hirschowitz, A., Maggesi, M.: Modules over monads and initial semantics. Information and Computation **208**(5), 545–564 (2010). https://doi.org/10.1016/j.ic.2009.07.003

16. Hoare, C.A.R.: Communicating Sequential Processes. Prentice-Hall (1985)
17. Hyland, M.: Game semantics. Semantics and logics of computation **14**, 131 (1997)
18. Jaber, G., Murawski, A.S.: Complete trace models of state and control. In: Yoshida, N. (ed.) Proc. 30th European Symposium on Programming. Lecture Notes in Computer Science, vol. 12648, pp. 348–374. Springer (2021). https://doi.org/10.1007/978-3-030-72019-3_13, https://doi.org/10.1007/978-3-030-72019-3_13
19. Jaber, G., Murawski, A.S.: Compositional relational reasoning via operational game semantics. In: 36th Annual ACM/IEEE Symposium on Logic in Computer Science, LICS. pp. 1–13. IEEE (2021). https://doi.org/10.1109/LICS52264.2021.9470524
20. Laird, J.: A fully abstract trace semantics for general references. In: Arge, L., Cachin, C., Jurdzinski, T., Tarlecki, A. (eds.) Proc. 34th International Colloquium on Automata, Languages and Programming. Lecture Notes in Computer Science, vol. 4596, pp. 667–679. Springer (2007). https://doi.org/10.1007/978-3-540-73420-8_58, https://doi.org/10.1007/978-3-540-73420-8_58
21. Laird, J.: A Curry-style semantics of interaction: From untyped to second-order lazy $\lambda\mu$-calculus. In: Goubault-Larrecq, J., König, B. (eds.) Proc. 23rd International Conference on Foundations of Software Science and Computation Structures. Lecture Notes in Computer Science, vol. 12077, pp. 422–441. Springer (2020). https://doi.org/10.1007/978-3-030-45231-5_22, https://doi.org/10.1007/978-3-030-45231-5_22
22. Lassen, S.B., Levy, P.B.: Typed normal form bisimulation. In: Duparc, J., Henzinger, T.A. (eds.) Proc. 21st International Workshop on Computer Science Logic. Lecture Notes in Computer Science, vol. 4646, pp. 283–297. Springer (2007). https://doi.org/10.1007/978-3-540-74915-8_23, https://doi.org/10.1007/978-3-540-74915-8_23
23. Levy, P.B., Staton, S.: Transition systems over games. In: Proc. 29th Symposium on Logic in Computer Science. pp. 64:1–64:10. ACM (2014). https://doi.org/10.1145/2603088.2603150
24. Mason, I.A., Talcott, C.L.: Equivalence in functional languages with effects. J. Funct. Program. **1**(3), 287–327 (1991). https://doi.org/10.1017/S0956796800000125, https://doi.org/10.1017/S0956796800000125
25. Milius, S.: Completely iterative algebras and completely iterative monads. Inf. Comput. **196**(1), 1–41 (2005). https://doi.org/10.1016/J.IC.2004.05.003, https://doi.org/10.1016/j.ic.2004.05.003
26. Milius, S., Litak, T.: Guard your daggers and traces: Properties of guarded (co-)recursion. Fundam. Informaticae **150**(3-4), 407–449 (2017). https://doi.org/10.3233/FI-2017-1475, https://doi.org/10.3233/FI-2017-1475
27. Milner, R.: Fully abstract models of typed *lambda*-calculi. Theor. Comput. Sci. **4**(1), 1–22 (1977). https://doi.org/10.1016/0304-3975(77)90053-6, https://doi.org/10.1016/0304-3975(77)90053-6
28. Milner, R.: Communication and concurrency. PHI Series in computer science, Prentice Hall (1989)
29. Xia, L., Zakowski, Y., He, P., Hur, C., Malecha, G., Pierce, B.C., Zdancewic, S.: Interaction trees: representing recursive and impure programs in coq. Proc. ACM Program. Lang. **4**(POPL), 51:1–51:32 (2020). https://doi.org/10.1145/3371119
30. Zeilberger, N.: The Logical Basis of Evaluation Order and Pattern-Matching. Ph.D. thesis, USA (2009), aAI3358066

Artifact Report: an Abstract, Certified Account of Operational Game Semantics

Peio Borthelle[1]([✉]), Tom Hirschowitz[2], Guilhem Jaber[3], and Yannick Zakowski[4]

[1] Université Savoie Mont Blanc, Chambéry, France
peio.borthelle@univ-smb.fr
[2] CNRS, Paris, France
[3] Nantes Université, Nantes, France
[4] Inria, Paris, France

This artifact report is a companion to the ESOP'25 paper *An abstract, certified account of operational game semantics* [3]. The paper describes the construction of a sound model for an abstract notion of language. The model is built using a semantic technique named *Operational Game Semantics (OGS)*.

All our results are mechanised in the Coq proof assistant: this mechanisation (The proof artifact is archived at https://doi.org/10.5281/zenodo.14697618.) constitutes the artifact we discuss in the present documentAs per Springer style, we are unable to fix footnote link in Abstract. So we have move the text within the brackets.. More specifically, our mechanisation covers our main result, the soundness of the abstract OGS model w.r.t. substitution equivalence (Theorem 8), as well as four example calculi: two variants of call-by-value λ-calculus and two variants of $\mu\tilde{\mu}$-calculus [4,5]. The only axiom used is the Axiom K [17] for equality proof irrelevance (To ease dependent pattern matching due to the intrinsically scoped representation.).

The README explains the installation process and the structure of the code. An online rendering (https://lapin0t.github.io/ogs/esop25/Readme.html.) is available thanks to Alectryon [12]. Furthermore, the main paper provides systematic hyperlinks from statements to their Coq counterparts. We encourage the interested reader to use these tools to navigate the code.

In this document, we focus first on users: how to read and instantiate our main result. We then detail salient technical aspects of our mechanisation.

1 The OGS Library from the Perspective of a User

Our library is intended to be reusable. In this section, we describe to the interested user how to understand our result, and how to instantiate it.

Soundness The main result, Theorem 8, is proven in OGS/Soundness.v. It quantifies over any suitable *language machine*, that is, an axiomatisation of substitution and evaluation in the style of abstract machines. Slightly unfolding the definitions, it is typed as follows.

```
Theorem ogs_correction {Γ} Ω (x y : conf Γ)
   : m_strat _ (inj_init_act Ω x) ≈ m_strat _ (inj_init_act Ω y)
   -> forall γ : Γ =[val]> Ω, eval_o (x ₜ⊛ γ) ≈ eval_o (y ₜ⊛ γ).
```

© The Author(s) 2025
V. Vafeiadis (Ed.): ESOP 2025, LNCS 15694, pp. 200–205, 2025.
https://doi.org/10.1007/978-3-031-91118-7_8

In plain words, for any final scope Ω and language machine configurations x and y, whenever the two OGS strategies obtained by embedding x and y into initial strategy states are weakly bisimilar, then, for any assignment γ, substituting x and y by γ and evaluating them to a final observation yields two weakly bisimilar computations. In other words, either both substituted configurations diverge or both return the same final result.

Language Machine Instantiation Several example language machines satisfying the OGS soundness hypotheses are provided in the `Examples/` folder. Instantiating our generic semantics and proof with one's favorite language always follows the same blueprint. First, define the standard syntax and substitution. Then, because the language evaluator must be presented as an abstract machine, define a family of configurations for this machine. Note that this abstract machine must reduce *open* configurations and these must also support substitution. For some languages such as $\mu\tilde{\mu}$-calculus [4], or say, Jump-With-Argument [10], configurations are already a standard notion, but for others such as λ-calculi, they are generally obtained by pairing a term with an evaluation context. Further, define the observation structure. This amounts to deciding which part of normal form *configurations* should be considered observable for the purpose of observational equivalence testing, and which part should be considered as a set of opaque *values*. Finally, when all these choices are made and the evaluator written, it suffices to check the theorem hypotheses. In our experience, they are always proven quite directly, without any surprising lemma required.

2   Inside the Beast: Implementation Details of Interest

We detail two salient aspects of our development. First, we have implemented strategies as shallow monadic computations, which led us to develop an indexed variant of the Interaction Tree (ITree) structure. Second, we have followed a well-scoped approach, relying on the `Equation` library and the `SProp` universe. This section is intended for expert readers familiar with the companion paper.

2.1   Strategies as Indexed Interaction Trees

Indexed Interaction Trees Library Rather than specifying labelled transition systems relationally in `Prop`, we have chosen a shallow Coq embedding for implementing strategies, understood as possibly non-terminating computations featuring uninterpreted actions (move exchanges). This suggests reusing the ITrees [18] library, which is designed for this purpose. It is also in line with Hancock and Hyvernat's similar construction of *interaction structures* [9], which represent agents in client-server protocols as coinductive trees.

However, the ITree format for specifying possible actions is not expressive enough for our purposes. In essence, it only captures games where the set of allowed client moves is constant throughout. To fix this, instead of describing possible actions by a polynomial functor on **Set**, we describe them by an *indexed* polynomial functor on $\mathbf{Set}^I$, for some set I representing active game positions. The `ITree/` folder thus contains a succinct port of the ITree library to this new indexed setting. This part of the artifact could certainly be useful independently of the OGS construction. We hope to extract it into a self-contained library.

This small library contains the coinductive definition of ITrees, their monadic structure, and the standard iteration operator. We provide definitions for weak and strong bisimilarity, together with the main reasoning principles: strong bisimulation up-to equivalence, and weak and strong bisimulation up-to monadic bind. Both bisimilarity relations are defined using the `Coinduction` [14] library, which provides enhanced coinduction principles based on a lattice-theoretic fixed point construction.[5] This relies on the impredicativity of the `Prop` universe.

Eventually Guarded Iteration Apart from indexing, the main novelty is a pair of new iteration operators, respectively for *guarded* and *eventually guarded* iteration (Prop. 5). They have been crucial in our OGS soundness proof and could certainly be backported to the unindexed ITree library.

The standard unguarded operator can iterate any "loop body", but it must insert a silent step after each iteration to be well-defined. Hence, it only produces a fixed point of the loop body w.r.t. weak bisimilarity, and it is in general not unique. By contrast, our two new operators do not insert any silent step after iteration, and produce unique fixed points w.r.t. strong bisimilarity. For this to work, they respectively require the loop body to feature a guard (a computation step) at each iteration or infinitely often, i.e., after a finite number of iterations.

Theoretically, unguarded iteration can be axiomatised as a complete Elgot monad structure [7] on ITrees quotiented by weak bisimilarity, while our new guarded iteration operators yield two completely iterative monad structures with different notions of guardedness on ITrees quotiented by strong bisimilarity [8].

Relationship with Transition Systems over Games Following Levy and Staton [11], in the paper (Def. 19), we define strategies over some game $\mathcal{G}$: `Game` IJ as a pair of active and waiting state families S^+: $\mathbf{Set}^I$ and S^-: $\mathbf{Set}^J$, together with action and reaction morphisms. This data is dubbed by Levy and Staton a *big-step system over* G and can be more succinctly expressed as a coalgebra for the following endofunctor on $\mathbf{Set}^I \times \mathbf{Set}^J$.

$$(S^+, S^-) \mapsto (\mathcal{D}(\mathtt{final}_{\mathcal{G}} + [\![\mathtt{client}_{\mathcal{G}}]\!]^+ S^-), [\![\mathtt{server}_{\mathcal{G}}]\!]^- S^+)$$

Instead of working with arbitrary coalgebras, we can equivalently see strategies as their image in the *final* coalgebra, whose states consist of coinductive trees. We do not construct this final coalgebra directly, but instead express it using our indexed interaction tree datatype. Given a polynomial endofunctor Σ on $\mathbf{Set}^I$ and an output family X, indexed interaction trees are given by the following final coalgebra:[6] $\mathtt{itree}_\Sigma(X) \coloneqq \nu S.\, X + S + \Sigma(S)$.

---

[5] `Coinduction` recently upgraded from the *companion* to a *tower induction* construction [15]. We have not made this port yet, and hence compile against Coq (8.17).

[6] Note that this is exactly the same construction as given by Xia et al. [18], simply taking place in the category $\mathbf{Set}^I$ instead of $\mathbf{Set}$.

The trick is to focus on strategies in some active position, by considering the sequence of choosing a client move and waiting for the next server move as one unit. Indeed, the composition $[\![\texttt{client}_\mathcal{G}]\!]^+ \circ [\![\texttt{server}_\mathcal{G}]\!]^-$ is a polynomial functor, and states of the final coalgebra of strategies over $\mathcal{G}$ may be computed as:[7]

$$\texttt{strat}_\mathcal{G}^+ := \texttt{itree}_{([\![\texttt{client}_\mathcal{G}]\!]^+ \circ [\![\texttt{server}_\mathcal{G}]\!]^-)} \texttt{final}_\mathcal{G}$$
$$\texttt{strat}_\mathcal{G}^- := [\![\texttt{server}_\mathcal{G}]\!]^- \texttt{strat}_\mathcal{G}^+.$$

Our implementation choices are then straightforward. We encode polynomial endofunctors on $\mathbf{Set}^I$ as *indexed containers* [2], which we dub *events*.

```
Record event (I : Type) := Event {
  e_qry : I -> Type ;
  e_rsp : forall i, e_qry i -> Type ;
  e_nxt : forall i (q : e_qry i), e_rsp i q -> I }.
```

For some indexed container E : event I and output family X : I -> Type, the interaction tree endofunctor and its final coalgebra are respectively:

```
Variant itreeF (REC : I -> Type) (i : I) :=
| RetF (r : X i)
| TauF (t : REC i)
| VisF (q : E.(e_qry) i) (k : forall r : E.(e_rsp) q, REC (E.(e_nxt) r)).
CoInductive itree (i : I) := go { observe : itreeF itree i }.
```

2.2   Scope Structures

Our development of intrinsically-typed-and-scoped syntax largely follows standard practice [6,1]. As this mechanisation style is heavy on dependent pattern matching, we make great use of the Equations plugin [16]. A notable novelty is that we abstract over the concrete representation of scopes and variables, which are usually fixed to lists of object language types and well-typed de Bruijn indices. Our motivation was pragmatic: using tailor-made variable representations drastically reduced the amount of boilerplate in complex $\mu\tilde{\mu}$-calculi instances.

The root cause is that most standard OGS examples involve separating object language types into so-called *positive* and *negative* classes, with only variables of negative types being shared and observed between OGS players. Given a *strict* predicate is_neg : ty -> SProp, negative types can be constructed as the strict subset { t : ty | is_neg t }. The prime benefit is that definitional equality of negative types is exactly definitional equality of the underlying "vanilla" types. For scopes containing only negative types, we lose this nice property if we represent them naively as list { t : ty | is_neg t }. It is vastly more convenient to work with the subset { ts : list ty | allS is_neg ts }, where allS denotes the strict universal quantifier on lists.

---

[7] We do not formally prove it computes the announced final coalgebra, but this can be shown by straightforward fixed point calculation, recalling that $\mathcal{D}(X) := \nu A.X + A$.

To allow for such "non-standard" scope representations and their custom notion of well-typed variable, we devise a notion of *scope structure*, close in spirit to the *Nameless, Painless* approach [13]. A scope structure on S: **Set** for object language types T consists of an element $\varnothing$: S, a binary operation $\oplus$: $S \to S \to S$ and a family of variables $\ni$: $S \to \mathbf{Set}^T$, equipped with two isomorphisms $\varnothing \ni t \approx \bot$ and $(\Gamma \oplus \Delta) \ni t \approx (\Gamma \ni t) \uplus (\Delta \ni t)$. The category of contexts is then taken to be the full image of $\ni$. In other words, objects are elements of S and renamings $\Gamma \to \Delta$ are given by functions $\forall t, \Gamma \ni t \to \Delta \ni t$. This interface can then be instantiated both by lists and de Bruijn indices as well as by our "subset scopes". The substitution metatheory is left mostly unchanged.

References

1. Allais, G., Atkey, R., Chapman, J., McBride, C., McKinna, J.: A type and scope safe universe of syntaxes with binding: their semantics and proofs. Proc. ACM Program. Lang. **2**(ICFP), 1–30 (Jul 2018). https://doi.org/10.1145/3236785
2. Altenkirch, T., Ghani, N., Hancock, P.G., McBride, C., Morris, P.: Indexed containers. J. Funct. Program. **25** (2015). https://doi.org/10.1017/S095679681500009X
3. Borthelle, P., Hirschowitz, T., Jaber, G., Zakowski, Y.: An abstract, certified account of operational game semantics. In: ESOP (2025)
4. Curien, P., Herbelin, H.: The duality of computation. In: ICFP. pp. 233–243. ACM (2000). https://doi.org/10.1145/351240.351262
5. Downen, P., Ariola, Z.M.: Compiling with classical connectives. Log. Methods Comput. Sci. **16**(3) (2020). https://doi.org/10.23638/LMCS-16(3:13)2020
6. Fiore, M., Szamozvancev, D.: Formal metatheory of second-order abstract syntax. Proc. ACM Program. Lang. **6**(POPL), 1–29 (2022). https://doi.org/10.1145/3498715
7. Goncharov, S., Milius, S., Rauch, C.: Complete elgot monads and coalgebraic resumptions. In: MFPS. Electron. Note Theor. Comput. Sci., vol. 325, pp. 147–168. Elsevier (2016). https://doi.org/10.1016/J.ENTCS.2016.09.036
8. Goncharov, S., Schröder, L., Rauch, C., Piróg, M.: Guarded and unguarded iteration for generalized processes. Log. Methods Comput. Sci. **15**(3) (2019). https://doi.org/10.23638/LMCS-15(3:1)2019
9. Hancock, P., Hyvernat, P.: Programming interfaces and basic topology. Ann. Pure Appl. Log. **137**(1-3), 189–239 (2006). https://doi.org/10.1016/J.APAL.2005.05.022
10. Levy, P.B.: Call-By-Push-Value: A Functional/Imperative Synthesis, Semant. Struct. Comput., vol. 2. Springer (2004)
11. Levy, P.B., Staton, S.: Transition systems over games. In: LICS. pp. 64:1–64:10. ACM (2014). https://doi.org/10.1145/2603088.2603150
12. Pit-Claudel, C.: Untangling mechanized proofs. In: SLE. pp. 155—174. ACM (2020). https://doi.org/10.1145/3426425.3426940
13. Pouillard, N.: Nameless, painless. In: ICFP. pp. 320–332. ACM (2011). https://doi.org/10.1145/2034773.2034817
14. Pous, D.: Coinduction all the way up. In: LICS. pp. 307–316. ACM (2016). https://doi.org/10.1145/2933575.2934564
15. Schäfer, S., Smolka, G.: Tower induction and up-to techniques for CCS with fixed points. In: RAMiCS. Lect. Note Comput. Sci., vol. 10226, pp. 274–289 (2017). https://doi.org/10.1007/978-3-319-57418-9_17

16. Sozeau, M., Mangin, C.: Equations reloaded: high-level dependently-typed functional programming and proving in coq. Proc. ACM Program. Lang. **3**(ICFP), 86:1–86:29 (2019). https://doi.org/10.1145/3341690
17. Streicher, T.: Investigations into intensional type theory. Habilitiation Thesis, Ludwig Maximilian Universität (1993)
18. Xia, L., Zakowski, Y., He, P., Hur, C., Malecha, G., Pierce, B.C., Zdancewic, S.: Interaction trees: representing recursive and impure programs in coq. Proc. ACM Program. Lang. **4**(POPL), 51:1–51:32 (2020). https://doi.org/10.1145/3371119

Neural Network Verification is a Programming Language Challenge

Lucas C. Cordeiro[1], Matthew L. Daggitt[2], Julien Girard-Satabin[3], Omri Isac[4],
Taylor T. Johnson[5], Guy Katz[4], Ekaterina Komendantskaya[6,7(✉)],
Augustin Lemesle[3], Edoardo Manino[1], Artjoms Šinkarovs[6], and Haoze Wu[8]

[1] University of Manchester, Manchester, UK
[2] University of Western Australia, Perth, Australia
[3] Atomic Energy and Alternative Energies Commission, Paris, France
[4] Hebrew University of Jerusalem, Jerusalem, Israel
[5] Vanderbilt University, Nashville, USA
[6] Southampton University, Southampton, UK
[7] Heriot-Watt University, Edinburgh, UK
ek1423@soton.ac.uk
[8] Amherst College, Amherst, USA

Abstract. Neural network verification is a new and rapidly developing field of research. So far, the main priority has been establishing efficient verification algorithms and tools, while proper support from the programming language perspective has been considered secondary or unimportant. Yet, there is mounting evidence that insights from the programming language community may make a difference in the future development of this domain. In this paper, we formulate neural network verification challenges as programming language challenges and suggest possible future solutions.

Keywords: Neural Networks · Verification · Domain Specific Languages.

1 Introduction

Traditionally, statistical machine learning has distinguished its methods from "algorithm-driven" programming: the consensus has been that machine learning is deployed when there is example input-output data but no general algorithm for computing outputs from inputs. Thus, neural networks are commonly seen as programs that emerge from data via training, without direct human guidance on how to perform the computation. This unfortunate dichotomy has led to a divide between programming language and machine learning research that is still awaiting resolution.

The first hint that this dichotomy is not as fundamental as was thought came from the machine learning community itself. The famous paper by Szegedy et al. [111] pointed out the "intriguing" problem that even the most accurate neural networks fail to satisfy the property of *robustness*, i.e. small perturbations of their inputs should result in small changes to their output. Szegedy's key

© The Author(s) 2025
V. Vafeiadis (Ed.): ESOP 2025, LNCS 15694, pp. 206–235, 2025.
https://doi.org/10.1007/978-3-031-91118-7_9

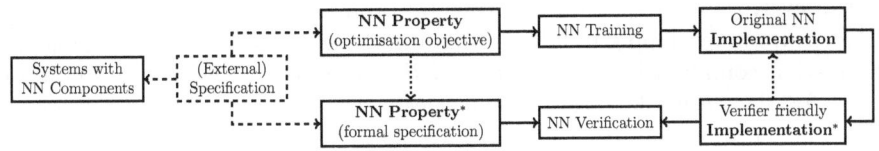

Fig. 1: *Schematic representation of the state of the art in training and verifying neural networks for properties. Solid lines denote methods widely accepted by the research communities, dashed lines mean "some experimental prototypes exist", dotted arrows mean the connection is desired but not established.*

example concerned imperceptible perturbations of pixels in an image that can sway the neural network's classification decisions. This lack of robustness can have safety and security implications: for example, an autonomous car's vision unit may fail to recognise pedestrians on the road. For that reason, the problem attracted significant attention [25] but remains unresolved to this day. Partial solutions often deploy methods of *adversarial training* — i.e., training based on computing *adversarial attacks* — which augment the training set with the worst-case perturbations of the input data points with respect to the output loss of the neural network [77].

The robustness of neural networks actually yields a formal specification [26]. Given a neural network $f : \mathbb{R}^m \to \mathbb{R}^n$, f is *robust around* $\hat{x} \in \mathbb{R}^m$, if

$$\forall x, \|\hat{x} - x\| \le \epsilon \implies \|f(\hat{x}) - f(x)\| \le \delta, \tag{1}$$

where $\epsilon, \delta \in \mathbb{R}$ are small constants and $\|.\|$ computes a vector distance. From the programming language perspective, robustness can be seen as a refinement type that refines input and output types of f, cf. [76]. At the same time, robustness is an example of a *desirable property* that neural networks cannot learn from data alone: note the quantification over vectors x that do not belong to the data set. This challenges the classical dichotomy between algorithm-driven and data-driven programming, demonstrating the inevitability of property specification in both cases.

Against this background, both the machine learning and verification communities proposed several useful methods of training for, or respectively verifying, *certain properties*[9]. Fig. 1 depicts these two groups of methods as two parallel pipelines. At the top, we include all adversarial training methods [77] that were generalised to account for arbitrary optimisation objectives, given a property informally expressed in (a fragment of) first-order logic [45,51]. At the bottom, we include the verification pipeline which is supported by more than a dozen neural network verifiers, such as Marabou [74,119], $\alpha\beta$-CROWN [118], PyRAT [50], to name but a few. Unlike the machine learning approaches, it features a formal language for property specification, VNN-LIB. Furthermore, an annual competition VNN-COMP develops common standards for this domain [20,19].

---

[9] We deliberately use the term "properties" rather than "specifications" here, as the latter means the presence of a sufficiently general specification language.

However, there are several fundamental problems that prevent these emerging ideas from developing to full fruition. Firstly, both the machine learning and verification communities assume that *in theory* a neural network can be optimised for the desirable verification property. However, without any programming language support to ensure this formally, discrepancies between machine learning objectives and verification objectives have been found in the literature, even for simple robustness properties [26]. In Fig. 1, this problem is depicted by distinguishing the two versions of **NN Property** and **NN Property***and a dotted line between them. The desirable solution is to have a single language with the relevant specification, which is then compiled down to either verification or machine learning backends.

Similarly, discrepancies have been reported between different representations of neural networks [70], e.g., using real numbers in verification and floating point numbers in training. In Fig. 1, this problem is depicted by showing two potentially disagreeing implementations, **Implementation** and **Implementation***. Ideally, we should be able to verify the actual programs, and not their idealised descriptions. Or, as an equally acceptable alternative, the solid arrow between two implementations in Fig. 1 should be reversed in the other direction – ensure that the guarantees concerning the verified neural networks extend to their actual implementations, thus establishing the connection along the bottom dotted arrow in Fig. 1.

Finally, neural networks are rarely implemented as stand-alone programs. More often, they are embedded into larger system development that, in turn, may have its own specification and verification regimes. Although the idea of a verified neural network controller is not itself new to the cyber-physical system research (cf. § 3.7), the programming language support for verification of such systems is a nascent field [114,88].

In this light, we believe it is time to discuss how the verification and synthesis of safe neural networks fit together with general programming practices. In this "Fresh Perspectives" paper, we give an overview of the current state of the art in implementing neural network verification and explain the challenges the neural network verification community currently faces (Sec. 3). We do so by tracing different parts of the diagram in Fig. 1, and explaining the nature of the discrepancies in its different parts, from the programming language point of view. We wrap up this paper by suggesting possible ways the programming language community can help improve the state of the art (Sec. 4).

2   Neural Network Verification Properties

The problem of defining verification properties for neural networks has received substantial attention. Verification approaches started with neural networks deployed as controllers in autonomous systems [101,73]. With time, they were generalised to cover data-dependent verification properties such as robustness [63,42,41,121]. A set of standard benchmarks is revised and updated annually at the VNN-COMP; the competition reports [21,18] provide a thorough overview of them.

Neural network verification properties can be divided into three categories.

1. **Geometric properties.** These properties are based on the geometry of the data manifold without any appeal to its possible semantic meaning. One such property is (local) *robustness*, whose definition is given in Equation 1 (see also the additional examples in [27]). Another related property is (local) *equivalence* [113], which constrains the output of two different networks to be similar under the same input, either in absolute value (ϵ-equivalence) or class prediction (top-k equivalence).

2. **Hyper-properties.** These properties require guarantees for any input, rather than just those close to the data manifold. Classic examples are global robustness [100] and global equivalence [81]. A more recent example of such properties is *confidence-based robustness* [8], which allows for some non-robust behaviour, but only for inputs close to the decision boundary. The latter complicates the specification and verification process in interesting ways (see Sec. 4).

3. **Domain-specific properties.** These properties are based on the presumed semantics of the data on which the neural network is trained. Usually, they take the form of admissible intervals on the input and output vector values.

The ACAS Xu challenge (the oldest neural network verification benchmark) best illustrates this third class of properties. It takes a neural network that models an aircraft controller: based on five input measurements between the own ship and an intruder (distance, angles, relative speeds), the neural network outputs one of five advisory actions (strong/weak left or right, clear of conflict).

When the benchmark was introduced in [73], nine properties were formulated by the engineers who designed the collision avoidance software. For instance, Property 3 states that *if the intruder is directly ahead and is moving towards the own ship, the network will not advise clear of conflict.* When written in the VNN-LIB query language [34] (see Sec. 3.1), the property is translated to real-valued intervals on the five input measurements and a constraint on the output prediction.

3   Neural Network Verification: State of the Art

In this section, we describe the state of the art in neural network verification, from the perspective of the existing programming language support, rather than the existing verification algorithms. For the latter, the tutorial [4] is available. We will proceed by tracing different arrows of Figure 1 and explaining the existing discrepancies and solutions.

3.1   Verification pipeline

Neural Network Verification Problem. Let us start with describing the common verification pipeline illustrated in Fig. 2. Given a trained neural network $f : \mathbb{R}^m \to \mathbb{R}^n$ and some network property Ξ, the *Neural Network Verification Problem* is the problem of deciding whether $\Xi(f)$ holds. Current verifiers

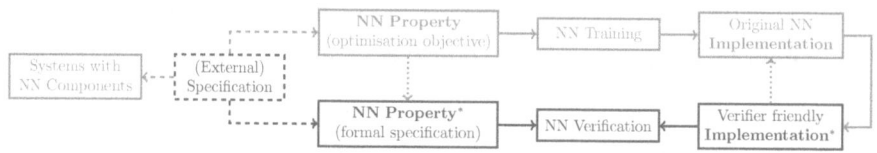

Fig. 2: *Schematic representation of the neural network verification pipeline.*

assume using a special format — ONNX (standing for *Open Neural Network Exchange*) [1] — to represent the neural networks. Thus, in reality, we verify $\Xi(f^*)$, where f^* is obtained from f by ONNX translation.

The verifiers typically consider properties defining a precondition on the network inputs and a postcondition on its outputs. Both conditions are most commonly linear (e.g., defined using linear bounds) and represent safe regions. Formally, let $\Xi := \langle P, Q \rangle$ where $P : \mathbb{R}^m \to \{\top, \bot\}$ and $Q : \mathbb{R}^n \to \{\top, \bot\}$. The neural network verification problem is then deciding whether $\forall x \in \mathbb{R}^m : P(x) \Rightarrow Q(f^*(x))$. Neural network verification algorithms then attempt to find a counterexample (i.e., $x \in \mathbb{R}^m$ such that $P(x) \wedge \neg Q(f^*(x))$) or conclude there is none. Several *neural network verifiers* are currently available to solve such verification problems: e.g. Marabou [74,119], $\alpha\beta$-CROWN [118], PyRAT [50], NNV [116,84] and ERAN [109]. Since 2020, an annual International Verification of Neural Networks Competition (VNN-COMP) has been held, and has played an important role in consolidating the new research community and developing standards for this domain [20,19].

Mainstream specification languages. Most neural network verifiers have a basic query language for representing individual queries. These formats are invariably simple enough so that the type-system is implicit rather than explicit and they possess no capability to abstract over definitions. The *de-facto* standard is the VNN-LIB query language [34] which is used in VNN-COMP [11]. The language is a subset of the QFLRA fragment of the SMT-LIB language, an S-expression based language widely used in the SMT verification community as a standard input for SMT provers [13]. The goal of VNN-LIB is to model first-order logic properties on the inputs and outputs of neural networks. Fig. 3 illustrates a snippet of robustness specification written in VNN-LIB. As can be seen, VNN-LIB specification itself does not explicitly talk about the functions f or f^*, rather it is assuming that the property will be used to verify the function f^* provided in a separate ONNX file. Thus, VNN-LIB and ONNX together serve as a specification for $\Xi(f^*)$.

From a programming language perspective, there are several issues with the VNN-LIB format as a language for expressing specifications.

1. **Lack of expressivity.** VNN-LIB and ONNX are simply not expressive enough to represent all the specifications users want to write. For example, the VNN-LIB and ONNX formats can only refer to a single neural network

```
(declare-const X_0 Real)        (assert (<= X_0 0.0))
(declare-const X_1 Real)        (assert (>= X_0 0.0))
. . .                           . . .
(declare-const X_791 Real)      (assert (<= X_791 -58.231295852661134))
(declare-const Y_0 Real)        (assert (>= X_791 -75.58388969421387))
. . .                           . . .
(declare-const Y_8 Real)        (assert (>= Y_5 Y_1))
(declare-const Y_9 Real)        (assert (>= Y_5 Y_3))
```

Fig. 3: *Snippet of robustness specification in VNN-Lib for an image data set that has input of dimension 792 and 10 classes. The specification assumes an external definition of $f^* : \mathbb{R}^{792} \to \mathbb{R}^{10}$.*

at a time, which makes encoding specifications where one needs to express properties on several neural networks at once impossible. Similarly, hyperproperties [8,27] cannot be specified in VNN-LIB without special tooling, and neither can properties involving hidden neurons. Finally, VNN-LIB only supports satisfaction queries, meaning the specification writer must manually negate universal queries before being encoded.

2. **Lack of conciseness.** The lack of abstraction and the limitation that variables cannot represent multi-dimensional tensors means that more complex properties cannot be represented concisely. Consequently, the length of the queries tend to scale with the dimensions of inputs and outputs of the network, even when the property can be expressed concisely in mathematics in constant space. For example, the full specification in Fig. 3 that encodes the single line of Eq. 1 is a couple of thousand lines long.

3. **Lack of rigour.** VNN-LIB does not have a formally defined semantics, nor does it even formally define its own syntax. Consequently, it is difficult for users to check whether their specification in VNN-LIB is correct or compliant, and impossible to prove the soundness of tools that either consume or generate VNN-LIB. Furthermore, the ONNX format that VNN-LIB relies on, also lacks a formal semantics. For example, the ONNX documentation for the convolution operator[10] has no proper mathematical specification for the semantics of the operator, describing it only with the single sentence "The convolution operator consumes an input tensor and a filter, and computes the output". Other ONNX operator descriptions like those of Convolution, Maxpool, or Add (for broadcasting) refer to external sources like Numpy, PyTorch or Tensorflow for more implementation details.

4. **Lack of dynamic bindings to datasets.** Crucial to most attempts to specify "correctness" of a neural network is the notion of the *data manifold*, i.e., the distribution of inputs that the neural network will actually encounter during operation. Usually, the data manifold is only a small subset of the actual input space. By definition, the network should never encounter inputs that lie off the data-manifold during normal operation. If it does, there is no reason to require any particular behaviour from the network, and con-

---

[10] https://onnx.ai/onnx/operators/onnx__Conv.html, accessed *21-09-2024*

sequently, specifications should only quantify over inputs that lie on the manifold. The problem is that, in most cases, there is no precise mathematical definition of the data manifold. Therefore, the most common approach is for the specification to approximate the manifold as the union of "small" regions around each input in the training dataset. Unfortunately, the training datasets themselves are frequently huge, anywhere from thousands to hundreds of millions of items. Therefore, it is infeasible to directly express the dataset in the specification.

This lack of rigour of the underlying specification format has been recognised as a major problem. A recent effort in the ONNX community has led to the creation of a ONNX Safety-Related Profile working group[11] which aims to elaborate a dedicated ONNX profile for safety-related systems. While still embryonic, this working group might answer some of the issues highlighted above.

To work around the remaining problems, the natural solution is to allow users to represent their specifications in a higher-level specification language, connecting the neural network specification to the language of the larger system in which it is embedded. Moreover, the specification language must provide some mechanism for dynamically binding variables to existing datasets in standard formats used by machine learning practitioners.

3.2   Prototypes of New Specification Languages

In response to the outlined problems, two major attempts have been made to design more principled specification languages for neural network verification. We outline the essence of both, in turn. Fig. 4 provides code snippets for illustration.

1. **CAISAR.** The CAISAR platform [50] incorporates a higher-level specification language deriving from WhyML [44]. WhyML is a typed first-order language with pattern-matching, polymorphism, and a module system. On top of that, CAISAR provides additional types of linear algebra structures common in machine learning and compiles the specification back to plain WhyML. Writing a compiler from WhyML to VNN-LIB is straightforward, allowing CAISAR to target all state-of-the-art solvers from one single specification. It can also deal with specifications involving multiple neural networks and dynamically bind variables to concrete datasets. However, it can be argued that the composability of WhyML is limited, and the lack of dependent types prevents the modelling of important properties (for instance, encoding the dimension of inputs directly in their types could prevent common runtime errors).

2. **Vehicle.** The Vehicle specification language [32,31,30] is a higher-order and dependently-typed functional language. The language aims to be able to express a full range of specifications and to that end it contains quantifiers as first class language constructs, conditionals and higher order functions over

---

[11] https://github.com/ericjenn/working-groups/blob/ericjenn-srpwg-wg1/safety-related-profile/README.md

```
theory MNIST

  use ieee_float.Float64
  use caisar.types.Float64WithBounds as Feature
  use caisar.types.IntWithBounds as Label
  use caisar.model.Model

  use caisar.dataset.CSV
  use caisar.robust.ClassRobustCSV

  constant model_filename: string
  constant dataset_filename: string

  constant label_bounds: Label.bounds =
    Label.{ lower = 0; upper = 9 }

  constant feature_bounds: Feature.bounds =
    Feature.{ lower = (0.0:t); upper = (1.0:t) }

[...]
  predicate robust (f_bounds: Feature.bounds)
                   (l_bounds: Label.bounds)
                   (m: model) (eps: t)
                   (l: Label.t)
                   (e: FeatureVector.t) =
    forall perturbed_e: FeatureVector.t.
      has_length perturbed_e (length e) ->
      FeatureVector.valid f_bounds perturbed_e ->
      let perturbation = perturbed_e - e in
      bounded_by_epsilon perturbation eps ->
      advises l_bounds m perturbed_e l

[...]
  goal robustness:
    let nn = read_model model_filename in
    let dataset = read_dataset dataset_filename in
    let eps = (0.010000000...:t) in
    robust feature_bounds label_bounds nn dataset eps

end
```

```
type Label = Index 10
type Image = Tensor Rat [28, 28]

@network
mnist : Image -> Tensor Rat [10]

validImage : Image -> Bool
validImage x = forall i j .
  0 <= x ! i ! j <= 1

advises : Image -> Label -> Bool
advises x i = forall j .
  j != i => mnist x ! i > mnist x ! j

@parameter
epsilon : Rat

boundedByEpsilon : Image -> Bool
boundedByEpsilon x = forall i j .
  -epsilon <= x ! i ! j <= epsilon

robust : Label -> Image -> Bool
robust label image = forall perturbation .
  boundedByEpsilon perturbation and
  validImage (perturbation + image) =>
  advises label (perturbation + image)

@parameter(infer=True)
n : Nat

@dataset
images : Tensor Image [n]

@dataset
labels : Tensor Label [n]

@property
robustness : Tensor Bool [n]
robustness = foreach i .
  robustAround (images ! i) (labels ! i)
```

(a) CAISAR   (b) Vehicle

Fig. 4: *An extract from a local robustness specification in CAISAR and Vehicle's input languages for the same image dataset described in Fig. 3. Note the ability to reuse predicates and definitions, the conciseness of vector-based operations, and the explicit data set bindings.*

tensors such as maps and folds. The language's dependently typed nature allows the user to encode richer properties and includes tensor size constraints that can be checked before verification by the type-checker. Vehicle also has a backend that allows connecting proofs of neural network properties to larger system specifications in Agda [31]. However, unlike CAISAR, it connects to far fewer tools and cannot allow multiple solvers to work together.

These two languages solve the problems outlined in Sec. 3.1 and provide a concrete implementation. Note, in particular, that both manage data set bindings, neural network bindings, and data validity checks in clear, explicit ways. By doing this, they are essentially building the specification languages on top of the

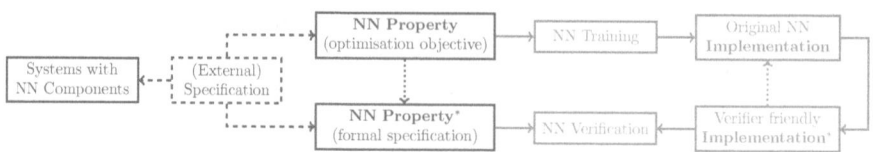

Fig. 5: *Schematic representation of the embedding gap.*

existing pipelines: in Figs. 1 and 2, this is depicted by a dashed "Specification" box towards the left side. Other specification languages exist, like NeSAL [122] (which has no implementation) or DNNP [106] (lacking quantifiers and strong typing).

3.3   The Embedding Gap

We now consider the influence of larger system verification on the neural network verification pipeline (see Fig. 5). Consider a purely symbolic program $s(\cdot)$, whose completion requires computing a complex, unknown function $\mathcal{H} : \mathcal{P} \to \mathcal{R}$ that maps objects in the *problem input space* $\mathcal{P}$ to those in the *problem output space* $\mathcal{R}$. Given an embedding function $e : \mathcal{P} \to \mathbb{R}^m$ and an unembedding function $u : \mathbb{R}^n \to \mathcal{R}$, we can approximate $\mathcal{H}$ by training a neural network $f : \mathbb{R}^m \to \mathbb{R}^n$ such that $u \circ f \circ e \approx \mathcal{H}$. We refer to $u \circ f \circ e$ as the *solution*, and refer to $\mathbb{R}^m$ and $\mathbb{R}^n$ as the *embedding input space* and *embedding output space* respectively. Unlike objects in the problem space, the vectors in the embedding space are often not directly interpretable. The complete program is then modelled as $s(u \circ f \circ e)$. Examples of u and e would be the normalization of inputs, resizing operations for images, or data augmentation operations that are commonplace in machine learning pipelines.

Our end goal is to prove that $s(u \circ f \circ e)$ satisfies a property Ψ, which we will refer to as the *program property*. The natural way to proceed is to establish a *solution property* Φ and a *network property* Ξ such that the proof of Ψ is decomposable into the following three lemmas:

$$\Xi(f) \tag{2}$$
$$\forall g : \Xi(g) \Rightarrow \Phi(u \circ g \circ e) \tag{3}$$
$$\forall h : \Phi(h) \Rightarrow \Psi(s(h)) \tag{4}$$

i.e. Lemma 2 proves that the network f obeys the network property Ξ, then Lemma 3 proves that this implies $u \circ f \circ e$, the neural network lifted to the problem space, obeys the solution property Φ, and finally Lemma 4 proves that this implies $s(u \circ f \circ e)$, the neuro-symbolic program, obeys the program property Ψ.

The first issue that we run into is what we call the *embedding gap*. In Ψ, users would like to be able to model data that potentially has non-trivial semantics (for example, featuring both continuous and discrete parameters of a cyber-physical system such as velocity, stopping distance, switches etc.). However, in

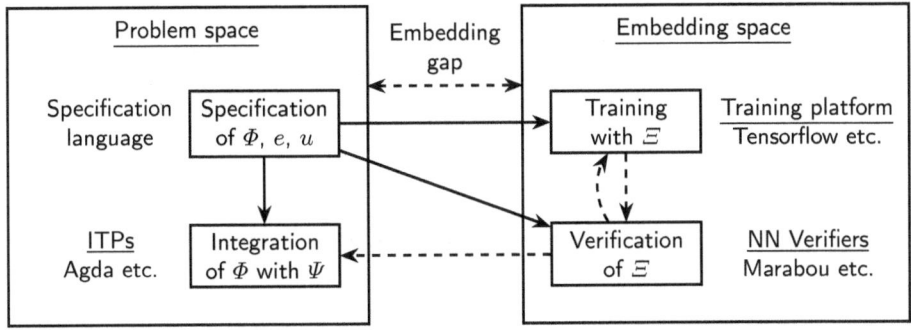

Fig. 6: *Outline of Vehicle compiler backends, bridging the Embedding Gap [32,31]. Dashed lines indicate information flow and solid lines automatic compilation.*

Ξ, all values must be represented as continuous real vectors (in actuality, at the training phase, floating-point vectors, cf. Sec. 3.4). A function from the latter to the former must be highly non-surjective.

For example, consider an input type with two values, 'Yes' and 'No', encoded as real values '0.0' and '1.0' correspondingly. In the low-level query, one can encode that this input variable can only take two possible values using a disjunctive constraint ($x = 0.0 \lor x = 1.0$), but this does not scale well as the number of constructors in the data type grows, as each disjunction drastically increases the cost of verification. Instead, the most common current solution is to encode this as a single non-disjunctive constraint, $0.0 \leq x \leq 1$. In this case, the problem is that floating-point numbers may contain other values (e.g., '0.005', '0.97'), which are meaningless in the chosen domain.

More generally, if users are to express specifications in Ψ, the high-level specification language must also allow users to specify the embedding and unembedding functions, e and u, as part of the specification. It should then be the responsibility of the compiler to generate suitable low-level queries representing Ξ. However, allowing the user to encode their specifications at the high-level Φ requires that the specification language compiler must be able to automatically translate from the former to the latter. The only existing attempt to provide programming language support for this was made by Vehicle [32,31,30] as shown in Fig. 6. In particular, Vehicle proposes a specification language to express Φ, e, u, and can compile the specification to Agda, in which more general properties of $s(\cdot)$ can be defined.

3.4   The Implementation Gap

In Sec. 3.1 we considered $\Xi(f^*)$, where f^* was an ONNX object, possibly obtained by conversion from the original implementation of f. The ONNX format has no backward translation from f^* to f, as the diagram in Fig. 7 shows. However, in the majority of neural network verification publications, authors implicitly assume that obtained verification guarantees about f^* extend to f. In

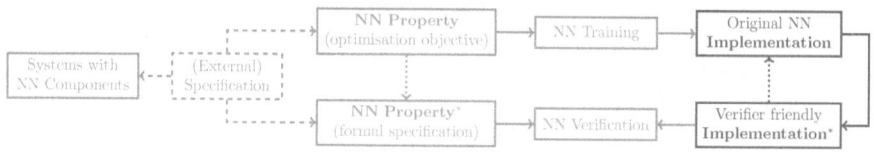

Fig. 7: *Schematic representation of the implementation gap.*

this section, we outline a range of problems caused by this and thus trace the right-most section of the diagram illustrated in Figs. 1 and 7.

Poor support for neural architecture conversion to ONNX. ONNX re-implementation of original neural networks remains a largely manual and un-verified procedure, which may be a source of errors. For example, neural networks contain different types of linear (e.g., fully connected, convolutional) and non-linear (e.g., ReLU, sigmoid, MaxPool) connections. Supporting the formal analysis of a new type of connection typically requires tool developers to add a new dedicated module to the codebase. For example, in verifiers based on abstract interpretation [109], this process would involve implementing the abstract transformer for the new type of connection. In SMT-based verification procedures [73,120], the developer would need to implement the encoding, simplification, and satisfiability checking of constraints corresponding to the new connection. This process is tedious, repetitive, and error-prone. For example, the verification code for two-phase activation functions such as ReLU, Leaky ReLU, and absolute values is very similar, yet developers typically need to hard-code separate verification modules for each of these connections. Ideally, there should be automated conversion procedures with correctness guarantees.

Mismatch in numerical types. Barring experimental architectures that rely on analog computing [123], most implementations of neural networks are based on digital platforms that operate with finite-precision types such as integer and floating-point numbers. Effective conversion between real-valued types and finite-precision ones is an active research direction in machine learning [48].

The most ubiquitous numerical type in machine learning is the floating-point number [80,14]. Indeed, the IEEE 754 single precision (32-bit) floating point type [64] is the de facto standard of libraries such as Tensorflow[12] and Pytorch[13]. Efforts to improve over the IEEE 754 standard exist, but they are often relegated to the context of hardware accelerators, where reducing the bit-size of numerical types may yield significant gains in terms of speed, memory and power consumption [117,23].

From the verification perspective, it is well known that the safety certificates produced by real-valued neural network verifiers do not hold for floating-point

---

[12] https://www.tensorflow.org
[13] https://pytorch.org/

implementations [70,128]. Indeed, Jia and Rinard [70] propose an algorithm to search for floating-point counterexamples to real-valued safety certificates, thus invalidating them. Similarly, Zombori et al. [128] construct neural networks that contain undetectable backdoors, as long as the effects of numerical precision are neglected. Furthermore, the counterexamples produced by real-valued verifiers may not exist on a floating-point implementation of the same neural network, a phenomenon that has been reported on some VNN-COMP benchmarks [90].

Other sources of non-determinism. The current machine learning workflow, from training to inference, is not reproducible across different hardware and software platforms [99,28,127,104]. This is due to a variety of reasons:

1. **Non-associativity of floating-point.** It is well-known that floating-point operations are not associative, i.e., $a + (b + c) \neq (a + b) + c$. As such, we can only verify the behaviour of a floating-point neural network if we know the *order* of all its operations. The existing *de-facto* standard ONNX does not include such a level of detail.

2. **Parallel execution.** Inference and training of neural networks are often sped up via parallel execution. Whether this is done via SIMD operations, multi-core CPUs, or GPU parallelism, it always introduces non-determinism in the results [99,104].

3. **Auto-selection of primitives.** Modern machine learning compilers like XLA[14] automatically select the most efficient algorithms depending on the computational load [99]. While PyTorch or Keras present ways to fix the behaviour of the algorithm, the ONNX runtime does not. For instance, Schögl et al. [104] report non-deterministic behaviour in the selection of convolutional algorithms on GPUs, which may alternate between explicit loop, GEMM-based, Winograd and FFT implementations.

4. **Runtime optimisations.** Machine learning frameworks may also implement runtime optimisation modifying the structure of the model itself to speed up inference or reduce memory usage, for example by fusing layers together (e.g. convolution and batch normalisation).

5. **Non-deterministic training.** The learning process itself is highly non-deterministic. Common sources include: parameter initialisation, data augmentation strategy, batch ordering, and dropout layers [99].

6. **Mathematical library rounding.** A long-standing issue in floating-point computation is incorrect roundings in the standard mathematical library `math.h`. Technically, the IEEE 754 standard recommends correct roundings [64], and there are efforts to create open-source implementations of `math.h` that abide by it [107]. However, mainstream compilers instead implement a variety of approximately-rounded algorithms [17].

7. **Low-level implementation details.** Furthermore, derived operators such as Softmax may leverage the fact that $\text{softmax}(x + c) = \text{softmax}(x)$ with constant c to increase the precision and avoid overflows. Such details can only be found in the low-level source code, even though they severely affect the precision of the computation.

---

[14] https://openxla.org/xla

Overall, the end-to-end effects of the above causes of non-determinism cannot be neglected. Indeed, Pham et al. [99] reports a 2.9% difference in accuracy while reproducing the same training run on different platforms. Similarly, Cidon et al. [28] reports a 6% difference in accuracy when considering the whole image recognition pipeline, including camera noise and image processing algorithms.

From the verification perspective, certifying the safety of neural network implementations requires a different approach than high-level neural network verifiers like Marabou [119] or $\alpha\beta$-CROWN [118]. Indeed, if we had access to the low-level implementation of every library in the machine learning pipeline, we could employ software verifiers [15] for this purpose. Unfortunately, existing software verifiers struggle to cope with the scale and complexity of neural network code [90,87,91]. In contrast, automated testing approaches are currently more effective [97,55,35], but cannot prove correctness.

Quantised neural networks. Switching to integer types (uniform quantisation) [48] can help alleviate some of the above problems (e.g. non-associativity of floating point, incorrect rounding) and improve reproducibility. From the machine learning perspective, a good quantisation scheme maintains the accuracy of the original floating-point neural network. Usually, 8-bit integers are used, but more aggressive quantisation schemes exist, down to ternary [57] and binary representations [102].

From the verification perspective, integer and binary data types require fundamentally different representations than the real-valued types used by mainstream verifiers such as Marabou [119] and $\alpha\beta$-CROWN [118]. Existing work on verifying quantised neural networks relies on either the bit-vector SMT theory [49,12,58] or (mixed) integer linear programming (ILP, MILP) [93,81,125,62]. In contrast, verifying the robustness of some binarised neural network architectures can be encoded as a satisfiability (SAT) problem [96,69]. Other binarised architectures can still be encoded as a real-valued verification instance [6].

3.5   Reliable Proof Production and Checking

To overcome some of the challenges raised above, neural network verifiers may accompany their results with proof certificates, attesting their soundness using an external and relatively simple checking program (the *proof checker*) [65]. Since neural network verifiers are complex software, optimised for performance and speed, their verification is commonly intractable. Thus, proof production replaces the need to directly verify the neural network verifiers, with the need to verify only the proof checker. When a safety property is violated, neural network verifiers often accompany their results with a counterexample, which can then be checked by its evaluation in the network. However, proving safety (i.e., absence of violation of the property) is not straightforward, as the DNN verification problem is NP-complete even for simple networks [73,103]. Therefore, proving safety is a greater challenge than proving a violation, and thus requires a more complicated proof and, consequently, a more complicated proof checker.

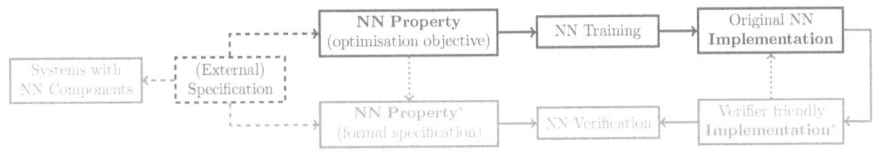

Fig. 8: *Schematic representation of the neural network training pipeline.*

Proof production mechanism, supporting several piecewise-linear activation functions, was implemented on top of Marabou [65,119]. The proofs produced by Marabou are checked by a proof checker implemented within Marabou. The Marabou proof checker is implemented in C++ and uses floating points arithmetic for its computations.

When using an external proof checker, the reliability of the neural network verifier is dependent on the reliability of the proof checker. Therefore, the proof checker is expected to meet higher standards of reliability, ideally provable soundness. Functional programming languages allow the implementation of a precise checker and formal verification of its soundness. For example, a simply-typed language Imandra was deployed to check proofs produced by Marabou [36,37]. This work also shows that computations with precise real arithmetic come at a price of limited performance. This opens up the possibility for a variety of implementations of the same checking algorithm in different programming languages, exploring the trade-off between precision and performance speed.

3.6   Property-Guided Training

Finally, we give a brief outline of the state-of-the-art in the property-guided training, which occupies the upper section of Fig. 8. This is a booming area in its own right, also known under the umbrella term of *neuro-symbolic AI*. By pointing out existing programming language discrepancies and solutions, we do not attempt to give a full survey of neuro-symbolic AI, but refer the reader to more comprehensive surveys [52,59].

In the introduction, we have already outlined the evolution from adversarial training (seen as training for the robustness property specifically) into a more general property-driven training (for any property of choice) [45,110,46]. It is noteworthy that, although robust training by *projected gradient descent* [53,86,78] predates verification, contemporary approaches are often related to, or derived from, the corresponding verification methods by optimizing verification-inspired regularization terms.

The weakest form of property-based training boils down to translating a specification written in a subset of first-order logic into a *loss function*, that serves directly as an optimisation objective within the implementation of a training algorithm. Thus, the training algorithm optimises the neural network to satisfy the desired property. This translation method is known under the name of *differentiable logic* (or DL) [45,110,46]. Vehicle implements DL as one of its backends [31] (cf. Fig. 6) and serves as a prototype of a compiler for neural network property specification languages (cf. Fig. 1). Recently, this inspired attempts at formalising different DLs in Coq [2].

There are other forms of training for robustness that come with stronger guarantees than DLs, e.g. IBP training [54,124] and certified training [95,126]. However, these usually have limited capacity for property specification; investigation of how these methods may fit into larger verification pipelines is warranted.

3.7   Other Directions

Verification of Cyber-Physical Systems. When following the diagram of Fig. 1, we did not impose any assumptions on the nature of properties we wish to ensure. In particular, we did not specify whether the "System" needs to be a cyber-physical system (CPS). However, CPS with machine learning components is an important safety-critical use case for neural network verification.

For example, a neural network may be utilized as a feedback controller for some plant model, typically represented as ordinary differential equations (ODEs) or generalizations thereof like hybrid automata. These are known as *neural networks control systems (NNCS)*. The introduction of constraints to describe the dynamics of a CPS requires revisiting several blocks of Fig. 1. Specifically, we need to replace the purely symbolic specifications and algorithms with those allowing for continuous variables and differential equations.

The annual International Competition on Verifying Continuous and Hybrid Systems (ARCH-COMP) has a category for this problem class, known as the AI and NNCS (AINNCS) category [85,72,71,82,83]. Several approaches for addressing the NNCS verification problem have been developed, such as implemented within software tools like CORA [75], JuliaReach [16], NNV [116,84], OVERT [108], POLAR [60], Sherlock [40,39], ReachNN* [61,43], VenMAS [3], and Verisig [68,67,66].

More broadly, researchers have considered several strategies for the specification of properties of CPS with neural network components [47,7,24]. These cover significant challenges in the CPS domain, ranging from classical software verification problems to real-time systems concerns, scalability, as well as finding suitable specifications [105,115,114,88]. Similarly to the standard neural network verification pipeline of Fig. 1, this area would benefit from a more principled programming language support.

Formal Specification of Probabilistic Properties. Program synthesis techniques can be valuable allies in producing correct-by-construction software and systems. In particular, the synthesis of logical formulas from a neural network and a dataset (e.g., via Inductive Logical Programming) received long-timed interest [98]. Also orthogonal to our work is Probabilistic Programming (as seen in [89]), which aims to provide a language and toolchain to express probabilistic properties of programs. It is clear that neural networks – seen as programs – would benefit from a probabilistic specification language. An early example in this direction is the ProbCompCert [112] project.

Existing Solutions	High-level		Low-level		Quantised		Software		Future	
PL Challenges Addressed	Vehicle [32]	CAISAR [50]	αβ-Crown [118]	Marabou [74]	QEBVerif [125]	Aster [81]	CBMC [79]	ESBMC [92]	Unified Language	Formal Interfaces
§3.1-3.2. Rigorous Semantics	✓	✓					✓	✓	✓	✓
§3.3. Embedding Gap	✓								✓	✓
§3.4. Implementation Gap		✓		✓	✓	✓	✓	✓	✓	
§3.5. Proof Certificates				✓			✓*		✓	✓
§3.6. Supports Training	✓								✓	✓

Table 1: *Examples of existing solutions and the PL challenges they (partially) address. For the sake of variety, we include the existing solutions in four distinct categories:* **high-level neural network verification DSLs** *(Vehicle, CAISAR); best-performing (according to VNNCOMP)* **low-level neural network verifiers** *(αβ-Crown, Marabou);* **formalisation and synthesis of quantised neural networks** *with mainstream MILP solvers (QEBVerif, Aster); and the use of* **general-purpose software verifiers** *(CBMC, ESBMC) in neural-network verification. For the latter, when we mark proof certificate production as ✓*, we refer to the generic proof production available for those verifiers, as opposed to the production of the* Farkas *witness for neural network* **UNSAT** *problems that is available in Marabou.*

Formalisation of Machine Learning. So far, research on formalisation of neural networks or optimisation algorithms has developed in isolation from the mainstream neural network verification pipelines summarised in Fig. 1. However, these two lines of research are bound to meet one day. Relevant work in formalisation of machine learning includes: verification of neural networks in Isabelle/HOL [22] and Imandra [38]; formalisation of piecewise affine activation functions in Coq [5]; providing formal guarantees of the degree to which the trained neural network will generalise to new data in Coq [10]; convergence, in this case of a single-layered perceptron in Coq [94]; verification of neural archetypes in Coq [33]. The two approaches that came the closest to unifying formalisation and verification in neural network domain are the Vehicle formalisation in Agda [9] and the formalisation of differentiable logics in Coq [2], relation of the latter to the verification pipeline of Fig. 1 is discussed in Sec. 3.6.

4   The Future Roadmap

The previous section identified five desirable programming language features that neural network verification could benefit from: rigorous semantics, support for handling the embedding and implementation gaps, generation of proof certificates, and rigorous integration of property-driven training into verification pipelines. Currently, no single neural network verification tool or framework possesses all five features (see Table 1). Moreover, some tools considered leaders in the neural network verification market do not satisfy any. The title of this paper reflects our belief that the desirable solution – global specifications that *formally* explain the expected properties and yield a *formal* proof that the given implementation respects the specification – is a challenge in programming language design. In this section, we overview a couple of possible directions that may play a role in future solutions.

4.1   A Unified Dependently Typed Language

We believe the idealised solution to be a single language that is expressive enough to implement the machine learning pipeline and, at the same time, encode the desired properties of both the neural networks created by the pipeline and the pipeline itself. The following are a non-exhaustive list of the types of properties that should be representable:

1. theoretical results about the convergence of the training process;
2. correctness of tensor operations that underlie the training;
3. rich properties of the input data, e.g., constraining inputs to a certain range;
4. relation between input data and the weights in the network produced, e.g., robustness;
5. properties of the floating point numbers being used.

Given the complexity of encoding some of these properties (e.g. numerical stability, robustness), we believe that the expressive power of dependent types is a natural fit. We now briefly argue how such a unified dependent-typed language would allow us to make progress towards the challenges outlined in Table 1.

1. **Rigorous semantics.** The meta-theory of dependent types is well studied [29] so defining rigorous semantics for the language should not be a significant challenge. Furthermore, by implementing all the components in a single language, the friction of aligning the semantics of the different components in the system is significantly reduced.
2. **Embedding gap.** In a dependently typed language, from one perspective there would be no embedding gap, as any representation changes must be stated explicitly as type conversions. However, from another perspective, working in such a language does not address the fundamental problem of translating the proofs from the problem space to the embedding space. It merely moves the work from the external proofs into the type-conversion functions. Nevertheless, the expressive power of dependent types is more than sufficient to implement the partial solutions proposed by Vehicle (Sec. 3.3).
3. **Implementation gap.** The implementation gap (Sec. 3.4) will be resolved, as implementations will respect their types. For example, consider numerical types. If our specification assumes infinite reals, there is no way to instantiate an implementation that uses machine floats, as we will not be able to prove that machine floats is a valid representation of reals. If our specification is

weak and we do not require properties of the operations or other equalities, then machine floats may be a valid data type for the chosen constraints. If we envision implementation to operate on machine floats, we can describe all the properties of interest (e.g., lack of associativity) in the data type. We must understand that we cannot use external libraries such as XLA or OpenBLAS without verifying them, as this will break all the formal guarantees in our specification. Either these libraries have to be verified formally or we can synthesise the code with similar runtime properties directly from our specification in a type-preserving way.

4. **Proof certificates.** In a dependently-typed language, where the specifications are encoded as types, there is no need for separate proof certificates or proof checkers. In particular, the terms themselves act as the proof certificates and the type-checker acts as the proof checker.

5. **Supports training.** Although at the moment training is carried out in non-dependently typed languages, there is nothing stopping training (e.g. automatic differentiation or similar algorithms) from being implemented in dependently-typed language. Not only would such an implemention significantly reduce the friction between training and verification, it would also facilitate the integrating property-driven training and verification by viewing it as code synthesis problem. The key idea here is that generating code from a formal specification is much easier than checking whether the given code respects the specification.

4.2 Formal Interfaces

However, we are not naive as to the difficulty of implementating such a unified framework. Firstly, it will be an uphill battle to overcome the significant first-mover advantage of existing tools in their respective domains, e.g. training frameworks in Python, C and others and neural network verifiers. Even leaving that aside, work has shown that checking such complex type-based specifications in an efficient manner is still a challenging problem (e.g. Kokke et al. [76]).

Therefore, we believe a more realistic short-term goal is to keep the overarching maximally expressive specification language, but design a compiler that can utilise existing tools to achieve certain subgoals. In particular, we should follow the approach of industry, where the use of many disparate systems is common. In such an environment, the designers of these individual components should not only rigorously pre-define their interfaces, but also provide full formal specifications about their behaviour and, ideally, provide proof certificates that the output satisfies the specification as part of the interface. This would allow the compiler to specify the expected behaviour of a given module and let the programmer choose the best implementation (provided it respects the specification) at that abstraction level.

One possible inspiration for the design of such interfaces could come from the rich literature of behavioural interface specification language (BISL) [56]. A BISL is a family of languages used to specify the expected behaviour of a program at the *function* level, providing a fine-grained level of control on how to precisely describe the function. BISLs usually follow a Hoare triplet-inspired formalism: the programmer should specify the precondition and the control flow; automated provers using weakest-precondition calculus or SAT can then automatically derive preconditions. Drawing from well-known languages like SPARK and Eiffel, it would then become easy to specify invariants on *several functions* at once. Such properties could then be translated back to the original program language (and then checked with the type system) or - if it results in a program that is impossible to represent - checked using external provers. This approach would be representative of what is being done in the industry for critical systems for decades, with JML, Why3 [44] or SPARK.

5   Conclusion

We have given some support for our main thesis – that *neural network verification is increasingly becoming a programming language challenge.* We hope this paper will provoke a stimulating discussion of this topic, helping the programming language community explore the opportunities presented by this new domain. Although we have supported our arguments with references to existing approaches, this is not a survey paper, and we make no claims of bibliographic completeness.

6   Acknowledgements

M. Daggitt and E. Komendantskaya acknowledge the partial support of the EPSRC grant AISEC: AI Secure and Explainable by Construction (EP/T026960/1). E. Komendantskaya was supported by ARIA: Mathematics for Safe AI grant. L. Cordeiro and E. Manino acknowledge the support of the EPSRC grant EnnCore: End-to-End Conceptual Guarding of Neural Architectures (EP/T026995/1). J. Girard-Satabin and Augustin Lemesle were supported by the French Agence Nationale de la Recherche (ANR) grant ANR-23-DEGR-0001 as part of the France 2030 programme. The work of Isac and Katz was partially funded by the European Union (ERC, VeriDeL, 101112713). Views and opinions expressed are however those of the author(s) only and do not necessarily reflect those of the European Union or the European Research Council Executive Agency. Neither the European Union nor the granting authority can be held responsible for them.

References

1. Open Neural Network Exchange format, https://onnx.ai/, accessed on 30.01.2022
2. Affeldt, R., Bruni, A., Komendantskaya, E., Slusarz, N., Stark, K.: Taming Differentiable Logics with Coq Formalisation. In: Interactive Theorem Provers (ITP) 2024 (2024)

3. Akintunde, M.E., Botoeva, E., Kouvaros, P., Lomuscio, A.: Formal verification of neural agents in non-deterministic environments. In: International Conference on Autonomous Agents and Multiagent Systems, AAMAS. pp. 25–33 (2020)

4. Albarghouthi, A.: Introduction to neural network verification (2021), https://arxiv.org/abs/2109.10317

5. Aleksandrov, A., Völlinger, K.: Formalizing piecewise affine activation functions of neural networks in Coq. In: 15th International NASA Symposium on Formal Methods (NFM 2023), Houston, TX, USA, May 16–18, 2023. Lecture Notes in Computer Science, vol. 13903, pp. 62–78. Springer (2023). https://doi.org/10.1007/978-3-031-33170-1_4, https://doi.org/10.1007/978-3-031-33170-1_4

6. Amir, G., Wu, H., Barrett, C., Katz, G.: An smt-based approach for verifying binarized neural networks. In: Groote, J.F., Larsen, K.G. (eds.) Tools and Algorithms for the Construction and Analysis of Systems. pp. 203–222. Springer International Publishing, Cham (2021)

7. Astorga, A., Hsieh, C., Madhusudan, P., Mitra, S.: Perception contracts for safety of ml-enabled systems. Proc. ACM Program. Lang. 7(OOPSLA2) (Oct 2023). https://doi.org/10.1145/3622875

8. Athavale, A., Bartocci, E., Christakis, M., Maffei, M., Nickovic, D., Weissenbacher, G.: Verifying global two-safety properties in neural networks with confidence (2024), https://arxiv.org/abs/2405.14400

9. Atkey, R., Daggitt, M.L., Kokke, W.: Vehicle formalisation (2024), https://github.com/vehicle-lang/vehicle-formalisation

10. Bagnall, A., Stewart, G.: Certifying the true error: Machine learning in Coq with verified generalization guarantees. In: Proceedings of the AAAI Conference on Artificial Intelligence. vol. 33, pp. 2662–2669 (2019)

11. Bak, S., Liu, C., Johnson, T.: The Second International Verification of Neural Networks Competition (VNN-COMP 2021): Summary and Results (2021), technical Report. http://arxiv.org/abs/2109.00498

12. Baranowski, M., He, S., Lechner, M., Nguyen, T.S., Rakamarić, Z.: An smt theory of fixed-point arithmetic. In: Peltier, N., Sofronie-Stokkermans, V. (eds.) Automated Reasoning. pp. 13–31. Springer International Publishing, Cham (2020)

13. Barrett, C., Fontaine, P., Tinelli, C.: The Satisfiability Modulo Theories Library (SMT-LIB). www.SMT-LIB.org (2016)

14. Baskin, C., Liss, N., Schwartz, E., Zheltonozhskii, E., Giryes, R., Bronstein, A.M., Mendelson, A.: Uniq: Uniform noise injection for non-uniform quantization of neural networks. ACM Trans. Comput. Syst. 37(1–4) (mar 2021). https://doi.org/10.1145/3444943, https://doi.org/10.1145/3444943

15. Beyer, D.: Competition on software verification and witness validation: Sv-comp 2023. In: Sankaranarayanan, S., Sharygina, N. (eds.) Tools and Algorithms for the Construction and Analysis of Systems. pp. 495–522. Springer Nature Switzerland, Cham (2023)

16. Bogomolov, S., Forets, M., Frehse, G., Potomkin, K., Schilling, C.: JuliaReach: A toolbox for set-based reachability. In: Proc. of the 22nd ACM International Conference on Hybrid Systems: Computation and Control. p. 39–44 (2019). https://doi.org/10.1145/3302504.3311804

17. Brisebarre, N., Hanrot, G., Muller, J.M., Zimmermann, P.: Correctly-rounded evaluation of a function: why, how, and at what cost? (2024), https://hal.science/hal-04474530/document

18. Brix, C., Bak, S., Johnson, T.T., Wu, H.: The fifth international verification of neural networks competition (vnn-comp 2024): Summary and results (2024), https://arxiv.org/abs/2412.19985

19. Brix, C., Bak, S., Liu, C., Johnson, T.T.: The Fourth International Verification of Neural Networks Competition (VNN-COMP 2023): Summary and Results. CoRR **abs/2312.16760** (2023). https://doi.org/10.48550/ARXIV.2312.16760, https://doi.org/10.48550/arXiv.2312.16760

20. Brix, C., Müller, M.N., Bak, S., Johnson, T.T., Liu, C.: First three years of the international verification of neural networks competition (VNN-COMP). Int. J. Softw. Tools Technol. Transf. **25**(3), 329–339 (2023). https://doi.org/10.1007/S10009-023-00703-4, https://doi.org/10.1007/s10009-023-00703-4

21. Brix, C., Müller, M.N., Bak, S., Johnson, T.T., Liu, C.: First three years of the international verification of neural networks competition (vnn-comp). International Journal on Software Tools for Technology Transfer **25**(3), 329–339 (2023)

22. Brucker, A.D., Stell, A.: Verifying feedforward neural networks for classification in Isabelle/HOL. In: 25th International Symposium on Formal Methods (FM 2023), Lübeck, Germany, March 6–10, 2023. Lecture Notes in Computer Science, vol. 14000, pp. 427–444. Springer (2023). https://doi.org/10.1007/978-3-031-27481-7_24, https://doi.org/10.1007/978-3-031-27481-7_24

23. Burgess, N., Milanovic, J., Stephens, N., Monachopoulos, K., Mansell, D.: Bfloat16 processing for neural networks. In: 2019 IEEE 26th Symposium on Computer Arithmetic (ARITH). pp. 88–91 (2019). https://doi.org/10.1109/ARITH.2019.00022

24. Calinescu, R., Imrie, C., Mangal, R., Rodrigues, G.N., Păsăreanu, C., Santana, M.A., Vázquez, G.: Controller synthesis for autonomous systems with deep-learning perception components. IEEE Transactions on Software Engineering **50**(6), 1374–1395 (2024). https://doi.org/10.1109/TSE.2024.3385378

25. Carlini, N.: A complete list of all (arxiv) adversarial example papers (2019)

26. Casadio, M., Komendantskaya, E., Daggitt, M.L., Kokke, W., Katz, G., Amir, G., Refaeli, I.: Neural network robustness as a verification property: A principled case study. In: Computer Aided Verification (CAV 2022). Lecture Notes in Computer Science, Springer (2022)

27. Christakis, M., Eniser, H.F., Hoffmann, J., Singla, A., Wüstholz, V.: Specifying and testing k-safety properties for machine-learning models (2022), https://arxiv.org/abs/2206.06054

28. Cidon, E., Pergament, E., Asgar, Z., Cidon, A., Katti, S.: Characterizing and taming model instability across edge devices. In: Smola, A., Dimakis, A., Stoica, I. (eds.) Proceedings of Machine Learning and Systems. vol. 3, pp. 624–636 (2021), https://proceedings.mlsys.org/paper_files/paper/2021/file/5190e987c46a346974e351f96997d640-Paper.pdf

29. Coquand, T., Huet, G.: The calculus of constructions. Ph.D. thesis, Inria (1986)

30. Daggitt, M.L., Kokke, W., Atkey, R., Arnaboldi, L., Komendantskya, E.: Vehicle: Interfacing neural network verifiers with interactive theorem provers (2022). https://doi.org/10.48550/ARXIV.2202.05207, https://arxiv.org/abs/2202.05207

31. Daggitt, M.L., Kokke, W., Atkey, R., Slusarz, N., Arnaboldi, L., Komendantskya, E.: Vehicle: Bridging the embedding gap in the verification of neuro-symbolic programs. CoRR **abs/2401.06379** (2024). https://doi.org/10.48550/ARXIV.2401.06379, https://doi.org/10.48550/arXiv.2401.06379

32. Daggitt, M.L., Kokke, W., Komendantskaya, E., Atkey, R., Arnaboldi, L., Slusarz, N., Casadio, M., Coke, B., Lee, J.: The vehicle tutorial: Neural network verification with vehicle. In: Narodytska, N., Amir, G., Katz, G., Isac, O. (eds.) Proceedings of the 6th Workshop on Formal Methods for ML-Enabled Autonomous Systems, FoMLAS@CAV 2023, Paris, France, July 17-18, 2023. Kalpa Publications in Computing, vol. 16, pp. 1–5. EasyChair (2023). `https://doi.org/10.29007/5S2X`, `https://doi.org/10.29007/5s2x`

33. De Maria, E., Bahrami, A., l'Yvonnet, T., Felty, A., Gaffé, D., Ressouche, A., Grammont, F.: On the use of formal methods to model and verify neuronal archetypes. Frontiers of Computer Science **16**(3), 1–22 (2022)

34. Demarchi, S., Guidotti, D., Pulina, L., Tacchella, A.: Supporting standardization of neural networks verification with vnn-lib and coconet. In: 6th Workshop on Formal Methods for ML-Enabled Autonomous Systems (Jul 2023)

35. Deng, Z., Meng, G., Chen, K., Liu, T., Xiang, L., Chen, C.: Differential testing of cross deep learning framework APIs: Revealing inconsistencies and vulnerabilities. In: 32nd USENIX Security Symposium (USENIX Security 23). pp. 7393–7410. USENIX Association, Anaheim, CA (Aug 2023), `https://www.usenix.org/conference/usenixsecurity23/presentation/deng-zizhuang`

36. Desmartin, R., Isac, O., Komendantskaya, E., Stark, K., Passmore, G., Katz, G.: A Certified Proof Checker for Deep Neural Network Verification. In: https://arxiv.org/abs/2405.10611 (2024)

37. Desmartin, R., Isac, O., Passmore, G.O., Stark, K., Komendantskaya, E., Katz, G.: Towards a Certified Proof Checker for Deep Neural Network Verification. In: Glück, R., Kafle, B. (eds.) Logic-Based Program Synthesis and Transformation - 33rd International Symposium, LOPSTR 2023, Cascais, Portugal, October 23-24, 2023, Proceedings. Lecture Notes in Computer Science, vol. 14330, pp. 198–209. Springer (2023). `https://doi.org/10.1007/978-3-031-45784-5_13`, `https://doi.org/10.1007/978-3-031-45784-5_13`

38. Desmartin, R., Passmore, G.O., Komendantskaya, E., Daggit, M.: Checkinn: Wide range neural network verification in imandra. In: PPDP 2022: 24th International Symposium on Principles and Practice of Declarative Programming, Tbilisi, Georgia, September 20 - 22, 2022. pp. 3:1–3:14. ACM (2022). `https://doi.org/10.1145/3551357.3551372`, `https://doi.org/10.1145/3551357.3551372`

39. Dutta, S., Chen, X., Sankaranarayanan, S.: Reachability analysis for neural feedback systems using regressive polynomial rule inference. In: ACM International Conference on Hybrid Systems: Computation and Control, HSCC. pp. 157–168 (2019). `https://doi.org/10.1145/3302504.3311807`

40. Dutta, S., Jha, S., Sankaranarayanan, S., Tiwari, A.: Learning and verification of feedback control systems using feedforward neural networks. IFAC-PapersOnLine **51**(16), 151 – 156 (2018). `https://doi.org/10.1016/j.ifacol.2018.08.026`, iFAC Conference on Analysis and Design of Hybrid Systems ADHS 2018

41. Dutta, S., Jha, S., Sankaranarayanan, S., Tiwari, A.: Output range analysis for deep feedforward neural networks. In: Dutle, A., Muñoz, C., Narkawicz, A. (eds.)

NASA Formal Methods. pp. 121–138. Springer International Publishing, Cham (2018)

42. Ehlers, R.: Formal verification of piece-wise linear feed-forward neural networks. In: D'Souza, D., Narayan Kumar, K. (eds.) Automated Technology for Verification and Analysis. pp. 269–286. Springer International Publishing, Cham (2017)

43. Fan, J., Huang, C., Li, W., Chen, X., Zhu, Q.: Reachnn*: A tool for reachability analysis of neural-network controlled systems. In: International Symposium on Automated Technology for Verification and Analysis (ATVA) (2020)

44. Filliâtre, J.C., Paskevich, A.: Why3 - Where Programs Meet Provers. In: Felleisen, M., Gardner, P. (eds.) Programming Languages and Systems. pp. 125–128. Lecture Notes in Computer Science, Springer, Berlin, Heidelberg (2013). https://doi.org/10.1007/978-3-642-37036-6_8

45. Fischer, M., Balunovic, M., Drachsler-Cohen, D., Gehr, T., Zhang, C., Vechev, M.T.: DL2: training and querying neural networks with logic. In: Chaudhuri, K., Salakhutdinov, R. (eds.) Proceedings of the 36th International Conference on Machine Learning, ICML 2019, 9-15 June 2019, Long Beach, California, USA. Proceedings of Machine Learning Research, vol. 97, pp. 1931–1941. PMLR (2019), http://proceedings.mlr.press/v97/fischer19a.html

46. Flinkow, T., Pearlmutter, B.A., Monahan, R.: Comparing differentiable logics for learning with logical constraints (2024), https://arxiv.org/abs/2407.03847

47. Fremont, D.J., Dreossi, T., Ghosh, S., Yue, X., Sangiovanni-Vincentelli, A.L., Seshia, S.A.: Scenic: a language for scenario specification and scene generation. In: Proceedings of the 40th ACM SIGPLAN Conference on Programming Language Design and Implementation. p. 63–78. PLDI 2019, Association for Computing Machinery, New York, NY, USA (2019). https://doi.org/10.1145/3314221.3314633

48. Gholami, A., Kim, S., Dong, Z., Yao, Z., Mahoney, M.W., Keutzer, K.: A survey of quantization methods for efficient neural network inference. In: Low-Power Computer Vision, pp. 291–326. Chapman and Hall/CRC (2022)

49. Giacobbe, M., Henzinger, T.A., Lechner, M.: How many bits does it take to quantize your neural network? In: Biere, A., Parker, D. (eds.) Tools and Algorithms for the Construction and Analysis of Systems. pp. 79–97. Springer International Publishing, Cham (2020)

50. Girard-Satabin, J., Alberti, M., Bobot, F., Chihani, Z., Lemesle, A.: Caisar: A platform for characterizing artificial intelligence safety and robustness. In: AISafety. CEUR-Workshop Proceedings, Vienne, Austria (Jul 2022), https://hal.archives-ouvertes.fr/hal-03687211

51. Giunchiglia, E., Stoian, M.C., Lukasiewicz, T.: Deep learning with logical constraints. In: Thirty-First International Joint Conference on Artificial Intelligence (IJCAI-22). pp. 5478–5485. International Joint Conferences on Artificial Intelligence Organization (7 2022). https://doi.org/10.24963/ijcai.2022/767, https://doi.org/10.24963/ijcai.2022/767, survey Track

52. Giunchiglia, E., Stoian, M.C., Lukasiewicz, T.: Deep learning with logical constraints. In: Raedt, L.D. (ed.) Proceedings of the Thirty-First International Joint Conference on Artificial Intelligence, IJCAI 2022, Vienna, Austria, 23-29 July 2022. pp. 5478–5485. ijcai.org (2022). https://doi.org/10.24963/ijcai.2022/767, https://doi.org/10.24963/ijcai.2022/767

53. Goodfellow, I.J., Shlens, J., Szegedy, C.: Explaining and harnessing adversarial examples (2015)

54. Gowal, S., Dvijotham, K.D., Stanforth, R., Bunel, R., Qin, C., Uesato, J., Arandjelovic, R., Mann, T., Kohli, P.: Scalable verified training for provably robust

image classification. In: Proceedings of the IEEE/CVF International Conference on Computer Vision. pp. 4842–4851 (2019)

55. Guo, Q., Xie, X., Li, Y., Zhang, X., Liu, Y., Li, X., Shen, C.: Audee: Automated testing for deep learning frameworks. In: Proceedings of the 35th IEEE/ACM International Conference on Automated Software Engineering. p. 486–498. ASE '20, Association for Computing Machinery, New York, NY, USA (2021). https://doi.org/10.1145/3324884.3416571, https://doi.org/10.1145/3324884.3416571

56. Hatcliff, J., Leavens, G.T., Leino, K.R.M., Müller, P., Parkinson, M.: Behavioral interface specification languages. ACM Comput. Surv. 44(3) (Jun 2012). https://doi.org/10.1145/2187671.2187678, https://doi.org/10.1145/2187671.2187678

57. He, Z., Fan, D.: Simultaneously optimizing weight and quantizer of ternary neural network using truncated gaussian approximation. In: Proceedings of the IEEE/CVF Conference on Computer Vision and Pattern Recognition (CVPR) (June 2019)

58. Henzinger, T.A., Lechner, M., Žikelić, Đ.: Scalable verification of quantized neural networks. In: Proceedings of the AAAI conference on artificial intelligence. vol. 35, pp. 3787–3795 (2021)

59. Hitzler, P., Sarker, M.: Neuro-symbolic Artificial Intelligence: The State of the Art. IOS Press (2022)

60. Huang, C., Fan, J., Chen, X., Li, W., Zhu, Q.: POLAR: A polynomial arithmetic framework for verifying neural-network controlled systems. In: International Symposium on Automated Technology for Verification and Analysis (ATVA) (2022)

61. Huang, C., Fan, J., Li, W., Chen, X., Zhu, Q.: Reachnn: Reachability analysis of neural-network controlled systems. ACM Transactions on Embedded Computing Systems (TECS) 18(5s), 1–22 (2019)

62. Huang, P., Wu, H., Yang, Y., Daukantas, I., Wu, M., Zhang, Y., Barrett, C.: Towards efficient verification of quantized neural networks. In: Proceedings of the AAAI Conference on Artificial Intelligence. vol. 38, pp. 21152–21160 (2024)

63. Huang, X., Kwiatkowska, M., Wang, S., Wu, M.: Safety verification of deep neural networks (2017)

64. IEEE: Ieee standard for floating-point arithmetic. IEEE Std 754-2019 (Revision of IEEE 754-2008) pp. 1–84 (2019). https://doi.org/10.1109/IEEESTD.2019.8766229

65. Isac, O., Barrett, C., Zhang, M., Katz, G.: Neural Network Verification with Proof Production. In: Proc. 22nd Int. Conf. on Formal Methods in Computer-Aided Design (FMCAD). pp. 38–48 (2022)

66. Ivanov, R., Carpenter, T., Weimer, J., Alur, R., Pappas, G.J., Lee, I.: Verisig 2.0: Verification of neural network controllers using taylor model preconditioning. In: International Conference on Computer-Aided Verification (2021)

67. Ivanov, R., Carpenter, T.J., Weimer, J., Alur, R., Pappas, G.J., Lee, I.: Verifying the safety of autonomous systems with neural network controllers. ACM Trans. Embed. Comput. Syst. 20(1) (Dec 2020). https://doi.org/10.1145/3419742

68. Ivanov, R., Weimer, J., Alur, R., Pappas, G.J., Lee, I.: Verisig: Verifying safety properties of hybrid systems with neural network controllers. In: International Conference on Hybrid Systems: Computation and Control. p. 169–178. HSCC, ACM (2019). https://doi.org/10.1145/3302504.3311806

69. Jia, K., Rinard, M.: Efficient exact verification of binarized neural networks. In: Larochelle, H., Ranzato, M., Hadsell, R., Balcan, M., Lin, H. (eds.) Advances in Neural Information Processing Systems. vol. 33, pp. 1782–1795. Curran

Associates, Inc. (2020), `https://proceedings.neurips.cc/paper_files/paper/2020/file/1385974ed5904a438616ff7bdb3f7439-Paper.pdf`

70. Jia, K., Rinard, M.: Exploiting verified neural networks via floating point numerical error. In: Drăgoi, C., Mukherjee, S., Namjoshi, K. (eds.) Static Analysis. pp. 191–205. Springer International Publishing, Cham (2021)

71. Johnson, T.T., Lopez, D.M., Benet, L., Forets, M., Guadalupe, S., Schilling, C., Ivanov, R., Carpenter, T.J., Weimer, J., Lee, I.: Arch-comp21 category report: Artificial intelligence and neural network control systems (ainncs) for continuous and hybrid systems plants. In: Frehse, G., Althoff, M. (eds.) 8th International Workshop on Applied Verification of Continuous and Hybrid Systems (ARCH21). EPiC Series in Computing, vol. 80, pp. 90–119. EasyChair (2021). `https://doi.org/10.29007/kfk9`, `https://easychair.org/publications/paper/Jq4h`

72. Johnson, T.T., Lopez, D.M., Musau, P., Tran, H.D., Botoeva, E., Leofante, F., Maleki, A., Sidrane, C., Fan, J., Huang, C.: Arch-comp20 category report: Artificial intelligence and neural network control systems (ainncs) for continuous and hybrid systems plants. In: Frehse, G., Althoff, M. (eds.) ARCH20. 7th International Workshop on Applied Verification of Continuous and Hybrid Systems (ARCH20). EPiC Series in Computing, vol. 74, pp. 107–139. EasyChair (2020). `https://doi.org/10.29007/9xgv`, `https://easychair.org/publications/paper/Jvwg`

73. Katz, G., Barrett, C., Dill, D.L., Julian, K., Kochenderfer, M.J.: Reluplex: An efficient smt solver for verifying deep neural networks. In: International conference on computer aided verification. pp. 97–117. Springer (2017)

74. Katz, G., Huang, D., Ibeling, D., Julian, K., Lazarus, C., Lim, R., Shah, P., Thakoor, S., Wu, H., Zeljić, A., Dill, D., Kochenderfer, M., Barrett, C.: The Marabou Framework for Verification and Analysis of Deep Neural Networks, pp. 443–452 (07 2019)

75. Kochdumper, N., Schilling, C., Althoff, M., Bak, S.: Open- and closed-loop neural network verification using polynomial zonotopes. In: NASA Formal Methods. pp. 16–36. Springer (2023)

76. Kokke, W., Komendantskaya, E., Kienitz, D., Atkey, R., Aspinall, D.: Neural networks, secure by construction - an exploration of refinement types. In: d. S. Oliveira, B.C. (ed.) Programming Languages and Systems - 18th Asian Symposium, APLAS 2020, Fukuoka, Japan, November 30 - December 2, 2020, Proceedings. Lecture Notes in Computer Science, vol. 12470, pp. 67–85. Springer (2020). `https://doi.org/10.1007/978-3-030-64437-6_4`, `https://doi.org/10.1007/978-3-030-64437-6_4`

77. Kolter, Z., Madry, A.: Adversarial robustness—theory and practice. NeurIPS 2018 tutorial (2018), available at `https://adversarial-ml-tutorial.org/`

78. Kolter, Z., Madry, A.: Adversarial robustness: Theory and practice. Tutorial at NeurIPS p. 3 (2018)

79. Kroening, D., Tautschnig, M.: CBMC–C bounded model checker. In: International Conference on Tools and Algorithms for the Construction and Analysis of Systems. pp. 389–391. Springer (2014)

80. Li, Y., Dong, X., Wang, W.: Additive powers-of-two quantization: An efficient non-uniform discretization for neural networks. In: International Conference on Learning Representations (2020), `https://openreview.net/forum?id=BkgXT24tDS`

81. Lohar, D., Jeangoudoux, C., Volkova, A., Darulova, E.: Sound mixed fixed-point quantization of neural networks. ACM Trans. Embed. Comput. Syst. **22**(5s) (sep 2023). https://doi.org/10.1145/3609118, https://doi.org/10.1145/3609118

82. Lopez, D.M., Althoff, M., Benet, L., Chen, X., Fan, J., Forets, M., Huang, C., Johnson, T.T., Ladner, T., Li, W., Schilling, C., Zhu, Q.: Arch-comp22 category report: Artificial intelligence and neural network control systems (ainncs) for continuous and hybrid systems plants. In: Frehse, G., Althoff, M., Schoitsch, E., Guiochet, J. (eds.) Proceedings of 9th International Workshop on Applied Verification of Continuous and Hybrid Systems (ARCH22). EPiC Series in Computing, vol. 90, pp. 142–184. EasyChair (2022). https://doi.org/10.29007/wfgr, https://easychair.org/publications/paper/C1J8

83. Lopez, D.M., Althoff, M., Forets, M., Johnson, T.T., Ladner, T., Schilling, C.: Arch-comp23 category report: Artificial intelligence and neural network control systems (ainncs) for continuous and hybrid systems plants. In: Frehse, G., Althoff, M. (eds.) Proceedings of 10th International Workshop on Applied Verification of Continuous and Hybrid Systems (ARCH23). EPiC Series in Computing, vol. 96, pp. 89–125. EasyChair (2023). https://doi.org/10.29007/x38n

84. Lopez, D.M., Choi, S.W., Tran, H.D., Johnson, T.T.: NNV 2.0: The neural network verification tool. In: Enea, C., Lal, A. (eds.) Computer Aided Verification. pp. 397–412. Springer Nature Switzerland, Cham (2023)

85. Lopez, D.M., Musau, P., Tran, H.D., Dutta, S., Carpenter, T.J., Ivanov, R., Johnson, T.T.: Arch-comp19 category report: Artificial intelligence and neural network control systems (ainncs) for continuous and hybrid systems plants. In: Frehse, G., Althoff, M. (eds.) ARCH19. 6th International Workshop on Applied Verification of Continuous and Hybrid Systems. EPiC Series in Computing, vol. 61, pp. 103–119. EasyChair (2019). https://doi.org/10.29007/rgv8, https://easychair.org/publications/paper/BFKs

86. Madry, A., Makelov, A., Schmidt, L., Tsipras, D., Vladu, A.: Towards deep learning models resistant to adversarial attacks. In: International Conference on Learning Representations (2018)

87. Magalhães, J.W.d.S., Woodruff, J., Polgreen, E., O'Boyle, M.F.P.: C2taco: Lifting tensor code to taco. In: Proceedings of the 22nd ACM SIGPLAN International Conference on Generative Programming: Concepts and Experiences. p. 42–56. GPCE 2023, Association for Computing Machinery, New York, NY, USA (2023). https://doi.org/10.1145/3624007.3624053, https://doi.org/10.1145/3624007.3624053

88. Mandal, U., Amir, G., Wu, H., Daukantas, I., Newell, F.L., Ravaioli, U.J., Meng, B., Durling, M., Ganai, M., Shim, T., Katz, G., Barrett, C.W.: Formally verifying deep reinforcement learning controllers with lyapunov barrier certificates. CoRR **abs/2405.14058** (2024). https://doi.org/10.48550/ARXIV.2405.14058, https://doi.org/10.48550/arXiv.2405.14058

89. Manhaeve, R., Dumančić, S., Kimmig, A., Demeester, T., De Raedt, L.: Neural probabilistic logic programming in deepproblog. Artificial Intelligence **298**, 103504 (2021). https://doi.org/https://doi.org/10.1016/j.artint.2021.103504, https://www.sciencedirect.com/science/article/pii/S0004370221000552

90. Manino, E., Menezes, R.S., Shmarov, F., Cordeiro, L.C.: NeuroCodeBench: a Plain C Neural Network Benchmark for Software Verification. In: Workshop on Automated Formal Reasoning for Trustworthy AI Systems (2023)

91. Matos, J.B.P., de Lima Filho, E.B., Bessa, I., Manino, E., Song, X., Cordeiro, L.C.: Counterexample guided neural network quantization refinement. IEEE Transac-

tions on Computer-Aided Design of Integrated Circuits and Systems **43**(4), 1121–1134 (2024). `https://doi.org/10.1109/TCAD.2023.3335313`

92. Menezes, R.S., Aldughaim, M., Farias, B., Li, X., Manino, E., Shmarov, F., Song, K., Brauße, F., Gadelha, M.R., Tihanyi, N., Korovin, K., Cordeiro, L.C.: Esbmc v7.4: Harnessing the power of intervals. In: Finkbeiner, B., Kovács, L. (eds.) Tools and Algorithms for the Construction and Analysis of Systems. pp. 376–380. Springer Nature Switzerland, Cham (2024)

93. Mistry, S., Saha, I., Biswas, S.: An milp encoding for efficient verification of quantized deep neural networks. IEEE Transactions on Computer-Aided Design of Integrated Circuits and Systems **41**(11), 4445–4456 (2022). `https://doi.org/10.1109/TCAD.2022.3197697`

94. Murphy, C., Gray, P., Stewart, G.: Verified perceptron convergence theorem. In: Proceedings of the 1st ACM SIGPLAN International Workshop on Machine Learning and Programming Languages. pp. 43–50 (2017)

95. Müller, M.N., Eckert, F., Fischer, M., Vechev, M.: Certified training: Small boxes are all you need (2023)

96. Narodytska, N., Kasiviswanathan, S., Ryzhyk, L., Sagiv, M., Walsh, T.: Verifying properties of binarized deep neural networks. In: Proceedings of the AAAI Conference on Artificial Intelligence. vol. 32 (2018)

97. Odena, A., Olsson, C., Andersen, D., Goodfellow, I.: TensorFuzz: Debugging neural networks with coverage-guided fuzzing. In: Chaudhuri, K., Salakhutdinov, R. (eds.) Proceedings of the 36th International Conference on Machine Learning. Proceedings of Machine Learning Research, vol. 97, pp. 4901–4911. PMLR (09–15 Jun 2019), `https://proceedings.mlr.press/v97/odena19a.html`

98. Payani, A., Fekri, F.: Inductive Logic Programming via Differentiable Deep Neural Logic Networks. Tech. rep. (Jun 2019). `https://doi.org/10.48550/arXiv.1906.03523`, `http://arxiv.org/abs/1906.03523`, zSCC: 0000039 arXiv:1906.03523 [cs] type: article

99. Pham, H.V., Qian, S., Wang, J., Lutellier, T., Rosenthal, J., Tan, L., Yu, Y., Nagappan, N.: Problems and opportunities in training deep learning software systems: an analysis of variance. In: Proceedings of the 35th IEEE/ACM International Conference on Automated Software Engineering. p. 771–783. ASE '20, Association for Computing Machinery, New York, NY, USA (2021). `https://doi.org/10.1145/3324884.3416545`, `https://doi.org/10.1145/3324884.3416545`

100. Prach, B., Brau, F., Buttazzo, G., Lampert, C.H.: 1-lipschitz layers compared: Memory speed and certifiable robustness. In: Proceedings of the IEEE/CVF Conference on Computer Vision and Pattern Recognition (CVPR). pp. 24574–24583 (June 2024)

101. Pulina, L., Tacchella, A.: An abstraction-refinement approach to verification of artificial neural networks. In: Touili, T., Cook, B., Jackson, P. (eds.) Computer Aided Verification. pp. 243–257. Springer Berlin Heidelberg, Berlin, Heidelberg (2010)

102. Qin, H., Gong, R., Liu, X., Bai, X., Song, J., Sebe, N.: Binary neural networks: A survey. Pattern Recognition **105**, 107281 (2020). `https://doi.org/https://doi.org/10.1016/j.patcog.2020.107281`, `https://www.sciencedirect.com/science/article/pii/S0031320320300856`

103. Sälzer, M., Lange, M.: Reachability Is NP-Complete Even for the Simplest Neural Networks. In: Proc. 15th Int. Conf. on Reachability Problems (RP). pp. 149–164 (2021)

104. Schlögl, A., Hofer, N., Böhme, R.: Causes and effects of unanticipated numerical deviations in neural network inference frameworks. In: Oh, A., Naumann, T., Globerson, A., Saenko, K., Hardt, M., Levine, S. (eds.) Advances in Neural Information Processing Systems. vol. 36, pp. 56095–56107. Curran Associates, Inc. (2023), https://proceedings.neurips.cc/paper_files/paper/2023/file/af076c3bdbf935b81d808e37c5ede463-Paper-Conference.pdf

105. Seshia, S.A., Sadigh, D., Sastry, S.S.: Toward verified artificial intelligence. Commun. ACM **65**(7), 46–55 (Jun 2022). https://doi.org/10.1145/3503914

106. Shriver, D., Elbaum, S., Dwyer, M.B.: DNNV: A framework for deep neural network verification. In: Silva, A., Leino, K.R.M. (eds.) Computer Aided Verification. pp. 137–150. Springer International Publishing, Cham (2021)

107. Sibidanov, A., Zimmermann, P., Glondu, S.: The core-math project. In: 2022 IEEE 29th Symposium on Computer Arithmetic (ARITH). pp. 26–34 (2022). https://doi.org/10.1109/ARITH54963.2022.00014

108. Sidrane, C., Kochenderfer, M.J.: OVERT: Verification of nonlinear dynamical systems with neural network controllers via overapproximation. Safe Machine Learning workshop at ICLR (2019)

109. Singh, G., Gehr, T., Püschel, M., Vechev, M.: An abstract domain for certifying neural networks. Proceedings of the ACM on Programming Languages **3**(POPL), 1–30 (2019)

110. Slusarz, N., Komendantskaya, E., Daggitt, M.L., Stewart, R.J., Stark, K.: Logic of differentiable logics: Towards a uniform semantics of DL. In: Piskac, R., Voronkov, A. (eds.) LPAR 2023: Proceedings of 24th International Conference on Logic for Programming, Artificial Intelligence and Reasoning, Manizales, Colombia, 4-9th June 2023. EPiC Series in Computing, vol. 94, pp. 473–493. EasyChair (2023). https://doi.org/10.29007/C1NT, https://doi.org/10.29007/c1nt

111. Szegedy, C., Zaremba, W., Sutskever, I., Bruna, J., Erhan, D., Goodfellow, I., Fergus, R.: Intriguing properties of neural networks (2014)

112. Tassarotti, J., Tristan, J.B.: Verified density compilation for a probabilistic programming language. Proc. ACM Program. Lang. **7**(PLDI) (Jun 2023). https://doi.org/10.1145/3591245, https://doi.org/10.1145/3591245

113. Teuber, S., Büning, M.K., Kern, P., Sinz, C.: Geometric path enumeration for equivalence verification of neural networks. In: 2021 IEEE 33rd International Conference on Tools with Artificial Intelligence (ICTAI). pp. 200–208 (2021). https://doi.org/10.1109/ICTAI52525.2021.00035

114. Teuber, S., Mitsch, S., Platzer, A.: Provably safe neural network controllers via differential dynamic logic. CoRR **abs/2402.10998** (2024). https://doi.org/10.48550/ARXIV.2402.10998, https://doi.org/10.48550/arXiv.2402.10998

115. Tran, H.D., Xiang, W., Johnson, T.T.: Verification approaches for learning-enabled autonomous cyber–physical systems. IEEE Design & Test **39**(1), 24–34 (2022). https://doi.org/10.1109/MDAT.2020.3015712

116. Tran, H.D., Yang, X., Lopez, D.M., Musau, P., Nguyen, L.V., Xiang, W., Bak, S., Johnson, T.T.: NNV: The neural network verification tool for deep neural networks and learning-enabled cyber-physical systems. In: 32nd International Conference on Computer-Aided Verification (CAV'20) (7 2020)

117. Wang, N., Choi, J., Brand, D., Chen, C.Y., Gopalakrishnan, K.: Training deep neural networks with 8-bit floating point numbers. In: Bengio, S., Wallach, H., Larochelle, H., Grauman, K., Cesa-Bianchi, N., Garnett, R. (eds.)

Advances in Neural Information Processing Systems. vol. 31. Curran Associates, Inc. (2018), https://proceedings.neurips.cc/paper_files/paper/2018/file/335d3d1cd7ef05ec77714a215134914c-Paper.pdf

118. Wang, S., Zhang, H., Xu, K., Lin, X., Jana, S., Hsieh, C.J., Kolter, J.Z.: Betacrown: Efficient bound propagation with per-neuron split constraints for neural network robustness verification. Advances in Neural Information Processing Systems **34**, 29909–29921 (2021)

119. Wu, H., Isac, O., Zeljic, A., Tagomori, T., Daggitt, M.L., Kokke, W., Refaeli, I., Amir, G., Julian, K., Bassan, S., Huang, P., Lahav, O., Wu, M., Zhang, M., Komendantskaya, E., Katz, G., Barrett, C.W.: Marabou 2.0: A Versatile Formal Analyzer of Neural Networks. In: Computer Aided Verification (CAV) (2024)

120. Wu, H., Zeljić, A., Katz, G., Barrett, C.: Efficient neural network analysis with sum-of-infeasibilities. In: International Conference on Tools and Algorithms for the Construction and Analysis of Systems. pp. 143–163. Springer (2022)

121. Xiang, W., Tran, H.D., Johnson, T.T.: Output reachable set estimation and verification for multilayer neural networks. IEEE transactions on neural networks and learning systems **29**(11), 5777–5783 (2018)

122. Xie, X., Kersting, K., Neider, D.: Neuro-symbolic verification of deep neural networks. In: Raedt, L.D. (ed.) Proceedings of the Thirty-First International Joint Conference on Artificial Intelligence, IJCAI-22. pp. 3622–3628. International Joint Conferences on Artificial Intelligence Organization (7 2022). https://doi.org/10.24963/ijcai.2022/503, https://doi.org/10.24963/ijcai.2022/503, main Track

123. Yao, P., Wu, H., Gao, B., Tang, J., Zhang, Q., Zhang, W., Yang, J.J., Qian, H.: Fully hardware-implemented memristor convolutional neural network. Nature **577**(7792), 641–646 (2020)

124. Zhang, H., Chen, H., Xiao, C., Gowal, S., Stanforth, R., Li, B., Boning, D., Hsieh, C.J.: Towards stable and efficient training of verifiably robust neural networks. In: 8th International Conference on Learning Representations, ICLR 2020 (2020)

125. Zhang, Y., Song, F., Sun, J.: Qebverif: Quantization error bound verification of neural networks. In: Enea, C., Lal, A. (eds.) Computer Aided Verification. pp. 413–437. Springer Nature Switzerland, Cham (2023)

126. Zhang, Y., Albarghouthi, A., D'Antoni, L.: Robustness to programmable string transformations via augmented abstract training. In: Proceedings of the 37th International Conference on Machine Learning. pp. 11023–11032 (2020)

127. Zhuang, D., Zhang, X., Song, S., Hooker, S.: Randomness in neural network training: Characterizing the impact of tooling. In: Marculescu, D., Chi, Y., Wu, C. (eds.) Proceedings of Machine Learning and Systems. vol. 4, pp. 316–336 (2022), https://proceedings.mlsys.org/paper_files/paper/2022/file/427e0e886ebf87538afdf0badb805b7f-Paper.pdf

128. Zombori, D., Bánhelyi, B., Csendes, T., Megyeri, I., Jelasity, M.: Fooling a complete neural network verifier. In: International Conference on Learning Representations (2021), https://openreview.net/forum?id=4IwieFS441

Stratified Type Theory

Jonathan Chan[1]($\boxtimes$) and Stephanie Weirich[1]

University of Pennsylvania, Philadelphia, PA 19104, USA
{jcxz,sweirich}@seas.upenn.edu

Abstract. A hierarchy of type universes is a rudimentary ingredient in the type theories of many proof assistants to prevent the logical inconsistency resulting from combining dependent functions and the type-in-type axiom. In this work, we argue that a universe hierarchy is not the *only* option for universes in type theory. Taking inspiration from Leivant's Stratified System F, we introduce **Stratified Type Theory** (StraTT), where rather than stratifying universes by levels, we stratify typing judgements and restrict the domain of dependent functions to strictly lower levels. Even with type-in-type, this restriction suffices to enforce consistency.

In StraTT, we consider a number of extensions beyond just stratified dependent functions. First, the subsystem subStraTT employs McBride's crude-but-effective stratification (also known as displacement) as a simple form of level polymorphism where global definitions with concrete levels can be displaced uniformly to any higher level. Second, to recover some expressivity lost due to the restriction on dependent function domains, the full StraTT includes a separate nondependent function type with a *floating* domain whose level matches that of the overall function type. Finally, we have implemented a prototype type checker for StraTT extended with datatypes and inference for level and displacement annotations, along with a small core library.

We have proven subStraTT to be consistent and StraTT to be type safe, but consistency of the full StraTT remains an open problem, largely due to the interaction between floating functions and cumulativity of judgements. Nevertheless, we believe StraTT to be consistent, and as evidence have verified the ill-typedness of some well-known type-theoretic paradoxes using our implementation.

Keywords: type theory · dependent types · stratification

1 Introduction

Every term in a dependent type theory has a type, including types such as Nat. Types are classified by the *type universes* to which they belong, and as type universes are themselves types, they must each belong to some type universe. In Martin-Löf Type Theory [28], these universes form a hierarchy: universe $\star_k$ has type $\star_{k+1}$ thus preventing any universe from classifying itself. Otherwise, the system would be inconsistent.

© The Author(s) 2025
V. Vafeiadis (Ed.): ESOP 2025, LNCS 15694, pp. 236–263, 2025.
https://doi.org/10.1007/978-3-031-91118-7_10

System F	*Stratified System F*	
	SF-POLY	SF-FUN
F-POLY	$j < k$	$\Gamma \vdash A$ **type** k
Γ, x **type** $\vdash B$ **type**	Γ, x **type** $j \vdash B$ **type** k	$\Gamma \vdash B$ **type** k
$\Gamma \vdash \forall x.\, B$ **type**	$\Gamma \vdash \forall x^j.\, B$ **type** k	$\Gamma \vdash A \to B$ **type** k

Fig. 1. Select rules from (Stratified) System F

Many contemporary proof assistants, such as Coq [10], Agda [33], Lean [32], F* [38], and Arend [9], include universe hierarchies. To make these systems easier to use, they often automatically infer the levels of each universe, so programmers can write, for instance, Type instead of Type 3. They also include forms of level polymorphism, so that definitions can be reused at multiple universe levels. However, supporting such generality means that the proof assistant must handle level variable constraints, level expressions, or both. As a result, programming with and especially debugging errors involving universe levels can be painful.

So we ask: can type universes and reusability coexist without resorting to level polymorphism?

In this work, we design **Stratified Type Theory** (StraTT), a new approach for type universes, and evaluate mechanisms for reusability that don't include level polymorphism. The key idea of our design is that we do not stratify universes into a hierarchy; instead, we stratify *typing judgements* themselves by levels. This approach is inspired by Leivant's *Stratified System F* [23], a predicative variant of System F [16,34].

Consider the formation rule F-POLY for System F's type polymorphism in Figure 1. The quantification is said to be *impredicative* because it quantifies over all types including itself. In contrast, the formation rule SF-POLY for Stratified System F disallows impredicativity by restricting polymorphic quantification to only types that are well formed at strictly lower stratification levels. The type well-formedness judgement tracks the stratification level with an index k.

To extend stratified polymorphism to dependent types, there are two ways to read this judgement form. We could interpret $\Gamma \vdash A$ **type** k as a type A living in some stratified type universe $\star_k$, which would correspond to a usual predicative type theory. Alternatively, we could continue to interpret the level k as a property of the judgement and annotate the dependent typing judgement form as $\Gamma \vdash a :^k A$. Analogously to stratified polymorphic types $\forall x^j.\, B$, we introduce stratified dependent function types $\Pi x :^j A.\, B$. They similarly quantify over arguments at the annotated level j, which must be strictly lower than the overall level of the type. This allows us to remove the level annotation from universes, so we have $\Gamma \vdash \star :^k \star$ for any k.

Moving levels off of universes and onto judgements and function domains opens up the opportunity to really take advantage of McBride's *crude but effective stratification* [30]. Following Favonia, Angiuli, and Mullanix [18], we refer to this as *displacement* to prevent confusion. Given some signature Δ of global definitions, we are permitted to use any definition with all of its concrete levels uniformly displaced upwards. Displacement is less effective than level polymorphism in MLTT for types that involve multiple universes, such as $\star_0 \to \star_3$, since we'd still be stuck with the relative difference of 3 between the two universes. With stratified functions, this type would look like $\Pi X :^0 \star. \star$, with only a single level annotation to displace.

However, we find that even with displacement, stratifying *all* function types is too restrictive and rules out terms that are otherwise typeable in MLTT even without level polymorphism. Going back to Stratified System F, we observe that with respect to the levels, ordinary function types are more flexible than polymorphic function types. Their formation rule SF-FUN in Figure 1 allows the level of the domain type to be equal to the overall level of the function type. It is this flexibility we're missing that would recover some lost expressivity, so we add an analogous separate function type that is nondependent but has no fixed domain level. If the overall level of the nondependent function type is raised, we say that the level of the domain *floats* to the same level.

We divide our design into two parts. The subsystem subStraTT features only stratified dependent functions and displacement, and the full system StraTT adds floating nondependent functions. We have proven in Agda the logical consistency of the former. Even with type-in-type, the stratification restriction on the domains of dependent functions prevents the kind of self-referential trickery that is needed for the usual paradoxes.

We conjecture, but have not proven, the consistency of the full StraTT. Floating functions permit covariant behaviour of the domain with respect to levels, and our existing Agda proof doesn't extend to this new feature. That doesn't mean that the system is inconsistent: it may be sufficiently different from usual predicative type theories to require an entirely different approach or an alternative foundation outside of Agda. Indeed, our experience with the system provides evidence that consistency does hold. We have found it impossible to use StraTT to encode some well-known type-theoretic paradoxes. We also have verified its syntactic metatheory, giving us further insight into its design.

The contributions of our paper are as follows:

- A subsystem subStraTT, featuring only stratified dependent functions and displacement, which is then extended to the full StraTT with floating nondependent functions. $\hookrightarrow$ Section 2
- Examples to demonstrate the expressivity of StraTT and especially to motivate floating functions. $\hookrightarrow$ Section 3
- Two major metatheorems: logical consistency for subStraTT, which is mechanized in Agda, and type safety for StraTT, which is mechanized in Coq. Consistency for the full StraTT remains an open problem. $\hookrightarrow$ Section 4
- A prototype implementation of a type checker, which extends StraTT to include datatypes to demonstrate the effectiveness of stratification and displacement in practical dependently-typed programming. $\hookrightarrow$ Section 5

We discuss potential avenues for proving consistency of the full StraTT and compare the useability of its design to existing proof assistants in terms of working with universe levels in Section 6 and conclude in Section 7. Our Agda and

Coq mechanizations along with the prototype implementation are available at https://github.com/plclub/StraTT, which is also archived as a paper artifact [8]. Where lemmas and theorems are first introduced, we include a footnote indicating the corresponding source file and lemma name in the development.

2 Stratified Type Theory

In this section, we present Stratified Type Theory in two parts. First is the subsystem subStraTT, which contains the two core features of stratified dependent function types and global definitions with level displacement. We then extend it to the full StraTT by adding floating nondependent function types. As the system is fairly small with few parts, we delay illustrative examples to Section 3, and begin with the formal description.

2.1 The subsystem subStraTT

The subsystem subStraTT is a cumulative, extrinsic type theory with types à la Russell, a single type universe, dependent functions, an empty type, and global definitions. The most significant difference between subStraTT and other type theories with these features is the annotation of the typing judgement with a level in place of universes in a hierarchy. We use the naturals and their usual strict order and addition operation for our levels, but they should be generalizable to any displacement algebra [18]. The syntax for terms, contexts Γ, and signatures Δ is given below, with x, y, z for variable and constant names and i, j, k for levels.

$$a, b, c, A, B, C ::= \star \mid x \mid x^i \mid \Pi x :^j A. B \mid \lambda x. b \mid b\, a \mid \bot \mid \mathsf{absurd}(b)$$

$$\Gamma ::= \varnothing \mid x :^k A$$

$$\Delta ::= \varnothing \mid x :^k A := a$$

A context consists of declarations $x :^k A$ of variables x of type A at level k; variables represent locations where an entire typing derivation may be substituted into the term, so they also need level annotations. A signature consists of global definitions $x :^k A := a$ of constants x of type A definitionally equal to a at level k; they represent complete typing derivations that will eventually be substituted into the term. The typing judgement $\boxed{\Delta; \Gamma \vdash a :^k A}$, whose derivation rules are given in Figure 2, states that the term a is well typed at level k with type A under the context Γ and signature Δ.

Because stratified judgements replace stratified universes, the type of the type universe $\star$ is itself at any level in rule DT-TYPE. Stratification is enforced in dependent function types in rule DT-PI: the domain type must be well typed at a strictly smaller level relative to the codomain type and the overall function type. Similarly, in rule DT-ABSTY, the body of a dependent function is well typed when its argument and its type are well typed at a strictly smaller level, and by rule DT-APPTY, a dependent function can only be applied to an argument at the strictly smaller domain level.

$$\boxed{\Delta;\Gamma \vdash a :^k A}$$ *(Typing)*

DT-TYPE
$$\dfrac{\Delta \vdash \Gamma}{\Delta;\Gamma \vdash \star :^k \star}$$

DT-PI
$$\dfrac{\begin{array}{c}\Delta;\Gamma \vdash A :^j \star \\ \Delta;\Gamma, x :^j A \vdash B :^k \star \\ j < k\end{array}}{\Delta;\Gamma \vdash \Pi x :^j A.\, B :^k \star}$$

DT-ABSTY
$$\dfrac{\begin{array}{c}\Delta;\Gamma \vdash A :^j \star \\ \Delta;\Gamma, x :^j A \vdash b :^k B \\ j < k\end{array}}{\Delta;\Gamma \vdash \lambda x.\, b :^k \Pi x :^j A.\, B}$$

DT-APPTY
$$\dfrac{\begin{array}{c}\Delta;\Gamma \vdash b :^k \Pi x :^j A.\, B \\ \Delta;\Gamma \vdash a :^j A \qquad j < k\end{array}}{\Delta;\Gamma \vdash b\, a :^k B\{a/x\}}$$

DT-VAR
$$\dfrac{\begin{array}{c}x :^j A \in \Gamma \\ \Delta \vdash \Gamma \qquad j \le k\end{array}}{\Delta;\Gamma \vdash x :^k A}$$

DT-CONST
$$\dfrac{\begin{array}{c}x :^j A := a \in \Delta \\ \vdash \Delta \qquad i + j \le k\end{array}}{\Delta;\Gamma \vdash x^i :^k A^{+i}}$$

DT-BOTTOM
$$\dfrac{\Delta \vdash \Gamma}{\Delta;\Gamma \vdash \bot :^k \star}$$

DT-ABSURD
$$\dfrac{\begin{array}{c}\Delta;\Gamma \vdash A :^k \star \\ \Delta;\Gamma \vdash b :^k \bot\end{array}}{\Delta;\Gamma \vdash \mathsf{absurd}(b) :^k A}$$

DT-CONV
$$\dfrac{\begin{array}{c}\Delta;\Gamma \vdash a :^k A \\ \Delta;\Gamma \vdash B :^k \star \\ \Delta \vdash A \equiv B\end{array}}{\Delta;\Gamma \vdash a :^k B}$$

Fig. 2. Typing rules (subStraTT)

Remark 1. The level annotation on dependent function types is necessary for consistency. Informally, suppose we have some unannotated type $\Pi X :\star.\, B$ and a function of this type, both at level 1. By cumulativity, we can raise the level of the function to 2, then apply it to its own type $\Pi X :\star.\, B$. In short, impredicativity is reintroduced, and stratification defeated.

Rules DT-BOTTOM and DT-ABSURD are the uninhabited type and its eliminator, respectively. The eliminator appears to only be able to eliminate a falsehood into the same level, but cumulativity, formally defined shortly, will permit raising the level of a falsehood, which can then be eliminated at that level.

Remark 2. More generally, the level of a well-typed term must match that of its type, which we prove later as Regularity (Lemma 9). Intuitively, the level of a typing judgement represents the level of all the subderivations (up to cumulativity) used to construct its derivation tree, which enforces predicativity at the derivation level. Since proving regularity amounts to constructing a derivation for the type out of the subderivations of the term, the level of the type could not possibly be any higher than that of the term.

In rules DT-VAR and DT-CONST, variables and constants at level j can be used at any larger level k, which we refer to as subsumption. This permits the following cumulativity lemma, allowing entire derivations to be used at higher levels.

Lemma 1 (Cumulativity).[1] *If* $\Delta;\Gamma \vdash a :^j A$ *and* $j \le k$ *then* $\Delta;\Gamma \vdash a :^k A$.

---

[1] `coq/restrict.v:DTyping_cumul`

Constants are further annotated with a superscript indicating how much they're displaced by. If a constant x is defined with a type A, then x^i is an element of type A but with all of its levels incremented by i. The metafunction a^{+i} performs this increment in the term a, defined recursively with $(\Pi x {:}^j A.\ B)^{+i} = \Pi x {:}^{i+j} A^{+i}.\ B^{+i}$ and $(x^j)^{+i} = x^{i+j}$. Constants come from signatures and variables from contexts, whose formation rules are given in Figure 3.

$$\boxed{\vdash \Delta} \qquad \boxed{\Delta \vdash \Gamma}$$

D-Cons
$$\vdash \Delta \qquad x \notin \operatorname{dom} \Delta$$
$$\Delta; \varnothing \vdash A {:}^k \star$$
$$\Delta; \varnothing \vdash a {:}^k A$$
$$\overline{\vdash \Delta, x {:}^k A := a}$$

D-Nil
$$\overline{\vdash \varnothing}$$

DG-Nil
$$\vdash \Delta$$
$$\overline{\Delta \vdash \varnothing}$$

DG-Cons
$$\Delta \vdash \Gamma \qquad \Delta; \Gamma \vdash A {:}^k \star$$
$$x \notin \operatorname{dom} \Gamma \qquad x \notin \operatorname{dom} \Delta$$
$$\overline{\Delta \vdash \Gamma, x {:}^k A}$$

Fig. 3. Signature and context formation rules (excerpt)

In rule DT-Conv, we use an untyped definitional equality $\boxed{\Delta \vdash a \equiv b}$ that is reflexive, symmetric, transitive, and congruent. The full set of rules are given in Figure 4, including β-equivalence for functions (rule DE-Beta) and δ-equivalence of constants x with their definitions (rule DE-Delta). When a constant is displaced as x^i, we must also increment the level annotations in their definitions by i.

$$\boxed{\Delta \vdash a \equiv b} \hspace{4cm} (\textit{Definitional equality})$$

DE-Refl
$$\overline{\Delta \vdash a \equiv a}$$

DE-Sym
$$\Delta \vdash b \equiv a$$
$$\overline{\Delta \vdash a \equiv b}$$

DE-Trans
$$\Delta \vdash a \equiv b \qquad \Delta \vdash b \equiv c$$
$$\overline{\Delta \vdash a \equiv c}$$

DE-Beta
$$\overline{\Delta \vdash (\lambda x.\ b)\ a \equiv b\{a/x\}}$$

DE-Delta
$$x {:}^k A := a \in \Delta$$
$$\overline{\Delta \vdash x^i \equiv a^{+i}}$$

DE-Pi
$$\Delta \vdash A \equiv A'$$
$$\Delta \vdash B \equiv B'$$
$$\overline{\Delta \vdash \Pi x {:}^k A.\ B \equiv \Pi x {:}^k A'.\ B'}$$

DE-Abs
$$\Delta \vdash b \equiv b'$$
$$\overline{\Delta \vdash \lambda x.\ b \equiv \lambda x.\ b'}$$

DE-App
$$\Delta \vdash a \equiv a'$$
$$\Delta \vdash b \equiv b'$$
$$\overline{\Delta \vdash b\ a \equiv b'\ a'}$$

DE-Absurd
$$\Delta \vdash b \equiv b'$$
$$\overline{\Delta \vdash \mathsf{absurd}(b) \equiv \mathsf{absurd}(b')}$$

Fig. 4. Definitional equality rules (subStraTT)

Given a well-typed, locally-closed term $\Delta; \varnothing \vdash a {:}^k A$, the entire derivation itself can be displaced upwards by some increment i. This lemma differs from cumulativity, since the level annotations in the term and its type are displaced as well, not just that of the judgement.

Lemma 2 (Displaceability (empty context))[2] *If $\Delta; \varnothing \vdash a {:}^k A$ then $\Delta; \varnothing \vdash a^{+i} {:}^{k+i} A^{+i}$.*

---

[2] `coq/incr.v:DTyping_incr`

With $x :^k A := a$ in the signature, x^i is definitionally equal to a^{+i}, so this lemma justifies rule DT-CONST, which would give this displaced constant the type A^{+i} at level $k + i$.

2.2 Floating functions

As we'll see in the next section, subStraTT alone is insufficiently expressive, with some examples being unexpectedly untypeable and others being simply clunky to work with as a result of the strict restriction on function domains. The full StraTT system therefore extends the subsystem with a separate nondependent function type, written $A \to B$, whose domain doesn't have the same restriction.

DT-ARROW
$$\frac{\Delta; \Gamma \vdash A :^k \star \qquad \Delta; \Gamma \vdash B :^k \star}{\Delta; \Gamma \vdash A \to B :^k \star}$$

DT-ABSTM
$$\frac{\Delta; \Gamma \vdash A :^k \star \qquad \Delta; \Gamma \vdash B :^k \star \qquad \Delta; \Gamma, x :^k A \vdash b :^k B}{\Delta; \Gamma \vdash \lambda x. b :^k A \to B}$$

DT-APPTM
$$\frac{\Delta; \Gamma \vdash b :^k A \to B \qquad \Delta; \Gamma \vdash a :^k A}{\Delta; \Gamma \vdash b\, a :^k B}$$

DE-ARROW
$$\frac{\Delta \vdash A \equiv A' \qquad \Delta \vdash B \equiv B'}{\Delta \vdash A \to B \equiv A' \to B'}$$

Fig. 5. Typing and definitional equality rules (floating functions)

The typing rules for nondependent function types, functions, and application are given in Figure 5. The domain, codomain, and entire nondependent function type are all typed at the same level. Functions take arguments of the same level as their bodies, and are thus applied to arguments of the same level.

This distinction between stratified dependent and unstratified nondependent functions corresponds closely to Stratified System F: type polymorphism is syntactically distinct from ordinary function types, and the former forces the codomain to be a higher level while the latter doesn't. From the perspective of Stratified System F, the dependent types of StraTT generalize stratified type polymorphism over types to include term polymorphism.

We say that the domain of these nondependent function types *floats* because unlike the stratified dependent function types, it isn't fixed to some particular level. The interaction between floating functions and cumulativity is where this becomes interesting. Given a function f of type $A \to B$ at level j, by cumulativity, it remains well typed with the same type at any level $k \geq j$. The level of the domain floats up from j to match the function at k, in the sense that f can be applied to an argument of type A at any greater level k. This is unusual because the domain isn't contravariant with respect to the ordering on the levels as expected, and is why, as we'll see shortly, the proof of consistency in Section 4.1 can't be straightforwardly extended to accommodate floating function types.

3   Examples

3.1   The identity function

In the following examples, we demonstrate why floating functions are essential. Below on the left is one way we could assign a type to the type-polymorphic identity function. For concision, we use a pattern syntax when defining global functions and place function arguments to the left of the definition. (The subscript is part of the constant name.)

$$\mathsf{id}_0 :^1 \Pi X :^0 \star. \Pi x :^0 X. X \qquad\qquad \mathsf{id} :^1 \Pi X :^0 \star. X \to X$$
$$\mathsf{id}_0 \, X \, x := x \qquad\qquad\qquad\qquad \mathsf{id} \, X \, x := x$$

Stratification enforces that the codomain of the function type and the function body have a higher level than that of the domain and the argument, so the overall identity function id_0 is well typed at level 1. While x and X have level 0 in the context of the body, by subsumption we can use x at level 1 as required.

Alternatively, since the return type doesn't depend on the second argument, we can use a floating function type instead, given above on the right. Since we still have a dependent type quantification, the function $X \to X$ is still typed at level 1. This means that x now has level 1 directly rather than through subsumption.

So far, there's no reason to pick one over the other, so let's look at a more involved example: applying an identity function to itself. This is possible due to cumulativity, and we'll follow the corresponding Coq example below.

```
Universes u0 u1.
Constraint u0 < u1.
Definition idid1 (id : forall (X : Type@{u1}), X -> X) :
  forall (X : Type@{u0}), X -> X :=
  id (forall (X : Type@{u0}), X -> X) (fun X => id X).
```

Here, since `forall (X : Type@{u0}), X -> X` can be assigned type `Type@{u1}`, it can be applied as the first argument to `id`. For the second argument, while `id` itself doesn't have this type, we can η-expand it to a function that does, since `Type@{u0}` is a subtype of `Type@{u1}`, so `X` can be passed to `id`.

If we try to write the analogous definition in subStraTT without using floating functions, we find that it doesn't type check! The problematic subterm is underlined in red below.

$$\mathsf{idid}_1 :^3 \Pi id :^2 (\Pi X :^1 \star. \Pi x :^1 X. X). \Pi X :^0 \star. \Pi x :^0 X. X$$
$$\mathsf{idid}_1 \, id := id \, (\Pi X :^0 \star. \Pi x :^0 X. X) \, \underline{(\lambda X. \lambda x. \, id \, X \, x)}$$

After η-expansion, $\lambda X. \lambda x. \, id \, X \, x$ has the correct type $\Pi X :^0 \star. \Pi x :^0 X. X$, but at level 0, the declared level of id itself. Meanwhile, the second argument of id expects an argument of that type but *at level 1*. We couldn't just raise the level annotation for that argument to 2, either, since that would raise the level of id to 3.

If we instead use floating functions for the nondependent argument, the analogous definition then *does* type check, since the second argument of type X can now be at level 2.

$$\text{idid}_1 :^2 (\Pi X :^1 \star. X \to X) \to \Pi X :^0 \star. X \to X$$
$$\text{idid}_1 \; id := id \; (\Pi X :^0 \star. X \to X) \; (\lambda X. \, id \; X)$$

This definition of idid_1 is now shaped the same as the Coq version, only with level annotations on domains where Coq has the corresponding level annotations on Type. If we were to turn on universe polymorphism in Coq, it would achieve the same kind of expressivity of being able to displace idid_1 in StraTT.

As an additional remark, even with floating functions, repeatedly nesting identity function self-applications is one way to non-trivially force the level to increase. The following definitions continue the pattern from idid_1; the corresponding Coq definitions would similarly require higher universe levels on their Type annotations.

$$\text{idid}_2 :^3 (\Pi X :^2 \star. X \to X) \to \Pi X :^0 \star. X \to X$$
$$\text{idid}_2 \; id := id \; ((\Pi X :^1 \star. X \to X) \to \Pi X :^0 \star. X \to X) \; \text{idid}_1 \; (\lambda X. \lambda x. \, id \; X \; x)$$
$$\text{idid}_3 :^4 (\Pi X :^3 \star. X \to X) \to \Pi X :^0 \star. X \to X$$
$$\text{idid}_3 \; id := id \; ((\Pi X :^2 \star. X \to X) \to \Pi X :^0 \star. X \to X) \; \text{idid}_2 \; (\lambda X. \lambda x. \, id \; X \; x)$$

In the untyped setting, these correspond to $\lambda id. \, id \; id$, $\lambda id. \, id \; (\lambda id. \, id \; id) \; id$, and $\lambda id. \, id \; (\lambda id. \, id \; (\lambda id. \, id \; id) \; id) \; id$. All of $\text{idid}_1 \; (\lambda X. \lambda x. \, x)$, $\text{idid}_2 \; (\lambda X. \lambda x. \, x)$, and $\text{idid}_3 \; (\lambda X. \lambda x. \, x)$ reduce to $\lambda X. \lambda x. \, x$.

3.2 Decidable types

The following example demonstrates a more substantial use of StraTT in the form of type constructors as floating functions and how they interact with cumulativity. Later in Section 5 we'll consider datatypes with parameters, but for now, consider the following Church encoding [6] of decidable types, which additionally uses negation defined as implication into the empty type.

$$\text{neg} :^0 \star \to \star \qquad\qquad \text{yes} :^1 \Pi X :^0 \star. X \to \text{Dec} \; X$$
$$\text{neg} \; X := X \to \bot \qquad\qquad \text{yes} \; X \; x := \lambda Z. \lambda f. \lambda g. \, f \; x$$
$$\text{Dec} :^1 \star \to \star \qquad\qquad \text{no} :^1 \Pi X :^0 \star. \text{neg} \; X \to \text{Dec} \; X$$
$$\text{Dec} \; X := \Pi Z :^0 \star. (X \to Z) \to (\text{neg} \; X \to Z) \to Z \qquad \text{no} \; X \; nx := \lambda Z. \lambda f. \lambda g. \, g \; nx$$

The yes X constructor decides X by a witness, while the no X constructor decides X by its refutation. We can show that deciding a given type is irrefutable[3]

---

[3] Note this differs from irrefutability of the law of excluded middle, $\text{neg} \; (\text{neg} \; (\Pi X :^0 \star. \text{Dec} \; X))$, which cannot be proven constructively.

$$\mathsf{irrDec} : \Pi X :^0 \star.\, \mathsf{neg}\ (\mathsf{neg}\ (\mathsf{Dec}\ X))$$
$$\mathsf{irrDec}\ X\ ndec := ndec\ (\mathsf{no}\ X\ (\lambda x.\, ndec\ (\mathsf{yes}\ X\ x)))$$

The same exercise of trying to define neg and Dec using only dependent functions and not floating functions has the same effect of no longer being able to type check irrDec, even if we allow ourselves to use displacement. More interestingly, let's now compare these definitions to more-or-less corresponding ones in Agda.

```
{-# OPTIONS --cumulativity #-}
open import Agda.Primitive using (lzero ; lsuc)
open import Data.Empty using (⊥)
neg : ∀ ℓ → Set ℓ → Set ℓ
neg ℓ X = X → ⊥
Dec : ∀ ℓ → Set (lsuc ℓ) → Set (lsuc ℓ)
Dec ℓ X = (Z : Set ℓ) → (X → Z) → (neg (lsuc ℓ) X → Z) → Z
yes : ∀ ℓ (X : Set ℓ) → X → Dec ℓ X
yes ℓ X x = λ Z f g → f x
no : ∀ ℓ (X : Set ℓ) → neg ℓ X → Dec ℓ X
no ℓ X nx = λ Z f g → g nx
```

Universe polymorphism is required to capture some of the expressivity of floating functions. For instance, to talk about the negation or the decidability of a type at level 1, by cumulativity it suffices to use neg and Dec respectively (without displacement!) in StraTT, but we must use neg (lsuc lzero) and Dec (lsuc lzero) in Agda. However, since the constructors for Dec use the type argument dependently, in StraTT the level of that argument is fixed at 0. The constructors must be displaced to yes[1] and no[1] to construct proofs of Dec[1], just as yes (lsuc lzero) and no (lsuc lzero) would construct proofs of Dec (lsuc lzero).

3.3   Leibniz equality

Although nondependent functions can often benefit from a floating domain, sometimes we don't want the domain to float. Here, we turn to a simple application of dependent types with Leibniz equality [22,27] to demonstrate a situation where the level of the domain needs to be fixed to a strictly lower level even when the codomain doesn't depend on the function argument.

$$\mathsf{eq} :^1 \Pi X :^0 \star.\, X \to X \to \star \qquad\qquad \mathsf{refl} :^1 \Pi X :^0 \star.\, \Pi x :^0 X.\, \mathsf{eq}\ X\ x\ x$$
$$\mathsf{eq}\ X\ x\ y := \Pi P :^0 X \to \star.\, P\ x \to P\ y \qquad \mathsf{refl}\ X\ x\ P\ px := px$$

An equality eq $A\ a\ b$ states that two terms are equal if given any predicate P, a proof of $P\ a$ yields a proof of $P\ b$; in other words, a and b are indiscernible. The proof of reflexivity should be unsurprising.

We might try to define a nondependent predicate stating that a given type X is a mere proposition, *i.e.* that all of its inhabitants are equal.

$$\mathsf{isProp} :^0 \star \to \star$$
$$\mathsf{isProp}\ X := \underline{\Pi x :^0 X . \Pi y :^0 X . \mathsf{eq}\ X\ x\ y}$$

But this doesn't type check, since the body contains an equality over elements of X, which necessarily has level 1 rather than the expected level 0. We must assign isProp a stratified function type, given below on the left; informally, stratification propagates dependency information not only from the codomain, but also from the function body.

$$\mathsf{isProp} :^1 \Pi X :^0 \star . \star \qquad\qquad \mathsf{isSet} :^2 \Pi X :^0 \star . \star$$
$$\mathsf{isProp}\ X := \Pi x :^0 X . \Pi y :^0 X . \mathsf{eq}\ X\ x\ y \qquad \mathsf{isSet}\ X := \Pi x :^0 X . \Pi y :^0 X .$$
$$\mathsf{isProp}^1\ (\mathsf{eq}\ X\ x\ y)$$

Going one further, we define above on the right a predicate isSet stating that X is an h-set [40], or that its equalities are mere propositions, by using a displaced isProp so that we can reuse the definition at a higher level; here, isProp^1 now has type $\Pi X :^1 \star . \star$ at level 2. Once again, despite the type of isSet not being an actual dependent function type, we need to fix the level of the domain.

4 Metatheory

4.1 Consistency of subStraTT

We use Agda to mechanize a proof of logical consistency — that no closed inhabitant of the empty type exists — for subStraTT, which excludes floating nondependent functions. For simplicity, the mechanization also excludes global definitions and displaced constants, which shouldn't affect consistency: if there is a closed inhabitant of the empty type that uses global definitions, then there is a closed inhabitant of the empty type under the empty signature by inlining all global definitions. The proof files are available at https://github.com/plclub/StraTT under the **agda/** directory. The only axiom we use is function extensionality[4].

The core construction of the consistency proof is a three-place logical relation $\boxed{a \in [\![A]\!]_k}$ among a term, its type, and its level, which we would aspirationally like to define as in Figure 6. Informally, this represents the interpretation of the type A as a set of closed terms which behave according to that type. For instance, a term f is in the interpretation of a function type if for every term y which behaves according to the domain, the term $f\ y$ behaves according to the codomain. Consistency follows from the fact that the interpretation of the empty type is empty. In our working metatheory, we use **0** for falsehood, **1** for truthhood, $\wedge$ for conjunction, $\longrightarrow$ for implication, and $\forall$ and $\exists$ for universal and existential quantification .

---

[4] `agda/accessibility.agda:`**funext,funext'**

$\boxed{a \in [\![A]\!]_k}$

$$\star \in [\![\star]\!]_k \triangleq 1 \qquad \Pi x\!:^j A.\, B \in [\![\star]\!]_k \triangleq j < k \wedge A \in [\![\star]\!]_j$$

$$\bot \in [\![\star]\!]_k \triangleq 1 \qquad \qquad \wedge\, (\forall y.\, y \in [\![A]\!]_j \longrightarrow B\{y/x\} \in [\![\star]\!]_k)$$

$$a \in [\![\bot]\!]_k \triangleq 0 \qquad f \in [\![\Pi x\!:^j A.\, B]\!]_k \triangleq \forall y.\, y \in [\![A]\!]_j \longrightarrow f\, y \in [\![B\{y/x\}]\!]_k$$

$$a \in [\![A]\!]_k \triangleq \exists B.\, A \equiv B \wedge a \in [\![B]\!]_k$$

Fig. 6. Ill-formed logical relation between terms and types

However, this definition isn't necessarily well formed. It isn't defined recursively on the structure of the terms or the types, because in the cases involving dependent functions, we need to talk about the substituted type $B\{y/x\}$. It isn't defined inductively, either, because again in the dependent function case, the inductive itself would appear to the left of an implication as $y \in [\![A]\!]_j$, making the inductive definition non-strictly-positive.

The solution is to define the logical relation as an inductive–recursive definition [14]. This design is adapted from a concise proof of consistency for MLTT in Coq by Liu [25], which uses an impredicative encoding in place of induction–recursion. This is a simplified and pared down adaptation of a proof of decidability of conversion for MLTT in Coq by Adjedj, Lennon-Bertrand, Maillard, Pédrot, and Pujet [2], which in turn uses a predicative encoding to adapt a proof of decidability of conversion for MLTT in Agda by Abel, Öhman, and Vezzosi [1] that uses induction–recursion.

Figure 7 sketches the inductive–recursive definition, which splits the logical relation into two parts: an inductive predicate on types and their levels $\boxed{[\![A]\!]_k}$, and a relation between types and terms defined recursively on the predicate on the type, which we continue to write as $\boxed{a \in [\![A]\!]_k}$.

$\boxed{[\![A]\!]_k} \qquad \boxed{a \in [\![A]\!]_k}$

$$\frac{}{[\![\star]\!]_k} \qquad \frac{}{[\![\bot]\!]_k} \qquad \frac{\begin{array}{c} j < k \qquad [\![A]\!]_j \\ \forall y.\, y \in [\![A]\!]_j \longrightarrow [\![B\{y/x\}]\!]_k \end{array}}{[\![\Pi x\!:^j A.\, B]\!]_k} \qquad \frac{A \Rightarrow B \qquad [\![B]\!]_k}{[\![A]\!]_k}$$

$$A \in [\![\star]\!]_k \triangleq [\![A]\!]_k \qquad f \in [\![\Pi x\!:^j A.\, B]\!]_k \triangleq \forall y.\, y \in [\![A]\!]_j \longrightarrow f\, y \in [\![B\{y/x\}]\!]_k$$

$$a \in [\![\bot]\!]_k \triangleq 0 \qquad a \in [\![A]\!]_k \triangleq a \in [\![B]\!]_k \quad (where\ A \Rightarrow B)$$

Fig. 7. Inductive–recursive logical relation between terms and types

In the last inductive rule, in place of $A \equiv B$, we instead use parallel reduction $\boxed{A \Rightarrow B}$, which is a reduction relation describing all visible reductions being performed in parallel from the inside out. This is justified by the following lemma, where $\boxed{A \Rightarrow^* B}$ is the reflexive, transitive closure of $A \Rightarrow B$.

Lemma 3 (Implementation of definitional equality).[5] $A \equiv B$ *iff there exists some C such that $A \Rightarrow^* C \ ^*\!\!\Leftarrow B$, which we write as* $\boxed{A \Leftrightarrow B}$.

Even now, this inductive–recursive definition is *still* not well formed. In particular, in the inductive rule for dependent functions, if A is $\star$, then by the recursive case for the universe, $[\![y]\!]_j$ could again appear to the left of an implication. However, we know that $j < k$, which we can exploit to stratify the logical relation just as we stratify typing judgements. We do so by parametrizing each logical relation at level k by an abstract logical relation defined at all strictly lower levels $j < k$, then at the end tying the knot by instantiating them via well-founded induction on levels. This technique is adapted from an Agda model of a universe hierarchy by Kovács [21], which originates from McBride's redundancy-free construction of a universe hierarchy [31, Section 6.3.1]. As the constructions are now fairly involved, we defer to the proof file[6] for the full definitions, in particular U for the inductive predicate and el for the recursive relation. For the purposes of exposition, we continue to use the old notation.

Because the logical relation only handles closed terms, we deal with contexts and simultaneous substitutions σ separately by relating the two via yet another inductive–recursive definition in Figure 8, with a predicate on contexts $\boxed{[\![\Gamma]\!]}$ and a relation between substitutions and contexts $\boxed{\sigma \in [\![\Gamma]\!]}$. $A\{\sigma\}$ denotes applying the simultaneous substitution σ to the term A, and $\sigma[x]$ denotes the term which σ substitutes for x.[7]

$$\boxed{[\![\Gamma]\!]} \qquad \boxed{\sigma \in [\![\Gamma]\!]}$$

$$\frac{}{[\![\varnothing]\!]} \qquad \frac{[\![\Gamma]\!] \qquad \forall \sigma.\, \sigma \in [\![\Gamma]\!] \longrightarrow [\![A\{\sigma\}]\!]_k}{[\![\Gamma, x :^k A]\!]} \qquad \begin{aligned} \sigma \in [\![\varnothing]\!] &\triangleq 1 \\ \sigma \in [\![\Gamma, x :^k A]\!] &\triangleq \sigma \in [\![\Gamma]\!] \wedge \sigma[x] \in [\![A\{\sigma\}]\!]_k \end{aligned}$$

Fig. 8. Inductive–recursive logical relation between substitutions and contexts

The most important lemmas that are needed are semantic cumulativity, semantic conversion, and backward preservation.

Lemma 4 (Cumulativity).[8] *Suppose $j < k$. If $[\![A]\!]_j$ then $[\![A]\!]_k$, and if $a \in [\![A]\!]_j$ then $a \in [\![A]\!]_k$.*

Lemma 5 (Conversion).[9] *Suppose $A \Leftrightarrow B$. If $[\![A]\!]_k$ then $[\![B]\!]_k$, and if $a \in [\![A]\!]_k$ then $a \in [\![B]\!]_k$.*

Lemma 6 (Backward preservation).[10] *If $a \Rightarrow^* b$ and $b \in [\![A]\!]_k$ then $a \in [\![A]\!]_k$.*

We can now prove the fundamental theorem of soundness of typing judgements with respect to the logical relation by induction on typing derivations, and consistency follows as a corollary.

---

[5] agda/typing.agda:≈-≈   [6] agda/semantics.agda   [7] The mechanization uses de Bruijn indexing; various index-shifting operations on substitutions are omitted for concision.   [8] agda/semantics.agda:cumU,cumEl   [9] agda/semantics.agda:≈-U,≈-el   [10] agda/semantics.agda:⇒*-el

Theorem 1 (Soundness).[11] *Suppose* $[\![\Gamma]\!]$ *and* $\sigma \in [\![\Gamma]\!]$. *If* $\Gamma \vdash a :^k A$, *then* $[\![A\{\sigma\}]\!]_k$ *and* $a\{\sigma\} \in [\![A\{\sigma\}]\!]_k$.

Corollary 1 (Consistency).[12] *There are no* b, k *such that* $\varnothing \vdash b :^k \bot$.

The problem with floating functions This proof can't be extended to the full StraTT. While floating nondependent function types can be added to the logical relation directly as below, cumulativity will no longer hold.

$$\frac{[\![A]\!]_k \qquad [\![B]\!]_k}{[\![A \to B]\!]_k} \qquad\qquad f \in [\![A \to B]\!]_k \triangleq \forall x.\, x \in [\![A]\!]_k \longrightarrow f\,x \in [\![B]\!]_k$$

In particular, given $j \leq k$ and $f \in [\![A \to B]\!]_j$, when trying to show $f \in [\![A \to B]\!]_k$, we have by definition $\forall x.\, x \in [\![A]\!]_j \longrightarrow f\,x \in [\![B]\!]_j$, a term x, and $x \in [\![A]\!]_k$, but no way to cast the latter into $x \in [\![A]\!]_j$ to obtain $f\,x \in [\![B]\!]_k$ as desired via the induction hypothesis, because such a cast would go *downwards* from a higher level k to a lower level j, rather than the other way around as provided by the induction hypothesis. Trying to incorporate the desired property into the relation, perhaps by defining it as $\forall \ell \geq k.\, \forall x.\, x \in [\![A]\!]_\ell \longrightarrow f\,x \in [\![B]\!]_k$, would break the careful stratification of the logical relation that we've set up.

The violation of cumulativity due to floating functions is independent of our method of logical relations. If we try to prove consistency via a translation into an existing type theory with a cumulative universe hierarchy, for instance Agda with cumulative universes, a similar direct translation of floating functions would cause the same issue. Concretely, suppose we translate the type $\star \to \star$ at some level k into the Agda function type Set k → Set k. To prove that the translation preserves StraTT's cumulativity, we would require a function of the type (Set k → Set k) → (Set (1suc k) → Set (1suc k)), which has the same problem of needing a downward cast. Such a translation would still need to be stratified by level to be well defined, so a universe-polymorphic translation to ∀ ℓ → Set ℓ ⊔ k → Set ℓ ⊔ k wouldn't be viable either.

4.2 Type safety of StraTT

While we haven't yet proven its consistency, we have proven type safety of the full StraTT. We use Coq to mechanize the syntactic metatheory of the typing, context formation, and signature formation judgements of StraTT, recalling that this covers all of stratified dependent functions, floating nondependent functions, and displaced constants. We also use Ott [36] along with the Coq tools LNgen [4] and Metalib [3] to represent syntax and judgements and to handle their locally-nameless representation in Coq. The proof scripts are available at https://github.com/plclub/StraTT under the coq/ directory.

We begin with some basic common properties of type systems, namely weakening, substitution, and regularity lemmas, as well as a generalized displaceability lemma. Next, we introduce a notion of *restriction*, which formalizes the

---

[11] agda/soundness.agda:soundness   [12] agda/consistency.agda:consistency

idea that lower judgements can't depend on higher ones, along with a notion of *restricted floating*, which is crucial for proving that floating function types are *syntactically* cumulative. Only then are we able to prove type safety.

As we haven't mechanized the syntactic metatheory of definitional equality $\Delta \vdash A \equiv B$, we state as axioms some standard, provable properties [5, Section 5.2], which are orthogonal to stratification and only used in the final proof of type safety. The equivalent lemmas for subStraTT, however, have been mechanized in Agda[13] as part of the consistency proof.

Axiom 1 (Function type injectivity).[14] *If* $\Delta \vdash A_1 \rightarrow B_1 \equiv A_2 \rightarrow B_2$ *then* $\Delta \vdash A_1 \equiv A_2$ *and* $\Delta \vdash B_1 \equiv B_2$. *If* $\Pi x :^{j_1} A_1. B_1 \equiv \Pi x :^{j_2} A_2. B_2$ *then* $\Delta \vdash A_1 \equiv A_2$ *and* $j_1 = j_2$ *and* $\Delta \vdash B_1 \equiv B_2$.

Axiom 2 (Consistency of definitional equality).[15] *If* $\Delta \vdash A \equiv B$ *then* A *and* B *do not have different head forms.*

Basic properties We extend the ordering between levels $j \leq k$ to an ordering between contexts $\boxed{\Gamma_1 \leq \Gamma_2}$ that also incorporates weakening in Figure 9. Stronger contexts have higher levels and fewer assumptions.

$\boxed{\Gamma_1 \leq \Gamma_2}$ (*Ordering on contexts*)

$$
\begin{array}{ccc}
\text{S-Nil} & \text{S-Cons} & \text{S-Weak} \\[4pt]
& \dfrac{j \leq k \quad \Gamma_1 \leq \Gamma_2}{\Gamma_1, x :^j A \leq \Gamma_2, x :^k A} & \dfrac{\Gamma_1 \leq \Gamma_2}{\Gamma_1, x :^k A \leq \Gamma_2} \\[12pt]
\dfrac{}{\varnothing \leq \varnothing} & &
\end{array}
$$

Fig. 9. Context subsumption rules

This ordering is contravariant in the typing judgement: we may lower the context without destroying typeability. This result subsumes a standard weakening lemma.

Lemma 7 (Weakening).[16] *If* $\Delta; \Gamma \vdash a :^k A$ *and* $\Delta \vdash \Gamma'$ *and* $\Gamma' \leq \Gamma$ *then* $\Delta; \Gamma' \vdash a :^k A$.

The substitution lemma reflects the idea that an assumption $x :^k B$ is a hypothetical judgement. The variable x stands for any typing derivation of the appropriate type and level.

Lemma 8 (Substitution).[17] *If* $\Delta; \Gamma_1, x :^j B, \Gamma_2 \vdash a :^k A$ *and* $\Delta; \Gamma_1 \vdash b :^j B$ *then* $\Delta; \Gamma_1, \Gamma_2\{b/x\} \vdash a\{b/x\} :^k A\{b/x\}$.

Typing judgements themselves ensure the well-formedness of their components: if a term type checks, then its type can be typed at the same level. Because our type system includes the non–syntax-directed rule DT-Conv, the proof of this lemma depends on several inversion lemmas, omitted here.

---

[13] agda/reduction.agda

[14] coq/axioms.v:DEquiv_{Arrow,Pi}_inj{1,2,3}

[15] coq/axioms.v:ineq_*

[16] coq/ctx.v:DTyping_SubG

[17] coq/subst.v:DCtx_DTyping_subst

Lemma 9 (Regularity).[18]   *If* $\Delta; \Gamma \vdash a :^k A$ *then* $\vdash \Delta$ *and* $\Delta \vdash \Gamma$ *and* $\Delta; \Gamma \vdash A :^k \star$.

Generalizing displaceability in an empty context, derivations can be displaced wholesale by also incrementing contexts, written Γ^{+i}, where $(\Gamma, x :^k A)^{+i} = \Gamma^{+i}, x :^{k+i} A^{+i}$.

Lemma 10 (Displaceability).[19]   *If* $\Delta; \Gamma \vdash a :^k A$ *then* $\Delta; \Gamma^{+j} \vdash a^{+j} :^{k+j} A^{+j}$.

If we displace a context, the result might not be stronger because displacement may modify the types in the assumptions. In other words, it is *not* the case that $\Gamma \leq \Gamma^{+k}$.

Restriction The key idea of stratification is that a judgement at level k is only allowed to depend on assumptions at the same or lower levels. One way to observe this property is through a form of strengthening result, which allows variables from higher levels to be removed from the context and contexts to be truncated at any level. Formally, we define the *restriction* operation, written $\lceil \Gamma \rceil^k$, which filters out all assumptions from the context with level greater than k. A restricted context may be stronger since it could contain fewer assumptions.

Definition 1 (Restriction).[20]
$$\lceil \varnothing \rceil^k = \varnothing$$
$$\lceil \Gamma, x :^j A \rceil^k = \begin{cases} \lceil \Gamma \rceil^k, x :^j A & \text{if } j \leq k \\ \lceil \Gamma \rceil^k & \text{if } k < j \end{cases}$$

Lemma 11 (Restriction).[21]   *If* $\Delta \vdash \Gamma$ *then* $\Delta \vdash \lceil \Gamma \rceil^k$ *for any* k, *and if* $\Delta; \Gamma \vdash a :^k A$ *then* $\Delta; \lceil \Gamma \rceil^k \vdash a :^k A$.

Lemma 12 (Restriction subsumption).[22] $\Gamma \leq \lceil \Gamma \rceil^k$.

Restricted floating Subsumption allows variables from one level to be made available to all higher levels using their current type. However, when we use this rule in a judgement, it doesn't change the context that is used to check the term. This can be restrictive — we can only substitute their assumptions with lower level derivations.

In some cases, we can raise the level of some assumptions in the context when we raise the level of the judgement without displacing their types or the rest of the context. For example, suppose we have a derivation for the judgement $f :^j \Pi x :^i A. B, x :^i A \vdash f \, x :^j B$ where $i < j$. We could derive the same judgement at a higher level $k > j$ where we also raise the level of f to k. However, we can't raise x from its lower level i because then it would be invalid as an argument

---

[18] coq/ctx.v:DCtx_DSig , coq/ctx.v:DTyping_DCtx , coq/inversion.v:DTyping_regularity

[19] coq/incr.v:DTyping_incr   [20] coq/ctx.v:restrict

[21] coq/ctx.v:DSig_DCtx_DTyping_restriction   [22] coq/restrict.v:SubG_restrict

to f. In general, we can only raise the level of variables at the *same* level as the entire judgement.

To prove this formally, we must work with judgements that don't have any assumptions above the current level by using the restriction operation to discard them. Next, to raise certain levels, we introduce a *floating* operation on contexts $\uparrow_j^k \Gamma$ that raises assumptions in Γ at level j to a higher level k without displacing their types.

Lemma 13 (Restricted Floating).[23]   *If $\Delta; \Gamma \vdash a :^j A$ and $j \leq k$ then $\Delta; \uparrow_j^k (\lceil \Gamma \rceil^j) \vdash a :^k A$.*

The restricted floating lemma is required to prove cumulativity of judgements.

Lemma 14 (Cumulativity).[24]   *If $\Delta; \Gamma \vdash a :^j A$ and $j \leq k$ then $\Delta; \Gamma \vdash a :^k A$.*

In the nondependent function case $\Delta; \Gamma \vdash \lambda x. b :^j A \to B$, where we want to derive the same judgement at level $k \geq j$, we get by inversion the premise $\Delta; \Gamma, x :^j A \vdash b :^j B$, while we need $\Delta; \Gamma, x :^k A \vdash b :^k B$. Restricted floating and weakening allows us to raise the level of b together with the single assumption x from level j to level k.

Type Safety We can now show that this language satisfies the preservation (*i.e.* subject reduction) and progress lemmas with respect to call by name $\beta\delta$-reduction $\boxed{\Delta \vdash a \rightsquigarrow b}$, whose rules are given in Figure 10. For progress, values are type formers and abstractions.

Theorem 2 (Preservation).[25]   *If $\Delta; \Gamma \vdash a :^k A$ and $\Delta \vdash a \rightsquigarrow a'$ then $\Delta; \Gamma \vdash a' :^k A$.*

Theorem 3 (Progress).[26]   *If $\Delta; \varnothing \vdash a :^k A$ then a is a value or $\Delta \vdash a \rightsquigarrow b$ for some b.*

$\boxed{\Delta \vdash a \rightsquigarrow b}$ *(Reduction)*

R-BETA
$$\frac{}{\Delta \vdash (\lambda x. b)\, a \rightsquigarrow b\{a/x\}}$$

R-DELTA
$$\frac{x :^k A := a \in \Delta}{\Delta \vdash x^i \rightsquigarrow a^{+i}}$$

R-APP
$$\frac{\Delta \vdash b \rightsquigarrow b'}{\Delta \vdash b\, a \rightsquigarrow b'\, a}$$

R-ABSURD
$$\frac{\Delta \vdash b \rightsquigarrow b'}{\Delta \vdash \mathsf{absurd}(b) \rightsquigarrow \mathsf{absurd}(b')}$$

Fig. 10. Call by name reduction rules

---

[23] coq/restrict.v:DTyping_float_restrict   [24] coq/restrict.v:DTyping_cumul
[25] coq/typesafety.v:Reduce_Preservation   [26] coq/typesafety.v:Reduce_Progress

5   Prototype implementation

We have implemented a prototype type checker, which can be found at `https://github.com/plclub/StraTT` under the `impl/` directory, including a brief overview of the concrete syntax.[27] This implementation is based on `pi-forall` [41], a simple bidirectional type checker for a dependently-typed programming language.

For convenience, displacements and level annotations on dependent types can be omitted; the type checker then generates level metavariables in their stead. When checking a single global definition, constraints on level metavariables are collected, which form a set of integer inequalities on metavariables. An SMT solver checks that these inequalities are satisfiable by the naturals and finally provides a solution that minimizes the levels. Therefore, assuming the collected constraints are correct, if a single global definition has a solution, then a solution will always be found. However, we don't know if this holds for a *set* of global definitions, because the solution for a prior definition might affect whether a later definition that uses it is solveable. Determining what makes a solution "better" or "more general" to maximize the number of global definitions that can be solved is part of future work.

The implementation additionally features stratified datatypes, case expressions, and recursion, used to demonstrate the practicality of programming in StraTT. Restricting the datatypes to inductive types by checking strict positivity and termination of recursive functions is possible but orthogonal to stratification and thus out of scope for this work. The parameters and arguments of datatypes and their constructors respectively can be either floating (*i.e.* nondependent) or fixed (*i.e.* dependent), with their levels following rules analogous to those of nondependent and dependent functions. Additionally, datatypes and constructors can be displaced like constants, in that a displaced constructor only belongs to its datatype with the same displacement.

We include with our implementation a small core library,[28] and all the examples that appear in this paper have been checked by our implementation.[29] In the subsections to follow, we examine three particular datatypes in depth: decidable types, propositional equality, and dependent pairs.

5.1   Decidable types

Revisiting an example from Section 3, we can define Dec as a datatype.

$$\textbf{data } \mathsf{Dec}\ (X : \star) :^0 \star \textbf{ where}$$
$$\mathsf{Yes} :^0 X \to \mathsf{Dec}\ X$$
$$\mathsf{No} :^0 \mathsf{neg}\ X \to \mathsf{Dec}\ X$$

The lack of annotation on the parameter indicates that it's a floating domain, so that $\lambda X.\ \mathsf{Dec}\ X$ can be assigned type $\star \to \star$ at level 0. Datatypes and

---

[27] `impl/README.md`   [28] `impl/pi/README.pi`   [29] `impl/pi/StraTT.pi`

their constructors, like variables and constants, are cumulative, so the aforementioned type assignment is valid at any level above 0 as well. When destructing a datatype, the constructor arguments of each branch are typed such that the constructor would have the same level as the level of the scrutinee. Consider the following proof that decidability of a type implies its double negation elimination, which requires inspecting the decision.

$$\mathsf{decDNE} :^1 \Pi X :^0 \star. \, \mathsf{Dec} \, X \rightarrow \mathsf{neg} \, (\mathsf{neg} \, X) \rightarrow X$$
$$\mathsf{decDNE} \, X \, dec \, nn := \mathbf{case} \, dec \, \mathbf{of}$$
$$\qquad \mathsf{Yes} \, y \Rightarrow y$$
$$\qquad \mathsf{No} \, x \Rightarrow \mathsf{absurd}(nn \, x)$$

By the level annotation on the function, we know that dec and nn both have level 1. Then in the branches, the patterns $\mathsf{Yes} \, y$ and $\mathsf{No} \, x$ must also be typed at level 1, so that y has type X and x has type $\mathsf{neg} \, X$ both at level 1.

5.2 Propositional equality

Datatypes and their constructors, like constants, can be displaced as well, uniformly raising the levels of their types. We again revisit an example from Section 3 and now define a propositional equality as a datatype with a single reflexivity constructor.

$$\mathbf{data} \, \mathsf{Eq} \, (X :^0 \star) :^1 X \rightarrow X \rightarrow \star \, \mathbf{where}$$
$$\mathsf{Refl} :^1 \Pi x :^0 X. \, \mathsf{Eq} \, X \, x \, x$$

This time, the parameter has a level annotation indicating that it's fixed at 0, while its indices are floating. Displacing Eq by 1 would then raise the fixed parameter level to 1, while the levels of Eq^1 itself and its floating indices always match but can be 2 or higher by cumulativity. Its sole constructor would be Refl^1 containing a single argument of type X at level 1. Displacement is needed to state and prove propositions about equalities between equalities, such as the uniqueness of equality proofs.[30]

$$\mathsf{UIP} :^2 \Pi X :^0 \star. \, \Pi x :^0 X. \, \Pi p :^1 \mathsf{Eq} \, X \, x \, x. \, \mathsf{Eq}^1 \, (\mathsf{Eq} \, X \, x \, x) \, p \, (\mathsf{Refl} \, x)$$
$$\mathsf{UIP} \, X \, x \, p := \mathbf{case} \, p \, \mathbf{of} \, \mathsf{Refl} \, x \Rightarrow \mathsf{Refl}^1 \, (\mathsf{Refl} \, x)$$

5.3 Dependent pairs

Because there are two different function types, there are also two different ways to define dependent pairs. Using a floating function type for the second component's type results in pairs whose first and second projections can be defined as usual,

---

[30] The provability of this principle, also known as UIP [17], is more a consequence of the quirks of unification in **pi-forall** than an intentional design.

while using the stratified dependent function type results in pairs whose second projection can't be defined using the first. We first take a look at the former.

> **data** NPair $(X :^0 \star)$ $(P : X \to \star) :^1 \star$ **where**
>
> MkPair $:^1 \Pi x :^0 X. P\ x \to$ NPair $X\ P$
>
> nfst $:^1 \Pi X :^0 \star. \Pi P :^0 X \to \star.$ NPair $X\ P \to X$
>
> nfst $X\ P\ p :=$ **case** p **of** MkPair $x\ y \Rightarrow x$
>
> nsnd $:^2 \Pi X :^0 \star. \Pi P :^0 X \to \star. \Pi p :^1$ NPair $X\ P. P$ (nfst $X\ P\ p$)
>
> nsnd $X\ P\ p :=$ **case** p **of** MkPair $x\ y \Rightarrow y$

Due to stratification, the projections need to be defined at level 1 and 2 respectively to accommodate dependently quantifying over the parameters at level 0 and the pair at level 1. Even so, the second projection is well typed, since P can be used at level 2 by subsumption to be applied to the first projection at level 2 also by subsumption in the return type of the second projection.

As the two function types are distinct, we do need both varieties of dependent pairs. In particular, with the above pairs alone, we aren't able to type check a universe of propositions NPair $\star$ isProp, as the predicate has type $\Pi X :^0 \star. \star.$

> **data** DPair $(X :^0 \star)$ $(P : \Pi x :^0 X. \star) :^1 \star$ **where**
>
> MkPair $:^1 \Pi x :^0 X. P\ x \to$ DPair $X\ P$
>
> dfst $:^2 \Pi X :^0 \star. \Pi P :^1 (\Pi x :^0 X. \star).$ DPair $X\ P \to X$
>
> dfst $X\ P\ p :=$ **case** p **of** MkPair $x\ y \Rightarrow x$
>
> dsnd $:^2 \Pi X :^0 \star. \Pi P :^1 (\Pi x :^0 X. \star). \Pi p :^1$ DPair $X\ P.$
>
> $\qquad$ **case** p **of** MkPair $x\ y \Rightarrow P\ x$
>
> dsnd $X\ P\ p :=$ **case** p **of** MkPair $x\ y \Rightarrow y$

In the second variant of dependent pairs where P is a stratified dependent function type, the domain of P is fixed to level 0, so in the type in dsnd, it can't be applied to the first projection, but it can still be applied to the first component by matching on the pair. Now we're able to type check DPair $\star$ isProp.

In both cases, the first component of the pair type has a fixed level, while the second component is floating, so using a predicate at a higher level results in a pair type at a higher level by subsumption. Consider the predicate isSet, which has type $\Pi X :^0 \star. \star$ at level 2: a universe of sets DPair $\star$ isSet is also well typed at level 2.

Unfortunately, the first projection dfst can no longer be used on an element of this pair, since the predicate is now at level 2, nor can its displacement dfst[1] since that would displace the level of the first component as well. Without proper level polymorphism, which would allow keeping the first argument's level fixed while setting the second argument's level to 2, we're forced to write a whole new first projection function.

In general, this limitation occurs whenever a datatype contains both dependent and nondependent parameters. Nevertheless, in the case of the pair type, the flexibility of a nondependent second component type is still preferable to a dependent one that fixes its level, since there would need to be entirely separate datatype definitions for different combinations of first and second component levels, *i.e.* one with levels 0 and 1 (as in the case of isProp), one with levels 0 and 2 (as in the case of isSet), and so on.

6   Discussion

6.1   On consistency

The consistency of subStraTT tells us that the basic premise of using stratification in place of a universe hierarchy is sensible. However, as we've seen that directly adding floating functions to the logical relation doesn't work, an entirely different approach may be needed to show the consistency of the full StraTT.

One possible direction is to take inspiration from the syntactic metatheory, especially Restricted Floating (Lemma 13), which is required specifically to show cumulativity of floating functions. Since cumulativity is exactly where the naïve addition of floating functions to the logical relation fails, the key may be to formulate this lemma more semantically.

Another possibility is based on the observation that due to cumulativity, floating functions appear to be parametric in their stratification level, at least starting from the smallest level at which it can be well typed. This observation suggests that some sort of relational model may help to interpret levels parametrically.

Nevertheless, we strongly believe that StraTT is indeed consistent. Restriction (Lemma 11) in particular intuitively tells us that nothing at higher levels could possibly be smuggled into a lower level to violate stratification. As a further confidence check, we have verified that four type-theoretic paradoxes which are possible in an ordinary type theory with type-in-type do *not* type check in our implementation. These paradoxes are Burali-Forti's paradox [7] and Russell's paradox [35] as formulated by Coquand [11], and Girard's paradox [16] as formulated by Hurkens [20]. In each case, the definitions reach a point where a higher-level term needs to fit into a lower-level position to proceed any further — exactly what stratification is designed to prevent. Appendix A examines these paradoxes in depth.

6.2   On useability

Useability comes down to the balance between practicality and expressivity. On the practicality side, our implementation demonstrates that if a definition is well typed, then its levels and displacements can be completely omitted and inferred, providing a workflow comparable to Coq or Lean. Additionally, constants are displaced uniformly, so StraTT doesn't exhibit the same kind of exponential blowup in levels and type checking time that can occur when using universe-polymorphic definitions in Coq or Lean.[31]

On the other hand, if a definition is *not* well typed, debugging it may involve wading through constraints among generated level metavariables in situations normally having nothing to do with universe levels, since stratification now involves levels everywhere, in particular when using dependent function types.

On the expressivity side, the displacement system of StraTT falls somewhere between level monomorphism and prenex level polymorphism; in some scenarios, it works just as well as polymorphism. For instance, to type check Hurkens' paradox as far as StraTT can, the Coq formulation of the paradox (without type-in-type) requires universe polymorphism, and the Agda formulation of the paradox (without type-in-type) requires definitions polymorphic over at least three universe levels. This is due to types that involve multiple syntactic universes, such as $\Pi X :^0 \star . (X \to \star) \to \star$, which only involves one level in StraTT, while the corresponding Agda type $(X : \mathsf{Set}\ \ell_1) \to (X \to \mathsf{Set}\ \ell_2) \to \mathsf{Set}\ \ell_3$ requires three. In Hurkens' paradox, these three Agda levels must vary independently, but StraTT achieves the same effect via displacement and floating.

However, in other scenarios, the expressivity of level polymorphism over multiple level variables is truly needed. In particular, merely having a type constructor with both a dependent domain and a nondependent domain interacts poorly with cumulativity. Suppose we have some type constructor $\mathsf{T} :^1 \Pi x :^0 X . Y \to \star$ and a function over elements of this type $\mathsf{f} :^1 \Pi x :^0 X . \Pi y :^0 Y . \mathsf{T}\ x\ y \to Z$. By cumulativity, if y has level 2, then $\mathsf{T}\ x\ y$ is still well typed by cumulativity at level 2, but f can no longer be applied to it, since the level of y is now too high. We would like the second argument of f to float along with T, but this isn't possible due to dependency. Making the level of the second argument polymorphic (subject to the expected constraints) would resolve this issue.

6.3   Related work

StraTT is directly inspired by Leivant's stratified polymorphism [23,24,12], which developed from Statman's ramified polymorphic typed λ-calculus [37]. Stratified System F, a slight modification of the original system, has since been used to demonstrate a normalization proof technique using hereditary substitution [15], which in turn has been mechanized in Coq as a case study for the Equations package [26]. More recently, an interpreter of an intrinsically-typed Stratified System F has been mechanized in Agda by Thiemann and Weidner [39], where stratification levels are interpreted as Agda's universe levels. Similarly, Hubers and Morris' Stratified R_ω, a stratified System F_ω with row types, has been mechanized in Agda as well [19]. Meanwhile, displacement comes from McBride's crude-but-effective stratification [30,29], and we specialize the displacement algebra (in the sense of Favonia, Angiuli, and Mullanix [18]) to the naturals.

---

[31] `impl/pi/Blowup.pi`

7   Conclusion

In this work, we have introduced Stratified Type Theory, a departure from a decades-old tradition of universe hierarchies without, we conjecture, succumbing to the threat of logical inconsistency. By stratifying dependent function types, we obstruct the usual avenues by which paradoxes manifest their inconsistencies; and by separately introducing floating nondependent function types, we recover some of the expressivity lost under the strict rule of stratification. Although proving logical consistency for the full StraTT remains future work, we *have* proven it for the subsystem subStraTT, and we have provided supporting evidence by proving its syntactic metatheory and showing how well-known type-theoretic paradoxes fail.

Towards demonstrating that StraTT isn't a mere theoretical exercise but could form a viable basis for theorem proving and dependently-typed programming, we have implemented a prototype type checker for the language augmented with datatypes, along with a small core library. The implementation also features inference for level annotations and displacements, allowing the user to omit them entirely. We leave formally ensuring that our rules for datatypes don't violate existing metatheoretical properties as future work as well.

Given the various useability tradeoffs discussed, as well as the incomplete status of its consistency, we don't see any particularly compelling reason for existing proof assistants to adopt a system based on StraTT. However, we don't see any showstoppers either, so we believe it to be suitable for further improvement and iteration. Ultimately, we hope that StraTT demonstrates that alternative treatments of type universes are feasibile and worthy of study, and opens up fresh avenues in the design space of type theories for proof assistants.

A   Paradoxes

A.1   Burali-Forti's paradox

Burali-Forti's paradox [7] in set theory concerns the simultaneous well-foundedness and non–well-foundedness of an ordinal. In type theory, we instead consider a particular datatype U due to Coquand [11][32,33] along with a well-foundedness predicate for U.

> **data** $U :^1 \star$ **where**
> > $\mathsf{MkU} :^1 \Pi X :^0 \star. (X \to U) \to U$
>
> **data** $\mathsf{WF} :^2 U \to \star$ **where**
> > $\mathsf{MkWF} :^2 \Pi X :^0 \star. \Pi f :^1 X \to U. (\Pi x :^1 X. \mathsf{WF}\ (f\ x)) \to \mathsf{WF}\ (\mathsf{MkU}\ X\ f)$

---

[32] Our thanks to Stephen Dolan for detailing to us this example.   [33] `impl/pi/WFU.pi`

Note that both of these definitions are strictly positive, so we aren't using any tricks relying on negative datatypes. We can show that all elements of U are well founded. If we ignore stratification and use type-in-type, we can also construct an element loop that is provably *not* well founded.

$\text{wf} :^2 \Pi u :^1 \text{U}.\, \text{WF}\ u$

$\text{wf}\ u := \textbf{case}\ u\ \textbf{of}$

$\quad \text{MkU}\ X\ f \Rightarrow \text{MkWF}\ X\ f\ (\lambda x.\, \text{wf}\ (f\ x))$

$\text{loop} :^1 \text{U}$

$\text{loop} := \text{MkU}\ \underline{\text{U}}\ (\lambda u.\, u)$

$\text{nwfLoop} :^2 \text{WF loop} \to \bot$

$\quad \text{MkWF}\ X\ f\ h \Rightarrow \text{nwfLoop}\ (h\ \text{loop})$

In the branch of nwfLoop, by pattern matching on the type of the scrutinee, X is bound to U and f to $\lambda u.\, u$, so h loop correctly has type WF loop. Note that this definition passes the usual structural termination check, since the recursive call is done on a subargument from h. Then nwfLoop (wf loop) is an inhabitant of the empty type.

However, with stratification, U with level 1 is too large to fit into the type argument of MkU, which demands level 0, so loop can't be constructed in the first place. This is also why the level of a datatype can't be strictly lower than that of its constructors, despite such a design not violating the regularity lemma.

A.2 Russell's paradox

The U above was originally used by Coquand [11] to express a variant of Russell's paradox [35].[34],[35] First, an element of U is said to be regular if it's provably inequal to its subarguments; this represents a set which doesn't contain itself.

$\text{regular} :^1 \text{U} \to \star$

$\text{regular}\ u := \textbf{case}\ u\ \textbf{of}$

$\quad \text{MkU}\ X\ f \Rightarrow \Pi x :^0 X.\, (f\ x = \text{MkU}\ X\ f) \to \bot$

The trick is to define a U that is both regular and nonregular. Normally, with type-in-type, this would be one that represents the set of all regular sets.

$\text{R} :^3 \text{U}^2$

$\text{R} := \text{MkU}^2\ (\text{NPair}^1\ \text{U regular})\ \underline{(\text{nfst}^1\ \text{U regular})}$

Stratification once again prevents R from type checking, since the pair projection returns a U and not a U^2 as required by the constructor MkU^2. The type contained in the pair can't be displaced to U^2 either, since that would make the pair's level too large to fit inside MkU^2.

---

[34] An Agda implementation [13] can be found at
https://github.com/agda/agda/blob/master/test/Succeed/Russell.agda.
[35] impl/pi/Russell.pi

A.3 Hurkens' paradox

Although we've seen that stratification thwarts the paradoxes above, they leverage the properties of datatypes and recursive functions, which we haven't formalized. Here, we turn to the failure of Hurkens' paradox [20] as further evidence of consistency, which in contrast can be formulated in pure StraTT without datatypes. Below is the paradox in Coq without universe checking.

```
Require Import Coq.Unicode.Utf8_core.
Unset Universe Checking.
Definition P (X : Type) : Type := X → Type.
Definition U : Type := ∀ (X : Type), (P (P X) → X) → P (P X).
Definition tau (t : P (P U)) : U := λ X f p, t (λ s, p (f (s X f))).
Definition sig (s : U) : P (P U) := s U tau.
Definition Delta (y : U) := (∀ p, sig y p → p (tau (sig y))) → False.
Definition Omega : U := tau (λ p, ∀ (x : U), sig x p → p x).
Definition M (x : U) (s : sig x Delta) : Delta x :=
  λ d, d Delta s (λ p, d (λ y, p (tau (sig y)))).
Definition D : Type := ∀ p, (∀ x, sig x p → p x) → p Omega.
Definition R : D := λ p d, d Omega (λ y, d (tau (sig y))).
Definition L (d : D) : False := d Delta M (λ p, d (λ y, p (tau (sig y)))).
Definition false : False := L R.
```

If we replace unsetting universe checking with `Set Universe Polymorphism.`, then the definitions check up to M. The corresponding StraTT code, too, checks up to M, using displacement as needed, and is verified in the implementation[36]

$$P :^0 \star \to \star := \lambda X. X \to \star$$

$$U :^1 \star := \Pi X :^0 \star. (P\ (P\ X) \to X) \to P\ (P\ X)$$

$$tau :^1 P\ (P\ U) \to U := t\ (\lambda s. p\ (f\ (s\ X\ f)))$$

$$sig :^2 U^1 \to P\ (P\ U) := \lambda s. s\ U\ tau$$

$$Delta :^2 P\ U^1 := \lambda y. (\Pi p :^1 P\ U. sig\ y\ p \to p\ (tau\ (sig\ y))) \to \bot$$

$$Omega :^3 U := tau\ (\lambda p. \Pi x :^2 U^1. sig\ x\ p \to p\ (\lambda X. x\ X))$$

$$M :^4 \Pi x :^3 U^2. sig^1\ x\ Delta \to Delta^1\ x :=$$
$$\lambda x. \lambda s. \lambda d. d\ Delta\ s\ (\lambda p. d\ (\lambda y. p\ (tau\ (sig\ y))))$$

$$D :^3 \star := \Pi p :^1 P\ U. (\Pi x :^1 U. sig\ \underline{x}\ p \to p\ x) \to p\ Omega$$

The next definition D doesn't type check, since sig takes a displaced U^1 and not a U. The type of x can't be displaced to fix this either, since p takes an undisplaced U and not a U^1. Being stuck trying to equate two different levels is reassuring, as conflating different universe levels is how we expect a paradox that exploits type-in-type to operate.

---

[36] `impl/pi/Hurkens.pi` (no annotations), `impl/pi/HurkensAnnot.pi` (all annotations)

References

1. Abel, A., Öhman, J., Vezzosi, A.: Decidability of Conversion for Type Theory in Type Theory. Proc. ACM Program. Lang. **2**(POPL) (Dec 2017). https://doi.org/10.1145/3158111

2. Adjedj, A., Lennon-Bertrand, M., Maillard, K., Pédrot, P.M., Pujet, L.: Martin-Löf à la Coq. In: Proceedings of the 13th ACM SIGPLAN International Conference on Certified Programs and Proofs. p. 230–245. CPP 2024 (2024). https://doi.org/10.1145/3636501.3636951

3. Aydemir, B., Charguéraud, A., Pierce, B.C., Pollack, R., Weirich, S.: Engineering formal metatheory. In: Proceedings of the 35th Annual ACM SIGPLAN-SIGACT Symposium on Principles of Programming Languages. p. 3–15. POPL '08, Association for Computing Machinery, New York, NY, USA (2008). https://doi.org/10.1145/1328438.1328443, https://doi.org/10.1145/1328438.1328443

4. Aydemir, B., Weirich, S.: LNgen: Tool Support for Locally Nameless Representations. Tech. rep., University of Pennsylvania (Jun 2010). https://doi.org/20.500.14332/7902

5. Barendregt, H.P.: Lambda calculi with types, p. 117–309. Oxford University Press, Inc. (1993). https://doi.org/10.5555/162552.162561

6. Böhm, C., Berarducci, A.: Automatic synthesis of typed λ-programs on term algebras. Theoretical Computer Science **39**, 135–154 (1985). https://doi.org/10.1016/0304-3975(85)90135-5

7. Burali–Forti, C.: Una questione sui numeri transfiniti. Rendiconti del Circolo matematico di Palermo **11** (1897)

8. Chan, J., Weirich, S.: Artifact for Stratified Type Theory (Jan 2025). https://doi.org/10.5281/zenodo.13958530, https://plclub/StraTT

9. Clifton, A.V.: Arend — Proof-assistant assisted pedagogy. Master's thesis, California State University, Fresno, California, USA (2015), https://staffwww.fullcoll.edu/aclifton/files/arend-report.pdf

10. Coq Development Team, T.: The Coq Proof Assistant (Jan 2022). https://doi.org/10.5281/zenodo.5846982, https://coq.github.io/doc/v8.15/refman

11. Coquand, T.: The paradox of trees in type theory. BIT Numerical Mathematics **32**, 10–14 (Mar 1992). https://doi.org/10.1007/BF01995104

12. Danner, N., Leivant, D.: Stratified polymorphism and primitive recursion. Mathematical Structures in Computer Science **9**(4), 507–522 (1999). https://doi.org/10.1017/S0960129599002868

13. Devriese, D.: [Agda] Simple contradiction from type-in-type (Mar 2013), https://lists.chalmers.se/pipermail/agda/2013/005164.html

14. Dybjer, P.: A general formulation of simultaneous inductive-recursive definitions in type theory. The Journal of Symbolic Logic **65**(2), 525–549 (Jun 2000). https://doi.org/10.2307/2586554

15. Eades III, H., Stump, A.: Hereditary substitution for stratified System F. In: International Workshop on Proof Search in Type Theories (2010), https://hde.design/includes/pubs/PSTT10.pdf

16. Girard, J.Y.: Interprétation fonctionnelle et élimination des coupures de l'arithmétique d'ordre supérieur. PhD dissertation, Université Paris VII (1972)

17. Hofmann, M., Streicher, T.: The groupoid model refutes uniqueness of identity proofs. In: Proceedings of the Ninth Annual IEEE Symposium on Logic in Computer Science (LICS 1994). pp. 208–212. IEEE Computer Society Press (July 1994). https://doi.org/10.1109/LICS.1994.316071

18. Hou (Favonia), K.B., Angiuli, C., Mullanix, R.: An Order-Theoretic Analysis of Universe Polymorphism. Proc. ACM Program. Lang. **7**(POPL) (Jan 2023). https://doi.org/10.1145/3571250

19. Hubers, A., Morris, J.G.: Generic Programming with Extensible Data Types: Or, Making Ad Hoc Extensible Data Types Less Ad Hoc. Proceedings of the ACM on Programming Languages **7**(ICFP), 356–384 (Aug 2023). https://doi.org/10.1145/3607843

20. Hurkens, A.J.C.: A simplification of Girard's paradox. In: Typed Lambda Calculi and Applications. pp. 266–278. Springer Berlin Heidelberg, Berlin, Heidelberg (1995). https://doi.org/10.1007/BFb0014058

21. Kovács, A.: Generalized Universe Hierarchies and First-Class Universe Levels. In: 30th EACSL Annual Conference on Computer Science Logic (CSL 2022). Leibniz International Proceedings in Informatics (LIPIcs), vol. 216, pp. 28:1–28:17. Schloss Dagstuhl – Leibniz-Zentrum für Informatik, Dagstuhl, Germany (2022). https://doi.org/10.4230/LIPIcs.CSL.2022.28, https://drops.dagstuhl.de/opus/volltexte/2022/15748

22. Leibniz, G.W.: Discours de métaphysique (1686)

23. Leivant, D.: Stratified polymorphism. In: [1989] Proceedings. Fourth Annual Symposium on Logic in Computer Science. pp. 39–47 (1989). https://doi.org/10.1109/LICS.1989.39157

24. Leivant, D.: Finitely stratified polymorphism. Information and Computation **93**(1), 93–113 (1991). https://doi.org/10.1016/0890-5401(91)90053-5, selections from 1989 IEEE Symposium on Logic in Computer Science

25. Liu, Y.: Mechanized consistency proof for MLTT (2024), https://github.com/yiyunliu/mltt-consistency/, Proof pearl under submission

26. Mangin, C., Sozeau, M.: Equations for Hereditary Substitution in Leivant's Predicative System F: A Case Study. In: Tenth International Workshop on Logical Frameworks and Meta Languages: Theory and Practice. EPTCS, vol. 185. Berlin, Germany (Aug 2015). https://doi.org/10.4204/EPTCS.185.5, https://hal.inria.fr/hal-01248807

27. Martin-Löf, P.: A theory of types (1971)

28. Martin-Löf, P.: An intuitionistic theory of types (1972)

29. McBride, C.: Crude but Effective Stratification (2002), https://personal.cis.strath.ac.uk/conor.mcbride/Crude.pdf

30. McBride, C.: Crude but Effective Stratification (2011), https://mazzo.li/epilogue/index.html%3Fp=857&cpage=1.html

31. McBride, C.: Datatypes of Datatypes (Jul 2015), https://www.cs.ox.ac.uk/projects/utgp/school/conor.pdf

32. de Moura, L., Kong, S., Avigad, J., van Doorn, F., von Raumer, J.: The Lean Theorem Prover (System Description). In: International Conference on Automated Deduction. Lecture Notes in Computer Science, vol. 9195, pp. 378–388 (Aug 2015). https://doi.org/10.1007/978-3-319-21401-6_26

33. Norell, U.: Towards a practical programming language based on dependent type theory. Ph.D. thesis, Chalmers University of Technology and Göteborg University, Göteborg, Sweden (2007), https://research.chalmers.se/en/publication/46311

34. Reynolds, J.C.: Towards a theory of type structure. In: Programming Symposium: Proceedings, Colloque sur la Programmation. pp. 408–425. Lecture Notes in Computer Science, Springer-Verlag Berlin, Berlin, Heidelberg (1974). https://doi.org/10.5555/647323.721503

35. Russell, B.: The Principles of Mathematics. Cambridge University Press (1903)

36. Sewell, P., Nardelli, F.Z., Owens, S., Peskine, G., Ridge, T., Sarkar, S., Strniša, R.: Ott: Effective tool support for the working semanticist. Journal of Functional Programming **20**(1), 71–122 (2010). https://doi.org/10.1017/S0956796809990293

37. Statman, R.: Number theoretic functions computable by polymorphic programs. In: 22nd Annual Symposium on Foundations of Computer Science (SFCS 1981). pp. 279–282 (1981). https://doi.org/10.1109/SFCS.1981.24

38. Swamy, N., Hriţcu, C., Keller, C., Rastogi, A., Delignat-Lavaud, A., Forest, S., Bhargavan, K., Fournet, C., Strub, P.Y., Kohlweiss, M., Zinzindohoue, J.K., Zanella-Béguelin, S.: Dependent Types and Multi-Monadic Effects in F*. In: Principles of Programming Languages. pp. 256–270 (Jan 2016). https://doi.org/10.1145/2837614.2837655

39. Thiemann, P., Weidner, M.: Towards Tagless Interpretation of Stratified System F. In: TyDe 2023: Proceedings of the 8th ACM SIGPLAN International Workshop on Type-Driven Development (2023), https://icfp23.sigplan.org/details/tyde-2023/12/

40. Univalent Foundations Program, T.: Homotopy Type Theory: Univalent Foundations of Mathematics. Institute for Advanced Study (2013), https://homotopytypetheory.org/book

41. Weirich, S.: Implementing Dependent Types in pi-forall (2023). https://doi.org/10.48550/arXiv.2207.02129, https://arxiv.org/abs/2207.02129

Coverage Semantics for Dependent Pattern Matching

Joseph Eremondi[1]($\boxtimes$)(iD) and Ohad Kammar[2](iD)

[1] Department of Computer Science, University of Regina, Regina, SK, Canada
`jeremondi@uregina.ca`
[2] Laboratory for the Foundations of Computer Science, University of Edinburgh,
Edinburgh, Scotland, UK
`ohad.kammar@ed.ac.uk`

Abstract. Dependent pattern matching is a key feature in dependently typed programming. However, there is a theory-practice disconnect: while many proof assistants implement pattern matching as primitive, theoretical presentations give semantics to pattern matching by elaborating to eliminators. Though theoretically convenient, eliminators can be awkward and verbose, particularly for complex combinations of patterns. This work aims to bridge the theory-practice gap by presenting a direct categorical semantics for pattern matching, which does not elaborate to eliminators. This is achieved using sheaf theory to describe when sets of arrows (terms) can be amalgamated into a single arrow. We present a language with top-level dependent pattern matching, without specifying which sets of patterns are considered covering for a match. Then, we give a sufficient criterion for which pattern-sets admit a sound model: patterns should be in the canonical coverage for the category of contexts. Finally, we use sheaf-theoretic saturation conditions to devise some allowable sets of patterns. We are able to express and exceed the status quo, giving semantics for datatype constructors, nested patterns, absurd patterns, propositional equality, and dot patterns.

Keywords: semantics, dependent pattern matching, sheaf, coverage

1 Introduction

Pattern matching is a core feature in dependently typed programming. With pattern matching one can specify a function consuming an input by giving functions for every possible way that input might have been constructed. For dependent types, the defined function can be a universally quantified proof, giving a Curry-Howard analogue of proof-by-cases.

However, there is a disconnect between the theory and practice of dependent pattern matching. Many dependently typed languages take pattern matching as a built-in user-facing construct: Coq [4], Agda [22], and Idris [5] all contain a form of dependent pattern matching in their core calculi. However, most theoretical treatments of dependent types deal with *eliminators* [19]: primitive recursors

© The Author(s) 2025
V. Vafeiadis (Ed.): ESOP 2025, LNCS 15694, pp. 264–291, 2025.
https://doi.org/10.1007/978-3-031-91118-7_11

with result types dependent on a value of the eliminated type. Eliminators and pattern matching are equally expressive, with or without with Axiom K [12, 6].

While it is possible to express all pattern matches using eliminators, it is not always convenient. Some pattern matching features require lengthy translations when converting to eliminators, such as overlapping patterns, catch-all branches, or matching on multiple values at once. Moreover, languages differ in which pattern matches they allow, so every variant of pattern matching requires a new eliminator-translation to prove consistency. Even the implementations of dependently typed languages are restricted by eliminators, since most pattern matches are elaborated into case trees with a 1:1 correspondence between branches and constructors of an inductive type.

The contribution of this paper is to narrow the theory-practice divide with a highly general syntax (Section 2) and categorical semantics for dependent pattern matching (Section 3). The semantics is direct and generic: pattern matches are translated directly into semantic objects without desugaring to eliminators or case trees, and the semantics is parameterized over an abstract coverage specifying which sets of patterns one can match against. We investigate the vision set forth by Epigram [20, 21] to enable diverse pattern-matching abstractions that go beyond the list of constructors declared by a datatype. We focus on non-overlapping patterns, but give a potential road map to supporting overlap.

In constructing our generic semantics, we present a general sufficient criterion for when a coverage leads to well-defined pattern matches without compromising logical consistency (Section 4), mechanized in Lean [11]. We define this criterion, drawing on parallels between dependent pattern matching and the theory of sheaves on a site, discovering that it is sufficient for each allowed set of patterns to correspond to a cover in the canonical coverage for the semantic category. Moreover, we use elementary results from sheaf theory to describe a group of closure operations which preserve the canonicity of a coverage (Section 5). These give a simple and direct way to model common features like multi-value matches, nested patterns, and matching on propositional equality proofs. With the exception of recursion, we achieve feature parity with the original presentation of dependent pattern matching by Coquand [9]. We conclude with an illustrative example (Section 6) and related and future work (Section 7).

A major contribution of our work is expressing pattern matching in the language of categories and sheaves. Our approach is semantic: instead of elaborating pattern matching syntax, we take pattern matches as primitive and work directly in the semantic domain, avoiding the need to consider eliminators as a syntactic primitive. The connection has been implicit for many decades, but we make it formal. That said, we only assume basic knowledge of functors, pullbacks, and slice categories, and we present all the required sheaf theory.

2   CoverTT: The Source Language

We begin with a variant of Martin Löf Type Theory, called CoverTT, parameterized over which sets of patterns can be matched against. Drawing from sheaf-theory terminology, when a set of patterns is permissible on the left-hand side of a pattern match we call it a **cover**, and say it is **covering**. The set of all covers together is called a **coverage**. The main distinct feature of COVERTT is that it is parameterized over a coverage.

2.1   The Anatomy of a Datatype

As they are presented in most dependently typed languages, inductively defined datatypes conflate four different concepts. Consider the quintessential inductive family of length-indexed vectors:

$$\text{data Vec } (A : \mathcal{U}) : (m : \mathbb{N}) \to \mathcal{U} \text{ where}$$
$$\text{nil} : \text{Vec } A \ 0$$
$$\text{cons} : (n : \mathbb{N}) \to A \to \text{Vec } A \ n \to \text{Vec } A \ (n+1)$$

This definition implicitly relies on the following concepts, the separation of which motivates the design COVERTT (as exhibited in Section 2.3).

- **Coproducts:** An inductive type behaves like the sum of its constructor types. For Vec, it behaves like $\mathbb{1} + (A \times \text{Vec } A \ n)$. In COVERTT, each inductive I is declared at the top level to have a finite collection of constructors $D_1^I \dots D_n^I$, each of which has a type ending in I.
- **Dependent fields:** each constructor has a dependent product type, so the arguments to a constructor are a curried dependent record, where the types of later fields can depend on the values of earlier ones. For Vec, in cons the return type and the type of the tail of the list depend on the earlier parameter n. In COVERTT, the type of a constructor is given as a telescope, where the types of later entries are allowed to depend on the values of previous entries.
- **Indexing:** each constructor implies a specific equation about the index values. For Vec, nil restricts that $m = 0$ and cons restricts that $m = n + 1$. In COVERTT, we use **Fording** [18], where each constructor has an identical return type, but may constrain type parameters using equality-proof fields. We treat equality as primitive and make it the only way to constrain indices of a constructor, simplifying the models of COVERTT.
- **Recursion:** inductive types can refer to themselves in fields, except to the left of a function arrow, a condition known as strict positivity. Typically, one can define structurally recursive functions over Vec. Here, Vec occurs as a field type for cons, which is allowed because it is not to the left of an arrow type. We omit recursion from COVERTT, as we believe it requires a separate toolkit of abstractions. In Section 7.2 we discuss its possible addition. In examples, we refer to some inductive types defined using self-reference, such as vectors or natural numbers.

Restricting to Top-Level Datatypes COVERTT only allows data types and pattern matches to be declared at the top level. The parameter and constructor types of datatypes must be typeable in the empty context, though they can refer to other data types. Likewise, the branches and motive of a pattern match must be typeable in the empty context. These assumptions simplify the presentation of CoverTT while reflecting how datatypes are implemented in languages like Agda, where declarations in a non-empty context are desugared into top level declarations with extra parameters. Treating nested patterns and arbitrary coverages is an interesting problem even with top-level matches, and requires substantial technical developments even to handle ordinary matching.

2.2 Syntax and Typing

The syntax for CoverTT below is standard, except for the separation of concerns from Section 2.1. Figure 1 gives the syntax, along with typing rules for CoverTT.

Overline arrows denote sequences, while bold metavariables denote dependent sequences, e.g. substitutions. Variables are assigned types from the context. Typing for dependent functions and equality is standard, with rules for their

$$\text{Term} \ni s, S, t, T ::= \quad x \mid \mathcal{U} \mid \Pi(x:S).T \mid \lambda x.t \mid t \, s \mid s =_T t \mid \mathbf{refl}_t$$

$$\mid I \, \mathbf{t} \mid D^I \, \mathbf{t} \mid \mathbf{case} \, (\mathbf{t}:\Gamma) \, \mathbf{to} \, T \, \mathbf{of} \, \{\overrightarrow{\Delta_i.\mathbf{s}_i \Rightarrow t}^i\}$$

$$\text{Ctx} \ni \Gamma, \Delta, \Xi ::= \quad \cdot \mid \Gamma,(x:T)$$

$$\text{Subst} \ni \mathbf{s}, \mathbf{t} ::= \quad \cdot \mid \mathbf{s}\,{}^\circ_9\, t$$

$$\boxed{\Gamma \vdash t : T \; \textit{(Well Typed Terms/Types)}} \qquad \boxed{\{t_i\}_i \triangleright \Xi \quad \textit{(Covering Patterns)}}$$

TypeConv
$$\frac{\Gamma \vdash t : S \qquad \Gamma \vdash S \equiv T : \mathcal{U}}{\Gamma \vdash t : T}$$

TyVar
$$\frac{\vdash \Gamma \, \mathsf{ctx} \qquad (x:T) \in \Gamma}{\Gamma \vdash x : T}$$

TyPi
$$\frac{\Gamma \vdash S : \mathcal{U} \qquad \Gamma,(x:S) \vdash T : \mathcal{U}}{\Gamma \vdash \Pi(x:S).T : \mathcal{U}}$$

TyApp
$$\frac{\Gamma \vdash t : \Pi(x:S).T \qquad \Gamma \vdash s : S}{\Gamma \vdash t \, s : [s/x]T}$$

TyLam
$$\frac{\Gamma,(x:S) \vdash t : T}{\Gamma \vdash \lambda x.t : \Pi(x:S).T}$$

TyRefl
$$\frac{\Gamma \vdash t : T}{\Gamma \vdash \mathbf{refl}_t : t =_T t}$$

TyInd
$$\frac{\mathsf{Params}(I) := \Delta \qquad \Gamma \vdash \mathbf{t} \Rightarrow \Delta}{\Gamma \vdash I \, \mathbf{t} : \mathcal{U}}$$

TyEq
$$\frac{\Gamma \vdash T : \mathcal{U} \qquad \Gamma \vdash s : T \qquad \Gamma \vdash t : T}{\Gamma \vdash s =_T t : \mathcal{U}}$$

TyCtor
$$\frac{\mathsf{Fields}(D^I) := \Delta, \Xi \qquad \Gamma \vdash \mathbf{s} \Rightarrow \Delta \qquad \Gamma \vdash \mathbf{t} \Rightarrow [\mathbf{s}/\Delta]\Xi}{\Gamma \vdash D^I \, \mathbf{t} : I \, \mathbf{s}}$$

TyCase
$$\frac{\vdash \Xi \, \mathsf{ctx} \quad \Gamma \vdash \mathbf{t_{scrut}} \Rightarrow \Xi \quad \Xi \vdash T_{motive} : \mathcal{U} \quad \overrightarrow{\vdash \Delta_i \, \mathsf{ctx}}^i \quad \overrightarrow{\Delta_i \vdash \mathbf{s}_i \Rightarrow \Xi}^i \quad \vdash \{\mathbf{s_i}\}_i \triangleright \Xi \quad \overrightarrow{\Delta_i \vdash t_i : [\mathbf{s}_i/\Xi]T_{motive}}^i}{\Gamma \vdash \mathbf{case} \, (\mathbf{t_{scrut}} : \Xi) \, \mathbf{to} \, T_{motive} \, \mathbf{of} \, [\overrightarrow{\Delta_i.\mathbf{s}_i \Rightarrow t_i}^i] : [\mathbf{t_{scrut}}/\Xi]T_{motive}}$$

Fig. 1. CoverTT: Term Typing

$$\boxed{\vdash \Gamma \; \mathsf{ctx} \quad \text{(Well Formed Contexts)}} \qquad \boxed{\Gamma \vdash \mathbf{t} \Rightarrow \Delta \quad \text{(Well Formed Substitutions)}}$$

$$\textsc{CtxNil} \qquad \frac{\textsc{CtxCons}}{\vdash \Gamma \; \mathsf{ctx} \quad \Gamma \vdash T : \mathcal{U}}{\vdash \Gamma, (x : T) \; \mathsf{ctx}} \qquad \textsc{EnvNil} \qquad \frac{\textsc{EnvCons}}{\Gamma \vdash \mathbf{s} \Rightarrow \Delta \quad \Gamma \vdash t : [\mathbf{s}/\Delta]T}{\Gamma \vdash \mathbf{s}\, \mathring{,}\, t \Rightarrow \Delta, (x : T)}$$

$$\frac{}{\vdash \cdot \; \mathsf{ctx}} \qquad\qquad\qquad\qquad \frac{}{\Gamma \vdash \cdot \Rightarrow \cdot}$$

Fig. 2. Typing: Contexts and Substitutions

types, introduction, and elimination. The equality type is intensional, and there is no reflection rule by which propositional equalities can be made judgmental equalities. Nevertheless, COVERTT is consistent with models that identify all propositionally-equal terms. We have no J-axiom, instead using the coverage to specify how to match on $\mathtt{refl}_t$. We have one universe which does not have a type, leaving a universe hierarchy for future work.

Contexts and Substitutions Figure 2 also specifies well-formedness rules for contexts and substitutions. Contexts are sequences of typed variables, where later types may refer to variables from earlier in the context. Substitutions are the inhabitants of contexts. The rules are like an iterated version of dependent pairs: the type of the later values in the substitutions may depend on the earlier values. We borrow the notation $\Gamma \vdash \mathbf{t} \Rightarrow \Delta$ from Hofmann [14], since such a substitution corresponds to a morphism $\Gamma \longrightarrow \Delta$ in the models we define. We use the notation $[\mathbf{s}/\Delta]t$ to denote the simultaneous substitution of the variables bound in Δ by the terms of $\mathbf{s}$ in t. If $\Gamma \vdash \mathbf{s} \Rightarrow \Delta$ and $\Delta \vdash t : T$, then $\Gamma \vdash [\mathbf{s}/\Delta]t : [\mathbf{s}/\Delta]T$.

Datatype and Pattern Matching Syntax We assume a fixed collection of inductive type constructors, along with data constructors. For each datatype there is a fixed context of parameters $\mathsf{Params}(I)$ and, for each constructor, fields $\mathsf{Fields}(D^I)$, such that $\vdash \mathsf{Params}(I), \mathsf{Fields}(D^I)$, i.e., both are well-formed, and the fields may depend on the parameters. The type $I\ \mathbf{t}$ denotes the type constructor I applied to parameters $\mathbf{t}$. $D^I\ \mathbf{t}$ is the data constructor D for the type I, given $\mathbf{t}$ for its fields. We omit I in D^I when it is clear from context.

The pattern matching form is a nameless version of defining functions by multiple pattern matching clauses, as in Agda or Idris. The term

$$\mathsf{case}\ (\mathbf{t} : \varXi)\ \mathsf{to}\ T\ \mathsf{of}\ \{\overrightarrow{\Delta_i.\, \mathbf{s}_i \Rightarrow t_i}^{\, i}\}$$

denotes a match on **scrutinees** $\mathbf{t}$ of context-type $\varXi$, producing a result of the **motive** type T, where T may refer to the variables bound in $\varXi$. The branches, indexed by i, each have a left–side pattern $\mathbf{s}_i$, which may contain pattern variables from the context Δ_i, and which produces a result t_i. The scrutinee is a substitution because pattern matching functions can take multiple arguments, and the types of later arguments can depend on the values of earlier ones.

Typing Pattern Matches The TYCASE typing rule (Fig. 1) is the most important rule. To type $\Gamma \vdash \mathbf{case} \ (\mathbf{t_{scrut}} : \Xi) \ \mathbf{to} \ T_{motive} \ \mathbf{of} \ \{\overrightarrow{\Delta_i.\mathbf{s}_i \Rightarrow t_i}^{\,i}\}$, the scrutinee inhabits some Ξ. Because pattern matching is dependent, the motive T_{motive} is indexed over the scrutinee type. The pattern $\mathbf{s}_i$ for each branch inhabit the scrutinee type Ξ in the context of its pattern variables Δ_i. Each branch is typed against the context of its pattern variables, and inhabits the motive for the scrutinee value given by that branch's pattern, e.g., $\mathbf{s}_i$. Finally, the entire match inhabits the motive type, instantiated to the scrutinee. Critically, the motive T_{motive} and each branch t_i must be typeable in the closed context Δ_i, making no reference to Γ. This restriction matches practice: in Agda and Idris, pattern matching elaborates to top level declarations. We give an example in Section 2.3.

The Generic Coverage Relation In a match, the patterns $\overline{\mathbf{s}_i}$ must be covering. At no point do we require the patterns of a match to correspond to constructors of an inductive type, or even that the matched upon type be inductive. Instead, we appeal to an arbitrary judgment $\{\mathbf{s}_i\}_i \triangleright \Xi$, relating sets of substitutions to contexts. This relation is to be read as "the patterns $\mathbf{s}_1 \ldots \mathbf{s}_n$ are a total decomposition of the context Ξ". This relation replaces the usual condition that there must be a case for each constructor of the datatype. It is the parameter by which we tune COVERTT, and can take many forms, from requiring a single scrutinee with exactly one branch per constructor, to allowing multiple scrutinees with arbitrary nested patterns and absurd branches omitted. Section 4.2 explores the conditions a coverage must satisfy to result in a well-behaved type theory. In general, we expect that a coverage will consist of a basis set of coverings, containing at least variables and constructors for each datatype, which can be closed under composition, concatenation, etc. For generality, we do not require closure conditions, but we show in Section 5 they are always permissible.

Computational Rules Figure 3 gives definitional equality for COVERTT, omitting structural (reflexivity, symmetry, transitivity) and congruence rules. Rule EQAPP is the usual β-reduction. In EQMATCH, we reduce a match when the scrutinee is $[\mathbf{t_{mat}}/\Delta_j]\mathbf{s}_j$ for some $\Gamma \vdash \mathbf{t_{mat}} \Rightarrow \Delta_j$, i.e., it is a pattern applied to values for the pattern variables of $\mathbf{s}_j$. This substitution $\mathbf{t_{mat}}$ instantiates the pattern variables in t_j, which is the value of the entire match.

2.3   Example: Vectors

To see these constructs concretely, we show how length-indexed vectors from Section 2.1 would be represented in our system, along with a type safe head function. In COVERTT, vectors can be defined using labelled sums. Notice the equality-type fields which encode the index constraints via Fording.

$\mathsf{Params}(\mathsf{Vec}) := \ , (\varLambda : \mathcal{U}), (n : \mathbb{N})$

$\mathsf{Fields}(\mathsf{Nil}^{\mathsf{Vec}}) := \cdot, (A : \mathcal{U}), (n : \mathbb{N}), (eq : n = 0)$

$\mathsf{Fields}(\mathsf{Cons}^{\mathsf{Vec}}) := \cdot, (A : \mathcal{U}), (n : \mathbb{N}), (m : \mathbb{N}), (h : A), \ (t : \mathsf{Vec}\,A\,m), (eq : n = m+1)$

$$\boxed{\Gamma \vdash t = s : T \;\; \textit{(Term Definitional Equality)}} \qquad \boxed{\vdash \Gamma \equiv \Delta \; \mathsf{ctx} \;\; \textit{(Equal Contexts)}}$$

$$\boxed{\Gamma \vdash \mathbf{t} \Rightarrow \Delta \;\; \textit{(Equal Substitutions)}}$$

EQMATCH

$$\dfrac{\vdash \Xi \; \mathsf{ctx} \quad \overrightarrow{\vdash \Delta_i \; \mathsf{ctx}}^{\,i} \quad j \in \{1 \ldots i\}}{\Gamma \vdash \mathbf{t_{mat}} \Rightarrow \Delta_j \quad \Xi \vdash T : \mathcal{U} \quad \overrightarrow{\Delta_i \vdash \mathbf{s}_i \Rightarrow \Xi}^{\,i} \quad \vdash \{\mathbf{s}_i\}_i \rhd \Xi \quad \overrightarrow{\Delta_i \vdash t_i : [\mathbf{s}_i/\Xi]T}^{\,i}}$$
$$\dfrac{}{\Gamma \vdash \mathsf{case}\; ([\mathbf{t_{mat}}/\Delta_i]\mathbf{s}_j : \Xi) \; \mathsf{to} \; T \; \mathsf{of} \; \{\overrightarrow{\Delta.\,\mathbf{s}_i \Rightarrow t_i}^{\,i}\} \equiv [\mathbf{t_{mat}}/\Delta_j]t_j : [\mathbf{t_{mat}}/\Delta_j][\mathbf{s}_j/\Xi]T}$$

EQAPP
$$\dfrac{\Gamma,(x:S) \vdash t : \Pi(x:S).T \qquad \Gamma \vdash s : S}{\Gamma \vdash (\lambda x.\,t)\,s \equiv [s/x]t : [s/x]T}$$

EQCTXNIL
$$\dfrac{}{\vdash \cdot \equiv \cdot \; \mathsf{ctx}}$$

SUBNIL
$$\dfrac{}{\Gamma \vdash \cdot \equiv \cdot : \cdot}$$

EQCTXCONS
$$\dfrac{\vdash \Gamma \equiv \Gamma' \; \mathsf{ctx} \qquad \Gamma \vdash T \equiv T' : \mathcal{U}}{\vdash \Gamma,(x:T) \equiv \Gamma',(x:T') \; \mathsf{ctx}}$$

SUBCONS
$$\dfrac{\Gamma \vdash \mathbf{s} \equiv \mathbf{s}' : \Delta \qquad \Gamma \vdash t \equiv t' : [\mathbf{s}/\Delta]T}{\Gamma \vdash \mathbf{s}\,\fatsemi\,t \equiv \mathbf{s}'\,\fatsemi\,t' : \Delta,(x:T)}$$

Fig. 3. Definitional Equality: Computational Rules

In Agda-style notation, a safe head function for vectors can be written:

head : $(A : \mathcal{U}) \to (n : \mathbb{N}) \to \mathsf{Vec}\, A\, (1+n) \to A$
head $A\; n\; (\mathsf{Cons}\; h\; t) = h$

In COVERTT this would be defined as:

head : $\Pi(A : \mathcal{U})(n : \mathbb{N})(x : \mathsf{Vec}\, A\, (n+1)).\, A$
head := $\lambda A.\, \lambda n.\, \lambda x.\, \mathsf{case}\; (\cdot\,\fatsemi\, n\,\fatsemi\, x : \cdot,(n : \mathbb{N}),(x : \mathsf{Vec}\, A\, (n+1)))\; \mathsf{to}\; A\; \mathsf{of}\; \{$
$\quad \cdot,(m : \mathbb{N}),(h : A),(t : \mathsf{Vec}\, A\, m).\, \cdot\,\fatsemi\, m\,\fatsemi\, \mathsf{Cons}\, A\, (m+1)\, m\, h\, t\, \mathbf{refl}_{m+1} \Rightarrow h\}$

That is, the function takes A, n, and x as type, number, and vector parameters. It then passes those parameters as the scrutinee of the pattern match, which is annotated with their types. The annotation is a telescope of types, so it introduces new names for the scrutinees. It happens that here we are passing names as the scrutinees, but this need not be the case, which is why we need new names for them. The result type is annotated as A. The match has a single branch, with a telescope of pattern variables m, h and t with their types. The pattern for the branch has $m+1$ as the value for scrutinee n and Cons applied to its arguments for scrutinee x. Finally, to the right of $\Rightarrow$ is the result for this case, which is h.

Implicit in this example is the need for the following to hold:

$$\{\cdot,(m : \mathbb{N})(h : A),(t : \mathsf{Vec}\, A\, m).\, \cdot\,\fatsemi\, m\,\fatsemi\, \mathsf{Cons}\, A\, (m+1)\, m\, h\, t\, \mathbf{refl}_{m+1}\}$$
$$\rhd\cdot,(n : \mathbb{N}),(x : \mathsf{Vec}\, A\, (n+1))$$

That is, the pattern for the single branch needs to cover the scrutinee type. Deducing that these patterns are a valid coverage involves seeing that $\mathtt{refl}_{m+1}$ constrains the value of n and that Nil has an absurd type.

The goal of this paper is to define direct semantics that justify such deductions, and give a broad framework to define valid coverages.

3   Categorical Models of CoverTT

In this section, we translate the syntactic constructs of CoverTT into the language of **Categories with Families** (CwFs). CwFs correspond almost exactly to the syntactic structure of dependent type theory, but with syntactic substitution replaced by a semantic operation, and with implicit liftings between contexts made explicit.

3.1   Background: Categories with Families

We recapitulate the definition and notation of CwFs, a categorical model for dependent type theory that follows the syntax fairly closely. See Hofmann [14] for more details.

Recall that a **family** X is a pair $(I_X, \underline{X})$ consisting of a set I_X and an I-indexed sequence of sets $(\underline{X}_i)_{i \in I}$. A **map** of families $f : X \to Y$ is a pair $(f_I, \underline{f})$ consisting of a function $f_I : I_X \to I_Y$ and an I-indexed sequence of functions $(f_i : \underline{X}_i \to \underline{Y}_{fi})_{i \in I}$. The category **Fam** has families as objects and maps of families as morphisms, with componentwise identity and composition structure.

A **basic CwF** $\mathcal{C}$ is a pair $(\mathcal{C}_o, F)$ consisting of a category $\mathcal{C}_o$ and a functor $F : \mathcal{C}_o^{\mathsf{op}} \to \mathbf{Fam}$. The functor F packs four pieces of structure which we'll unpack using the following notation:

- Objects $\Gamma \in \mathcal{C}_o$ are **contexts**, and morphisms $\theta : \Gamma \to \Delta$ are **substitutions**.
- For every context $\Gamma \in \mathcal{C}_o$, we denote the family $F\Gamma$ by $(\mathsf{Ty}(\Gamma), \mathsf{Tm}_\Gamma(\_))$. We call the elements of its indexing set $\mathsf{Ty}(\Gamma)$ the **types** in context Γ. For each type in $T \in \mathsf{Ty}(\Gamma)$, we call the element of the component $\mathsf{Tm}_\Gamma(T)$ the **terms** of type T in context Γ. We omit Γ when it is clear from context.
- For every substitution $\theta : \Gamma \to \Delta$, we have a map of families $F\theta : F\Gamma \leftarrow F\Delta$, and we use the same notation for both its components $F\theta = (\_\{\theta\}, \_\{\theta\})$ and call both **substitution functions**. The first component is the substitution function on **types** $\_\{\theta\} : \mathsf{Ty}(\Gamma) \leftarrow \mathsf{Ty}(\Delta)$. The second component is a sequence of substitution functions on the terms of each type $\_\{\theta\} : \mathsf{Tm}_\Gamma(T\{\theta\}) \leftarrow \mathsf{Tm}_\Delta(T)$.
- The functoriality of F amounts to the following four properties, which we call the **substitution lemma** for this CwF, where T ranges over $\mathsf{Ty}(\Gamma)$, t ranges over $\mathsf{Tm}_\Gamma(T)$:

$$T\{\mathsf{id}_\Gamma\} = T \quad t\{\mathsf{id}_\Gamma\} = t \quad T\{\theta \circ \sigma\} = (T\{\theta\})\{\sigma\} \quad t\{\theta \circ \sigma\} = (t\{\theta\})\{\sigma\}$$
$$(\text{where } \Xi \xrightarrow{\theta} \Delta \xrightarrow{\sigma} \Gamma)$$

A basic CwF includes only the bare bones of semantic models for a dependent type theory. In order to model dependent type theories of interests we need to equip them with additional structure.

We start with context extension. Let $\mathcal{C}$ be a basic CwF, and assume $\mathcal{C}_o$ has a terminal object $\cdot$. A **comprehension structure** $(\triangleright, p, v)$ over $\mathcal{C}$ consists of, for each context $\Gamma \in \mathcal{C}_o$ and type $T \in \mathsf{Ty}(\Gamma)$:

- A context $\Gamma \triangleright T$, the context Γ **extended by** T.
- A substitution $p_T : \Gamma \triangleright T \to \Gamma$, the **weakening** of Γ by T. We say that we **weaken** a type or a term by T when we apply the corresponding substitution function for the weakening p_T.
- A term $v_T \in \mathsf{Tm}_{\Gamma \triangleright T}(T)$, the **variable** we extend the context Γ with.
- Moreover, for every substitution $\theta : \Delta \to \Gamma$ and term $t \in \mathsf{Tm}_\Delta(T\{\theta\})$ there is a unique substitution $\langle \theta, t : T \rangle : \Delta \to \Gamma \triangleright T$ satisfying:

$$p_T \circ \langle \theta, t \rangle = \theta \qquad v_T\{\langle \theta, t \rangle\} = t$$

We call this substitution the **extension** of the substitution θ by t. In the sequel we omit the type ascription and write $\langle \theta, t \rangle$ for $\langle \theta, t : T \rangle$ when T is clear from context. Likewise, we omit the subscript on p and v when clear.

A CwF is a basic CwF together with comprehension structure. For a CwF $\mathcal{C} = (\mathcal{C}_o, F)$, we refer to $\mathcal{C}_o$ as $\mathcal{C}$ when doing so will cause no ambiguity.

3.2   Sections, Slices, and Dependent Types

Let $\mathcal{C}$ be a category and $\Gamma \in \mathcal{C}$ an object in it. Recall the slice category $\mathcal{C}/\Gamma$ whose objects (T, d) consist of an object $T \in \mathcal{C}$ and a morphism $d : T \to \Gamma$. Morphisms $f : (T, d) \to (S, e)$ in the slice are morphisms $f : T \to S$ that lift d through e, i.e.: $e \circ f = d$. For example, a section of Γ is a morphism out of (Γ, id) in the slice $\mathcal{C}/\Gamma$, i.e., an object $T \in \mathcal{C}$, and a pair of morphisms $f : \Gamma \to T$ and $d : T \to \Gamma$ such that $d \circ f = \mathrm{id}$.

We can use the slices of a category $\mathcal{C}$ to model dependent type theory by requiring $\mathcal{C}$ to be locally Cartesian closed (LCCC). The intuition behind this structure is that the object (T, d) in the slice $\mathcal{C}/\Gamma$ represent types T in context Γ, and d represents the dependency of terms of this type on their context. We will not recapitulate the LCCC conditions explicitly. We will, however, spell the induced LCCC structure needed for a CwF, for two reasons. First, we indicate what we have formalized in LEAN. Second, we rely on this relationship between type families and slice objects in Section 4. It lets us use core results of sheaf theory to model dependencies in pattern matching.

Lemma 1. ($\checkmark$ LEAN) *Let $\mathcal{C}$ be a CwF.*

- *The weakening $p_T : (\Gamma \triangleright T) \to \Gamma$ encodes the type T as the slice object $((\Gamma \triangleright T), p_T)$, in the sense that sections of Γ correspond to terms in context Γ:*

$$\mathsf{Tm}_\Gamma(T) \cong \mathsf{Hom}_{(\mathcal{C}/\Gamma)}\Big((\Gamma, \mathrm{id}), (\Gamma \triangleright T, p_T) \Big)$$

- *The morphisms in $\mathcal{C}$ encode indexed types—for all $\Gamma, \Delta \in \mathcal{C}$, $T \in \mathsf{Ty}(\Gamma)$, and $\theta : \Delta \to \Gamma$:*

$$\mathsf{Tm}_\Delta(T\{\theta\}) \cong \mathsf{Hom}_{(\mathcal{C}/\Gamma)}\Big((\Delta, \theta), (\Gamma \triangleright T, \mathsf{p}_T)\Big)$$

For $t \in \mathsf{Tm}_\Gamma(T)$ we write $\bar{t} : \Gamma \to \Gamma \triangleright T$ for $\langle id, t \rangle$, the corresponding p-section.

3.3   Semantic Type Formers and Closedness

CwFs give the core structure of type dependency, but give no indication of what types a model supports. Here we give semantic closedness conditions which postulate the existence of type and term constructors corresponding to common features of a dependent type theory.

Dependent Functions   We say that a CwF $\mathcal{C}$ supports dependent functions if it has:

- For each $S \in \mathsf{Ty}(\Gamma)$ and $T \in \mathsf{Ty}(\Gamma \triangleright S)$, a type $\Pi(S, T) \in \mathsf{Ty}(\Gamma)$;
- For each $T \in \mathsf{Ty}(\Gamma \triangleright S)$ and $t \in \mathsf{Ty}(T)$, a term $\lambda(t) \in \mathsf{Tm}(\Pi(S, T))$;
- For each $T \in \mathsf{Ty}(\Gamma \triangleright S)$, $s \in \mathsf{Tm}(S)$ and $t \in \mathsf{Tm}(\Pi(S, T))$, a term $\mathsf{App}(t, s) \in \mathsf{Tm}(T\{\langle id, s \rangle\})$;

such that the usual structural substitution rules hold, as well as the β-reduction equality $\mathsf{App}(\lambda(t), s) = t\{\langle id, s \rangle\}$. We could impose a version of an η rule, but this is not required for our results.

Equality   A CwF $\mathcal{C}$ supports propositional equality types [14] if, for every type $T \in \mathsf{Ty}(\Gamma)$, there exists substitution-stable terms as follows:

- A type $\mathsf{Id}(T) \in \mathsf{Ty}(\Gamma \triangleright T \triangleright T\{\mathsf{p}\})$;
- A morphism $\mathsf{Refl}_T : \Gamma \triangleright T \to \Gamma \triangleright T \triangleright T\{\mathsf{p}\} \triangleright \mathsf{Id}(T)$, such that $\mathsf{p} \circ \mathsf{Refl} = \langle id, \mathsf{v}_T \rangle$;
- For each $S \in \mathsf{Ty}(\Gamma \triangleright T \triangleright T\{\mathsf{p}\} \triangleright \mathsf{Id}(T))$, a function (on sets) $J_{T,S}$ which is in $\mathsf{Tm}(T\{\mathsf{Refl}_T\}) \to \mathsf{Tm}(S)$, where, for any $t \in \mathsf{Tm}(S\{\mathsf{Refl}_T\})$, $J(t)\{\mathsf{Refl}_T\} = t$.

We have analogues of COVERTT terms using substitution. For $T \in \mathsf{Ty}(\Gamma)$ and $s, t \in \mathsf{Tm}(T)$:

- $\mathsf{Id}(T, s, t) := \mathsf{Id}(T)\{\langle \langle id, s \rangle, t \rangle\} \in \mathsf{Tm}(\Gamma)$;
- $\mathsf{Refl}_T(t) := \mathsf{v}\{\mathsf{Refl}_T \circ \bar{t}\} \in \mathsf{Tm}(\mathsf{Id}(T)\{\mathsf{p} \circ \mathsf{Refl}_T \circ \bar{t}\}) = \mathsf{Tm}(\mathsf{Id}(T, t, t))$.

We say that a CwF supports **extensional equality** when $\mathsf{Tm}(\mathsf{Id}(T, s, t)) \neq \emptyset$ iff $s = t$, such as in presheaf or set-theoretic models. Note that this condition does not require COVERTT to soundly model an equality reflection rule. Intensional equality in COVERTT can be modelled extensionally, so long as one does not augment COVERTT with axioms like univalence, which are inconsistent with equality reflection. We focus on extensional models, discussing alternatives in Section 7.2.

Labelled Variants Next we define what it means for a category to support **labelled variants**, so that we can interpret datatypes as coproducts of their constructor types. Labelled variants are simply coproducts with extra structure to mediate the type-context relationship. Assume:

- a fixed set of type constructors $\textsc{TyCon}$;
- for each $I \in \textsc{TyCon}$, a set of data constructors $\textsc{DataCon}_I$;
- for each $I \in \textsc{TyCon}$, an object $\mathsf{Params}_I \in \mathcal{C}$ specifying types of arguments to the type constructor;
- for each $D^I \in \textsc{DataCon}_I$ a type $\mathsf{Fields}_{D^I} \in \mathsf{Ty}(\mathsf{Params}_I)$ specifying the types of arguments to the data constructor.

The last condition will usually rely on having some sort of dependent pair to encode multiple fields. Then a CwF supports the labelled variants for I if there exists some $\mathsf{TyCon}_I \in \mathsf{Ty}(\mathsf{Params}_I)$, such that for each $\theta : \Gamma \to \mathsf{Params}_I$, there exists an isomorphism

$$\iota : \Gamma \triangleright \mathsf{TyCon}_I\{\theta\} \cong \coprod_i (\Gamma \triangleright \mathsf{Fields}_{D^I_i}\{\theta\}) \quad \text{s.t. } \forall i,\, \mathsf{p}_{\mathsf{Fields}_{D^I_i}\{\theta\}} = \mathsf{p}_{\mathsf{TyCon}_I\{\theta\}} \circ \iota^{-1} \circ \mathrm{inj}_i$$

That is, projecting out the context of from the fields' type is the same as converting into TyCon_I with ι and then projecting the context. Then, for each $t \in \mathsf{Tm}(\mathsf{Fields}_{D^I_i}\{\theta\})$, the arrow $\iota^{-1} \circ \mathrm{inj}_i \circ \bar{t}$ is a section of $\mathsf{p}_{\mathsf{TyCon}_I\{\theta\}}$, and hence denotes a term in $\mathsf{Tm}(\mathsf{TyCon}_I\{\theta\})$. We call this term $\mathsf{DataCon}_{D^I_i}(t)$, since it denotes the ith data constructor applied to field values t.

3.4 Pattern Matching

Here we give a semantic presentation of $\textsc{CoverTT}$-style pattern matching. In the CwF framework, we can follow the definition of $\textsc{CoverTT}$. This serves as a statement of what we need to define pattern matching semantically. We show how to fulfill those requirements in Section 4.

Consider a semantic coverage relation $\triangleright$ whose elements are sets containing arrows into Δ. We say $\mathcal{C}$ supports matching over the semantic coverage $\triangleright$ if, for every, $\Delta \in \mathcal{C}$, $T \in \mathsf{Ty}(\Delta)$, index set $\mathcal{I}$, covering $\{\theta_i : \Delta_i \to \Delta\}_i \triangleright \Delta$ for $i \in \mathcal{I}$, branch results $t_i \in \mathsf{Tm}(T\{\theta_i\})$ for $i \in \mathcal{I}$, and scrutinee $\theta : \Gamma \to \Delta$, there exists a term $\mathsf{match}_{\overrightarrow{(\Delta_i,\theta_i,t_i)}}(\theta) \in \mathsf{Tm}(T\{\theta\})$ such that:

- for any $\sigma_i : \Gamma \to \Delta_i$, if $\theta = \theta_i \circ \sigma_i$, then $\mathsf{match}_{\overrightarrow{(\Delta_i,\theta_i,t_i)}}(\theta) = t_i\{\sigma_i\}$;
- The above choice commutes with substitution, i.e., for $\theta_1 : \Gamma_1 \to \Gamma_2$ and $\theta_2 : \Gamma_2 \to \Delta$, we have $\mathsf{match}_{\overrightarrow{(\Delta_i,\theta_i,t_i)}}(\theta_2 \circ \theta_1) = (\mathsf{match}_{\overrightarrow{(\Delta_i,\theta_i,t_i)}}(\theta_2))\{\theta_1\}$;

To see this concretely, consider the head function from Section 2.3 in the CwF structure of $\textsc{CoverTT}$. The scrutinee type Δ is $\cdot, (A : \mathcal{U}), (n : \mathbb{N}), (x : \mathsf{Vec}\ A\ n)$. The cover is the singleton $\{\cdot \fatsemi (m+1) \fatsemi \mathsf{Cons}\ m\ h\ t\ \mathbf{refl}_{m+1}\}$, where syntactic extension $\fatsemi$ corresponds to $\langle \_, \_ \rangle$. This pattern corresponds to θ_1. The pattern context $\Delta_1 := \cdot, (m : \mathbb{N}), (h : A), (t : \text{Vec } A \ m)$, so the pattern in the cover corresponds to an arrow $\cdot, (m : \mathbb{N}), (h : A), (t : \text{Vec } A \ m) \rightarrow \cdot, (A : \mathcal{U}), (n : \mathbb{N}), (x : \text{Vec } A \ n)$. There is one branch, whose result t_1 is $h : A$ (which matches the overall result because the result type is not dependent). Finally, the scrutinees are the variables $\cdot \, \mathbin{\mathring{,}} n \, \mathbin{\mathring{,}} x$, which have context-type Δ in the empty context.

The pattern matching condition says that, if $\rhd$ is supported by a model of CoverTT, and $\{\cdot \, \mathbin{\mathring{,}} (m+1) \, \mathbin{\mathring{,}} \text{Cons } m \ h \ t \ \text{refl}_{m+1}\} \rhd \Delta$, then there exists a term $\text{match}_{\Delta_1, \theta_1, t_1}$ such that, for any m, h, t, applying the substitution yields t, i.e. $[\cdot \, \mathbin{\mathring{,}} (m+1) \, \mathbin{\mathring{,}} \text{Cons } m \ h \ t \ \text{refl}_{m+1} / \Delta]\text{match}_{\Delta_1, \theta_1, t_1} = t$. In the case of our term model, this is given by the pattern match:

case $(x : \cdot \, \mathbin{\mathring{,}} n \, \mathbin{\mathring{,}} x \ : \ \cdot, (n' : \mathbb{N}), (x' : \text{Vec } A \ n'))$ to A of $\{$

$\cdot, (m : \mathbb{N})(h : A), (t : \text{Vec } A \ m). \cdot \, \mathbin{\mathring{,}} (m+1) \, \mathbin{\mathring{,}} \text{Cons } m \ h \ t \ \text{refl}_{m+1} \Rightarrow h\}$

However, in other models, there may not be an obvious way to form $\text{match}_{\Delta_1, \theta_1, t_1}$. We provide a general way of forming such a term in Section 4.

3.5   Model compatibility and soundness

The correspondence between the type formers we have introduced and the constructs of CoverTT is fairly direct, but we must account for some technical details to make the connection formal.

Not every possible syntactic cover of CoverTT leads to a non-trivial model. For example, if $\{(x : 0). \text{inl } x\} \rhd (0 + \mathbb{N})$, then we can write an inhabitant for the empty type:

bad $: 0 := \text{case } (\text{inr } 3 : (0 + \mathbb{N}))$ to 0 of $\{(x : 0). (\text{inl } x) \Rightarrow x\}$

If we have a CwF structure on a category $\mathcal{C}$ supporting functions, labelled variants, and pattern matching in the sense of Section 3.4 with a coverage relation $\rhd$, then we can soundly model CoverTT in $\mathcal{C}$ so long as the syntactic $\rhd$ is compatible with the semantic $\rhd$.

In Fig. 4 we define partial translations $[\![\Gamma]\!] \in \mathcal{C}$, $[\![\Gamma \vdash T]\!] \in \text{Ty}(\Gamma)$, $[\![\Gamma \vdash t : T]\!] \in \text{Tm}_\Gamma(T)$. We omit the cases other than pattern matching, as they are standard. The translation for pattern matches checks if the patterns translate to a semantic cover, which is well founded because each pattern is syntactically smaller than the entire match.

We have the following soundness result, characterizing how the syntactic coverage must correspond to a semantic coverage supporting pattern matching.

Theorem 1 (soundness). *If every* CoverTT *syntactic cover* $\{\Delta_i. \mathbf{s}_i\}_i \rhd \Xi$ *has* $[\![\Delta_i]\!]$ *and* $[\![\mathbf{s}_i]\!]$ *defined, and* $\{[\![\mathbf{s}_i]\!]\}_i \rhd [\![\Xi]\!]$, *then* $[\![\_]\!]$ *is a total mapping on terms/types/environments/contexts that are well typed with respect to* $\rhd$. *Moreover, the model is sound with respect to definitional equality.*

Proof. If all covers are compatible, then straightforward induction shows that the undefined case never arises on well-typed terms. The argument follows the standard CwF model of type theory, except for pattern matching, where the equations from Section 3.4 directly satisfy EqMatch.

$$[\![\cdot]\!] = \mathbb{1} \qquad [\![\Gamma, (x : T)]\!] = [\![\Gamma]\!] \triangleright [\![T]\!]$$

$$[\![\Gamma \vdash \cdot \Rightarrow \cdot]\!] = !_{[\![\Gamma]\!]} : \Gamma \to \mathbb{1} \qquad [\![\Gamma \vdash \mathbf{s}\,\mathring{,}\,t \Rightarrow \Delta, (x : T)]\!] = \langle [\![\mathbf{s}]\!], [\![t]\!] \rangle : [\![\Gamma]\!] \to [\![\Delta]\!] \triangleright [\![T]\!]$$

$$[\![\Gamma \vdash \mathsf{case}\ (\mathbf{t_{scrut}} : \varXi)\ \mathsf{to}\ T_{motive}\ \mathsf{of}\ \{\overrightarrow{\Delta_i.\,\mathbf{s}_i \Rightarrow t_i}^{\,i}\}]\!]$$

$$= \mathsf{match}_{\overline{([\![\Delta_i]\!], [\![\mathbf{s}_i]\!], [\![t_i]\!])}^{\,i}}([\![\mathbf{t_{scrut}}]\!]) \in \mathsf{Tm}(T\{[\![\mathbf{t_{scrut}}]\!]\})$$

when $[\![t_i]\!]$ *are defined for all* i *and* $\{[\![\mathbf{s}_i]\!]\}_i \triangleright [\![\varXi]\!]$

$$[\![\Gamma \vdash \mathsf{case}\ (\mathbf{t_{scrut}} : \varXi)\ \mathsf{to}\ T_{motive}\ \mathsf{of}\ \{\overrightarrow{\Delta_i.\,\mathbf{s}_i \Rightarrow t_i}^{\,i}\}]\!] \ \textit{undefined otherwise}$$

Fig. 4. Model of Pattern Matching in COVERTT

4   Coverages and Sheaves to Model COVERTT

Theorem 1 lists conditions that ensure we can soundly interpret COVERTT. What categories and coverages can we find that fulfill our criteria?

   In this section we connect some core concepts of sheaf theory to pattern matching. Specifically, we provide a sufficient condition for when a coverage on a category $\mathcal{C}$ admits semantic pattern matching as in Section 3.4.

4.1   Coverages and Sheaves

Alongside our contribution we provide a brief introduction to sheaves and sites for completeness. Systematic overviews of sheaves are given, for example, by Johnstone [15, C2] or MacLane and Moerdijk [17].

Coverages and Sites A **sheaf-theoretic coverage** on a category $\mathcal{C}$ is, for each $\Delta \in \mathcal{C}$, a set of subsets of $\mathsf{Hom}_\mathcal{C}(\_, \Delta)$, called **covers**, which fulfill the following closure condition [15, C2.1.1]: For each cover $\{f_i : \Gamma_i \to \Delta\}_{i \in 1 \ldots n}$, and other morphism $g : \varXi \to \Delta$ there exists a $\varXi$-cover $\{h_j : \varXi_j \to \varXi\}_{j \in 1 \ldots m}$ such that, for each j, there exists an f_i such $g \circ h_j$ lifts along f_i. That is, there exists a k_j making the diagram to the right commute.

$$\begin{array}{ccc} \varXi_j & \xrightarrow{\ k_j\ } & \Gamma_i \\ {\scriptstyle h_j}\downarrow & & \downarrow{\scriptstyle f_i} \\ \varXi & \xrightarrow{\ g\ } & \Delta \end{array}$$

   This condition is weaker than requiring covers to be closed under pullback by any arrow. In particular, we do not require $\mathcal{C}$ to have all pullbacks. If $\mathcal{C}$ does have all pullbacks, one can saturate the coverage so that the property of being a cover is preserved under pullbacks.

   A sheaf-theoretic coverage on $\mathcal{C}$ gives a coverage J for each object $\Delta \in \mathcal{C}$. Arrows in a J-cover share a common codomain, so it is clear to which object a cover belongs. A **site** $(\mathcal{C}, J)$ is a category $\mathcal{C}$ equipped with a coverage J.

   We refer to "sheaf theoretic coverages" specifically to distinguish them from coverages in the sense of Sections 2 and 3, i.e. the sets of patterns that we allow. Both denote the sets of morphisms/patterns that cover a given context, but we don't require pattern coverages to fulfill the sheaf-theoretic closure conditions. In Section 7.2 we show that a constructive syntactic model cannot fulfill them.

Sheaves The next conceptual tools we need are those of a presheaf and a sheaf. A **presheaf** P is a functor $P : \mathcal{C}^{op} \to \mathbf{Set}$. Sheaf theorists think of presheaves as abstract collection of functions/terms, with $P\Delta \in \mathbf{Set}$ being the set of functions out of Δ/terms in context Δ. A **sheaf** is a collection that 'thinks' all pattern matches over every cover uniquely defines a term. Formulating sheaves precisely involves multiple nested quantifiers, and we break it down in stages.

For any presheaf P and cover $\overline{\theta_i : \Delta_i \to \Delta} \in J$, a **matching family** is a collection $x_i \in P(\Delta_i)$ such that for every $\sigma : \varXi \to \Delta_i$ and $\sigma' : \varXi \to \Delta_j$, if $\theta_i \circ \sigma = \theta_j \circ \sigma'$, then $P(\sigma)(x_i) = P(\sigma')(x_j)$. I.e., a matching family assigns a P value for all arrows in a cover, while agreeing in overlapping cases.

An **amalgamation** of a matching family $\overrightarrow{x_i}^{i}$ over $\overline{\theta_i : \Delta_i \to \Delta} \in J$ is an $x \in P\Delta$ such that $P(\theta_i)(x) = x_i$, i.e., it is a value in the covered object that is compatible with the matching family.

A **sheaf** on $(\mathcal{C}, J)$ for a cover $\overline{\theta_i : \Delta_i \to \Delta} \in J$ is a presheaf P such that every matching family has a unique amalgamation. A presheaf is a J-sheaf, or just a sheaf, when it is a sheaf for each cover in J. It is in this way that a J-sheaf is a presheaf that 'thinks' all covers admit pattern-matching.

Let $\mathbf{y} : \mathcal{C} \to (\mathcal{C}^{op} \to \mathbf{Set})$ denote the **Yoneda embedding** that maps each $\Gamma \in \mathcal{C}$ to the presheaf $\mathrm{Hom}_{\mathcal{C}}(\_, \Gamma)$. A coverage is **subcanonical** when for every $\Delta \in \mathcal{C}$, $\mathbf{y}\Delta$ is a sheaf. There is a largest such coverage $J_{canonical}$—the **canonical coverage**. We say a cover is **canonical** when it is in the canonical coverage. Every representable is a sheaf for a canonical cover, though in Section 7.2 we disprove the converse: there are models which support pattern matching, so every representable is a sheaf for each allowed pattern, but where the allowed patterns do not fulfill the necessary conditions to be a sheaf-theoretic coverage.

4.2   Pattern Matching via Sheaves

The similarity between amalgamation and pattern matching is apparent, and was informally established by Coquand [9]: since morphisms in $\mathcal{C}$ correspond to substitutions (sequences of terms) in COVERTT, the sheaf condition gives a way to merge arrows (branches) with the same codomain (return type). However, to model dependent pattern matching, we need to handle the dependency of the branch result type on the scrutinee's value. Thankfully, slices give us the tools to model type dependency, and sheaf theory lets us convert subcanonical coverages on a category to coverages on a slice. The key properties, which we have mechanized in Lean [11], are as follows (see, e.g. Johnstone [15, C2.2.17]):

Theorem 2. ($\checkmark$LEAN) *If $(\mathcal{C}, J)$ is a subcanonical site, then for $\Gamma \in \mathcal{C}$, the site $(\mathcal{C}/\Gamma, J_\Gamma)$ is subcanonical, where we define $\{f_i : (\Delta_i, \theta_i) \to (\varXi, \sigma)\}_i \in J_\Gamma$ if and only if $\{f_i : \Delta_i \to \varXi\}_i \in J$. In particular, if $\{f_i : \Delta_i \to \Gamma\}_i$ is canonical, then $\{f_i : (\Delta_i, f_i) \to (\Gamma, id)\}_i$ is too.*

These properties are related to the **fundamental theorem of topos theory**, which says that a slice of a sheaf category is equivalent to a category of sheaves over the slice.

We now have what we need to state and prove the main result of this section: a criterion ensuring that a coverage can model pattern matching. The following theorem has been mechanized in the Lean 4 theorem prover [11]; work is underway to mechanize the model's soundness and the coverage building rules of Section 5.

Theorem 3. ($\checkmark$ LEAN) *Consider a CwF $\mathcal{C}$ and, for each $\Delta \in \mathcal{C}$, a relation $\{\theta_i\}_i \triangleright \Delta$ where the θ_i are disjoint monomorphisms into Δ. If all covers in $\triangleright$ are canonical, then $\mathcal{C}$ supports pattern matching (in the sense of Section 3.4).*

Proof. Let $(C, J_{canonical})$ be a canonical site with a CwF structure and a relation $\triangleright \subseteq J_{canonical}$. Consider a scrutinee type $\Delta : \mathcal{C}$, dependent result type $T \in \mathsf{Ty}(\Delta)$, canonical cover $\{\theta_i : \Delta_i \to \Delta\}_i \triangleright \Delta$ of non-overlapping monos, branch results $t_i \in \mathsf{Tm}(T\{\theta_i\})$, and scrutinee $\theta : \Gamma \to \Delta$. To construct $\mathsf{match}\overrightarrow{{}_{(\Delta_i, \theta_i, t_i)}}{}^i(\theta) \in \mathsf{Tm}(T\{\theta\})$, we build $t'_{match} \in \mathsf{Tm}_\Delta(T\{id\})$ with which we compose the scrutinee θ. We will show how the sheaf condition corresponds to the pattern match.

Matches as Arrows Recall from Lemma 1 that there is a **Set**-isomorphism $\mathsf{Tm}_\Delta(T\{\theta\}) \cong \mathsf{Hom}_{(\mathcal{C}/\Gamma)}((\Delta, \theta), (\Gamma \triangleright T, \mathsf{p}_T))$. To find a term in $\mathsf{Tm}_\Delta(T\{id\})$, we use an arrow in $\mathsf{Hom}_{(\mathcal{C}/\Delta)}((\Delta, id), (\Delta \triangleright T, \mathsf{p})) = \mathbf{y}(\Delta \triangleright T, \mathsf{p})(\Delta, id)$.

Pattern Sets as Slice Covers The patterns $\{\theta_i : \Delta_i \to \Delta\}_i$ correspond to a canonical $\mathcal{C}$-cover by our premise, so by Thm. 2 the cover $\{\theta'_i : (\Delta_i, \theta_i) \to (\Delta, id)\}_i$ is canonical in $\mathcal{C}/\Delta$.

Branches as Matching Families The branch results of the pattern match form a matching family for $\mathbf{y}((\Gamma \triangleright T, \mathsf{p}))$. Our branches are $\overrightarrow{t_i \in \mathsf{Tm}_{\Delta_i}(T\{\theta_i\}}{}^i$. By Lem. 1, this family yields a sequence $\overrightarrow{x_i \in \mathsf{Hom}_{(\mathcal{C}/\Delta)}((\Delta_i, \theta_i), (\Delta \triangleright T, \mathsf{p}))}{}^i$, i.e., $\overrightarrow{x_i \in \mathbf{y}((\Delta \triangleright T, \mathsf{p}))((\Delta_i, \theta_i))}{}^i$, which is a matching family for the presheaf $\mathbf{y}(\Delta \triangleright T, \mathsf{p})$ and the cover $\{\theta_i : (\Delta_i, \theta_i) \to (\Delta, id)\}_i$.

Amalgamating Branches Because the cover is canonical, then $\mathbf{y}(\Delta \triangleright T, \mathsf{p})$ is a sheaf for it. The sheaf condition states that the above matching family has an amalgamation $x \in \mathbf{y}(\Delta \triangleright T, \mathsf{p})(\Delta, id)$, such that $\theta_i \circ x = x_i$. So Lem. 1 yields a term $t'_{match} \in \mathsf{Tm}(T\{id\})$ such that $t'_{match}\{\theta_i\} = t_i$.

Equations and the Scrutinee Finally, given a scrutinee $\theta : \Gamma \to \Delta$, we choose $t'_{match}\{\theta\}$ as $\mathsf{match}\overrightarrow{{}_{(\Delta_i, \theta_i, t_i)}}{}^i(\theta) \in \mathsf{Tm}(T\{\theta\})$. It is in $\mathsf{Tm}_\Gamma(T\{\theta\})$, so it has the correct type. It satisfies the requisite equations. Indeed, since $t'_{match}\{\theta_i\} = t_i$, whenever $\theta = \theta_i \circ \sigma_i$ for some σ_i, we have $t'_{match}\{\theta\} = t'_{match}\{\theta_i \circ \sigma_i\} = (t'_{match}\{\theta_i\})\{\sigma_i\} = t_i\{\sigma_i\}$ just as Section 3.4 requires. For substitution, given $\theta = \theta_2 \circ \theta_1$, we have $t'_{match}\{\theta_2 \circ \theta_1\} = (t'_{match}\{\theta_2\})\{\theta_1\} = \mathsf{match}\overrightarrow{{}_{(\Delta_i, \theta_i, t_i)}}{}^i(\theta_2)\{\theta_1\}$.

The above construction lets us model pattern matching for any canonical cover, where the motive type corresponds to a representable sheaf. If J is subcanonical, then every representable is a sheaf, so we can define dependent pattern matching for any motive type. Moreover, the canonical coverage contains the covers from every subcanonical coverage, so it suffices that each allowed pattern set is a canonical cover. The disjointness and injectivity conditions ensure that the branches of a match follow the sheaf-theoretic definition of a matching family. One could instead require that branches agree on their overlap [7], which is suited to matching on real numbers [25].

We conclude this section by recalling a property characterizing subcanonical covers [15, C2.1.11], which we will utilize in Section 5.

Theorem 4. *A set of arrows $\{\theta_i : U_i \to U\}_i$ is canonical for $\mathcal{C}$ if and only if, for every $\sigma : V \to U$ and every object $T \in \mathcal{C}$, the presheaf $\mathbf{y}(T)$ is a sheaf for the pulled back family $\{\sigma^*\theta_i : \sigma^*U_i \to V\}_i$.*

We can use this theorem to form basic subcanonical coverages. To build new coverages from old ones, we employ **saturation conditions:** operations on coverages which do not change which presheaves are sheaves for that coverage. This is of interest to us because the canonical coverage is invariant under every saturation: it is already the largest possible subcanonical coverage, so no covers can be added without changing its notion of sheaf. The next section gives several examples of useful saturation conditions.

5   Tools for Building Coverages

In this section, we take the abstract canonicity condition and derive concrete rules for forming canonical covers. This section justifies the idea that COVERTT can begin with a basic set of covers for each type and obtain a language of patterns by allowing nesting, variables, and multiple scrutinees. We provide base coverages, along with composition rules for building complex coverages from simpler ones. This recreates commonly supported features of dependent pattern matching: variables, constructors for labelled variants, pruning absurd branches, and matching on `refl` with inaccessible (dot) patterns. In Section 7.2 we discuss potential novel coverages that can be supported using coverage semantics.

5.1   Identity and Isomorphism

The most basic canonical covers are singletons consisting of an isomorphism. If two contexts are isomorphic, then moving from one to the other covers all cases.

Lemma 2. *A presheaf is a sheaf for a singleton cover containing an isomorphism $\iota : \Gamma \overset{\cong}{\to} \Delta$, so every isomorphism is a canonical singleton cover.* [3]

---

[3] In a category with pullbacks, sheaves may be defined for Grothendieck pretopologies, in which all isomorphisms definitionally yield singleton covers.

As a consequence, identity arrows are in singleton canonical covers:

Corollary 1. *The singleton cover* $\{id : \Gamma \to \Gamma\}$ *is canonical for any category, so a pattern consisting entirely of variables* $x_1, x_2, \ldots x_n$ *can be safely included in any coverage for* COVERTT.

Supporting identity arrows is the bare minimum we need for pattern matching. They are the base case out of which other patterns are built, where no discrimination or computation happens at all. Likewise, a catch-all pattern, commonly written as an underscore '_', is just an unnamed variable that does not occur in the right-hand side of the branch.

More generally, the canonical coverage contains all isomorphisms. So we can devise a sound semantics for COVERTT where any isomorphism is a valid cover of a type. This allows for operations such as rearranging variables in a dependency-respecting way or re-bracketing nested sums and products.

Functions written by the programmer can even be used as patterns if they are isomorphisms, opening the door for user-defined views into a type. Of course, the existence of a sound semantics does not guarantee a language we can actually implement. Checking whether a term is a definitional isomorphism is undecidable without being explicitly given its inverse. Moreover, depending on how extensional the model is, there may be terms that are isomorphisms in the model, but are not definitional isomorphisms in COVERTT.

5.2   Coproducts and Wadler Views

With variables as patterns, the next primitive patterns we need are constructors for a datatype. As we saw in Section 3.3, one way to model datatypes is with labelled variants. So if $\mathcal{C}$ has coproducts, we can model datatype constructors as injections into a coproduct context, and we can amalgamate branches that match on all the constructors of a datatype using the universal property of a coproduct.

Labelled variants are only coproducts up to isomorphism, but we have seen that isomorphisms are always singleton covers, and below in Section 5.3 we see that composition preserves canonical covers. So it suffices to consider coproducts directly. Unfortunately, in an arbitrary category, coproduct injections are not guaranteed to form a canonical cover. Thm. 4 requires each representable to be a sheaf for the pullback of every cover, so we need coproducts to be stable under pullback, i.e. the pullback of a coproduct is the coproduct of pullbacks. Thankfully, pullback stability of coproducts holds if $\mathcal{C}$ is **Set**, a presheaf category, a topos, or any other locally cartesian closed category (LCCC). We already want $\mathcal{C}$ to be LCCC in order to support dependent functions.

Theorem 5. *Suppose* $\mathcal{C}$ *has all pullbacks and that coproducts are disjoint and stable under pullback. Then* $\{\mathsf{inj}_j : \Delta_i \to \coprod_{i \in I} \Delta_i\}_j$ *canonically cover* $\coprod_{i \in I} \Delta_i$.

The immediate result of this theorem is that for every inductive type, the constructors are covering for that type, so long as the inductive type is modelled as the labelled variants of its constructor types. However, it is important to realize that this theorem applies for any decomposition of a type into the coproduct of other types, regardless of whether the injections correspond to constructors or not. Such a coverage introduces the possibility for views as introduced by Wadler [27], which act as first class pattern synonyms:

Corollary 2. *Consider a finite $I : \mathcal{U}$, a family $S : I \to \mathcal{U}$ and an indexed function $f : (i : I) \to S\ i \to T$ in* COVERTT. *Suppose we have a category C with a CwF model of* COVERTT *supporting pattern matching as in Section 3.4 over a coverage $\_ \triangleright \_$. If $[\![T]\!] \cong [\![\Sigma(t : T)(i : I)(s : S\ i).t =_T f\ i\ s)]\!]$, then there is also a model of* COVERTT *with coverage $(\_ \triangleright \_ \cup \{f\ i\}_i)$*

That is, if T is isomorphic to the sum of some types $S\ i$ over finite i, we can safely match on a value from T, where the ith pattern is the $S\ i$ value that it corresponds to, regardless of whether T is defined as an inductive type or the $S\ i$ are its constructor types.

5.3   Nesting and Composition

With variables and constructors as primitive covers, we now need a way to combine them to build more complex covers. Adding the composition of different coverages does not change their sheaves. Every cover has the same sheaves as the sieve it generates, i.e., the closure of the cover under precomposition with any arrow in C [15, C2.1.3]. So canonical covers are closed under composition:

Theorem 6. *For a cover J of C, If $\{f_i : \Delta_i \to \Delta\}_i \in J$, and for each i, we have $\{g_{ij} : \Delta_{ij} \to \Delta_i\}_{ij} \in J$, then the sheaves of (C, J) are identical to the sheaves of $(C, J \cup \{f_i \circ g_{ij} : \Delta_{ij} \to \Delta\}_i)$. So if $\{f_i : \Delta_i \to \Delta\}_i$ is canonical, and for each i, $\{g_{ij} : \Delta_{ij} \to \Delta_i\}_{ij}$ is canonical, then $\{f_i \circ g_{ij} : \Delta_{ij} \to \Delta\}_{ij}$ is canonical.*

This allows patterns to be nested: if $\{f_i\}_i$ are covering for Δ, and for each set of variables in those covering patterns, $\{g_{ij}\}_{ij}$ is covering, then we can case split each variable in the f_i into j cases corresponding to the g_{ij} patterns, and the entire resulting set can still be covering. This property gives semantic justification for the case-split operation of the Agda and Idris editor modes, where the programmer selects a variable in a pattern match, and the pattern containing the variable is replaced by the sequence of patterns that has each possible constructor application in place of the variable.

When we combine the closure of the canonical coverage under identity (isomorphisms), sum injections, and composition, we can recreate dependent pattern matching on non-indexed datatypes. However, we see in the next sections that the language of coverages also gives us the tools to handle indexing.

5.4   Pruning Absurd Contexts

If we allow ourselves some extensionality, then we can use sheaves to model absurd branches and empty cases. Suppose that C has an initial object $\mathbb{0}$, with a unique arrow $0_\Gamma : \mathbb{0} \to \Gamma$ for every Γ. The initial context denotes an empty or absurd context, since we can derive a term of any type from it. It turns out that we do not ever need to include branches for patterns whose contexts are empty. If we can amalgamate for a cover where one pattern has an empty context, we can amalgamate for the same cover with that arrow deleted, since any matching family for the smaller cover can be turned into one for the larger cover by adding the unique arrow out of the initial context.

Theorem 7. *Let c be a canonical cover with $\theta : \Delta \to \Gamma \in c$. If there exists an arrow $\iota : \Delta \to \mathbb{0}$, then $c \setminus \{\theta\}$ is canonical.*

This property mirrors how Agda and Idris allow for the omission of empty cases. In some cases, these languages only allow branch right-hand sides to be removed after the programmer specifies an empty pattern, marking which part of the scrutinee has an impossible type. We view this empty pattern as a syntactic aid to tell the type checker when a context is isomorphic to the initial context, so we do not directly model the empty pattern.

Like our assumption about equality, the condition of having a (strong) initial object does not hold in the term model, since not all eliminations of the empty type are definitionally equal. So long as COVERTT does not contain any axioms that specifically distinguish empty eliminations, our model is still sound.

5.5   Propositional Equality

Since isomorphisms are always canonical singleton covers (Lem. 2), we can create a coverage for a sufficiently-extensional equality type.

Corollary 3. *If $\langle \mathsf{v}, \langle \mathsf{v}, \mathsf{Refl}_A \rangle \rangle : \Gamma \rhd A \to \Gamma \rhd A \rhd A\{\mathsf{p}\} \rhd \mathsf{Id}(A\{\mathsf{p}^2\}, \mathsf{v}, \mathsf{v}\{\mathsf{p}\})$ is an isomorphism, then $\{\langle \mathsf{v}, \langle \mathsf{v}, \mathsf{Refl}_A \rangle \rangle\}$ is canonical.*

In more readable, non CwF notation: if A is isomorphic to $\Sigma(x : A)(y : A). x =_A y$ in the model via the projections, then $\{(x, x, \mathtt{refl}_x)\}$ can be a singleton cover for $\Sigma(x : A)(y : A). x =_A y$. Such an isomorphism holds if $\mathcal{C}$ has extensional equality, since it asserts that there is a unique, internally constructible proof of equality between two equal terms.

For a dependent match targeting $(x : A), (y : A), (pf : x =_A y) \vdash P(x, y, pf) : \mathcal{U}$, the above cover only requires we provide a branch result with type $P(x, x, \mathsf{Refl}_A)$. The variable y was replaced by x in the goal type. This captures "inaccessible" or "forced" patterns [22], known as dot-patterns in Agda and Idris. By matching on the propositional equality, we work with refined information about the context. Here, we match y against the variable x rather than a constructor. No branching or discrimination happening, since the cover is a singleton. Rather, x is the only possible value for y given the equality proof. Agda writes $.x$ to express this pattern. Section 5.6 extends this to equality proof between arbitrary terms, rather than variables.

5.6   Pullbacks and Unification

We have seen that the canonical coverage includes isomorphisms and injections and that it allows for composition. However, the definition of a sheaf-theoretic coverage enables stability under pullback: for any coverage, a sheaf for that coverage is still a sheaf if we add the pullback of any cover by any arrow. Closure under pullback is the key condition that separates a coverage from a set of arrows. The definition in Section 4.1 is presented in the style of Johnstone [15, C2], in a general way that does not assume the existence of pullbacks. However, when each arrow in a cover has a pullback along some morphism, we get the following saturation condition:

Theorem 8. *For a cover J of $\mathcal{C}$, if $\{\theta_i : \Delta_i \to \Delta\}_i \in J$, and $g : \Gamma \to \Delta$, where the pullback of each θ_i along g exists, then $J \cup \{\{g^*\theta_i : g^*\Delta_i \to \Gamma\}_i\}$ has the same sheaves as J. So if $\{\theta_i : \Delta_i \to \Delta\}_i$ is canonical, then so is $\{g^*\theta_i : g^*\Delta_i \to \Gamma\}_i$.*

This abstract property, known as **stability under base change**, can be exploited to build interesting covers.

Context Extension Base change lets us add new scrutinees to a pattern match. In any CwF, for $\theta : \Gamma \to \Delta$ and $T \in \mathsf{Ty}(\Delta)$, pulling back by $\mathsf{p} : \Delta \triangleright T \to \Delta$ yields a morphism $\langle \theta \circ \mathsf{p}, \mathsf{v} \rangle : \Gamma \triangleright T\{\theta\} \to \Delta \triangleright T$ [14]. Combining this with Thm. 8 gives:

Theorem 9. *For canonical $\{\theta_i : \Delta_i \to \Delta\}_i$ and a type $T \in \mathsf{Ty}(\Delta)$, there is also a canonical cover $\{\langle \theta_i \circ \mathsf{p}, \mathsf{v} \rangle : \Delta_i \triangleright T\{\theta_i\} \to \Delta \triangleright T\}_i$.*

So we can build a covering pattern for a context Δ and immediately obtain a covering context on $\Delta \triangleright T$ by appending a new variable $\mathsf{v} \in \mathsf{Tm}(T\{\theta_i\})$ to each pattern in the cover. In a dependent match the new variable might have a different type in each branch: T may be indexed by variables in Δ, but each θ_i is a value for Δ with variables from Δ_i. Further case-splitting on the newly introduced variable can be achieved using composition à la Section 5.3.

Matching on Equality Suppose that for some $\Gamma \in \mathcal{C}$ and $T \in \mathsf{Ty}(\Gamma)$, and that: $\{\mathsf{Refl}_T : \Gamma \triangleright T \to \Gamma \triangleright T \triangleright T\{\mathsf{p}\} \triangleright \mathsf{Id}(T\{\mathsf{p}^2\}, \mathsf{v}, \mathsf{v}\{\mathsf{p}\})\}$ is canonical. As in Section 5.5, such a property holds for an extensional model. With such a cover on equality, we can apply the base change theorem, the CwF laws, and the properties of equality (Section 3.3) to obtain a cover on contexts containing equalities by matching:

Theorem 10. *Suppose $\mathcal{C}$ has all pullbacks. Consider $\Gamma \in \mathcal{C}$ with $T \in \mathsf{Ty}(\Gamma)$, $t_1, t_2 \in \mathsf{Tm}(T)$. Then pulling back Refl_T by $\langle \langle t_1\{\mathsf{p}\}, t_2\{\mathsf{p}\} \rangle, \mathsf{v} \rangle$ yield a context Δ and an arrow $\langle \theta, \mathsf{Refl}_T(t_{12}) \rangle$, where $\theta : \Delta \to \Gamma$, $t_{12} \in \mathsf{Tm}(T[\theta])$, and $t_1\{\theta\} = t_2\{\theta\} = t_{12}$. Moreover, if $\{\mathsf{Refl}_T\}$ is canonical, then so is the cover $\{\langle \theta, \mathsf{Refl}_T(t_{12}) \rangle : \Delta \to \Gamma \triangleright \mathsf{Id}(T, t_1, t_2)\}$.*

For the intuition behind this, consider the pullback square to the right, translated to COVERTT-style notation for clarity. First, because the square commutes, we know that θ is a substitution that equates (t_1, t_2, pf) and

$$\Delta \xrightarrow{\theta \, \fatsemi \, t_{12}} \Gamma, (x:T)$$

$$\Big\downarrow{\theta \, \fatsemi \, \mathtt{refl}_{t_{12}}} \qquad\qquad \Big\downarrow{(x \, \fatsemi \, x \, \fatsemi \, \mathtt{refl}_x)}$$

$$\Gamma, (pf : x =_T y) \xrightarrow{(t_1 \, \fatsemi \, t_2 \, \fatsemi \, \fatsemi)} \Gamma, (x:T), (y:T), (x =_T y)$$

$(x, x, \mathtt{refl}_x)$, i.e., it is a **unifier** of t_1 and t_2. Since a pullback is a limit, it is universal, so any other unifiers for t_1 and t_2 necessarily factor through θ. Thus, it is the **most general unifier** for t_1 and t_2. This is precisely what the usual rule for pattern matching on equality uses: it unifies the two sides of the equality, treating syntactic variables as unification variables, and generates a substitution that is then applied to the goal. The context Δ consists of the variables that were in common between t_1 and t_2 which remain free in the unification t_{12}. In the case that t_1 and t_2 do not unify, then the pullback is an arrow out of an initial context, and the branch can be omitted completely (because absurd covers can be omitted, as in Section 5.4).

6   Example: Folding Without a Starting Value

We now have specified everything we need (sans recursion) for feature-parity with the original presentation of dependent pattern matching by Coquand [9]. Our sheaf-centric view generalizes the elaboration process of Goguen et al. [12], but directly within the model instead of as a syntactic elaboration. Constructors for a coproduct form a cover and variables form a singleton cover, acting as the basis from which other covers are generated. Covers can be composed, extended, refined by matching on an equality, or pared down by pruning absurd branches. Indexed data types can be handled using fording and matching on equality.

To see a non-trivial example of how to build a cover in the canonical coverage, consider the foldr_1 function found in the Agda standard library [10].

$\mathsf{foldr}_1 : (A \to A \to A) \to \mathsf{Vec}\, A\, (\mathsf{suc}\, n) \to A$

$\mathsf{foldr}_1\, f\, (\mathsf{cons}\, x\, \mathsf{nil}) = x \ \mid\ \mathsf{foldr}_1\, f\, (\mathsf{cons}\, x\, (\mathsf{cons}\, y\, ys)) = f\, x\, (\mathsf{foldr}_1\, f\, (\mathsf{cons}\, y\, ys))$

Because the argument vector has length at least one, the case for nil can be omitted. The base case is then a vector of length one, and the inductive case is a vector of length two or more.

Assume an extensional CwF model of COVERTT in a LCCC $\mathcal{C}$ where inductive types are labelled variants. We show how the patterns for foldr_1 are in the canonical coverage for $\mathcal{C}$, and hence foldr_1 can be modelled. Note that because labelled variants are defined in terms of isomorphism, we do not preclude initial algebra semantics for modelling the self-reference part of inductive types.

6.1   Translating to COVERTT

First, we translate the function to COVERTT-style by making the length argument explicit and replacing the indexed constructors with ones taking explicit equality proofs. The datatype becomes:

$$\text{data Vec } (A : \mathcal{U}) : (n : \mathbb{N}) \to \mathcal{U} \text{ where}$$
$$\text{nil} : (n = 0) \to \text{Vec } A \ n$$
$$\text{cons} : (m : \mathbb{N}) \to A \to \text{Vec } A \ m \to n = m + 1 \to \text{Vec } A \ n.$$

We also abstract out the recursive calls, since we have not included them in CoverTT and have not required that our model category $\mathcal{C}$ support them. Despite using recursion, foldr_1 is an ideal example because it is not contrived, and uses all the main saturation conditions we developed in Section 5. Since foldr_1 is decreasing in the length of the lists, its recursion can be modelled with well-known techniques orthogonal to our contribution.

$$\text{foldr}_1 : (n : \mathbb{N}) \to (A \to A \to A) \to \text{Vec } A \ (\text{suc } n)$$
$$\to (\text{self} : (A \to A \to A) \to \text{Vec } A \ (\text{suc } n) \to A) \to A$$
$$\text{foldr}_1 \ 0 \ f \ (\text{cons } 0 \ x \ (\text{nil Refl}) \ \text{Refl}) \ \text{self} = x$$
$$\text{foldr}_1 \ (m + 1) \ f \ (\text{cons } (m + 1) \ x \ (\text{cons } m \ y \ ys \ \text{Refl}) \ \text{Refl}) \ \text{self}$$
$$= f \ x \ (\text{self } f \ (\text{cons } y \ ys \ \text{Refl}) \ \text{Refl})$$

6.2 Building the Coverage

Using CoverTT notation rather than CwF notation for clarity and space reasons, we now show how the rules of Section 5 can be used to build a cover:

$$\{((m + 1) \ f \ (\text{cons } (m + 1) \ x \ (\text{nil Refl}) \ \text{Refl}) \ \text{self}),$$
$$((m + 1) \ f \ (\text{cons } (m + 1) \ x \ (\text{cons } m \ y \ ys \ \text{Refl}) \ \text{Refl}) \ \text{self})\}$$
$$\triangleright (n : \mathbb{N}), (f : A \to A \to A), (v : \text{Vec } A \ (\text{suc } n)), (\text{self} : \dots)$$

- Identity (Cor. 1) has variables $(n)(f)(v)(\text{self})$ covering the scrutinee type;
- Coproduct (Cor. 2) has $\{(\text{nil } eq_{nil}), (\text{cons } m' \ x \ xs \ eq_{cons})\} \triangleright \text{Vec A q}$ for any q;
- Composition (Thm. 6) allows us to construct the canonical cover
  $\{(n \ f \ (\text{nil } eq_{nil}) \ \text{self}), (n \ f \ (\text{cons } m' \ x \ xs \ eq_{cons}) \ \text{self})\}$;
- We have $eq_{nil} : n + 1 = 0$, but this type is empty, so applying the absurd rule (Thm. 7) gives a singleton cover $\{(n \ f \ (\text{cons } m' \ x \ xs \ eq_{cons}) \ \text{self})\}$;
- $eq_{cons} : n + 1 = m' + 1$, so we get a pullback substitution mapping m' to n and all other variables to themselves. Applying the Refl rule (Cor. 3), $n \ n \ \text{Refl}$ is a cover of $(m' : \mathbb{N}) \triangleright (n : \mathbb{N}) \triangleright (n + 1 = m' + 1)$. By composition, the scrutinee context has singleton cover $\{(n \ f \ (\text{cons } n \ x \ xs \ \text{Refl}) \ \text{self})\}$ in the canonical coverage;
- The coproduct property for Vec and composition yield a cover
  $\{(n \ f \ (\text{cons } n \ x \ (\text{nil } eq_{nil}) \ \text{Refl}) \ \text{self}), (n \ f \ (\text{cons } n \ x \ (\text{cons } m \ y \ ys \ eq_{cons}) \ \text{Refl}) \ \text{self})\}$;
- Finally, since $eq_{nil} : n = 0$ and $eq_{cons} : n = m + 1$, we apply the Refl rule for each proof, along with composition, to obtain the desired cover above.

Then, we can use the sheaf condition model how $f \ x \ (\text{self } f \ (\text{cons } y \ ys \ \text{Refl}) \ \text{Refl})$ and x are amalgamated into a denotation for the entire function.

7 Discussion

7.1 Related Work

Dependent pattern matching was first proposed by Coquand [9]. While this work contains no explicit mentions of sheaf theory, it originated the idea that patterns could be thought of in terms of coverings and partitions of a space, which greatly inspired our work. The theory and practice of both pattern matching and eliminators foundational developments in proof assistants: McBride [19] developed elimination for LEGO, and later EPIGRAM [20]. This was extended to views and with-clauses by Mcbride and Mckinna [21].

Goguen et al. [12] show how pattern matching can be elaborated to primitive eliminators, and hence given semantics in any model that had semantics for eliminators. These are in turn given semantics using initial algebras [1, 2]. Cockx et al. [6] extend this to work with univalent theories. Elaboration is similar to amalgamation using the sheaf condition, but amalgamation occurs strictly in the model. Elaborating to eliminators also handles recursion, which is not yet explicitly included in our sheaf semantics.

To our knowledge, the first explicit connection between the sheaves and pattern matching was by Sherman et al. [25], which gave a framework for pattern-matching on real numbers using topological spaces. The thesis version of this work [24] generalizes the approach from topological spaces to Grothendieck topologies. Cockx et al. [7] give similar semantics to overlapping patterns by treating them as definitional equalities, using confluence rather than sheaves. Using equalizers or pullbacks to represent unification was originated by Rydeheard and Burstall [23], as well as Goguen [13].

7.2 Future Work

First-Class Pattern Synonyms An immediate application of this work would be to implement an enhanced version of pattern synonyms in a language like Agda. Currently, Agda lets the programmer declare pattern synonyms, but each name must map to a syntactic pattern i.e., a set of nested constructor applications. Agda checks if a definition is covering by elaborating to these patterns. Our framework could be used to build direct coverage checking for pattern synonyms, so the programmer could build their own alternate, extensible covers of a type, using sheaf theory to justify their coverage. This would provide direct semantics for the user-defined views of Wadler [27] and Mcbride and Mckinna [21]. Further research is needed to extract a constructive procedure for amalgamating branches that can be implemented in practice.

Overlapping Pattern Matches Our semantics require non-overlapping, injective patterns, but our framework suggests a way to lift this restriction. Recall that the sheaf condition only requires that a matching family agrees on the overlap between covering patterns. This suggests two ways to give semantics to overlapping patterns: by ensuring that the right-hand sides of each pattern match agree on the overlap of their left-hand sides, or by adding information to each pattern to ensure they are actually non-overlapping.

The latter approach matches current implementations: catch-all patterns are elaborated into multiple branches whose left-hand patterns are the constructors that have not yet been used. Unfortunately, to prove anything about a function defined this way, the programmer needs a proof case for each branch in the elaboration, even if they correspond to a single branch in the function as written. Our framework may support canonical covers which contain extra information preventing overlap, such as proofs that previous branches had not matched. These could be used to develop covers for matches with overlapping patterns that do not require creating additional cases during elaboration, enabling more succinct proofs about overlapping cases.

Inductive Datatypes and Termination Checking When patterns are not restricted to constructors, it is not immediately apparent which recursive pattern matching functions can be soundly modelled, since pattern variables may not be structurally smaller than the patterns in which they occur. Further study is needed to devise criteria for which recursive definitions are well founded with non-constructor patterns.

Beyond Top-Level Matches Our semantics only support top level pattern matches. Many of the results we used, such as the fundamental theorem of topos theory, are well suited to top-level matches but do not directly translate to terms in an arbitrary context. Additionally, if the scrutinee type of a pattern match is in a non-empty context, then matching affects not only the motive, but may refine the values or types of variables in the context on the left. These technical issues suggest a semantic theory of *telescopes*, which are objects representing extensions to a given context by some number of types, and *environments*, which extend substitutions by some number of terms.

With Clauses Our approach to matching on equality proofs gives an intuition for modelling Agda-style with-clauses and views [21], though a full account is beyond the scope of this paper. Suppose we are defining a pattern match with scrutinees of type Δ and result type $\Delta \vdash T : \mathcal{U}$, and we want to match on some intermediate expression $\Delta \vdash s : S$. There is an isomorphism $\iota : \Delta \cong \Delta, (x : S), (pf : x =_S s)$. So if we have a cover of $\{s_i : \Delta_i \to \Delta\}_i$ to match s against, we can use composition and extension to obtain a cover $\{s_i : \Delta, (pf : s_i = s) \to \Delta\}_i$. In the case that s_i and s unify, the Refl rule from above can be used to match on the equality, and in an extensional model, the goal type can be safely rewritten due to the existence of the equality proof.

Intensional Models Our current approach relies on extensional models, where equality proofs correspond with equality in the model. We can define models of CoverTT in terms of canonical coverages and non-syntactic equality, and we can give a CwF term model for CoverTT because syntactic pattern matching fulfills the criteria of Section 3.4, but the term model for CoverTT cannot be described in terms of sheaf-theoretic coverages.

To show the issue, we show that {true, false} is not a canonical cover of Bool for the CwF given by well-typed CoverTT terms quotiented by definitional equality. Consider a function haltsInN : SyntaxTree $\to \mathbb{N} \to$ Bool, that looks at a syntax tree of an untyped lambda calculus term and checks whether it halts in n or fewer steps. Consider also Ω : SyntaxTree, a representation of $(\lambda x.\, x\ x)(\lambda x.\, x\ x)$. If {true, false} is a canonical cover, it is also a sieve in the canonical topology [15, C2.1.8], so pulling the sieve back by haltsInN Ω produces the set of arrows $\{h_j \circ !_{V_j} : V_j \to \mathbb{N} \mid h_j : \mathbb{1} \to \mathbb{N}\}$. This contains each arrow in $\mathbb{1} \to \mathbb{N}$, i.e., each natural number. For the cover to be canonical, for any type T there must be a way to amalgamate $\{t_j : T \mid h_j : \mathbb{1} \to \mathbb{N}\}$ into $\mathbb{N} \to T$. Then all set-theoretic infinite sequences of natural numbers could be amalgamated into type-theoretic functions $\mathbb{N} \to \mathbb{N}$, which is impossible.

The above example relies on the existence of an infinite cover. While infinite covers are allowed in sheaf theory, they do not correspond directly to pattern matches that a programmer can write down. So further exploration of finite and infinite covers may resolve the issue.

Another issue is that extensional models typically imply that all equality proofs of a given type are equal. As such our approach is incompatible with univalent theories like Homotopy or Cubical Type Theory [26, 8]. Both of these issues might be addressed by replacing sheaves with stacks or, even more generally, ∞-stacks [16]. These replace the strict equality of the sheaf condition with higher structure. However, the technical and theoretical overhead of switching to stacks is considerable, and utilizing them for pattern matching will be a significant undertaking.

Toposes and Quasi-toposes Apart from pattern matching, the theory of sheaves plays a central role in categorical logic, since categories of sheaves over a coverage form *Grothendieck toposes*, which serve as models of constructive logic. Quasi-toposes relax the sheaf conditions to only require uniqueness of amalgamations. Future work should search for deeper connections to toposes or quasi-toposes. Two-level type theories [3] may yield some answers, since they describe the interactions between a model of a type theory and the category of presheaves over that model.

7.3   Conclusion

This work formalizes the connection between dependent pattern matching and the notion of sheaves over a site. We have provided a framework which is expressive enough to capture the semantics of current pattern matching implementations, while laying the groundwork for future enhancements. Our work demonstrates that elaboration to eliminators is not the only feasible semantics for dependent pattern matching, and that there is perspective to be gained from treating pattern matching as a core feature and using the lens of sheaf theory.

References

[1] Abbott, M., Altenkirch, T., Ghani, N.: Containers: Constructing strictly positive types. Theor. Comput. Sci. **342**(1), 3–27 (2005), ISSN 0304-3975, https://doi.org/10.1016/j.tcs.2005.06.002

[2] Altenkirch, T., Ghani, N., Hancock, P., Mcbride, C., Morris, P.: Indexed containers. J. Funct. Program. **25**, e5 (Jan 2015), ISSN 0956-7968, 1469-7653, https://doi.org/10.1017/S095679681500009X

[3] Annenkov, D., Capriotti, P., Kraus, N., Sattler, C.: Two-level type theory and applications. Math. Struct. Comput. Sci. **33**(8), 688–743 (Sep 2023), ISSN 0960-1295, 1469-8072, https://doi.org/10.1017/S0960129523000130

[4] Bertot, Y., Castéran, P.: Interactive Theorem Proving and Program Development. Springer-Verlag (2004)

[5] Brady, E.: Idris 2: Quantitative Type Theory in Practice. In: 35th Eur. Conf. Object-Oriented Program. ECOOP 2021, Schloss Dagstuhl – Leibniz-Zentrum für Informatik (2021), https://doi.org/10.4230/LIPIcs.ECOOP.2021.9

[6] Cockx, J., Devriese, D., Piessens, F.: Pattern matching without K. In: Proc. 19th ACM SIGPLAN Int. Conf. Funct. Program., pp. 257–268, ICFP '14, ACM, New York, NY, USA (2014), ISBN 978-1-4503-2873-9, https://doi.org/10.1145/2628136.2628139

[7] Cockx, J., Piessens, F., Devriese, D.: Overlapping and Order-Independent Patterns. In: Shao, Z. (ed.) Program. Lang. Syst., pp. 87–106, Springer, Berlin, Heidelberg (2014), ISBN 978-3-642-54833-8, https://doi.org/10.1007/978-3-642-54833-8_6

[8] Cohen, C., Coquand, T., Huber, S., Mörtberg, A.: Cubical type theory: A constructive interpretation of the univalence axiom. In: Uustalu, T. (ed.) 21st Int. Conf. Types Proofs Programs TYPES 2015, Leibniz International Proceedings in Informatics (LIPIcs), vol. 69, pp. 5:1–5:34, Schloss Dagstuhl–Leibniz-Zentrum fuer Informatik, Dagstuhl, Germany (2018), ISBN 978-3-95977-030-9, ISSN 1868-8969, https://doi.org/10.4230/LIPIcs.TYPES.2015.5

[9] Coquand, T.: Pattern matching with dependent types. In: Informal Proc. Log. Framew., vol. 92, pp. 66–79 (1992)

[10] Documentation for Agda: Data.Vec.Base. https://github.com/agda/agda-stdlib/blob/196766082e913de0d7cd98e3b672935a3b4528b8/src/Data/Vec/Base.agda (2024)

[11] Eremondi, J.: Joeyeremondi/lean-cwf: Lean proof for esop 2025 "coverage semantics for dependent pattern matching" (Jan 2025), https://doi.org/10.5281/zenodo.14768609, URL https://doi.org/10.5281/zenodo.14768609

[12] Goguen, H., McBride, C., McKinna, J.: Eliminating dependent pattern matching. In: Futatsugi, K., Jouannaud, J.P., Meseguer, J. (eds.) Algebra, Meaning, and Computation: Essays Dedicated to Joseph A. Goguen

on the Occasion of His 65th Birthday, pp. 521–540, Springer Berlin Heidelberg, Berlin, Heidelberg (2006), ISBN 978-3-540-35464-2, https://doi.org/10.1007/11780274_27

[13] Goguen, J.A.: What is unification?: A categorical view of substitution, equation and solution. In: Algebraic Techniques, pp. 217–261, Elsevier (1989)

[14] Hofmann, M.: Syntax and Semantics of Dependent Types. In: Pitts, A.M., Dybjer, P. (eds.) Semantics and Logics of Computation, pp. 79–130, Publications of the Newton Institute, Cambridge University Press, Cambridge (1997), ISBN 978-0-521-58057-1, https://doi.org/10.1017/CBO9780511526619.004

[15] Johnstone, P.T.: Sketches of an Elephant: A Topos Theory Compendium. Oxford Logic Guides, Oxford University Press, Oxford, New York (Jul 2003), ISBN 978-0-19-852496-0

[16] Lurie, J.: Higher Topos Theory. No. no. 170 in Annals of Mathematics Studies, Princeton University Press, Princeton, N.J (2009), ISBN 978-0-691-14048-3 978-0-691-14049-0

[17] MacLane, S., Moerdijk, I.: Sheaves in Geometry and Logic: A First Introduction to Topos Theory. Springer, New York, NY, UNITED STATES (1992), ISBN 978-1-4612-0927-0

[18] McBride, C.: Dependently Typed Functional Programs and Their Proofs. Ph.D. thesis, University of Edinburgh, UK (2000)

[19] McBride, C.: Elimination with a Motive. In: Callaghan, P., Luo, Z., McKinna, J., Pollack, R., Pollack, R. (eds.) Types Proofs Programs, pp. 197–216, Lecture Notes in Computer Science, Springer, Berlin, Heidelberg (2002), ISBN 978-3-540-45842-5, https://doi.org/10.1007/3-540-45842-5_13

[20] McBride, C.: Epigram: Practical Programming with Dependent Types. In: Vene, V., Uustalu, T. (eds.) Adv. Funct. Program., pp. 130–170, Springer, Berlin, Heidelberg (2005), ISBN 978-3-540-31872-9, https://doi.org/10.1007/11546382_3

[21] Mcbride, C., Mckinna, J.: The view from the left. J. Funct. Prog. **14**(1), 69–111 (Jan 2004), ISSN 0956-7968, 1469-7653, https://doi.org/10.1017/S0956796803004829

[22] Norell, U.: Dependently typed programming in Agda. In: Proc. 4th Int. Workshop Types Lang. Des. Implement., pp. 1–2, TLDI '09, ACM, New York, NY, USA (2009), ISBN 978-1-60558-420-1, https://doi.org/10.1145/1481861.1481862

[23] Rydeheard, D.E., Burstall, R.M.: Computational category theory. Prentice Hall International (UK) Ltd., GBR (1988), ISBN 0131627368

[24] Sherman, B.: Making Discrete Decisions Based on Continuous Values. Master of Science, Massachusetts Institute of Technology (2017)

[25] Sherman, B., Sciarappa, L., Chlipala, A., Carbin, M.: Computable decision making on the reals and other spaces: Via partiality and nondeterminism. In: Proc. 33rd Annu. ACMIEEE Symp. Log. Comput. Sci., pp. 859–868, ACM, Oxford United Kingdom (Jul 2018), ISBN 978-1-4503-5583-4, https://doi.org/10.1145/3209108.3209193

[26] Univalent Foundations Program, T.: Homotopy Type Theory: Univalent Foundations of Mathematics. https://homotopytypetheory.org/book, Institute for Advanced Study (2013)

[27] Wadler, P.: Views: A way for pattern matching to cohabit with data abstraction. In: Proc. 14th ACM SIGACT-SIGPLAN Symp. Princ. Program. Lang., pp. 307–313, POPL '87, Association for Computing Machinery, New York, NY, USA (Oct 1987), ISBN 978-0-89791-215-0, https://doi.org/10.1145/41625.41653

Variable Elimination as Rewriting in a Linear Lambda Calculus

Thomas Ehrhard[1] , Claudia Faggian[1]([✉]), and Michele Pagani[2]

[1] Université de Paris Cité, CNRS, IRIF, F-75013 Paris, France
{ehrhard,faggian}@irif.fr
[2] École Normale Supérieure, LIP, F-69342 Lyon, France
michele.pagani@ens-lyon.fr

Abstract. Variable Elimination (VE) is a classical *exact inference* algorithm for probabilistic graphical models such as Bayesian Networks, computing the marginal distribution of a subset of the random variables in the model. Our goal is to understand Variable Elimination as an algorithm acting *on programs* in an idealized probabilistic functional language—a linear simply-typed λ-calculus suffices for our purpose. Precisely, we express VE as *a term rewriting process*, which transforms a global definition of a variable into a local definition, by swapping and nesting let-in expressions. We exploit in an essential way linear types.

Keywords: Linear Logic · Lambda Calculus · Bayesian Inference · Probabilistic Programming · Denotational Semantics

1 Introduction

Probabilistic programming languages (PPLs) provide a rich and expressive framework for stochastic modeling and Bayesian reasoning. The crucial but computationally hard task is that of inference, *i.e.* computing explicitly the probability distribution which is implicitly specified by the probabilistic program. Most PPLs focus on continuous random variables—in this setting the inference engine typically implements *approximate* inference algorithms based on sampling methods (such as importance sampling, Markov Chain Monte Carlo, Gibbs sampling). However, several domains of application (*e.g.* network verification, ranking and voting, text or graph analysis) are naturally discrete, yielding to an increasing interest in the challenge of *exact inference* [21,19,44,35,46,17,34,39]. A good example is Dice [21], a *first-order* functional language whose inference algorithm exploits *the structure of the program* in order to factorise inference, making it possible to scale exact inference to large distributions. A common ground to most exact approaches is to be inspired by techniques for exact inference on discrete graphical models, which typically exploit probabilistic independence as the key for compact representation and efficient inference.

Indeed, specialized formalisms do come with highly efficient algorithms for *exact inference*; a prominent example is that of Bayesian networks, which enable

---

Supplementary Information The online version contains supplementary material available at https://doi.org/10.1007/978-3-031-91118-7_12

V. Vafeiadis (Ed.): ESOP 2025, LNCS 15694, pp. 292–321, 2025.
https://doi.org/10.1007/978-3-031-91118-7_12

algorithms such as Message Passing [37] and Variable Elimination [45]—to name two classical ones—and a variety of approaches for exploiting local structure, such as reducing inference to Weighted Model Counting [3,4]. General-purpose programming language do provide a rich expressiveness, which allows in particular for the encoding of Bayesian networks, however, the corresponding algorithms are often lost when leaving the realm of graphical models for PPLs, leaving an uncomfortable gap between the two worlds. Our goal is shedding light in this gray area, understanding exact inference as an algorithm acting *on programs*.

In pioneering work, Koller et al. [27] define a general purpose functional language which not only is able to encode Bayesian networks (as well as other specialized formalisms), but also comes with an algorithm which mimics Variable Elimination (VE for short) by means of *term transformation*. VE is arguably the simplest algorithm for exact inference, which is factorised into smaller intermediate computations, by eliminating the irrelevant variables according to a specific order. The limit in [27] is that unfortunately, the algorithm there can only implement a specific elimination ordering (the one determined by the lazy evaluation implicit in the algorithm), which might not be the most efficient: a different ordering might result in smaller intermediate factors. The general problem to be able to deal with any possible ordering, hence producing any possible factorisation, is there left as an open challenge for further investigation. The approach that is taken by the authors in a series of subsequent papers will go in a different direction from term rewriting; eventually in [39] programs are compiled into an intermediate structure, and it is on this graph structure that a sophisticated variant of VE is performed. The question of understanding VE as a *transformation on programs* remains still open; we believe it is important for a foundational understanding of PPLs.

In this paper, we provide an answer, defining an inference algorithm which *fully* formalizes the classical VE algorithm as rewriting of programs, expressed in an idealized probabilistic functional language—a linear simply-typed λ-calculus suffices for our purpose. Formally, we prove *soundness and completeness* of our algorithm with respect to the standard one. Notice that the choice of the elimination order is not part of a VE algorithm—several heuristics are available in the literature to compute an efficient elimination order (see *e.g.* [8]). As wanted, we prove that *any* given elimination ordering can be implemented by our algorithm. When we run it on a stochastic program representing a Bayesian network, its computational behaviour is the same as that of standard VE for Bayesian networks, and the cost is of the same complexity order. While the idea behind VE is simple, crafting an algorithm on terms which is able to implement any elimination order is non-trivial— our success here relies on the use of linear types $P \multimap T$ enabled by linear logic [18], accounting for the interdependences generated by a specific elimination order. Let us explain the main ideas.

Factorising Inference, via the graph structure. Bayesian networks describe a set of random variables and their conditional (in)dependencies. Let us restrict ourselves to boolean random variables, *i.e.* variables x representing a boolean

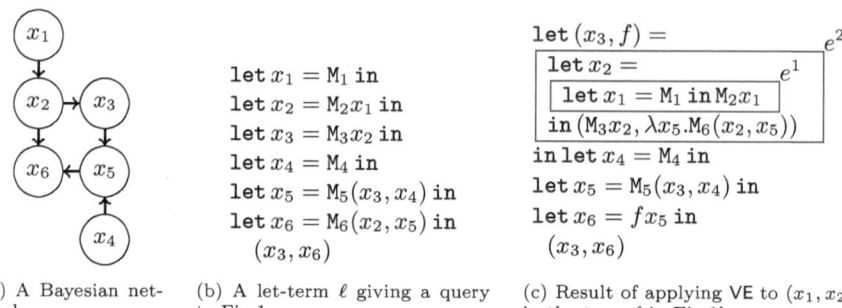

(a) A Bayesian network.

(b) A let-term ℓ giving a query to Fig.1a.

(c) Result of applying VE to (x_1, x_2) in the term ℓ in Fig.1b.

Fig. 1: Example of running the VE algorithm on a let-term ℓ.

value t or f with some probability.[3] Such a variable can be described as a vector of two non-negative real numbers (ρ_t, ρ_f) quantifying the probability ρ_t (resp. ρ_f) of sampling t (resp. f) from x.

Fig. 1a depicts an example of Bayesian network. It is a directed acyclic graph $\mathcal{G}$ where the nodes are associated with random variables and where the arrows describe conditional dependencies between these variables. For instance, in Fig. 1a the variable x_5 depends on the values sampled from x_3 and x_4, and, in turn, it affects the probability of which boolean we can sample from x_6. The network does not give a direct access to a vector (ρ_t, ρ_f) describing x_5 by its own, but only to a stochastic matrix M_5 quantifying the conditional dependence of x_5 with respect to x_3 and x_4. Formally, M_5 is a matrix with four rows, representing the four possible outcomes of a joint sample of x_3 and x_4 (*i.e.* (t, t), (t, f), (f, t), (f, f)), and two columns, representing the two possible outcomes for x_5. The matrix is *stochastic* in the sense that each line represents a probabilistic distribution of booleans: for instance, $(M_5)_{(t,f),t} = 0.4$ and $(M_5)_{(t,f),f} = 0.6$ mean that t can be sampled from x_5 with a 40% chance, while f with 60%, whenever x_3 has been observed to be t and x_4 to be f.

Having such a graph $\mathcal{G}$ and the stochastic matrices M_1, M_2, M_3, *etc.* associated with its nodes, a typical query is to compute the joint probability of a subset of the variables of $\mathcal{G}$. For example, the vector $\Pr(x_3, x_6) = (\rho_{(t,t)}, \rho_{(t,f)}, \rho_{(f,t)}, \rho_{(f,f)})$ giving the marginal over x_3 and x_6, *i.e.* the probability of the possible outcomes of x_3 and x_6. A way to obtain this is first computing the joint distributions of all variables in the graph in a single shot and then summing out the variable we are not interested in. This will give, for every possible boolean value b_3, b_6 in $\{t, f\}$ taken by, respectively, x_3 and x_6, the following expression:

$$\sum_{b_1, b_2, b_4, b_5 \in \{t, f\}} (M_1)_{b_1} (M_2)_{b_1, b_2} (M_3)_{b_2, b_3} (M_4)_{b_4} (M_5)_{(b_3, b_4), b_5} (M_6)_{(b_2, b_5), b_6}. \quad (1)$$

For each of the 2^2 possible values of the indexes (b_3, b_6) we have a sum of 2^4 terms. That is, to compute the joint probability of (x_3, x_6), we have to compute 2^6 entries. This method is unfeasible in general as it requires a number of

---
[3] The results trivially extends to random variables over *countable* sets of outcomes.

operations exponential in the size of $\mathcal{G}$. Luckily, one can take advantage of the conditional (in)dependencies underlined by $\mathcal{G}$ to get a better factorisation than in (1), breaking the computation in that of factors of smaller size. For example:

$$\sum_{b_5}\left(\sum_{b_2}\left(\sum_{b_1}(\mathsf{M}_1)_{b_1}(\mathsf{M}_2)_{b_1,b_2}\right)(\mathsf{M}_3)_{b_2,b_3}(\mathsf{M}_6)_{(b_2,b_5),b_6}\right)\left(\sum_{b_4}(\mathsf{M}_4)_{b_4}(\mathsf{M}_5)_{(b_3,b_4),b_5}\right). \quad (2)$$

Let us denote by ϕ^i the intermediate factor in (2) identified by the sum over b_i: for example ϕ^2 is the sum $\sum_{b_2}\phi^1_{b_2}(\mathsf{M}_3)_{b_2,b_3}(\mathsf{M}_6)_{(b_2,b_5),b_6}$. Notice that if we suppose to have memorised the results of computing ϕ^1, to obtain ϕ^2 requires to compute 2^4 entries, *i.e.* the cost is exponential in the number of the different indexes b_j's appearing in the expression defining ϕ^2. By applying the same reasoning to all factors in (2), one notices that in the whole computation we never need to compute more than 2^4 entries: we have gained a factor of 2^2 with respect to (1).

The Variable Elimination algorithm performs factorisations like (2) in order to compute more efficiently the desired marginal distribution. The factorisation is characterised by an ordered sequence of unobserved (or marginalised) variables to eliminate, *i.e.* to sum out. The factorisation in (2) is induced by the sequence (x_1, x_2, x_4, x_5): ϕ^1 eliminates variable x_1, ϕ^2 then eliminates variable x_2, and so on. Different orders yield different factorisations with different performances, *e.g.* the inverse order (x_5, x_4, x_2, x_1) is less efficient, as the largest factor here requires to compute 2^5 entries.

Factorising Inference, via the program structure. In the literature, factorisations are usually described as collections of factors (basically vectors) and the VE algorithm is presented as an iterative algorithm acting on such collections. In this paper we propose a framework that gives more *structure* to this picture, expressing VE as a program transformation, building a factorisation by induction on the structure of a program, *compositionally*. More precisely:

- we define a fragment $\mathcal{L}$ of the linear simply-typed λ-calculus, which is able to represent *any factorisation* of a Bayesian network query as a λ-term. Random variables are associated with term variables of ground type;
- we express the VE algorithm as rewriting over the λ-terms in $\mathcal{L}$, consisting in reducing the scope of the variables that have to be eliminated.

Our approach integrates and is grounded on the denotational semantics of the terms, which directly *reflects and validates the factorisation* algorithm—yielding soundness and completeness. We stress that inference is computing the semantics of the program (the marginal distribution defined by it).

The reader can easily convince herself that the query about the joint marginal distribution (x_3, x_6) to the Bayesian network in Fig. 1a can be expressed by the let-term ℓ in Fig. 1b, where we have enriched the syntax of λ-terms with the constants representing the stochastic matrices. We consider $\mathtt{let}\, x = e\,\mathtt{in}\, e'$ as a syntactic sugar for $(\lambda x.e')e$, so the term ℓ can be seen as a λ term, which is moreover typable in a linear type system like the one in Fig. 2. The fact that some variables x_i have more free occurrences in sub-terms of ℓ is not in contrast with the linearity feature of the term, as let-expressions are supposed to be evaluated following a call-by-value strategy, and ground values (as e.g. booleans) can be duplicated in linear systems (see Ex. 1 and Remark 2 for more details).

Terms of this type are associated in *quantitative* denotational semantics such as [7,29] with algebraic expressions which give the joint distribution of the output variables. Here, in the same spirit as [11], we adopt a variant of the quantitative denotation (Sect. 3), which can be seen as a compact reformulation of the original model, and is more suitable to deal with factorised inference. It turns out that when we compositionally compute the semantics of ℓ following the structure of the program, we have a more efficient computation than in (1). This is because *the inductive interpretation yields intermediate factors of smaller size*, similarly to what algorithms for exact inference do. Indeed, the inductive interpretation of ℓ behaves like VE with the elimination order (x_5, x_4, x_2, x_1), see Ex. (5).

Notice that *different programs* may encode the *same model* and query, but with a significantly *different inference cost*, due to their different structure. A natural question is then to wonder if we can directly act on the structure of the program, in such a way that *the semantics is invariant, but inference is more efficient*. In fact, we show that the language $\mathcal{L}$ is sufficiently expressive to represent *all* possible factorisations of (1), *e.g.* (2). The main idea for such a representation arises from the observation that summing-out variables in the semantics corresponds in the syntax to make a let-in definition local to a subexpression. For example, the factor $\phi^1 = \sum_{b_1} (\mathsf{M}_1)_{b_1} (\mathsf{M}_2)_{b_1,b_2}$ of (2) can be easily obtained by making the variable x_1 local to the definition of x_2, creating a λ-term e^1 of the shape $\mathtt{let}\, x_1 = \mathsf{M}_1 \,\mathtt{in}\, \mathsf{M}_2 x_1$ and replacing the first two definitions of ℓ with $\mathtt{let}\, x_2 = e^1 \,\mathtt{in} \ldots$. In fact, the denotation of e^1 is exactly ϕ^1. What about ϕ^2? Here the situation is subtler as in order to make local the definition of x_2 one should gather together the definitions of x_3 and x_6, but the definition of x_6 depends on a variable x_5 which in turn depends on x_3, so a simple factor of ground types (*i.e.* tensors of booleans) will generate a dependence cycle. Luckily, we can use a (linear) functional type, defining a λ-term e^2 as $\mathtt{let}\, x_2 = e^1 \,\mathtt{in}\, (\mathsf{M}_3 x_2, \lambda x_5.\mathsf{M}_6(x_2, x_5))$ and then transforming ℓ into Fig. 1c. Again, we can notice that the denotation of e^2 is exactly ϕ^2. Fig. 7 details[4] the whole rewriting mimicking the elimination of the variables (x_1, x_2, x_4, x_5) applied to ℓ. This paper shows how to generalise this reasoning to any let-term.

Contents of the paper. We present an algorithm which is able to *fully* perform VE *on programs*: for any elimination order, program ℓ is *rewritten* by the algorithm into program ℓ', representing—possibly in a more efficient way—the same model. As stressed, our investigation is of *foundational nature*; we focus on a theoretical framework in which we are able to prove the *soundness and completeness* (Th. 1, Cor. 1) of the VE algorithm on terms. To do so, we leverage on the quantitative denotation of the terms. The structure of the paper is as follows.

---

[4] Actually, the expressions e^1 and e^2 in Fig. 7 are a bit more cumbersome that the ones here discussed because of some bureaucratic let-in produced by a more formal treatment. This difference is inessential and can be avoided by adding a post-processing.

– Sect. 2 defines the linear λ-calculus $\mathcal{L}$, and its semantics. In particular, Fig. 2 gives the linear typing system, which is a fragment of multiplicative linear logic [18] (Remark 2). Fig. 4 sketches the denotational semantics of $\mathcal{L}$ as weighted relations [29]. At first, the reader who wishes to focus on VE can skip the formal details about the semantics, and just read the intuitions in Sect. 2.2.

– Sect. 3 formalises the notion of factorisation as a set of factors (Def. 1) and shows how to associate a factorisation to the *let-terms* in $\mathcal{L}$ (Def. 4). Def. 5 recalls the standard VE algorithm—acting on sets of factors—denoted by VE^F.

– Sect. 4 is the *core of our paper*, capturing VE as a let-term transformation (Def. 8), denoted here by $VE^{\mathcal{L}}$, using the rewriting rules of Fig. 6. We prove the correspondence between the two versions of VE in Th. 1 and Cor. 1, stating our main result, the soundness and completeness of $VE^{\mathcal{L}}$ with respect to VE^F.

As an extra bonus, an enrichment of the semantics—based on probabilistic coherence spaces [7]—yields a neat property of the terms of $\mathcal{L}$, namely that the total mass of the denotation is easily computable from the terms type (Prop. 1).

Missing proofs and more technical details are in the extended version [12].

Related work. Variants of factorisation algorithms were invented independently in multiple communities (see [28] for a survey). The algorithm of Variable Elimination (VE) was first formalised in [45]. The approach to VE which is usually taken by PPLs is to compile a program into an *intermediate structure*, on which VE is performed. Our specific contribution is to provide the first algorithm which *fully* performs VE *directly on programs*. As explained, by this we mean the following. First, we observe that the inductive interpretation of a term behaves as VE, for an ordering of the variables to eliminate which is implicit in the structure of the program—possibly a non-efficient one. Second, our algorithm transforms the program in such a way that its structure reflects VE according to any arbitrary ordering, while the semantics (the denoted model) is invariant.

As we discussed before, our work builds on the programme put forward in [27]. Pfeffer [39](page 417) summarizes this way the limits of the algorithm in [27]: "The the solution is only partial. Given a BN encoded in their language, the algorithm can be viewed as performing Variable Elimination using *a particular elimination order*: namely, from the last variable in the program upward. It is well-known that the cost of VE is highly dependent on the elimination order, so the algorithm is exponentially more expensive for some families of models than an algorithm that can use *any order*." The algorithm we present here achieves a full solution: any elimination order can be implemented.

The literature on probabilistic programming languages and inference algorithms is vast, even restricting attention to *exact inference*. At the beginning of the Introduction we have mentioned several relevant contributions. Here we briefly discuss two lines of work which are especially relevant to our approach.

– *Rewriting the program to improve inference efficiency, as in [19]*. A key goal of PPLs is to separate the model description (the program) from the inference task. As pointed out by [19], such a goal is hard to achieve in practice. To improve inference efficiency, users are often forced to re-write the program by hand.

– *Exploiting the local structure of the program to achieve efficient inference, as in [21].* This road is taken by the authors of the language Dice—here the algorithm does not act on the program itself.

Our work incorporates elements from both lines: we perform inference compositionally, following the inductive structure of the program; to improve efficiency, our rewriting algorithm modifies the program structure (modelling the VE algorithm),while keeping the semantics invariant.

As a matter of fact, our first-order language is very similar to the language Dice [21], and has similar expressiveness. In order to keep presentation and proofs simple, we prefer to omit a conditioning construct such as `observe`, but it could easily be accommodated (see Sect. 5). There are however significant differences. We focus on VE, while Dice implements a different inference algorithm, compiling programs to weighted Boolean formulas, then performing Weighted Model Counting [3]. Moreover, as said, Dice exploits the local structure of the *given* program, without program transformations to improve the inference cost, which is instead at the core of our approach.

Rewriting is central to [19]. The focus there is on probabilistic programs with *mixed* discrete and continuous parameters: by eliminating the discrete parameters, general (gradient-based) algorithms can then be used. To *automate* this process, the authors introduce an information flow type system that can detect conditional independencies; rewriting uses VE techniques, even though the authors are not directly interested in the equivalence with the standard VE algorithm (this is left as a conjecture). In the same line, we mention also a very recent work [31] which tackle a similar task as [19]; while using similar ideas, a new design in both the language and the information flow type system allows the authors to deal with bounded recursion. The term transformations have a different goal than ours, compiling a probabilistic program into a pure one. However, some key elements there resonate with our approach: program transformations are based on continuation passing style (we use arrow variables in a similar fashion); the language in [31] is not defined by an operational semantics, instead the authors —like us— adopt a compositional, *denotational* treatment.

Denotational semantics versus cost-awareness. Our approach integrates and is grounded on a quantitative *denotational semantics*. Pioneering work by [24,25] has paved the way for a logical and semantical comprehension of Bayesian networks and inference from a categorical perspective, yielding an extensive body of work based on the setting of string diagrams, *e.g.* [5,23,22]. A denotational take on Bayesian networks is also at the core of [36], and underlies the categorical framework of [43]. These lines of research however do not take into consideration the *computational cost*, which is the very reason motivating the introduction and development of Bayesian networks, and inference algorithms such as VE. In the literature, foundational understanding tends to focus on either a compositional semantics or on efficiency, but the two worlds are separated, and typically explored as *independent* entities. This dichotomy stands in stark contrast to Bayesian networks, where the representation, the semantics (*i.e.* the underlying joint distribution), and the inference algorithms are deeply *intertwined*. A new perspective has been recently propounded by [11], advocating the need for a quantitative semantical approach more attentive to the resource consumption and to the actual cost of computing the semantics, which here exactly corresponds to performing inference. Our contribution fits in this line, which inspires also the cost-aware semantics in [16]. The latter introduces a higher-order language —in the idealized form of a λ-calculus—which is sound and complete w.r.t. Bayesian networks, together with a type system which computes the cost of (inductively performed) inference. Notice that [16] does not deal with terms transformations to rewrite a program into a more efficient one. Such transformations, reflecting the essence of the VE algorithm, is exactly the core of our paper — our algorithm easily adapts to the first-order fragment of [16].

2 $\mathcal{L}$ Calculus and Let-Terms

We consider a linear simply typed λ-calculus extended with stochastic matrices over tuples of booleans. Our results can be extended to more general systems, but here we focus on the core fragment able to represent Bayesian networks and the factorisations produced by the VE algorithm. In particular, we adopt a specific class of types, where arrow types are restricted to *linear* maps from (basically) tuples of booleans (i.e. the values of positive types in the grammar below) to pairs of a tuple of booleans and, possibly, another arrow.

2.1 Syntax

We consider the following grammar of types:

$$
\begin{array}{lll}
P, Q, \ldots ::= \mathsf{Bool} \mid P \otimes Q & \text{(positive types)} \\
A, B, \ldots ::= P \multimap T & \text{(arrow types)} \\
T, S, \ldots ::= P \mid A \mid P \otimes T & \text{(let-term types)}
\end{array}
$$

It is convenient to adopt a typing system *à la Church*, i.e. we will consider type annotated variables, meaning that we fix a set of variables and a function ty from this set to the set of positive and arrow types (see e.g. [20, ch.10], this style is opposed to the typing system *à la Curry*, where types should be associated to variables by typing contexts). We call a variable v positive (resp. arrow) whenever ty(v) is a positive (resp. arrow) type. We use metavariables x, y, z (resp. f, g, h) to range over positive (resp. arrow) variables. The letters v, w will be used to denote indistinctly positive or arrow variables.

The syntax of $\mathcal{L}$ is given by the following 3-sorted grammar, where M is a metavariable corresponding to a stochastic matrix between tuples of booleans:

$$
\begin{array}{lll}
\boldsymbol{v} ::- v \mid (\boldsymbol{v}, \boldsymbol{v}') & \text{if } \mathsf{FV}(\boldsymbol{v}) \cap \mathsf{\Gamma V}(\boldsymbol{v}') - \emptyset & \text{(patterns)} \\
e ::= v \mid \mathsf{M}(\boldsymbol{x}) \mid f\boldsymbol{x} \mid (e, e') \mid \lambda \boldsymbol{x}.e \mid \mathtt{let}\ \boldsymbol{v} = e\ \mathtt{in}\ e' & \text{(expressions)} \\
\ell ::= \boldsymbol{v} \mid \mathtt{let}\ \boldsymbol{v} = e\ \mathtt{in}\ \ell & \text{(let-terms)}
\end{array}
$$

Notice that a pattern is required to have pairwise different variables. We allow 0-ary stochastic matrices, representing random generators of boolean tuples, which we will denote simply by M, instead of M(). We can assume to have two 0-ary stochastic matrices t and f representing the two boolean values.

We denote by $\mathsf{FV}(e)$ the set of free variables of an expression e. As standard, λ-abstractions $\lambda v.e$ and let-in $\mathtt{let}\, v = e'\,\mathtt{in}\, e$ bind in the subexpression e all occurrences of the variables in the pattern v. In fact, $\mathtt{let}\, v = e'\,\mathtt{in}\, e$ can be thought as syntactic sugar for $(\lambda v.e)e'$. Given a set of variables $\mathcal{V}$, we denote by $\mathcal{V}^a$ (resp. $\mathcal{V}^+$) the subset of the arrow variables (resp. positive variables) in $\mathcal{V}$, in particular $\mathsf{FV}(e)^a$ denotes the set of arrow variables free in e.

Patterns are a special kind of let-terms and these latter are a special kind of expressions. A pattern is called *positive* if all its variables are positive. We use metavariables x, y, z to range over positive patterns. A let-term is *positive* if its rightmost pattern is positive, *i.e.*: $\mathtt{let}\, v = e\,\mathtt{in}\,\ell$ is positive if ℓ is positive.

$$\frac{\mathsf{ty}(v)\ \text{positive or arrow}}{v : \mathsf{ty}(v)} \qquad \frac{f : P \multimap T \quad x : P}{fx : T} \qquad \frac{\mathsf{M} : P \multimap Q \quad x : P}{\mathsf{M}x : Q}$$

$$\frac{x : P \quad e : T}{\lambda x.e : P \multimap T} \qquad \frac{e : P \quad e' : T \quad \mathsf{FV}(e)^a \cap \mathsf{FV}(e')^a = \emptyset}{(e, e') : P \otimes T}$$

$$\frac{v : T \quad e : T \quad e' : S \quad \mathsf{FV}(e)^a \cap \mathsf{FV}(e')^a = \emptyset \quad \text{if } f \in \mathsf{FV}(v) \text{ then } f \in \mathsf{FV}(e')^a}{\mathtt{let}\, v = e\,\mathtt{in}\, e' : S}$$

Fig. 2: Typing rules: the binary rules suppose that the set of the free arrow variables of the subterms are disjoint; the let-rule binding an arrow variable f requires also that this variable f is free in the expression e'.

Fig. 2 gives the rules generating the set of well-typed expressions (and so including patterns and let-terms). As standard in typing systems *à la Church*, we omit an explicit typing environment of the typing judgment $e : T$, as this can be recovered from the typing of the free variables of e, i.e. if $\mathsf{FV}(e) = \{x_1, \ldots, x_n\}$, then *à la Curry* we would write $e : T$ by $x_1 : \mathsf{ty}(x_1), \ldots, x_n : \mathsf{ty}(x_1) \vdash e : T$. See Fig. 3 for an *example of typing derivation* in both styles.

The binary rules suppose the side condition $\mathsf{FV}(e)^a \cap \mathsf{FV}(e')^a = \emptyset$ and the let-in rule binding an arrow variable f has also the condition $f \in \mathsf{FV}(e')^a$. These conditions guarantee that arrow variables are used *linearly*, ensuring the linear feature of the typing system.

Church style (our system):

$$\frac{v : P \quad v' : P \quad \dfrac{v : P \quad v' : P}{(v, v') : P \otimes P}}{\mathtt{let}\, v' = v\,\mathtt{in}\,(v, v') : P \otimes P}$$

Curry style:

$$\frac{v : P \vdash v : P \quad \dfrac{v : P \vdash v : P \quad v' : P \vdash v' : P}{v : P, v' : P \vdash (v, v') : P \otimes P}}{v : P \vdash \mathtt{let}\, v' = v\,\mathtt{in}\,(v, v') : P \otimes P}$$

Fig. 3: An example of type derivation, in both Church and Curry style.

Example 1. Consider the term $\mathtt{let}\, v' \,=\, v \,\mathtt{in}\,(v, v')$, which will duplicate any value assigned to the free variable v. If v has *positive type* (*e.g.* boolean), it admits the type derivation in Fig. 3. On the contrast, if v has *arrow type*, no type derivation is possible, in agreement with the fact that arrows can only occur linearly. See also the discussion in Ex. 4.

Notice that λ-abstractions are restricted to positive patterns. Also, a typing derivation of conclusion $e : T$ is completely determined by its expression. This means that if an expression can be typed, then its type is unique. Because of that, we can extend the function ty to all expressions, *i.e.* $\mathsf{ty}(e)$ is the unique type such that $e : \mathsf{ty}(e)$ is derivable, whenever e is well-typed.

Notice that well-typed patterns $\boldsymbol{v}$ have at most one occurrence of an arrow variable (which is moreover in the rightmost position of the pattern). By extension of notation, we write $\boldsymbol{v}^a$ as the only arrow variable in $\boldsymbol{v}$, if it exists, otherwise we consider it as undefined. We also write by $\boldsymbol{v}^+$ for the pattern obtained from $\boldsymbol{v}$ by removing the arrow variable $\boldsymbol{v}^a$, if any. In particular $\boldsymbol{x}^+ = \boldsymbol{x}$.

Remark 1. The readers acquainted with linear logic [18] may observe that the above grammar of types identifies a special fragment of this logic. In fact, the boolean type Bool may be expressed as the additive disjunction of the tensor unit: $\mathbf{1} \oplus \mathbf{1}$. Since $\otimes$ distributes over $\oplus$, positive types are isomorphic to n-ary booleans, for some $n \in \mathbb{N}$, *i.e.* $\bigoplus_n \mathbf{1}$, which is a notation for $\mathbf{1} \oplus \cdots \oplus \mathbf{1}$ n-times.

Moreover, by the isomorphisms $(\bigoplus_i \mathbf{1}) \multimap T \simeq \&_i (\mathbf{1} \multimap T) \simeq \&_i T$, where $\&$ denotes the additive conjunction, we deduce that the grammar of $\mathcal{L}$ types is equivalent to an alternation of *balanced* additive connectives, *i.e.* it can be presented by the grammar: $T := \mathbf{1} \mid \bigoplus_n T \mid \&_n T$, for $n \in \mathbb{N}$. The typing system hence identifies a fragment of linear logic with non-trivial regularity (the alternation), expressing more than just the set of arrows between tuples of booleans.

Remark 2. Notice that the binary rules might require to contract some positive types in the environment, as the expressions in the premises might have positive variables in common. In fact, it is well-known that contraction and weakening rules are derivable for the positive formulas in the environment, *e.g.* $\mathbf{1} \oplus \mathbf{1} \vdash (\mathbf{1} \oplus \mathbf{1}) \otimes (\mathbf{1} \oplus \mathbf{1})$ is provable in linear logic. From a categorical point of view, this corresponds to the fact that positive types define co-algebras, and, operationally, that positive *values* can be duplicated or erased without the need of being promoted (see *e.g.* [15] in the setting of PPLs).

In the following we will represent a let-term $\ell := \mathtt{let}\, \boldsymbol{v}_1 \,=\, e_1 \,\mathtt{in} \ldots \mathtt{let}\, \boldsymbol{v}_n \,=\, e_n \,\mathtt{in}\, \boldsymbol{v}_{n+1}$ by the more concise writing: $\ell := (\boldsymbol{v}_1 = e_1; \ldots; \boldsymbol{v}_n = e_n \,\mathtt{in}\, \boldsymbol{v}_{n+1})$. By renaming we can always suppose, if needed, that the patterns $\boldsymbol{v}_1, \ldots, \boldsymbol{v}_n$ are pairwise disjoint sequences of variables and that none of these variables has occurrences (free or not) outside the scope of its binder. We call $\{\boldsymbol{v}_1 = e_1, \ldots, \boldsymbol{v}_n - e_n\}$ the set of the *definitions* of ℓ (which has exactly n elements thanks to the convention of having $\boldsymbol{v}_1, \ldots, \boldsymbol{v}_n$ pairwise disjoint), and $\biguplus_{i=1}^n \boldsymbol{v}_i$ the set of the *defined variables of* ℓ. The final pattern $\boldsymbol{v}_{n+1}$ is called the *output of* ℓ. Notice that ℓ is positive if its output is positive.

Example 2. A Bayesian network of n nodes can be represented by a closed let-term ℓ having all variables positive and n definitions of the form $x = \texttt{M}(\boldsymbol{y})$. The variables are associated with the edges of the graph and the definitions with the nodes such that $x = \texttt{M}(y_1, \ldots, y_k)$ represents a node with stochastic matrix $\texttt{M}$, an outgoing edge associated with x and k incoming edges associated with, respectively, $y_1, \ldots, y_k$. The output pattern contains the variables associated with a specific query to the Bayesian network.

For instance, the Bayesian network in Fig. 1a is represented by the let-term:
$(x_1 = \texttt{M}_1; x_2 = \texttt{M}_2 x_1; x_3 = \texttt{M}_3 x_2; x_4 = \texttt{M}_4; x_5 = \texttt{M}_5(x_3, x_4); x_6 = \texttt{M}_6(x_2, x_5) \texttt{ in } (x_3, x_6))$,
which is the succinct notation for the let-term ℓ in Fig. 1b. Notice that ℓ induces a linear order on the nodes of the graph. The same graph can be represented by other let-terms, differing just from the order of its definitions. For example, by swapping the definitions of x_3 and x_4 we get a different let-term representing the same Bayesian network. We will consider this "swapping" invariance in full generality by defining the swapping rewriting γ in Fig. 6 and stating Lemma 1.

As discussed in the Introduction, let-terms with arrow variables and λ-abstractions might be needed to represent the result of applying the VE algorithm to a Bayesian network. For instance, Fig. 7 details the let-term produced by the elimination of the variables (x_1, x_2, x_4, x_5). For example the closed subexpression e_2 in Fig. 7 keeps local the variables x_1 and x_2 and has type $\mathsf{Bool} \otimes (\mathsf{Bool} \multimap \mathsf{Bool})$.

2.2   Semantics

We omit to detail an operational semantics of $\mathcal{L}$, which can be defined in a standard way by using a sample-based or distribution-based semantics, in the spirit of *e.g.* [2]. We prefer to focus on the denotational semantics, which is more suitable to express the variable elimination algorithm in a compositional way. Below, examples 3 and 4 informally illustrate the *denotational* and *operational* behavior of a `let`-term, highlighting the *linearity* of its nature.

Semantics, a gentle presentation. We consider the semantics of weighted relations [29], which is an example of quantitative semantics of linear logic interpreting programs as matrices over non-negative real numbers. The intuition behind this semantics is quite simple: each type T is associated with a finite set $|T|$ of indexes, called the *web of T* (see (3)). In case of a positive type, the web is the set of all possible outcomes of a computation of that type: the web of the boolean type $|\mathsf{Bool}|$ is the set of the two booleans $\{\mathtt{t}, \mathtt{f}\}$, the web of a tensor $P \otimes Q$ is the cartesian product $|P| \times |Q|$ of the web of its components. An arrow type $P \multimap T$ is also associated with the cartesian product $|P| \times |Q|$, intuitively representing the elements of the trace of a function of type $P \multimap T$. To sum up, in this very simple fragment, webs are sets of nesting tuples of booleans, e.g. $|(\mathsf{Bool} \times \mathsf{Bool}) \multimap \mathsf{Bool}| = \{((b_1, b_2), b_3) \mid b_i \in |\mathsf{Bool}|\}$.

The denotation $[\![e]\!]$ of an expression e is then a matrix (sometimes called weighted relation) whose rows are indexed by the sequences of the elements in the web of the free variables in e and the columns are indexed by the elements in the web of the type of e. Eg, consider the expression e_0 given by $\mathtt{let}\ y\ =\ f x\ \mathtt{in}\ (z, y)$, with free variables $f : \mathsf{Bool} \multimap \mathsf{Bool}$, $x : \mathsf{Bool}$ and $z : \mathsf{Bool}$ and type $\mathsf{Bool} \times \mathsf{Bool}$. The matrix $[\![e_0]\!]$ will have rows indexed by tuples $((b_1, b_2), b_3, b_4)$ and columns by (b_5, b_6) for b_i's in $\{\mathtt{t}, \mathtt{f}\}$. Intuitively, the entry $[\![e_0]\!]_{((b_1, b_2), b_3, b_4),(b_5, b_6)}$ gives a weight to the possibility of a computation where the free variables of e will "behave" as (b_1, b_2) for f, b_3 for y and b_4 for z and the output will be (b_5, b_6).

The matrix $[\![e]\!]$ is defined by structural induction on the expression e by using matrix composition (for let-construction and application) and tensor product (for tuples), plus the diagonalisation of the indexes in the variables common to sub-expressions. Fig. 4 details this definition, giving a precise meaning to each programming construct. For example, taking the notation of Fig. 4, the definition of $[\![(e', e'')]\!]_{\overline{a},(b',b'')}$ states that the weight of getting (b', b'') supposing $\overline{a}$ is the product of the weights of getting b' from e' and b'' from e'', supposing $\overline{a}$ in both cases. The sharing of $\overline{a}$ in the two components of the tuple characterises the linearity of this calculus. Let us discuss this point with another example.

Example 3 (Linearity, denotationally). Let us write $\mathsf{coin}_{0.3}$ for a random generator of boolean values (a 0-ary stochastic matrix), modeling a biased coin. In our setting $[\![\mathsf{coin}_{0.3}]\!]$ is a row vector $(0.3, 0.7)$ modeling the probability of sampling $\mathtt{t}$ or $\mathtt{f}$. Let e be the closed term $\mathtt{let}\ v\ =\ \mathsf{coin}_{0.3}\ \mathtt{in}\ \mathtt{let}\ v'\ =\ v\ \mathtt{in}\ (v, v')$, of type $\mathsf{Bool} \otimes \mathsf{Bool}$, well-typed because v is positive $(\mathsf{ty}(v) = \mathsf{Bool})$. Since e is closed, $[\![e]\!]$ is also a row vector, now of dimension 4. One can easily check that $[\![e]\!] = (0.3, 0, 0, 0.7)$, stating that the only possible outcomes are the couples $(\mathtt{t}, \mathtt{t})$ and $(\mathtt{f}, \mathtt{f})$, while $(\mathtt{t}, \mathtt{f})$, $(\mathtt{f}, \mathtt{t})$ have probability zero to happen.

Notice that $[\![e]\!]$ is different from $[\![(\mathsf{coin}_{0.3}, \mathsf{coin}_{0.3})]\!] = (0.3^2, 0.21, 0.21, 0.7^2)$. In fact, $[\![e]\!]$ is *linear* in $\mathsf{coin}_{0.3}$, while $[\![(\mathsf{coin}_{0.3}, \mathsf{coin}_{0.3})]\!]$ is quadratic.

Example 4 (Linearity and $\mathtt{let}$-reduction). Let us give an operational intuition for the term e in Ex. 3. There are two possibilities: we can first sample a boolean from $\mathsf{coin}_{0.3}$ and then replace v for the result of this sampling, or first replace v for the sampler $\mathsf{coin}_{0.3}$, then sampling a boolean from each copy of $\mathsf{coin}_{0.3}$. The semantics states that we follow the former possibility and not the latter (as usual in a setting with effects). Intuitively, $\mathsf{coin}_{0.3}$ reduces to a probabilistic sum $0.3\,\mathtt{t} + 0.7\,\mathtt{f}$, and so e first reduces to the sum $0.3\ \mathtt{let}\ v\ =\ \mathtt{t}\ \mathtt{in}\ \mathtt{let}\ v'\ =\ v\ \mathtt{in}\ (v, v') + 0.7\ \mathtt{let}\ v\ =\ \mathtt{f}\ \mathtt{in}\ \mathtt{let}\ v'\ =\ v\ \mathtt{in}\ (v, v')$, eventually yielding $0.3(\mathtt{t}, \mathtt{t}) + 0.7(\mathtt{f}, \mathtt{f})$. In contrast, duplicating the sampler would yield $(\mathsf{coin}_{0.3}, \mathsf{coin}_{0.3})$ whose semantics is different, as discussed in Ex. 3. Finally, notice that replacing in e the argument $\mathsf{coin}_{0.3}$ with an expression $\lambda x.u$ (of arrow type) yields a term which is *not typable* in our system (see Ex. 1).

Remark 3. In standard Call-by-Value λ-calculus, the abstraction plays two roles: defining functions and acting as a thunk (so allowing duplication). Please notice that linear abstraction does not act as a thunk. This is common in refinement such as [30] and [41], and in calculi based on Linear Logic [1,42,33,9,10,15].

The rest of the subsection recalls from [29] the definitions and notations of the denotational semantics, but the reader can jump to the next section if already satisfied with these intuitions and willing to focus on variable elimination.

$$[\![v]\!]_{\bar{a},b} := \delta_{\bar{a},b}$$

$$[\![(e',e'')]\!]_{\bar{a},(b',b'')} := [\![e']\!]_{\bar{a}|_{\mathsf{FV}(e')},b'} \, [\![e'']\!]_{\bar{a}|_{\mathsf{FV}(e'')},b''}$$

$$[\![(v=e' \text{ in } e'')]\!]_{\bar{a},b} := \sum_{\bar{c} \in |v|} [\![e']\!]_{\bar{a}|_{\mathsf{FV}(e')},\bar{c}} [\![e'']\!]_{(\bar{a} \uplus \bar{c})|_{\mathsf{FV}(e'')},b}$$

$$[\![\lambda v.e']\!]_{\bar{a},(b',b'')} := [\![e']\!]_{\bar{a} \uplus b'|_{\mathsf{FV}(e')},b''}$$

$$[\![\mathsf{M}(x)]\!]_{\bar{a},b} := \mathsf{M}_{\bar{a},b}$$

$$[\![fx]\!]_{\bar{a},b} := \delta_{a',\bar{a}'''} \delta_{a'',b} \qquad\qquad \text{where } \bar{a}|_f = (a',a'') \text{ and } \bar{a}|_x = \bar{a}'''.$$

Fig. 4: Denotation of e as a matrix $[\![e]\!]$ giving a linear map from $|\mathsf{FV}(e)|$ to $|\mathsf{ty}(e)|$, so $\bar{a} \in |\mathsf{FV}(e)|$ and $b \in |\mathsf{ty}(e)|$. In the tuple and λ cases, we suppose $b = (b',b'')$.

Semantics, formally. Let us fix some basic notation from linear algebra. Metavariables S,T,U range over finite sets. We denote by $\mathsf{s}(S)$ the cardinality of a set S. We denote by $\mathbb{R}_{\geq 0}$ the cone of non-negative real numbers. Metavariables ϕ,ψ,ξ will range over vectors in $\mathbb{R}_{\geq 0}^S$, for S a *finite* set, ϕ_a denoting the scalar associated with $a \in S$ by $\phi \in \mathbb{R}_{\geq 0}^S$. Matrices will be vectors indexed by pairs, e.g. in $\mathbb{R}_{\geq 0}^{S \times T}$ for S and T two finite sets. We may write $\phi_{a,b}$ instead of $\phi_{(a,b)}$ for $(a,b) \in S \times T$ if we wish to underline that we are considering indexes that are pairs. Given $\phi \in \mathbb{R}_{\geq 0}^{S \times T}$ and $\psi \in \mathbb{R}_{\geq 0}^{T \times U}$, the standard matrix multiplication is given by $\phi\psi \in \mathbb{R}_{\geq 0}^{S \times U}$: $(\phi\psi)_{a,c} := \sum_{b \in T} \phi_{a,b} \psi_{b,c} \in \mathbb{R}_{\geq 0}$. The identity matrix is denoted $\delta \in \mathbb{R}_{\geq 0}^{S \times S}$ and defined by $\delta_{a,a'} = 1$ if $a = a'$, otherwise $\delta_{a,a'} = 0$.

A less standard convention, but common in this kind of denotational semantics, is to consider the rows of a matrix ϕ as the *domain* and the columns as the *codomain* of the underlined linear map. Hence, a vector in $\mathbb{R}_{\geq 0}^S$ is considered as a *one line* matrix $\mathbb{R}_{\geq 0}^{1 \times S}$, and the application of a vector $\psi \in \mathbb{R}_{\geq 0}^S$ to a matrix $\phi \in \mathbb{R}_{\geq 0}^{S \times T}$, is given by $\phi \cdot \psi := \psi\phi \in \mathbb{R}_{\geq 0}^{1 \times T} \cong \mathbb{R}_{\geq 0}^T$.

The model denotes a type T with a set $|T|$, called the *web* of T, as follows:

$$|\mathsf{Bool}| := \{\mathsf{t},\mathsf{f}\}, \qquad\qquad |P \otimes T| := |P \multimap T| := |P| \times |T|. \qquad (3)$$

To denote an expression e, we must associate a web with the set of free variables occurring in e. Given a finite set of variables $\mathcal{V}$, we define $|\mathcal{V}|$ by using indexed products: $|\mathcal{V}| := \prod_{v \in \mathcal{V}} |\mathsf{ty}(v)|$. Metavariables $\bar{a},\bar{b},\bar{c}$ denote elements in such webs $|\mathcal{V}|$. In fact, $\bar{a} \in |\mathcal{V}|$ can be seen as a function mapping any variable $v \in \mathcal{V}$ to an element $\bar{a}_v \in |\mathsf{ty}(v)|$. We denote by $\star$ the empty function, which is the only element of $|\emptyset| = \prod_{\emptyset}$. Given a subset $\mathcal{V}' \subseteq \mathcal{V}$, we denote by $\bar{a}|_{\mathcal{V}'}$ the restriction of $\bar{a}$ to $\mathcal{V}'$, i.e. $\bar{a}|_{\mathcal{V}'} \in |\mathcal{V}'|$. Also, given two disjoint sets of variables $\mathcal{V}$ and $\mathcal{W}$ we denote by $\bar{a} \uplus \bar{b}$ the union of an element $\bar{a} \in |\mathcal{V}|$ and an element $\bar{b} \in |\mathcal{W}|$, i.e. $\bar{a} \uplus \bar{b} \in |\mathcal{V} \uplus \mathcal{W}|$ and: $(\bar{a} \uplus \bar{b})_v := \bar{a}_v$ if $v \in \mathcal{V}$, and $(\bar{a} \uplus \bar{b})_v := \bar{b}_v$ if $v \in \mathcal{W}$.

An expression e of type T will be interpreted as a linear map $[\![e]\!]$ from $\mathbb{R}_{\geq 0}^{|\mathsf{FV}(e)|}$ to $\mathbb{R}_{\geq 0}^{|T|}$. As such, $[\![e]\!]$ can then be presented as a matrix in $\mathbb{R}_{\geq 0}^{|\mathsf{FV}(e)| \times |T|}$. Fig. 4 recalls the definition of $[\![e]\!]$ by structural induction on e. In the case of $\mathsf{M}(x)$, we take the liberty to consider an element $\bar{a} \in |x|$ as actually the tuple of its components, ordered according to the order of the variables in the pattern x. Similarly, when we compare $\bar{a}'''$ with a' in $[\![fx]\!]$.

Example 5. Recall the term ℓ in Ex. 2. It is closed and of type $\mathsf{Bool} \otimes \mathsf{Bool}$, hence $[\![\ell]\!]$ is a one-row matrix in $\mathbb{R}_{\geq 0}^{|\emptyset| \times |\mathsf{Bool} \otimes \mathsf{Bool}|} \simeq \mathbb{R}_{\geq 0}^4$. By unfolding the definition in Fig. 4, we get the following expression for $[\![\ell]\!]_{*,(b_3,b_6)}$ with $b_3, b_6 \in \{\mathsf{t}, \mathsf{f}\}$, where all b_i vary over $\{\mathsf{t}, \mathsf{f}\}$, the index i referring to the corresponding variable in ℓ:

$$\sum_{b_1}(M_1)_{b_1}\left(\sum_{b_2}(M_2)_{b_1,b_2}\left(\sum_{b_3'}(M_3)_{b_2,b_3'}\left(\sum_{b_4}(M_4)_{b_4}\left(\sum_{b_5}(M_5)_{(b_3,b_4),b_5}\right.\right.\right.\right.$$
$$\left.\left.\left.\left.\left(\sum_{b_6'}(M_6)_{(b_2,b_5),b_6'}\delta_{b_3',b_3}\delta_{b_6',b_6}\right)\right)\right)\right). \quad (4)$$

Expression (4) describes a way of computing $[\![\ell]\!]$ in a number of basic operations which is of order 2^3 terms for each possible 2^2 values of b_3, b_6.

For a more involved example, let us consider the let-term ℓ' in line (L8) of Fig. 7, which is the result of the elimination of the variables (x_1, x_2). We first calculate the semantics $[\![e_2]\!]$ of the sub-expression keeping local (x_1, x_2). Notice that e_2 is a closed expression of type $\mathsf{Bool} \otimes (\mathsf{Bool} \multimap \mathsf{Bool})$, so consider $b_3 \in |\mathsf{Bool}|$ and $(b_f, b_f') \in |\mathsf{Bool} \multimap \mathsf{Bool}|$, we have (after some simplification of δ's):

$$[\![e_2]\!]_{*,(b_3,(b_f,b_f'))} = \sum_{b_2}\left(\sum_{b_1}(M_1)_{b_1}(M_2)_{b_1,b_2}\right)(M_3)_{b_2,b_3}(M_6)_{(b_2,b_f),b_f'}. \quad (5)$$

We can then associate $[\![\ell']\!]_{*,(b_3,b_6)}$ with the following algebraic expression:

$$\sum_{b_3',(b_f,b_f')}[\![e]\!]_{*,(b_3,(b_f,b_f'))}\left(\sum_{b_4}(M_4)_{b_4}\left(\sum_{b_5}(M_5)_{b_4,b_5}\left(\sum_{b_6'}\delta_{b_5,b_f}\delta_{b_f',b_6'}\right)\delta_{b_3',b_3}\delta_{b_6',b_6}\right)\right) \quad (6)$$

Expression (6) reduces to a number of basic operations which is of order 2^2. By one memoizing the computation of $[\![e]\!]$, Expression 6 offers a way of computing the matrix $[\![\ell']\!]$ in a time linear in $2^2 \times 2^2$. Indeed, Proposition 6 guarantees that ℓ and ℓ' (in fact all let-terms in Fig. 7) have the same denotational semantics: so the computation of $[\![\ell']\!]$ gains a factor of 2 with respect to (4).

Let us conclude this subsection by observing that the type of a closed expression allows for computing the total mass of the denotational semantics of that expression. With any positive type P we associate its dimension $\dim(P) \in \mathbb{N}$ by $\dim(\mathsf{Bool}) = 2$ and $\dim(P \otimes Q) = \dim(P)\dim(Q)$. This means that $\dim(P)$ is the cardinality of $|P|$. And with any type T we associate its height $\mathsf{ht}(T) \in \mathbb{N}$, the definition is: $\mathsf{ht}(P) = 1$, $\mathsf{ht}(P \multimap T) = \dim(P) \times \mathsf{ht}(T)$ and $\mathsf{ht}(P \otimes T) = \mathsf{ht}(T)$.

Proposition 1. *For any closed expression e, one has $\sum_{a \in |\mathsf{ty}(e)|}[\![e]\!]_{*,a} = \mathsf{ht}(\mathsf{ty}(e))$.*

Example 6. Take the type $\mathsf{Bool} \otimes \mathsf{Bool}$ of the let-terms ℓ and ℓ' discussed in Example 5. We have that $\mathsf{ht}(\mathsf{Bool} \otimes \mathsf{Bool}) = 1$, in accordance with the fact that all closed expressions of that type (such as ℓ and ℓ') describe joint probability distributions, so are denoted with vectors of total mass 1. On the contrast, consider the type $\mathsf{Bool} \otimes (\mathsf{Bool} \multimap \mathsf{Bool})$ of the expression e_2 keeping local the variables x_1 and x_2. We have $\mathsf{ht}(\mathsf{Bool} \otimes (\mathsf{Bool} \multimap \mathsf{Bool})) = \mathsf{ht}(\mathsf{Bool} \multimap \mathsf{Bool}) = 2$, which is the expected total mass of a stochastic matrix over booleans. However notice that the type $\mathsf{Bool} \otimes (\mathsf{Bool} \multimap \mathsf{Bool})$ is subtler than that of a stochastic matrix $\mathsf{Bool} \multimap \mathsf{Bool}$: in fact, by using the isomorphisms discussed in Remark 1, we have $\mathsf{Bool} \otimes (\mathsf{Bool} \multimap \mathsf{Bool}) \simeq (\mathsf{Bool} \multimap \mathsf{Bool}) \oplus (\mathsf{Bool} \multimap \mathsf{Bool})$, which is the type of a probabilistic distribution of stochastic matrices.

3 Variable Elimination VE^F over Let-Terms Factors

As mentioned in the Introduction, variable elimination is an iterative procedure transforming sets of factors (one can think of these as originally provided by a Bayesian network). We recall this procedure, adapting it to our setting—in particular, we start from a set $\mathsf{Fs}(\ell)$ of factors generated by a let-term ℓ representing a Bayesian network. Subsect. 3.1 defines factors and the main operations on them (product and summing-out). Subsect. 3.2 shows how to associate a let-term ℓ with a set of factors $\mathsf{Fs}(\ell)$ such that from their product one can recover $[\![\ell]\!]$ (Prop. 3). Finally, Subsect. 3.3 presents the variable elimination algorithm as a transformation VE^F over $\mathsf{Fs}(\ell)$ (Def. 5) and Prop. 4 gives the soundness of the algorithm. This latter result is standard from the literature (see e.g. [8]), and the contribution of this section is the definition of $\mathsf{Fs}(\ell)$ which is essential to link this variable elimination VE^F on factors to our main contribution given in the next section: the variable elimination $\mathsf{VE}^\mathcal{L}$ as a term-rewriting process.

3.1 Factors

Definition 1 (Factor). *A factor ϕ is a pair $(\mathsf{Var}(\phi), \mathsf{Fun}(\phi))$ of a finite set $\mathsf{Var}(\phi)$ of typed variables and a function $\mathsf{Fun}(\phi)$ from the web $|\mathsf{Var}(\phi)|$ to $\mathbb{R}_{\geq 0}$.*

We will shorten the notation $\mathsf{Fun}(\phi)$ by writing just ϕ when it is clear from the context that we are considering the function associated with a factor and not the whole pair $(\mathsf{Var}(\phi), \mathsf{Fun}(\phi))$. We often consider $\mathsf{Fun}(\phi)$ as a vector indexed by the elements of its domain, so that $\phi_{\overline{a}}$ stands for $\mathsf{Fun}(\phi)(\overline{a})$, for every $\overline{a} \in |\mathsf{Var}(\phi)|$.

The degree of ϕ, written d_ϕ, is the cardinality of $\mathsf{Var}(\phi)$, and the base of ϕ, written b_ϕ, is the maximal cardinality of $|v|$ for every $v \in \mathsf{Var}(\phi)$. Notice that $\mathsf{b}_\phi^{\mathsf{d}_\phi}$ is an upper bound to the dimension of $\mathsf{Fun}(\phi)$, i.e. the cardinality of $|\mathsf{Var}(\phi)|$.

Example 7. Sect. 3.2 formalises how to associate the definitions of a let-expression with factors. Let us anticipate a bit and see as an example the factor ϕ that will be associated with the definition $x_5 = \mathsf{M}_5(x_3, x_4)$ in the let-term in Ex. 2. We have $\mathsf{Var}(\phi) = \{x_3, x_4, x_5\}$ and for every $a, b, c \in |\mathsf{Bool}|$ we have $\mathsf{Fun}(\phi)(a, b, c) = (\mathsf{M}_5)_{(a,b),c}$. Notice that ϕ forgets the input/output (or rows/columns) distinction carried by the indexes of the stochastic matrix M_5.

$$\mathsf{Var}(\textstyle\sum_{\mathcal{V}}(\phi)) := \mathsf{Var}(\phi) \setminus \mathcal{V}, \qquad\qquad \textstyle\sum_{\mathcal{V}}(\phi)_{\overline{a}} := \sum_{\overline{b} \in |\mathcal{V} \cap \mathsf{Var}(\phi)|} \phi_{\overline{a} \uplus \overline{b}}$$

$$\mathsf{Var}(\phi \odot \psi) := \mathsf{Var}(\phi) \cup \mathsf{Var}(\psi), \qquad (\phi \odot \psi)_{\overline{c}} := \phi_{\overline{c}|_{\mathsf{Var}(\phi)}} \psi_{\overline{c}|_{\mathsf{Var}(\psi)}}$$

Fig. 5: *Summing-out* $\sum_{\mathcal{V}}(\phi)$ of a set of variables $\mathcal{V}$ in a factor ϕ and *product* $\phi \odot \psi$ of two factors ϕ, ψ. We suppose $\overline{a} \in |\mathsf{Var}(\phi) \setminus \mathcal{V}|$ and $\overline{c} \in |\mathsf{Var}(\phi \odot \psi)|$.

A factor $(\mathsf{Var}(\phi), \mathsf{Fun}(\phi))$ involves two "levels" of indexing: one is given by the variables $v_1, v_2, \cdots \in \mathsf{Var}(\phi)$ tagging the different sets of the product $|\mathsf{Var}(\phi)| := \prod_{v \in \mathsf{Var}(\phi)} |v|$, and the other "level" is given by $\overline{a}, \overline{b}, \cdots \in |\mathsf{Var}(\phi)|$ labelling the different components of the vector $\mathsf{Fun}(\phi)$, which we call web elements.

Recall that the set of variables $\mathsf{Var}(\phi)$ endows $|\mathsf{Var}(\phi)|$ with a cartesian structure, so that we can project a web element $\overline{a} \in |\mathsf{Var}(\phi)|$ on some subset of variables $\mathcal{V}' \subseteq \mathsf{Var}(\phi)$ by writing $\overline{a}|_{\mathcal{V}'}$, as well as we can pair two web elements $\overline{a} \uplus \overline{a}'$ whenever $\overline{a} \in |\mathsf{Var}(\phi)|$ and $\overline{a}' \in |\mathsf{Var}(\phi)'|$ and $\mathsf{Var}(\phi) \cap \mathsf{Var}(\phi)' = \emptyset$.

Fig. 5 defines the two main operations on factors: summing-out and binary products. We illustrate them with some examples and remarks.

Example 8. By recalling the factor ϕ of Ex. 7, we have that $\mathsf{Var}(\sum_{\{x_3\}}(\phi)) = \{x_4, x_5\}$ and for every $a, b \in |\mathsf{Bool}|$, $\sum_{\{x_3\}}(\phi)_{(a,b)} = \mathsf{M}_{(\mathsf{t},a),b} + \mathsf{M}_{(\mathsf{f},a),b}$. In fact, we can do weirder summing-out, as for example $\mathsf{Var}(\sum_{\{x_3, x_5\}}(\phi)) = \{x_4\}$, so that $\sum_{\{x_3, x_5\}}(\phi)_a = \mathsf{M}_{(\mathsf{t},a),\mathsf{t}} + \mathsf{M}_{(\mathsf{t},a),\mathsf{f}} + \mathsf{M}_{(\mathsf{f},a),\mathsf{t}} + \mathsf{M}_{(\mathsf{f},a),\mathsf{f}}$ may be a scalar greater than one, no more representing a probability.

With the notations of Fig. 5, if ϕ is a join distribution over $|\mathsf{Var}(\phi)|$, the summing out of $\mathcal{V}$ in ϕ gives the marginal distribution over $|\mathsf{Var}(\phi) \setminus \mathcal{V}|$. In the degenerate case where $\mathsf{Var}(\phi) \subseteq \mathcal{V}$, then $\mathsf{Var}(\sum_{\mathcal{V}}(\phi))$ is the empty set and $\sum_{\mathcal{V}}(\phi)_{\star}$ is the total mass of ϕ, *i.e.* $\sum_{\overline{b} \in |\mathsf{Var}(\phi)|} \phi_{\overline{b}}$.

Example 9. Recall the factor $\phi = (\{x_3, x_4, x_5\}, (a, b, c \mapsto (\mathsf{M}_5)_{(a,b),c}))$ of Ex. 7, representing the definition $x_5 = \mathsf{M}_5(x_3, x_4)$ in the let-term in Ex.2, and consider a factor $\psi = (\{x_3, x_4\}, (a, b \mapsto \mathsf{M}'_{a,b}))$ representing some definition $x_4 = \mathsf{M}'(x_3)$. Then, $\mathsf{Var}(\phi \odot \psi) = \{x_3, x_4, x_5\}$ and for every $a, b, c \in |\mathsf{Bool}|$, we have $\mathsf{Fun}(\phi \odot \psi)(a, b, c) = (\mathsf{M}_5)_{(a,b),c} \mathsf{M}'_{a,b}$. Notice that the factor product $\phi \odot \psi$ is *not* the tensor product $\otimes$ of the vectors $\mathsf{Fun}(\phi)$ and $\mathsf{Fun}(\psi)$, as variables can be shared between the different factors. In fact, the dimension of $\mathsf{Fun}(\phi) \otimes \mathsf{Fun}(\psi)$ is $2^3 \times 2^2 = 2^5$, while $\mathsf{Fun}(\phi \odot \psi)$ is 2^3.

Notice that the computation of the sum out $\sum_{\mathcal{V}}(\phi)$ is in $O(\mathsf{b}_\phi^{\mathsf{d}_\phi})$, as $\mathsf{b}_\phi^{\mathsf{d}_\phi}$ is an upper bound to the cardinality of $|\mathsf{Var}(\phi)|$ which gives the number of basic operations needed to define $\sum_{\mathcal{V}}(\phi)$. Analogously, the computation of $\phi \odot \psi$ is in $O(\mathsf{b}_{\phi \odot \psi}^{\mathsf{d}_{\phi \odot \psi}}) = O(\max(\mathsf{b}_\phi, \mathsf{b}_\psi)^{\mathsf{d}_\phi + \mathsf{d}_\psi})$, as $\mathsf{b}_{\phi \odot \psi}^{\mathsf{d}_{\phi \odot \psi}}$ is an upper bound to the cardinality of $|\psi \odot \psi|$, which gives the number of basic operations needed to define $\phi \odot \psi$.

Proposition 2. *Factor product is associative and commutative, with neutral element the empty factor* $(\emptyset, 1)$. *Moreover:*

1. $\sum_V(\sum_W(\phi)) = \sum_{V \cup W}(\phi)$;
2. $\sum_V(\phi \odot \psi) = (\sum_V(\phi)) \odot \psi$, whenever $\mathsf{Var}(\psi) \cap V = \emptyset$.

Definition 2 (*I*-factor product). *Let I be a finite set. Given a collection of factors $(\phi_i)_{i \in I}$, we define their* factor product *as the factor $\bigodot_{i \in I} \phi_i := \phi_{i_1} \odot \cdots \odot \phi_{i_n}$, for some enumeration of I. This is well-defined independently from the chosen enumeration because of Prop. 2.*

By iterating our remark on the complexity for computing binary products, we have that the computation of the whole vector $\mathsf{Var}(\bigodot_{i \in I} \phi_i)$ is in $O(\mathsf{s}(I)\mathsf{b}^{\mathsf{d}_{\bigodot_{i \in I} \phi_i}}_{\bigodot_{i \in I} \phi_i})$, where we recall $\mathsf{s}(I)$ denotes the cardinality of I.

3.2 Let-terms as Sets of Factors

Let us introduce some convenient notation. Metavariables Γ, Δ, Ξ will range over finite sets of factors. We lift the notation for factors to sets of factors: we write $\mathsf{Var}(\Gamma)$ for the union $\bigcup_{\phi \in \Gamma} \mathsf{Var}(\phi)$, so we can speak about a variable of Γ meaning a variable of one (or more) factor in Γ; hence, the degree d_Γ (resp. the base b_Γ) of Γ is the cardinality of $\mathsf{Var}(\Gamma)$ (resp. the maximal cardinality of a set $|v|$ for $v \in \mathsf{Var}(\Gamma)$). Also, the operations of the sum-out and product with a factor are lifted component-wise, *i.e.* $\sum_V(\Gamma) := \{\sum_V(\phi) \mid \phi \in \Gamma\}$ and $\psi \odot \Gamma := \{\psi \odot \phi \mid \phi \in \Gamma\}$. In contrast, the *I*-factor product $\bigodot \Gamma$ returns the single factor result of the products of all factors in Γ, according to Def. 2.

Given a set of variables V, it will be convenient to partition Γ into Γ_V and $\Gamma_{\neg V}$, depending on whether a factor in Γ has common labels with V or not, *i.e.*:

$$\Gamma_V := \{\phi \in \Gamma \mid \mathsf{Var}(\phi) \cap V \neq \emptyset\}, \qquad \Gamma_{\neg V} := \{\phi \in \Gamma \mid \mathsf{Var}(\phi) \cap V = \emptyset\}. \tag{7}$$

Notice that $\Gamma = \Gamma_V \uplus \Gamma_{\neg V}$, as well as $\mathsf{Var}(\Gamma) \cap V \subseteq \mathsf{Var}(\Gamma_V)$ and $\mathsf{Var}(\Gamma_{\neg V}) \subseteq \mathsf{Var}(\Gamma) \setminus V$. In the case of singletons $\{v\}$, we can simply write Γ_v and $\Gamma_{\neg v}$.

Definition 3 ($\mathsf{F}(v = e)$). *Given a pattern v and expression e s.t. $\mathsf{FV}(v) \cap \mathsf{FV}(e) = \emptyset$, we define $\mathsf{F}(v = e)$, by: $\mathsf{Var}(\mathsf{F}(v = e)) := \mathsf{FV}(e) \uplus \mathsf{FV}(v)$ and $\mathsf{Fun}(\mathsf{F}(v = e)) := \overline{a} \uplus \overline{b} \mapsto [\![e]\!]_{\overline{a},\overline{b}}$, for $\overline{a} \in |\mathsf{FV}(e)|$, $\overline{b} \in |\mathsf{FV}(v)|$.*

In a definition $v = e$, e's free variables can be seen as input channels, while v's variables as output channels. This is also reflected in the matrix $[\![e]\!]$ where rows are associated with inputs and columns with outputs. In contrast, a factor forgets such a distinction, mixing all indexes in a common family.

Let us warn that Def. 3 as well as the next Def. 4 are not compatible with renaming of bound variables (a.k.a. α-equivalence), as they use bound variables as names for the variables of factors. Of course, one can define an equivalence of factors by renaming their variables, but this must be done consistently on all factors taken in consideration.

Definition 4 (Fs(ℓ)). *Given a let-term ℓ with output pattern $\boldsymbol{w}$, we define the set of factors Fs(ℓ), by induction on the number of definitions of ℓ:*

$$\mathsf{Fs}(\boldsymbol{w}) := (\mathsf{FV}(\boldsymbol{w}), \boldsymbol{a} \mapsto 1)$$

$$\mathsf{Fs}((\boldsymbol{v} = e \,\mathbf{in}\, \ell)) := \begin{cases} \left\{ \sum_f (\mathsf{F}(\boldsymbol{v} = e) \odot \mathsf{Fs}(\ell)_f) \right\} \uplus \mathsf{Fs}(\ell)_{\neg f} & \text{if } f \in \mathsf{FV}(\boldsymbol{v})^a \setminus \mathsf{FV}(\boldsymbol{w}), \\ \{\mathsf{F}(\boldsymbol{v} = e)\} \uplus \mathsf{Fs}(\ell) & \text{otherwise.} \end{cases}$$

The definition of $\mathsf{Fs}((\boldsymbol{v} = e \,\mathbf{in}\, \ell))$ is justified by the linear status of the arrow variables, assured by the typing system. In a let-term $((\boldsymbol{x}, f) = e \,\mathbf{in}\, \ell)$, we have two disjoint cases: either the arrow variable f occurs free exactly once in one of the definitions of ℓ, or f is free in the output $\boldsymbol{w}$ of ℓ. In the former case, $\mathsf{Fs}(\ell)_f$ is a singleton $\{\phi\}$, and we can sum-out f once multiplied $\mathsf{F}((\boldsymbol{x}, f) = e)$ with ϕ, as no other factor will use f. In the latter case, we keep f in the family of the factors associated with the let-term, as this variable will appear in its output.

Example 10. Let us consider Fig. 7. The let-term ℓ in (L1) has exactly 7 factors, the 1-constant factor associated with the output and one factor for each definition, carrying the corresponding stochastic matrix M_i. For a less obvious example, consider the term ℓ' in (L8). The set $\mathsf{Fs}(\ell')$ has 4 factors: one for the output, two associated with the definitions of, respectively, x_4 and x_5 and the last one defined as $\sum_f (\mathsf{F}(x_3, f = e_2) \odot \mathsf{F}(x_6 = fx_5))$. Notice that $\mathsf{F}(x_6 = fx_5)_{\bar{a}} = 1$ if $\bar{a}_f = (\bar{a}_{x_5}, \bar{a}_{x_6})$ otherwise $\mathsf{F}(x_6 = fx_5)_{\bar{a}} = 0$. Therefore the sum-out on f produces a sum of only one term, whenever fixed $b_5 \in |x_5|$ and $b_6 \in |x_6|$.

Notice also that all let-terms from line (L12) have a set of factors of cardinality two, although they may have more than one definition.

The following proposition shows how to recover the quantitative semantics $[\![\ell]\!]$ of a let-term ℓ out of the set of factors $\mathsf{Fs}(\ell)$: take the product of all factors in $\mathsf{Fs}(\ell)$ and sum-out all variables that are not free in ℓ nor occurs in the output. The proposition is proven by induction on ℓ.

Proposition 3. *Consider a let-term ℓ with output v. Let $\mathcal{F} = \mathsf{Var}(\mathsf{Fs}(\ell))$, and consider $\bar{a} \in |\mathsf{FV}(\ell)|$, $\bar{b} \in |\mathsf{FV}(v)|$. If $\bar{a}|_{\mathsf{FV}(\ell) \cap \mathsf{FV}(v)} = \bar{b}|_{\mathsf{FV}(\ell) \cap \mathsf{FV}(v)}$, with $\bar{a}' = \bar{a}|_{\mathsf{FV}(\ell) \setminus \mathsf{FV}(v)}$, $\bar{b}' = \bar{b}|_{\mathsf{FV}(v) \setminus \mathsf{FV}(\ell)}$, and $\bar{c} = \bar{a}|_{\mathsf{FV}(\ell) \cap \mathsf{FV}(v)} = \bar{b}|_{\mathsf{FV}(\ell) \cap \mathsf{FV}(v)}$, we have $[\![\ell]\!]_{\bar{a}, \bar{b}} = \sum_{\mathcal{F} \setminus (\mathsf{FV}(\ell) \cup \mathsf{FV}(v))} (\odot \mathsf{Fs}(\ell)) (\bar{a}' \uplus \bar{c} \uplus \bar{b}')$. Otherwise $[\![\ell]\!]_{\bar{a}, \bar{b}} = 0$. In particular, if ℓ is closed, then $[\![\ell]\!]_{\star, \bar{b}} = \sum_{\mathcal{F} \setminus v} (\odot \mathsf{Fs}(\ell)) (\bar{b})$.*

3.3   Variable Elimination VE^F over Sets of Factors

We recall the definition of the variable elimination algorithm as acting on sets of factors. Prop. 4 states its soundness, which is a standard result that we revisit here just to fix our notation. We refer to [8, ch.6] for more details.

Definition 5 (Variable elimination over sets of factors). *The elimination of a variable v in a set of factors Γ is the set of factors $\mathsf{VE}^{\mathsf{F}}(\Gamma, v)$ defined by:*

$$\mathsf{VE}^{\mathsf{F}}(\Gamma, v) := \{\textstyle\sum_v \odot \Gamma_v\} \uplus \Gamma_{\neg v} \tag{8}$$

This definition extends to finite sequences of variables $(v_1, \ldots, v_h)$ by iteration:

$$\mathsf{VE}^{\mathsf{F}}(\Gamma, (v_1, \ldots, v_h)) := \mathsf{VE}^{\mathsf{F}}(\mathsf{VE}^{\mathsf{F}}(\Gamma, v_1), (v_2, \ldots, v_h)) \tag{9}$$

if $h > 0$, otherwise $\mathsf{VE}^{\mathsf{F}}(\Gamma, ()) = \Gamma$.

Example 11. Recall the sets of factors $\mathsf{Fs}(\ell)$ and $\mathsf{Fs}(\ell')$ of Ex. 10. An easy computation gives: $\mathsf{Fs}(\ell') = \mathsf{VE}^{\mathsf{F}}(\mathsf{Fs}(\ell), (x_1, x_2))$.

The soundness of $\mathsf{VE}^{\mathsf{F}}(\Gamma, (v_1, \ldots, v_h))$ follows by induction on the length h of the sequence $(v_1, \ldots, v_h)$, using Prop. 2 :

Proposition 4 (Soundness). *We have:* $\odot\,\mathsf{VE}^{\mathsf{F}}(\Gamma, (v_1, \ldots, v_h)) = \sum_{\{v_1, \ldots, v_h\}} \odot\, \Gamma$. *In particular,* $\mathsf{Var}(\mathsf{VE}^{\mathsf{F}}(\Gamma, (v_1, \ldots, v_h))) = \mathsf{Var}(\Gamma) \setminus \{v_1, \ldots, v_h\}$.

Soundness states that the VE^{F} transformation corresponds to summing-out the variables to eliminate from the product of the factors into consideration. This means that if the factors in Γ represent random variables, then $\odot\,\mathsf{VE}^{\mathsf{F}}(\Gamma, (v_1, \ldots, v_h))$ computes the join distribution over the variables in $\mathsf{Var}(\Gamma) \setminus (v_1, \ldots, v_h)$.

4   Variable Elimination $\mathsf{VE}^{\mathcal{L}}$ as Let-Term Rewriting

This section contains our main contribution, expressing the variable elimination algorithm syntactically, as a rewriting of let-terms, transforming the "eliminated" variables from global variables (*i.e.* defined by a definition of a let-term and accessible to the following definitions), into local variables (*i.e.* private to some subexpression in a specific definition). Subsect. 4.1 defines such a rewriting $\rightarrow$ of let-terms (Fig. 6) and states some of its basic properties. Subsect. 4.2 introduces the $\mathsf{VE}^{\mathcal{L}}$ transformation as a deterministic strategy to apply $\rightarrow$ in order to make local the variable to be eliminated (Def. 8), without changing the denotational semantics of the term (Prop. 6). Theorem 1 and Corollary 1 prove that $\mathsf{VE}^{\mathcal{L}}$ and VE^{F} are equivalent, showing that $\mathsf{Fs}(\cdot)$ commutes over the two transformations. Finally, Subsect. 4.2 briefly discusses some complexity properties, namely that the $\mathsf{VE}^{\mathcal{L}}$ increases the size of a let-term quite reasonably, keeping a linear bound.

4.1   Let-Term Rewriting

Fig. 6 gives the rewriting rules of let-terms that we will use in the sequel. The rewriting steps $\gamma_1, \gamma_2, \gamma_3$ are called *swapping* and we write $\ell \xrightarrow{\gamma} \ell'$ whenever ℓ' is obtained from ℓ by applying any such swapping step. The rewriting step μ is called *multiplicative* and it is used to couple two definitions. The reason why γ_3 is classified as swapping rather than multiplicative reflects the role of arrow

(γ_1) $(\boldsymbol{v}_1 = e_1; \boldsymbol{v}_2 = e_2 \text{ in } \ell) \rightarrow (\boldsymbol{v}_2 = e_2; \boldsymbol{v}_1 = e_1 \text{ in } \ell)$
$$\text{if } \mathsf{FV}(\boldsymbol{v}_1) \cap \mathsf{FV}(e_2) = \emptyset,$$

(γ_2) $(\boldsymbol{v}_1 = e_1; \boldsymbol{v}_2 = e_2 \text{ in } \ell) \rightarrow (f = \lambda \boldsymbol{x}.e_2; \boldsymbol{v}_1 = e_1; \boldsymbol{v}_2 = f\boldsymbol{x} \text{ in } \ell)$
$$\text{if } \boldsymbol{x} = \mathsf{FV}(\boldsymbol{v}_1) \cap \mathsf{FV}(e_2) \text{ positive and not empty,}$$

(γ_3) $(\boldsymbol{v}_1 = e_1; \boldsymbol{v}_2 = e_2 \text{ in } \ell) \rightarrow ((\boldsymbol{v}_1^+, \boldsymbol{v}_2) = (\boldsymbol{v}_1 = e_1 \text{ in } (\boldsymbol{v}_1^+, e_2)) \text{ in } \ell)$
$$\text{if } \boldsymbol{v}_1^a = f, \text{ with } f \in \mathsf{FV}(e_2),$$

(μ) $(\boldsymbol{v}_1 = e_1; \boldsymbol{v}_2 = e_2 \text{ in } \ell) \rightarrow ((\boldsymbol{v}_1, \boldsymbol{v}_2) = (\boldsymbol{v}_1 = e_1 \text{ in } (\boldsymbol{v}_1, e_2)) \text{ in } \ell)$
$$\text{if } \boldsymbol{v}_1 \text{ positive,}$$

(ϵ_x) $(\boldsymbol{v} = e_1 \text{ in } \ell) \rightarrow (\boldsymbol{v}' = (\boldsymbol{v} = e_1 \text{ in } \boldsymbol{v}') \text{ in } \ell)$
$$\text{if } x \notin \mathsf{FV}(\ell) \text{ and } \boldsymbol{v}' \text{ is not empty and removes } x \text{ in } \boldsymbol{v}.$$

Fig. 6: Let-terms rewriting rules. We recall that x's variables (f's variables) are supposed positive (resp. arrow), while v's may be positive or arrow. We also recall from Section 2 that $\boldsymbol{v}^a$ denotes the only arrow variable in a pattern $\boldsymbol{v}$, if it exists, and $\boldsymbol{v}^+$ denotes the pattern obtained from $\boldsymbol{v}$ by removing the arrow variable $\boldsymbol{v}^a$, if any. In the case $\boldsymbol{v}^+$ is empty, the notation $(\boldsymbol{v}^+, e)$ stands for e.

variables in the definition of $\mathsf{Fs}(\ell)$. Finally, the rewriting step ϵ_x *eliminates* a positive variable x from the outermost definitions, supposing this variable is not used in the sequel. The conditions in each rule guarantee that the rewriting $\rightarrow$ preserves typing as stated by the following proposition.

Proposition 5 (Subject reduction). *The rewriting $\rightarrow$ of Fig. 6 preserves typing, i.e. if $\ell \rightarrow \ell'$ and ℓ is of type T, then so is ℓ', as well as $\mathsf{FV}(\ell) = \mathsf{FV}(\ell')$.*

Proposition 6 (Semantics invariance). *The rewriting $\rightarrow$ of Fig. 6 preserves the denotational interpretation, i.e. if $\ell \rightarrow \ell'$ then $[\![\ell]\!] = [\![\ell']\!]$.*

Moreover, $\mathsf{Fs}(\ell)$ is invariant under commutative rewriting:

Lemma 1. *If $\ell \xrightarrow{\gamma} \ell'$, then $\mathsf{Fs}(\ell') = \mathsf{Fs}(\ell)$.*

4.2 Variable Elimination Strategy

The $\mathsf{VE}^{\mathcal{L}}$ transformation can be seen as a deterministic strategy of applying the rewriting $\rightarrow$ in order to make local a variable in a let-term. The idea of $\mathsf{VE}^{\mathcal{L}}(\ell, x)$ is the following: first, we gather together of definitions $(\boldsymbol{v}_i = e_i)$ of ℓ having x free in e_i into a common huge definition $\boldsymbol{v} = e$ and we move this latter close to the definition of x in ℓ; then, we make the definition of x local to e. To formalise this rewriting sequence we define two auxiliary transformations: the swapping definitions SD (Def. 6) and the variable anticipation VA (Def. 7).

The *swapping definition* procedure rewrites a let-term ℓ with at least two definitions by swapping (or gathering) the first definition with the second one, without changing the factor representation.

Definition 6 (Swapping definitions). *We define* $\mathsf{SD}(\ell)$ *for a let-term* $\ell :=$ $(\boldsymbol{v}_1 = e_1, \boldsymbol{v}_2 = e_2 \text{ in } \ell')$ *with at least two definitions. The definition splits in the following cases, depending on the dependence of* e_2 *with respect to* $\boldsymbol{v}_1$.
1. *If* $\mathsf{FV}(\boldsymbol{v}_1) \cap \mathsf{FV}(e_2) = \emptyset$, $\mathsf{SD}(\ell) := (\boldsymbol{v}_2 = e_2; \boldsymbol{v}_1 = e_1 \text{ in } \ell')$.
2. *If* $\mathsf{FV}(\boldsymbol{v}_1) \cap \mathsf{FV}(e_2) = \boldsymbol{x}$ *is a non-empty sequence of positive variables,* $\mathsf{SD}(\ell) :=$ $(g = \lambda \boldsymbol{x}.e_2; \boldsymbol{v}_1 = e_1; \boldsymbol{v}_2 = g\boldsymbol{x} \text{ in } \ell')$.
3. *If* $\boldsymbol{v}_1^a = f$ *and* $f \in \mathsf{FV}(e_2)$, $\mathsf{SD}(\ell) := ((\boldsymbol{v}_1^+, \boldsymbol{v}_2) = (\boldsymbol{v}_1 = e_1 \text{ in } (\boldsymbol{v}_1^+, e_2)) \text{ in } \ell')$, *if* $\boldsymbol{v}_1^+$ *is non-empty, otherwise:* $\mathsf{SD}(\ell) := (\boldsymbol{v}_2 = (\boldsymbol{v}_1 = e_1 \text{ in } e_2) \text{ in } \ell')$.

Notice that the above cases are exhaustive. In particular, if $\boldsymbol{v}_1$ has some variables in common with $\mathsf{FV}(e_2)$ then either all such common variables are positive or one of them is an arrow variable f. By case inspection and Lemma 1, we get:

Lemma 2 (SD soundness). *Given a let-term* ℓ *with at least two definitions, then* $\ell \xrightarrow{\gamma} \mathsf{SD}(\ell)$, *for the swap reduction* γ *defined in Fig. 6. In particular,* $\mathsf{SD}(\ell)$ *is a well-typed let-term having the same type of* ℓ *and such that* $\mathsf{Fs}(\ell) = \mathsf{Fs}(\mathsf{SD}(\ell))$.

Given a set of variables $\mathcal{V}$, the *variable anticipation* procedure rewrites a let-term ℓ into $\mathsf{VA}(\ell, \mathcal{V})$ by "gathering" in the first position all definitions having free variables in $\mathcal{V}$ or having arrow variables defined by one of the definitions already "gathered". This definition is restricted to positive let-terms.

Definition 7 (Variable anticipation). *We define a let-term* $\mathsf{VA}(\ell, \mathcal{V}) := (\boldsymbol{v}' = e' \text{ in } \ell')$, *given a positive let-term* $\ell := (\boldsymbol{v}_1 = e_1 \text{ in } \ell_1)$ *with at least one definition and a set of variables* $\mathcal{V} \subseteq \mathsf{FV}(\ell)$ *disjoint from the output variables of* ℓ. *The definition is by structural induction on* ℓ *and splits in the following cases.*
1. *If* $\mathcal{V} = \emptyset$, *then define:* $\mathsf{VA}(\ell, \mathcal{V}) := \ell$.
2. *If* $\mathcal{V} \cap \mathsf{FV}(e_1) = \emptyset$, *so that* $\mathcal{V} \subseteq \mathsf{FV}(\ell_1)$, *then define:*
   $\mathsf{VA}(\ell, \mathcal{V}) := \mathsf{SD}((\boldsymbol{v}_1 = e_1 \text{ in } \mathsf{VA}(\ell_1, \mathcal{V})))$.
3. *If* $\mathcal{V} \cap \mathsf{FV}(e_1) \neq \emptyset$ *and* $\boldsymbol{v}_1$ *is positive, then consider* $\mathsf{VA}(\ell_1, \mathcal{V} \cap \mathsf{FV}(\ell_1)) :=$ $(\boldsymbol{v}' = e' \text{ in } \ell')$ *and set:* $\mathsf{VA}(\ell, \mathcal{V}) := ((\boldsymbol{v}_1, \boldsymbol{v}') = (\boldsymbol{v}_1 = e_1 \text{ in } (\boldsymbol{v}_1, e')) \text{ in } \ell')$.
4. *If* $\mathcal{V} \cap \mathsf{FV}(e_1) \neq \emptyset$ *and* $\boldsymbol{v}_1^a = f$. *Notice that, by hypothesis,* f *does not appear in the output of* ℓ_1, *as* ℓ *(and hence* ℓ_1*) is positive. So we can consider* $\mathsf{VA}(\ell_1, (\mathcal{V} \cap \mathsf{FV}(\ell_1)) \cup \{f\}) := (\boldsymbol{v}' = e' \text{ in } \ell')$ *and define:* $\mathsf{VA}(\ell, \mathcal{V}) := ((\boldsymbol{v}_1^+, \boldsymbol{v}') = (\boldsymbol{v}_1 = e_1 \text{ in } (\boldsymbol{v}_1^+, e')) \text{ in } \ell')$, *if* $\boldsymbol{v}_1^+$ *is non-empty, otherwise:* $\mathsf{VA}(\ell, \mathcal{V}) := (\boldsymbol{v}' = (\boldsymbol{v}_1 = e_1 \text{ in } e') \text{ in } \ell')$.

Finally, we can define the procedure $\mathsf{VE}^{\mathcal{L}}(\ell, x)$. This procedure basically consists in three steps: (i), it uses VA for gathering in a unique definition all expressions having a free occurrence of x or a free occurrence of an arrow variable depending from x; then (ii), it performs μ and ϵ rewriting so to make x local to a definition, and finally (iii), it uses SD to move the obtained definition as the first definition of the let-term. This latter step is not strictly necessary but it is convenient in order to avoid free arrow variables of the expression having x local, so getting a simple representation of the factor obtained after x "elimination".

Definition 8 (Variable elimination strategy). *The let-term* $\mathsf{VE}^{\mathcal{L}}(\ell, x)$ *is defined from a positive let-term* $\ell := \text{let } \boldsymbol{v}_1 = e_1 \text{ in } \ell_1$ *and a positive variable* x

defined in ℓ but not in the output of ℓ. The definition is by induction on ℓ and splits in the following cases.

1. *If $x \in \mathsf{FV}(v_1)$ and $x \notin \mathsf{FV}(\ell_1)$, then write by v_1' the pattern obtained from v_1 by removing x and define: $\mathsf{VE}^{\mathcal{L}}(\ell, x) := (v_1' = (v_1 = e_1 \text{ in } v_1') \text{ in } \ell_1)$.*
2. *If $x \in \mathsf{FV}(v_1)$ and $x \in \mathsf{FV}(\ell_1)$, then write by v_1' the pattern obtained from v_1 by removing x. Remark that ℓ_1 has at most one definition, as x is not in the output of ℓ_1. We split in two subcases:*
   1. *if v_1' is positive, then set $(v' = e' \text{ in } \ell') := \mathsf{VA}(\ell_1, \{x\})$ and define: $\mathsf{VE}^{\mathcal{L}}(\ell, x) := ((v_1', v') = (v_1 = e_1 \text{ in } (v_1', e')) \text{ in } \ell')$.*
   2. *if $(v_1')^a = f$, then set $(v' = e' \text{ in } \ell') := \mathsf{VA}(\ell_1, \{x, f\})$ and define: $\mathsf{VE}^{\mathcal{L}}(\ell, x) := ((v_1^+, v') = (v_1 = e_1 \text{ in } (v_1^+, e')) \text{ in } \ell')$.*
   In both sub-cases, if $v_1'^+$ is empty, we mean $\mathsf{VE}^{\mathcal{L}}(\ell, x) := (v' = (v_1 = e_1 \text{ in } e') \text{ in } \ell')$.
3. *If $x \notin \mathsf{FV}(v_1)$, then x is defined in ℓ_1, and we can set: $\mathsf{VE}^{\mathcal{L}}(\ell, x) := \mathsf{SD}((v_1 = e_1 \text{ in } \mathsf{VE}^{\mathcal{L}}(\ell_1, x)))$.*
   As for VE^{F}, we extend $\mathsf{VE}^{\mathcal{L}}$ to sequences of (positive) variables, by

$$\mathsf{VE}^{\mathcal{L}}(\ell, (x_1, \ldots, x_h)) := \mathsf{VE}^{\mathcal{L}}(\mathsf{VE}^{\mathcal{L}}(\ell, x_1), (x_2, \ldots, x_h)).$$

with the identity on ℓ for the empty sequence.

Example 12. Consider Fig. 7 and denote by ℓ_i the let-term in line (Li). This figure details the rewriting sequence of the term ℓ_1 into $\ell_{15} = \mathsf{VE}^{\mathcal{L}}(\ell_1, (x_1, x_2, x_4, x_5))$. Namely, $\ell_3 = \mathsf{VE}^{\mathcal{L}}(\ell_1, x_1)$, $\ell_8 = \mathsf{VE}^{\mathcal{L}}(\ell_3, x_2)$, $\ell_{11} = \mathsf{VE}^{\mathcal{L}}(\ell_8, x_4)$, $\ell_{15} = \mathsf{VE}^{\mathcal{L}}(\ell_{11}, x_5)$.

Proposition 7 (Rewriting into $\mathsf{VE}^{\mathcal{L}}$). *Let ℓ be a let-term with n definitions: $\mathsf{VE}^{\mathcal{L}}(\ell, x)$ is obtained from ℓ by at most n steps of the $\to$ rewriting of Fig. 6. In particular, $\mathsf{VE}^{\mathcal{L}}(\ell, x)$ has the same type and free variables of ℓ.*

The following theorem states both the soundness and completeness of our syntactic definition of $\mathsf{VE}^{\mathcal{L}}$ with respect to the more standard version defined on factors. The soundness is because any syntactic elimination variable is equivalent to the semantic $\mathsf{VE}^{\mathcal{L}}$ modulo the map $\mathsf{Fs}(\ell)$. Completeness is because this holds for *any* chosen variable, so all variable elimination sequences can be simulated in the syntax (Corollary 1).

Theorem 1. *Given ℓ and x as in Def. 8, we have: $\mathsf{Fs}(\mathsf{VE}^{\mathcal{L}}(\ell, x)) = \mathsf{VE}^{\mathsf{F}}(\mathsf{Fs}(\ell), x)$.*

From Theorem 1 and Def. 5 and 8, the following is immediate.

Corollary 1. *Given a let-term ℓ with all output variables positive and given a sequence $(x_1, \ldots, x_n)$ of positive variables defined in ℓ and not appearing in the output of ℓ, we have that: $\mathsf{VE}^{\mathsf{F}}(\mathsf{Fs}(\ell), (x_1, \ldots, x_n)) = \mathsf{Fs}(\mathsf{VE}^{\mathcal{L}}(\ell, (x_1, \ldots, x_n)))$.*

Recall from Ex. 2 that Bayesian networks can be represented by let-terms, so the above result shows that $\mathsf{VE}^{\mathcal{L}}$ implements in $\mathcal{L}$ the elimination of a set of random variables of a Bayesian network in any possible order. It is well-known that the variable elimination algorithm may produce intermediate factors that are not stochastic matrices. The standard literature on probabilistic graphical

$\ell = (x_1 = \mathsf{M}_1; x_2 = \mathsf{M}_2 x_1; x_3 = \mathsf{M}_3 x_2; x_4 = \mathsf{M}_4; x_5 = \mathsf{M}_5(x_3, x_4); x_6 = \mathsf{M}_6(x_2, x_5) \text{ in } (x_3, x_6))$ (L1)

$\xrightarrow{\mu} ((x_1, x_2) = (x_1 = \mathsf{M}_1 \text{ in } (x_1, \mathsf{M}_2 x_1)); x_3 = \mathsf{M}_3 x_2; x_4 = \mathsf{M}_4; x_5 = \mathsf{M}_5(x_3, x_4); x_6 = \mathsf{M}_6(x_2, x_5) \text{ in } (x_3, x_6))$ (L2)

$\xrightarrow{e_{x_1}} (x_2 = ((x_1, x_2) = \underline{(x_1 = \mathsf{M}_1 \text{ in } (x_1, \mathsf{M}_2 x_1))} \text{ in } x_2); x_3 = \mathsf{M}_3 x_2; x_4 = \mathsf{M}_4; x_5 = \mathsf{M}_5(x_3, x_4); x_6 = \mathsf{M}_6(x_2, x_5) \text{ in } (x_3, x_6))$
$\underbrace{\phantom{(x_1 = \mathsf{M}_1 \text{ in } (x_1, \mathsf{M}_2 x_1))}}_{e_1}$ (L3)

$\xrightarrow{\gamma_2} (x_2 = e_1; x_3 = \mathsf{M}_3 x_2; x_4 = \mathsf{M}_4; f = \lambda y.\mathsf{M}_6(x_2, y); x_5 = \mathsf{M}_5(x_3, x_4); x_6 = f x_5; \text{ in } (x_3, x_6))$ (L4)

$\xrightarrow{\gamma_1} (x_2 = e_1; x_3 = \mathsf{M}_3 x_2; f = \lambda y.\mathsf{M}_6(x_2, y); x_4 = \mathsf{M}_4; x_5 = \mathsf{M}_5(x_3, x_4); x_6 = f x_5; \text{ in } (x_3, x_6))$ (L5)

$\xrightarrow{\mu} (x_2 = e_1; (x_3, f) = (x_3 = \mathsf{M}_3 x_2 \text{ in } (x_3, \lambda y.\mathsf{M}_6(x_2, y))); x_4 = \mathsf{M}_4; x_5 = \mathsf{M}_5(x_3, x_4); x_6 = f x_5; \text{ in } (x_3, x_6))$ (L6)

$\xrightarrow{\mu} ((x_2, (x_3, f)) = (x_2 = e_1 \text{ in } (x_2, (x_3 = \mathsf{M}_3 x_2 \text{ in } (x_3, \lambda y.\mathsf{M}_6(x_2, y))))); x_4 = \mathsf{M}_4; x_5 = \mathsf{M}_5(x_3, x_4); x_6 = f x_5; \text{ in } (x_3, x_6))$ (L7)

$\xrightarrow{e_{x_2}} ((x_3, f) = ((x_2, (x_3, f)) = \underline{(x_2 = e_1 \text{ in } (x_2, (x_3 = \mathsf{M}_3 x_2 \text{ in } (x_3, \lambda y.\mathsf{M}_6(x_2, y)))))} \text{ in } (x_3, f)); x_4 = \mathsf{M}_4; x_5 = \mathsf{M}_5(x_3, x_4); x_6 = f x_5; \text{ in } (x_3, x_6))$
$\underbrace{}_{e_2}$ (L8)

$\xrightarrow{\mu} ((x_3, f) = e_2; (x_4, x_5) = (x_4 = \mathsf{M}_4 \text{ in } (x_4, \mathsf{M}_5(x_3, x_4))); x_6 = f x_5; \text{ in } (x_3, x_6))$ (L9)

$\xrightarrow{e_{x_4}} ((x_3, f) = e_2; (x_4, x_5) = ((x_4, x_5) = \underline{(x_4 = \mathsf{M}_4 \text{ in } (x_4, \mathsf{M}_5(x_3, x_4)))} \text{ in } x_5); x_6 = f x_5; \text{ in } (x_3, x_6))$ (L10)

$\xrightarrow{\gamma_2} (g = \lambda z.((x_4, x_5) = \underline{(x_4 = \mathsf{M}_4 \text{ in } (x_4, \mathsf{M}_5(z, x_4)))} \text{ in } x_5); (x_3, f) = e_2; x_5 = g x_3; x_6 = f x_5; \text{ in } (x_3, x_6))$
$\underbrace{}_{e_4}$ (L11)

$\xrightarrow{\mu} (g = e_4; (x_3, f) = e_2; (x_5, x_6) = (x_5 = g x_3 \text{ in } (x_5, f x_5)) \text{ in } (x_3, x_6))$ (L12)

$\xrightarrow{e_{x_5}} (g = e_4; (x_3, f) = e_2; x_6 = ((x_5, x_6) = (x_5 = g x_3 \text{ in } (x_5, f x_5)) \text{ in } x_6) \text{ in } (x_3, x_6))$ (L13)

$\xrightarrow{\gamma_3} (g = e_4; (x_3, x_6) = ((x_3, f) = e_2 \text{ in } (x_3, ((x_5, x_6) = (x_5 = g x_3 \text{ in } (x_5, f x_5)) \text{ in } x_6))) \text{ in } (x_3, x_6))$ (L14)

$\xrightarrow{\gamma_3} ((x_3, x_6) = (g = e_4; \text{ in } ((x_3, f) = e_2 \text{ in } (x_3, ((x_5, x_6) = (g x_3 \text{ in } (x_5, f x_5)) \text{ in } x_6)))) \text{ in } (x_3, x_6))$
$\underbrace{}_{e_5}$ (L15)

Fig. 7: Rewriting of ℓ into $\mathsf{VE}^{\mathcal{L}}(\ell, ((x_1, x_2, x_4, x_5)) = \ell'$ for ℓ, ℓ' given in Ex. 2. We underline in blue the fired redex in the following reduction step. We also name e_1, e_2, e_4, e_5, the expressions keeping local the corresponding variable (i.e. e_i keeps local x_i).

models refer to the intermediate factors simply as vectors of non-negative real numbers, missing any finer characterisation. We stress that our setting allows for a more precise characterisation of such factors, as they are represented by *well-typed* terms of $\mathcal{L}$: not all non-negative real numbers vectors fit in. In particular, the typing system suggests a hierarchy of the complexity of a factor that, by recalling Remark 1, can by summarised by the alternation between direct sums $\oplus$ and products $\&$: the simplest factors have type $\oplus_n 1$, i.e. probabilistic distributions over n values, then we have those of type $\&_m \oplus_n 1$, i.e. stochastic matrices describing probabilities over n values conditioned from observations over m values, then we have more complex factors of type $\oplus_k \&_m \oplus_n 1$, i.e. probabilistic distributions over stochastic matrices, and so forth.

Complexity Analysis. Prop. 7 gives a bound to the number of $\rightarrow$ steps needed to rewrite ℓ into $\mathsf{VE}^{\mathcal{L}}(\ell, x)$, however some of these steps adds new definitions in the rewritten let-term. The size of $\mathsf{VE}^{\mathcal{L}}(\ell, x)$, although greater in general than that of ℓ, stays reasonable, in fact it has an upper bound linear in the degree of $\mathsf{Fs}(\ell)_x$ (Prop. 8). We define the size of an expression as follows:

$$\mathsf{s}(v) := 1 \qquad \mathsf{s}(\lambda v.e) := \mathsf{s}(v) + \mathsf{s}(e) \qquad \mathsf{s}((e, e')) := \mathsf{s}(e) + \mathsf{s}(e')$$
$$\mathsf{s}(f\boldsymbol{x}) := 1 + \mathsf{s}(\boldsymbol{x}) \quad \mathsf{s}(\mathsf{M}(\boldsymbol{x})) := 1 + \mathsf{s}(\boldsymbol{x}) \qquad \mathsf{s}((v = e \text{ in } e')) := \mathsf{s}(v) + \mathsf{s}(e) + \mathsf{s}(e')$$

By induction on ℓ, we obtain the following:

Proposition 8. *Given a let-term ℓ and a positive variable x as in Def. 8, we have that* $\mathsf{s}(\mathsf{VE}^{\mathcal{L}}(\ell, x)) \leq \mathsf{s}(\ell) + 4 \times \mathsf{s}(\mathsf{Var}(\mathsf{Fs}(\ell)_x) \setminus \mathsf{FV}(\ell))$.

5 Conclusions and discussion

We have identified a fragment $\mathcal{L}$ of the linear simply-typed λ-calculus which can express syntactically *any* factorisation induced by a run of the variable elimination algorithm over a Bayesian network. In particular, we define a rewriting (Fig. 6) and a reduction strategy $\mathsf{VE}^{\mathcal{L}}$ (Def. 8) that, given a sequence $(x_1, \ldots, x_n)$ of variables to eliminate, transforms in $O(ns(\ell))$ steps a let-term ℓ into a let-term $\mathsf{VE}^{\mathcal{L}}(\ell, (x_1, \ldots, x_n))$ associated with the factorisation generated by the $(x_1, \ldots, x_n)$ elimination (Corollary 1). We have proven that the size of $\mathsf{VE}^{\mathcal{L}}(\ell, (x_1, \ldots, x_n))$ is linear in the size of ℓ and in the number of variables involved in the elimination process (Prop. 8).

Our language is a fragment of a more expressive one [15], in which several classes of stochastic models can be encoded. Our work is therefore a step towards defining standard exact inference algorithms on a general-purpose stochastic language, as first propounded in [27] with the goal is to have general-purpose algorithms of *reasonable* cost, usable on any model expressed in the language.

While it is known (see [26], Sect. 9.3.1.3) that VE produces intermediate factors that are not conditional probabilities—*i.e.* not stochastic matrices— our approach is able to associate *a term and a type* to such factors. In fact, the types of the calculus $\mathcal{L}$ give a logical description of the interdependences between the factors generated by the VE algorithm: the grammar is more expressive than just the types of stochastic matrices between tuples of booleans (Remark 1).

Discussion and perspectives. Since our approach is theoretical, the main goal has been to give a formal framework for proving *the soundness and the completeness* of VE$^{\mathcal{L}}$. For that sake, the rewriting rules of Fig. 6 are reduced to a minimum, in order to keep reasonable the number of cases in the proofs. The drawback is that the rewritten terms have a lot of bureaucratic code, as the reader may realize by looking at Fig. 7. Although this fact is not crucial from the point of view of the asymptotic complexity, when aiming at a prototypical implementation, one may enrich the rewriting system with more rules to avoid useless code.

The grammar of let-terms recalls the notion of administrative normal form (abbreviated ANF), which is often used as an intermediate representation in the compilation of functional programs. In particular, let-terms and ANF share in common the restriction of applications to variables, so suggesting a precise evaluation order. Several optimisations are defined as transformations over ANF, even considering some *let-floating* rules analogous to the ones considered in Fig. 6, see e.g. [38]. Comparing these optimisations is not trivial as the cost model is different. E.g. [38] aims to reduce heap allocations, while here we are factoring algebraic expressions to minimise floating-point operations. We plan to investigate more in detail the possible interplay/interference between these techniques.

The quest for optimal factorisations is central not only to Bayesian programming. In particular, these techniques can be applied to large fragments of λ-calculus, suggesting heuristics for making tractable the computation of the quantitative semantics of other classes of λ-terms than the one identified by $\mathcal{L}$. This is of great interest in particular because these semantics are relevant in describing quantitative observational equivalences, as hinted for example by the full-abstraction results achieved in probabilistic programming, *e.g.* [13,14,6].

Finally, while we have stressed that our work is theoretical, we do not mean to say that foundational understanding in general, and this work in particular, is irrelevant to the practice. Let us mention one such perspective. Factored inference is central to inference in graphical models, but scaling it up to the more complex problems expressible as probabilistic programs proves difficult—research in this direction is beginning, mainly guided by implementation techniques [40,32,21]. We believe that a foundational understanding of factorisation on the structure of the program—starting from the most elementary algorithms, as we do here— is also important to allow progress in this direction.

On dealing with evidence. We have focused on the computation of marginals, without explicitly treating *posteriors*. Our approach could easily be adapted to deal with evidence (hence, posteriors), by extending syntax and rewriting rules to include an `observe` construct as in [21] or in [16].

Acknowledgments. We are deeply grateful to Marco Gaboardi for suggesting investigating the link between variable elimination and linear logic, as well as to Robin Lemaire, with whom we initiated this research. We also thank the anonymous referees for their many valuable suggestions to improve the paper.

This work has been supported by the ANR grant PPS ANR-19-CE48-0014 and ENS de Lyon research grant.

References

1. Benton, P.N., Wadler, P.: Linear logic, monads and the lambda calculus. In: Proceedings, 11th Annual IEEE Symposium on Logic in Computer Science, New Brunswick, New Jersey, USA, July 27-30, 1996. pp. 420–431. IEEE Computer Society (1996). https://doi.org/10.1109/LICS.1996.561458
2. Borgström, J., Lago, U.D., Gordon, A.D., Szymczak, M.: A lambda-calculus foundation for universal probabilistic programming. In: Garrigue, J., Keller, G., Sumii, E. (eds.) Proceedings of the 21st ACM SIGPLAN International Conference on Functional Programming, ICFP 2016, Nara, Japan, September 18-22, 2016. pp. 33–46. ACM (2016). https://doi.org/10.1145/2951913.2951942
3. Chavira, M., Darwiche, A.: Compiling bayesian networks with local structure. In: Kaelbling, L.P., Saffiotti, A. (eds.) IJCAI-05, Proceedings of the Nineteenth International Joint Conference on Artificial Intelligence, Edinburgh, Scotland, UK, July 30 - August 5, 2005. pp. 1306–1312. Professional Book Center (2005), http://ijcai.org/Proceedings/05/Papers/0931.pdf
4. Chavira, M., Darwiche, A.: On probabilistic inference by weighted model counting. Artif. Intell. **172**(6-7), 772–799 (2008). https://doi.org/10.1016/J.ARTINT.2007.11.002
5. Cho, K., Jacobs, B.: Disintegration and bayesian inversion via string diagrams. Math. Struct. Comput. Sci. **29**(7), 938–971 (2019). https://doi.org/10.1017/S0960129518000488
6. Clairambault, P., Paquet, H.: Fully Abstract Models of the Probabilistic λ-calculus. In: 27th EACSL Annual Conference on Computer Science Logic (CSL 2018). Birmingham, United Kingdom (Sep 2018). https://doi.org/10.4230/LIPIcs.CSL.2018.16, https://hal.archives-ouvertes.fr/hal-01886956
7. Danos, V., Ehrhard, T.: Probabilistic coherence spaces as a model of higher-order probabilistic computation. Information and Computation **209**(6), 966–991 (2011)
8. Darwiche, A.: Modeling and Reasoning with Bayesian Networks. Cambridge University Press (2009), http://www.cambridge.org/uk/catalogue/catalogue.asp?isbn=9780521884389
9. Egger, J., Møgelberg, R.E., Simpson, A.: The enriched effect calculus: syntax and semantics. J. Log. Comput. **24**(3), 615–654 (2014). https://doi.org/10.1093/logcom/exs025
10. Ehrhard, T.: Call-by-push-value from a linear logic point of view. In: Thiemann, P. (ed.) Programming Languages and Systems - 25th European Symposium on Programming, ESOP 2016, Held as Part of the European Joint Conferences on Theory and Practice of Software, ETAPS 2016, Eindhoven, The Netherlands, April 2-8, 2016, Proceedings. Lecture Notes in Computer Science, vol. 9632, pp. 202–228. Springer (2016). https://doi.org/10.1007/978-3-662-49498-1_9
11. Ehrhard, T., Faggian, C., Pagani, M.: The sum-product algorithm for quantitative multiplicative linear logic. In: Gaboardi, M., van Raamsdonk, F. (eds.) 8th International Conference on Formal Structures for Computation and Deduction, FSCD 2023, July 3-6, 2023, Rome, Italy. LIPIcs, vol. 260, pp. 8:1–8:18. Schloss Dagstuhl - Leibniz-Zentrum für Informatik (2023). https://doi.org/10.4230/LIPICS.FSCD.2023.8

12. Ehrhard, T., Faggian, C., Pagani, M.: Variable elimination as rewriting in a linear lambda calculus. extended version. CoRR **abs/2501.15439** (2025), https://arxiv.org/abs/2501.15439

13. Ehrhard, T., Pagani, M., Tasson, C.: Probabilistic Coherence Spaces are Fully Abstract for Probabilistic PCF. In: Sewell, P. (ed.) The 41th Annual ACM SIGPLAN-SIGACT Symposium on Principles of Programming Languages, POPL14, San Diego, USA. ACM (2014)

14. Ehrhard, T., Pagani, M., Tasson, C.: Full abstraction for probabilistic pcf. J. ACM **65**(4) (Apr 2018). https://doi.org/10.1145/3164540

15. Ehrhard, T., Tasson, C.: Probabilistic call by push value. Log. Methods Comput. Sci. **15**(1) (2019). https://doi.org/10.23638/LMCS-15(1:3)2019

16. Faggian, C., Pautasso, D., Vanoni, G.: Higher order bayesian networks, exactly. Proc. ACM Program. Lang. **8**(POPL), 2514–2546 (2024). https://doi.org/10.1145/3632926

17. Gehr, T., Misailovic, S., Vechev, M.T.: PSI: exact symbolic inference for probabilistic programs. In: Chaudhuri, S., Farzan, A. (eds.) Computer Aided Verification - 28th International Conference, CAV 2016, Toronto, ON, Canada, July 17-23, 2016, Proceedings, Part I. Lecture Notes in Computer Science, vol. 9779, pp. 62–83. Springer (2016). https://doi.org/10.1007/978-3-319-41528-4_4

18. Girard, J.Y.: Linear logic. Theor. Comput. Sci. **50**, 1–102 (1987)

19. Gorinova, M.I., Gordon, A.D., Sutton, C., Vákár, M.: Conditional independence by typing. ACM Trans. Program. Lang. Syst. **44**(1), 4:1–4:54 (2022). https://doi.org/10.1145/3490421

20. Hindley, J.R., Seldin, J.P.: Lambda-Calculus and Combinators: An Introduction. Cambridge University Press, USA, 2 edn. (2008)

21. Holtzen, S., den Broeck, G.V., Millstein, T.D.: Scaling exact inference for discrete probabilistic programs. Proc. ACM Program. Lang. **4**(OOPSLA), 140:1–140:31 (2020). https://doi.org/10.1145/3428208

22. Jacobs, B.: Structured probabilitistic reasoning (2023), http://www.cs.ru.nl/B.Jacobs/PAPERS/ProbabilisticReasoning.pdf, draft

23. Jacobs, B., Kissinger, A., Zanasi, F.: Causal inference by string diagram surgery. In: Bojanczyk, M., Simpson, A. (eds.) Foundations of Software Science and Computation Structures - 22nd International Conference, FOSSACS 2019, Held as Part of the European Joint Conferences on Theory and Practice of Software, ETAPS 2019, Prague, Czech Republic, April 6-11, 2019, Proceedings. Lecture Notes in Computer Science, vol. 11425, pp. 313–329. Springer (2019). https://doi.org/10.1007/978-3-030-17127-8_18

24. Jacobs, B., Zanasi, F.: A predicate/state transformer semantics for bayesian learning. In: Birkedal, L. (ed.) The Thirty-second Conference on the Mathematical Foundations of Programming Semantics, MFPS 2016, Carnegie Mellon University, Pittsburgh, PA, USA, May 23-26, 2016. Electronic Notes in Theoretical Computer Science, vol. 325, pp. 185–200. Elsevier (2016). https://doi.org/10.1016/j.entcs.2016.09.038

25. Jacobs, B., Zanasi, F.: The logical essentials of bayesian reasoning. In: Foundations of Probabilistic Programming, pp. 295 – 332. Cambridge University Press (2020)

26. Koller, D., Friedman, N.: Probabilistic Graphical Models: Principles and Techniques. The MIT Press (2009)

27. Koller, D., McAllester, D.A., Pfeffer, A.: Effective bayesian inference for stochastic programs. In: Kuipers, B., Webber, B.L. (eds.) Proceedings of the Fourteenth National Conference on Artificial Intelligence and Ninth Innovative Applications of Artificial Intelligence Conference, AAAI 97, IAAI 97, July 27-31, 1997, Providence, Rhode Island, USA. pp. 740–747. AAAI Press / The MIT Press (1997), http://www.aaai.org/Library/AAAI/1997/aaai97-115.php

28. Kschischang, F.R., Frey, B.J., Loeliger, H.: Factor graphs and the sum-product algorithm. IEEE Trans. Inf. Theory **47**(2), 498–519 (2001). https://doi.org/10.1109/18.910572

29. Laird, J., Manzonetto, G., McCusker, G., Pagani, M.: Weighted relational models of typed lambda-calculi. In: 28th Annual ACM/IEEE Symposium on Logic in Computer Science, LICS 2013, New Orleans, LA, USA, June 25-28, 2013. IEEE Computer Society (Jun 2013)

30. Levy, P.B.: Call-by-push-value: A subsuming paradigm. In: Girard, J. (ed.) Typed Lambda Calculi and Applications, 4th International Conference, TLCA'99, L'Aquila, Italy, April 7-9, 1999, Proceedings. Lecture Notes in Computer Science, vol. 1581, pp. 228–242. Springer (1999). https://doi.org/10.1007/3-540-48959-2_17

31. Li, J., Wang, E., Zhang, Y.: Compiling probabilistic programs for variable elimination with information flow. Proc. ACM Program. Lang. **8**(PLDI), 1755–1780 (2024). https://doi.org/10.1145/3656448

32. Mansinghka, V.K., Schaechtle, U., Handa, S., Radul, A., Chen, Y., Rinard, M.C.: Probabilistic programming with programmable inference. In: Foster, J.S., Grossman, D. (eds.) Proceedings of the 39th ACM SIGPLAN Conference on Programming Language Design and Implementation, PLDI 2018, Philadelphia, PA, USA, June 18-22, 2018. pp. 603–616. ACM (2018). https://doi.org/10.1145/3192366.3192409

33. Melliès, P., Tabareau, N.: Resource modalities in tensor logic. Ann. Pure Appl. Log. **161**(5), 632–653 (2010). https://doi.org/10.1016/j.apal.2009.07.018

34. Narayanan, P., Carette, J., Romano, W., Shan, C., Zinkov, R.: Probabilistic inference by program transformation in hakaru (system description). In: Kiselyov, O., King, A. (eds.) Functional and Logic Programming - 13th International Symposium, FLOPS 2016, Kochi, Japan, March 4-6, 2016, Proceedings. Lecture Notes in Computer Science, vol. 9613, pp. 62–79. Springer (2016). https://doi.org/10.1007/978-3-319-29604-3_5

35. Obermeyer, F., Bingham, E., Jankowiak, M., Pradhan, N., Chiu, J.T., Rush, A.M., Goodman, N.D.: Tensor variable elimination for plated factor graphs. In: Chaudhuri, K., Salakhutdinov, R. (eds.) Proceedings of the 36th International Conference on Machine Learning, ICML 2019, 9-15 June 2019, Long Beach, California, USA. Proceedings of Machine Learning Research, vol. 97, pp. 4871–4880. PMLR (2019), http://proceedings.mlr.press/v97/obermeyer19a.html

36. Paquet, H.: Bayesian strategies: probabilistic programs as generalised graphical models. In: Yoshida, N. (ed.) Programming Languages and Systems - 30th European Symposium on Programming, ESOP 2021, Held as Part of the European Joint Conferences on Theory and Practice of Software, ETAPS 2021, Luxembourg City, Luxembourg, March 27 – April 1, 2021, Proceedings. Lecture Notes in Computer Science, vol. 12648, pp. 519–547. Springer (2021). https://doi.org/10.1007/978-3-030-72019-3_19

37. Pearl, J.: Probabilistic reasoning in intelligent systems - networks of plausible infer-
    ence. Morgan Kaufmann series in representation and reasoning, Morgan Kaufmann
    (1989)
38. Peyton Jones, S., Partain, W., Santos, A.: Let-floating: moving bindings to give
    faster programs. In: Proceedings of the First ACM SIGPLAN International Con-
    ference on Functional Programming. p. 1–12. ICFP '96, Association for Computing
    Machinery, New York, NY, USA (1996). https://doi.org/10.1145/232627.232630
39. Pfeffer, A.: The design and implementation of ibal:a general-purpose probabilistic
    language. Introduction to Statistical Relational Learning p. 399 (2019)
40. Pfeffer, A., Ruttenberg, B.E., Kretschmer, W., O'Connor, A.: Structured fac-
    tored inference for probabilistic programming. In: Storkey, A.J., Pérez-Cruz, F.
    (eds.) International Conference on Artificial Intelligence and Statistics, AISTATS
    2018, 9-11 April 2018, Playa Blanca, Lanzarote, Canary Islands, Spain. Pro-
    ceedings of Machine Learning Research, vol. 84, pp. 1224–1232. PMLR (2018),
    http://proceedings.mlr.press/v84/pfeffer18a.html
41. Sabry, A., Wadler, P.: A reflection on call-by-value. ACM Trans. Program. Lang.
    Syst. **19**(6), 916–941 (1997)
42. Simpson, A.K.: Reduction in a linear lambda-calculus with applications to opera-
    tional semantics. In: Giesl, J. (ed.) Term Rewriting and Applications, 16th Interna-
    tional Conference, RTA 2005, Nara, Japan, April 19-21, 2005, Proceedings. Lecture
    Notes in Computer Science, vol. 3467, pp. 219–234. Springer (2005). https://doi.
    org/10.1007/978-3-540-32033-3_17
43. Stein, D., Staton, S.: Compositional semantics for probabilistic programs with ex-
    act conditioning. 2021 36th Annual ACM/IEEE Symposium on Logic in Computer
    Science (LICS) pp. 1–13 (2021)
44. Zaiser, F., Murawski, A.S., Ong, C.L.: Exact bayesian inference on discrete models
    via probability generating functions: A probabilistic programming approach. In:
    Oh, A., Naumann, T., Globerson, A., Saenko, K., Hardt, M., Levine, S. (eds.)
    Advances in Neural Information Processing Systems 36: Annual Conference on
    Neural Information Processing Systems 2023, NeurIPS 2023, New Orleans, LA,
    USA, December 10 - 16, 2023 (2023), http://papers.nips.cc/paper_files/paper/
    2023/hash/0747af6f877c0cb555fea595f01b0e83-Abstract-Conference.html
45. Zhang, N., Poole, D.: A simple approach to bayesian network computations. In:
    Proceedings of the 10th Biennial Canadian Artificial Intelligence Conference. p.
    171–178. AAAI Press / The MIT Press (1994)
46. Zhou, Y., Yang, H., Teh, Y.W., Rainforth, T.: Divide, conquer, and combine: a new
    inference strategy for probabilistic programs with stochastic support. In: Proceed-
    ings of the 37th International Conference on Machine Learning, ICML 2020, 13-18
    July 2020, Virtual Event. Proceedings of Machine Learning Research, vol. 119, pp.
    11534–11545. PMLR (2020), http://proceedings.mlr.press/v119/zhou20e.html

A Program Logic for Concurrent Randomized Programs in the Oblivious Adversary Model

Weijie Fan[1], Hongjin Liang[1]✉, Xinyu Feng[1], and Hanru Jiang[2]

[1] State Key Laboratory for Novel Software Technology, Nanjing University,
Nanjing 210023, Jiangsu, China
weijiefan@smail.nju.edu.cn, {hongjin, xyfeng}@nju.edu.cn
[2] Beijing Institute of Mathematical Sciences and Applications,
Beijing 101408, Beijing, China
hanru@bimsa.cn

Abstract. Concurrent randomized programs in the oblivious adversary model are extremely difficult for modular verification because the interaction between threads is very sensitive to the program structure and the execution steps. We propose a new program logic supporting thread-local verification. With a novel "split" mechanism, one can split the state distribution into smaller partitions, and the reasoning can be done based on each partition independently, which allows us to avoid considering different execution paths of branch statements simultaneously. The logic rules are compositional and are natural extensions of their sequential counterparts. Using our program logic, we verify four typical algorithms in the oblivious adversary model.

1 Introduction

Randomization has become an important and powerful technique in the design of concurrent and distributed algorithms. By introducing probabilistic coin-flip operations, problems like consensus and leader election can be solved efficiently (e.g. [12,2,3]), despite being inherently difficult or even impossible to solve in a non-probabilistic concurrent setting.

To understand the semantics of concurrent randomized programs, one has to take into account the interplay between concurrency and randomization. In particular, one must answer the question: can the result of a coin-flip operation affect the choice of scheduling (i.e. which thread will perform the next operation)? For this, algorithm designers propose a spectrum of *adversary models* specifying the knowledge about the past execution that a scheduler (a.k.a. an adversary) can use for choosing the next thread. Different adversary models differs in the amount of knowledge they assume, varying from none to all.

At one end of the spectrum is the *oblivious adversary* (OA) model, where an adversary has no knowledge and must fix the entire schedule prior to the execution. The OA model is a natural abstraction of most real-world scheduling

Supplementary Information The online version contains supplementary material available at https://doi.org/10.1007/978-3-031-91118-7_13

V. Vafeiadis (Ed.): ESOP 2025, LNCS 15694, pp. 322–348, 2025.
https://doi.org/10.1007/978-3-031-91118-7_13

algorithms, including the round-robin scheduling and the priority-based scheduling. It reflects the scheduling in almost all real general infrastructures such as operating systems or programming languages (e.g. as in golang) where the scheduling does not rely on the specific behaviors of the threads being scheduled.

Designing algorithms for the OA model has gained lots of attention and more than ten algorithms have been proposed over the years (see [4,5] for a comprehensive introduction). As a concrete example, consider Chor et al. [12]'s *conciliator* algorithm. A conciliator is a weak consensus object that guarantees probabilistic agreement, namely that with a high probability the return values of all threads are equal. In Chor et al. [12]'s conciliator algorithm, each thread i executes C_i:

$$C_i \stackrel{\text{def}}{=} (\textbf{while } (s = 0) \textbf{ do } \langle s := i \rangle \oplus_p \langle \textbf{skip} \rangle) \, ; y_i := s$$

Here s is a shared variable initialized to 0, y_i is the local variable for thread i that records its return value. The probabilistic choice $\langle s := i \rangle \oplus_p \langle \textbf{skip} \rangle$ says that thread i writes i to s with probability p and does nothing ($\textbf{skip}$) with probability $1 - p$. It repeats until the thread observes $s \neq 0$, then it loads s to y_i. Given n threads running the conciliator code in the OA model, the algorithm ensures the postcondition $\textbf{Pr}(y_1 = y_2 = \cdots = y_n) \geq (1 - p)^{n-1}$, i.e., the probability for the threads to reach a consensus (thus $y_1 = y_2 = \cdots = y_n$) is no less than $(1 - p)^{n-1}$.

However, there has been little attention paid to verifying algorithms in the OA model. Existing program logics for verifying concurrent randomized programs [20,18,14] work with only the *strong adversary* (SA) model, which is at the other end of the spectrum of adversary models. A strong adversary has the full knowledge of the past execution, including outcomes of past coin-flips, thread-local states and shared states. Consequently, any algorithm which is correct under SA must still be correct under OA, but not vice versa. For instance, the aforementioned conciliator algorithm is *not* correct in SA and we will explain why in Sec. 6. None of the existing program logics can apply to the conciliator, or more generally, to any algorithms which are correct only with weaker adversaries such as OA.

On the one hand, it is unclear how to *take advantage of* the OA model in the verification. On the other hand, the OA model brings its own verification challenges. As we will see in Sec. 3, the program behaviors in the OA model seem sensitive to the number of execution steps in different program branches, but the verification with program logics should be modular, syntax-directed and insensitive to the number of execution steps.

The good news is, from the existing algorithms designed for the OA model, we observe that the correctness properties of these algorithms usually follow certain common patterns and can be specified by what we call "closed" assertions, which will be introduced in Sec. 3.2. To verify these properties, we do not need to prove they hold over the whole state distribution, which may contain states resulting from the execution of different program branches. Instead, we can prove there exists a partition of the distribution such that the property holds over every part. For *closed* assertions, the validity over every part implies the validity over the whole distribution.

Based on this observation, we propose the first program logic for concurrent randomized programs targeting the OA model. Our work makes the following new contributions:

- We take advantage of the OA model by proposing an abstract small-step operational semantics over state distributions, which allows us to apply classical concurrency reasoning techniques (such as invariants) by interpreting assertions over state distributions.
- We propose a novel proof technique called *split* to support modular reasoning and overcome the problem with branch statements. By splitting a state distribution into several smaller ones, we can reason about the different program branches independently. This leaves us only to prove the postcondition holds over a partition of the final state distribution. Then we can derive it for the whole distribution as long as the postcondition is closed.
- We design a set of logic rules for compositional reasoning about concurrent randomized programs with the split mechanism. Thanks to the split idea, our rules for sequential composition, **if**-statements and **while**-loops are simple and natural extensions of their classical (non-probabilistic) counterparts.
- We prove that our logic ensures partial correctness of concurrent randomized programs where the adversaries are also randomized. Since we focus on closed assertions as postconditions, the verification is independent of the distribution of schedules. The partial correctness verified by the logic holds over arbitrary probabilistic distributions of oblivious adversaries.
- Using our logic, we report the first formal verification of four typical algorithms in the OA model, including the aforementioned conciliator [12], group election (the core phase of Alistarh and Aspnes' randomized test-and-set algorithm [2]), a shared three-sided dice and a multiplayer level-up game.

Outline. Below we first review mathematical preliminaries in Sec. 2. Then we informally explain our key ideas in Sec. 3. We present the language setting including our abstract semantics in Sec. 4. We develop our program logic in Sec. 5, and verify conciliator as a case study in Sec. 6. We discuss related work in Sec. 7. The accompanying technical report (TR) [13] contains the full formal details, including semantics rules, logic rules and soundness proofs, and examples.

2   Preliminaries

Below we review the background on probability theory and sketch the basic mathematical notations used in our work for describing probabilities, expected values, etc. Readers who are not interested in mathematics can safely skip this section and come back later when the notations are used.

A *sub-distribution* over a set A is defined as a function $\mu: A \to [0, 1]$ such that

- the support $supp(\mu) \overset{\text{def}}{=} \{a \in A \mid \mu(a) > 0\}$ is countable; and
- the weight $|\mu| \overset{\text{def}}{=} \sum_{a \in A} \mu(a)$ is less than or equal to 1.

If we have $|\mu| = 1$, we say μ is a *distribution* over A. We use $\mathbb{SD}_A$ to denote the set of sub-distributions over A, and $\mathbb{D}_A$ to denote the set of distributions. For $\mu \in \mathbb{SD}_A$, intuitively $\mu(a)$ represents the *probability* of drawing a from μ.

We define the *probability of an event* $E : A \to \text{Prop}$ and the *expected value of a random variable* $V : A \to \mathbb{R}$ as follows, denoted by $\mathbf{Pr}_{a \sim \mu}[E(a)]$ and $\mathbb{E}_{a \sim \mu}[V(a)]$ respectively (where a is a bound variable, just like $\sum_{a \in A} f(a)$). Here Prop represents the set of propositions, and $\mathbb{R}$ is the set of real numbers.

$$\mathbf{Pr}_{a \sim \mu}[E(a)] \stackrel{\text{def}}{=} \sum_{a \in A} \{ \mu(a) \mid E(a) \} \qquad \mathbb{E}_{a \sim \mu}[V(a)] \stackrel{\text{def}}{=} \sum_{a \in A} \mu(a) \cdot V(a) \qquad (1)$$

For instance, suppose μ is a state distribution, and $\mathbf{q}$ is a state assertion (we write $\sigma \models \mathbf{q}$ if $\mathbf{q}$ holds at the state σ). Then $\mathbf{Pr}_{\sigma \sim \mu}[\sigma \models \mathbf{q}]$ represents the probability that $\mathbf{q}$ is satisfied. If $[\![e]\!]_\sigma$ is the evaluation of the expression e on σ, then $\mathbb{E}_{\sigma \sim \mu}[[\![e]\!]_\sigma]$ represents the expected value of e in μ.

For an event E with non-zero probability in μ (i.e. $\mathbf{Pr}_{a \sim \mu}[E(a)] > 0$), we define the *conditional sub-distribution* $\mu|_E$ as follows:

$$\mu|_E \stackrel{\text{def}}{=} \lambda a. \begin{cases} \frac{\mu(a)}{\mathbf{Pr}_{a \sim \mu}[E(a)]}, & \text{if } E(a) \text{ holds} \\ 0, & \text{otherwise} \end{cases} \qquad (2)$$

Given two sub-distributions $\mu_1, \mu_2 \in \mathbb{SD}_A$ and a probability $p \in [0, 1]$, we define the *mixture sub-distribution* $\mu_1 \oplus_p \mu_2 \in \mathbb{SD}_A$ as follows:

$$\mu_1 \oplus_p \mu_2 \stackrel{\text{def}}{=} \lambda a. \ p \cdot \mu_1(a) + (1 - p) \cdot \mu_2(a) \qquad (3)$$

Given two sub-distributions $\mu_1 \in \mathbb{SD}_A$ and $\mu_2 \in \mathbb{SD}_B$, we define the *product sub-distribution* $\mu_1 \otimes \mu_2 \in \mathbb{SD}_{A \times B}$ as follows:

$$\mu_1 \otimes \mu_2 \stackrel{\text{def}}{=} \lambda(a, b). \ \mu_1(a) \cdot \mu_2(b) \qquad (4)$$

In Sec. 4.2, we will use the product $\otimes$ to compute the initial distribution of program configurations, from the initial program $\mathbb{C}$ and an initial state distribution. When $\mathbb{C}$'s execution ends, we will extract the final state distribution from the final distribution of program configurations by projection. Specifically, given $\mu \in \mathbb{SD}_{A \times B}$, the *projection* of μ with the sets A and B is defined as:

$$\mu^{(A)} \stackrel{\text{def}}{=} \lambda a'. \mathbf{Pr}_{(a,b) \sim \mu}[a = a'] \qquad \mu^{(B)} \stackrel{\text{def}}{=} \lambda b'. \mathbf{Pr}_{(a,b) \sim \mu}[b = b'] \qquad (5)$$

For *almost surely terminating* programs (i.e. programs which have infinite executions with zero probability and terminate with probability 1), we define the "final" state distribution as the limit of an infinite sequence of state distributions. In general, we define the limit of a convergent sequence of sub-distributions in Def. 6.

Definition 6 (convergent sequence of sub-distributions). Let A be a set, $\overrightarrow{\mu}$ be an infinite sequence of sub-distributions over A. We say $\overrightarrow{\mu}$ *converges to a* sub-distribution μ, represented as $\lim \overrightarrow{\mu} = \mu$, if and only if $\lim_{n \to \infty} \sum_{a \in A} |\overrightarrow{\mu}[n](a) - \mu(a)| = 0$ (where $\overrightarrow{\mu}[n]$ means the n-th element of the sequence $\overrightarrow{\mu}$). We say $\overrightarrow{\mu}$ diverges and $\lim \overrightarrow{\mu}$ is undefined if $\overrightarrow{\mu}$ does not converge to any μ.

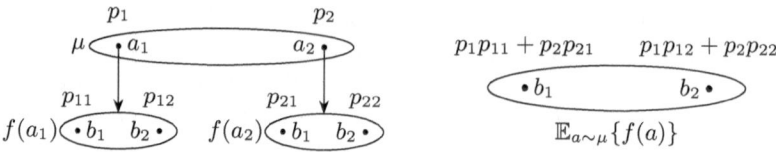

Fig. 1: Expected sub-distribution

Definition 7 (expected sub-distribution). Let $\mu \in \mathbb{SD}_A$ and $f : A \to \mathbb{SD}_B$. The *expected sub-distribution* $\mathbb{E}_{a \sim \mu}\{f(a)\} \in \mathbb{SD}_B$ is defined as

$$\mathbb{E}_{a \sim \mu}\{f(a)\} \stackrel{\text{def}}{=} \lambda b. \sum_{a \in A} \mu(a) \cdot f(a)(b)$$

Definition 7 computes the sub-distributions' expectation. As illustrated in Fig. 1, the function f transforms each element a_i in the support of μ to a sub-distribution $f(a_i)$, and then the expected sub-distribution (see the right side of the figure) is the mixture of all $f(a_i)$.

Also, from a sub-distributions' sub-distribution $\mu \in \mathbb{SD}_{\mathbb{SD}_A}$, we can compute the *flattened sub-distribution* $\overline{\mu} \in \mathbb{SD}_A$ as the mixture of all the sub-distributions in the support of μ:

$$\overline{\mu} \stackrel{\text{def}}{=} \lambda a. \sum_{\nu \in supp(\mu)} \mu(\nu) \cdot \nu(a) . \tag{8}$$

3   Informal Development

Below we start with reasoning about sequential randomized programs (Sec. 3.1). For concurrent randomized programs, we introduce the oblivious adversary (OA) model and define the correctness of programs with randomized schedules (Sec. 3.2). Then we show how to do thread-local reasoning by taking advantage of OA (Sec. 3.3). To address the challenges posed by branch statements (Sec. 3.4), we propose the split mechanism (Sec. 3.5).

3.1   Sequential Randomized Programs and Their Correctness

Randomized programs can be viewed as programs in a classical (non-probabilistic) programming language (e.g. WHILE) extended with probabilistic choice statements $\langle C_1 \rangle \oplus_p \langle C_2 \rangle$. It makes a random choice to execute $\langle C_1 \rangle$ or $\langle C_2 \rangle$, with probability p and $1 - p$, respectively. Here we use $\langle C \rangle$ to represent an *atomic* statement that executes C in one step (see the formal semantics in Sec. 4.1).

The execution of a *sequential* randomized program starting from a particular initial state forms a tree. For instance, Fig. 2a shows the execution tree for

$$Coins \stackrel{\text{def}}{=} \langle x := 0 \rangle \oplus_{\frac{1}{2}} \langle x := 1 \rangle; \ \langle y := 0 \rangle \oplus_{\frac{1}{2}} \langle y := 1 \rangle;$$

starting from the initial state where x and y are both 0. Each branching in the tree corresponds to a probabilistic choice. If we consider all possible initial states, the execution becomes a forest (where each node represents a program state σ), as shown in Fig. 2b.

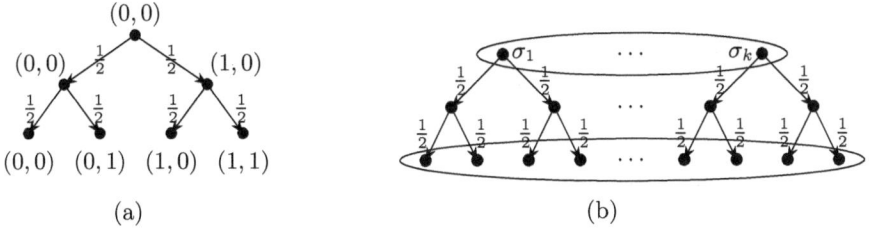

Fig. 2: Execution of a sequential program. In (a), a pair at a node specifies x and y's values in the state.

Correctness. Although the execution model based on the view of state transitions is similar to the model of classical sequential programs, the properties of randomized programs can be significantly different. For the program *Coins*, one may want to derive properties like "the probability that x equals y at the end of the program is 0.5". Unlike a postcondition in Hoare-style logics for classical sequential programs, which is expected to hold over *every* leaf node of the forest, the above property describes *the collection of all the leaf nodes* as a whole, i.e. the state distribution at the end of the program.

Therefore, in the Hoare-style specification $\{P\}C\{Q\}$ for randomized programs, P and Q are assertions over distributions of initial states and final states, respectively. For the example *Coins*, we can specify the aforementioned property as $\{\textbf{true}\}\,Coins\{\textbf{Pr}(x = y) = 0.5\}$ or $\{\textbf{true}\}\,Coins\{\lceil x = y\rceil \oplus_{0.5} \lceil x \neq y\rceil\}$. Here $\lceil \textbf{p}\rceil$ lifts the state assertion $\textbf{p}$ to an assertion over *state distributions* μ, requiring that $\textbf{p}$ holds at all states in $supp(\mu)$. The assertion $P \oplus_p Q$ holds at μ, if μ is a *mixture* of two distributions μ_0 and μ_1, which are associated with probabilities p and $1-p$, and satisfy P and Q respectively. We can give the following Hoare-logic rule to probabilistic choices:

$$\frac{\vdash_{\text{sq}} \{P\}C_1\{Q_1\} \qquad \vdash_{\text{sq}} \{P\}C_2\{Q_2\}}{\vdash_{\text{sq}} \{P\}\langle C_1\rangle \oplus_p \langle C_2\rangle\{Q_1 \oplus_p Q_2\}} \ (\text{SQ-PCH})$$

In this view, a program C transforms a state distribution μ satisfying P to another state distribution μ' satisfying Q (an alternative view is expectation-based, where P and Q are expectations [17,8]). The resulting logic rules (e.g. [6]) are almost the same as the classical (non-probabilistic) ones — we just need to lift the assertions from predicates over states to predicates over state distributions.

3.2   Concurrent Randomized Programs and the OA Model

A concurrent randomized program $C_1 \parallel \cdots \parallel C_n$ (denoted by $\mathbb{C}$) has two sources of nondeterminism: the probabilistic choices (in each thread C_i) and the scheduling. Its correctness usually assumes a certain class of scheduling, specified by an *adversary model*.

The *oblivious* adversary (OA) model considered in this paper requires that the scheduling must be determined prior to the execution, regardless of the outcomes of a thread's local coin-flip operations. For example, Fig. 3 shows all

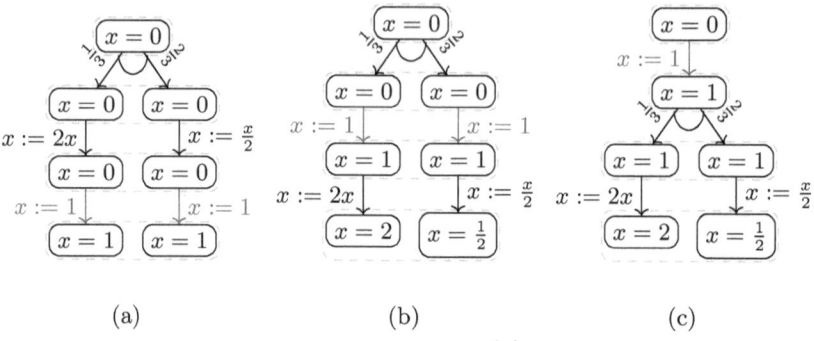

Fig. 3: Execution trees in OA model for $\mathbb{C}_x \overset{\text{def}}{=} ((\langle x := 2x \rangle \oplus_{\frac{1}{3}} \langle x := \frac{x}{2} \rangle \parallel x := 1)$

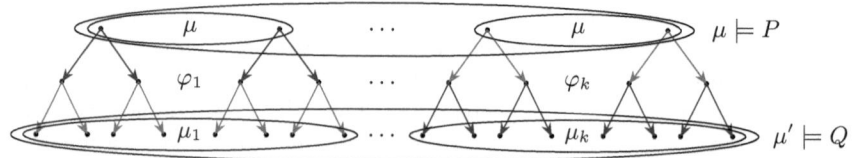

Fig. 4: Illustration of $\models \{P\}\mathbb{C}\{Q\}$

the possible executions in the OA model for a simple program $\mathbb{C}_x$ consisting of two threads: $\langle x := 2x \rangle \oplus_{\frac{1}{3}} \langle x := \frac{x}{2} \rangle \parallel x := 1$. In the concurrent setting, the probabilistic choice $\langle C_1 \rangle \oplus_p \langle C_2 \rangle$ is executed in *two steps*: it first flips a coin, getting heads with probability p and tails with probability $1 - p$, and then executes either the atomic statement $\langle C_1 \rangle$ for heads, or $\langle C_2 \rangle$ for tails.

Therefore, in OA, there are only three possible schedules for $\mathbb{C}_x$: $t_1\ t_1\ t_2$ (Fig. 3a); $t_1\ t_2\ t_1$ (Fig. 3b); and $t_2\ t_1\ t_1$ (Fig. 3c). In the figure, state transitions by different threads are in different colors (in black for t_1, and in red for t_2). We can see that, by fixing a specific OA schedule, the transitions at the same layer of an execution tree must be made by the *same* thread.

In contrast, the *strong* adversary (SA) model allows arbitrary scheduling. An SA scheduler has the full knowledge of machine states, especially including the outcomes of coin-flip operations, and can rely on that knowledge to schedule threads. For the example $\mathbb{C}_x$, in addition to the three schedules in Fig. 3, the SA model also allows two additional schedules, where t_1 and t_2 are scheduled in different orders for different outcomes of the coin flip. As such, the transitions at the same layer of an execution tree could be made by *different* threads.

This example also demonstrates that, thanks to the restriction of the scheduling, one can derive stronger properties of programs in the OA model that do not hold in the SA model. As shown in Fig. 3, in the OA model, the expected value of x at the end of execution is 1, which is not true considering the two more schedules in the SA model.

Correctness and closed assertions. What is the meaning of the Hoare triple $\{P\}\mathbb{C}\{Q\}$ now? Figure 4 shows the execution of a concurrent program, where μ

is the distribution of the initial states. We use $\mu \models P$ to denote that μ satisfies P, which will be formally defined in Sec. 5.1. The execution under each (OA) schedule φ_i corresponds to a forest, as in the case for sequential programs. Edges of different colors represent execution steps from different threads. The execution under all schedules forms *a set of forests*. It is obvious that P specifies μ, but what about Q?

Here we have two choices. We can either view the schedules as being *non-deterministic*, or as being *probabilistic*. For the former, we require that Q holds over every μ_i (the leaf node distribution of the forest generated with the schedule φ_i). However, this result is not strong enough — if we sample the execution of $\mathbb{C}$ and observe the final results, the sampled executions may not be generated with the same schedule, that is, the final states we observe may come from different μ_i. So it is more natural to take the latter (probabilistic) view of schedule and consider the mixture distribution μ' of $\mu_1, \ldots, \mu_k, \ldots$, where the weight of each μ_i is the probability of the schedule φ_i. Since we do not know the distribution of schedules in advance, Q needs to hold for all schedule distributions, that is, Q holds over μ' obtained by taking an *arbitrary* probability distribution for $\mu_1, \ldots, \mu_k, \ldots$.

We use $\models_{\text{ND}} \{P\}\mathbb{C}\{Q\}$ to represent the semantics of the Hoare triple under the *non-deterministic* view, and $\models_{\text{PR}} \{P\}\mathbb{C}\{Q\}$ for the *probabilistic* view. It is easy to prove the latter implies the former. The reverse does not hold in general, but it holds if Q is "closed". Here $\mathbf{closed}(Q)$ requires that the mixture of any (potentially countably infinite) number of distributions satisfies Q if each of these distributions satisfies Q. (We will formally define $\mathbf{closed}(Q)$ in Sec. 5.1.) As a result, for a closed postcondition, we can reduce the proof of $\models_{\text{PR}} \{P\}\mathbb{C}\{Q\}$ to the proof of $\models_{\text{ND}} \{P\}\mathbb{C}\{Q\}$.

As far as we know, most concurrent randomized algorithms have closed postconditions. As examples of closed assertions, $\lceil b \rceil$, $\mathbf{Pr}(b) = 0.5$ and $\mathbb{E}(x) = 1 \wedge \lceil x \geq 0 \rceil$ are all closed. So, for the earlier example $\mathbb{C}_x$, it suffices to prove that the leaf distribution of each execution tree in Fig. 3 satisfies $\mathbb{E}(x) = 1 \wedge \lceil x \geq 0 \rceil$.

We give the formal definition of $\models_{\text{ND}} \{P\}\mathbb{C}\{Q\}$ in Sec. 4.1. We show the formal definition of $\models_{\text{PR}} \{P\}\mathbb{C}\{Q\}$ and prove that they are equivalent when Q is closed in the TR [13]. In this paper we focus on closed Q's only and omit the subscript ND/PR henceforth. Note that $\mathbf{closed}(Q)$ is *not* an overly strong requirement for practical programs, because it is needed only for the postcondition Q of the *whole program* $\mathbb{C}$. The postconditions for individual statements and threads do not need to be closed.

3.3   Thread-Local Reasoning in OA

The question is, *how to take advantage of the OA model and verify the stronger correctness guarantee of a program by thread-local reasoning, i.e., verifying one thread at a time.*

A natural thought is to extend the sequential reasoning in Sec. 3.1 to concurrency. To this end, we hope to view the execution of a concurrent program as transitions over state distributions, as we do for sequential reasoning. However,

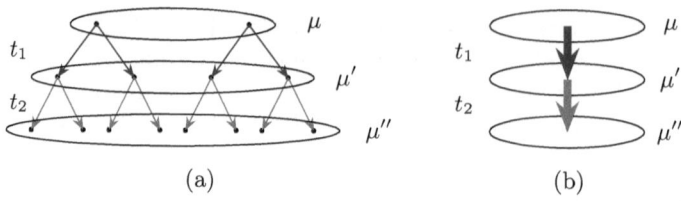

t_1
μ
t_2
μ'
μ''

(a)

t_1
μ
t_2
μ'
μ''

(b)

Fig. 5: Concrete *vs.* Abstract Operational Semantics in OA

unlike sequential semantics that are usually *big-step* (see e.g. [6,19]) and care about only the initial and final state distributions, the transitions in a concurrent setting need to be small-step, to reflect the interleaving between threads.

One might also consider to migrate the existing approaches for the SA model to the OA setting. However, the interleaving pattern between threads in the OA model is very different from that in the SA model. The SA model allows that different threads may be scheduled for different outcomes of a probabilistic choice operation, while the OA model does not allow it. As a result, program logics for SA (e.g. [18,14]) adopt *weak* assumptions on the environment behaviors in the thread view: for different states in the support of the current state distribution, different environment threads may interrupt and take very different steps. Therefore, they model the environment behaviors as transitions from states to state distributions (e.g. [18]) or transitions from states to states (e.g. [14]).

However, this idea may not be as useful in the OA setting as in the SA setting (thought it is still sound). Algorithms in the OA model usually rely on the assumption that the scheduling cannot depend on the results of probabilistic choices, so the weak assumption that different states may be interrupted by different environment threads is too weak in the OA setting, and it is not obvious how to forbid the impossible interleavings in the OA model if we still model the environment behaviors as transitions from states to state distributions or transitions from states to states.

To address this problem, we exploit the stronger assumption on the environment behaviors: for different states in the support of the current distribution, it must be the same environment thread that interrupts and take steps. Therefore, we propose an abstract operational semantics and layer-based reasoning.

Abstract operational semantics. In the OA model, we observe that, for all the states at the same layer of the execution forest (i.e. nodes of the same depths, as shown in Fig. 5a), it is always the same thread picked to execute the next step, since the schedule is predetermined. That is, the edges with the same depth are always of the same color, representing steps from the same thread. Naturally, we can view the states of the same layer as a whole, forming a state distribution. If we also view the edges between two layers as a whole, then Fig. 5a is abstracted to Fig. 5b. This gives us an *abstract operational semantics* with small-step transitions over state distributions. The execution looks like an interleaving execution of a classical (non-probabilistic) concurrent program.

Consequently, we can apply classical concurrency reasoning techniques (e.g. invariants) to reason about executions in our abstract semantics. Our abstraction is sound in that the Hoare-triple $\{P\}\mathbb{C}\{Q\}$ valid in our abstract semantics also holds with the concrete semantics.

Invariants. To do thread-local reasoning, one needs to specify the interference between the current thread and its environment (i.e. the other threads), which can be modeled by an invariant I. For classical concurrent programs, I is a state assertion that needs to hold at all times. The current thread can assume that I holds before each of its steps, but it must also ensure that I still holds after each step. For a randomized program, we define I over state distributions. It holds at all the μ's in executions in our abstract semantics (e.g. μ, μ' and μ'' in Fig. 5b). Since every such μ corresponds to a layer in the concrete semantics, we call I a *layer invariant* and the reasoning layer-based.

In addition to layer invariants I, our logic also uses *non-probabilistic rely-guarantee conditions* (R and G), to simplify the formulation of I in proofs of programs. By "non-probabilistic", we mean that R and G specify state transitions in the concrete semantics (but do not specify the probability of the transitions). Their treatment is the same as in classical rely-guarantee reasoning [15].

Unfortunately, we need to address one more challenge to make this nice abstraction work. To define the abstract operational semantics, we view all the edges (program steps) at the same layer in Fig. 5a as a whole to get Fig. 5b. However, although these edges are from the same thread, they may still correspond to the execution of *different code*, due to the branch statements in the thread. Below we explain the challenges and our solution in detail.

3.4   Problems with Branch Statements

A program may contain branch statements such as **if**-statements and **while**-loops, which condition on random variables (i.e. variables whose values are probabilistic). Different branches may take different numbers of steps to execute, making it difficult to do layer-based reasoning.

For instance, we consider the program $C \parallel c_4$, where:

$$C \overset{\text{def}}{=} (\textbf{if } (x = 0) \textbf{ then } (c_{11}; c_{12}) \textbf{ else } c_{21}); c_3;$$

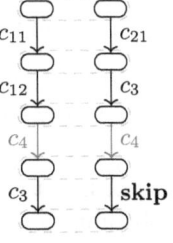

Here each $c_\square$ stands for an atomic command. Assume the initial values of x are assigned in a probabilistic choice, which is either 0 or 1. Figure 6 shows a possible execution, where we need to consider the two possibilities corresponding to the two initial values of x. Note that we allow the right branch to execute **skip** when it reaches the end while the left branch executes c_3.

Fig. 6

Thread t_1 switches to t_2 after executing two steps (we omit the step evaluating the boolean condition). The layer-based reasoning asks us to find some invariant and prove that it holds over the distribution of every layer (i.e. every green dashed box). This forces us to consider the simultaneous execution of c_{11} in the **then**-branch and c_{21} in the **else**-branch. Even worse, since the two branches have different lengths, we have to consider the simultaneous execution of c_{12} and c_3. This looks particularly unreasonable if we consider the fact that c_3 actually sequentially follows c_{12} in the program structure! This makes it almost impossible to design structural and compositional Hoare-style logic rules. The problem is exacerbated by **while**-loops, where the number of rounds of loops may rely on random variables.

Note that this problem does not show up in the deterministic setting where there is no randomization and we prove properties of individual states. In the execution of **if**-statements, a state either enters the **then**-branch or enters the **else**-branch, but not both. So we only need to verify the two cases respectively.

We also do not have to worry about the problem with branch statements in the sequential probabilistic setting. Since there is no interleaving, we can reason about probabilistic properties in a "big-step" flavor where we only consider the initial state distribution and the final one. To reason about the branch statement, we can reason about the different branches (on the corresponding sub-distributions) separately and then do a mixture at the join point, as shown by the (COND) rule in Barthe et al. [6]'s sequential logic:

$$\frac{\{P_1 \wedge \lceil b \rceil\}C_1\{Q_1\} \qquad \{P_2 \wedge \lceil \neg b \rceil\}C_2\{Q_2\}}{\{(P_1 \wedge \lceil b \rceil) \oplus (P_2 \wedge \lceil \neg b \rceil)\}\textbf{if } (b) \textbf{ then } C_1 \textbf{ else } C_2\{Q_1 \oplus Q_2\}} \text{ (COND)}$$

The (COND) rule in [6] is sound for sequential programs, but not for the concurrent OA setting. If C_1 and C_2 have different numbers of steps, then $Q_1 \oplus Q_2$ specifies a state distribution where states are not at the same "layer", which will make it difficult to reason about subsequent statements.

Below we use an interesting example to further demonstrate the problem and then introduce our solution.

Example: a shared three-sided dice. To see the problem with branch statements more concretely, we consider a simple program $\mathbb{C}_{Dice}$ of n threads, where the code of each thread is *Dice*:

$$Dice \stackrel{\text{def}}{=} \textbf{while } (x = 0) \textbf{ do } Roll, \quad \text{where } Roll \stackrel{\text{def}}{=} (x \stackrel{\$}{:=} \{1 : \tfrac{1}{2} \mid 2x : \tfrac{1}{6} \mid \tfrac{x}{2} : \tfrac{1}{3}\})$$

Here x is a shared variable initialized to 0. The loop body *Roll* is a random assignment, which is short for the atomic probabilistic choice $\langle\langle x := 1 \rangle \oplus_{\frac{1}{2}} (\langle x := 2x \rangle \oplus_{\frac{1}{3}} \langle x := \frac{x}{2} \rangle)\rangle$. That is, the thread atomically rolls a 3-sided dice and updates x according to the outcome: it sets x to 1 with probability $\frac{1}{2}$, doubles x with probability $\frac{1}{6}$ and halves x with probability $\frac{1}{3}$.

We want to verify that $\mathbb{C}_{Dice}$ satisfies the postcondition $\mathbb{E}(x) = 1$. As we explained, to do thread-local reasoning, we first find out the invariant I_{Dice} to model the interference:

$$I_{Dice} \stackrel{\text{def}}{=} I_0 \oplus I_1, \quad \text{where } I_0 \stackrel{\text{def}}{=} \lceil x = 0 \rceil \text{ and } I_1 \stackrel{\text{def}}{=} (\lceil x \neq 0 \rceil \wedge \mathbb{E}(x) = 1)$$

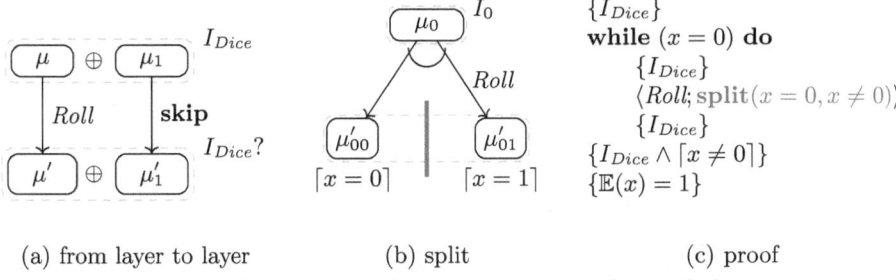

(a) from layer to layer   (b) split   (c) proof

Fig. 7: Executions of *Dice* and Its Proof with Split

It says, every whole state distribution μ (at every layer of an execution forest) is a mixture $\mu_0 \oplus \mu_1$ (formed by taking μ_0 with arbitrary probability and taking μ_1 with the remaining probability) in which μ_0 and μ_1 satisfy I_0 and I_1 respectively.

To check I_{Dice} is indeed an invariant, one may consider showing that I_{Dice} is preserved by *Roll*. However, even if I_{Dice} is preserved by *Roll* (which is indeed true), it is still unclear whether I_{Dice} is preserved layer by layer. Specifically, after executing *Roll*, we will reach a state distribution whose support contains both the states satisfying $x = 0$ and those satisfying $x \neq 0$. From the former, the thread will enter the next round of the loop; but from the latter, the thread will exit the loop and execute the code after the loop (or **skip** if there is no subsequent code). Consequently, *Roll* may be executed "at the same time" with **skip**, as shown in Fig. 7a. What we need to prove is that I_{Dice} is preserved by a *mixture* of executing *Roll* and **skip** at the same layer.

However, it is difficult to design logic rules to compose the proofs of *Roll* and **skip** for their mixture, because *Roll* as the loop body is actually syntactically sequenced before **skip**, the code after the loop. We face a similar problem as the problem with the **if**-statement, as explained above.

3.5   Our Key Idea: Split

Instead of trying to reason about the mixture of the behaviors of different statements at the whole layer, we *split* the state distribution of the layer, and reason about the different statements separately. In detail, we introduce an auxiliary command $\text{split}(b_1, \ldots, b_k)$. It divides the current state distribution μ into k disjoint parts $\mu_1, \ldots, \mu_k$, such that each smaller distribution μ_i satisfies $\lceil b_i \rceil$ and μ is their mixture $\mu_1 \oplus \ldots \oplus \mu_k$. In our abstract operational semantics the thread *non-deterministically* picks a μ_i and continues its execution. One can instrument the code being verified with proper **split** commands so that each μ_i corresponds to a distinct branch in the control flow. Note that the **split** commands only affects the abstract semantics. In the concrete semantics, **split** has no effect and can be viewed as a no-op.

With split, the invariant I no longer needs to specify the whole layer μ, but instead it specifies only the smaller distributions μ_i generated by split. This I must be preserved by the execution at every μ_i. For instance, if we instrument

split$(b, \neg b)$ before **if** (b) **then** C_1 **else** C_2, then it suffices to prove that I is preserved by the executions of C_1 and C_2 at distributions satisfying $\lceil b \rceil$ and $\lceil \neg b \rceil$ respectively.

Split is physical and irreversible. We do not provide any command to mix back the smaller distributions that result from split. Instead of directly verifying $\vdash_A \{P\}\mathbb{C}\{Q\}$, where $\mathbb{C}$ contains no **split** commands and thus Q holds at the whole leaf layer, we verify $\vdash_A \{P\}\mathbb{C}'\{Q\}$ for $\mathbb{C}'$ that results from instrumenting $\mathbb{C}$ with auxiliary **split** commands. Therefore Q needs to hold at every smaller distribution at the leaf layer. That said, we do provide the following logic rule to convert $\vdash_A \{P\}\mathbb{C}'\{Q\}$ back to $\vdash_A \{P\}\mathbb{C}\{Q\}$:

$$\frac{\vdash_A \{P\}\mathbb{C}'\{Q\} \quad \mathbf{closed}(Q)}{\vdash_A \{P\}\mathbf{RemoveSplit}(\mathbb{C}')\{Q\}} \quad (\text{REMOVESPLIT})$$

Here **RemoveSplit**$(\mathbb{C}')$ removes all the **split** commands from $\mathbb{C}'$, and **closed**(Q) (introduced at the end of Sec. 3.2) allows us to re-establish Q at the mixture of smaller distributions that all satisfy Q. The subscript "A" in the judgement indicates that the reasoning is based on the *abstract* semantics.

Proof for the shared three-sided dice. To verify *Dice*, we split the state distributions so that the states at which the thread enters the next round of the loop and those at which the thread exits the loop are always separate. As such, the invariant I_{Dice} is revised to be a *disjunction*:

$$I_{Dice} \stackrel{\text{def}}{=} I_0 \vee I_1, \quad \text{where } I_0 \stackrel{\text{def}}{=} \lceil x = 0 \rceil \text{ and } I_1 \stackrel{\text{def}}{=} (\lceil x \neq 0 \rceil \wedge \mathbb{E}(x) = 1)$$

In contrast to the earlier $I_0 \oplus I_1$ which holds at a mixture, this new I_{Dice} holds at a state distribution μ satisfying *either* I_0 or I_1. If μ satisfies I_0, the thread enters the next round of the loop; otherwise it exits the loop.

We instrument the loop body with the **split** command, as shown in red color in Fig. 7c. This **split** command ensures that the new I_{Dice} is indeed an invariant. As the blue assertions indicate, if I_{Dice} holds before the loop body, which means either I_0 or I_1 holds, then I_{Dice} still holds after atomically executing *Roll* and **split**. In particular, as shown in Fig. 7b, if I_0 holds before the loop body, executing *Roll* gives us a state distribution satisfying $\lceil x = 0 \rceil \oplus \lceil x = 1 \rceil$, and then executing **split**$(x = 0, x \neq 0)$ (see the red vertical bar) results in two separate state distributions μ'_{00} satisfying $\lceil x = 0 \rceil$ and μ'_{01} satisfying $\lceil x = 1 \rceil$. Both μ'_{00} and μ'_{01} satisfy I_{Dice}. The full proof is given in the TR [13].

Logic rules for split and branch statements. Below we introduce our logic rules for **split**, if-statements and **while**-loops to show how the split mechanism works.

$$\frac{G \vdash_{sq} \{I \wedge P\}C\{(I \wedge Q \wedge \lceil b_1 \rceil) \oplus \cdots \oplus (I \wedge Q \wedge \lceil b_k \rceil)\} \quad \cdots}{R, G, I \vdash \{P\}\langle C \rangle \, \mathbf{split}(b_1, \ldots, b_k)\{(Q \wedge \lceil b_1 \rceil) \vee \ldots \vee (Q \wedge \lceil b_k \rceil)\}} \quad (\text{ATOM-SPLIT})$$

As in the *Dice* example, **split** is usually inserted after and executed atomically with some code $\langle C \rangle$. As such, we provide the command $\langle C \rangle \, \mathbf{split}(b_1, \ldots, b_k)$, which has the same meaning as $\langle C; \mathbf{split}(b_1, \ldots, b_k)\rangle$. The (ATOM-SPLIT) rule requires us to prove the $\vdash_{\mathsf{sq}}$ judgement, which reasons about C as sequential code, and ensures that the state distribution at the end is a mixture of smaller distributions satisfying $\lceil b_1 \rceil, \ldots, \lceil b_n \rceil$ respectively. Since **split** turns the big distribution into these smaller ones as separate parts, the postcondition of the conclusion is a disjunctive assertion. We can see that split essentially turns $\oplus$ into $\vee$. The disjunction can be the precondition of the subsequent **if** and **while** statements as required by the (COND) and (WHILE) rules below. Here we omit the side conditions which says that the pre/post-conditions are stable with respect to R and I. The definition of rely/guarantee conditions and stability will be explained in Sec. 5.1 and the complete rule will be presented in Sec. 5.2.

$$\frac{P_1 \Rightarrow \lceil b \rceil \quad P_2 \Rightarrow \lceil \neg b \rceil \quad R, G, I \vdash \{P_1\}C_1\{Q\} \quad R, G, I \vdash \{P_2\}C_2\{Q\} \quad \cdots}{R, G, I \vdash \{P_1 \vee P_2\}\mathbf{if}\ (b)\ \mathbf{then}\ C_1\ \mathbf{else}\ C_2\{Q\}} \quad \text{(COND)}$$

$$\frac{P_1 \Rightarrow \lceil b \rceil \quad P_2 \Rightarrow \lceil \neg b \rceil \wedge Q \quad R, G, I \vdash \{P_1\}C\{P_1 \vee P_2\} \quad \cdots}{R, G, I \vdash \{P_1 \vee P_2\}\mathbf{while}\ (b)\ \mathbf{do}\ C\{Q\}} \quad \text{(WHILE)}$$

Our (COND) rule assumes that, before the **if**-statement, the state distributions have already been split into smaller distributions for executing the **then**- and **else**-branches separately. Therefore, the precondition is supposed to be the disjunction $P_1 \vee P_2$, where $P_1 \Rightarrow \lceil b \rceil$ and $P_2 \Rightarrow \lceil \neg b \rceil$. Recall that $\lceil b \rceil$ says b holds with probability 1, i.e., all the states in the support of the distribution satisfy b. So, $\lceil b \rceil \vee \lceil \neg b \rceil$ is not implied by $\lceil b \vee \neg b \rceil$. The latter holds always, but for the former to hold, we must do split first. Then the branches can be verified independently, as we do in classical Hoare logic.

Similarly, in the (WHILE) rule, the loop invariant is the disjunction $P_1 \vee P_2$. Resulting from a split, the part satisfying P_1 ensures that the loop always continues with its next round since $P_1 \Rightarrow \lceil b \rceil$, while the part satisfying P_2 terminates the loop as $P_2 \Rightarrow \lceil \neg b \rceil$. If the value of b is probabilistic and can be modified by the code before the loop and by the loop body C, one need to insert **split** before the loop *and* inside the loop body C, so that $P_1 \vee P_2$ holds before every round of the loop.

4   The Programming Language

The syntax of the language is defined in Fig. 8. The whole program $\mathbb{C}$ consists of n sequential threads. The statements C of each thread are mostly standard. The *atomic statements* $\langle C \rangle$ and *the probabilistic choices* $\langle C_1 \rangle \oplus_p \langle C_2 \rangle$ are explained in Sec. 3. For verification purposes, we also append the atomic statements with split statements to get $(\langle C \rangle\ sp)$ where sp is in the form of $\mathbf{split}(b_1, \ldots, b_k)$.

Below we give two operational semantics to the language. The concrete one follows the standard interleaving semantics and models program steps as *probabilistic* transitions over program states. *The split statements are ignored in this semantics.* That is, they are viewed as annotations for verification only and have no operational effects.

$$(Nat)\ n, k\ \in \mathbb{N} \qquad\qquad (Real)\ p, r\ \in\ \mathbb{R} \qquad\qquad (PVar)\ x\ \in\ String$$

$$(Expr)\ e\ ::= n \mid x \mid e_1 + e_2 \mid e_1 - e_2 \mid e_1 * e_2 \mid \ldots$$

$$(Bexp)\ b\ ::= \mathbf{true} \mid \mathbf{false} \mid e_1 < e_2 \mid e_1 = e_2 \mid e_1 \le e_2 \mid \neg b \mid b_1 \wedge b_2 \mid b_1 \vee b_2 \mid \ldots$$

$$(SplitInstr)\ sp\ ::= \mathbf{split}(b_1, \ldots, b_k)$$

$$(Stmt)\ C\ ::= \mathbf{skip} \mid x := e \mid C_1; C_2 \mid \mathbf{if}\ (b)\ \mathbf{then}\ C_1\ \mathbf{else}\ C_2 \mid \mathbf{while}\ (b)\ \mathbf{do}\ C$$
$$\mid \langle C \rangle \mid \langle C \rangle\ sp \mid \langle C_1 \rangle \oplus_p \langle C_2 \rangle$$

$$(Prog)\ \mathbb{C}\ ::= C_1 \parallel \cdots \parallel C_n$$

Fig. 8: The Programming Language

Thread IDs, schedules, states and states distributions:

$$(ThreadId)\ t \in \mathbb{N}_+ \qquad\qquad (Schedule)\ \varphi ::= t :: \varphi \qquad (\text{coinductive})$$
$$(State)\ \sigma \in PVar \to \mathbb{R} \qquad (DState)\ \mu\ \in\ \mathbb{D}_{State}$$

Global transitions: $(\mathbb{C}, \sigma) \xrightarrow[t]{p} (\mathbb{C}', \sigma')$

$$\frac{(C_t, \sigma) \xrightarrow{p} (C_t', \sigma')}{(C_1 \parallel \cdots \parallel C_t \parallel \cdots \parallel C_n, \sigma) \xrightarrow[t]{p} (C_1 \parallel \cdots \parallel C_t' \cdots \parallel C_n, \sigma')}$$

Thread-local transitions: $(C, \sigma) \xrightarrow{p} (C', \sigma')$

$$\frac{[\![e]\!]_\sigma = n}{(x := e, \sigma) \xrightarrow{1} (\mathbf{skip}, \sigma\{x \rightsquigarrow n\})} \qquad (\mathbf{skip}, \sigma) \xrightarrow{1} (\mathbf{skip}, \sigma)$$

$$\frac{C_1 \neq \mathbf{skip} \quad (C_1, \sigma) \xrightarrow{p} (C_1', \sigma')}{(C_1; C_2, \sigma) \xrightarrow{p} (C_1'; C_2, \sigma')} \qquad \frac{}{(\mathbf{skip}; C_2, \sigma) \xrightarrow{1} (C_2, \sigma)}$$

$$\frac{}{(\langle C_1 \rangle \oplus_p \langle C_2 \rangle, \sigma) \xrightarrow{p} (\langle C_1 \rangle, \sigma)} \qquad \frac{}{(\langle C_1 \rangle \oplus_p \langle C_2 \rangle, \sigma) \xrightarrow{1-p} (\langle C_2 \rangle, \sigma)}$$

$$\frac{\exists k. \forall n \ge k.\ (C, \sigma) \xrightarrow{p}^n (\mathbf{skip}, \sigma')}{(\langle C \rangle, \sigma) \xrightarrow{p} (\mathbf{skip}, \sigma')} \qquad \frac{(\langle C \rangle, \sigma) \xrightarrow{p} (\mathbf{skip}, \sigma')}{(\langle C \rangle\ \mathbf{split}(b_1, \ldots, b_k), \sigma) \xrightarrow{p} (\mathbf{skip}, \sigma')}$$

Fig. 9: Concrete Operational Semantics

The abstract semantics models program steps as transitions over distributions of program configurations. We also assign operational semantics to **split** statements. We prove that Hoare-triples valid in the abstract semantics are also valid in the concrete semantics (Thm 1 below).

4.1   Concrete Operational Semantics

We show selected semantics rules in Fig. 9 and give the full set of rules in the TR [13]. The single-step transition of the whole program is defined through the thread-local transitions. Each step is decorated with a p, the probability that the step may occur. For most thread-local transitions except the probabilistic choices and atomic statements, p is simply 1. Note that we allow the **skip** command at the end of execution to stutter with probability 1, but it cannot stutter if it is sequenced before some C. That is, "**skip**; C" can only step to C. $\langle C_1 \rangle \oplus_p \langle C_2 \rangle$

chooses to execute the left or right branches, with probability p and $1 - p$, respectively. The atomic statement $\langle C \rangle$ is always done in one step, no matter how complicated C is. We assume C in the atomic statement never contains **while**-loops, so it always terminates in a bounded number of steps. Note that the need of atomicity of the branches in $\langle C_1 \rangle \oplus_p \langle C_2 \rangle$ is not overly idealistic, because we mainly use $\langle C_1 \rangle \oplus_p \langle C_2 \rangle$ to encode a random assignment, thus C_1 and C_2 themselves may correspond to single instructions at the machine level anyway (in this case, the atomic wrappers $\langle \cdot \rangle$ are unnecessary). In the proofs of algorithms, we may insert auxiliary statements (a.k.a. ghost code) to be executed with the probabilistic choice together in one step. This is actually the only case when C_1 or C_2 is non-atomic and needs to be wrapped by $\langle \cdot \rangle$. The more general form of $C_1 \oplus_p C_2$ can be encoded as $\langle x := \text{true} \rangle \oplus_p \langle x := \text{false} \rangle; \textbf{if } (x) \textbf{ then } C_1 \textbf{ else } C_2$.

Before giving semantics to $\langle C \rangle$, we first introduce the n-step thread-local transition, represented as $(C, \sigma) \xrightarrow{p}^n (C', \sigma')$. Informally, if there is only one n-step execution path from (C, σ) to (C', σ'), the probability p in $(C, \sigma) \xrightarrow{p}^n (C', \sigma')$ is the product of the probability of every step on the path. If there are more than one execution paths, we need to sum up the probabilities of all the paths. We present the formal definition of the n-step thread-local transition and an illustrative example in the TR [13].

Then the operational semantics rule for $\langle C \rangle$ says it finishes the execution of C in one step (that is, the execution of C cannot be interrupted by other threads). Note that $\langle C \rangle$ may lead to different states with different probabilities, since C may contain probabilistic choices.

The multi-step transition $((\mathbb{C}, \sigma) \xrightarrow[\varphi]{p}^n (\mathbb{C}'', \sigma''))$ of the whole program $\mathbb{C}$ under the schedule φ is similar to the multi-step thread-local transitions. The schedule φ is an infinite sequence of thread IDs. It decides which thread t is to be executed next. The accumulated probability of an n-step transition is the *sum* of the probability of every possible execution path.

Below we define $[\![\mathbb{C}]\!]_\varphi$ as a function that maps an *initial state* σ to a sub-distribution of *final states*. We also lift the function to the distribution μ of the initial states.

$$[\![\mathbb{C}]\!]_\varphi(\sigma) \overset{\text{def}}{=} \lambda\sigma'. \lim \vec{p}_{\sigma'}, \quad \text{where } \forall n.\, (\mathbb{C}, \sigma) \xrightarrow[\varphi]{\vec{p}_{\sigma'}[n]}^n (\textbf{skip} \parallel \cdots \parallel \textbf{skip}, \sigma')$$

$$[\![\mathbb{C}]\!]_\varphi(\mu) \overset{\text{def}}{=} \mathbb{E}_{\sigma \sim \mu}\{[\![\mathbb{C}]\!]_\varphi(\sigma)\} \quad \text{(see Def. 7 for the expected sub-distribution)}$$

Here $\vec{p}_{\sigma'}$ is an infinite sequence of probabilities and $\vec{p}_{\sigma'}[n]$ is the n-th element of the sequence. Note $\lim \vec{p}_{\sigma'}$ always exists as we can prove $\vec{p}_{\sigma'}$ always converges.

Then we can give a simple definition of the partial correctness of $\mathbb{C}$ with respect to the precondition P and the postcondition Q, which are assertions over state distributions and are defined in Sec. 5.1.

Definition 9. $\models \{P\}\mathbb{C}\{Q\}$ iff, for all μ and φ, if $\mu \models P$, and $|[\![\mathbb{C}]\!]_\varphi(\mu)| = 1$, then $[\![\mathbb{C}]\!]_\varphi(\mu) \models Q$.

The premise $|[\![\mathbb{C}]\!]_\varphi(\mu)| = 1$ requires the execution of $\mathbb{C}$ (with the schedule φ and the initial state distribution μ) *terminates with probability 1*.

$$W \quad \in \mathbb{D}_{Prog \times State} \qquad W|_b \overset{\text{def}}{=} W|_{\lambda(\mathbb{C},\sigma).\sigma \models b}$$

$$\delta(\mathbb{C}) \overset{\text{def}}{=} \lambda \mathbb{C}_1. \begin{cases} 1, & \text{if } \mathbb{C}_1 = \mathbb{C} \\ 0, & \text{otherwise} \end{cases}$$

$$init(\mathbb{C}, \mu) \overset{\text{def}}{=} \delta(\mathbb{C}) \otimes \mu \qquad (\text{see Eqn. (4) for the definition of } \otimes)$$

$$nextsplit(C) \overset{\text{def}}{=} \begin{cases} \mathbf{split}(b_1, \dots, b_k), & \text{if } C = \langle C_1 \rangle \ \mathbf{split}(b_1, \dots, b_k) \\ nextsplit(C_1), & \text{if } C = C_1; C_2 \\ \mathbf{split}(\text{true}), & \text{otherwise} \end{cases}$$

$$nextsplit(W, t) \overset{\text{def}}{=} \{ nextsplit(C_t) \mid (C_1 \| \cdots \| C_n, \sigma) \in supp(W) \}$$

$$W \overset{t}{\leadsto} W' \quad \text{iff } W' = \lambda(\mathbb{C}', \sigma'). \sum_{\mathbb{C},\sigma} \{ p \cdot W(\mathbb{C}, \sigma) \mid (\mathbb{C}, \sigma) \overset{p}{\underset{t}{\to}} (\mathbb{C}', \sigma') \}$$

$$\dfrac{W \overset{t}{\leadsto} W' \quad nextsplit(W, t) = \{ \mathbf{split}(b_1, \dots, b_k) \} \quad W'|_{b_i} = W''}{W \overset{t}{\hookrightarrow} W''}$$

$$\dfrac{W \overset{t}{\leadsto} W' \quad \#nextsplit(W, t) > 1}{W \overset{t}{\hookrightarrow} W'}$$

Fig. 10: Abstract Operational Semantics

4.2   Abstract Operational Semantics

The abstract semantics, shown in Fig. 10, models each step as a transition between distributions W of the whole program configurations $(\mathbb{C}, \sigma)$. Also we give semantics to **split** statements.

Below we use $nextsplit(W, t)$ to represent the set consisting of the next **split** statements to be executed in the thread t of the program configurations in $supp(W)$. The next **split** statement of the thread t is sp if the next statement to be executed is in the form of $\langle C \rangle \ sp$, otherwise the next split is defined as **split**(true). Throughout this paper, we assume all the splits $\mathbf{split}(b_1, \dots, b_k)$ satisfy the following validity check, which says for any state there is always one and only one b_i that holds.

Definition 10. A split statement is valid, i.e., **validsplit**$(\mathbf{split}(b_1, \dots, b_k))$ holds, if and only if for any state σ, $\forall i, j. \ i \neq j \implies \sigma \models \neg(b_i \wedge b_j)$ and $\sigma \models b_1 \vee \dots \vee b_k$.

The transition $W \overset{t}{\hookrightarrow} W''$ is done in two steps. First we make the transition $W \overset{t}{\leadsto} W'$ based on the concrete semantics, without considering splits. Then the splits in $nextsplit(W, t)$ are executed. We expect $nextsplit(W, t)$ to be a singleton set, i.e., threads t in different program configurations in $supp(W)$ all have the same subsequent **split** statement. We non-deterministically pick a b_i from $b_1 \dots b_k$, and let W'' be the filtered distribution $W'|_{b_i}$ (see Fig. 10 and Eqn. (2) for the definition of $W|_b$). If the **split** statement is **split**(true), we know W'' is the same as W'. If $nextsplit(W, t)$ contains more than one **split** statements, then we view the program as inappropriately instrumented. In this case we ignore all the split statements in $nextsplit(W, t)$ and let W'' be W'.

Figure 11 illustrates the execution. The dashed arrows represent state transitions in the concrete semantics, while the solid arrows represent the transitions $W \overset{t}{\leadsto} W'$ in the abstract semantics. Like before, we use different colors to represent actions of different threads. The vertical bars represent splits. The solid arrow

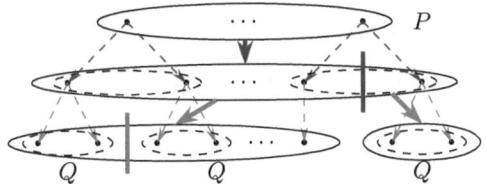

Fig. 11: Illustration of $\models_{\text{A}} \{P\}\mathbb{C}\{Q\}$

and the split together correspond to the transition $W \overset{t}{\leadsto} W''$. The branching shown by the two solid red arrows reflects the *non-deterministic* choice of the cases of the split.

Before giving the partial correctness under the abstract semantics, we first define the termination of W_0 in Def. 11: if the execution sequence of W_0 under the abstract semantics converges with the limit W, we say W_0 terminates at W.

Definition 11 (Termination of W). Given W_0 and a schedule φ. We say W_0 *terminates at W under the schedule φ*, represented as $W_0 \Downarrow_\varphi W$, if and only if there is an infinite sequence $\overrightarrow{W}$ such that **History**$(W_0, \varphi, \overrightarrow{W})$, $\lim \overrightarrow{W} = W$ and $W^{(Prog)}(\textbf{skip} \parallel \cdots \parallel \textbf{skip}) = 1$.

Here **History**$(W_0, \varphi, \overrightarrow{W})$ says that $\overrightarrow{W}$ is a possibly infinite sequence $W_0, W_1, \ldots$ where $W_i \overset{\varphi[i]}{\leadsto} W_{i+1}$ for every i. The formal definition of **History** can be found in the TR [13]. The limit $(\lim \overrightarrow{W})$ is defined by Def. 6. The projection of W over code $(W^{(Prog)})$ and state $(W^{(State)})$ are defined by Eqn. (5).

Next we define the partial correctness under the abstract semantics, $\models_{\text{A}} \{P\}\mathbb{C}\{Q\}$. The initial distribution of program configurations is $init(\mathbb{C}, \mu)$. As defined in Fig. 10, $init(\mathbb{C}, \mu)$ says the initial program is always $\mathbb{C}$ and the state distribution is μ. Figure 11 illustrates the meaning of $\models_{\text{A}} \{P\}\mathbb{C}\{Q\}$: if P holds over the initial distribution, Q must hold over *every* final distribution. Theorem 1 shows that the partial correctness in the abstract semantics implies the partial correctness in the concrete semantics when the postcondition is closed. Below we develop our program logic based on this abstract semantics.

Definition 12. $\models_{\text{A}} \{P\}\mathbb{C}\{Q\}$ iff for all μ, if $\mu \models P$, then for all φ and W, if $init(\mathbb{C}, \mu) \Downarrow_\varphi W$, then $W^{(State)} \models Q$.

Theorem 1. For all $P, \mathbb{C}, Q$, if $\models_{\text{A}} \{P\}\mathbb{C}\{Q\}$ and **closed**(Q), then $\models \{P\}\mathbb{C}\{Q\}$.

5   The Program Logic

We present the assertion language and the logic rules in this section.

(Assertion)	$\mathbf{p}, \mathbf{q}$	$::= b \mid \neg\mathbf{q} \mid \mathbf{q}_1 \wedge \mathbf{q}_2 \mid \mathbf{q}_1 \vee \mathbf{q}_2 \mid \forall X.\mathbf{q} \mid \exists X.\mathbf{q} \mid \ldots$
(Pexp)	ξ	$::= r \mid \mathbb{E}(e) \mid \mathbf{Pr}(\mathbf{q}) \mid \xi_1 + \xi_2 \mid \xi_1 - \xi_2 \mid \xi_1 * \xi_2 \mid \ldots$
(PAssertion)	P, Q, M, I	$::= \lceil \mathbf{q} \rceil \mid \xi_1 < \xi_2 \mid \xi_1 = \xi_2 \mid \xi_1 \le \xi_2 \mid \neg Q \mid Q_1 \wedge Q_2 \mid Q_1 \vee Q_2$
		$\mid \forall X.Q \mid \exists X.Q \mid Q_1 \oplus_p Q_2 \mid Q_1 \oplus Q_2 \mid \ldots$
(Action)	R, G	$::= \mathbf{p} \ltimes \mathbf{q} \mid [\mathbf{q}] \mid \neg R \mid R_1 \wedge R_2 \mid R_1 \vee R_2 \mid \forall X.R \mid \exists X.R \mid R_1 \circ R_2 \mid \ldots$

Fig. 12: The Assertion Language

Evaluation of probabilistic expressions:

$$[\![\mathbb{E}(e)]\!]_\mu \stackrel{\text{def}}{=} \mathbb{E}_{\sigma\sim\mu}[[\![e]\!]_\sigma] \qquad\qquad [\![\mathbf{Pr}(\mathbf{q})]\!]_\mu \stackrel{\text{def}}{=} \mathbf{Pr}_{\sigma\sim\mu}[\sigma \models \mathbf{q}]$$

Semantics of probabilistic assertions:

$\mu \models \lceil \mathbf{q} \rceil$ iff for all $\sigma \in supp(\mu)$, $\sigma \models \mathbf{q}$

$\mu \models Q_1 \oplus_p Q_2$ iff $p = 1$ and $\mu \models Q_1$, or $p = 0$ and $\mu \models Q_2$, or $0 < p < 1$ and there exists μ_1 and μ_2 such that $\mu = \mu_1 \oplus_p \mu_2$, $\mu_1 \models Q_1$ and $\mu_2 \models Q_2$

$\mu \models Q_1 \oplus Q_2$ iff there exists p such that $\mu \models Q_1 \oplus_p Q_2$

Fig. 13: Semantics of Assertions

5.1 The Assertion Language

We show the syntax of assertions in Fig. 12 and their semantics in Fig. 13. We use $\mathbf{p}$ and $\mathbf{q}$ to represent classical assertions over states, and P, Q and I for *probabilistic assertions* over state distributions. We also use ξ to denote *probabilistic expressions* such as the expected value of an arithmetic expression or the probability of a classical assertion. The expression ξ evaluates to a real number under the state distribution μ, represented as $[\![\xi]\!]_\mu$. $\mathbb{E}(e)$ evaluates to the expected value of $[\![e]\!]_\sigma$ (where $\sigma \in supp(\mu)$). $\mathbf{Pr}(\mathbf{q})$ evaluates to the probability of $\sigma \models \mathbf{q}$ (where $\sigma \in supp(\mu)$). The key definitions of expected values and probability of assertions are shown in Eqn. (1).

The assertion $\lceil \mathbf{q} \rceil$ lifts the state assertion $\mathbf{q}$ to a probabilistic assertion. It says $\mathbf{q}$ holds on all states in the support of the state distribution. The assertion $P \oplus_p Q$ holds at μ, if μ is a *mixture* of two distributions μ_0 and μ_1, which are associated with probabilities p and $1-p$, and satisfy P and Q respectively. $Q_1 \oplus Q_2$ says there exists p such that $Q_1 \oplus_p Q_2$ holds. The semantics of $\forall X.Q$ and $\exists X.Q$ are given in the TR [13]. Throughout this paper, we use capital letters X to indicate that X is a logical variable and lowercase letters x to indicate that x is a program variable. We define **true** as a syntactic sugar of $\lceil \text{true} \rceil$ which holds on all state distributions.

Actions R and G are assertions over state transitions. Their semantics, $(\sigma, \sigma') \models R$, is the same as that in classical (non-probabilistic) rely-guarantee logics. We use $[\![R]\!]$ to denote the set of state transitions that satisfy R.

Stability We define the stability of a probabilistic assertion Q with respect to the environment interference (specified by I and R) in Fig. 14. We first define

$$\mu \overset{R}{\hookrightarrow} \mu' \quad \text{iff} \ \exists \theta \in \mathcal{P}(State \times State). \, \theta \subseteq \llbracket R \rrbracket \wedge supp(\mu) = dom(\theta) \wedge supp(\mu') = range(\theta)$$

$$\mu \overset{R}{\underset{I}{\to}} \mu'' \quad \text{iff} \ \mu \models I \wedge (\exists \mu'. \, \mu \overset{R}{\hookrightarrow} \mu' \wedge supp(\mu'') \subseteq supp(\mu')) \wedge \mu'' \models I$$

$$\mathbf{Sta}(Q, R, I) \ \text{iff} \ \forall \mu, \mu'. \, \mu \models Q \wedge \mu \overset{R}{\underset{I}{\to}} \mu' \implies \mu' \models Q$$

Fig. 14: Stability

$\mu \overset{R}{\underset{I}{\to}} \mu''$ to describe that the current state distribution is changed from μ to μ'' due to the environment interference. As we can see in the abstract operational semantics, every transition made by a thread is done in two steps. The first step is normal execution without splits and the second step is the execution of **split**. Similarly, we model the execution of the environment in two steps. The first step is $\mu \overset{R}{\hookrightarrow} \mu'$. It requires us to find a set θ of state transitions allowed by R (i.e. $\theta \subseteq \llbracket R \rrbracket$), such that θ transforms the states of $supp(\mu)$ to those of $supp(\mu')$. The second step is the execution of **split** statements by the environment. The condition $supp(\mu'') \subseteq supp(\mu')$ abstracts the behaviors of **split**. In addition, the environment needs to preserve the invariant I, so $\mu \models I \wedge \mu'' \models I$. Then we can give a simple definition of $\mathbf{Sta}(Q, R, I)$ in Fig. 14.

In general, it is not easy to prove the stability of a probabilistic assertion with respect to classical rely conditions. But in practice, the thread-local pre/post-conditions and intermediate assertions P are usually "non-probabilistic", in the form of $\lceil b_1 \rceil \vee \ldots \vee \lceil b_n \rceil$. This is because the probabilistic information is often about the shared resource and has already been specified by the global invariant I. For such P, proving stability $\mathbf{Sta}(P, R, I)$ is not much harder than proving stability in the classical rely-guarantee reasoning. We give some rules to syntactically proving $\mathbf{Sta}(P, R, I)$ in the TR [13].

Closed Assertions As explained in Sec. 3.5, we need the postcondition of the whole program to be closed for applying split. $\mathbf{closed}(Q)$ means that the mixture of any (maybe countably infinite) number of state distributions satisfies Q if each of them satisfies Q.

Definition 13. An assertion Q is closed, i.e., $\mathbf{closed}(Q)$ holds, if and only if, for all $\nu \in \mathbb{D}_{\mathbb{D}_{State}}$, if $\mu \models Q$ holds for all $\mu \in supp(\nu)$, then $\overline{\nu} \models Q$ (see Eqn. (8) for the definition of $\overline{\nu}$).

Many assertions are closed, such as $\lceil x = 1 \rceil$, $\mathbf{Pr}(y > 2) = 0.5$, $\lceil x = 0 \rceil \oplus \lceil x = 1 \rceil$. We give syntactic rules in the TR [13] to prove closedness of assertions. There do exist non-closed assertions, such as $\lceil x = 1 \rceil \vee \lceil x = 2 \rceil$ and $\mathbf{Pr}(x = 0) \neq 0.5$. In this work, we focus on the class of randomized algorithms whose correctness is about the bound of the probability of a random event or the expected value of a random variable. For this kind of algorithms, our syntactic rules for closedness are useful enough.

Limit-Closed Assertions To verify almost surely terminating programs, we require the invariant I and the postconditions of all threads are limit-closed assertions. Below we define limit-closed assertions (see Def. 6 for the definition of $\lim \vec{\mu}$).

Definition 14. An assertion Q is limit-closed, i.e., **lclosed**(Q) holds, if and only if, for all infinite sequences $\vec{\mu}$, if $\lim \vec{\mu} = \mu$, and $\vec{\mu}[n] \models Q$ holds for all n, then $\mu \models Q$.

We also give syntactic rules in the TR [13] to prove that an assertion is limit-closed. They are similar to those for closedness and thus are also useful in verifying algorithms whose correctness is about the bound of the probability of a random event or the expected value of a random variable.

5.2 Inference Rules

Our inference rules are organized into three layers for the whole program, the thread local reasoning, and sequential reasoning, as shown in Fig. 15. The top-level judgement for the whole program is in the form of $\vdash_A \{P\}\mathbb{C}\{Q\}$ where "A" means abstract. One can use the parallel composition rule (PAR) to decompose the verification of concurrent programs into the verification of each thread. The judgement for thread-local reasoning is in the form of $R, G, I \vdash \{P\}C\{Q\}$ where R and G are rely/guarantee conditions and I is the layer invariant. To verify atomic blocks, one can use the (ATOM) and (ATOM-SPLIT) rules to apply sequential reasoning to the code in the atomic blocks. The judgement for sequential reasoning is in the form of $\vdash_{SQ} \{P\}C\{Q\}$ where "SQ" means sequential.

Whole-Program Rules The top-level rules are used to verify whole programs. The judgement is in the form of $\vdash_A \{P\}\mathbb{C}\{Q\}$. Here P and Q are probabilistic assertions, which specify the initial state distributions and the terminating state distributions respectively.

The parallel composition rule (PAR) is (mostly) standard. The invariant I and the postcondition of each thread $Q_1, \ldots, Q_n$ are required to be limit-closed assertions, which ensures that the limit state distribution of the infinite sequence produced by $\mathbb{C}$ under the abstract operational semantics satisfies I and $Q_1, \ldots, Q_n$.

The (LAZYCOIN) rule is used to verify probabilistic choices. Note that the execution of $\langle C_1 \rangle \oplus_p \langle C_2 \rangle$ is *not* atomic, and its two steps (i.e. the coin flip and the execution of $\langle C_1 \rangle$ or $\langle C_2 \rangle$) can interleave with the environment steps. The (LAZYCOIN) rule allows us to verify **lazycoin**$(\mathbb{C})$ instead of $\mathbb{C}$, where **lazycoin**$(\mathbb{C})$ replaces every $\langle C_1 \rangle \oplus_p \langle C_2 \rangle$ in $\mathbb{C}$ with **skip**; $\langle\langle C_1 \rangle \oplus_p \langle C_2 \rangle\rangle$. We can view **lazycoin** as a transformation that defers the coin flip step to be executed with $\langle C_1 \rangle$ or $\langle C_2 \rangle$ together. This transformation is sound because, in the OA model, the scheduler and the environment threads should not be aware of the outcome of the coin flip, so we can soundly swap the coin-flip step and the environment steps, and reason about the atomic probabilistic choice $\langle\langle C_1 \rangle \oplus_p \langle C_2 \rangle\rangle$ instead. The extra **skip** is to ensure that the new code has the same number of steps as the non-atomic

Whole program rules: $\vdash_A \{P\}\mathbb{C}\{Q\}$

$$\frac{\forall i.\ R_i, G_i, I \vdash \{P_i\}C_i\{Q_i\} \quad \forall i, j.\ i \neq j \implies (G_i \Rightarrow R_j)}{\vdash_A \{P\}C_1 \parallel \cdots \parallel C_n\{Q\}} \text{ (PAR)}$$

with $P \Rightarrow I \wedge P_1 \wedge \cdots \wedge P_n \quad I \wedge Q_1 \wedge \cdots \wedge Q_n \Rightarrow Q \quad \textbf{lclosed}(\{I, Q_1, \ldots, Q_n\})$

$$\frac{\vdash_A \{P\}\mathbb{C}\{Q\} \quad \textbf{closed}(Q)}{\vdash_A \{P\}\textbf{RemoveSplit}(\mathbb{C})\{Q\}} \text{ (REMOVESPLIT)} \qquad \frac{\vdash_A \{P\}\textbf{lazycoin}(\mathbb{C})\{Q\}}{\vdash_A \{P\}\mathbb{C}\{Q\}} \text{ (LAZYCOIN)}$$

Thread-local rules: $R, G, I \vdash \{P\}C\{Q\}$

$$\frac{G \vdash_{sq} \{I \wedge P\}C\{I \wedge Q\} \quad \textbf{Sta}(\{P, Q\}, R, I)}{R, G, I \vdash \{P\}\langle C\rangle\{Q\}} \text{ (ATOM)} \qquad \frac{R, G, I \vdash \{P\}C_1\{M\} \quad R, G, I \vdash \{M\}C_2\{Q\}}{R, G, I \vdash \{P\}C_1; C_2\{Q\}} \text{ (SEQ)}$$

$$\frac{G \vdash_{sq} \{I \wedge P\}C\{(I \wedge Q \wedge \lceil b_1 \rceil) \oplus \cdots \oplus (I \wedge Q \wedge \lceil b_k \rceil)\} \quad \textbf{Sta}(\{P, Q \wedge (\lceil b_1 \rceil \vee \cdots \vee \lceil b_k \rceil)\}, R, I)}{R, G, I \vdash \{P\}\langle C\rangle \textbf{ split}(b_1, \ldots, b_k)\{(Q \wedge \lceil b_1 \rceil) \vee \ldots \vee (Q \wedge \lceil b_k \rceil)\}} \text{ (ATOM-SPLIT)}$$

$$\frac{P_1 \Rightarrow \lceil b \rceil \quad P_2 \Rightarrow \lceil \neg b \rceil \quad \textbf{Sta}(P_1 \vee P_2, R, I) \quad R, G, I \vdash \{P_1\}C_1\{Q\} \quad R, G, I \vdash \{P_2\}C_2\{Q\}}{R, G, I \vdash \{P_1 \vee P_2\}\textbf{if } (b) \textbf{ then } C_1 \textbf{ else } C_2\{Q\}} \text{ (COND)}$$

$$\frac{P_1 \Rightarrow \lceil b \rceil \quad P_2 \Rightarrow \lceil \neg b \rceil \wedge Q \quad R, G, I \vdash \{P_1\}C\{P_1 \vee P_2\} \quad \textbf{Sta}(\{P_1 \vee P_2, Q\}, R, I)}{R, G, I \vdash \{P_1 \vee P_2\}\textbf{while } (b) \textbf{ do } C\{Q\}} \text{ (WHILE)}$$

Fig. 15: Selected Logic Rules

$\langle C_1 \rangle \oplus_p \langle C_2 \rangle$, and thus to ensure that **lazycoin**$(\mathbb{C})$ and $\mathbb{C}$ generate the same behaviors in the OA model. Note that (LAZYCOIN) is *unsound* in the SA model.

The (REMOVESPLIT) rule has been explained in Sec. 3. We also support the standard consequence rule, conjunction rule and disjunction rule for whole programs, which are shown in the TR [13].

Thread-Local Rules The thread-local judgement is in the form of $R, G, I \vdash \{P\}C\{Q\}$. The rely/guarantee conditions R and G are non-probabilistic and their meaning are the same as in the traditional rely-guarantee reasoning. The invariant I specifies the probabilistic property that is preserved by both the thread and its environment at every layer. The rely/guarantee conditions need to be reflexive in well-formed thread-local judgements.

To verify $\langle C \rangle$, the (ATOM) rule asks one to verify C as sequential code, and requires I is preserved at the end if it holds at the beginning, and the whole state transitions resulting from the sequential execution C satisfy the guarantee G. The pre/post-conditions need to be stable with respect to R and I. We use $\textbf{Sta}(\{P, Q\}, R, I)$ as a shorthand for $\textbf{Sta}(P, R, I) \wedge \textbf{Sta}(Q, R, I)$. Similar representations are used in the remaining part of the paper.

Our (SEQ) rule for sequential composition is standard. The (ATOM-SPLIT), (COND) and (WHILE) rules have been explained in Sec. 3.5. Note that (ATOM-

SPLIT) cannot be replaced by (ATOM), since only **split** can turn $\oplus$ into $\vee$ (see the first premise and conclusion's postconditions in (ATOM-SPLIT)).

Sequential Rules The judgement for sequential rules is in the form of $G \vdash_{\text{SQ}} \{P\}C\{Q\}$. Note that the guarantee G does not specify the state transition of every single step of C. Instead it specifies the state transitions from initial states to the corresponding final states at the end of C. The rules for sequential reasoning are simple extensions of those in [6] and are presented in the TR [13].

Soundness The following theorem shows that our logic is sound with respect to the abstract operational semantics, where $\models_A \{P\}\mathbb{C}\{Q\}$ is given in Def. 12.

Theorem 2. *For all $P, \mathbb{C}, Q$, if $\vdash_A \{P\}\mathbb{C}\{Q\}$, then $\models_A \{P\}\mathbb{C}\{Q\}$.*

6   Case Study: Conciliator

As introduced in Sec. 1, Chor et al. [12] give a probabilistic-write based conciliator for *probabilistic agreement* between n threads, each thread i executing C_i below, where s is a shared variable and y_i is the local variable for thread i that records its return value.

$$C_i \overset{\text{def}}{=} (\textbf{while } (s = 0) \textbf{ do } \langle s := i \rangle \oplus_p \langle \textbf{skip} \rangle) \, ; y_i := s$$

We want to prove $\{\lceil s = 0 \rceil\}C_1 \parallel \cdots \parallel C_n\{\textbf{Pr}(y_1 = \cdots = y_n) \geq (1 - p)^{n-1}\}$. Intuitively the postcondition holds because, when there is exactly one thread i which succeeds in writing to s, all threads will return i. This ideal case happens with probability no less than $(1 - p)^{n-1}$ in OA, because (i) for the program to terminate, at least one thread has updated s, and (ii) after the first update to s, each of the other $n - 1$ threads has at most one chance to update s, and such an update happens with probability no more than $1 - p$. Note that this algorithm does *not* work in SA, where different threads can be scheduled for different outcomes of coin flips. For example, a strong adversary may behave as follows: It first non-deterministically selects a thread and keeps scheduling it until it flips heads. It then selects another thread and schedules it in the same manner, until all threads have flipped heads. After that, it schedules each thread for two consecutive steps, so that each returns its own number. In this case, the probability of agreement is 0.

To formulate the intuition, we introduce a shared auxiliary variable c that counts how many threads have updated s and insert the auxiliary code $c := c+1$ which is executed atomically with $s := i$. We also introduce flag variables d_i to formalize the "at most one chance" update to s. When d_i is set, it means thread i can no longer update s. We insert the auxiliary code $SetFlag_i$ to set d_i at the proper time. At the whole-program level, we apply (LAZYCOIN) and (REMOVESPLIT) to wrap the probabilistic choice in an atomic block, and to instrument $\textbf{split}(s = 0, s \neq 0)$ at the end of the loop body such that the resulting smaller distributions either enter or exit the loop, respectively. Using the (PAR) rule, our goal becomes to thread-locally verify the code below.

(**while** $(s = 0)$ **do** (**skip**; $\langle PWrite_i \rangle$ **split**$(s = 0, s \neq 0)$)); $\langle\ SetFlag_i\ ; y_i := s \rangle$,

where $PWrite_i \stackrel{\text{def}}{=} \langle s := i;\ c := c + 1; SetFlag_i\ \rangle \oplus_p \langle\ SetFlag_i\ \rangle$

and $\quad SetFlag_i \stackrel{\text{def}}{=}$ **if** $(s \neq 0)$ **then** $d_i := 1$ **else skip**

We define the invariant I below, which says that either $s = 0$ (and thus $c = 0$ and each thread has chance to update s), or $s \neq 0$ (and thus $c > 0$) and the probability of $c = 1$ has a lower bound.

$$I \stackrel{\text{def}}{=} I_0 \vee I_1, \text{ where } I_0 \stackrel{\text{def}}{=} \lceil s = 0 \wedge c = 0 \wedge \forall i.\, d_i = 0 \rceil, \ I_1 \stackrel{\text{def}}{=} \lceil s \neq 0 \wedge c > 0 \rceil \wedge \mathsf{PBound},$$
$$\text{and } \mathsf{PBound} \stackrel{\text{def}}{=} \exists K \leq n. \lceil \textstyle\sum_{i=1}^{n} d_i = K \rceil \wedge \mathbf{Pr}(c = 1) \geq (1 - p)^{K-1}$$

We give the detailed proofs in the TR [13]. The logic presented in the paper requires us to split in each round of the while-loop. This technique is sufficient to prove conciliator and *Dice*. However, for more advanced examples such as group election and multiplayer level-up game (in the TR), their loops require split in the first few rounds only. Thus, we extend the logic with a new while rule for while loops and a new sequential composition rule for sequential statements. With the two new rules, we can prove the two advanced examples. The full logic and the proofs of the advanced examples can be found in the TR.

7   Related Work and Discussions

McIver et al. [18] develop the probabilistic rely-guarantee calculus, which, to our knowledge, is the first program logic for concurrent randomized programs. Their semantics assume arbitrary schedules, i.e. the strong adversary (SA) model, and their reasoning rules use probabilistic rely/guarantee conditions. Their logic does not apply to the algorithms of conciliator and group election verified in our work, whose correctness assumes weaker adversary models. Besides, we encode probabilistic properties in the invariant and use only non-probabilistic rely-guarantee conditions, which enable simple stability proofs.

Tassarotti and Harper [20] extend the concurrent program logic Iris [16] with probabilistic relational reasoning, to establish refinements between concurrent randomized programs and monadic models. They also give rules for reasoning about probabilistic properties on monadic models. On the one hand, their program semantics assumes the SA model. On the other hand, their logic soundness only holds for schedules under which the program is guaranteed to certainly terminate (i.e. terminate in a finite number of steps). As a result, they cannot verify the examples in our work.

Fesefeldt et al. [14] propose a concurrent quantitative separation logic for reasoning about lower-bound probabilities of realizing a postcondition of a concurrent randomized program in the SA model. Like us, they require program executions to preserve invariants on shared states. But their invariants are limited to *qualitative* expectations, which map states to either 0 or 1, so they cannot specify probabilistic distributions as ours can. Moreover, they can only verify lower bounds of probabilities, while we can verify exact probabilities and expectations.

For the part of *sequential* reasoning, our rules mostly follow Barthe et al. [6]. Our **lclosed** condition (see the (PAR) rule in Fig. 15) is similar to their "t-closed" condition, both introduced for supporting almost surely terminating programs. Our assertion language for invariants and pre/post-conditions is similar to theirs too, where an assertion is a predicate over state distributions. They provide a (SPLIT) rule which is very different from our split mechanism. Using their (SPLIT) rule, one can logically split the initial distribution into two parts, reason about the execution of the same code on the two parts separately, and mix the two final distributions back. Our (SQ-OPLUS) rule for sequential reasoning in the TR [13], is almost the same as their (SPLIT) rule. It is interesting to extend our assertion language with separating conjunctions, to specify spatial disjointness of state distributions and probabilistic independence (following [7]). There are also (sequential) program logics (e.g. [9,8,1]) where assertions denote functions from program states to probabilities or expected values.

Bertrand et al. [10,11] apply model checking techniques for verifying randomized algorithms in weak adversary models. However, Bertrand et al.'s approach does not apply to the algorithms we have verified. Their work focuses on the class of algorithms with some form of "symmetry" regarding the local control flow. Such an algorithm must execute "symmetric" code for different outcomes of a coin flip. But none of the algorithms verified here satisfies this property. Instead they all have probabilistic branch statements that take different numbers of steps, which is the main challenge to our logic design. We conjecture that our split idea may still be helpful when developing automata-based approaches to verify these algorithms.

Verification overhead and scalability. One may be concerned about the verification overhead caused by adding auxiliary variables and auxiliary code, and the scalability of our logic to large algorithms. In our proofs, auxiliary variables and code are introduced to capture the key intuition of the probabilistic properties that we care about, so they are usually highly related to the random variables and the probabilistic operations (coin flips) in the original algorithms. As a result, the overhead of the auxiliary variables and code is usually proportional to the number of random variables and probabilistic operations rather than the number of lines of code. For large-scale randomized algorithms, the number of probabilistic operations may not be that large, thus the proof overhead of adding auxiliary variables and splits statements should be acceptable.

In our current setting, the auxiliary variables and split statements are added manually during the verification process, which requires a good understanding of the algorithm, i.e., how the algorithm works and why it is correct. We leave it as future work to support automated code instrumentation and verification.

Acknowledgments. We thank anonymous referees for their suggestions and comments on earlier versions of this paper. This work is supported in part by National Natural Science Foundation of China (NSFC) under Grant No. 61232015.

Disclosure of Interests. The authors have no competing interests to declare that are relevant to the content of this article.

References

1. Aguirre, A., Barthe, G., Hsu, J., Kaminski, B.L., Katoen, J.P., Matheja, C.: A pre-expectation calculus for probabilistic sensitivity. Proc. ACM Program. Lang. 5(POPL) (jan 2021). https://doi.org/10.1145/3434333, https://doi.org/10.1145/3434333

2. Alistarh, D., Aspnes, J.: Sub-logarithmic test-and-set against a weak adversary. In: Proceedings of the 25th International Conference on Distributed Computing. pp. 97–109. DISC'11, Springer-Verlag, Berlin, Heidelberg (2011). https://doi.org/10.1007/978-3-642-24100-0_7

3. Aspnes, J.: Randomized protocols for asynchronous consensus. Distributed Comput. 16(2-3), 165–175 (2003). https://doi.org/10.1007/s00446-002-0081-5, https://doi.org/10.1007/s00446-002-0081-5

4. Aspnes, J.: Notes on randomized algorithms (2023), https://www.cs.yale.edu/homes/aspnes/classes/469/notes.pdf

5. Aspnes, J.: Notes on theory of distributed systems (2023), https://www.cs.yale.edu/homes/aspnes/classes/465/notes.pdf

6. Barthe, G., Espitau, T., Gaboardi, M., Grégoire, B., Hsu, J., Strub, P.: An assertion-based program logic for probabilistic programs. In: Proceedings of the 27th European Symposium on Programming (ESOP 2018). pp. 117–144. Springer (2018). https://doi.org/10.1007/978-3-319-89884-1_5, https://doi.org/10.1007/978-3-319-89884-1_5

7. Barthe, G., Hsu, J., Liao, K.: A probabilistic separation logic. Proc. ACM Program. Lang. 4(POPL), 55:1–55:30 (2020)

8. Batz, K., Kaminski, B.L., Katoen, J.P., Matheja, C.: Relatively complete verification of probabilistic programs: An expressive language for expectation-based reasoning. Proc. ACM Program. Lang. 5(POPL) (jan 2021). https://doi.org/10.1145/3434320, https://doi.org/10.1145/3434320

9. Batz, K., Kaminski, B.L., Katoen, J.P., Matheja, C., Noll, T.: Quantitative separation logic: A logic for reasoning about probabilistic pointer programs. Proc. ACM Program. Lang. 3(POPL) (jan 2019). https://doi.org/10.1145/3290347, https://doi.org/10.1145/3290347

10. Bertrand, N., Konnov, I., Lazic, M., Widder, J.: Verification of randomized consensus algorithms under round-rigid adversaries. In: Fokkink, W.J., van Glabbeek, R. (eds.) Proceedings of the 30th International Conference on Concurrency Theory (CONCUR 2019). LIPIcs, vol. 140, pp. 33:1–33:15. Schloss Dagstuhl - Leibniz-Zentrum für Informatik (2019). https://doi.org/10.4230/LIPIcs.CONCUR.2019.33, https://doi.org/10.4230/LIPIcs.CONCUR.2019.33

11. Bertrand, N., Lazic, M., Widder, J.: A reduction theorem for randomized distributed algorithms under weak adversaries. In: Henglein, F., Shoham, S., Vizel, Y. (eds.) Proceedings of the 22nd International Conference on Verification, Model Checking, and Abstract Interpretation (VMCAI 2021). Lecture Notes in Computer Science, vol. 12597, pp. 219–239. Springer (2021). https://doi.org/10.1007/978-3-030-67067-2_11, https://doi.org/10.1007/978-3-030-67067-2_11

12. Chor, B., Israeli, A., Li, M.: Wait-free consensus using asynchronous hardware. SIAM Journal on Computing 23(4), 701–712 (1994). https://doi.org/10.1137/S0097539790192035, https://doi.org/10.1137/S0097539790192035

13. Fan, W., Liang, H., Feng, X., Jiang, H.: A program logic for concurrent randomized programs in the oblivious adversary model. Tech. rep. (2025), https://plax-lab.github.io/publications/randoa/randoa-tr.pdf

14. Fesefeldt, I., Katoen, J., Noll, T.: Towards concurrent quantitative separation logic. In: Proceedings of 33rd International Conference on Concurrency Theory (CONCUR 2022). pp. 25:1–25:24 (2022). https://doi.org/10.4230/LIPIcs.CONCUR.2022.25, https://doi.org/10.4230/LIPIcs.CONCUR.2022.25

15. Jones, C.B.: Tentative steps toward a development method for interfering programs. ACM Trans. Program. Lang. Syst. 5(4), 596–619 (oct 1983). https://doi.org/10.1145/69575.69577, https://doi.org/10.1145/69575.69577

16. Jung, R., Swasey, D., Sieczkowski, F., Svendsen, K., Turon, A., Birkedal, L., Dreyer, D.: Iris: Monoids and invariants as an orthogonal basis for concurrent reasoning. In: Proceedings of the 42nd Annual ACM SIGPLAN-SIGACT Symposium on Principles of Programming Languages. p. 637–650. POPL '15, Association for Computing Machinery, New York, NY, USA (2015). https://doi.org/10.1145/2676726.2676980, https://doi.org/10.1145/2676726.2676980

17. McIver, A., Morgan, C.: Abstraction, Refinement and Proof for Probabilistic Systems. Monographs in Computer Science, Springer (2005). https://doi.org/10.1007/b138392, https://doi.org/10.1007/b138392

18. McIver, A., Rabehaja, T.M., Struth, G.: Probabilistic rely-guarantee calculus. Theor. Comput. Sci. 655, 120–134 (2016). https://doi.org/10.1016/j.tcs.2016.01.016, https://doi.org/10.1016/j.tcs.2016.01.016

19. Rand, R., Zdancewic, S.: VPHL: A verified partial-correctness logic for probabilistic programs. In: Ghica, D.R. (ed.) Proceedings of the 31st Conference on the Mathematical Foundations of Programming Semantics (MFPS 2015). Electronic Notes in Theoretical Computer Science, vol. 319, pp. 351–367. Elsevier (2015). https://doi.org/10.1016/j.entcs.2015.12.021, https://doi.org/10.1016/j.entcs.2015.12.021

20. Tassarotti, J., Harper, R.: A separation logic for concurrent randomized programs. Proc. ACM Program. Lang. 3(POPL) (jan 2019). https://doi.org/10.1145/3290377, https://doi.org/10.1145/3290377

Iso-Recursive Multiparty Sessions and Their Automated Verification

Marco Giunti(✉) ⓘD and Nobuko Yoshida(✉) ⓘD

University of Oxford, Oxford, UK
{marco.giunti,nobuko.yoshida}cs.ox.ac.uk

Abstract. Most works on session types take an equi-recursive approach and do not distinguish among a recursive type and its unfolding. This becomes more important in recent type systems which do not require global types, also known as *generalised multiparty session types* (GMST). In GMST, in order to establish properties as deadlock-freedom, the environments which type processes are assumed to satisfy extensional properties holding in all infinite sequences. This is a problem because: (1) the mechanisation of GMST and equi-recursion in proof assistants is utterly complex and eventually requires co-induction; and (2) the implementation of GMST in type checkers relies on model checkers for environment verification, and thus the program analysis is not self-contained.
In this paper, we overcome these limitations by providing an *iso-recursive typing system* that computes the *behavioural properties of environments*. The type system relies on a terminating function named *compliance* that computes all final redexes of an environment, and determines when these redexes do not contain mismatches or deadlocks: *compliant environments cannot go wrong*. The function is defined theoretically by introducing the novel notions of deterministic LTS of environments and of environment closure, and can be implemented in mainstream programming languages and compilers. We showcase an implementation in OCaml by using exception handling to tackle the inherent non-determinism of synchronisation of branching and selection types. We assess that the implementation provides the desired properties, namely absence of mismatches and of deadlocks in environments, by resorting to automated deductive verification performed in tools of the OCaml ecosystem relying on Why3.

1   Introduction

Session types [32,51,33] are an effective method to control the behaviour of software components that run in message-passing distributed systems. *Multiparty session types* (MPST) [34,35] enhance session types by providing support for sessions involving multiple participants, thus representing more expressive scenarios. Various theories of MPST have been deployed in programming languages [55] allowing verification of industrial code at compile or run-time [21].

In most works on session types, recursive types follow an *equi-recursive* view [47] and represent infinite trees that are manipulated co-inductively. This representation does not have a direct counterpart in non-lazy programming languages, which typically resort to *iso-recursive* types [1,47] that are manipulated

ⓒ The Author(s) 2025
V. Vafeiadis (Ed.): ESOP 2025, LNCS 15694, pp. 349–378, 2025.
https://doi.org/10.1007/978-3-031-91118-7_14

inductively. Moreover, lazy evaluation of predicates on equi-recursive trees might not terminate, and is thus not effective for static program analysis. In practice, MPST are embedded in non-lazy languages by encoding equi-recursive types; for instance, [37] defines infinite sequence of types as polymorphic lenses [20] by using OCaml generalised algebraic data types.

Our proposal to overcome this problem consists in introducing a theory of *iso-recursive multiparty session types* relying on a type system that *computes the deadlock-freedom* of type environments.

Lately, there have been several advances in MPST that can establish deadlock-freedom without using global types, e.g. [38,50,49,5,24,46,30,7]: this bottom-up approach is known as *generalised multiparty session types (GMST)*. However, the price to pay in GMST is that environments must satisfy extensional predicates requiring that a certain property holds for all infinite sequences. This is a non-integrated feature in GMST, which resort to external tools as model checkers to assess these predicates. Moreover, mechanising equi-recursive GMST in proof assistants is quite complex, and eventually relies on co-induction [17]. Specifically, formulations based on GMST are difficult to implement in programming languages because of the interplay among equi-recursive types and the verification of the semantic properties of environments. Another possibility is to proceed top-down by using global types and ensure deadlock freedom without verifying environments, while the analysis' expressiveness is affected by projectability [52].

In this paper, we propose a formal system to compute the deadlock-freedom of type environments *compositionally* at the typing of parallel processes, and we provide an implementation that is automatically verified by using automated deductive tools of the OCaml ecosystem [45,44,9] relying on Why3 [19].

1.1   Equi-recursive vs Iso-recursive Types: SSH/OAuth2 Example

We illustrate our methodology using a recursive variant of the OAuth 2.0 protocol (cf. [49]) which provides support for *ssh* [10]. Let us indicate *send to* and *receive from* participant p as the *types* $\mathsf{p}!l(S).T$ and $\mathsf{p}?l(S).T$, respectively, where l is a *label* indicating the nature of the communication, S is the *sort* of the payload, and T is the type of the continuation. Selection among (branching on) different output (input) types is done by means of the binary operator $+$. Recursion is provided by the construct $\mu X.T$, which binds the type variable X in T. Termination is represented by type end. *Sorts* describe the types of string, boolean, and unit values. The session types of the service (s), of the client (c), and of the authorisation server (a) are:

$$T_{\mathsf{s}} \stackrel{\text{def}}{=} \mu X.(\mathsf{c}!\mathsf{login}(\mathsf{unit}).\mathsf{a}?\mathsf{auth}(\mathsf{bool}).X + \mathsf{c}!\mathsf{cancel}(\mathsf{unit}).\mathsf{end})$$

$$T_{\mathsf{c}} \stackrel{\text{def}}{=} \mu X.(\mathsf{s}?\mathsf{login}(\mathsf{unit}).(\mathsf{a}!\mathsf{pwd}(\mathsf{str}).X + \mathsf{a}!\mathsf{ssh}(\mathsf{unit}).X) + $$
$$\qquad\qquad \mathsf{s}?\mathsf{cancel}(\mathsf{unit}).\mathsf{a}!\mathsf{quit}(\mathsf{unit}).\mathsf{end})$$

$$T_{\mathsf{a}} \stackrel{\text{def}}{=} \mu X.R_{\mathsf{a}}$$

$$R_{\mathsf{a}} \stackrel{\text{def}}{=} \mathsf{c}?\mathsf{pwd}(\mathsf{str}).\mathsf{s}!\mathsf{auth}(\mathsf{bool}).X + \mathsf{c}?\mathsf{ssh}(\mathsf{unit}).\mathsf{s}!\mathsf{auth}(\mathsf{bool}).X + \mathsf{c}?\mathsf{quit}(\mathsf{unit}).\mathsf{end}$$

The protocol says that the service (s) sends to the client (c) either a request to login, or cancel; in the first case, c continues by sending the password (pwd, carrying a string), or by sending ssh, to a, who in turn sends authentication to s (auth, with a boolean, telling whether the client is authorised), and the session restarts; in the second case, c sends quit to a, and the session ends.

A problem of equi-recursive GMST, e.g. [49], is that types are defined co-inductively (cf. [17]). Recursive types can be infinitely folded and unfolded: for instance, we have the following *equi-recursive equations*:

$$T_a = T_a^* = T_a^{**} = \cdots$$

$$T_a^* \stackrel{\text{def}}{=} \text{c?pwd(str).s!auth(bool)}.T_a + \text{c?ssh(unit).s!auth(bool)}.T_a + \text{c?quit(unit).end}$$

$$T_a^{**} \stackrel{\text{def}}{=} \text{c?pwd(str).s!auth(bool)}.T_a^* + \text{c?ssh(unit).s!auth(bool)}.T_a^* + \text{c?quit(unit).end}$$

This is particularly relevant when establishing the properties of the typing system, e.g. safety [49, Definition 4.1], which are based on a notion of *transition of session environments*. To illustrate, the idea is to interpret *types as processes*, cf. [41], and consider transitions of *session environments* mapping participants p to types T. The environment $\Gamma_1 \stackrel{\text{def}}{=} \text{s: c!login(unit).a?auth(bool)}.T_s + \text{c!cancel(unit).end}$ can fire an output action c!login(unit) and reach s: a?auth(bool). T_s, or can fire an output action c!cancel(unit) and reach s: end. The environment $\Gamma_2 \stackrel{\text{def}}{=} \text{c: s?login(unit)}.T_c' + \text{s?cancel(unit).a!quit(unit).end}$ can fire an input action s?login(unit) and reach c: T_c', where $T_c' \stackrel{\text{def}}{=} \text{a!pwd(str)}.T_c + \text{a!ssh(unit)}.T_c$, or can fire an input action s?cancel(unit) and reach c: a!quit(unit).end. The environment Γ_1, Γ_2 can fire two synchronisation actions: (1) login@s⋈c, which indicates a synchronisation on the label login by the input participant s and the output participant c, and reach the environment s: a?auth(bool). T_s, c: T_c'; and (2) cancel@s⋈c, and reach the environment s: end, c: a!quit(unit).end.

In particular, the rule for recursive types in [49, Definition 2.8] states that a recursive type $\mu X.T$ inherits the transitions from its unfolding, that is the type $T\{\mu X.T/X\}$. For instance, the rule can be instantiated with type T_a as

$$[\Gamma\text{-}\mu] \frac{\Gamma, a: T_a^* \xrightarrow{\alpha} \Gamma'}{\Gamma, a: T_a \xrightarrow{\alpha} \Gamma'}$$

and allows for inferring the following transitions:

$$\Gamma, a: T_a \xrightarrow{\text{c?ssh(unit)}} \Gamma, a: \text{s!auth(bool)}.T_a$$

$$\Gamma, a: T_a \xrightarrow{\text{c?ssh(unit)}} \Gamma, a: \text{s!auth(bool)}.T_a^* \cdots$$

We note that this elegant approach is appropriate for the theory, but less suited for mechanising GMST in theorem provers, and for automated verification.

More specifically, the approach introduced in [49] and followed in many subsequent papers on GMST, e.g. [38,49,5,24,46,30,7], requires to type check sessions with environments having certain *extensional properties*. Crucially, such properties must be established *before typing* by analysing all possible infinite transitions of session environments. To illustrate, the paper [49] provides a companion artefact by using mCRL2 [29] featuring μ-calculus formulae that represent the safety and deadlock freedom properties of environments [49, Figure 5], which are defined by least and greatest fixed points.

Our solution. In this paper, we *compute the semantic properties* of the session environment in the rule for *type checking the session composition*, hence achieving *decidable type checking*. This is possible because our types are iso-recursive and have a finite structure.

In our setting, the types T_a, T_a^*, and T_a^{**} are all different, but isomorphic. A recursive type $\mu X.T$ can only be used to type-check a recursive process, or a type variable. To type check an input or output process, we need to unfold $\mu X.T$ by applying the substitution $\mu X.T/X$ to type T, denoted as $T\{\mu X.T/X\}$. That is, we have the following *iso-recursive equations*:

$$T_a^* = R_a\{T_a/X\} \quad T_a^{**} = R_a\{T_a^*/X\} = R_a\{(R_a\{T_a/X\})/X\} \cdots$$

For instance, consider the authorisation process Q_a below, whose syntax mirrors the one of its type T_a^*, but that the payload of input and output are (bound) variables and expressions, respectively, and that there is a process variable χ:

$$Q_a \stackrel{\text{def}}{=} c?\mathsf{pwd}(x).\mathsf{s!auth}\langle\mathsf{false}\rangle.\chi + c?\mathsf{ssh}(x).\mathsf{s!auth}\langle\mathsf{true}\rangle.\chi + c?\mathsf{quit}(x).\mathbf{0}$$

In order to type check the recursive process $\mu\chi.Q_a$ we use the typing judgement:

$$\text{T-Rec} \frac{\chi: T_a \vdash Q_a: T_a^*}{\emptyset \vdash \mu\chi.Q_a: T_a}$$

Now consider the process obtained by substituting χ in Q_a with $\mu\chi.Q_a$, that is process $P_a^* \stackrel{\text{def}}{=} Q_a\{\mu\chi.Q_a/\chi\}$, and the parallel execution of $a \lhd P_a^*$ with $s \lhd P_s$ and $c \lhd P_c$, where P_s, P_c are recursive processes implementing the service s typed by T_s, and the client c typed by T_c, respectively. This session should be accepted by the type system, since at runtime it behaves correctly, independently of the fact that the authorisation service P_a^* has been "unrolled" once.

That is, we want to infer the following judgement by using the rule for session composition of the typing system for sessions, denoted $\Vdash$:

$$\text{T-Ses} \frac{\emptyset \vdash P_s: T_s \quad \emptyset \vdash P_c: T_c \quad \emptyset \vdash P_a^*: T_a^* \quad \Delta = s: T_s, c: T_c, a: T_a^* \quad \mathsf{comp}(\Delta)}{\emptyset \Vdash s \lhd P_s \parallel c \lhd P_c \parallel a \lhd P_a^* \rhd \Delta}$$

The predicate $\mathsf{comp}(\Delta)$ establishes *compliance* by using the *computable function* comp. The goal is to calculate all possible *final environments* that are reachable from Δ, and verify that they are not errors. Intuitively, an environment is final when is stuck, or when it has already been encountered, reaching a fixed point.

Since we are interested in mechanising compliance, the calculation should be achieved by relying on the novel notion of *deterministic transition*, denoted $\longrightarrow_d$, such that $\Delta \stackrel{\alpha_1}{\longrightarrow}_d \Delta_1$ and $\Delta \stackrel{\alpha_2}{\longrightarrow}_d \Delta_2$ imply $\alpha_1 = \alpha_2$ and $\Delta_1 = \Delta_2$. The key point is that a deterministic transition system can be encoded as a computable function that can be deployed in type checkers and compilers. Moreover, the properties of the function can be verified with automated deductive verification tools as Why3 [19]. In particular, we propose the idea of *closure of an environment* Δ: the function receives Δ in input and returns in output a finite set of final environments reachable from Δ by multiple applications of $\longrightarrow_d$.

The compliance function decides when in all final environments reached by transitions starting from Δ, there is not a *communication mismatch* or a *deadlock*. A communication mismatch arises when a participant p has a single I/O type receiving from/sending to participant q, and q has a single I/O type receiving from/sending to participant p, and one of the following cases arise: (i) both p and q are sending or receiving; (ii) the intersection among the labels used by p and q is empty; (iii) p and q agree on a label but disagree on the label's sort. A deadlock arises when the environment Δ cannot fire any transition and there is at least a participant p s.t. $\Delta(p) \neq$ end.

To see an example of environment rejected by the compliance function comp, consider Δ'' below. An authorisation server typed by T_a'' only allows two subsequent attempts for ssh authentication: after that, it ends. Conversely, a client typed by T_c performs an infinite number of requests of ssh authentication: for this very reason, a system typed by Δ'' can deadlock and must be rejected.

$$T_a' \stackrel{\text{def}}{=} \mu X.(\text{c?pwd(str).s!auth(bool)}.X + \text{c?ssh(unit).s!auth(bool).end} +$$
$$\text{c?quit(unit).end})$$

$$T_a'' \stackrel{\text{def}}{=} \text{c?pwd(str).s!auth(bool)}.T_a + \text{c?ssh(unit).s!auth(bool)}.T_a' + \text{c?quit(unit).end}$$

$$\Delta'' \stackrel{\text{def}}{=} \text{s}: T_s, \text{c}: T_c, \text{a}: T_a''$$

The closure of Δ'' does return a set of environments containing the deadlocked environment Δ_{lock}, which depicts the scenario discussed above. Since $\Delta_{\text{lock}} \in$ closure(Δ'') and Δ_{lock} is a deadlock, we have $\neg\,\text{comp}(\Delta'')$:

$$\Delta_{\text{lock}} \stackrel{\text{def}}{=} \text{s}: \text{a?auth(bool)}.T_s, \text{c}: \text{a!pwd(str)}.T_c + \text{a!ssh(unit)}.T_c, \text{a}: \text{end}$$

Outline. § 2 introduces the syntax and semantics of multiparty sessions. § 3 presents the non-deterministic labelled transition semantics of session environments (cf. § 3.1), and its deterministic counterpart (cf. § 3.2): the former is used to define deadlocks and to prove subject reduction; the latter is used in § 3.3 to define closure and in turn to mechanise compliance. § 4 introduces the typing system. We first analyse the typing rules for processes. Second, we analyse the rule for typing sessions, which relies on a computable function calculating compliance that is defined in § 4.1. Last, in § 4.2 we provide the proof of subject reduction and we state a progress result. § 5 is devoted to the automated deductive verification of compliance. We start in § 5.1 by outlining few details of the implementation of compliance and of closure of deterministic transitions in OCaml. § 5.2 verifies the behavioural specification of the implementation in automated deductive verification tools of the OCaml ecosystem relying on Why3. § 6 concludes by presenting related work and next directions. The full proofs and omitted definitions can be found in [27] and the accompanying artefact can be found at https://doi.org/10.5281/zenodo.14621028.

2   Multiparty Sessions

The syntax of types and processes is in Definition 1. We consider *iso-recursive* types of the form $\mu X.T$ where $\mu X.T$ and its unfolding are not equal, but isomorphic. We stress that types have a *finite representation* rather than abstract infinite trees (cf. equi-recursive types).

Definition 1 (Syntax of types and processes).

$$S := \mathsf{nat} \mid \mathsf{int} \mid \mathsf{str} \mid \mathsf{bool} \mid \mathsf{unit} \qquad\qquad \text{Sorts}$$
$$T := \mathbf{r}!l(S).T \mid \mathbf{r}?l(S).T \mid T + T \mid \mathsf{end} \mid \mu X.T \mid X \qquad \text{Types}$$
$$P := \mathbf{r}!l\langle e\rangle.P \mid \mathbf{r}?l(x).P \mid P + P \mid \mu\chi.P \mid \chi \mid \mathsf{if}\ e\ \mathsf{then}\ P\ \mathsf{else}\ Q \mid \mathbf{0} \quad \text{Processes}$$
$$\mathcal{M} := \mathbf{p} \lhd P \mid \|_{i\in I}\ \mathbf{p}_i \lhd P_i \qquad\qquad \text{Sessions}$$

We require all terms to be contractive, i.e. $\mu X_1.\mu X_2.\ldots.\mu X_n.X_1$ is not allowed as a sub-term for any $n \geq 1$ [47, p. 300], which can be alternatively stated as type variables occur guarded (by input or output prefixes) [14].[1]

We use $\mathbf{p}, \mathbf{q}, \mathbf{r}$ to range over *participants*, l to range over *labels*, and i, j to range over indexes (natural numbers). X, Y range over *type variables*, e, e' range over *expressions*, v, w range over *values*, x, y range over *variables*, and χ range over *process variables*. *Sessions* $\mathcal{M}$ belong to the set $\mathbb{M}$. A single session or *thread* is a process P indexed by a participant, denoted $\mathbf{p} \rhd P$. A *multiparty session* is a composition of all threads, denoted $\|_{i\in I}\ \mathbf{p}_i \lhd P_i$ or $\mathbf{p}_1 \lhd P_1 \| \cdots \| \mathbf{p}_n \lhd P_n$.

The constructor μ is a *binder* in types and processes, respectively: we let X be bound in $\mu X.T$ and *free* in T; similarly, χ is bound in $\mu\chi.P$ and free in P. The remaining binder for processes is input: variable x is bound in $\mathbf{r}?l(x).P$ and free in P. *Closed* terms are those without free variables.

We assume the *substitution* of free occurrences of a type variable X in a type T_1 with a closed type T_2, written $T_1\{T_2/X\}$. We assume the substitution of free occurrences of a process variable χ in process P_1 with a closed process P_2, written $P_1\{P_2/\chi\}$, and the substitution of free occurrences of variable x in process P with a value v, written $P\{v/x\}$. A type R is *μ-guarded* (*guarded*, for short) if it is a sub-term of T in the definition $\mu X.T$.

The symbol $=$ is reserved for Leibniz equality.

Definition 2 (Session notation).

$$\oplus_{i\in I}\mathbf{r}!l_i(S_i).T_i \overset{def}{=} \mathbf{r}!l_1(S_1).T_1 + \cdots + \mathbf{r}!l_n(S_n).T_n \quad I = (1,\ldots,n), n \geq 1$$
$$\&_{i\in I}\mathbf{r}?l_i(S_i).T_i \overset{def}{=} \mathbf{r}?l_1(S_1).T_1 + \cdots + \mathbf{r}?l_n(S_n).T_n \quad I = (1,\ldots,n), n \geq 1$$

The next step towards the definition of the typing system is to identify *well-formed* types that correctly abstract multiparty sessions. The definition is in the technical report [27]. We collect the labels of types in multi-sets, and the polarities and the participants of types in sets. Intuitively, a sum type $T_1 + T_2$ is *well-behaved* when it has not duplicated labels, T_1 and T_2 have the same

---

[1] Formally, contractiveness is mechanised in Coq [11] by relying on the reflexive-transitive closure of the transition system of types introduced in § 3.

$$\text{R-Inp} \frac{}{\mathsf{p} \lhd \mathsf{q}?l(x).P \xrightarrow{\mathsf{q}?l(v)} \mathsf{p} \lhd P\{v/x\}} \qquad \text{R-Out} \frac{e \downarrow v}{\mathsf{p} \lhd \mathsf{q}!l\langle e\rangle.P \xrightarrow{\mathsf{q}!l\langle v\rangle} \mathsf{p} \lhd P}$$

$$\text{R-Sum-L} \frac{\mathsf{r} \lhd P \xrightarrow{\alpha} \mathsf{r} \lhd P'}{\mathsf{r} \lhd P + Q \xrightarrow{\alpha} \mathsf{r} \lhd P'}$$

$$\text{R-Com} \frac{\mathsf{p} \lhd P \xrightarrow{\mathsf{q}?l(v)} \mathsf{p} \lhd P' \qquad \mathsf{q} \lhd Q \xrightarrow{\mathsf{p}!l\langle v\rangle} \mathsf{q} \lhd Q'}{\mathsf{p} \lhd P \parallel \mathsf{q} \lhd Q \parallel_{i \in I} \mathsf{r}_i \lhd R_i \xrightarrow{l@\mathsf{p}\bowtie\mathsf{q}} \mathsf{p} \lhd P' \parallel \mathsf{q} \lhd Q' \parallel_{i \in I} \mathsf{r}_i \lhd R_i}$$

$$\text{R-Rec} \frac{}{\mathsf{r} \lhd \mu\chi.P \parallel_{i \in I} \mathsf{r}_i \lhd R_i \xrightarrow{\tau} \mathsf{r} \lhd P\{\mu\chi.P/\chi\} \parallel_{i \in I} \mathsf{r}_i \lhd R_i}$$

$$\text{R-IfT} \frac{e \downarrow \text{true}}{\mathsf{r} \lhd \text{if } e \text{ then } P \text{ else } Q \parallel_{i \in I} \mathsf{r}_i \lhd R_i \xrightarrow{\tau} \mathsf{r} \lhd P \parallel_{i \in I} \mathsf{r}_i \lhd R_i}$$

$$\text{R-Str} \frac{\mathcal{M}'_1 \equiv \mathcal{M}_1 \qquad \mathcal{M}_1 \xrightarrow{\alpha} \mathcal{M}_2 \qquad \mathcal{M}_2 \equiv \mathcal{M}'_2}{\mathcal{M}'_1 \xrightarrow{\alpha} \mathcal{M}'_2}$$

Fig. 1. Labelled transition rules for multiparty sessions (we omit R-IfF)

unique polarity, and the same unique participant. These assumptions eliminate ill-types of the form e.g. $\mathsf{p}!l(S_1).T_1 + \mathsf{p}!l(S_2).T_2$ or of the form e.g. $\mathsf{p}_1?l_1(S_1).T_1 + \mathsf{p}_2?l_2(S_2).T_2$ with $\mathsf{p}_1 \neq \mathsf{p}_2$, as well as mixed choice types, e.g. $\mathsf{p}!l_1(S_1).T_1 + \mathsf{p}?l_2(S_2).T_2$. A type T is well-formed, denoted $\text{WF}(T)$, when it is well-behaved, contractive, and closed.

Operational semantics of multiparty sessions. We assume an *evaluation* function $\downarrow$ transforming expressions e into boolean, integer and unit values v, written $e \downarrow v$. The operational semantics of multiparty sessions are defined modulo a *structural congruence* relation over sessions $\mathcal{M}$, denoted $\equiv \subseteq \text{M} \times \text{M}$. We let $\equiv$ be the least reflexive relation that satisfies the axiom

$$\parallel_{i \in I} \mathsf{p}_i \lhd P_i \equiv \parallel_{j \in J} \mathsf{p}_j \lhd P_j \qquad (\text{permutation}(I, J))$$

The *labelled transition rules* are defined in Figure 1; we just present the left rules. A *computation* is a sequence of α-transitions, $\alpha \in \{\tau, l@\mathsf{p}\bowtie\mathsf{q}\}$, or *reductions* $\mathcal{M}_1 \xrightarrow{\alpha} \mathcal{M}_2 \xrightarrow{\alpha} \cdots$. We are mainly interested in analysing computations of well-typed sessions (cf. § 4).

Rule R-Inp says that a participant p waiting for a value from q on the label l can do a transition labelled by $\mathsf{q}?l(v)$ and instantiate the formal parameter x with the value v in the continuation P, noted as $P\{v/x\}$. Rule R-Out allows a participant p sending to q on label l an expression e that can be evaluated as v to do a transition labelled by $\mathsf{q}!l\langle v\rangle$ and continue as P. Non-deterministic reductions are allowed by means of rule R-Sum-L, which says that a participant r

non-deterministically choosing among process P and Q, denoted $P + Q$, can do a transition labelled by α and reach $\mathbf{r} \lhd P'$ whenever $\mathbf{r} \lhd P$ can fire the same transition and reach the same redex.

Communication among two participants $\mathbf{p}$ and $\mathbf{q}$ is performed by means of rule R-COM. Whenever $\mathbf{p} \lhd P$ can do a transition labelled by the input action $\mathbf{q}?l(v)$ and reach the redex $\mathbf{p} \lhd P'$, and $\mathbf{q} \lhd Q$ can do a transition labelled by the output action $\mathbf{p}!l\langle v\rangle$ and reach the redex $\mathbf{q} \lhd Q'$, we can infer a transition labelled with $l@\mathbf{p}\bowtie\mathbf{q}$ from the composition of $\mathbf{p} \lhd P$ and $\mathbf{q} \lhd Q$ and a session $\|_{i \in I} \mathbf{r}_i \lhd R_i$ to the composition of $\mathbf{p} \lhd P'$ and $\mathbf{q} \lhd Q'$ and $\|_{i \in I} \mathbf{r}_i \lhd R_i$. Rule R-REC allows a participant $\mathbf{r}$ recursively defined as $\mu\chi.P$ and running in parallel with a session $\|_{i \in I} \mathbf{r}_i \lhd R_i$, to do an internal transition τ and unfold the body P while instantiating the occurrences of χ in P with $\mu\chi.P$, thus reaching the redex $\mathbf{r} \lhd P\{\mu\chi.P/\chi\} \|_{i \in I} \mathbf{r}_i \lhd R_i$. Rule R-IFT (R-IFF) says that a participant $\mathbf{r}$ with the body if e then P else Q and running in parallel with a session $\|_{i \in I} \mathbf{r}_i \lhd R_i$, can do a τ-transition and reach the redex $\mathbf{r} \lhd P \|_{i \in I} \mathbf{r}_i \lhd R_i$ ($\mathbf{r} \lhd Q \|_{i \in I} \mathbf{r}_i \lhd R_i$) whenever the expression e evaluates to true (false). Rule R-STR rearranges processes with structural congruence.

Example 1. Consider the authorisation protocol in § 1.1 and

$$Q_{\mathbf{a}} \stackrel{\text{def}}{=} \mathbf{c}?\mathsf{pwd}(x).\mathbf{s}!\mathsf{auth}\langle\mathsf{false}\rangle.\chi + \mathbf{c}?\mathsf{ssh}(x).\mathbf{s}!\mathsf{auth}\langle\mathsf{true}\rangle.\chi + \mathbf{c}?\mathsf{quit}(x).\mathbf{0}$$

$$P_{\mathbf{s}} \stackrel{\text{def}}{=} \mu\chi.(\mathbf{c}!\mathsf{login}\langle\rangle.\mathbf{a}?\mathsf{auth}(x).\chi + \mathbf{c}!\mathsf{cancel}\langle\rangle.\mathbf{0})$$

$$P_{\mathbf{c}} \stackrel{\text{def}}{=} \mu\chi.(\mathbf{s}?\mathsf{login}(x).(\mathbf{a}!\mathsf{pwd}\langle\text{``fido''}\rangle.\chi + \mathbf{a}!\mathsf{ssh}\langle\rangle.\chi) + \mathbf{s}?\mathsf{cancel}(x).\mathbf{a}!\mathsf{quit}\langle\rangle.\mathbf{0})$$

$$\mathcal{M} \stackrel{\text{def}}{=} \mathbf{s} \lhd P_{\mathbf{s}} \parallel \mathbf{c} \lhd P_{\mathbf{c}} \parallel \mathbf{a} \lhd P_{\mathbf{a}}^*$$

where process $P_{\mathbf{a}}^* \stackrel{\text{def}}{=} Q_{\mathbf{a}}\{\mu\chi.Q_{\mathbf{a}}/\chi\}$ implements the (unfolding of the) authorisation server $\mathbf{a}$, and processes $P_{\mathbf{s}}$ and $P_{\mathbf{c}}$ implement the service $\mathbf{s}$ and the client $\mathbf{c}$, respectively. We analyse transitions of the session introduced in § 1.1 and composing the service $\mathbf{s}$, the client $\mathbf{c}$, and the server $\mathbf{a}$, here referred as $\mathcal{M}$.

We want to analyse a communication of the server $\mathbf{s}$ with the client $\mathbf{c}$ depicting a login transaction. A first application of rule R-REC unfolds the service $\mathbf{s}$:

$$\mathcal{M} \xrightarrow{\tau} \mathbf{s} \lhd P_{\mathbf{s}}^* \parallel \mathbf{c} \lhd P_{\mathbf{c}} \parallel \mathbf{a} \lhd P_{\mathbf{a}}^* \stackrel{\text{def}}{=} \mathcal{M}_1$$

where $P_{\mathbf{s}}^* \stackrel{\text{def}}{=} \mathbf{c}!\mathsf{login}\langle\rangle.\mathbf{a}?\mathsf{auth}(x).P_{\mathbf{s}} + \mathbf{c}!\mathsf{cancel}\langle\rangle.\mathbf{0}$.

The next step consists in unfolding the client $\mathbf{c}$. Since the client thread does not occur in the left, we need to first apply R-REC and then apply structural congruence in rule R-STR:

$$\text{R-STR} \cfrac{\text{R-REC} \cfrac{}{\mathbf{c} \lhd P_{\mathbf{c}} \parallel \mathbf{s} \lhd P_{\mathbf{s}}^* \parallel \mathbf{a} \lhd P_{\mathbf{a}}^* \xrightarrow{\tau} \mathbf{c} \lhd P_{\mathbf{c}}^* \parallel \mathbf{s} \lhd P_{\mathbf{s}}^* \parallel \mathbf{a} \lhd P_{\mathbf{a}}^*}}{\mathcal{M}_1 \xrightarrow{\tau} \mathbf{s} \lhd P_{\mathbf{s}}^* \parallel \mathbf{c} \lhd P_{\mathbf{c}}^* \parallel \mathbf{a} \lhd P_{\mathbf{a}}^* \stackrel{\text{def}}{=} \mathcal{M}_2}$$

where $P_{\mathbf{c}}^* \stackrel{\text{def}}{=} \mathbf{s}?\mathsf{login}(x).(\mathbf{a}!\mathsf{pwd}\langle\text{``fido''}\rangle.P_{\mathbf{c}} + \mathbf{a}!\mathsf{ssh}\langle\rangle.P_{\mathbf{c}}) + \mathbf{s}?\mathsf{cancel}(x).\mathbf{a}!\mathsf{quit}\langle\rangle.\mathbf{0}$. Now we apply rule R-COM to infer a communication among the service $\mathbf{s}$ and the client $\mathbf{c}$ on the label login, followed by R-STR:

$$\text{R-Str}\dfrac{\text{R-Com}\dfrac{(A)\quad(B)}{c\lhd P_c^*\,\|\,s\lhd P_s^*\,\|\,a\lhd P_a^*\xrightarrow{\text{login}@c\bowtie s}c\lhd P_c'\,\|\,s\lhd P_s'\,\|\,a\lhd P_a^*}}{\mathcal{M}_2\xrightarrow{\text{login}@c\bowtie s}\mathcal{M}_3}$$

where $\mathcal{M}_3\stackrel{\text{def}}{=}s\lhd a?\text{auth}(x).P_s\;\|\;c\lhd P_c'\;\|\;a\lhd P_a^*$, $P_s'\stackrel{\text{def}}{=}a?\text{auth}(x).P_s$, $P_c'\stackrel{\text{def}}{=}a!\text{pwd}\langle\text{"fido"}\rangle.P_c+a!\text{ssh}\langle\rangle.P_c$, and

$$(A)\ \text{R-Sum-L}\dfrac{\text{R-Inp}\dfrac{}{s?\text{login}(x).P_c'\xrightarrow{s?\text{login}()}P_c'}}{c\lhd P_c^*\xrightarrow{s?\text{login}()}c\lhd P_c'}$$

$$(B)\ \text{R-Sum-L}\dfrac{\text{R-Out}\dfrac{}{s\lhd c!\text{login}\langle\rangle.P_s'\xrightarrow{c!\text{login}\langle\rangle}s\lhd P_s'}}{s\lhd P_s^*\xrightarrow{c!\text{login}\langle\rangle}s\lhd P_s'}$$

As you can see, in session $\mathcal{M}_3$ the client c is ready to communicate the *password*, or to send a ssh request, to the authorisation server a. □

3 Session Environment Reduction, Algorithmically

A central notion of multiparty session types is the interaction among parties. We model this abstraction by depicting the behaviour of *session environments* Δ assigning types T to participants p.

Our aim is to define a *function* that decides at *compile-time* when it is safe to type-check a group of participants running in parallel and willing to communicate with each other. This is reminiscent of the notion of type duality in binary session types (e.g. [22,26]), but encompasses multiple participants. We will use the function in the typing system introduced in § 4.

Definition 3 (Labelled transition system). *A labelled transition system (LTS) is a tuple* $(\tilde{A},\mathcal{S}_1,\mathcal{A},\mathcal{S}_2,\rightarrow)$, *noted as* $\tilde{A}\rhd\sigma_1\xrightarrow{\alpha}\sigma_2$, *whenever* $\sigma_1\in\mathcal{S}_1$ *and* $\sigma_2\in\mathcal{S}_2$ *and* $\alpha\in\mathcal{A}$, *where* $\tilde{A}$ *is a (possibly empty) tuple of parameters,* $\mathcal{S}_i$ *are set of states,* $i=1,2$, $\mathcal{A}$ *is a set of actions, and* $\rightarrow$ *is a transition relation s.t.* $\rightarrow\subseteq\tilde{A}\times\mathcal{S}_1\times\mathcal{A}\times\mathcal{S}_2$. *A transition relation* $\rightarrow$ *is a partial function whenever* $\tilde{A}\rhd\sigma_1\xrightarrow{\alpha'}\sigma_2'$ *and* $\tilde{A}\rhd\sigma_1\xrightarrow{\alpha''}\sigma_2''$ *imply* $\alpha'=\alpha''$ *and* $\sigma_2'=\sigma_2''$. *A LTS is deterministic whenever its transition relation is a partial function.*

3.1 Non-deterministic Transition System

We first define a non-deterministic LTS of session environments, and then in § 3.2 we outline its transformation to a deterministic LTS. Non-deterministic transitions are used in the notion of deadlock (cf. Definition 10), and in the proof of

Transition rules for types: $\boxed{T \xrightarrow{\alpha} T}$

$$\text{E-Out}\frac{\emptyset \vdash v : S}{\mathbf{r}!l(S).T \xrightarrow{\mathbf{r}!l\langle v \rangle} T} \qquad \text{E-In}\frac{\emptyset \vdash v : S}{\mathbf{r}?l(S).T \xrightarrow{\mathbf{r}?l\langle v \rangle} T} \qquad \text{E-Sel-L}\frac{T_1 \xrightarrow{\mathbf{r}!l\langle v \rangle} T'}{T_1 + T_2 \xrightarrow{\mathbf{r}!l\langle v \rangle} T'}$$

$$\text{E-Bra-L}\frac{T_1 \xrightarrow{\mathbf{r}?l\langle v \rangle} T'}{T_1 + T_2 \xrightarrow{\mathbf{r}?l\langle v \rangle} T'} \qquad \text{E-Rec}\frac{}{\mu X.T \xrightarrow{\tau} T\{\mu X.T/X\}}$$

Transition rules for session environments: $\boxed{\Delta \xrightarrow{\alpha} \Delta}$

$$\text{Se-Rec}\frac{T \xrightarrow{\tau} T'}{\Delta, \mathbf{p} : T \xrightarrow{\tau} \Delta, \mathbf{p} : T'} \qquad \text{Se-Com}\frac{T_{\mathbf{p}} \xrightarrow{\mathbf{q}?l\langle v \rangle} T'_{\mathbf{p}} \quad T_{\mathbf{q}} \xrightarrow{\mathbf{p}!l\langle v \rangle} T'_{\mathbf{q}}}{\Delta, \mathbf{p} : T_{\mathbf{p}}, \mathbf{q} : T_{\mathbf{q}} \xrightarrow{l@\mathbf{p}\bowtie\mathbf{q}} \Delta, \mathbf{p} : T'_{\mathbf{p}}, \mathbf{q} : T'_{\mathbf{q}}}$$

Transition rule for configurations: $\boxed{D \diamond \Delta \xrightarrow{\alpha} D \diamond \Delta}$

$$\text{Se-Top}\frac{\Delta \in D \quad \Delta \xrightarrow{\alpha} \Delta'}{D \diamond \Delta \xrightarrow{\alpha} D\backslash_\Delta \diamond \Delta'}$$

Fig. 2. Labelled transition system of session environments

subject reduction (cf. § 4.2). In the non-deterministic setting, the parameters $\widetilde{A}$ are empty and $\mathcal{S}_1 = \mathcal{S}_2$.

We start by defining a non-deterministic LTS of types. Since we will also use the transition system to match the actions of processes, it is practical to use the same labels of the LTS of Figure 1. The left rules for types are in Figure 2. The rules are designed for well-formed types (cf. § 2), as we discuss below (cf. rules E-Sel-L, fitsE-Bra-L). Rule E-Out says that a type doing an output to the participant $\mathbf{r}$ on label l with payload S and continuing as T can fire the action $\mathbf{r}!l\langle v \rangle$ and reach the redex T whenever v is a value of sort S. Dually, rule E-In allows an input type from $\mathbf{r}$ on label l with payload S and continuing as T to do an action $\mathbf{r}?l(v)$ and reach the redex T, if v has sort S. Rule E-Sel-L allows a sum type $T_1 + T_2$ to do an output action $\mathbf{r}!l\langle v \rangle$ and reach the redex T' whenever T_1 can fire this action and reach T'. Dually, rule E-Bra-L allows a sum type $T_1 + T_2$ to do an input action $\mathbf{r}?l(v)$ and reach the redex T' if T_1 can fire this action and reach T'. Note that input and output are the only actions that a sum type can fire. This is because types as e.g. $T_1 + \mu X.T$ or $T_1 + (\mu X.T + T_2)$ are not well-formed.

The non-deterministic transition rules for session environments follow in Figure 2, and are the counterpart of the non-deterministic rules of the form $\Gamma \xrightarrow{\alpha} \Gamma$ used in GMST (cf. [49]) to analyse the *safety* and *deadlock freedom* of multiparty protocols. We consider a top-level rule of the form $D \diamond \Delta \xrightarrow{\alpha} D \diamond \Delta$, where we refer to $D \diamond \Delta$ as a *configuration*, and use C to range over it. D is a set of type environments representing a *decreasing set* which is a *subset of a fixed point*: a step can be taken only if Δ is in the decreasing set D. The idea is the following: since we are interested in computing all possible redexes of session environments, we avoid to further analyse the same environment twice by removing the visited environments from the (possibly infinite) set of all possible environments.

Rule SE-TOP applies to configurations and checks that an environment Δ is in the decreasing set D, and Δ can move to Δ' with label α: in such case the configuration $D \diamond \Delta$ moves to the configuration $D\backslash_\Delta \diamond \Delta'$, where $D\backslash_\Delta$ notes the decreasing set D less the environment Δ.

Rule SE-REC applies to session environments and says that $\Delta, \mathsf{p} \colon \mu X.T$ can do an internal action τ and reach the environment $\Delta, \mathsf{p} \colon T\{\mu X.T/X\}$, thus unfolding the type of the participant p. Rule SE-COM applies to session environments and depicts a communication: when a participant p has a type T_p that can fire an input action $\mathsf{q}?l(v)$ and move to T'_p, and a participant q has a type T_q that can fire an output action $\mathsf{p}!l\langle v\rangle$ and move to T'_q, then $\Delta, \mathsf{p} \colon T_\mathsf{p}, \mathsf{q} \colon T_\mathsf{q}$ can fire a synchronisation action $l@\mathsf{p}{\bowtie}\mathsf{q}$ and move to $\Delta, \mathsf{p} \colon T'_\mathsf{p}, \mathsf{q} \colon T'_\mathsf{q}$.

Example 2. Consider the protocol introduced in § 1.1 and take $\Delta \overset{\text{def}}{=} \mathsf{s} \colon T_\mathsf{s}, \mathsf{c} \colon T_\mathsf{c}, \mathsf{a} \colon T^*_\mathsf{a}$. Consider a fixed point D such that $\Delta \in D$. A first application of E-REC, SE-REC, SE-TOP allows for unfolding the type of the service s, where we let $T^*_\mathsf{s} \overset{\text{def}}{=} \mathsf{c}!\mathsf{login}(\mathsf{unit}).\mathsf{a}?\mathsf{auth}(\mathsf{bool}).T_\mathsf{s} + \mathsf{c}!\mathsf{cancel}(\mathsf{unit}).\mathsf{end}$:

$$D \diamond \Delta \xrightarrow{\tau} D\backslash_\Delta \diamond \Delta, \mathsf{s} \colon T^*_\mathsf{s}, \mathsf{c} \colon T_\mathsf{c}, \mathsf{a} \colon T^*_\mathsf{a} \overset{\text{def}}{=} \Delta_1$$

To continue and unfold the type of the client c, we need to verify that $\Delta_1 \in D\backslash_\Delta$: this follows indeed from the property of a fixed point, that is to be closed under transition, and from the fact $\Delta_1 \neq \Delta$, which holds because types are iso-recursive, and in turn $T^*_\mathsf{s} \neq T_\mathsf{s}$. We proceed as above and infer the following transition, where $T^*_\mathsf{c} \overset{\text{def}}{=} \mathsf{s}?\mathsf{login}(\mathsf{unit}).(\mathsf{a}!\mathsf{pwd}(\mathsf{str}).T_\mathsf{c} + \mathsf{a}!\mathsf{ssh}(\mathsf{unit}).T_\mathsf{c}) + \mathsf{s}?\mathsf{cancel}(\mathsf{unit}).\mathsf{a}!\mathsf{quit}(\mathsf{unit}).\mathsf{end}$:

$$D\backslash_\Delta \diamond \Delta_1 \xrightarrow{\tau} D\backslash_{\Delta,\Delta_1} \diamond \Delta, \mathsf{s} \colon T^*_\mathsf{s}, \mathsf{c} \colon T^*_\mathsf{c}, \mathsf{a} \colon T^*_\mathsf{a} \overset{\text{def}}{=} \Delta_2$$

Two non-deterministic transitions are available from Δ_2, and involve the synchronisation of s and c: one over the label login and the other over the label cancel. The interaction below corresponds to the label login and is obtained by applying E-OUT, E-SEL-L, E-IN, E-BRA-L, SE-COM, SE-TOP, where $T'_\mathsf{c} \overset{\text{def}}{=} \mathsf{a}!\mathsf{pwd}(\mathsf{str}).T_\mathsf{c} + \mathsf{a}!\mathsf{ssh}(\mathsf{unit}).T_\mathsf{c}$ and $D_2 \overset{\text{def}}{=} D\backslash_{\Delta,\Delta_1}$ and $D_3 \overset{\text{def}}{=} D_2\backslash_{\Delta_2}$:

$$D_2 \diamond \Delta_2 \xrightarrow{\mathsf{login}@\mathsf{c}{\bowtie}\mathsf{s}} D_3 \diamond \Delta, \mathsf{s} \colon \mathsf{a}?\mathsf{auth}(\mathsf{bool}).T_\mathsf{s}, \mathsf{c} \colon T'_\mathsf{c}, \mathsf{a} \colon T^*_\mathsf{a} \overset{\text{def}}{=} \Delta_3$$

The interaction over the label cancel is obtained by applying E-OUT, E-SEL-R, E-IN, E-BRA-R, SE-COM, SE-TOP, where E-SEL-R and E-BRA-R are the right rules of E-SEL-L and E-BRA-L, respectively:

$$D_2 \diamond \Delta_2 \xrightarrow{\mathsf{cancel}@\mathsf{c}{\bowtie}\mathsf{s}} D_3 \diamond \Delta, \mathsf{s} \colon \mathsf{end}, \mathsf{c} \colon \mathsf{a}!\mathsf{quit}(\mathsf{unit}).\mathsf{end}, \mathsf{a} \colon T^*_\mathsf{a} \overset{\text{def}}{=} \Delta'_3$$

We conclude by noting that the transition system $D \diamond \Delta \xrightarrow{\alpha} D \diamond \Delta$ is indeed non-deterministic (Definition 3) by $\mathtt{login@c \bowtie s} \neq \mathtt{cancel@c \bowtie s}$ and $\Delta_3 \neq \Delta_3'$.

$\square$

3.2 Deterministic Session Environment Transitions

In this section, we define a deterministic LTS for environments that is the basis for the definition of *closure* in § 3.3, and in turn for the mechanisation of *compliance* (cf. § 4.1) in deductive tools of the OCaml ecosystem (cf. § 5).

The transition system $D \diamond \Delta \xrightarrow{\alpha} D' \diamond \Delta'$ is non-deterministic, for two reasons: (1) threads can reduce or interact in any order; (2) label synchronisation among two participants can occur on multiple labels and in any order.

To make the LTS deterministic (cf. Definition 3), we need four ingredients: (i) To partition the environment into minimal environments, and invoke the LTS on each minimal environment; (ii) To collect information about discarded branches and selections in synchronisations; (iii) To pass an oracle Ω that given an environment Δ returns the next two engaging participants, or the next participant firing a τ action, or nothing; (iv) To define a scheduling policy for labels of communicating participants.

We discuss (i) and (iii), and provide the signature of the deterministic LTS. Feature (i) relies on following definition; see [27] forall details.

Let $\mathsf{parties}(\mathsf{p}?l(S).T) \overset{\text{def}}{=} \mathsf{parties}(T) \cup \{\mathsf{p}\} = \mathsf{parties}(\mathsf{p}!l(S).T)$, $\mathsf{parties}(\mu X.T) \overset{\text{def}}{=} \mathsf{parties}(T)$, $\mathsf{parties}(T_1 + T_2) \overset{\text{def}}{=} \mathsf{parties}(T_1) \cup \mathsf{parties}(T_2)$, and $\mathsf{parties}(T) \overset{\text{def}}{=} \emptyset$ otherwise. Let $\mathsf{parties}(\emptyset) \overset{\text{def}}{=} \emptyset$, $\mathsf{parties}(\Delta, \mathsf{p} \colon T) \overset{\text{def}}{=} \{\mathsf{p}\} \cup \mathsf{parties}(T) \cup \mathsf{parties}(\Delta)$. Let $\Delta \backslash_{\mathsf{End}}$ project all non-ended participants of Δ.

Definition 4 (Minimal partition and environments). *A set* $\{\Delta_1, \ldots, \Delta_n\} \neq \emptyset$ *is a partition of* $\Delta_1 \cup \cdots \cup \Delta_n$ *whenever* $\Delta_i \neq \emptyset$ *and* $\mathsf{parties}(\Delta_i) \cap \mathsf{parties}(\Delta_j) = \emptyset$ *for all* $\{i, j\} \subseteq \{1, \ldots, n\}$, $i \neq j$. *Let* $\mathcal{P}_{\mathcal{R}}(\Delta)$ *be the set of all partitions of* Δ. *We say that* Δ *is minimal if there not exists* $\mathcal{P}_{\mathcal{R}}(\Delta \backslash_{\mathsf{End}}) \ni S \neq \{\Delta \backslash_{\mathsf{End}}\}$ *s.t.* $\Delta \backslash_{\mathsf{End}} = \bigcup_{\Delta' \in S} \Delta'$. *A partition* $\{\Delta_1, \ldots, \Delta_n\}$ *of* Δ *is minimal, denoted as* $\mathsf{minPartition}_\Delta(\Delta_1, \ldots, \Delta_n)$, *whenever* Δ_i *is minimal, for all* $i \in \{1, \ldots, n\}$.

The aim of invoking the LTS on minimal environments is to avoid the non-determinism coming from sub-systems executing unrelated behaviours. The fixed point mechanism based on decreasing sets assumes that once we re-encounter the same environment twice, we can stop since we already explored all possible computations. This is no longer sound if the system contain unrelated sub-systems. For instance, if an environment contains two participants p and q communicating with each other and reaching a fixed point after few steps, and *also* two participants r and s communicating with each other, then, depending on the oracle (see (iii)), it might be the case that the computation finishes without analysing r and s (cf. [28]). On contrast, if we consider a minimal environment, all parties are properly parsed, because the oracle is forced to analyse all sub-processes of the interacting participants. As we shall see in § 4, the minimality assumption does not pose any limitation because we perform the compliance analysis on all environments of a minimal partition.

Feature (iii) is implemented by adding a *fair* oracle returning participants willing to reduce or communicate when this option is available. The top level participant of a well-formed type T, denoted $\mathrm{top}(T)$, is a partial function indicating the unguarded participant of a branching or of a selection:

$$\mathrm{top}(\mathsf{p}?(S).T) \overset{\mathrm{def}}{=} \mathsf{p} \qquad \mathrm{top}(\mathsf{p}!(S).T) \overset{\mathrm{def}}{=} \mathsf{p} \qquad \mathrm{top}(T_1 + T_2) \overset{\mathrm{def}}{=} \mathrm{top}(T_1)$$

Definition 5 (Oracle fairness). *A oracle Ω is fair whenever:*

1. *$\Omega(\Delta) = (\mathsf{p}, \mathsf{q})$ implies $\mathrm{top}(\Delta(\mathsf{p})) = \mathsf{q}$ and $\mathrm{top}(\Delta(\mathsf{q})) = \mathsf{p}$*
2. *$\Omega(\Delta) = \mathsf{p}$ implies $\Delta(\mathsf{p}) = \mu X.T$*
3. *$\Omega(\Delta)$ undefined implies*
   (a) forall $\mathsf{p} \in \mathrm{dom}(\Delta)$ we have $\Delta(\mathsf{p}) \neq \mu X.T$
   (b) there not exists $\{\mathsf{p}, \mathsf{q}\} \subseteq \mathrm{dom}(\Delta)$ s.t. $\mathrm{top}(\Delta(\mathsf{p})) = \mathsf{q}$ and $\mathrm{top}(\Delta(\mathsf{q})) = \mathsf{p}$

Deterministic transitions of session environments have the following form:

$$\Omega \triangleright D \diamond \Delta \overset{\alpha}{\longrightarrow}_d D \diamond \Delta \blacktriangleright \Delta$$

where Δ is minimal (i), Ω is a fair oracle (iii), we assume a label scheduling policy (iv), α is a synchronisation label $l@\mathsf{p}\bowtie\mathsf{q}$ or a τ action decorated with the originating participant, denoted τ_p, and Δ after the symbol $\blacktriangleright$ is called the *sum continuation* and is a type environment or an environment placeholder, denoted ∇° (ii). We note that, w.r.t. to Definition 3, we have that $\widetilde{A} = \Omega$, the set of states $\mathcal{S}_1$ contains $D \diamond \Delta$, and the set of states $\mathcal{S}_2$ contains $D \diamond \Delta \blacktriangleright \Delta$. Moreover, $\longrightarrow_d$ is a partial function: $\Omega \triangleright D \diamond \Delta \overset{\alpha'}{\longrightarrow}_d D' \diamond \Delta'_1 \blacktriangleright \Delta'_2$ and $\Omega \triangleright D \diamond \Delta \overset{\alpha''}{\longrightarrow}_d D'' \diamond \Delta''_1 \blacktriangleright \Delta''_2$ imply $\alpha' = \alpha''$, and $D' = D''$, $\Delta'_i = \Delta''_i$, $i = 1, 2$.

Example 3. Consider $D \diamond \Delta$ defined in Example 2. We note that Δ is minimal. Take a fair oracle Ω, and assume that the scheduling of labels follows the *lexicographic order*. First, we note that $\Omega(\Delta)$ undefined gives rise to a contradiction, because e.g. $\Delta(\mathsf{s}) = \mu X.T$. Depending on the oracle Ω, we may have $\Omega(\Delta) = \mathsf{s}$ or $\Omega(\Delta) = \mathsf{c}$, because any other combination would contradict Definition 5.

Assume $\Omega(\Delta) = \mathsf{s}$. A first step let us infer the reduction of the service, where $\Delta_1 \overset{\mathrm{def}}{=} \Delta, \mathsf{s}: T_\mathsf{s}^*, \mathsf{c}: T_\mathsf{c}, \mathsf{a}: T_\mathsf{a}^*$, and $\mathrm{minimal}(\Delta_1)$.

$$\Omega \triangleright D \diamond \Delta \overset{\tau_\mathsf{s}}{\longrightarrow}_d D\backslash_\Delta \diamond \Delta_1 \blacktriangleright \nabla^\circ$$

Next, we assume that $\Omega(\Delta_1) = \mathsf{c}$, where $\Delta_2 \overset{\mathrm{def}}{=} \Delta, \mathsf{s}: T_\mathsf{s}^*, \mathsf{c}: T_\mathsf{c}^*, \mathsf{a}: T_\mathsf{a}^*$.

$$\Omega \triangleright D\backslash_\Delta \diamond \Delta_1 \overset{\tau_\mathsf{c}}{\longrightarrow}_d D\backslash_{\Delta,\Delta_1} \diamond \Delta_2 \blacktriangleright \nabla^\circ$$

In the next round we have $\mathrm{minimal}(\Delta_2)$ and $\Omega(\Delta_2) = (\mathsf{c}, \mathsf{s})$, and the algorithm picks the first label in the intersection of the labels of c and s, that is cancel:

$$\Omega \triangleright D_2 \diamond \Delta_2 \overset{\mathtt{cancel}@\mathsf{c}\bowtie\mathsf{s}}{\longrightarrow}_d D_3 \diamond \Delta'' \blacktriangleright \Delta'$$

where D_2, D_3 are defined in Example 2 and

$$\Delta'' \stackrel{\text{def}}{=} \text{s: end, c: a!quit(unit).end, a: } T_\text{a}^*$$

$$\Delta' \stackrel{\text{def}}{=} \text{s: c!login(unit).a?auth(bool).}T_\text{s}\text{, c: s?login(unit).}T_\text{c}'\text{, a: } T_\text{a}^*$$

$$T_\text{c}' \stackrel{\text{def}}{=} \text{a!pwd(str).}T_\text{c} + \text{a!ssh(unit).}T_\text{c}$$

After this sequence of transitions, we have two minimal environments Δ'' and Δ' corresponding to the redex of the interaction of the service s and the client c over the label cancel, and to the environment prompt to let s and c interact over the label login, respectively. The idea is to deterministically visit all the binary trees spawned by further transitions starting from $D_3 \diamond \Delta''$ and from $D_3 \diamond \Delta'$, respectively, as we discuss in the next section.   □

3.3   Closure

The aim of the deterministic LTS presented in § 3.2 is to be used by the function that computes the *compliance* of session environments in the typing system (cf. § 4). Compliance analyses all final environments computed by the closure of the deterministic transitions originating from a type environment.

More specifically, we consider the *semireflexive-transitive closure* of the deterministic lts $\longrightarrow_d$, denoted $\Longrightarrow$. Semireflexivity means that a configuration is related with itself only if is stuck, that is it cannot fire any transition.

We are interested in applying closure to environments preserving minimality.

Definition 6 (Stuck environment). *A minimal environment Δ is stuck w.r.t. an oracle Ω and a decreasing set D, denoted $\text{stuck}_{\Omega,D}(\Delta)$, if there not exists $\alpha, \Delta_1, \Delta_2$ such that $\Omega \rhd D \diamond \Delta \xrightarrow{\alpha}_d D' \diamond \Delta_1 \blacktriangleright \Delta_2$.*

Definition 7 (Closure). *Define:*

$$\text{C-Rfl} \frac{\text{stuck}_{\Omega,D}(\Delta)}{\Omega \rhd D \diamond \Delta \Longrightarrow D \diamond \Delta} \qquad \text{C-Err} \frac{\neg\text{minimal}(\Delta)}{\Omega \rhd D \diamond \Delta \Longrightarrow \text{err}}$$

$$\text{C-Tra} \frac{\Omega \rhd D \diamond \Delta \xrightarrow{\alpha}_d D' \diamond \Delta_1 \blacktriangleright \Delta_2 \quad \Omega \rhd D' \diamond \Delta_1 \Longrightarrow \widetilde{E_1} \quad \Omega \rhd D' \diamond \Delta_2 \Longrightarrow \widetilde{E_2}}{\Omega \rhd D \diamond \Delta \Longrightarrow \widetilde{E_1}, \widetilde{E_2}}$$

The closure of a minimal environment Δ w.r.t. a decreasing set D s.t. $\Delta \in D$ and a fair oracle Ω is defined by the following rule:

$$\text{C-Top} \frac{\Omega \rhd D \diamond \Delta \Longrightarrow D_1 \diamond \Delta_1, \cdots, D_n \diamond \Delta_n}{\text{closure}_{\Omega,D}(\Delta) = \Delta_1, \dots, \Delta_n}$$

Given a a fair oracle Ω, the relation $\Longrightarrow$ associates a configuration C to a *non-empty* tuple of e-configurations $E_1, \dots, E_n$, denoted as $\widetilde{E}$, where each E_i is a configuration C or the *failure* err. Given a configuration $C = D \diamond \Delta$, three cases may arise. If C is stuck, that is C cannot fire any transition, then we apply rule [C-Rfl] and relate C with itself, else if C is not minimal, then we we apply rule [C-Err] and relate C with err. Otherwise we have that C fires an action and reaches the redex $\Delta' \diamond \Delta_1 \blacktriangleright \Delta_2$: we apply rule [C-Tra] and whenever $\Delta' \diamond \Delta_1$ is related by $\Longrightarrow$ to the e-configurations $\widetilde{E_1}$, and $\Delta' \diamond \Delta_2$ is related by $\Longrightarrow$ to $\widetilde{E_2}$, we let C be related by $\Longrightarrow$ to $\widetilde{E_1}, \widetilde{E_2}$.

The `closure` of a session environment Δ is defined iff $\Longrightarrow$ does not relate Δ with failures. If this is the case, then $\Longrightarrow$ relates Δ with configurations $\widetilde{C}$: the function strips off all decreasing sets and associates Δ to a set of minimal stuck environments. It is worth noting that `closure` is a *terminating function*, because it is deterministic and it has $|D|$ as decreasing measure.

Example 4. We continue the analysis started in Example 3 and find a subset of $\mathsf{closure}_{\Omega,D}(\Delta)$, which is defined because Δ and its redexes are minimal. Remember T_{a}^* defined in § 1.1: $T_{\mathsf{a}}^* \overset{\text{def}}{=} \mathsf{c}?\mathsf{pwd}(\mathsf{str}).\mathsf{s}!\mathsf{auth}(\mathsf{bool}).T_{\mathsf{a}} + \mathsf{c}?\mathsf{ssh}(\mathsf{unit}).\mathsf{s}!\mathsf{auth}$ $(\mathsf{bool}).T_{\mathsf{a}} + \mathsf{c}?\mathsf{quit}(\mathsf{unit}).\mathsf{end}$. Consider $D_3 \diamond \Delta'' \blacktriangleright \Delta'$ defined in Example 3:

$$\Omega \triangleright D \diamond \Delta \xrightarrow{\tau_s}_d \xrightarrow{\tau_c}_d \xrightarrow{\mathsf{cancel}@\mathsf{c}\bowtie\mathsf{s}}_d D_3 \diamond \Delta'' \blacktriangleright \Delta'$$

To calculate the closure of Δ w.r.t. D, we need to analyse the closures of Δ'' and Δ' w.r.t. D_3, respectively. We have that Δ'' and Δ' are minimal: we analyse the former closure, and note that $D_3 \diamond \Delta''$ is not stuck, i.e. the client c and the server a can communicate on quit. Assume $\Omega(\Delta'') = (\mathsf{a}, \mathsf{c})$. We have:

$$\text{C-Tra} \frac{\Omega \triangleright D_3 \diamond \Delta'' \xrightarrow{\mathsf{quit}@\mathsf{a}\bowtie\mathsf{c}}_d D_3\backslash_{\Delta''} \diamond \mathsf{s}\colon \mathsf{end}, \mathsf{c}\colon \mathsf{end}, \mathsf{a}\colon \mathsf{end} \blacktriangleright \nabla^\circ \quad (A)}{\Omega \triangleright D_3 \diamond \Delta'' \Longrightarrow D_3\backslash_{\Delta''} \diamond \mathsf{s}\colon \mathsf{end}, \mathsf{c}\colon \mathsf{end}, \mathsf{a}\colon \mathsf{end}}$$

$$(A) \ \text{C-Rfl} \frac{}{\Omega \triangleright D_3\backslash_{\Delta''} \diamond \mathsf{s}\colon \mathsf{end}, \mathsf{c}\colon \mathsf{end}, \mathsf{a}\colon \mathsf{end} \Longrightarrow D_3\backslash_{\Delta''} \diamond \mathsf{s}\colon \mathsf{end}, \mathsf{c}\colon \mathsf{end}, \mathsf{a}\colon \mathsf{end}}$$

We can thus infer $(\mathsf{s}\colon \mathsf{end}, \mathsf{c}\colon \mathsf{end}, \mathsf{a}\colon \mathsf{end}) \in \mathsf{closure}_{\Omega,D}(\Delta)$. $\qquad\square$

4 Iso-Recursive Multiparty Type System

The typing rules for processes and sessions are defined in Figure 3; we refer to the technical report [27] for the rules for expressions.

Typing judgements for processes have the form $\Gamma \vdash P\colon T$, where Γ maps variables to sorts and process variables to types:

$$\Gamma := \emptyset \mid \Gamma, x\colon S \mid \Gamma, \chi\colon T$$

Typing judgements for sessions have the form $\Gamma \Vdash \mathcal{M}\colon \Delta$, where Δ is the session environment introduced in § 3, that is a map from participants to types, and invoke the type system $\vdash$. The type system for sessions $\Vdash$ only invokes the type system for processes $\vdash$ with well-formed types (cf. § 2): for this reason, the typing rules for processes involving type sums can be simplified (cf. rules T-Sum,T-Sum-L,T-Sum-R).

The rule depicting the essence of iso-recursive multiparty session types is T-Rec. In order to allow Γ to type a recursion process $\mu\chi.P$ with a type $\mu X.T$, it must be the case that $\Gamma, \chi\colon \mu X.T$ types the continuation P with the unfolded type $T\{\mu X.T/X\}$. That is, in our iso-recursive setting the continuation must be typed by explicitly unfolding the recursive type. This is different from the equi-recursive approach, e.g. [23], where the type of $\mu\chi.P$ and the type of the

Sorting rules: $\boxed{\Gamma \vdash e \colon S}$

Typing rules for processes: $\boxed{\Gamma \vdash P \colon T}$

$$\text{T-End} \frac{}{\Gamma \vdash 0 \colon \mathsf{end}} \qquad \text{T-Rec} \frac{\Gamma, \chi \colon \mu X.T \vdash P \colon T\{\mu X.T/X\}}{\Gamma \vdash \mu\chi.P \colon \mu X.T}$$

$$\text{T-Var} \frac{\Gamma(\chi) = \mu X.T}{\Gamma \vdash \chi \colon \mu X.T} \qquad \text{T-Inp} \frac{\Gamma, x \colon S \vdash P \colon T}{\Gamma \vdash \mathbf{r}?l(x).P \colon \mathbf{r}?l(S).T}$$

$$\text{T-Out} \frac{\Gamma \vdash e \colon S \qquad \Gamma \vdash P \colon T}{\Gamma \vdash \mathbf{r}!l\langle e\rangle.P \colon \mathbf{r}!l(S).T} \qquad \text{T-Sum} \frac{\Gamma \vdash P \colon T_1 \qquad \Gamma \vdash Q \colon T_2}{\Gamma \vdash P + Q \colon T_1 + T_2}$$

$$\text{T-Sum-L} \frac{\Gamma \vdash P \colon T_1}{\Gamma \vdash P \colon T_1 + T_2} \qquad \text{T-Sum-R} \frac{\Gamma \vdash P \colon T_2}{\Gamma \vdash P \colon T_1 + T_2}$$

$$\text{T-If} \frac{\Gamma \vdash e \colon \mathsf{bool} \qquad \Gamma \vdash P \colon T \qquad \Gamma \vdash Q \colon T}{\Gamma \vdash \mathsf{if}\ e\ \mathsf{then}\ P\ \mathsf{else}\ Q \colon T}$$

Typing rules for sessions: $\boxed{\Gamma \Vdash \mathcal{M} \colon \Delta}$

$$\text{T-Thr} \frac{\Gamma \vdash P \colon T \qquad \mathrm{WF}(T)}{\Gamma \Vdash \mathbf{p} \lhd P \colon \mathbf{p} \colon T}$$

$$\text{T-Ses} \frac{\begin{array}{c}\Gamma \Vdash \mathbf{p}_1 \lhd P_1 \colon \mathbf{p}_1 \colon T_1 \quad \cdots \quad \Gamma \Vdash \mathbf{p}_n \lhd P_n \colon \mathbf{p}_n \colon T_n \quad \Delta = \mathbf{p}_1 \colon T_1, \ldots, \mathbf{p}_n \colon T_n \\ \mathsf{minPartition}_\Delta(\Delta_1, \ldots, \Delta_k) \qquad \forall j \in \{1, \ldots, k\}.\,\mathsf{comp}(\Delta_j)\end{array}}{\Gamma \Vdash \|_{i \in \{1,..,n\}} \mathbf{p}_i \lhd P_i \colon \Delta}$$

Fig. 3. Type system

continuation P can be equal, because types $\mu X.T$ and $T\{\mu X.T/X\}$ are equal. For the same reason, in rule T-Var an environment $\Gamma, \chi \colon \mu X.T$ assigns the type $\mu X.T$ to the process variable χ: note that it is not possible to assign a non-recursive type to process variables.

Rule T-Inp allows Γ to type a input process $\mathbf{r}?l(x).P$ with type $\mathbf{r}?l(S).T$ whenever $\Gamma, x \colon S$ assigns the type T to the continuation P. Dually, rule T-Out allows Γ to type an output process $\mathbf{r}!l\langle e\rangle.P$ with type $\mathbf{r}?l(S).T$ whenever the expression has sort S and Γ assigns the type T to the continuation P.

Rule T-Sum is used for branching and selection, that are sums containing only input types from the same participant and without duplicated labels, or output types from the same participant and without duplicated labels, respectively (cf. Well-Formed Types in § 2, and Definition 2). Note indeed that well-formed types do not contain types of the form e.g. $T_1 + \mu X.T_2$, or $\mathsf{end} + T$. The rule says that if Γ can be used to type a process P_1 with type T_1, and a process P_2 with type T_2, then Γ types $P_1 + P_2$ with type $T_1 + T_2$.

While rule T-Sum types exactly each input and output with their corresponding input and output type singletons, rule T-Sum-L allows for typing a process P having type T_1 with the type $T_1 + T_2$. For instance, if P is the branch-

$P_{\mathsf{a}} \overset{\text{def}}{=} \mu\chi.(P_1 + P_2) \quad P_1 \overset{\text{def}}{=} \mathsf{c}?\mathsf{pwd}(x).Check_{\mathsf{a}}$

$P_2 \overset{\text{def}}{=} \mathsf{c}?\mathsf{ssh}(x).\mathsf{s}!\mathsf{auth}\langle\mathsf{true}\rangle.\chi + \mathsf{c}?\mathsf{quit}(x).\mathbf{0}$

$Check_{\mathsf{a}} \overset{\text{def}}{=} \mathsf{if}\, x = \text{``miau''}\, \mathsf{then}\, \mathsf{s}!\mathsf{auth}\langle\mathsf{true}\rangle.\chi\, \mathsf{else}\, \mathsf{s}!\mathsf{fail}\langle\rangle.\mathbf{0}$

$T' \overset{\text{def}}{=} \mathsf{c}?\mathsf{pwd}(\mathsf{str}).(\mathsf{s}!\mathsf{auth}(\mathsf{bool}).X + \mathsf{s}!\mathsf{fail}(\mathsf{unit}).\mathsf{end})$

$T'' \overset{\text{def}}{=} \mathsf{c}?\mathsf{ssh}(\mathsf{unit}).\mathsf{s}!\mathsf{auth}(\mathsf{bool}).X + \mathsf{c}?\mathsf{quit}(\mathsf{unit}).\mathsf{end} \quad T \overset{\text{def}}{=} T' + T''$

Fig. 4. Variant of authorisation server in § 1.1

ing process $\mathsf{r}?l_1(x).P_1 + \cdots + \mathsf{r}?l_n(x).P_n$ then we can use T-SUM-L to assign to P the type $\&_{i\in\{1,\ldots,n+1\}}\mathsf{r}?l_i(S_i).T_i$. Rule T-SUM-R does the same thing, on the right: if P has type T_2 then we can use the rule to assign to P the type $T_1 + T_2$.

The increased flexibility offered by rules T-SUM-L, T-SUM-R is used in the rule for if-then-else, that is T-IF. In order to type process if e then P else Q with type T we require that e has a boolean sort, and that both P and Q have type T. To allow P and Q to use different labels to communicate in input/output with a participant, we use rules T-SUM-L and T-SUM-R in the premises of T-IF, thus mimicking a simple form of subtyping. The next example illustrates this idea.

Example 5. Consider the variant of Figure 4 of the authorisation server a in § 1.1 such that a verifies the password sent by the client c while allowing only one attempt: if the password is wrong, a sends fail to the service s and stops. We informally discuss the typing of the authorisation server P_{a}, and omit the types of the other participants. A formal derivation is included in [27].

Let $\Gamma \overset{\text{def}}{=} \chi\colon \mu X.T, x\colon \mathsf{str}$, consider the two branches of $Check_{\mathsf{a}}$, and let $T_{\mathsf{if}} \overset{\text{def}}{=} \mathsf{s}!\mathsf{auth}(\mathsf{bool}).\mu X.T + \mathsf{s}!\mathsf{fail}(\mathsf{unit}).\mathsf{end}$. The left branch $\mathsf{s}!\mathsf{auth}\langle\mathsf{true}\rangle.\chi$ can be assigned to T_{if} under Γ by using T-SUM-L, T-OUT, T-VAR. The right branch $\mathsf{s}!\mathsf{fail}\langle\rangle.\mathbf{0}$ can be assigned to T_{if} under Γ by using T-SUM-R, T-OUT, T-END. By applying T-IF we thus assign T_{if} to $Check_{\mathsf{a}}$ under Γ; in turn, process P_1 is assigned to $T_1 \overset{\text{def}}{=} \mathsf{c}?\mathsf{pwd}(\mathsf{str}).T_{\mathsf{if}}$ under $\chi\colon \mu X.T$ by using T-INP. We note that $T_1 = T'\{\mu X.T/X\}$. Process P_2 is assigned to $T_2 \overset{\text{def}}{=} \mathsf{c}?\mathsf{ssh}(\mathsf{unit}).\mathsf{s}!\mathsf{auth}(\mathsf{bool}).\mu X.T + \mathsf{c}?\mathsf{quit}(\mathsf{unit}).\mathsf{end}$ under $\chi\colon \mu X.T$: we omit all details. We note that $T_2 = T''\{\mu X.T/X\}$.

We use T-SUM to assign $T'\{\mu X.T/X\} + T''\{\mu X.T/X\} = T\{\mu X.T/X\}$ to $P_1 + P_2$ under $\chi\colon \mu X.T$. We conclude by using T-REC to assign $\mu X.T$ to P_{a} under the empty environment, thus typing the authorisation server. □

Type checking sessions. The typing rules for sessions of Figure 3 have the form $\Gamma \Vdash \mathcal{M}\colon \Delta$ and use the rules for processes $\Gamma \vdash P\colon T$. The system relies on the notion of *minimal partition* (cf. Definition 4).

Rule T-THR is used for single threads and says that if the type system for processes $\vdash$ can be used to type a process P with a well-formed type T (cf. § 2), then the type system $\Vdash$ assigns the typing $\mathsf{p}\colon T$ to the thread $\mathsf{p} \lhd P$.

Rule T-SES is the top-level rule used to type-check the multiparty session. In order to type-check a session composing the threads $\mathsf{p}_1 \lhd P_1, \ldots, \mathsf{p}_n \lhd P_n$ with the session environment $\Delta = \mathsf{p}_1\colon T_1, \ldots, \mathsf{p}_n\colon T_n$, we require two things:

1. Each thread $\mathsf{p}_i \lhd P_i$ is typed with the environment $\mathsf{p}_i \colon T_i$, for $i = 1, \ldots n$;
2. Each environment Δ_j of the minimal partition $\{\Delta_1, \ldots, \Delta_k\}$ of Δ satisfies *compliance*, denoted $\mathsf{comp}(\Delta_j)$.

Compliance resembles the approach based on safe contexts (e.g. [49, Definition 4.1]), although is fully computational.

4.1   Compliance

Intuitively, a session typed by a compliant environment never reaches an *error*, that is a deadlocked system, or a redex containing two participants p and q that are willing to communicate, e.g. p is sending an output to q, and q is receiving an input from p, or vice-versa, but they mismatch the communication label and/or the type payload, or both p and q are sending (receiving) a value to each other: that is, there is a mismatch that makes the two participants stuck.

The formal definition of compliance relies on the *closure* of $\longrightarrow_d$ introduced in § 3, and of the formal definition of error below. Let the *tagged labels* of a type T, denoted $\mathcal{L}(T)$, be defined inductively as follows: $\mathcal{L}(\mathsf{r}!l(S).T) \overset{\text{def}}{=} \{l@S\}$, $\mathcal{L}(\mathsf{r}?l(S).T) \overset{\text{def}}{=} \{l@S\}$, $\mathcal{L}(T_1 + T_2) \overset{\text{def}}{=} \mathcal{L}(T_1) \cup \mathcal{L}(T_2)$, $\mathcal{L}(T) \overset{\text{def}}{=} \emptyset$ otherwise.

Definition 8 (Well-formed environment). *A session environment Δ is well-formed, denoted $WF(\Delta)$, whenever $\mathsf{p} \in \mathrm{dom}(\Delta)$ implies $WF(\Delta(\mathsf{p}))$.*

Definition 9 (Communication mismatch). *A well-formed session environment Δ is a communication mismatch whenever there exists $\{\mathsf{p}, \mathsf{q}\} \subseteq \mathrm{dom}(\Delta)$ such that one of the following cases arise:*

$$\Delta(\mathsf{p}) = \oplus_{i \in I}\mathsf{q}!l_i(S_i).T_i \quad \Delta(\mathsf{q}) = \oplus_{j \in J}\mathsf{p}!l_j(S_j).T_j$$
$$\Delta(\mathsf{p}) = \&_{i \in I}\mathsf{q}?l_i(S_i).T_i \quad \Delta(\mathsf{q}) = \&_{j \in J}\mathsf{p}?l_j(S_j).T_j$$
$$\Delta(\mathsf{p}) = \oplus_{i \in I}\mathsf{q}!l_i(S_i).T_i \quad \Delta(\mathsf{q}) = \&_{j \in J}\mathsf{p}?l_j(S_j).T_j \quad \mathcal{L}(\Delta(\mathsf{p})) \cap \mathcal{L}(\Delta(\mathsf{q})) = \emptyset$$
$$\Delta(\mathsf{p}) = \&_{i \in I}\mathsf{q}?l_i(S_i).T_i \quad \Delta(\mathsf{q}) = \oplus_{j \in J}\mathsf{p}!l_j(S_j).T_j \quad \mathcal{L}(\Delta(\mathsf{p})) \cap \mathcal{L}(\Delta(\mathsf{q})) = \emptyset$$

The notion of deadlock is insensitive to decreasing sets and determinism, and is based on the non-deterministic transition system $\Delta \overset{\alpha}{\longrightarrow} \Delta$ of Figure 2.

Definition 10 (Deadlock). *Let $\mathsf{consumed}(\Delta) \overset{\text{def}}{=} \forall \mathsf{p} \in \mathrm{dom}(\Delta) . \Delta(\mathsf{p}) = \mathsf{end}$. A session environment Δ is a deadlock when both (1) there not exists α, Δ' such that $\Delta \overset{\alpha}{\longrightarrow} \Delta'$, and (2) $\neg\mathsf{consumed}(\Delta)$.*

Definition 11 (Error). *A well-formed environment Δ is an error whenever Δ is a communication mismatch, or Δ is a deadlock.*

Definition 12 (Compliance). *Let Δ be a minimal well-formed environment. Define $\mathsf{comp}(\Delta)$ whenever for all fair oracles Ω and fixed points D including Δ, if $\mathsf{closure}_{\Omega,D}(\Delta) = \Delta_1, \ldots, \Delta_n$ then Δ_i is not an error, for all $i \in \{1, \ldots, n\}$.*

Example 6. Consider the minimal well-formed environment Δ'' introduced at the end of § 1.1, and the claim $\neg\mathsf{comp}(\Delta'')$, which follows from Δ'' reaching the dead-locked environment $\Delta_{\mathtt{lock}} = \mathtt{s}: \mathtt{a}?\mathsf{auth}(\mathsf{bool}).T_\mathtt{s},\ \mathtt{c}: \mathtt{a}!\mathsf{pwd}(\mathsf{str}).T_\mathtt{c} + \mathtt{a}!\mathsf{ssh}(\mathsf{unit}).T_\mathtt{c},\ \mathtt{a}: \mathsf{end}$. We prove the claim by using a Lemma mapping non-deterministic transitions to deterministic transitions. We start by a sequence of (non-deterministic) transitions from Δ'' that lead to $\Delta_{\mathtt{lock}}$, and use the result to find a fair oracle Ω mimicking the sequence:

$$D \diamond \Delta'' \xrightarrow{\tau_\mathtt{s}} \xrightarrow{\tau_\mathtt{c}} \xrightarrow{\text{login@c}\bowtie\text{s}} \xrightarrow{\text{ssh@a}\bowtie\text{c}} \xrightarrow{\text{auth@s}\bowtie\text{a}} \tag{1}$$

$$D_1 \diamond \mathtt{s}: T_\mathtt{s}, \mathtt{c}: T_\mathtt{c}, \mathtt{a}: T_\mathtt{a}' \xrightarrow{\tau_\mathtt{s}} \xrightarrow{\tau_\mathtt{c}} \xrightarrow{\text{login@c}\bowtie\text{s}} \xrightarrow{\tau_\mathtt{a}} \xrightarrow{\text{ssh@a}\bowtie\text{c}} \xrightarrow{\text{auth@s}\bowtie\text{a}} \tag{2}$$

$$D_2 \diamond \mathtt{s}: T_\mathtt{s}, \mathtt{c}: T_\mathtt{c}, \mathtt{a}: \mathsf{end} \xrightarrow{\tau_\mathtt{s}} \xrightarrow{\tau_\mathtt{c}} \xrightarrow{\text{login@c}\bowtie\text{s}} D_3 \diamond \Delta_{\mathtt{lock}} \tag{3}$$

The transitions in (1) correspond to a first round of the protocol, which leads the service $\mathtt{s}$ and the client $\mathtt{c}$ to re-initialise, while the authorisation server $\mathtt{a}$ reaches the type $T_\mathtt{a}' = \mu X.(\mathtt{c}?\mathsf{pwd}(\mathsf{str}).\mathtt{s}!\mathsf{auth}(\mathsf{bool}).X + \mathtt{c}?\mathsf{ssh}(\mathsf{unit}).\mathtt{s}!\mathsf{auth}(\mathsf{bool}).\mathsf{end} + \mathtt{c}?\mathsf{quit}(\mathsf{unit}).\mathsf{end})$. The transitions in (2) correspond to a second round of the protocol, which leads the service $\mathtt{s}$ and the client $\mathtt{c}$ to re-initialise, while the authorisation server $\mathtt{a}$ reaches the type end. The transitions in (3) correspond to the starting of the protocol where the service $\mathtt{s}$ sends a login request to the client $\mathtt{c}$. After that, both the service and the client waits to interact with the server $\mathtt{a}$, which has ended. Note that $\mathsf{stuck}_{\Omega,D_3}(\Delta_{\mathtt{lock}})$.

We apply a multi-step Lemma (see [27]) and infer $\Omega \triangleright D \diamond \Delta'' \implies \widetilde{C_1}, D_3 \diamond \Delta_{\mathtt{lock}}, \widetilde{C_2}$. By Definition 7, we have $\Delta_{\mathtt{lock}} \in \mathsf{closure}_{\Omega,D}(\Delta'')$. To prove $\neg\mathsf{comp}(\Delta'')$, we show that $\Delta_{\mathtt{lock}}$ is an error. In fact, $\Delta_{\mathtt{lock}}$ is a deadlock (cf. Definition 10), because it cannot fire any action, and because there is a participant that has not finished, e.g. $\Delta_{\mathtt{lock}}(\mathtt{s}) \neq \mathsf{end}$. By Definition 11, $\Delta_{\mathtt{lock}}$ is an error. □

Example 7. Consider the minimal well-formed environment Δ of the authorisation protocol in § 1.1. We claim that for any fair oracle Ω and fixed point $D \ni \Delta$, the closure of Δ returns two environments, where $\Delta^{\mathsf{end}} \overset{\mathsf{def}}{=} \mathtt{s}: \mathsf{end}, \mathtt{c}: \mathsf{end}, \mathtt{a}: \mathsf{end}$: $\mathsf{closure}_{\Omega,D}(\Delta) = \{\Delta, \Delta^{\mathsf{end}}\}$. Following this claim, we have $\mathsf{comp}(\Delta)$. In fact, both Δ and Δ^{end} are not errors. By definition, neither Δ nor Δ^{end} is a mismatch: the latter case is clear; in the former case, the unique unguarded sum of prefixes is the branching of the authorisation service $\mathtt{a}$ below, while the type of $\mathtt{c}$ is guarded:

$\mathtt{c}?\mathsf{password}(\mathsf{str}).\mathtt{s}!\mathsf{auth}(\mathsf{bool}).T_\mathtt{a} + \mathtt{c}?\mathsf{ssh}(\mathsf{unit}).\mathtt{s}!\mathsf{auth}(\mathsf{bool}).T_\mathtt{a} + \mathtt{c}?\mathsf{quit}(\mathsf{unit}).\mathsf{end}$

Moreover, neither Δ nor Δ^{end} is a deadlock. Δ can indeed take a step: the environment is in the closure because it is first contained in the initial decreasing set D and then re-encountered after a sequence of interactions. The claim can be verified by using the certified implementation in § 5. □

Remark 1. In [49] an environment is deadlock-free if for all redexes Γ reachable in multiple steps we have that if Γ does not move then its range contains only the type end. Conversely, Definition 10 expresses a negative property, and in turn we transform the implication $\mathsf{stuck}(\Gamma) \to \mathsf{consumed}(\Gamma)$ of [49] into its negation: $\mathsf{stuck}(\Gamma) \wedge \neg\mathsf{consumed}(\Gamma)$. □

4.2 Subject Reduction and Progress

We conclude this section by showing that the typing system satisfies subject reduction and progress. We outline the sketch of the proof of subject reduction, and refer to [27] for all details, including the proof of progress.

The purpose of the subject reduction theorem is to establish that if a session $\mathcal{M}$ is well-typed and does a step α and reaches the session $\mathcal{M}'$, then $\mathcal{M}'$ is well-typed. Assume that $\Gamma \Vdash \mathcal{M}: \Delta$. To assess subject reduction, we provide an environment Δ' s.t. $\Gamma \Vdash \mathcal{M}': \Delta'$. Since the step $\mathcal{M} \xrightarrow{\alpha} \mathcal{M}'$ is non-deterministic, we match this step with a non-deterministic environment transition (cf. Figure 2).

A key result to establish subject reduction is that compliance (cf. Definition 12) is preserved by non-deterministic transitions of session environments.

Lemma 1. *Let Δ be minimal. If $D \diamond \Delta \xrightarrow{\alpha} D' \diamond \Delta'$ then there exists a fair oracle Ω and environment Δ'' s.t. $\Omega \triangleright D \diamond \Delta \xrightarrow{\alpha}_d D' \diamond \Delta' \blacktriangleright \Delta''$.*

Lemma 2. *If $\mathsf{comp}(\Delta)$ and $\Omega \triangleright D \diamond \Delta \xrightarrow{\alpha}_d D' \diamond \Delta' \blacktriangleright \Delta''$ then $\mathsf{comp}(\Delta')$.*

Corollary 1 (Compliance preservation). *If $\mathsf{comp}(\Delta)$ and $D \diamond \Delta \xrightarrow{\alpha} D' \diamond \Delta'$ then $\mathsf{comp}(\Delta')$.*

Lemma 3. *If $\Gamma \Vdash \mathcal{M}_1: \Delta$ and $\mathcal{M}_1 \equiv \mathcal{M}_2$ then $\Gamma \Vdash \mathcal{M}_2: \Delta$.*

Proof. If follows from the inversion of $\Gamma \Vdash \mathcal{M}_1: \Delta$ and the definition of $\equiv$. The result is mechanised in Coq. □

Theorem 1 (Subject Reduction). *Let $\mathcal{M}$ be a closed session, and let D be a fixed point including Δ. Assume (1) $\Gamma \Vdash \mathcal{M}: \Delta$ and (2) $\mathcal{M} \xrightarrow{\alpha} \mathcal{M}'$. We have $\Gamma \Vdash \mathcal{M}': \Delta$ or $D \diamond \Delta \xrightarrow{\alpha} D' \diamond \Delta'$ and $\Gamma \Vdash \mathcal{M}': \Delta'$.*

Proof. By induction on (2), using value and process substitution (mechanised in Coq), Lemma 3, and Corollary 1. □

Let $\mathsf{Ended}(\|_{i \in I}\ \mathsf{p}_i \lhd P_i)$ when for all $i \in I$ we have $P_i = \mathbf{0}$.

Theorem 2 (Progress). *Let $\mathcal{M}$ be a closed session. If $\Gamma \Vdash \mathcal{M}: \Delta$ and does not exist $\mathcal{M}'$ s.t. $\mathcal{M} \xrightarrow{\tau} \mathcal{M}'$ or $\mathcal{M} \xrightarrow{l@\mathsf{p}\bowtie\mathsf{q}} \mathcal{M}'$, for all $l, \mathsf{p}, \mathsf{q}$, then $\mathsf{Ended}(\mathcal{M})$.*

5   Automated Deductive Verification of Compliance

The typing system presented in § 4 relies on the notion of *compliance*, which is defined theoretically by relying on the novel definitions of *deterministic session environment transitions* and *closure* introduced in § 3. In this section, we showcase how these theoretical notions can de deployed *soundly* in mainstream programming languages and compilers by presenting a *reference implementation of compliance* and by mechanising the properties of the implementation, which are that compliant environment are mismatch-free and deadlock-free.

Our goal is to define *compliance* as a computable function that decides when a session environment has a "good behaviour", and in turn can be assigned by the typing system to a session. We note that computability is an essential prerequisite for decidable type checking while assigning non-compliant environments to sessions is unsound because it invalidates progress, and must be avoided.

Towards this aim, we need to (1) deploy the function; (2) provide a mechanised proof that the function terminates; (3) provide a mechanised proof that the function decides freedom from mismatches and deadlocks. This result is established once (by the type system designer): after that, the function can be used each time we invoke the type checker on a session process.

The proofs and their mechanisation in (2) and (3) are necessary because the designer can deploy a wrong implementation, e.g. it could have forgotten a case leading to an environment deadlock, thus allowing to type check sessions that deadlock at runtime. By providing a computer-assisted proof that the implementation rules out errors and deadlocks in environments, we can rely on Theorem 2 to obtain that sessions typed by accepted environments do not deadlock.

In the remainder of the section, we tackle the requirements (1), (2) and (3) by defining function *compliance* and its *behavioural specification*, that is the contract of the function [40]. We choose OCaml as target language and use tools of the OCaml ecosystem relying on Why3 [19] to enable automated deductive verification of behavioural specifications by using constraint solvers, e.g. [16,42,4], while supporting imperative features, ghost code [18], and interactive proofs.

The verification has been done by using Cameleer [45,44], which in turn relies on [9,19]. Proofs of lemmas requiring induction are done interactively in Why3.

5.1   Structure of the Implementation

To implement *closure* (cf. Definition 7) in OCaml, we use function `cstep` receiving a fair oracle Ω, a decreasing set D, a (ghost) fixed point $\mathcal{W}$, a session environment Δ, and a (ghost) list of environments $\mathcal{H}$ representing the *history* of the visited environments; the function returns an environment. Function `compliance` invokes `cstep` in order to accept or reject the environment Δ:

```
let[@ghost] rec cstep (o : oracle) (d : typEnv list)
  (( w : typEnvRedexes )[ @ghost ]) (delta: typEnv )
  (( history : typEnv list )[ @ghost ]): typEnv = ···
let[@ghost] compliance (o : oracle) (d : typEnv list)
  (( w : typEnvRedexes )[ @ghost ]) (delta : typEnv ) :bool =
  try let m = cstep o d w delta [] in consumed m
  with | Fixpoint h → (* h = h0, e *) let e = last h in let h0 = pre h
  in mem_typEnv e h0 && sound e next | _ → raise NotCompliant
```

The behavioural specification of the functions is described in § 5.2. Ghost parameters are used both to provide a semantics to the fixed point mechanism and to prove the soundness of the accepted environments, and do not have computational interest: all ghost code referring to such parameters should be erased from the regular code after providing the proof effort [18,45].

In function `cstep` we use exceptions to tackle different behaviours of environments. In all cases but for exception `Fixpoint`, termination by raising an exception determines failure of establishing compliance.

Definition 13 (Positive exits). *Positive exits of function* `cstep` *are listed below. A positive exit implies that the parameter* Δ *of* `cstep` *satisfies compliance.*

name	param	exit	exception	positive
cstep	$\Omega, D, \mathcal{W}, \Delta, \mathcal{H}$	✓		✓
			Fixpoint	✓

W.r.t. the signatures of `cstep` and of closure in Definition 7, the non-ghost parameters are the same while the return type is different, because closure returns a set of environments. Remember that the aim of the returned set of environments is to establish *compliance* by verifying that all the final environments are not a communication mismatch, or a deadlock (cf. Definition 12). Function `cstep` achieves the same result by using exception handling and ghost parameters.

The body of `cstep` is recursive, and contains sub-calls of the form `cstep`$(\Omega, D\backslash_\Delta, \mathcal{W}, \Delta', (\mathcal{H}, \Delta))$: the first parameter Ω is the oracle and is the same in all calls; the second parameter $D\backslash_\Delta$ corresponds to the removal of Δ from the decreasing set D; the third parameter $\mathcal{W}$ is the fixed point and is the same in all calls; the fourth parameter Δ' is obtained by updating the type of one or of two participants returned by the oracle Ω (cf. Definition 5); the last parameter appends Δ to the history $\mathcal{H}$: in the remainder of the section, the *notation* $\mathcal{H}, \Delta$ indicates that Δ is the last environment visited in $\mathcal{H} \cup \{\Delta\}$.

5.2   Verification

The verification of function `compliance` relies on the behavioural specification and verification of function `cstep`, which in turn relies on auxiliary lemmas.

Figure 5 presents the behavioural specification of the implementation. The column **param** lists the input arguments of each function. The column **result** lists the result returned by each function. The column **variant** indicates the decreasing argument of `cstep`; note that `compliance` is not recursive. The column **requires** indicates the pre-conditions stated in terms of the parameters. The column **raises** indicates the formula holding for the argument carried by the exception; in the specification of `cstep` we omit exceptions asserting true. The column **ensures** indicates the post-condition stated in terms of the result.

There are two positive exits of function `cstep` establishing the *compliance* of the environment Δ received in input (cf. Definition 13): termination, and raising `Fixpoint`. The conditions holding when `cstep` raises an exception (cf. keyword **raises**) are discussed below while illustrating the verification process. Note that exceptions `Fixpoint`, `Deadlock`, `Wrongbranch`, `DecrNotFix` and `NotMinimal` carry the history $\mathcal{H}', \Delta'$, where Δ' is the last visited environment.

The predicate $\mathrm{sound}_\Omega(\Delta')$ relies on the result of the oracle and on Definition 9: if the oracle receives Δ' and returns one (cf. rule SD-REC) or two (cf. rule SD-COM) participants, and Δ' is not a mismatch, then Δ' is sound. The predicate $\mathrm{cons}(\Delta')$ says that all participants in the environment Δ' have type end.

name	param	result	variant	requires	raises	ensures
cstep	Ω	Δ_o	$|D|$	fair(Ω)	OracleNotFair $\Rightarrow$ false	cons(Δ_o)
	D			isFix($\mathcal{W}, \Delta, |D| * 2$)	Fixpoint($\mathcal{H}', \Delta'$) $\Rightarrow$ $\Delta' \in \mathcal{H}' \wedge$ sound$_\Omega(\Delta')$	
	$\mathcal{W}$			$D \cap \mathcal{H} = \emptyset$	Deadlock($\mathcal{H}', \Delta'$) $\Rightarrow$ $\Delta' \in \mathcal{H}' \wedge$ mismatch(Δ') $\vee$ $\Omega(\Delta') = \text{Ret}_0 \wedge \neg\text{cons}(\Delta')$	
	Δ			$D \cup \mathcal{H} = \text{comb}(\mathcal{W})$	WrongBranch($\mathcal{H}', \Delta'$) $\Rightarrow$ $\exists \text{p}, \text{q} . \Omega(\Delta') = \text{Ret}_2(\text{p}, \text{q}) \wedge$ mismatch$_2(\Delta'(\text{p}), \Delta'(\text{q}))$	
	$\mathcal{H}$			$\Delta \in \text{comb}(\mathcal{W})$	DecrNotFix($\mathcal{H}', \Delta'$) $\Rightarrow$ $\Delta' \notin \mathcal{H}'$	
					NotMinimal($\mathcal{H}', \Delta'$) $\Rightarrow$ $\neg\text{minimal}(\Delta')$	

$$\text{SD-REC} \frac{\Omega(\Delta) = \text{Ret}_1(\text{p}) \quad \neg\text{mismatch}(\Delta)}{\text{sound}_\Omega(\Delta)} \qquad \text{SD-COM} \frac{\Omega(\Delta) = \text{Ret}_2(\text{p}, \text{q}) \quad \neg\text{mismatch}(\Delta)}{\text{sound}_\Omega(\Delta)}$$

name	param	result	requires	raises	ensures
compliance	Ω	b	fair(Ω)	NotCompliant $\Rightarrow$ true	$b = $ true
	D		isFix($\mathcal{W}, \Delta, |D| * 2$)		
	$\mathcal{W}$		$D = \text{comb}(\mathcal{W})$		
	Δ		$\Delta \in D$		

Fig. 5. Behavioural specification of the implementation

The post-condition (cf. keyword **ensures**) of `cstep` says that the returned environment is consumed: all participants have type end. For what concerns the pre-conditions of `cstep` (cf. keyword **requires**), the predicate fair(Ω) implements Definition 5 by relying on constructors Ret_2, Ret_1 and Ret_0:

$$\text{fair}(\Omega) \stackrel{\text{def}}{=} \forall \Delta . (\forall \text{p} \, \text{q} . \Omega(\Delta) = \text{Ret}_2(\text{p}, \text{q}) \Rightarrow \text{top}(\Delta(\text{p})) = \text{q} \wedge \text{top}(\Delta(\text{q})) = \text{p}) \wedge$$
$$(\forall \text{p} . \Omega(\Delta) = \text{Ret}_1(\text{p}) \Rightarrow \exists X \, T . \Delta(\text{p}) = \mu X.T) \wedge$$
$$(\forall X \, T \, \text{r} \, \text{p} \, \text{q} . \Omega(\Delta) = \text{Ret}_0 \Rightarrow \Delta(\text{r}) \neq \mu X.T \wedge$$
$$\neg(\text{top}(\Delta(\text{p})) = \text{q} \wedge \text{top}(\Delta(\text{q}) = \text{p})))$$

The predicate isFix($\mathcal{W}, \Delta, n$) says that $\mathcal{W}$ is a fixed point of Δ (up-to depth n). The core mechanism to analyse iso-recursive types and environments is to rely on fixed points $\mathcal{W}$ of type `typEnvRedexes`, that is a map from participants to all type redexes up-to depth n, and on the projection of all combinations of these mappings into a set of environments, denoted comb($\mathcal{W}$). The depth n indicates how many type transitions $T \xrightarrow{\alpha_1} \cdots \xrightarrow{\alpha_n} T'$ are considered (cf. Figure 2); these include the unfolding of iso-recursive types $\mu X.T$ into $T\{\mu X.T/X\}$. Given a fixed point $\mathcal{W}$, we require that the decreasing set D and the history $\mathcal{H}$ partition the set comb($\mathcal{W}$) (cf. Figure 5, function `cstep`, keyword requires, lines 3-4).

The pre-conditions of `compliance` mirror those of `cstep`, modulo the fact that there is no history. The post-condition of `compliance` ensures that the function returns true by exploiting (1) the post-condition of cstep and (2) the formula holding when cstep raises Fixpoint. The exceptional exit of compliance occurs when raising NonCompliant, thus rejecting the input environment Δ.

Termination. The first result establishes that function cstep terminates. We instruct [45] to use $|D|$ as decreasing measure, cf. the keyword variant in the function specification of Figure 5, and obtain the desired result automatically.

Absence of communication mismatches. In order to show that environments accepted by compliance are mismatch-free, we ensure that positive exits of function cstep (cf. Definition 13) carry environments that are not communication mismatches (cf. Definition 9) by inspecting cstep's contract in Figure 5.

The first positive exit is termination: cstep returns Δ_o. The contract's clause with keyword ensures establishes that Δ_o is consumed: by definition, Δ_o is not a mismatch. The second positive exit corresponds to the exception Fixpoint: the exceptions carries the history $\mathcal{H}', \Delta'$, where Δ' is the last visited environment. The clause raises establishes that $\Delta' \in \mathcal{H}'$ and that Δ' is sound. By inversion of rules SD-REC, SD-COM, we obtain that Δ' is not a mismatch.   □

The automated verification is performed in [45] and relies on the predicate $\mathsf{mismatch}_2(T_1, T_2)$ (cf. Figure 5) to deal with wrong choices of sums: intuitively, the predicate follow Definition 9 by using types rather than participants.

Absence of deadlocks. Similarly, we show that positive exits of cstep of Definition 13 correspond to absence of deadlocks of Definition 10.

The first positive exit occurs when function cstep returns Δ_o. The clause with keyword ensures establishes that Δ_o is consumed: by definition, Δ_o is not a deadlock. The second positive exit is raising exception Fixpoint; the exception carries the history $\mathcal{H}', \Delta'$, where Δ' is the last visited environment. From the contract's clause with keyword raises, we infer that $\Delta' \in \mathcal{H}'$ and that Δ' is sound.

By inversion of rules SD-REC, SD-COM, we obtain that two cases arise: (1) there is a participant p s.t. $\Omega(\Delta') = \mathsf{Ret}_1(\mathsf{p})$ and Δ' is not a mismatch; (2) there are participants p, q such that $\Omega(\Delta') = \mathsf{Ret}_2(\mathsf{p}, \mathsf{q})$ and Δ' is not a mismatch. We show that in both cases (1) and (2) we have that Δ' can do a transition.

1. By the fairness pre-condition of cstep, we obtain

$$\Omega(\Delta') = \mathsf{Ret}_1(\mathsf{p}) \Rightarrow \exists X\,T\,.\,\Delta'(\mathsf{p}) = \mu X.T$$

We apply E-REC, SE-REC of Figure 2 and find Δ'' s.t. $\Delta' \xrightarrow{\tau} \Delta''$.

2. By the fairness pre-condition of cstep, we obtain

$$\Omega(\Delta') = \mathsf{Ret}_2(\mathsf{p}, \mathsf{q}) \Rightarrow \mathsf{top}(T_\mathsf{p}) = \mathsf{q} \wedge \mathsf{top}(T_\mathsf{q}) = \mathsf{p}$$

where $\Delta'(\mathsf{p}) \stackrel{\mathrm{def}}{=} T_\mathsf{p}$ and $\Delta'(\mathsf{q}) \stackrel{\mathrm{def}}{=} T_\mathsf{q}$.
By inversion of $\mathsf{top}(T_\mathsf{p})$ and $\mathsf{top}(T_\mathsf{q})$ (cf. Definition 5), we obtain that $T_\mathsf{p} = \&_{i \in I}\mathsf{q}?l_i(S_i).T_i$ or $T_\mathsf{p} = \oplus_{i \in I}\mathsf{q}!l_i(S_i).T_i$, and $T_\mathsf{q} = \&_{j \in J}\mathsf{p}?l_j(S_j).T_j$ or $T_\mathsf{q} = \oplus_{j \in J}\mathsf{p}!l_j(S_j).T_j$.
By hypothesis, Δ' is not a mismatch: Definition 9 ensures that two sub-cases arise: $T_\mathsf{p} = \&_{i \in I}\mathsf{q}?l_i(S_i).T_i$ and $T_\mathsf{q} = \oplus_{j \in J}\mathsf{p}!l_j(S_j).T_j$ and $\mathcal{L}(T_\mathsf{p}) \cap \mathcal{L}(T_\mathsf{q}) \neq \emptyset$, or $T_\mathsf{p} = \oplus_{i \in I}\mathsf{q}!l_i(S_i).T_i$, and $T_\mathsf{q} = \&_{j \in J}\mathsf{p}?l_j(S_j).T_j$ and $\mathcal{L}(T_\mathsf{p}) \cap \mathcal{L}(T_\mathsf{q}) \neq \emptyset$. In both cases we apply SE-COM of Figure 2 and find α, Δ'' s.t. $\Delta' \xrightarrow{\alpha} \Delta''$.   □

6   Related Work

To the best of our knowledge, only few works follow an iso-recursive approach to session types. [31] proposes a decentralized analysis of multiparty protocols that is based on a typed asynchronous π-calculus relying on the notion of router processes; deadlock-freedom is established by following the priority-based approach of session types [13]. The rule to type check recursion types the continuation by unfolding iso-recursive types and lifting priorities to a common greater highest priority. Finally, type preservation holds up to unfolding (cf. [31, Theorem 2]).

[36] studies iso-recursive and equi-recursive subtyping for binary sessions. Session types are interpreted as propositions of multiplicative/additive linear logic extended with least and greatest fixed points (cf. [8,54]). The typing rules correspond to the proof rules in [3], and include the unfolding of least and greatest fixed points. The authors compare the two subtyping relations, and note that the relations preserve not only the usual safety properties, but also termination.

Many recent papers [56,57,58,59,48,43,39] rely on iso-recursive types for variants of the λ-calculus, following the seminal work on Amber rules [1]. While the setting is different from ours, these papers provide several insights on the advantage of iso-recursive types and on their algorithmic implementation and mechanised verification. Previous papers [6,2] studied iso-recursive types for a concurrent λ-calculus that can be seen as the foundational theory of core $F^{\sharp}$.

As mentioned above, iso-recursive types have been first studied formally in the setting of Amber rules [1]. Pierce's book [47] further discusses the differences between iso-recursive and equi-recursive types.

Future Work. Our plans go along two directions: completing the study in the paper and extending the language model and the type analysis.

Towards completion, we plan to conclude the mechanisation of subject reduction in Coq, and to compare the performance of compliance checking in OCaml with the verification of deadlock freedom in bottom-up approaches (cf. [52]) relying on model-checking [49], eventually considering a realistic testing suite involving multiple participants and interactions (cf. [49, Table 2]).

For what concerns extensions, there are two main features we are interested in: session delegation and asynchronous subtyping for multiparty session types.

Handling session delegation in session types is challenging and might require type constructors [25] or session channel decorations [22,15,53] to preserve type soundness. Our plan is to enforce soundness at the type level, without affecting the programmer's syntax.

Asynchronous subtyping (e.g. [24]) is known to be undecidable for more than two participants. We envision to overcome this obstacle to an algorithmic solution by considering a maximal depth of the search of the asynchronous outputs that can be anticipated, similarly to the bound on recursion in [12].

Acknowledgements. We thank the reviewers for detailed and helpful comments. This work is partially supported by EPSRC EP/T006544/2, EP/N027833/2, EP/T014709/2, EP/Y005244/1, EP/V000462/1, Horizon EU TaRDIS 101093006, Advanced Research and Invention Agency (ARIA), and a grant from the Simons Foundation.

References

1. Abadi, M., Cardelli, L.: A Theory of Objects. Monographs in Computer Science, Springer (1996). https://doi.org/10.1007/978-1-4419-8598-9
2. Backes, M., Hritcu, C., Maffei, M.: Union, intersection and refinement types and reasoning about type disjointness for secure protocol implementations. J. Comput. Secur. **22**(2), 301–353 (2014). https://doi.org/10.3233/JCS-130493
3. Baelde, D., Doumane, A., Kuperberg, D., Saurin, A.: Bouncing threads for circular and non-wellfounded proofs: Towards compositionality with circular proofs. In: Baier, C., Fisman, D. (eds.) LICS '22: 37th Annual ACM/IEEE Symposium on Logic in Computer Science, Haifa, Israel, August 2 - 5, 2022. pp. 63:1–63:13. ACM (2022). https://doi.org/10.1145/3531130.3533375
4. Barrett, C.W., Conway, C.L., Deters, M., Hadarean, L., Jovanovic, D., King, T., Reynolds, A., Tinelli, C.: CVC4. In: Gopalakrishnan, G., Qadeer, S. (eds.) Computer Aided Verification - 23rd International Conference, CAV 2011, Snowbird, UT, USA, July 14-20, 2011. Proceedings. Lecture Notes in Computer Science, vol. 6806, pp. 171–177. Springer (2011). https://doi.org/10.1007/978-3-642-22110-1_14
5. Barwell, A.D., Scalas, A., Yoshida, N., Zhou, F.: Generalised multiparty session types with crash-stop failures. In: Klin, B., Lasota, S., Muscholl, A. (eds.) 33rd International Conference on Concurrency Theory, CONCUR 2022, September 12-16, 2022, Warsaw, Poland. LIPIcs, vol. 243, pp. 35:1–35:25. Schloss Dagstuhl - Leibniz-Zentrum für Informatik (2022). https://doi.org/10.4230/LIPICS.CONCUR.2022.35
6. Bengtson, J., Bhargavan, K., Fournet, C., Gordon, A.D., Maffeis, S.: Refinement types for secure implementations. ACM Trans. Program. Lang. Syst. **33**(2), 8:1–8:45 (2011). https://doi.org/10.1145/1890028.1890031
7. Brun, M.A.L., Dardha, O.: Magπ: Types for failure-prone communication. In: Wies, T. (ed.) Programming Languages and Systems - 32nd European Symposium on Programming, ESOP 2023, Held as Part of the European Joint Conferences on Theory and Practice of Software, ETAPS 2023, Paris, France, April 22-27, 2023, Proceedings. Lecture Notes in Computer Science, vol. 13990, pp. 363–391. Springer (2023). https://doi.org/10.1007/978-3-031-30044-8_14
8. Caires, L., Pfenning, F.: Session types as intuitionistic linear propositions. In: Gastin, P., Laroussinie, F. (eds.) CONCUR 2010 - Concurrency Theory, 21th International Conference, CONCUR 2010, Paris, France, August 31-September 3, 2010. Proceedings. Lecture Notes in Computer Science, vol. 6269, pp. 222–236. Springer (2010). https://doi.org/10.1007/978-3-642-15375-4_16
9. Charguéraud, A., Filliâtre, J., Lourenço, C., Pereira, M.: GOSPEL - providing OCaml with a formal specification language. In: ter Beek, M.H., McIver, A., Oliveira, J.N. (eds.) Formal Methods - The Next 30 Years - Third World Congress, FM 2019, Porto, Portugal, October 7-11, 2019, Proceedings. Lecture Notes in Computer Science, vol. 11800, pp. 484–501. Springer (2019). https://doi.org/10.1007/978-3-030-30942-8_29
10. ContainerSSH: DevLog: SSH authentication via OAuth2, https://containerssh.io/v0.5/blog/2021/04/13/devlog-oauth2/
11. Coq development team: Reference manual, https://coq.inria.fr/doc/V8.20.0/refman/
12. Cutner, Z., Yoshida, N., Vassor, M.: Deadlock-free asynchronous message reordering in rust with multiparty session types. In: Lee, J., Agrawal, K., Spear, M.F. (eds.) PPoPP '22: 27th ACM SIGPLAN Symposium on Principles and Practice of

Parallel Programming, Seoul, Republic of Korea, April 2 - 6, 2022. pp. 246–261. ACM (2022). https://doi.org/10.1145/3503221.3508404

13. Dardha, O., Gay, S.J.: A new linear logic for deadlock-free session-typed processes. In: Baier, C., Lago, U.D. (eds.) Foundations of Software Science and Computation Structures - 21st International Conference, FOSSACS 2018, Held as Part of the European Joint Conferences on Theory and Practice of Software, ETAPS 2018, Thessaloniki, Greece, April 14-20, 2018, Proceedings. Lecture Notes in Computer Science, vol. 10803, pp. 91–109. Springer (2018). https://doi.org/10.1007/978-3-319-89366-2_5

14. Demangeon, R., Honda, K.: Full abstraction in a subtyped pi-calculus with linear types. In: Katoen, J., König, B. (eds.) CONCUR 2011 - Concurrency Theory - 22nd International Conference, CONCUR 2011, Aachen, Germany, September 6-9, 2011. Proceedings. Lecture Notes in Computer Science, vol. 6901, pp. 280–296. Springer (2011). https://doi.org/10.1007/978-3-642-23217-6_19

15. Dezani-Ciancaglini, M., Drossopoulou, S., Mostrous, D., Yoshida, N.: Objects and session types. Inf. Comput. **207**(5), 595–641 (2009). https://doi.org/10.1016/J.IC.2008.03.028

16. Dross, C., Conchon, S., Kanig, J., Paskevich, A.: Adding decision procedures to SMT solvers using axioms with triggers. J. Autom. Reason. **56**(4), 387–457 (2016). https://doi.org/10.1007/S10817-015-9352-2

17. Ekici, B., Yoshida, N.: Completeness of asynchronous session tree subtyping in coq. In: Bertot, Y., Kutsia, T., Norrish, M. (eds.) 15th International Conference on Interactive Theorem Proving, ITP 2024, September 9-14, 2024, Tbilisi, Georgia. LIPIcs, vol. 309, pp. 13:1–13:20. Schloss Dagstuhl - Leibniz-Zentrum für Informatik (2024). https://doi.org/10.4230/LIPICS.ITP.2024.13

18. Filliâtre, J., Gondelman, L., Paskevich, A.: The spirit of ghost code. Formal Methods Syst. Des. **48**(3), 152–174 (2016). https://doi.org/10.1007/S10703-016-0243-X

19. Filliâtre, J., Paskevich, A.: Why3 - where programs meet provers. In: Felleisen, M., Gardner, P. (eds.) Programming Languages and Systems - 22nd European Symposium on Programming, ESOP 2013, Held as Part of the European Joint Conferences on Theory and Practice of Software, ETAPS 2013, Rome, Italy, March 16-24, 2013. Proceedings. Lecture Notes in Computer Science, vol. 7792, pp. 125–128. Springer (2013). https://doi.org/10.1007/978-3-642-37036-6_8

20. Foster, J.N., Greenwald, M.B., Moore, J.T., Pierce, B.C., Schmitt, A.: Combinators for bidirectional tree transformations: A linguistic approach to the view-update problem. ACM Trans. Program. Lang. Syst. **29**(3), 17 (2007). https://doi.org/10.1145/1232420.1232424

21. Gay, S., Ravara, A. (eds.): Behavioural Types: from Theory to Tools. River Publishers (2017), https://doi.org/10.13052/rp-9788793519817

22. Gay, S.J., Hole, M.: Subtyping for session types in the pi calculus. Acta Informatica **42**(2-3), 191–225 (2005). https://doi.org/10.1007/S00236-005-0177-Z

23. Ghilezan, S., Jaksic, S., Pantovic, J., Scalas, A., Yoshida, N.: Precise subtyping for synchronous multiparty sessions. J. Log. Algebraic Methods Program. **104**, 127–173 (2019). https://doi.org/10.1016/J.JLAMP.2018.12.002

24. Ghilezan, S., Pantović, J., Prokić, I., Scalas, A., Yoshida, N.: Precise subtyping for asynchronous multiparty sessions. ACM Trans. Comput. Logic **24**(2) (nov 2023). https://doi.org/10.1145/3568422

25. Giunti, M., Vasconcelos, V.T.: A linear account of session types in the pi calculus. In: Gastin, P., Laroussinie, F. (eds.) CONCUR 2010 - Concurrency Theory, 21th

International Conference, CONCUR 2010, Paris, France, August 31-September 3, 2010. Proceedings. Lecture Notes in Computer Science, vol. 6269, pp. 432–446. Springer (2010). https://doi.org/10.1007/978-3-642-15375-4_30

26. Giunti, M., Vasconcelos, V.T.: Linearity, session types and the pi calculus. Math. Struct. Comput. Sci. **26**(2), 206–237 (2016). https://doi.org/10.1017/S0960129514000176

27. Giunti, M., Yoshida, N.: Iso-Recursive Multiparty Sessions and their Automated Verification – Technical Report (2025). https://doi.org/10.48550/ARXIV.2501.17778

28. van Glabbeek, R., Höfner, P., Horne, R.: Assuming just enough fairness to make session types complete for lock-freedom. In: 36th Annual ACM/IEEE Symposium on Logic in Computer Science, LICS 2021, Rome, Italy, June 29 - July 2, 2021. pp. 1–13. IEEE (2021). https://doi.org/10.1109/LICS52264.2021.9470531

29. Groote, J.F., Mousavi, M.R.: Modeling and Analysis of Communicating Systems. MIT Press (2014), https://mitpress.mit.edu/books/modeling-and-analysis-communicating-systems

30. Harvey, P., Fowler, S., Dardha, O., Gay, S.J.: Multiparty session types for safe runtime adaptation in an actor language. In: Møller, A., Sridharan, M. (eds.) 35th European Conference on Object-Oriented Programming, ECOOP 2021, July 11-17, 2021, Aarhus, Denmark (Virtual Conference). LIPIcs, vol. 194, pp. 10:1–10:30. Schloss Dagstuhl - Leibniz-Zentrum für Informatik (2021). https://doi.org/10.4230/LIPIcs.ECOOP.2021.10

31. van den Heuvel, B., Pérez, J.A.: A decentralized analysis of multiparty protocols. Sci. Comput. Program. **222**, 102840 (2022). https://doi.org/10.1016/J.SCICO.2022.102840

32. Honda, K.: Types for dyadic interaction. In: Best, E. (ed.) CONCUR '93, 4th International Conference on Concurrency Theory, Hildesheim, Germany, August 23-26, 1993, Proceedings. Lecture Notes in Computer Science, vol. 715, pp. 509–523. Springer (1993). https://doi.org/10.1007/3-540-57208-2_35

33. Honda, K., Vasconcelos, V.T., Kubo, M.: Language primitives and type discipline for structured communication-based programming. In: Hankin, C. (ed.) Programming Languages and Systems - ESOP'98, 7th European Symposium on Programming, Held as Part of the European Joint Conferences on the Theory and Practice of Software, ETAPS'98, Lisbon, Portugal, March 28 - April 4, 1998, Proceedings. Lecture Notes in Computer Science, vol. 1381, pp. 122–138. Springer (1998). https://doi.org/10.1007/BFB0053567

34. Honda, K., Yoshida, N., Carbone, M.: Multiparty asynchronous session types. In: Necula, G.C., Wadler, P. (eds.) Proceedings of the 35th ACM SIGPLAN-SIGACT Symposium on Principles of Programming Languages, POPL 2008, San Francisco, California, USA, January 7-12, 2008. pp. 273–284. ACM (2008). https://doi.org/10.1145/1328438.1328472

35. Honda, K., Yoshida, N., Carbone, M.: Multiparty asynchronous session types. J. ACM **63**(1), 9:1–9:67 (2016). https://doi.org/10.1145/2827695

36. Horne, R., Padovani, L.: A logical account of subtyping for session types. J. Log. Algebraic Methods Program. **141**, 100986 (2024). https://doi.org/10.1016/J.JLAMP.2024.100986

37. Imai, K., Neykova, R., Yoshida, N., Yuen, S.: Multiparty session programming with global protocol combinators. In: Hirschfeld, R., Pape, T. (eds.) 34th European Conference on Object-Oriented Programming, ECOOP 2020, November 15-17, 2020, Berlin, Germany (Virtual Conference). LIPIcs, vol. 166,

pp. 9:1–9:30. Schloss Dagstuhl - Leibniz-Zentrum für Informatik (2020). https://doi.org/10.4230/LIPICS.ECOOP.2020.9

38. Lange, J., Ng, N., Toninho, B., Yoshida, N.: A static verification framework for message passing in go using behavioural types. In: Chaudron, M., Crnkovic, I., Chechik, M., Harman, M. (eds.) Proceedings of the 40th International Conference on Software Engineering, ICSE 2018, Gothenburg, Sweden, May 27 - June 03, 2018. pp. 1137–1148. ACM (2018). https://doi.org/10.1145/3180155.3180157

39. Ligatti, J., Blackburn, J., Nachtigal, M.: On subtyping-relation completeness, with an application to iso-recursive types. ACM Trans. Program. Lang. Syst. **39**(1), 4:1–4:36 (2017). https://doi.org/10.1145/2994596

40. Meyer, B.: Applying "design by contract". Computer **25**(10), 40–51 (1992). https://doi.org/10.1109/2.161279

41. Milner, R.: Communication and concurrency. PHI Series in computer science, Prentice Hall (1989)

42. de Moura, L.M., Bjørner, N.S.: Z3: an efficient SMT solver. In: Ramakrishnan, C.R., Rehof, J. (eds.) Tools and Algorithms for the Construction and Analysis of Systems, 14th International Conference, TACAS 2008, Held as Part of the Joint European Conferences on Theory and Practice of Software, ETAPS 2008, Budapest, Hungary, March 29-April 6, 2008. Proceedings. Lecture Notes in Computer Science, vol. 4963, pp. 337–340. Springer (2008). https://doi.org/10.1007/978-3-540-78800-3_24

43. Patrignani, M., Martin, E.M., Devriese, D.: On the semantic expressiveness of recursive types. Proc. ACM Program. Lang. **5**(POPL), 1–29 (2021). https://doi.org/10.1145/3434302

44. Pereira, M.: Practical Deductive Verification of OCaml Programs. In: Platzer, A., Rozier, K.Y., Pradella, M., Rossi, M. (eds.) Formal Methods - 26th International Symposium, FM 2024, Milan, Italy, September 9-13, 2024, Proceedings, Part II. Lecture Notes in Computer Science, vol. 14934, pp. 518–542. Springer (2024). https://doi.org/10.1007/978-3-031-71177-0_29

45. Pereira, M., Ravara, A.: Cameleer: A deductive verification tool for OCaml. In: Silva, A., Leino, K.R.M. (eds.) Computer Aided Verification - 33rd International Conference, CAV 2021, Virtual Event, July 20-23, 2021, Proceedings, Part II. Lecture Notes in Computer Science, vol. 12760, pp. 677–689. Springer (2021). https://doi.org/10.1007/978-3-030-81688-9_31

46. Peters, K., Yoshida, N.: Separation and encodability in mixed choice multiparty sessions. In: Sobocinski, P., Lago, U.D., Esparza, J. (eds.) Proceedings of the 39th Annual ACM/IEEE Symposium on Logic in Computer Science, LICS 2024, Tallinn, Estonia, July 8-11, 2024. pp. 62:1–62:15. ACM (2024). https://doi.org/10.1145/3661814.3662085

47. Pierce, B.C.: Types and programming languages. MIT Press (2002)

48. Rossberg, A.: Mutually iso-recursive subtyping. Proc. ACM Program. Lang. **7**(OOPSLA2), 347–373 (2023). https://doi.org/10.1145/3622809

49. Scalas, A., Yoshida, N.: Less is more: multiparty session types revisited. Proc. ACM Program. Lang. **3**(POPL), 30:1–30:29 (2019). https://doi.org/10.1145/3290343

50. Scalas, A., Yoshida, N., Benussi, E.: Verifying message-passing programs with dependent behavioural types. In: McKinley, K.S., Fisher, K. (eds.) Proceedings of the 40th ACM SIGPLAN Conference on Programming Language Design and Implementation, PLDI 2019, Phoenix, AZ, USA, June 22-26, 2019. pp. 502–516. ACM (2019). https://doi.org/10.1145/3314221.3322484

51. Takeuchi, K., Honda, K., Kubo, M.: An interaction-based language and its typing system. In: Halatsis, C., Maritsas, D.G., Philokyprou, G., Theodoridis, S. (eds.) PARLE '94: Parallel Architectures and Languages Europe, 6th International PARLE Conference, Athens, Greece, July 4-8, 1994, Proceedings. Lecture Notes in Computer Science, vol. 817, pp. 398–413. Springer (1994). https://doi.org/10.1007/3-540-58184-7_118

52. Udomsrirungruang, T., Yoshida, N.: Top-down or bottom-up? Complexity analyses of synchronous multiparty session types. In: Proceedings of the ACM on Programming Languages, vol. 9, no. POPL, pp. 1040–1071 (2025). https://doi.org/10.1145/3704872

53. Vasconcelos, V.T.: Fundamentals of session types. Inf. Comput. **217**, 52–70 (2012). https://doi.org/10.1016/J.IC.2012.05.002

54. Wadler, P.: Propositions as sessions. J. Funct. Program. **24**(2-3), 384–418 (2014). https://doi.org/10.1017/S095679681400001X

55. Yoshida, N.: Programming language implementations with multiparty session types. In: de Boer, F.S., Damiani, F., Hähnle, R., Johnsen, E.B., Kamburjan, E. (eds.) Active Object Languages: Current Research Trends, Lecture Notes in Computer Science, vol. 14360, pp. 147–165. Springer (2024). https://doi.org/10.1007/978-3-031-51060-1_6

56. Zhou, L., Oliveira, B.C.d.S.: QuickSub: efficient iso-recursive subtyping. In: Proceedings of the ACM on Programming Languages, vol. 9, no. POPL, pp. 954–985 (2025). https://doi.org/10.1145/3704869

57. Zhou, L., Wan, Q., d. S. Oliveira, B.C.: Full iso-recursive types. Proc. ACM Program. Lang. **8**(OOPSLA2), 192–221 (2024). https://doi.org/10.1145/3689718

58. Zhou, L., Zhou, Y., d. S. Oliveira, B.C.: Recursive subtyping for all. Proc. ACM Program. Lang. **7**(POPL), 1396–1425 (2023). https://doi.org/10.1145/3571241

59. Zhou, Y., Zhao, J., d. S. Oliveira, B.C.: Revisiting iso-recursive subtyping. ACM Trans. Program. Lang. Syst. **44**(4), 24:1–24:54 (2022). https://doi.org/10.1145/3549537

Verifying Algorithmic Versions of the Lovász Local Lemma

Rongen Lin, Hongjin Liang[✉], and Xinyu Feng

State Key Laboratory for Novel Software Technology, Nanjing University,
Nanjing, Jiangsu, China
relin@smail.nju.edu.cn, {hongjin,xyfeng}@nju.edu.cn

Abstract. Algorithmic versions of the Lovász Local Lemma (ALLLs), or rather, the Moser-Tardos algorithm and its variants, are impactful in both theory and practice. In this paper, we take the first step towards the goal of formally verifying ALLLs by applying programming language techniques. We propose two proof recipes, called loop truncation and resampling-table-based coupling, for bridging the gap between Hoare-style program logics and ALLLs' original informal proofs. We formally verify six existing important results related to ALLLs, and propose a new result which generalizes several existing results. Our proof recipes can also be used to verify general properties of other probabilistic programs in addition to ALLLs.

1 Introduction

The Lovász Local Lemma [19, 57] (LLL) is a powerful tool in combinatorics. It guarantees the existence of a combinatorial object with certain properties in a probability space. It has also been helpful for proving the existence of solutions to numerous significant problems in computer science, such as the Boolean Satisfiability Problem and the Graph Coloring Problem, since these problems can be viewed as instances of the problem of finding some combinatorial objects.

Besides proving the solution's existence, we also want to *efficiently construct* a solution. To this end, people have devised algorithmic versions of the Lovász Local Lemma (ALLLs). The most notable one is the Moser-Tardos (MT) algorithm proposed by Moser and Tardos in their Gödel Prize-winning paper [50]. The algorithm searches the probability space for the desired combinatorial object iteratively, bringing us a constructive proof for LLL. It is efficient in that the expected total number of iterations is bounded. Since then, a huge number of works have emerged, some explore the power of the MT algorithm [53, 42, 31, 43, 1, 37], some find variants of the MT algorithm [31, 16, 34, 30, 25, 36, 29, 13], and some utilize the MT algorithm to solve problems in various areas of computer science [31, 43, 33, 9, 26, 55, 15, 14, 27, 23], including applications in real-world systems [2, 39].

Therefore it is of great importance to formally verify the (total) correctness of ALLLs, in particular, that the MT algorithm and its variants almost surely terminate (i.e. terminate with probability 1) and their expected iteration times

© The Author(s) 2025
V. Vafeiadis (Ed.): ESOP 2025, LNCS 15694, pp. 379–407, 2025.
https://doi.org/10.1007/978-3-031-91118-7_15

have certain upper bounds. Previous works (e.g. [50]) have given proofs for the correctness of ALLLs, though these proofs are rather informal. Therefore, a natural choice is to formally verify ALLLs by formalizing existing informal proofs.

However, we encounter a challenge when verifying ALLLs by following existing proofs. We propose *Proof Recipe 1* to circumvent this challenge, and propose *Proof Recipe 2* for completing the verification after applying *Proof Recipe 1*.

Challenge: Handling infinite execution traces. It is challenging to formulate some subgoals in ALLLs' existing informal proofs using distribution-based semantics, which is commonly used in the literature of probabilistic program verification. The reason is that, on the one hand, these subgoals are about complex properties of the algorithm's execution traces, and we have to take *infinite* traces into account until we prove their absence. On the other hand, distribution-based semantics can only describe certain simple properties of these infinite traces, e.g. their overall probability.

Proof Recipe 1. We propose a proof recipe called *loop truncation* to circumvent the above challenge. For a loop in an ALLL, we transform it to a set of arbitrarily truncated loops. Now we have a set of "truncated algorithms", which can only generate *finite* execution traces. Then, instead of directly verifying the original algorithm, we prove a common bound of the expected iteration times for all the truncated algorithms. The latter can be proved following existing proofs, and now we do not have to handle infinite traces when formulating the subgoals.

Proof Recipe 2. A crucial step commonly found in many proofs of ALLLs, is to prove *an inequality between probabilities involving two programs*. Specifically, for the original ALLL program C_1 and a property $\mathbf{p}$, one constructs a program C_2 and a property $\mathbf{q}$, and shows that the probability of $\mathbf{p}$ holding after C_1's execution is not greater than the probability of $\mathbf{q}$ holding after C_2's execution.

To prove this inequality, existing informal proofs introduce variants of C_1 and C_2, say C_1' and C_2', that use a new random source called *resampling table*. By assuming that C_1 and C_2 are respectively equivalent to C_1' and C_2', they reduce the original inequality to a similar inequality that involves C_1' and C_2', and prove the latter. We elaborate on these proofs in Sec. 2.1.

Following the above proof idea, we propose a proof recipe called *resampling-table-based coupling* to formally prove the aforementioned inequality. At the core of this proof recipe is a new measure-theoretic semantics for probabilistic programs, which we call a *resampling-table-based semantics*. This semantics formalizes the *resampling table* in existing proofs as a built-in structure. We formulate C_1' (C_2') by giving C_1 (C_2) this new semantics without changing its syntax, and express the equivalence between C_1 and C_1' (C_2 and C_2') as the equivalence between a classic probabilistic semantics and the new semantics. We prove the semantics equivalence once and for all, instead of repeatedly proving the equivalence between every pair of programs. Then it remains to prove the inequality involving C_1' and C_2', which is now an inequality on the new semantics.

Our proof recipe, resampling-table-based coupling, further reduces the problem to verifying the two programs C_1' and C_2' individually. The idea is to introduce an intermediate assertion specifying the resampling table as the common random source to bridge the two programs' unary verification. The unary verification can be done using a simple Hoare-style program logic.

Contributions. Using the above two proof recipes, we have successfully verified several ALLL-related results. In summary, we make the following contributions:

- We verify six important results from [50, 53, 42, 31] for the first time. They include all the three "probabilistic" results from Moser and Tardos's Gödel Prize-winning paper [50].
- We propose a proof recipe called *loop truncation*, which circumvents the challenge when verifying ALLLs with classic distribution-based semantics.
- We propose a proof recipe called *resampling-table-based coupling*. It expresses the informal proof idea of an important inequality in a formal and concise way, taking a perspective of semantics equivalence and Hoare-style reasoning.
- We propose a new result related to the Moser-Tardos algorithm, with results from [50, 53, 42] as its corollaries. The statement and the proof of this result are formal, and the proof is done by applying our proof recipes.

Our proof recipes can also be used to prove general properties (i.e. total correctness and inequalities between probabilities) of probabilistic programs *beyond* ALLLs (see Ex. 1 and Ex. 2). We also discuss the relationship between our proof recipes and existing formal proof methods for *positive almost sure termination* and *asynchronous coupling* in Sec. 7.

Outline. We review the original informal proof of the MT algorithm, and introduce the challenge and our main ideas in Sec. 2. We then give the mathematical preliminaries in Sec. 3, and define the programming language, including our new semantics, in Sec. 4. Then we introduce our two proof recipes in Sec. 5. By applying these recipes, we verify six existing important ALLL-related results and a new result in Sec. 6. We finally discuss related work in Sec. 7.

The technical report [46] contains the full formal details of this work, including all the definitions and all the proofs for lemmas, theorems and examples.

2   Informal Development

To formally verify the ALLL-related results, a natural choice is to follow their original informal proofs. Below we first provide a brief overview of the original informal proof of Moser and Tardos's seminal result [50], which serves as an example for understanding the ideas behind the original proofs of many ALLL-related results. We then explain the verification challenge and our proof recipes.

Independently sample $X_1, \ldots, X_N$	$succ := 1$
while $\exists j \in [1, M].\ \eta_j$ holds **do**	**for all** $\eta_j \in g_{\mathsf{WT}}(wt)$ **do**
Choose such an η_j	**for all** X_i that η_j depends on **do**
for all X_i that η_j depends on **do**	Resample X_i
Resample X_i	**if** η_j does not hold **then** $succ := 0$
Output the current values of $X_1, \ldots, X_N$	Output $succ$

Fig. 1. The MT algorithm   **Fig. 2.** The check(wt) algorithm

2.1 Moser and Tardos's Proof

The Moser-Tardos (MT) algorithm efficiently constructs a solution for the following problem. Given N program variables $X_1, \ldots, X_N$ and M events $\eta_1, \ldots, \eta_M$, where each variable is associated with some random distribution and each event depends on some of $X_1, \ldots, X_N$, we would like to construct an assignment of $X_1, \ldots, X_N$ such that none of the M events occurs. The Lovász Local Lemma [19, 57] provides the Erdős-Lovász condition which sufficiently ensures the existence of such assignments. The MT algorithm finds such an assignment as shown in Fig. 1. Here "(re-)sample X_i" means the following: sample from the random distribution with which X_i is associated, and assign the result to X_i.

Moser and Tardos prove that, under the Erdős-Lovász condition, the expectation of the total iteration number of the algorithm's outer loop is no more than a real number r_{EL}, and thus the algorithm almost surely terminates. (Here we do not expose the definitions of the Erdős-Lovász condition and r_{EL}, which can be found in Thm. 4.) In the remainder of this subsection, we sketch their proof.

Restatement of the proof goal. Moser and Tardos restate their proof goal using *execution logs*. For every execution of the algorithm, its execution log Λ is a sequence of events η_j, which are dynamically chosen at the beginning of the outer loop iterations. We write $\Lambda\langle i \rangle$ for the i-th element of Λ, which is the event chosen at the i-th iteration. We write $|\Lambda|$ for the length of Λ, so it specifies the total number of the outer loop iterations. If the loop does not terminate in an execution, then $|\Lambda| = \infty$. Now, Moser and Tardos restate their proof goal as

$$\mathbb{E}[|\Lambda|] \leq r_{\mathsf{EL}}. \tag{1}$$

That is, the expected length of the execution log has an upper bound r_{EL}, where the randomness of Λ comes from the randomness of the MT algorithm. From (1), Moser and Tardos conclude that the program almost surely terminates. The proof of (1) can be divided into three stages, which will be discussed in turn.

Stage 1. In this stage, Moser and Tardos rewrite $\mathbb{E}[|\Lambda|]$ by defining a special mathematical structure called *witness trees*. A witness tree wt is a tree with some special properties, where each node is labeled with an event from $\eta_1, \ldots, \eta_M$. One can construct a witness tree wt from an execution log Λ following some specific procedure, and we write $wt = f_{\mathsf{WT}}(\Lambda)$ for this. From the concrete definitions and properties of wt and f_{WT} (which we omit here), Moser and Tardos rewrite

$\mathbb{E}[\|A\|]$ as the infinite series in (2). It enumerates all witness trees wt, and sums the probabilities that wt can be constructed from some prefix of A (that is, there exists a sequence A' such that: A' is a prefix of A, and $wt = f_{\mathsf{WT}}(A')$ holds).

$$\mathbb{E}[\|A\|] = \sum_{wt} \Pr[wt = f_{\mathsf{WT}}(\text{some prefix of } A)] \tag{2}$$

Stage 2. Next, Moser and Tardos give an upper bound of the probability in (2). That is, for all witness trees wt, they prove that

$$\Pr[wt = f_{\mathsf{WT}}(\text{some prefix of } A)] \leq p(wt), \tag{3}$$

where $p(wt)$ is a specific real number related to wt, whose definition we omit. Instead of directly proving (3) (which is challenging), Moser and Tardos construct a program check(wt), which outputs either 0 or 1, and then prove the following:

(a) The check(wt) algorithm outputs 1 with probability $p(wt)$.
(b) $\Pr[wt = f_{\mathsf{WT}}(\text{some prefix of } A)] \leq \Pr[\text{check}(wt) \text{ outputs } 1]$.

(3) then follows from the above two properties. The proof of (a) is not difficult. What is really interesting is the proof of (b). To see this, we present the check(wt) algorithm in Fig. 2, where $g_{\mathsf{WT}}(wt)$ gives us an event sequence collecting the labels of wt's nodes in a certain order (in fact, a reversed BFS ordering of wt).

To prove (b), Moser and Tardos observe that whenever wt can be generated by the MT algorithm and check(wt) is run on the *same* random source, check(wt) outputs 1. They capture this observation by specifying the random sources using *resampling tables* (RT) and letting the algorithms explicitly use the tables.

Specifically, Moser and Tardos give an RT-MT algorithm[1], and assume that it is "equivalent" to the MT algorithm, i.e., the two algorithms produce the same distribution of execution logs. The idea of the RT-MT algorithm is to transfer the lazy samplings in the MT algorithm to eager ones: the RT-MT algorithm performs all the samplings ahead of time and stores the results in an table (the RT) so that it can interpret all subsequent samplings as *deterministic* table queries.

The RT-MT algorithm is shown in Fig. 3, where we highlight the difference with Fig. 1 in blue. At the beginning, the RT-MT algorithm randomly generates a resampling table RT, which has N rows and an infinite number of columns. For all $i \in [1, N]$, this step independently samples X_i an infinite number of times, and fills the i-th row of RT with these samples. Subsequently, every sampling step of the MT algorithm is replaced by a table-query step in the RT-MT algorithm. For instance, resampling X_i is replaced by reading the leftmost unread element from the i-th row of RT, and assigning the result to X_i.

Similarly, Moser and Tardos give the RT-check(wt) algorithm as shown in Fig. 4, and assume that it is "equivalent" to check(wt), i.e., the two algorithms have the same output distribution.

---

[1] In [50], Moser and Tardos did *not* explicitly introduce new algorithms (RT-MT and RT-check). The algorithm here is a possible interpretation of their prose description.

Randomly generate an RT	Randomly generate an RT
Assign the first col. of RT to $X_1, \ldots, X_N$	$succ := 1$
while $\exists j \in [1, M]$. η_j holds **do**	**for all** $\eta_j \in g_{\mathsf{WT}}(wt)$ **do**
Choose such an η_j	**for all** X_i that η_j depends on **do**
for all X_i that η_j depends on **do**	Assign the next number of
Assign the next number of	the i-th row of RT to X_i
the i-th row of RT to X_i	**if** η_j does not hold **then** $succ := 0$
Output the current values of $X_1, \ldots, X_N$	Output $succ$

Fig. 3. The RT-MT algorithm   **Fig. 4.** The RT-check(wt) algorithm

Since the MT algorithm and check(wt) are "equivalent" to their RT-based counterparts respectively, to prove (b), we only need to show that,

(b') $\Pr[wt = f_{\mathsf{WT}}(\text{some prefix of } \Lambda \text{ of RT-MT})] \leq \Pr[\text{RT-check}(wt) \text{ outputs } 1]$.

Note that the first lines of the RT-MT algorithm and RT-check(wt) are the same, and all other parts of these two programs are non-probabilistic. Thus, we couple the random sources of the RT-MT algorithm and RT-check(wt), or rather, let the first lines of these two programs generate the same RT. Then it remains to prove that, for any RT, if wt can be generated from the RT-MT algorithm using this RT, then RT-check(wt) with the same RT must output 1.

The proof is based on the following observation. If wt can be generated from the RT-MT algorithm using RT, then *in retrospect* RT must have some crucial properties, and these properties will make RT-check(wt) output 1. More precisely, for all events η_j in wt, at the time η_j is chosen in the execution of the RT-MT algorithm, it must hold under the current assignment formed by some of RT's entries. Then, during the execution of RT-check(wt), when the program tests η_j, the test passes because the current assignment must be formed by (almost) the same entries of RT.

Stage 3. Finally, Moser and Tardos prove that,

$$\sum_{wt} p(wt) \leq r_{\mathsf{EL}}, \quad \text{if the Erdős-Lovász condition holds.} \tag{4}$$

It can be proved in a purely mathematical (i.e. program-independent) yet simple way, as pointed out by Srinivasan [58].

Combining all three stages above, Moser and Tardos obtain (1):

$$\mathbb{E}[|\Lambda|] = \sum_{wt} \Pr[wt = f_{\mathsf{WT}}(\text{some prefix of } \Lambda)] \qquad \text{Stage 1, (2)}$$

$$\leq \sum_{wt} p(wt) \qquad \text{Stage 2, (3)}$$

$$\leq r_{\mathsf{EL}}. \qquad \text{Stage 3, (4)}$$

Two parts in Moser and Tardos's reasoning that need more careful formalization. First, Moser and Tardos restate their ultimate proof goal as (1) using $|\Lambda|$, the length of the execution log Λ. However, their restatement is ambiguous, since without defining the program semantics, it is unclear how programs are executed and generate execution logs. Similar ambiguity arises when stating those subgoals that also involve quantities related to Λ, e.g. (2) and (3).

Second, Moser and Tardos's original proof of *Stage 2* is far from rigorous. To prove (b), they assume that the MT algorithm and check(wt) are "equivalent" to their RT-based variants, but they did not strictly define and prove the "equivalences". Besides, they did not give a rigorous proof of (b') with these RT-based variants strictly defined.

In the next subsections, we show how we formally state and verify Moser and Tardos's result. We illustrate the proof path in Fig. 5, which is also explained below.

2.2   Stating Proof Goals Using Distribution-Based Semantics

To formally state Moser and Tardos's ultimate proof goal, we must formulate the program semantics and the expected total number of iterations (or equivalently, the expected length of the execution log Λ).

We use a classic distribution-based semantics as the formal program semantics. This semantics (and other equivalent semantics, e.g. the probabilistic wp-semantics [45, 48] and Kozen's "Semantics 2" [44]) is commonly used in the literature of probabilistic program verification (e.g. [45, 48, 3, 7, 21]). It interprets the execution result of a program C as a sub-distribution μ over states. For any state σ, this final state sub-distribution μ specifies the probability that the program C terminates at σ.

For specifying the expected total number of iterations, we introduce a fresh program variable cnt that records the number of iterations. Our code of the MT algorithm, $C_{\mathsf{MT}}(cnt)$, sets cnt to zero at the beginning, and increments it in each iteration of the outer loop. Consequently, when $C_{\mathsf{MT}}(cnt)$ terminates, the value of cnt is the total number of iterations.

Now, our proof goal can be stated as the following *total correctness* Hoare triple (assuming that the Erdős-Lovász condition holds on the probability space):

$$\vDash [\mathbf{true}]\, C_{\mathsf{MT}}(cnt)\, [\mathbb{E}[cnt] \leq r_{\mathsf{EL}}]. \tag{5}$$

Informally it says, the execution of $C_{\mathsf{MT}}(cnt)$ in the distribution-based semantics almost surely terminates (i.e., terminates with probability 1), and the expectation of the value of cnt (represented as $\mathbb{E}[cnt]$) at the final state sub-distribution is no greater than r_{EL}. The goal is shown on the top of Fig. 5.

For proving (5), we follow the original proof. That is, we formulate the subgoals in the three stages in Sec. 2.1 using distribution-based semantics, and then prove them. However, we encounter a challenge when formulating (2) and (3).

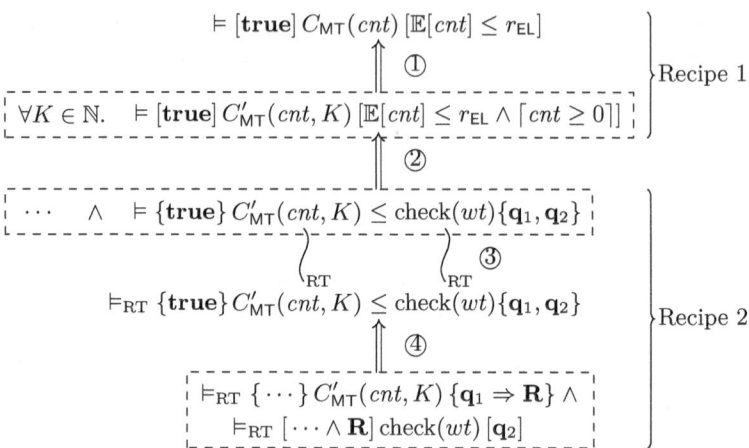

Fig. 5. Our proof path of Moser and Tardos's result, where $\mathbf{q_1} = \mathsf{Gen}(wt, cnt, K)$ and $\mathbf{q_2} = \mathsf{Succ}$

Challenge: Handling infinite execution traces. The problem arises when formulating the probability (6), which appears in both (2) and (3).

$$\Pr[wt = f_{\mathsf{WT}}(\text{some prefix of } \varLambda)] \qquad (6)$$

Let μ be the final state sub-distribution of $C_{\mathsf{MT}}(cnt)$. Then, it is challenging to formulate (6) using μ. Note that (6) can be positive even when $C_{\mathsf{MT}}(cnt)$ never terminates. But if we simply define (6) as the probability of some event on μ, this probability must be 0 if $C_{\mathsf{MT}}(cnt)$ never terminates, since μ is now a null sub-distribution (which specifies that $C_{\mathsf{MT}}(cnt)$ terminates at σ with probability 0 for any σ). Other definition attempts using μ may also fail.

The difficulty in formulating (6) lies in the following facts. On the one hand, (6) is the total probability of $C_{\mathsf{MT}}(cnt)$'s possibly infinite execution traces on which $wt = f_{\mathsf{WT}}(\text{some prefix of } \varLambda)$ holds. This is a complex property that may involve only some of $C_{\mathsf{MT}}(cnt)$'s infinite traces. On the other hand, distribution-based semantics can only express certain simple properties of infinite traces, and thus cannot express (6). From μ, all we know about $C_{\mathsf{MT}}(cnt)$'s infinite traces is their overall probability $1 - |\mu|$, where $|\mu|$ is the weight of μ (see Sec. 3.1).

One should not simply rule out infinite traces by strengthening (2) and (3) to include almost sure termination of $C_{\mathsf{MT}}(cnt)$, since in Sec. 2.1 the termination has not been derived until the ultimate goal is fully proved (also, it is not easy to prove the termination alone, as discussed in Sec. 7).

2.3 Proof Recipe 1: Loop Truncation

We circumvent the aforementioned challenge by proposing *loop truncation*. Our idea is to do a code transformation on loops, so that the codes after transformation do not generate infinite traces. For the main loop in $C_{\mathsf{MT}}(cnt)$, our transformation introduces a loop bound K whose value is an arbitrary natural number, and turns the original loop **while** (b) **do** C into a set of truncated loops $\{$ **while** $(b \wedge cnt < K)$ **do** $C \mid K \in \mathbb{N}\}$. Since we increment cnt in the loop body C, each truncated loop **while** $(b \wedge cnt < K)$ **do** C terminates in at most K rounds, and thus can only generate finite execution traces.

Soundness of this transformation can be captured by Lem. 1 below (we will show the more general form in Thm. 2 in Sec. 5.1). It says, the original loop guarantees almost sure termination and its expected total iteration number is bounded by r, as long as all the truncated loops terminate and their expected total iteration numbers have the same upper bound r. Here $\lceil cnt \geq 0 \rceil$ says, cnt, the number of iterations, is always non-negative after **while** $(b \wedge cnt < K)$ **do** C's execution. Without this condition the transformation is unsound.

Lemma 1. *For all* P, b, C, r, *if*

$$\forall K \in \mathbb{N}. \quad \vDash [P]\,\mathbf{while}\,(b \wedge cnt < K)\,\mathbf{do}\,C\,[\mathbb{E}[cnt] \leq r \wedge \lceil cnt \geq 0 \rceil],$$

then $\vDash [P]\,\mathbf{while}\,(b)\,\mathbf{do}\,C\,[\mathbb{E}[cnt] \leq r]$.

Using this transformation, we can reduce (5) to proving the total correctness of $C'_{\mathsf{MT}}(cnt, K)$ for all K, where $C'_{\mathsf{MT}}(cnt, K)$ is the resulting code after transforming the main loop of $C_{\mathsf{MT}}(cnt)$ to a truncated one. That is, we prove (7) for all K.

$$\vDash [\mathbf{true}]\,C'_{\mathsf{MT}}(cnt, K)\,[\mathbb{E}[cnt] \leq r_{\mathsf{EL}} \wedge \lceil cnt \geq 0 \rceil] \tag{7}$$

We show this as Step ① in Fig. 5. The double arrow represents logical implication. Then we can prove (7) following Moser and Tardos's proof ideas explained in Sec. 2.1. We formulate subgoals (2) and (3) for $C'_{\mathsf{MT}}(cnt, K)$; however, we will not encounter the aforementioned challenge, since $C'_{\mathsf{MT}}(cnt, K)$ does not have infinite execution traces.

Serving as a proof method for PAST. Lem. 1 is itself a general proof method for positive almost sure termination (PAST) [11], whenever we use cnt to record the number of program steps. The PAST property says, the program terminates not only almost surely, but also within finite number of steps in expectation. We give an example in Ex. 1 in Sec. 5.1.

2.4 Proof Recipe 2: Resampling-Table-Based Coupling

Following the ideas in Sec. 2.1, we prove (7) in three stages. The most challenging part is proving (b) in *Stage 2*, which is an inequality between probabilities involving two programs.

We first formally specify the inequality. To this end, we introduce the tuple $\vDash \{P\}C_1 \leq C_2\{\mathbf{q}_1, \mathbf{q}_2\}$. Here P is a predicate specifying state distributions μ, while $\mathbf{q}_1$ and $\mathbf{q}_2$ are predicates over states σ. The tuple says that, the probability of $\mathbf{q}_1$ holding at the terminating states of C_1 is not greater than the probability of $\mathbf{q}_2$ holding at the terminating states of C_2, where C_1 and C_2's executions start from the same μ satisfying P and use the distribution-based semantics. Then, we can formulate (b) for $C'_{\mathsf{MT}}(cnt, K)$ and check(wt) as follows.

$$\vDash \{\mathbf{true}\}C'_{\mathsf{MT}}(cnt, K) \leq \text{check}(wt)\{\mathsf{Gen}(wt, cnt, K),\ \mathsf{Succ}\} \qquad (8)$$

Here $\mathsf{Gen}(wt, cnt, K)$ roughly says that wt can be generated and is well-formed with respect to cnt and K. The predicate Succ says that the output $succ$ is 1. See Step ② in Fig. 5.

Following Moser and Tardos's proof in Sec. 2.1, we introduce the RT-MT algorithm (now with a truncated loop) and the RT-check(wt) algorithm. We need to give strict definitions of these variants, and to prove that they are indeed equivalent to the original $C'_{\mathsf{MT}}(cnt, K)$ and check(wt) respectively.

Resampling-table-based semantics. Instead of introducing the RT-MT algorithm and the RT-check(wt) algorithm with explicit statements for generating the RT and accessing it, our approach is to *keep the program syntax unchanged but reinterpret the code using a new semantics.* Our RT is a built-in structure of the new semantics, and it is randomly generated before programs start execution.

More specifically, we re-interpret (8) using the novel *RT-based semantics.* In this semantics, we let a program execute with a resampling table RT, which stores all sampling results of the program in advance, and serves as an oracle for the sampling statements in the program. Each sampling statement is interpreted as a query to RT. So this semantics is deterministic given a specific RT.

Our RT-based semantics is equivalent to the classic distribution-based semantics explained in Sec. 2.2. By specifying and proving the semantics equivalence, we essentially show that all programs (including the MT algorithm and check(wt) in Sec. 2.1) are "equivalent" to their RT-based variants.

Based on the semantics equivalence, we can show the equivalence between $\vDash \{P\}C_1 \leq C_2\{\mathbf{q}_1, \mathbf{q}_2\}$ and $\vDash_{\mathrm{RT}} \{P\}C_1 \leq C_2\{\mathbf{q}_1, \mathbf{q}_2\}$. The latter specifies the same relational property as the former but uses the RT-based semantics for execution. See Step ③ in Fig. 5.

Resampling-table-based coupling. Our proof recipe reduces the relational verification for $\vDash_{\mathrm{RT}} \{P\}C_1 \leq C_2\{\mathbf{q}_1, \mathbf{q}_2\}$ to unary verification of each of C_1 and C_2 in the RT-based semantics.

Specifically, we couple the random sources of C_1 and C_2, i.e. let them use the same RT in their executions. We prove: for all RT, if C_1 using RT terminates on a state satisfying $\mathbf{q}_1$, then C_2 using the same RT must also terminate on a state satisfying $\mathbf{q}_2$.

To prove this, we introduce an intermediate assertion $\mathbf{R}$ to describe what kind of RT can make $\mathbf{q}_1$ hold after the execution of C_1. Usually $\mathbf{R}$ specifies that "some entries in RT have some properties". With $\mathbf{R}$, we can split the goal into the following two subgoals:

- For all RT, if C_1 using RT terminates at a state satisfying $\mathbf{q}_1$, then *in retrospect RT must satisfy $\mathbf{R}$*. This is formulated as the Hoare-triple

$$\vDash_{\mathrm{RT}} \{\cdots\} C_1 \{\mathbf{q}_1 \Rightarrow \mathbf{R}\}. \qquad (9)$$

The post-condition reflects this retrospective reasoning. We omit the pre-condition, which usually degenerates to a regular state assertion. Then we only need classical (non-probabilistic) Hoare-style proofs for the Hoare triple.

– Starting with any RT satisfying $\mathbf{R}$, the execution of C_2 must terminate at a final state satisfying $\mathbf{q_2}$, that is,

$$\vDash_{\mathrm{RT}} [\cdots \wedge \mathbf{R}] \, C_2 \, [\mathbf{q_2}]. \tag{10}$$

Here $\mathbf{R}$ is in the precondition. We omit the rest parts of the precondition.

Note that the first subgoal (9) only needs to be *partial correctness*. It says, for any execution of C_1, if it terminates and the final state satisfies $\mathbf{q_1}$, RT must satisfy $\mathbf{R}$. Then the *total correctness* of C_2 (the second subgoal (10)) says, starting from the same RT, C_2 terminates at a final state satisfying $\mathbf{q_2}$. This way we can prove that the probability of $\mathbf{q_1}$ at the end of C_1 is not greater than the probability of $\mathbf{q_2}$ at the end of C_2. Step ④ in Fig. 5 shows this reduction of the relational reasoning to unary proofs of the two programs separately.

Our reasoning above benefits from a key novelty of our RT-based semantics with respect to existing random-source-based semantics (e.g. Kozen's "Semantics 1" [44] and those in [10, 17]). That is, our RT is an immutable structure that never changes during program execution. In particular, used samples are not popped out of RT. Therefore the assertion $\mathbf{R}$ derived from the post-condition of (9) must also hold over the RT at the beginning of the execution. So we can use it in the precondition in (10).

Finding such an $\mathbf{R}$ is not difficult in many cases, especially when verifying ALLLs. We give another example in Sec. 5.2.

3 Preliminaries

In this section, we review some fundamentals of probability theory in two stages. We first introduce some basics of discrete probability theory without mentioning their measure-theoretic extensions, serving as the foundation of our distribution-based semantics in Sec. 4.1. Then we turn to the measure-theoretic probability theory, which forms the basis of our RT-based semantics in Sec. 4.2.

3.1 Discrete Probability Theory

We use notations from [21, 3]. A (discrete) *sub-distribution* over a set A is defined as a function $\mu : A \rightarrow [0, 1]$ that satisfies the following two conditions: (1) the support of μ, denoted by $supp(\mu) = \{a \in A : \mu(a) > 0\}$, is countable; (2) $|\mu| \leq 1$, where $|\mu| = \sum_{a \in A} \mu(a)$ is μ's weight.

A sub-distribution μ is called a *distribution* if $|\mu| = 1$. We denote by $\mathbb{SD}_A$ all of the sub-distributions over A, and by $\mathbb{D}_A$ all of the distributions over A. We write $\mathrm{Pr}_{a \sim \mu}[E(a)]$, which is defined as $\sum_{a \in A : E(a)} \mu(a)$, for the probability of $E : A \rightarrow \mathrm{Prop}$ on the sub-distribution μ. We write $\mathbb{E}_{a \sim \mu}[V(a)]$, which is defined as $\sum_{a \in A} \mu(a) \cdot V(a)$, for the expected value of $V : A \rightarrow \mathbb{R}$ on μ.

$$(\textit{Dsts}) \ \mathcal{D} ::= (\kappa_1, \ldots, \kappa_N) \qquad (\textit{Evts}) \ \mathcal{E} \ ::= \ (\eta_1, \ldots, \eta_M)$$

$$(\textit{Dst}) \ \kappa \ \in \ \mathbb{D}_{Real} \qquad (\textit{Evt}) \ \eta \ \in \ \underbrace{Real \times \cdots \times Real}_{N \ Real's} \to \{\text{true}, \text{false}\}$$

$$\text{vbl}(\eta, j) \ \text{iff} \ \exists r_1, \ldots, r_N, r'. \ \eta(r_1, \ldots, r_N) \neq \eta(r_1, \ldots, r_{j-1}, r', r_{j+1}, \ldots, r_N)$$

$$P(\eta) \ \triangleq \ \sum_{\substack{r_1 \in supp(\mathcal{D}[1]), \ldots, r_N \in supp(\mathcal{D}[N]) \\ \eta(r_1, \ldots, r_N) = \text{true}}} \ \prod_{i \in [1,N]} \mathcal{D}[i](r_i)$$

$$\Gamma(j) \ \triangleq \ \{k : \exists i. \ \text{vbl}(\mathcal{E}[j], i) \wedge \text{vbl}(\mathcal{E}[k], i))\} \setminus \{j\}$$

$(\textit{Expr}) \ e \ ::= \ v \ | \ x \ | \ e_1 + e_2 \ | \ a[e] \ | \ e_1\langle e_2 \rangle \ | \ \text{len}(e) \ | \ \text{app}(e_1, e_2) \ | \ \ldots$

$(\textit{Bexp}) \ b \ ::= \ \text{true} \ | \ \text{false} \ | \ e_1 = e_2 \ | \ b_1 \wedge b_1 \ | \ \text{hold}(e, e_1, \ldots, e_N) \ | \ \text{vbl}(e_1, e_2) \ | \ \ldots$

$(\textit{Stmt}) \ C \ ::= \ \textbf{skip} \ | \ x := e \ | \ x := \text{Sample}(e) \ | \ a[e_1] := e_2$
$\qquad\qquad | \ C_1; C_2 \ | \ \textbf{if} \ (b) \ \textbf{then} \ C_1 \ \textbf{else} \ C_2 \ | \ \textbf{while} \ (b) \ \textbf{do} \ C \ | \ \ldots$

Fig. 6. Syntax of the programming language

For an infinite sequence $\vec{\mu}$, we define $\lim \vec{\mu}$ as the sub-distribution μ such that $\lim_{n \to \infty} \sum_{a \in A} |\vec{\mu}[n](a) - \mu(a)| = 0$. One can prove that such a μ is unique if it exists, otherwise we leave $\lim \vec{\mu}$ undefined.

For $\mu \in \mathbb{SD}_A$ and function $f \in A \to \mathbb{SD}_B$, we define the *expected sub-distribution* $\mathbb{E}_{a \sim \mu}\{f(a)\} \in \mathbb{SD}_B$ as $\lambda b. \ \sum_{a \in A} \mu(a) \cdot f(a)(b)$.

3.2   Measure-Theoretic Probability Theory

A set of subsets of a set Ω, say $\mathcal{F}$, is a σ-algebra on Ω if it contains Ω and is closed under complement and countable union. A measurable space is defined as a pair $(\Omega, \mathcal{F})$, where $\mathcal{F}$ is a σ-algebra on Ω. We call Ω the *sample space*.

A function $\mathcal{M} : \mathcal{F} \to [0, \infty)$ is called a (finite) *measure* on measurable space $(\Omega, \mathcal{F})$ if it satisfies $\mathcal{M}(\varnothing) = 0$ and is countably additive. A *measure space* is defined as a triple $(\Omega, \mathcal{F}, \mathcal{M})$, where $\mathcal{M}$ is a measure on measurable space $(\Omega, \mathcal{F})$. $(\Omega, \mathcal{F}, \mathcal{M})$ is called a *probability space* if $\mathcal{M}(\Omega) = 1$.

A discrete distribution μ can be lifted to a measure-theoretic probability space $(\Omega, \mathcal{F}, \mathcal{M})$, where $\Omega = supp(\mu)$, $\mathcal{F} = \mathcal{P}(supp(\mu))$, and $\mathcal{M}(A) = \sum_{a \in A} \mu(a)$ for all $A \subseteq supp(\mu)$.

Let $\{(\Omega_i, \mathcal{F}_i, \mathcal{M}_i) : i \in I\}$ be a collection of probability spaces for some possibly infinite set I. We denote by $\prod_{i \in I}(\Omega_i, \mathcal{F}_i, \mathcal{M}_i)$ the *product probability space* of $\{(\Omega_i, \mathcal{F}_i, \mathcal{M}_i) : i \in I\}$, defined as $(\Omega, \mathcal{F}, \mathcal{M})$, where: (1) $\Omega = \prod_{i \in I} \Omega_i$, (2) $\mathcal{F}$ is the smallest σ-algebra containing all $\prod_{i \in I} A_i$ such that $A_i \in \mathcal{F}_i$ and $\{j : A_j \subsetneq \Omega_j\}$ is finite, and (3) $\mathcal{M}(\prod_{i \in I} A_i) = \prod_{j \in J} \mathcal{M}_j(A_j)$ when $A_i \in \mathcal{F}_i$ and $J = \{j : A_j \subsetneq \Omega_j\}$ is finite. The above $(\Omega, \mathcal{F}, \mathcal{M})$ exists and is unique (see [54]).

4   Two Semantics of the Language

In this section we define the programming language. We first define the language syntax, and then give two equivalent semantics in Sec. 4.1 and Sec. 4.2.

Global parameters. Throughout the paper, we assume four global parameters for programs: N, M, $\mathcal{D}$ and $\mathcal{E}$. They are viewed as meta-variables, and can be configured differently for different programs.

As defined at the top of Fig. 6, $\mathcal{D}$ and $\mathcal{E}$ represent the "N distributions" and "M events" in ALLL's setting (see Sec. 2.1) respectively. Each event η_j in $\mathcal{E}$ takes N reals as input, and outputs a boolean value. Each κ_i in $\mathcal{D}$ is a distribution over reals, and is associated with the i-th argument of every η_j in $\mathcal{E}$.

Fig. 6 also gives important notations related to $\mathcal{D}$ and $\mathcal{E}$, which are used in the statements and the formal proofs of ALLL-related results. $\mathrm{vbl}(\eta, j)$ holds iff the event η depends on its j-th argument.[2] $\mathrm{P}(\eta)$ is the probability of the event η occurring, given that its N arguments are independently distributed according to $\mathcal{D}[1], \ldots, \mathcal{D}[N]$ respectively. $\Gamma(j)$ is the index set of events that depend on some argument that $\mathcal{E}[j]$ also depends on, except $\mathcal{E}[j]$ itself.

Syntax of the programming language. As shown at the bottom of Fig. 6, we use customized program statements, expressions and boolean expressions to formulate ALLLs' code. We write $x := \mathsf{Sample}(e)$ to sample from the distribution $\mathcal{D}[e]$ and store the result in the program variable x. The boolean expression $\mathsf{hold}(e, e_1, \ldots, e_N)$ tests if the event $\mathcal{E}[e]$ holds with arguments $e_1, \ldots, e_N$. Moreover, $\mathsf{vbl}(e_1, e_2)$ tests if the event $\mathcal{E}[e_1]$ depends on its e_2-th argument.

We use arrays to formulate the N variables $X_1, \ldots, X_N$ in ALLLs. We use $a[e]$ to represent the element of array a with index e, and use $a[e_1] := e_2$ for the in-place update.

We use lists to formulate the execution logs in ALLLs. To access and manipulate the execution log, we introduce list-related expressions. We use $e_1 \langle e_2 \rangle$ for the e_2-th element of list e_1, use $\mathsf{len}(e)$ for the length of list e, and use $\mathsf{app}(e_1, e_2)$ for appending an element e_2 to list e_1.

Using the syntax in Fig. 6, we can formulate the code of the MT algorithm, $C_{\mathsf{MT}}(cnt)$, in Fig. 12 in Sec. 6.

States and state distributions. As defined below, a state σ maps each program variable in $PVar$ to some value v. For simplicity, we view each array element as a program variable. A value v is either a real r or a list Λ of natural numbers.

$$(State) \quad \sigma \ \in \ PVar \rightarrow Val \qquad (DState) \quad \mu \ \in \ \mathbb{D}_{State}$$

State distributions μ are used to specify that, with probability $\mu(\sigma)$, the program state before or after the execution of a program is exactly σ. We write $\llbracket e \rrbracket_\sigma$ and $\llbracket b \rrbracket_\sigma$ for the evaluation of e and b in a state σ.

Below we give two equivalent probabilistic semantics of our language, a classic distribution-based semantics and an RT-based semantics. We use n for natural numbers and p, r for reals. Throughout this paper, we assume that the program's execution does not get stuck, and the evaluation of expressions does not abort.

---

[2] The name "vbl" is short for "variables". Moser and Tardos [50] used $\mathrm{vbl}(\eta)$ as the minimal set of variables (i.e. arguments of the event) that determine η.

r_{10}	r_{11}	r_{12}	r_{13}	$\cdots$
r_{20}	r_{21}	r_{22}	r_{23}	$\cdots$

Fig. 7. A resampling table RT with $N = 2$

4.1   Distribution-Based Semantics

Following [21, 3], we first define the semantic function $[\![C]\!](\sigma) \in \mathbb{SD}_{State}$. Here $[\![C]\!](\sigma)(\sigma')$ represents the probability of C's execution from σ finally reaching σ'. For example, for the sampling operation $x := \mathsf{Sample}(e)$ that samples from the distribution $\mathcal{D}[i]$ and gets r as the result, the probability is $\mathcal{D}[i](r)$. That is,

$$[\![x := \mathsf{Sample}(e)]\!](\sigma)(\sigma') = \begin{cases} \mathcal{D}[i](r) & \text{if } [\![e]\!]_\sigma = i \in [1, N] \text{ and } \sigma' = \sigma\{x \rightsquigarrow r\} \\ 0 & \text{otherwise} \end{cases}.$$

We give the full definition in [46]. We further define $[\![C]\!](\mu) \in \mathbb{SD}_{State}$ (where $\mu \in DState$) by lifting $[\![C]\!](\sigma)$, using the expected sub-distribution in Sec. 3.1:

$$[\![C]\!](\mu) \triangleq \mathbb{E}_{\sigma \sim \mu}\{[\![C]\!](\sigma)\}.$$

4.2   Resampling-Table-Based Semantics

Informally, in our new RT-based semantics, a program first randomly generates a resampling table (RT); with this table, the program then starts its deterministic execution. Below we first give the definition of an RT, and specify how the semantics "generates" an RT. Then we define an RT-based operational semantics, which describes the deterministic execution of the program with a certain RT. Finally, we combine all the above definitions into the RT-based semantic functions $[\![C]\!]_{RT}(\sigma)$ and $[\![C]\!]_{RT}(\mu)$.

The resampling table is defined as follows.

$$(RTable) \quad RT \quad \in \quad [1, N] \times Nat \to Real \quad \text{where generable}(RT)$$
$$\text{generable}(RT) \quad \text{iff} \quad \forall i, j. \ RT[i][j] \in supp(\mathcal{D}[i])$$

A resampling table RT is a matrix with size $N \times \infty$. An example of such table is shown in Fig. 7, where $N = 2$ and $RT[i][j] = r_{ij}$ for $i \in [1, 2]$ and $j \in Nat$. Intuitively, as described in Sec. 2.1, the i-th row of RT stores the ahead-of-time samples from the distribution $\mathcal{D}[i]$. Additionally, we require that generable(RT) holds. That is, every entry in the i-th row of RT must be able to be sampled from the distribution $\mathcal{D}[i]$. This accords with the intuition of the RT.

We specify how the semantics "generates" an RT. To this end, we define the probability space of all (generable) RTs as $(\Omega, \mathcal{F}, \mathcal{M})$, and thus $\mathcal{M}(\{RT \mid \cdots\})$ represents the probability of some RT from set $\{RT \mid \cdots\}$ being generated. The definition is shown below:

$$(\Omega, \mathcal{F}, \mathcal{M}) \quad \triangleq \quad \prod_{(i,j) \in [1,N] \times Nat} (\Omega_{i,j}, \mathcal{F}_{i,j}, \mathcal{M}_{i,j}),$$

$$\frac{[\![e]\!]_\sigma = v}{RT \vdash (x := e, \sigma, \iota) \to (\mathbf{skip}, \sigma\{x \rightsquigarrow v\}, \iota)}$$

$$\frac{[\![e]\!]_\sigma = i \in [1, N] \qquad \iota' = (\iota[1], \ldots, \iota[i-1], \iota[i]+1, \iota[i+1], \ldots, \iota[N])}{RT \vdash (x := \mathsf{Sample}(e), \sigma, \iota) \to (\mathbf{skip}, \sigma\{x \rightsquigarrow RT[i][\iota[i]]\}, \iota')}$$

Fig. 8. RT-based operational semantics

where $(\Omega_{i,j}, \mathcal{F}_{i,j}, \mathcal{M}_{i,j})$ is lifted from the discrete distribution $\mathcal{D}[i]$ (see Sec. 3.2). Note that $\Omega = RTable$, i.e., the sample space is indeed the set of all RTs.

Below we explain our construction of $(\Omega, \mathcal{F}, \mathcal{M})$. The probability space of all RTs is the *infinite product* of probability spaces of all entries, since an RT is generated by filling all of its entries by an infinite number of independent samples. For the entry in row i and (arbitrary) column j, its probability space is lifted from $\mathcal{D}[i]$, from which the entry is sampled.

We then define the RT-based operational semantics, with selected semantics rules shown in Fig. 8. The definition is almost standard, except that it interprets sampling operations to table queries. Recall that, when the program performs a sampling from the distribution $\mathcal{D}[i]$, it reads the leftmost unread entry in the i-th row of RT as the result. To keep track of these entries, we maintain the heads ι in the program configuration to record their column numbers.

$$(Heads) \quad \iota \ ::= \ (n_1, \ldots, n_N)$$

ι is an N-tuple. Its i-th component, $\iota[i]$, represents the column number of the leftmost unread entry in the i-th row of RT. Now, $RT \vdash (C, \sigma, \iota) \to^* (C', \sigma', \iota')$ says that, starting from the program state σ, with the leftmost unread entries of RT initially specified by ι, C deterministically executes to C' using RT, where the result state is σ' and finally the leftmost unread entries in RT are specified by ι'. When the program performs a sampling from $\mathcal{D}[i]$, it takes $RT[i][\iota[i]]$ as the result and increments $\iota[i]$. In other program steps, ι remains unchanged.

Now the RT-based semantic functions are defined below, where $\iota_{\mathsf{init}} = (0, \ldots, 0)$ represents the initial positions of heads.

$$[\![C]\!]_{\mathrm{RT}}(\sigma) \ \triangleq \ \lambda\sigma'. \ \mathcal{M}(\{RT \mid RT \vdash (C, \sigma, \iota_{\mathsf{init}}) \to^* (\mathbf{skip}, \sigma', \_)\})$$

$$[\![C]\!]_{\mathrm{RT}}(\mu) \ \triangleq \ \mathbb{E}_{\sigma \sim \mu}\{[\![C]\!]_{\mathrm{RT}}(\sigma)\}$$

Informally, the probability of C's execution from σ finally reaching σ', say $[\![C]\!]_{\mathrm{RT}}(\sigma)(\sigma')$, is the probability of some RT, which satisfies the following property, being generated: starting from σ, C's execution using RT finally reaches σ'. This property is formally stated as $RT \vdash (C, \sigma, \iota_{\mathsf{init}}) \to^* (\mathbf{skip}, \sigma', \_)$, with the help of the operational semantics.

Lem. 2 shows that the RT-based semantics is indeed well-defined.

Lemma 2. *For all* $C, \sigma, \sigma', \iota, \ \{RT \mid RT \vdash (C, \sigma, \iota) \to^* (\mathbf{skip}, \sigma', \_)\} \in \mathcal{F}$

To conclude this subsection, we give the following theorem, which states the equivalence between the distribution-based semantics defined in Sec. 4.1 and the RT-based semantics.

$(Assn)\ \mathbf{p}, \mathbf{q}, \mathbf{r} ::= b \mid \neg\mathbf{q} \mid \mathbf{q}_1 \wedge \mathbf{q}_2 \mid \mathbf{q}_1 \vee \mathbf{q}_2 \mid \forall X.\mathbf{q} \mid \exists X.\mathbf{q} \mid \ \ldots$

$(PExp)\quad \xi\quad ::= r \mid \mathbb{E}[e] \mid \Pr[\mathbf{q}] \mid \xi_1 + \xi_2 \mid \xi_1 - \xi_2 \mid \ \ldots$

$(PAssn)\ P, Q, R ::= \lceil \mathbf{q} \rceil \mid \xi_1 = \xi_2 \mid \neg Q \mid Q_1 \wedge Q_2 \mid \forall X.Q \mid \exists X.Q \mid \ \ldots$

$\llbracket r \rrbracket_\mu \triangleq r$ $\qquad\qquad\qquad \mu \vDash \lceil \mathbf{q} \rceil \ \text{ iff } \forall \sigma.\ \sigma \in supp(\mu) \implies \sigma \vDash \mathbf{q}$

$\llbracket \mathbb{E}[e] \rrbracket_\mu \triangleq \mathbb{E}_{\sigma \sim \mu}[\llbracket e \rrbracket_\sigma]$ $\qquad\quad \mu \vDash \xi_1 = \xi_2 \ \text{ iff } \ \llbracket \xi_1 \rrbracket_\mu = \llbracket \xi_2 \rrbracket_\mu$

$\llbracket \Pr[\mathbf{q}] \rrbracket_\mu \triangleq \Pr_{\sigma \sim \mu}[\sigma \vDash \mathbf{q}]$ $\qquad\ \ \mu\{X \rightsquigarrow v\} \triangleq \mathbb{E}_{\sigma \sim \mu}\{\delta(\sigma\{X \rightsquigarrow v\})\}$

$\llbracket \xi_1 + \xi_2 \rrbracket_\mu \triangleq \llbracket \xi_1 \rrbracket_\mu + \llbracket \xi_2 \rrbracket_\mu$ $\qquad \mu \vDash \exists X.Q \ \text{ iff } \ \exists v.\ \mu\{X \rightsquigarrow v\} \vDash Q$

Fig. 9. Assertions over states and state distributions

Theorem 1 (Semantics Equivalence). *For all C and μ, $\llbracket C \rrbracket(\mu) = \llbracket C \rrbracket_{\mathrm{RT}}(\mu)$.*

5   Proof Recipes

Our ultimate proof goals are formulated as total correctness Hoare triples $\vDash [P]C[Q]$ using the distribution-based semantics of Sec. 4.1.

Before showing the definition of $\vDash [P]C[Q]$, we first define assertions in Fig. 9, following the assertion language in [21]. We write $\mathbf{p}, \mathbf{q}, \mathbf{r}$ for non-probabilistic assertions on program states, and P, Q, R for probabilistic assertions on state distributions. The assertion $\lceil \mathbf{q} \rceil$ holds on the distribution μ iff $\mathbf{q}$ holds on all states in the support of μ. We write **true** as a shorthand for $\lceil \text{true} \rceil$. The expression $\Pr[\mathbf{q}]$ represents the probability that $\mathbf{q}$ holds, and $\mathbb{E}[e]$ represents the expected value of e. The assertion $\exists X.Q$ holds on μ, if Q holds on μ' obtained by assigning some constant v to X in all states in μ (here δ gives the Dirac distribution).

Then, $\vDash [P]C[Q]$ says that, starting from a state distribution satisfying P, C's execution terminates with probability 1, and thus the sub-distribution of the result states is actually a state distribution, which satisfies Q. We show the definition in Def. 1.

Definition 1 (Total Correctness). *For all P, C, Q, $\vDash [P]C[Q]$ holds iff*

$$\forall \mu.\ \mu \vDash P \implies |\llbracket C \rrbracket(\mu)| = 1 \wedge \llbracket C \rrbracket(\mu) \vDash Q.$$

In the following subsections, we formalize our two proof recipes, loop truncation and RT-based coupling.

5.1   Loop Truncation

We have explained a specialized form of loop truncation in Lem. 1 in Sec. 2.3. Below we show the more general theorem (Thm. 2).

Theorem 2 (Loop Truncation). *For all $P, b, C, \mathbf{E}, Q, e$ and r, if*

$$\forall K \in \mathbb{N}.\ \ \vDash [P]\ \mathbf{E}[\textbf{while } (b \wedge e < K) \textbf{ do } C]\ [Q \wedge \mathbb{E}[e] \leq r \wedge \lceil e \geq 0 \rceil],$$

modbf$(\mathbf{E}, e)$ *and* t**-closed**(Q)*, then* $\vDash [P]\ \mathbf{E}[\textbf{while } (b) \textbf{ do } C]\ [Q]$.

Here $\mathbf{E}$ is a program context, and $\mathbf{E}[\mathbf{while}\ (b)\ \mathbf{do}\ C]$ fills the hole in $\mathbf{E}$ with the loop $\mathbf{while}\ (b)\ \mathbf{do}\ C$.

$$(Ctx)\ \ \mathbf{E}\ ::=\ [\,]\ \mid\ C;\mathbf{E}\ \mid\ \mathbf{E};C\ \mid\ \mathbf{while}\ (b)\ \mathbf{do}\ \mathbf{E}$$
$$\mid\ \mathbf{if}\ (b)\ \mathbf{then}\ C\ \mathbf{else}\ \mathbf{E}\ \mid\ \mathbf{if}\ (b)\ \mathbf{then}\ \mathbf{E}\ \mathbf{else}\ C$$

Thm. 2 says that, to prove total correctness of $\mathbf{E}[\mathbf{while}\ (b)\ \mathbf{do}\ C]$, we transform the code to $\mathbf{E}[\mathbf{while}\ (b \wedge e < K)\ \mathbf{do}\ C]$ with a specific e. How to choose e is application-dependent. Usually we choose as e the loop counter incremented in the loop body, such as cnt in $C_{\mathsf{MT}}(cnt)$ (see Sec. 2.2 and Fig. 12). With an inappropriate e, the first premise of the theorem may be invalid or still hard to prove, though how e is chosen does not affect the validity of the theorem.

In addition to e, the first premise also asks users to find a common bound r (a real number) that can bound $\mathbb{E}[e]$ at the end of $\mathbf{E}[\mathbf{while}\ (b \wedge e < K)\ \mathbf{do}\ C]$ for all K. Usually the postcondition Q can help us find such an r. Besides the upper bound r, we require that evaluating e at the end of $\mathbf{E}[\mathbf{while}\ (b \wedge e < K)\ \mathbf{do}\ C]$ must result in a *non-negative* real number. These two bounds are crucial for ensuring almost sure termination of $\mathbf{E}[\mathbf{while}\ (b)\ \mathbf{do}\ C]$.

The second premise, $\mathbf{modbf}(\mathbf{E}, e)$, rules out those contexts $\mathbf{E}$ that make $\mathbb{E}[e] \leq r$ hold at the end of $\mathbf{E}[\mathbf{while}\ (b \wedge e < K)\ \mathbf{do}\ C]$ vacuously, e.g. those that modify the program variables in e at the end of the context and make $e = r$ hold. $\mathbf{modbf}(\mathbf{E}, e)$ syntactically restricts $\mathbf{E}$ such that the variables in e can be modified in $\mathbf{E}$ only before the code in the hole of $\mathbf{E}$ is executed. For example, $\mathbf{modbf}(C'; [\,], e)$ holds for any C' and e, since only C', which is executed before the hole, can modify the variables in e in the context. Similarly, $\mathbf{modbf}([\,], e)$ holds. We give the definition of $\mathbf{modbf}(\mathbf{E}, e)$ in [46].

The third premise, $t\text{-}\mathbf{closed}(Q)$, is for deriving the postcondition Q of $\mathbf{E}[\mathbf{while}\ (b)\ \mathbf{do}\ C]$ from the same Q of $\mathbf{E}[\mathbf{while}\ (b \wedge e < K)\ \mathbf{do}\ C]$. We say an assertion Q is t-closed [3], denoted by $t\text{-}\mathbf{closed}(Q)$, if for all infinite state distribution sequences $\vec{\mu}$, if Q holds on $\vec{\mu}[i]$ for each i and $\lim \vec{\mu} = \mu$, then Q holds on μ. Many assertions are t-closed. For example, we can prove that $t\text{-}\mathbf{closed}(\mathbb{E}[e] \leq r \wedge \lceil e \geq 0 \rceil)$ always holds for any e and any r.

Since $\mathbf{modbf}([\,], e)$ and $t\text{-}\mathbf{closed}(\mathbb{E}[e] \leq r \wedge \lceil e \geq 0 \rceil)$ both hold, Lem. 1 can be derived from Thm. 2.

Proof Sketch of Thm. 2. Due to the space limit, below we only show the case of $\mathbf{E} = [\,]$. We prove 1) almost sure termination and 2) the establishment of the postcondition Q, respectively.

For 1), assuming that $\mathbf{while}\ (b)\ \mathbf{do}\ C$ terminates with probability $p < 1$, we derive a contradiction. From the premise we know $\mathbf{while}\ (b \wedge e < K)\ \mathbf{do}\ C$ almost surely terminates, so it terminates in a state where $e \geq K$ with probability at least $1 - p$. Thus, by the semantics of $\mathbb{E}[e]$ (and since the value of e is non-negative), we know $\mathbb{E}[e] \geq (1-p)K$ holds at the end of $\mathbf{while}\ (b \wedge e < K)\ \mathbf{do}\ C$. Therefore, we can find a sufficiently large K such that $\mathbb{E}[e] \geq (1-p)K > r$, which contradicts the premise.

For 2), the key is proving that, for all $\mu \models P$,

$$[\![\mathbf{while}\ (b)\ \mathbf{do}\ C]\!](\mu) = \lim_{K \to \infty} [\![\mathbf{while}\ (b \wedge e < K)\ \mathbf{do}\ C]\!](\mu).$$

Then, we can establish Q for **while** (b) **do** C, from t-**closed**(Q) and that Q is the postcondition for each **while** $(b \land e < K)$ **do** C.   □

We apply Thm. 2 for the verification of the MT algorithm and its variants in Sec. 6. Here we show another example beyond ALLLs, which is taken from [41] (with slight modifications).

Example 1. Let $N = 1$ and $\mathcal{D}[1] = \{(0, \frac{1}{2}), (1, \frac{1}{2})\}$. The code C_{flip} is defined as **while** $(y = 1)$ **do** $\{ y := \mathsf{Sample}(1); cnt := cnt + 1; \}$. We prove:

$$\vDash [\lceil cnt = 0 \land y = 1 \rceil] \, C_{\text{flip}} \, [\mathbb{E}[cnt] \leq 2]. \tag{11}$$

Here C_{flip} repeatedly flips a fair coin by sampling from $\mathcal{D}[1]$, until it gets heads $(y = 0)$. We use cnt to record the number of coin flips. Then our proof goal (11) says that C_{flip} almost surely terminates, and it flips at most twice in expectation.

To prove (11), by Thm. 2 (or Lem. 1), we only need to prove that, for all $K \in \mathbb{N}$, $\vDash [\lceil cnt = 0 \land y = 1 \rceil] \, C'_{\text{flip}}(K) \, [\mathbb{E}[cnt] \leq 2 \land \lceil cnt \geq 0 \rceil]$, where $C'_{\text{flip}}(K)$ is defined as **while** $(y = 1 \land cnt < K)$ **do** $\{y := \mathsf{Sample}(1); cnt := cnt + 1; \}$. We adapt the program logic ELLORA [3] to complete the proof.

5.2   Resampling-Table-Based Coupling

As informally explained in Sec. 2.4, our RT-based coupling is for proving the relational tuple $\vDash \{P\}C_1 \leq C_2\{\mathbf{q}_1, \mathbf{q}_2\}$, an intermediate proof goal that appears in ALLLs' verification. We show the formal definition of $\vDash \{P\}C_1 \leq C_2\{\mathbf{q}_1, \mathbf{q}_2\}$ in Def. 2. Note that in this definition we neither require nor assume the termination of C_1 and C_2's executions.

Definition 2 (Inequality between Probabilities). *For all* $P, C_1, C_2, \mathbf{q}_1, \mathbf{q}_2$, $\vDash \{P\}C_1 \leq C_2\{\mathbf{q}_1, \mathbf{q}_2\}$ *holds iff*

$$\forall \mu. \ \ \mu \vDash P \implies \mathrm{Pr}_{\sigma \sim [\![C_1]\!](\mu)}[\sigma \vDash \mathbf{q}_1] \leq \mathrm{Pr}_{\sigma \sim [\![C_2]\!](\mu)}[\sigma \vDash \mathbf{q}_2].$$

Our RT-based coupling reduces the verification of the relational tuple to proving unary properties of C_1 and C_2's executions in the RT-based semantics respectively (i.e. the subgoals (9) and (10) in Sec. 2.4). We show the formal theorem in Thm. 3.

Theorem 3 (RT-Based Coupling). *For all* $\mathbf{p}, C_1, C_2, \mathbf{q}_1, \mathbf{R}, \mathbf{q}_2$, *if*

- **RTonly**$(\mathbf{R})$;
- $\vDash_{\mathrm{RT}} \{\mathbf{p} \land \mathsf{hdinit}\}C_1\{\mathbf{q}_1 \Rightarrow \mathbf{R}\}$;
- $\vDash_{\mathrm{RT}} [\mathbf{p} \land \mathbf{R} \land \mathsf{hdinit}]C_2[\mathbf{q}_2]$;

then $\vDash \{\lceil \mathbf{p} \rceil\}C_1 \leq C_2\{\mathbf{q}_1, \mathbf{q}_2\}$.

We apply Thm. 3 for verifying ALLLs, which we will explain in Sec. 6. Below we explain Thm. 3 in four aspects: (1) requiring $\lceil \mathbf{p} \rceil$ as the precondition in the relational tuple; (2) the assertions $\mathbf{R}$, hdinit and the requirement **RTonly**$(\mathbf{R})$; (3) the RT-based unary triples $\vDash_{\mathrm{RT}}$; and (4) its proof ideas. We also show another example beyond ALLLs, and briefly discuss an extension of Thm. 3 at the end.

$(RTExpr)$ E $::= e \mid \mathsf{RT}[E_1][E_2] \mid \mathsf{hd}_1 \mid \ldots \mid \mathsf{hd}_N \mid E_1 + E_2 \mid \ldots$

$(RTBexp)$ B $::= b \mid E_1 = E_2 \mid E_1 < E_2 \mid \ldots$

$(RTAssn)$ $\mathbf{P}, \mathbf{Q}, \mathbf{R} ::= \mathbf{q} \mid B \mid \neg\mathbf{Q} \mid \mathbf{Q}_1 \wedge \mathbf{Q}_2 \mid \mathbf{Q}_1 \vee \mathbf{Q}_2 \mid \forall X. \mathbf{Q} \mid \exists X. \mathbf{Q} \mid \ldots$

$(\sigma, RT, \iota) \vDash \mathbf{q}$ iff $\sigma \vDash \mathbf{q}$ $[\![\mathsf{hd}_n]\!]_{(\sigma, RT, \iota)} \triangleq \iota[n]$

$[\![\mathsf{RT}[E_1][E_2]]\!]_{(\sigma, RT, \iota)} \triangleq RT[i][j],$ if $[\![E_1]\!]_{(\sigma, RT, \iota)} = i, [\![E_2]\!]_{(\sigma, RT, \iota)} = j$

$\mathsf{hdinit} \triangleq \bigwedge_{i \in [1,N]} \cdot \mathsf{hd}_i = 0$

$\mathbf{RTonly}(\mathbf{R})$ iff $\forall \sigma, RT, \iota. \ (\sigma, RT, \iota) \vDash \mathbf{R} \implies \forall \sigma', \iota'. \ (\sigma', RT, \iota') \vDash \mathbf{R}$

Fig. 10. Non-probabilistic assertions on RT-extended states

Lifting state assertions as preconditions. The relational tuples we prove are in a restricted form, namely that the precondition P is in the form of $\lceil \mathbf{p} \rceil$, where $\mathbf{p}$ is an assertion over states. Recall that $\lceil \mathbf{p} \rceil$ holds over μ iff $\mathbf{p}$ holds over any σ such that $\sigma \in supp(\mu)$ (see Fig. 9). Therefore the precondition $\lceil \mathbf{p} \rceil$ says we are only interested in the executions of C_1 and C_2 with the initial states satisfying $\mathbf{p}$. So we can fill the omitted part of the two subgoals (9) and (10) with $\mathbf{p}$, and turn them into classical (*deterministic*) Hoare triples $\vDash_{\mathsf{RT}} \{\mathbf{p}\} C_1 \{\mathbf{q}_1 \Rightarrow \mathbf{R}\}$ and $\vDash_{\mathsf{RT}} [\mathbf{p} \wedge \mathbf{R}] C_2 [\mathbf{q}_2]$.

Assertions over RT-extended states. Thm. 3 requires us to find an "intermediate assertion" $\mathbf{R}$ that describes (and *only* describes) the (non-probabilistic) properties of the resampling table RT. Since we need explicit reasoning about RT, the assertions used in the classical reasoning of $\vDash_{\mathsf{RT}}$ actually specify RT and the heads ι as well as the states σ.

In Fig. 10, we define non-probabilistic assertions $\mathbf{P}, \mathbf{Q}, \mathbf{R}$ over the extended states (σ, RT, ι). Besides using $\mathbf{q}$ to describe σ in the extended states, we introduce RT-expressions to specify RT and ι. We use $\mathsf{RT}[E_1][E_2]$ to represent the entry at row E_1 and column E_2 of RT, and use hd_n to represent the n-th head $\iota[n]$, where $n \in [1, N]$.

The assertion hdinit (defined as a shorthand in Fig. 10) says that all of the heads ι point to the first column of RT. It specifies the initial heads before program execution, so it appears in the preconditions of the two $\vDash_{\mathsf{RT}}$ triples in Thm. 3.

The requirement $\mathbf{RTonly}(\mathbf{R})$ (defined in Fig. 10) says that changing σ and/or ι in the extended state does not affect whether $\mathbf{R}$ holds. That is, $\mathbf{R}$ describes RT only. One can check that $\mathbf{RTonly}(\mathbf{R})$ holds if $\mathbf{R}$ does not syntactically contain any free variables and hd_n's.

RT-based unary triples. Now we can define the RT-based unary triples, $\vDash_{\mathsf{RT}} [\mathbf{P}]C[\mathbf{Q}]$ and $\vDash_{\mathsf{RT}} \{\mathbf{P}\}C\{\mathbf{Q}\}$. They are standard Hoare triples for total correctness and partial correctness respectively, using the RT-based operational semantics (in Fig. 8 of Sec. 4.2) for program execution.

Definition 3 (Total Correctness in RT-Based Operational Semantics).
For all $\mathbf{P}, C, \mathbf{Q}, \vDash_{\mathsf{RT}} [\mathbf{P}]C[\mathbf{Q}]$ *holds iff*

```
1    L := []; d := 1;
2    bad := 0;
3    while (d ≤ k) do
4        if (¬findkey(L, x[d])) then
5            y := Sample(1);
6            if (findval(L, y)) then bad := 1;
7            L := app(L, (x[d], y));
8        d := d + 1
```

Fig. 11. The code $C_{\mathrm{PRF}}^{\mathrm{bad}}$ in Ex. 2

$$\forall \sigma, RT, \iota. \quad (\sigma, RT, \iota) \vDash \mathbf{P} \implies$$
$$\exists \sigma', \iota'. \ RT \vdash (C, \sigma, \iota) \to^* (\mathbf{skip}, \sigma', \iota') \wedge (\sigma', RT, \iota') \vDash \mathbf{Q}.$$

Definition 4 (Partial Correctness in RT-Based Operational Semantics). *For all* $\mathbf{P}, C, \mathbf{Q},$ $\vDash_{\mathrm{RT}} \{\mathbf{P}\}C\{\mathbf{Q}\}$ *holds iff*

$$\forall \sigma, RT, \iota, \sigma', \iota'. \quad (\sigma, RT, \iota) \vDash \mathbf{P} \wedge RT \vdash (C, \sigma, \iota) \to^* (\mathbf{skip}, \sigma', \iota')$$
$$\implies (\sigma', RT, \iota') \vDash \mathbf{Q}.$$

For total correctness, Def. 3 says there exists a terminating execution of (C, σ, ι) under RT. This essentially ensures the absence of non-terminating executions, because the RT-based operational semantics is *deterministic*.

We can use a classical Hoare-style program logic to prove the $\vDash_{\mathrm{RT}}$ triples. We show the logic in [46].

Proof ideas of the theorem. To prove Thm. 3, we need to bridge two gaps between the $\vDash_{\mathrm{RT}}$ triples in the premises and the $\vDash$ tuple in the conclusion. First, the $\vDash_{\mathrm{RT}}$ triples use the RT-based semantics, while the $\vDash$ tuple uses the distribution-based semantics. Second, the $\vDash_{\mathrm{RT}}$ triples are unary, while the $\vDash$ tuple is relational.

The key to bridging the gaps is reduction through the following RT-based tuple as an intermediate form, which is the counterpart of Def. 2 in the RT-based semantics.

Definition 5 (Inequality between Pr. in RT-Based Semantics). *For all* $P, C_1, C_2, \mathbf{q}_1, \mathbf{q}_2,$ $\vDash_{\mathrm{RT}} \{P\}C_1 \leq C_2\{\mathbf{q}_1, \mathbf{q}_2\}$ *holds iff*

$$\forall \mu. \ \mu \vDash P \implies \mathrm{Pr}_{\sigma \sim [\![C_1]\!]_{\mathrm{RT}}(\mu)}[\sigma \vDash \mathbf{q}_1] \leq \mathrm{Pr}_{\sigma \sim [\![C_2]\!]_{\mathrm{RT}}(\mu)}[\sigma \vDash \mathbf{q}_2].$$

Lemma 3 shows the equivalence between the two relational tuples, which follows from the semantics equivalence (Thm. 1). This lemma bridges the first gap, and is interesting in its own right.

Lemma 3. *For all* $P, C_1, C_2, \mathbf{q}_1, \mathbf{q}_2,$

$$\vDash \{P\}C_1 \leq C_2\{\mathbf{q}_1, \mathbf{q}_2\} \iff \vDash_{\mathrm{RT}} \{P\}C_1 \leq C_2\{\mathbf{q}_1, \mathbf{q}_2\}.$$

Our "intermediate assertion" $\mathbf{R}$ allows us to split the $\vDash_{\mathrm{RT}}$ relational tuple into two unary $\vDash_{\mathrm{RT}}$ triples, bridging the second gap.

Example 2. This example is adapted from an intermediate goal in [6]'s proof of the PRP/PRF switching lemma.[3] Let $k \geq 1$. For any $n_1, \ldots, n_k$, we prove that

$$\vDash \{\lceil \mathsf{inp} \rceil\} C_{\mathrm{PRF}}^{\mathsf{bad}} \leq C_{\mathrm{PRF}} \\ \{bad = 1, \quad \exists X_1, X_2, Y. \ X_1 \neq X_2 \wedge \mathsf{find}(L, (X_1, Y)) \wedge \mathsf{find}(L, (X_2, Y))\}. \quad (12)$$

We show the code of $C_{\mathrm{PRF}}^{\mathsf{bad}}$ in Fig. 11, and the code of C_{PRF} results from removing lines 2 and 6 from the figure. The assertion inp says that $n_1, \ldots, n_k$ are the inputs stored in $x[1], \ldots, x[k]$, which is defined as $\bigwedge_{i \in [1,k]} \cdot x[i] = n_i$.

By extending the programming language, we implement a map in the program variable L, which stores some key-value pairs. One can insert a pair into the map by writing $\mathsf{app}(L, (e_1, e_2))$, and query for the existence of a key, a value or a pair by writing $\mathsf{findkey}(L, e)$, $\mathsf{findval}(L, e)$ or $\mathsf{find}(L, (e_1, e_2))$.

$C_{\mathrm{PRF}}^{\mathsf{bad}}$ and C_{PRF} do the following: for $n = x[1], \ldots, x[k]$, the programs check if n has been inserted in L as a key; if not, they sample a value y from $\mathcal{D}[1]$, and then insert the key-value pair (n, y) into L; if y has been inserted in L as a value, $C_{\mathrm{PRF}}^{\mathsf{bad}}$ marks bad.

(12) then says that, the probability of $C_{\mathrm{PRF}}^{\mathsf{bad}}$ terminating with $bad = 1$ is no more than the probability of C_{PRF} terminating with two key-value pairs with the same value left in L.

To prove (12), we apply Thm. 3. We take $\mathbf{R} = \mathsf{coll}$, where

$$\mathsf{coll} \triangleq \bigvee_{0 \leq i < j < |\{n_1, \ldots, n_k\}|} \cdot \mathsf{RT}[1][i] = \mathsf{RT}[1][j].$$

coll says that, there exist two identical entries in the first row of RT, which are picked as samples in the executions of both $C_{\mathrm{PRF}}^{\mathsf{bad}}$ and C_{PRF}. Therefore coll specifies the kind of RT that can make $bad = 1$ hold after the execution of $C_{\mathrm{PRF}}^{\mathsf{bad}}$.

We can check that $\mathbf{RTonly}(\mathsf{coll})$ holds. Then, by applying Thm. 3, it remains to prove the following two unary $\vDash_{\mathrm{RT}}$ triples.

$\vDash_{\mathrm{RT}} \{\mathsf{inp} \wedge \mathsf{hdinit}\} C_{\mathrm{PRF}}^{\mathsf{bad}} \{bad = 1 \Rightarrow \mathbf{R}\}$

$\vDash_{\mathrm{RT}} [\mathsf{inp} \wedge \mathbf{R} \wedge \mathsf{hdinit}] C_{\mathrm{PRF}} [\exists X_1, X_2, Y. \ X_1 \neq X_2 \wedge \mathsf{find}(L, (X_1, Y)) \wedge \mathsf{find}(L, (X_2, Y))]$

We prove them using a simple Hoare-style program logic.

An extension of RT-based coupling. In [46], we give another relational proof recipe that extends Thm. 3. It asks users to provide two intermediate assertions $\mathbf{R}_1$ and $\mathbf{R}_2$ for splitting the $\vDash_{\mathrm{RT}}$ relational tuple, and provides more flexibility for reasoning about inequalities between probabilities.

6 Case Studies

We show the usefulness of our proof recipes (Thm. 2 and Thm. 3) by verifying several representative existing results about ALLLs and a new result about the MT algorithm. Below we first give a brief survey of several important research lines on ALLLs. Then we summarize the existing ALLL-related results that we have verified, and show how we verify Theorem 1.2 of [50] as an example. Finally, we explain our new result about the MT algorithm.

---

[3] In [6], $C_{\mathrm{PRF}}^{\mathsf{bad}}$ and C_{PRF} are defined using procedure calls. We adapt the code here.

```
1     d := 1; while (d≤N) do {a:=Sample(d); x[d]:=a; d:=d+1;}
2     flag := 0; cnt := 0; lst := [];
3     while (flag = 0) do
4         z := 0; h := 1;
5         while (h ≤ M) do
6             if (hold(h, x[1],...,x[N])) then z := h;
7             h := h + 1;
8         if (z = 0) then flag := 1;
9         else
10            cnt := cnt + 1; lst := app(lst, z); d := 1;
11            while (d ≤ N) do
12                if (vbl(z, d)) then {a := Sample(d); x[d] := a;}
13                d := d + 1;
```

Fig. 12. The code of the MT algorithm, $C_{MT}(cnt)$

Research lines of ALLLs. The MT algorithm is first proposed in [50], where the expected iteration number of the algorithm is bounded under the Erdős-Lovász condition [19, 57] and the Erdős-Spencer condition [20]. Following [50], some works [53, 42, 31, 1, 43, 37] further analyze the termination property and the iteration times of the MT algorithm under other conditions. Besides analyzing the iteration times of the MT algorithm, a number of works (including [50]) also analyze other sequential ALLLs [31, 34, 36, 29], explore properties of output distributions of ALLLs [31, 35, 29, 32], or design parallel and distributed ALLLs [50, 16, 30, 25, 13]. However, the proofs in all these works are relatively informal.

Existing results we verify. As listed below, we verify *six* representative results that cover the aforementioned research lines.

First, we verify the termination and the expected iteration times of the MT algorithm, under the Erdős-Lovász condition [19, 57], the cluster expansion condition [8], the Shearer's condition [56], and the Erdős-Spencer condition [20]. These four results are proposed and informally proved in **Theorem 1.2** of [50], **Theorem 1.4** of [53], **Theorem 4** of [42] and **Theorem 6.1** of [50].

Second, we verify (the second part of) **Theorem 2.2** of [31] that estimates the output distribution of the MT algorithm under the Erdős-Lovász condition. This result can also be viewed as estimating the output distribution of a sequential ALLL that only executes on core events (see **Theorem 3.3** of [31]).

Finally, we verify the termination and a tail bound of the iteration times of a parallelizable version of the MT algorithm, under the Erdős-Lovász condition with ϵ-slack. This variant and the tail bound are given in **Theorem 1.3** of [50].

It is worth noting that we verify all the three "probabilistic" results from Moser and Tardos's Gödel Prize-winning paper [50].[4]

Verifying Theorem 1.2 of [50]. As an example, we explain in more detail how we verify Theorem 1.2 of [50], which we informally described in Sec. 2.

---

[4] In [50], Moser and Tardos propose four results, three related to the MT algorithm and its probabilistic variants, and one related to a deterministic variant.

Fig. 12 shows $C_{\mathsf{MT}}(cnt)$, the code of the MT algorithm that we verify. It first does independent samplings and stores the results in $x[1], \ldots, x[N]$ (line 1), where d and a are temporal variables. For the main loop (lines 3-13), we introduce *flag* to indicate whether a required assignment is found, *cnt* to record the number of iteration times, and *lst* to collect the indexes of the events in the execution log. They are initialized at line 2. In the main loop (lines 3-13), we use z to represent the index of the chosen event, which is an event that holds under the current $x[1], \ldots, x[N]$ (lines 4-7). If no such event exists, the code marks *flag* (line 8) and exits the loop (line 3). Otherwise, it resamples from $\mathcal{D}[d]$ for every d such that $\mathsf{vbl}(z, d)$ holds, and updates the corresponding $x[d]$ (lines 10-13).

Having defined the code of the MT algorithm, Moser and Tardos's result (Theorem 1.2 of [50]) is formally stated in Thm. 4. Note that $N, M, \mathcal{D}$ and $\mathcal{E}$ are global parameters and thus not fixed in Thm. 4, and r_{EL} is parametrized by M.

Theorem 4. *For all reals* $\alpha_1, \ldots, \alpha_M \in (0, 1)$, *if the Erdős-Lovász condition [19, 57] holds, i.e.* $\forall i \in [1, M]$. $\mathrm{P}(\mathcal{E}[i]) \le \alpha_i \prod_{j \in \Gamma(i)} (1 - \alpha_j)$, *and let* $r_{\mathsf{EL}} = \sum_{i \in [1, M]} \alpha_i (1 - \alpha_i)^{-1}$, *then* $\models [\mathbf{true}] \, C_{\mathsf{MT}}(cnt) \, [\mathbb{E}[cnt] \le r_{\mathsf{EL}}]$.

Proof Sketch. Our proof follows the path in Fig. 5. Due to the space limit, here we only explain our construction of **R**, used in the two RT-triples at the bottom of Fig. 5. Let $\Lambda = g_{\mathsf{WT}}(wt)$. Then,

$$\mathbf{R} \triangleq \forall l \in [1, |\Lambda|]. \, \forall V_1, \ldots V_N. \, \mathsf{RTAssign}(V_1, \ldots V_N, l, \Lambda) \Rightarrow \mathsf{hold}(\Lambda\langle l \rangle, V_1, \ldots, V_N),$$

where $\mathsf{RTAssign}(V_1, \ldots, V_N, l, \Lambda) \triangleq \forall i \in [1, N]. \, \mathsf{vbl}(\Lambda\langle l \rangle, i) \Rightarrow V_i = \mathsf{RT}[i][\mathsf{ve}(i, \Lambda, l - 1)]$,

$\mathsf{ve}(i, \Lambda, l) \triangleq \sum_{l' \in [1, l]} [\mathsf{vbl}(\Lambda\langle l' \rangle, i)]$.

Informally **R** says that, every event in wt (denoted by $\Lambda\langle l \rangle$) must hold under any assignment of $V_1, \ldots, V_N$ satisfying $\mathsf{RTAssign}$. $\mathsf{RTAssign}$ says, the assignment contains the "relevant" entries of RT which make the event $\Lambda\langle l \rangle$ hold when it is chosen in the execution of $C'_{\mathsf{MT}}(cnt, K)$. For each such entry, its row number i corresponds to a variable that the event depends on (i.e. $\mathsf{vbl}(\Lambda\langle l \rangle, i)$ holds), and its column number is computed by $\mathsf{ve}(i, g_{\mathsf{WT}}(wt), l - 1)$. Note our **R** only talks about the RT (and the wt), not about the actual execution of $C'_{\mathsf{MT}}(cnt, K)$.

We prove the remaining intermediate proof goals in Fig. 5 by adapting the program logic Ellora [3] (for proving $\models$ triples) and using a classical Hoare-style logic (for proving $\models_{\mathsf{RT}}$ triples). □

Our new result. Thm. 4 shows the MT algorithm's total correctness with r_{EL} as the upper bound of expected iteration times, under the Erdős-Lovász condition. There are many works [53, 42, 1, 43, 37] that informally study similar properties of the MT algorithm under other conditions. Most of these results use similar ideas with Moser and Tardos to analyze the algorithm, except that they introduce other witness-tree-like structures for analysis and derive various bounds. Like [50], they generate their witness-tree-like structures ds from prefixes of the execution log, enumerate the events in ds in some specific order, and bound a sum over all such structures to get their final upper bounds.

We unify these results to a general one. Our new result enables that, when proving the expected iteration number of the MT algorithm, without doing the complete proof following Moser and Tardos's idea, one only needs to instantiate the required witness-tree-like structures and prove some relevant mathematical side conditions. We show that Theorem 1.2 of [50], Theorem 1.4 of [53] and Theorem 4 of [42] are corollaries of our new result. We give details of our new result and proofs in [46].

7   Related Work

(Positive) almost sure termination. Existing proof methods for almost sure termination (AST) can be roughly classified into the following two categories: "direct" methods [48, 11, 12, 24, 49, 38, 47], which prove termination by constructing probabilistic ranking functions, and "indirect" methods [41, 52, 51, 40], which infer finite bounds on the expected runtime and then imply the termination.

However, these methods may not apply to ALLLs' termination. To construct the structures (e.g. ranking supermatingales [12, 24] and upper ω-invariants [41]) required by these methods, we need to understand what occurs during *each iteration* of the algorithm's outer loop, which is, however, not yet well understood. For example, [50] only analyzes the properties of the *entire* MT algorithm (e.g. (2)), not of each individual iteration.

In Sec. 2.3, we emphasize Lem. 1 as a general proof method for positive almost sure termination (PAST) [11]. Lem. 1 also serves as a *fallback plan* for proving (P-)AST. Informally, a part of existing methods [12, 24, 49, 41] provide stronger premises than Lem. 1's. These premises are easier to prove in most scenarios, except for ALLLs. For most programs, one can still apply these existing methods; for programs like ALLLs, one should take a step back and apply Lem. 1.

Asynchronous coupling. In Sec. 2.4, we apply the RT-based coupling proof recipe to (8), which involves $C'_{\mathsf{MT}}(cnt, K)$ and check(wt). Existing probabilistic relational program logics [4, 5, 6] support couplings, but none of them can prove (8). Specifically, these works only provide proof rules for *synchronous* couplings. Their rules say that, when the two programs sample from the same distribution synchronously, we can reason as if the two sampling statements return the same value. But, it may *not* be possible to synchronize the sampling statements in $C'_{\mathsf{MT}}(cnt, K)$ and check(wt) for the following reason. Given an execution log's prefix Λ and the corresponding witness tree $wt = f_{\mathsf{WT}}(\Lambda)$, $C'_{\mathsf{MT}}(cnt, K)$ resamples the variables that η_j depends on for every event η_j in Λ, and check(wt) does similar resamplings but its events are taken from the sequence $g_{\mathsf{WT}}(wt)$. However, $g_{\mathsf{WT}}(wt)$ can be different from Λ, since the construction of wt (i.e. $f_{\mathsf{WT}}(\Lambda)$) may drop some events in Λ and lose some ordering information of Λ, which $g_{\mathsf{WT}}(wt)$ cannot recover.

Recently [28] proposes a probabilistic relational program logic that supports *asynchronous* coupling. They introduce *presampling tapes*, a new kind of ghost state, which store the sampling results ahead of time. Our work is developed independently, with a more focused goal of verifying ALLLs. Technically, our RTs look similar to their tapes, but there are two key differences as follows.

First, we give an RT-based operational semantics, where all the samples (which could be infinitely many) are generated at once and stored in the *RT* *before programs start execution*, and the *RT* is immutable during the program execution. By contrast, sample values are added into their tapes *one at a time* and *on demand* by ghost operations in the logical reasoning, and are popped out at sampling statements. We think their approach is more flexible, but ours is more suitable for complicated examples like ALLLs. In particular, as we explain at the end of Sec. 2.4, we can use an intermediate assertion **R** to specify *the whole sampling history*. **R** can be derived as the post-condition of the unary reasoning of one program, and then used as the pre-condition of the other, thanks to the immutability of *RT*. With dynamically changing tapes, they would need ghost variables to track the popped samples, and write complicated assertions to describe the correspondence between the tapes used by the two programs. We give a more detailed comparison in [46].

Second, the two works have different focuses. We mainly focus on verifying ALLLs, so we verify almost sure termination as well as a restricted form of relational properties (like (8)). Their work verifies contextual refinement, but does not verify termination.

Other related works. [22] proposes the *guard strengthening* proof rule for verifying lower bounds of expected values at the end of while loops. This rule introduces a loop with strengthened loop guard, which is similar to the truncated one in the premise of our loop truncation (Lem. 1 and Thm. 2). However, these two methods have different focuses. Their rule focuses on proving *lower bounds*, while our loop truncation focuses on proving general total correctness and PAST. The PAST is about an *upper bound* of the expected runtime.

We have discussed other related works in Sec. 2.2 and Sec. 2.4, including: the semantics that are equivalent to the distribution-based semantics [45, 48, 44], and the semantics with explicit random sources [44, 10, 17]. In the future, we would like to test our proof recipes with more applications, such as the other ALLL-related results mentioned in Sec. 6. We also plan to mechanize our work in a proof assistant like Coq, as [18] has mechanized the classical (i.e. non-constructive) proof of the Lovász Local Lemma in Isabelle/HOL. Mechanizing our work requires a measure-theoretic library that supports infinite product of measure spaces, which, to the best of our knowledge, is still lacking for Coq.

Acknowledgments. We thank anonymous referees for their suggestions and comments on earlier versions of this paper. This work is supported in part by National Natural Science Foundation of China (NSFC) under Grant No. 62232015.

Disclosure of Interests. The authors have no competing interests to declare that are relevant to the content of this article.

References

1. Achlioptas, D., Gouleakis, T.: Algorithmic improvements of the Lovász local lemma via cluster expansion. In: FSTTCS 2012. pp. 16–23 (2012). https://doi.org/10.4230/LIPIcs.FSTTCS.2012.16
2. Anderson, E., Phillips, C., Sicker, D., Grunwald, D.: Optimization decomposition for scheduling and system configuration in wireless networks. IEEE/ACM Trans. Netw. **22**(1), 271–284 (2014). https://doi.org/10.1109/TNET.2013.2289980
3. Barthe, G., Espitau, T., Gaboardi, M., Grégoire, B., Hsu, J., Strub, P.Y.: An assertion-based program logic for probabilistic programs. In: ESOP 2018. pp. 117–144 (2018). https://doi.org/10.1007/978-3-319-89884-1_5
4. Barthe, G., Espitau, T., Grégoire, B., Hsu, J., Stefanesco, L., Strub, P.Y.: Relational reasoning via probabilistic coupling. In: LPAR 2015. p. 387–401 (2015). https://doi.org/10.1007/978-3-662-48899-7_27
5. Barthe, G., Gaboardi, M., Grégoire, B., Hsu, J., Strub, P.Y.: Proving differential privacy via probabilistic couplings. In: LICS 2016. p. 749–758 (2016). https://doi.org/10.1145/2933575.2934554
6. Barthe, G., Grégoire, B., Zanella Béguelin, S.: Formal certification of code-based cryptographic proofs. In: POPL 2009. p. 90–101 (2009). https://doi.org/10.1145/1480881.1480894
7. Batz, K., Kaminski, B.L., Katoen, J.P., Matheja, C.: Relatively complete verification of probabilistic programs: an expressive language for expectation-based reasoning. Proc. ACM Program. Lang. **5**(POPL), 1–30 (2021). https://doi.org/10.1145/3434320
8. Bissacot, R., Fernández, R., Procacci, A., Scoppola, B.: An improvement of the Lovász local lemma via cluster expansion. Comb. Probab. Comput. **20**(5), 709–719 (2011). https://doi.org/10.1017/S0963548311000253
9. Boissonnat, J., Dyer, R., Ghosh, A.: A probabilistic approach to reducing algebraic complexity of delaunay triangulations. In: ESA 2015. pp. 595–606 (2015). https://doi.org/10.1007/978-3-662-48350-3_50
10. Borgström, J., Dal Lago, U., Gordon, A.D., Szymczak, M.: A lambda-calculus foundation for universal probabilistic programming. In: ICFP 2016. pp. 33–46 (2016). https://doi.org/10.1145/2951913.2951942
11. Bournez, O., Garnier, F.: Proving positive almost-sure termination. In: RTA 2005. pp. 323–337 (2005). https://doi.org/10.1007/978-3-540-32033-3_24
12. Chakarov, A., Sankaranarayanan, S.: Probabilistic program analysis with martingales. In: CAV 2013. pp. 511–526 (2013). https://doi.org/10.1007/978-3-642-39799-8_34
13. Chang, Y.J., He, Q., Li, W., Pettie, S., Uitto, J.: Distributed edge coloring and a special case of the constructive Lovász local lemma. ACM Trans. Algorithms **16**(1), 8:1–8:51 (2020). https://doi.org/10.1145/3365004
14. Chen, A., Harris, D.G., Srinivasan, A.: Partial resampling to approximate covering integer programs. Random Struct. Algorithms **58**(1), 68–93 (2021). https://doi.org/10.1002/rsa.20964
15. Cheng, K., Haeupler, B., Li, X., Shahrasbi, A., Wu, K.: Synchronization strings: Highly efficient deterministic constructions over small alphabets. In: SODA 2019. pp. 2185–2204 (2019). https://doi.org/10.1137/1.9781611975482.132
16. Chung, K.M., Pettie, S., Su, H.H.: Distributed algorithms for the Lovász local lemma and graph coloring. In: PODC 2014. p. 134–143 (2014). https://doi.org/10.1145/2611462.2611465

17. Culpepper, R., Cobb, A.: Contextual equivalence for probabilistic programs with continuous random variables and scoring. In: ESOP 2017. pp. 368–392 (2017). https://doi.org/10.1007/978-3-662-54434-1_14
18. Edmonds, C., Paulson, L.C.: Formal probabilistic methods for combinatorial structures using the Lovász local lemma. In: CPP 2024. pp. 132–146 (2024). https://doi.org/10.1145/3636501.3636946
19. Erdős, P., Lovász, L.: Problems and results on 3-chromatic hypergraphs and some related questions. Infinite and finite sets 10(2), 609–627 (1975)
20. Erdős, P., Spencer, J.: Lopsided Lovász local lemma and latin transversals. Discrete Applied Mathematics 30(151-154), 10–1016 (1991). https://doi.org/10.1016/0166-218X(91)90040-4
21. Fan, W., Liang, H., Feng, X., Jiang, H.: A program logic for concurrent randomized programs in the oblivious adversary model. To appear in ESOP 2025.
22. Feng, S., Chen, M., Su, H., Kaminski, B.L., Katoen, J., Zhan, N.: Lower bounds for possibly divergent probabilistic programs. Proc. ACM Program. Lang. 7(OOPSLA1), 696–726 (2023). https://doi.org/10.1145/3586051
23. Fernández, M., Livieratos, J., Martín, S.: Bounds and constructions of parent identifying schemes via the algorithmic version of the Lovász local lemma. IEEE Trans. Inf. Theory 69(11), 7049–7069 (2023). https://doi.org/10.1109/TIT.2023.3282452
24. Ferrer Fioriti, L.M., Hermanns, H.: Probabilistic termination: Soundness, completeness, and compositionality. In: POPL 2015. p. 489–501 (2015). https://doi.org/10.1145/2676726.2677001
25. Fischer, M., Ghaffari, M.: Sublogarithmic distributed algorithms for Lovász local lemma, and the complexity hierarchy. In: DISC 2017. pp. 18:1–18:16 (2017). https://doi.org/10.4230/LIPIcs.DISC.2017.18
26. Gebauer, H., Szabó, T., Tardos, G.: The local lemma is asymptotically tight for SAT. J. ACM 63(5), 43:1–43:32 (2016). https://doi.org/10.1145/2975386
27. Graf, A., Harris, D.G., Haxell, P.: Algorithms for weighted independent transversals and strong colouring. ACM Trans. Algorithms 18(1), 1:1–1:16 (2022). https://doi.org/10.1145/3474057
28. Gregersen, S.O., Aguirre, A., Haselwarter, P.G., Tassarotti, J., Birkedal, L.: Asynchronous probabilistic couplings in higher-order separation logic. Proc. ACM Program. Lang. 8(POPL), 753–784 (2024). https://doi.org/10.1145/3632868
29. Guo, H., Jerrum, M., Liu, J.: Uniform sampling through the Lovász local lemma. J. ACM 66(3), 18:1–18:31 (2019). https://doi.org/10.1145/3310131
30. Haeupler, B., Harris, D.G.: Parallel algorithms and concentration bounds for the Lovász local lemma via witness dags. ACM Trans. Algorithms 13(4), 53:1–53:25 (2017). https://doi.org/10.1145/3147211
31. Haeupler, B., Saha, B., Srinivasan, A.: New constructive aspects of the Lovász local lemma. J. ACM 58(6), 28:1–28:28 (2011). https://doi.org/10.1145/2049697.2049702
32. Harris, D.G.: New bounds for the Moser-Tardos distribution. Random Struct. Algorithms 57(1), 97–131 (2020). https://doi.org/10.1002/rsa.20914
33. Harris, D.G., Srinivasan, A.: Constraint satisfaction, packet routing, and the Lovász local lemma. In: STOC 13. p. 685–694 (2013). https://doi.org/10.1145/2488608.2488696
34. Harris, D.G., Srinivasan, A.: A constructive algorithm for the Lovász local lemma on permutations. In: SODA 2014. pp. 907–925 (2014). https://doi.org/10.1137/1.9781611973402.68

35. Harris, D.G., Srinivasan, A.: Algorithmic and enumerative aspects of the Moser-Tardos distribution. ACM Trans. Algorithms **13**(3), 33:1–33:40 (2017). https://doi.org/10.1145/3039869

36. Harris, D.G., Srinivasan, A.: The Moser-Tardos framework with partial resampling. J. ACM **66**(5), 36:1–36:45 (2019). https://doi.org/10.1145/3342222

37. He, K., Li, Q., Sun, X.: Moser-Tardos algorithm: Beyond Shearer's bound. In: SODA 2023. pp. 3362–3387 (2023). https://doi.org/10.1137/1.9781611977554.CH129

38. Huang, M., Fu, H., Chatterjee, K., Goharshady, A.K.: Modular verification for almost-sure termination of probabilistic programs. Proc. ACM Program. Lang. **3**(OOPSLA), 129:1–129:29 (2019). https://doi.org/10.1145/3360555

39. Jiang, N., Gu, Y., Xue, Y.: Learning Markov random fields for combinatorial structures via sampling through Lovász local lemma. In: AAAI 2023. pp. 4016–4024 (2023). https://doi.org/10.1609/AAAI.V37I4.25516

40. Kaminski, B.L.: Advanced weakest precondition calculi for probabilistic programs. Ph.D. thesis, RWTH Aachen University, Germany (2019). https://doi.org/10.18154/RWTH-2019-01829

41. Kaminski, B.L., Katoen, J., Matheja, C., Olmedo, F.: Weakest precondition reasoning for expected run-times of probabilistic programs. In: ESOP 2016. pp. 364–389 (2016). https://doi.org/10.1007/978-3-662-49498-1_15

42. Kolipaka, K.B.R., Szegedy, M.: Moser and Tardos meet Lovász. In: STOC 2011. p. 235–244 (2011). https://doi.org/10.1145/1993636.1993669

43. Kolipaka, K.B.R., Szegedy, M., Xu, Y.: A sharper local lemma with improved applications. In: APPROX-RANDOM 2012. pp. 603–614 (2012). https://doi.org/10.1007/978-3-642-32512-0_51

44. Kozen, D.: Semantics of probabilistic programs. J. Comput. Syst. Sci. **22**(3), 328–350 (1981). https://doi.org/10.1016/0022-0000(81)90036-2

45. Kozen, D.: A probabilistic PDL. J. Comput. Syst. Sci. **30**(2), 162–178 (1985). https://doi.org/10.1016/0022-0000(85)90012-1

46. Lin, R., Liang, H., Feng, X.: Verifying algorithmic versions of the Lovász local lemma – technical report. https://plax-lab.github.io/publications/alll/alll-tr.pdf (2024)

47. Majumdar, R., Sathiyanarayana, V.R.: Positive almost-sure termination: Complexity and proof rules. Proc. ACM Program. Lang. **8**(POPL), 1089–1117 (2024). https://doi.org/10.1145/3632879

48. McIver, A., Morgan, C.: Abstraction, Refinement and Proof for Probabilistic Systems. Springer (2005). https://doi.org/10.1007/B138392

49. McIver, A., Morgan, C., Kaminski, B.L., Katoen, J.: A new proof rule for almost-sure termination. Proc. ACM Program. Lang. **2**(POPL), 33:1–33:28 (2018). https://doi.org/10.1145/3158121

50. Moser, R.A., Tardos, G.: A constructive proof of the general Lovász local lemma. J. ACM **57**(2), 11:1–11:15 (2010). https://doi.org/10.1145/1667053.1667060

51. Ngo, V.C., Carbonneaux, Q., Hoffmann, J.: Bounded expectations: Resource analysis for probabilistic programs. In: PLDI 2018. p. 496–512 (2018). https://doi.org/10.1145/3192366.3192394

52. Olmedo, F., Kaminski, B.L., Katoen, J.P., Matheja, C.: Reasoning about recursive probabilistic programs. In: LICS 2016. p. 672–681 (2016). https://doi.org/10.1145/2933575.2935317

53. Pegden, W.: An extension of the Moser-Tardos algorithmic local lemma. SIAM J. Discret. Math. **28**(2), 911–917 (2014). https://doi.org/10.1137/110828290

54. Saeki, S.: A proof of the existence of infinite product probability measures. The American Mathematical Monthly **103**(8), 682–683 (1996). https://doi.org/10.1080/00029890.1996.12004804
55. Sarkar, K., Colbourn, C.J., Bonis, A.D., Vaccaro, U.: Partial covering arrays: Algorithms and asymptotics. Theory Comput. Syst. **62**(6), 1470–1489 (2018). https://doi.org/10.1007/S00224-017-9782-9
56. Shearer, J.B.: On a problem of Spencer. Combinatorica **5**, 241–245 (1985). https://doi.org/10.1007/BF02579368
57. Spencer, J.: Asymptotic lower bounds for Ramsey functions. Discrete Mathematics **20**, 69–76 (1977). https://doi.org/10.1016/0012-365X(77)90044-9
58. Srinivasan, A.: Progress on algorithmic versions of the Lovász local lemma. https://www.ias.edu/sites/default/files/video/Aravind.pdf (2013)

Elucidating Type Conversions in SQL Engines

Wenjia Ye[1,2(✉)], Matías Toro[3], Claudio Gutierrez[3], Bruno C. d. S. Oliveira[2],
and Éric Tanter[3]

[1] National University of Singapore, Singapore, Singapore
`yewenjia@connect.hku.hk`
[2] The University of Hong Kong, Hong Kong, China
`bruno@cs.hku.hk`
[3] Computer Science Department, University of Chile and IMFD, Santiago, Chile
{`mtoro,cgutierr,etanter`}`@dcc.uchile.cl`

Abstract. Practical SQL engines differ in subtle ways in their handling
of typing constraints and implicit type casts. These issues, usually not
considered in formal accounts of SQL, directly affect the portability of
queries between engines. To understand this problem, we present a formal
typing semantics for SQL, named **TRAF**, that explicitly captures both
static and dynamic type behavior. The system **TRAF** is expressed in
terms of abstract operators that provide the necessary leeway to precisely
model different SQL engines (PostgreSQL, MS SQL Server, MySQL,
SQLite, and Oracle).
We show that this formalism provides formal guarantees regarding the
handling of types. We provide practical conditions on engines to prove
type safety and soundness of queries. In this regard, **TRAF** can serve
as precise documentation of typing in existing engines and potentially
guide their evolution, as well as provide a formal basis to study type-
aware query optimizations, and design provably-correct query transla-
tors. Additionally, we test the adequacy of the formalism, implementing
TRAF in Python for these five engines, and tested them with thousands
of randomly-generated queries.

Keywords: SQL, Typing Semantics, Databases

1 Introduction

Query translation between different SQL engines is a common practice arising in different scenarios, like database migration (to reduce costs, mainte-
nance, changes in software, etc.) [6, 20, 22] and prototyping (code in lightweight
databases like SQLlite and then port to a more robust database). Today there
are many tools addressing this task [1, 18].

Translation between SQL engines could bring many surprises. One that particularly captures attention is the semantic discrepancy between SQL engines
related to typing behavior, the problem we study in this paper. This problem

Supplementary Information The online version contains supplementary material
available at https://doi.org/10.1007/978-3-031-91118-7_16

V. Vafeiadis (Ed.): ESOP 2025, LNCS 15694, pp. 408–435, 2025.
https://doi.org/10.1007/978-3-031-91118-7_16

is mainly due to differences in datatypes, type checking, when to perform the checks, and explicit and implicit type casts that may or may not be performed by the engines. This poses substantial challenges for developers and database administrators. Existing migration tools, whether paid or open source, often fall short of addressing these differences, tending to prioritize syntax over behavioral disparities.[4]

For illustration purposes, consider a table R. In the query SELECT 'a' + '2b' FROM R, the engine PSQL reports a static error and Oracle a runtime error (in both engines, addition is not defined for strings); MSSQL interprets the operation as string concatenation, yielding 'a2b'; and MySQL and SQLite yield 2. On the other hand, the query SELECT 1 FROM R WHERE '1' < 2 shows that MySQL and SQLite do not always exhibit identical behavior: the first yields 1, while the other an empty result. In Table 1 we present further (minimal) examples of this wide difference in behavior, which are explained in detail in Section 2.

As these examples show, database engines have different treatment of types, following different design models, like some being statically typed while others embrace dynamic typing, and different approaches to overloading basic arithmetic and comparison operations.

Understanding and addressing these anomalies is not a simple task. A first issue is that SQL standards do not cover many issues related to typing or leave the interpretation rather open.[5] In addition, many of the design decisions of the engines are hidden under optimization mechanisms that either are not public or complex to find in the code. Furthermore, the problem has not been addressed by the research literature. Although there is solid work on the formalization of the semantics of SQL [19,31], they assume that all comparisons and operations apply to the right types. Typing in SQL have been explored [3,13,24,26,32]. Nonetheless, the problem of type constraints and casts potentially raising errors at runtime, which is addressed in this paper, has not been dealt with before.

In this paper we address the problem of discrepant type related behavior by proposing a general formal framework, called TRAF, that models both common behavior and the intricate behavioral discrepancies across SQL database engines. TRAF was designed to explicitly capture the semantics of types, both static and dynamic, of a core fragment of relational algebra. The selected minimal core (already presented in other works like [8,19,27]) is designed to include the minimal features and operators that generate the indicated anomalies, as well as being flexible enough to model different SQL engines. It comprises booleans, numbers, selections, cross-products, nested queries within FROM clauses, and set operations. We also add support for arithmetic operators and type casts. Although features

---

[4] Some examples: https://en.wikibooks.org/wiki/Converting_MySQL_to_PostgreSQL http://www.sqlines.com/online https://www.rebasedata.com/convert-bmysql-bto-bpostgres-bonline

[5] A good example is the following: To cast an exact number to an exact numeric type, e.g. from a real to int, the specification says: "If there is a representation of SV [source value] in the data type TV [target value] that does not lose any leading significant digits after rounding or truncating if necessary, then TV is that representation. The choice of whether to round or truncate is implementation-defined." ANSI SQL 1992, Sec. 6.10, Case 3)a)i))

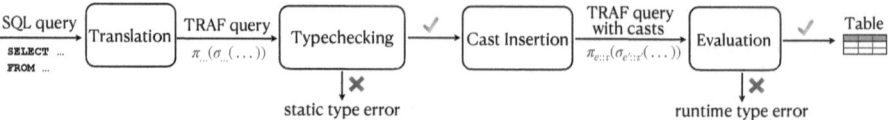

Fig. 1: Overview of TRAF. Some abstract operators in the typechecking, cast insertion, and evaluation phases must be instantiated to implement a particular engine. We provide sample instantiations for PSQL, MSSQL, Oracle, MySQL and SQLite.

such as nulls, aggregation, or EXISTS, are not supported within this core, it serves to illustrate the primary distinctions, leaving the extension to these additional features as potential future work.

We study two kinds of different behavior among engines: (1) different results due to type conversions, and (2) different behavior related to type errors. Regarding the latter, we identify two kinds of type errors: *static errors*, which happen during compilation/before running the query; and *runtime errors* that occur during the execution of the query. We say that two engines differ in behavior if, for a given query, the results are different (including different kinds of errors).

TRAF involves four sequential phases as illustrated in Figure 1: translation, typechecking, cast insertion, and evaluation. In the **translation** step (which is standard and can be found in the extended version of the paper), an SQL query is (1) analyzed to rule out syntactically invalid queries such as SELECT FROM FROM and (2) transformed to a TRAF query, that is, essentially a typed relational algebra query. Next, in the **typechecking** phase, a typechecker validates the query before evaluation (Section 3.3).[6] This typechecker is responsible for identifying mismatches between types and the number of columns of subqueries in set operations, and to ensure proper access to column names in scope. More importantly, it validates the appropriate usage of both implicit and explicit casts, rejecting operations that may result in casts known to always fail during evaluation. If the typechecker rejects the query, the process terminates and reports a static type error to the user. However, if the query is deemed well-typed, it proceeds to the third phase.

The **cast insertion** phase (Section 3.4) transforms a TRAF query by making all implicit type casts explicit. The purpose of this phase is to circumvent the complexities that would arise from handling implicit casts in the evaluation phase, thereby simplifying the dynamic semantics of TRAF. The **evaluation** phase (Section 3.5) interprets the transformed TRAF query. For this purpose, we present a monadic evaluator expressed using denotational semantics, cleanly encompassing the management of explicit type conversions and runtime errors. Should a type error arise during evaluation, the evaluation process is halted, and a runtime type error is reported. In the absence of runtime type errors, the outcome of evaluating a query is a table.

---

[6] TRAF does not assume the absence of type mismatches; users can write queries such as SELECT R.A from R WHERE 'Bob' = 1.

TRAF is designed to be flexible enough to model different real-world engines (PSQL, MSSQL, Oracle, MySQL and SQLite) in order to facilitate understanding of different behaviors and thus enable informed decisions when translating queries. Specifically, typechecking, cast insertion, and evaluation are parameterized in terms of abstract operators that need to be instantiated (Section 4).

The formal model is coherent and comprehensive, making it possible to precisely formulate and prove properties satisfied by all or some engines (Section 5). First, we prove a type safety result that ensures that well typed queries either reduce to a table or raise a (controlled) type error. In other words, evaluation of well-typed queries does not get stuck. Second, we enhance this result proving that the resulting table can be typed to the same type of the query. Third, the instantiation of the model to PSQL, MySQL and SQLite satisfies a theorem stating that if the programmer does not use explicit casts in well-typed queries, then the queries will evaluate without errors. Fourth, regarding cast insertion, independently of the engine (the proofs are parameterized by light constraints on abstract operators), translated queries preserve types, and the translation is unique.

Finally, to validate the adequacy of our formal framework, and following other approaches that also validate semantics by testing them against real-world implementations [19, 29, 30], we developed multiple database interpreters, and tested them with thousands of randomly-generated queries, comparing their results with those obtained from actual database engines. Additionally, we shed light on the impact and challenges of query optimizations on the evaluation process.

In summary, our contributions includes the identificacion of practical semantic discrepancies due to typing between SQL engines; the description of TRAF, a formal framework to reason about types both statically and dynamically, which can model different SQL engines; the metatheory of TRAF, indicating precise constraints on abstract operators required for properties to hold; and an empirical validation of our formal model, by building several interpreters tested against real engines. Additional material, including proofs and full definitions, can be found in the extended version. Also, we made available a prototype implementation as supplementary material.

The rest of the paper is organized as follows. Section 2 explains the discrepancies illustrated in Table 1. Section 3 presents the TRAF formal framework. Section 4 describes the instantiation of TRAF to practical SQL engines. Section 5 presents and proves formal properties of the model and its instantiations. Section 6 summarizes the experimental validation. In Section 7 we discuss related work, and Section 8 presents brief conclusions.

2   Typing semantic discrepancies

In this section we explain the source of discrepancies of Table 1, which we use as a starting point and develop (and justify) TRAF. For clarity, we categorize

	Query	PSQL	MSSQL	Oracle	MySQL	SQLite
E1	`SELECT 1.1 + 1 FROM R`	2.1	2.1	2.1	2.1	2.1
E2	`SELECT '1' + 1 FROM R`	2	2	2	2	2
E3	`SELECT '1.1' + 1 FROM R`	✗	↛	2.1	2.1	2.1
E4	`SELECT '1.1' + 1.1 FROM R`	2.2	2.2	2.2	2.2	2.2
E5	`SELECT '1' + '1' FROM R`	✗	'11'	2	2	2
E6	`SELECT 'a' + '2b' FROM R`	✗	'a2b'	↛	2	2
E7	`SELECT 1+A FROM R WHERE B=20`	✗	2	2	2	2
E8	`SELECT 1+A FROM R WHERE B=10`	✗	↛	↛	1	1
E9	`SELECT 1 + A FROM (SELECT '2' AS A) B`	✗	3	3	3	3
E10	`SELECT 1 FROM R WHERE '1' < 2`	1	1	1	1	∅
E11	`SELECT 1 FROM R WHERE '1.1' < 2`	✗	↛	1	1	∅
E12	`SELECT '1.1' FROM R INTERSECT SELECT 1.1 FROM R`	1.1	1.1	✗	1.1	∅
E13	`SELECT '1.1' FROM R INTERSECT SELECT 1 FROM R`	✗	↛	✗	∅	∅

Table 1: Examples of discrepant behaviors of different database engines, considering the table R(A,B) = {('Bob', 10), ('1', 20), ('1.1', 30)}. The queries are purposely chosen to exhibit minimal cases of typing issues. For simplicity we show only one element of the result. We use ✗ to denote a static error (before execution), and ↛ to denote a runtime error.

the examples of discrepancies into three groups: arithmetic, boolean, and set operations.

2.1   Arithmetic operations

For the first set of examples we focus on the expression being selected rather than the tables or the conditions.

E1 and E2. To begin, we present two examples that behave uniformly across the engines. For simplicity, we say that the result is 2.1, to denote a bag of uniform elements {2.1, 2.1, 2.1}.

E3. This is the first example that illustrates a difference in behavior. PSQL and MSSQL throw a type error, whereas the other engines return 2.1. The reason for the error is that in PSQL and MSSQL we can implicitly cast a string to an integer if the string is an integer, but not if the string is a real number. To fix this problem in PSQL, we must explicitly *cast* the string to a real number: `SELECT CAST('1.1' as FLOAT) + 1 FROM R.`

E4. If we take example 3, and change 1 for a real number, such as 1.1, then the result is now 2.2 for every engine. The difference with respect to the previous example is that the plus operation is defined for both integers and real numbers, and now '1.1' can be cast directly to a real number.

E5. PSQL reports an static error due to the lack of an addition operator between two strings. MSSQL returns '11' as addition is overloaded for string. The other engines return 2 as addition is only defined between numbers, thus implicit casting '1' to 1.

E6. Both PSQL and Oracle report an error, MSSQL uses string concatenation yielding 'a2b', and MySQL and SQLite yield 2. The reason for the latter is due

Operation	SQLite	Other engines
0 < 1	1	t
'0' < 1	0	t
'1' < 0	0	f
'0'+0 < 1	1	t
'0' < CAST(1 AS INT)	1	t
'0' < 1 + 0	0	t

Table 2: Behavior of the comparison operator in SQLite

to the way these engines cast strings to numbers: they search for a number in the prefix of the string (if nothing is found then 0 is returned).

E7. PSQL rejects this query as column A is of type String, and the addition between numbers and strings is not defined. This behavior is more conservative than E2, as now it cannot determine statically if the given string can be cast to number or not. Other engines defer the check to runtime and return 2. To fix this query in PSQL we can explicitly cast column A to integer: SELECT 1+CAST(A as INT) FROM R WHERE B=20.

E8. PSQL (statically) rejects this query similarly to E7. MSSQL and Oracle now fail dynamically as they cannot convert 'Bob' to a number. MySQL and SQLite on the other hand do not fail and return 1 as 'Bob' is cast to 0. Casting A to INT in PSQL would make the error dynamic, and a runtime type error would be reported instead, similarly to MySQL and SQLite.

E9. Contrary to E2, PSQL raises a static error as the nested query hides the actual String returned by the subquery. All other engines yield 3 as conversions are optimistically performed at runtime. To fix this query in PSQL an explicit cast must be inserted SELECT 1 + CAST(A AS INT) FROM (SELECT '2' AS A) B.

2.2   Boolean operations

The following examples illustrate difference in behavior related to comparison operators on conditionals. Note that 1 and 0 are used to represent true and false in SQLite and MySQL.

E10. Almost every engine is able to cast '1' to INT, returning 1. SQLite, on the other hand, returns a empty result as the condition is false. This is because SQLite does not perform implicit conversions at the boundaries of comparisons. SQLite has a type hierarchy where every string is bigger than any number.

E11. Now, if the left operand is a string representing a real, then PSQL and MSSQL return a type error. This is because the best type of the comparison operator is the one that takes two integers as argument (because 2 is an integer). As there is no direct implicit conversion between a string representing a real and an integer the query is rejected. SQLite still returns an empty result, and MySQL and Oracle return 1.

Comparison operator in SQLite. SQLite warrants special attention to illustrate unique cases related to the comparison operator, as exemplified in Table 2.

Notably, operations '0' < 1 and '1' < 1 yields 0. This behavior is attributed to the fact that strings are considered larger than integers, as previously explained. However, when a cast is introduced the expressions now yields 1. For instance, '0' < CAST(1 as INT) yields 1. Since when the type of one operand is explicitly specified, an implicit conversion to that type is performed on the other operand.

2.3 Set operations

E12. PSQL, MSSQL and MySQL, yield 1.1. This is because, during intersection, two conditions are checked: (1) the number of columns of both subqueries must match, and (2) the types of the columns must also be consistent. To achieve the second condition, an implicit conversion from string to real is inserted in the left subquery (the other direction is forbidden). However, Oracle encounters a type error since the column types do not match. On the other hand, SQLite returns an empty result as 1.1 is not the same as '1.1'.

E13. Now as '1.1' cannot be implicitly cast to an integer (the column type of the right subquery), this program is rejected by PSQL, MSSQL and Oracle. Both MySQL and SQLite return an empty result.

Having illustrated the various discrepancies between SQL engines in handling queries, it becomes evident that a more structured approach is necessary to fully understand and model these differences. To achieve this, we now turn to the formalism of TRAF.

3 The (**TRAF**) formal framework

In this section we present the syntax, type system, cast insertion, dynamic semantics, and translation of a typed core fragment of relational algebra, supporting projections, selection, set operations, arithmetic and boolean operations, and implicit and explicit casts. The formalism captures common behavior between engines while providing leeway to model different concrete engines, and thus is parametrized by abstract operators (detailed and instantiated in Section 3.2).

3.1 Syntax

The syntax of Typed Relational Algebra Framework (TRAF) is presented in Figure 2. The formalization is inspired by the work of Guagliardo and Libkin [19], except that here we deal with typing instead of assuming a prior (unstudied) typing phase. Types play a central role in this work, because as we illustrated, typing discrepancies are a source of important behavioral differences between engines. This section first presents types and schemas, then values and expressions, and finally queries.

Types and Schemas. There are two categories of types, *value types* τ for expressions (and values), and *relation types* T for queries and tables (relations). For simplicity, we only consider reals $\mathbb{R}$, integers $\mathbb{Z}$, booleans $\mathbb{B}$ and strings String. To avoid dealing with precision issues inherent in floating-point representations,

Types and	$\tau ::=$	$\mathbb{R} \mid \mathbb{Z} \mid \mathbb{B} \mid$ String $\mid$?	(value types)
Schemas	$T ::=$	$N \mapsto \tau \mid T, N \mapsto \tau$	(relation types)
	$\Gamma ::=$	$\emptyset \mid \Gamma, R \mapsto T$	(schema)
Values and	$0_A \in$	$\{+\}$	(arithmetic ops)
Expressions	$0_C \in$	$\{<, =\}$	(comparison ops)
	$0_B \in$	$\{\wedge, \vee\}$	(boolean ops)
	$w ::=$	$d \mid n \mid b \mid s$	(simple values)
	$v ::=$	$w \mid w :: ?$	(values)
	$e ::=$	$N \mid v \mid e\,0_A\,e \mid e :: \tau$	(general expressions)
	$\theta ::=$	$e\,0_C\,e \mid \theta\,0_B\,\theta \mid \neg\theta$	(boolean expressions)
	$\beta ::=$	e as $N \mid \beta, e$ as N	(aliased expressions)
Queries	$0_S \in$	$\{\cup, \cap, \times, -\}$	(set query ops)
	$Q ::=$	$R \mid \pi_\beta(Q) \mid \sigma_\theta(Q) \mid Q\,0_S\,Q \mid \varepsilon(Q)$	(queries)
Rows and	$r ::=$	$\overline{v_i}$	
Tables	$t ::=$	$\{\!\{\overline{r_i}\}\!\}$	

Fig. 2: Syntax of TRAF. n, b, s denote respectively an integer number, a boolean value and a string. N is a name. R a relation.

we use the abstract type $\mathbb{R}$ to represent decimal numbers. In addition, we use the symbol ? for the unknown type, used by PSQL to type string literals [17], and to model flexible typing in SQLite. A relation type T is an ordered list of pairs of column names and their corresponding value type. A schema Γ is a list of pairs of relation names and their relation type. We assume that both T and Γ do not contain duplicated column names and relation names, respectively (and thus behave as mappings). Intuitively, schemas represent types of databases.

Values and expressions. We represent tables as bags of *rows*, where each row is a list of *values*. A *simple value* w, which represent atomic data (integers, booleans, strings). Values v are either a simple value w, or a simple value cast to the unknown type $w :: ?$ (the latter is not used directly by programmers, and it is used exclusively in engines such as SQLite). There are three kinds of expressions: general, boolean and aliased. A general expression e, used in projections and selections, is either a column name N (e.g. Name or Age), a value v, an arithmetic operation (for simplicity we only use $+$), or an explicit cast $e :: \tau$. Boolean expressions θ as usual are comparison operations or logical combinations of them.[7] As a standard, an aliased expression is a slight extension of the classical renaming, allowing binding of names to expressions, instead of only to queries. For example, in SELECT A.C FROM (SELECT 1+1 AS C FROM R) A, the expression 1+1 gets a name C that can be used in the outer query.

Queries. A query is either a relation R, a projection $\pi_\beta(Q)$, a selection $\sigma_\theta(Q)$, or a set operation, that is, cross product $(Q \times Q)$, intersection $(Q \cap Q)$, union $(Q \cup Q)$, difference $(Q - Q)$, and the removal of duplication $(\varepsilon(Q))$.

---

[7] Note that we do not include boolean expressions as general expressions, because some engines do not support selecting boolean values in queries (e.g. in MSSQL and Oracle, SELECT 1 < 2 FROM R is a syntactically invalid query while it is valid in PSQL, MySQL and SQLite).

The only novelty is that a projection here is parametrized by a list of aliased expressions, instead of a list of names. This allows to model SQL queries like SELECT 1+1 AS C FROM R as $\pi_{(1+1)\text{ as }C}(R)$.

Rows and Tables. A table t is a bag of *rows* $\{\!\{r_i\}\!\}$, where a row r is an ordered list of values $\overline{v_i}$.

3.2   Abstract operators

As mentioned in Section 1, certain key operators in TRAF are left abstract, as they depend on the specific engine being used. We mark with (*) the partial operators.

Bidirectional Implicit Cast(*). Operator $biconv(e_1, \tau_1, e_2, \tau_2) = \tau_3$ determines the optimal implicit type cast for a set operator applied to two columns of (possibly) different types. The *biconv* operator takes as argument two expressions (e_1, e_2) and their corresponding types (τ_1, τ_2), returning a type. It either returns τ_2 or τ_1 by testing if e_1 can be implicitly cast to τ_2, or if e_2 can be implicitly cast to τ_1 respectively.

Explicit Cast(*). Operator $cast(v, \tau) = v'$ attempts to cast value v to a value v' of type τ. This function is primarily used to evaluate casts at runtime.

Overloading Resolution(*). Operator $resolve(e_1, \tau_1, e_2, \tau_2, \mathsf{O}) = \tau_3$ determines which specific operation among a set of overloaded ones should be called based on the provided arguments during invocation. More specifically, given an operator it tries to find the best candidate type for expressions e_1 and e_2, typed as τ_1 and τ_2 respectively.

Explicit Cast Feasibility. This operator takes one expression and two types, and returns a boolean. For simplicity, it is presented as a relation $e : \tau' \rightrightarrows \tau$, and rules out explicit casts that are known to fail at runtime. It tests if it is possible to explicitly cast expression e of type τ', to an expression of type τ.

Type of Values. Operator $ty(v) = \tau$ computes the type of values (constants).

Type Cleaning. The operator $clean(T) = T'$ performs post-processing on the relation type T, returning a new relation type T'. This is primarily used in PSQL, where literal strings are initially typed as ?, a type that is later converted to String when determining the type of a subquery.

Annotation Insertion. The operator $insert(e, \tau, \mathsf{O}) = e'$ returns either an explicitly cast expression e to type τ or simply e, depending on the operation O. For instance, in SQLite, comparison operations do not implicitly cast their operands, whereas addition operations do perform such casts.

Value Operation Application. Operator $apply(\mathsf{O}, v_1, v_2) = v_3$ performs arithmetic or comparison operation O to values v_1 and v_2, yielding value v_3.

In the next subsections, we use these operators to define the dynamic semantics, the type system and the cast insertion procedure. Examples of instantiation of these abstract operators can be found in Section 4.

$$(\mathrm{T}v)\dfrac{\boxed{T \vdash e : \tau}}{T \vdash v : \; ty(v)}$$

$$(\mathrm{TO_B})\dfrac{T \vdash \theta_1 : \mathbb{B} \qquad T \vdash \theta_2 : \mathbb{B}}{T \vdash \theta_1 \; \mathsf{O_B} \; \theta_2 : \mathbb{B}}$$

$$(\mathrm{T}N)\dfrac{(N \mapsto \tau) \in T}{T \vdash N : \tau}$$

$$(\mathrm{T}\neg)\dfrac{T \vdash \theta : \mathbb{B}}{T \vdash \neg \theta : \mathbb{B}}$$

$$(\mathrm{T}::)\dfrac{T \vdash e : \tau' \qquad e : \tau' \nrightarrow \tau}{T \vdash (e :: \tau) : \tau}$$

$$(\mathrm{TO})\dfrac{T \vdash e_1 : \tau_1 \qquad T \vdash e_2 : \tau_2 \qquad \mathsf{O} \in \mathsf{O_A} \cup \mathsf{O_C}}{\qquad resolve(e_1, \tau_1, e_2, \tau_2, \mathsf{O}) = \tau_3 \times \tau_4 \to \tau_5 \qquad}{T \vdash e_1 \; \mathsf{O} \; e_2 : \tau_5}$$

$$\boxed{T \vdash \beta : T'}$$

$$(\mathrm{T}\beta)\dfrac{\forall i. T \vdash e_i : \tau_i \qquad unique(\overline{N_i})}{T \vdash \overline{e_i \; \mathbf{as} \; N_i} : \overline{N_i \mapsto \tau_i}}$$

$$\boxed{\Gamma \vdash Q : T}$$

$$(\mathrm{T}\pi)\dfrac{\Gamma \vdash Q : T \qquad clean(T) \vdash \beta : T'}{\Gamma \vdash \pi_\beta(Q) : T'}$$

$$(\mathrm{T}\sigma)\dfrac{\Gamma \vdash Q : T \qquad T \vdash \theta : \mathbb{B}}{\Gamma \vdash \sigma_\theta(Q) : T}$$

$$(\mathrm{T}\times)\dfrac{\ell(\Gamma, Q_1) \cap \ell(\Gamma, Q_2) = \emptyset \qquad \Gamma \vdash Q_1 : T_1 \qquad \Gamma \vdash Q_2 : T_2}{\Gamma \vdash Q_1 \times Q_2 : T_1, T_2}$$

$$(\mathrm{T}R)\dfrac{\Gamma(R) = T}{\Gamma \vdash R : T}$$

$$(\mathrm{TO_S})\dfrac{\Gamma \vdash \pi_{\beta_1}(Q_1) : T_1 \qquad \Gamma \vdash \pi_{\beta_2}(Q_2) : T_2}{biconv^*(\beta_1, T_1, \beta_2, T_2) = T \qquad \mathsf{O_S} \in \{\cup, \cap, -\}}{\Gamma \vdash \pi_{\beta_1}(Q_1) \; \mathsf{O_S} \; \pi_{\beta_2}(Q_2) : T}$$

$$(\mathrm{T}\varepsilon)\dfrac{\Gamma \vdash Q : T}{\Gamma \vdash \varepsilon(Q) : T}$$

Fig. 3: Type System of TRAF. Abstract operators are highlighted in gray.

3.3   Type System

The type system of TRAF is presented in Figure 3, and in the following, we briefly explain the rationale behind each rule. Boxes in gray indicate abstract operators, and we can provide specific implementations for modeling an engine (Section 3.2).

Expressions. Rule (Tv) assigns types to values based on the specific database engine (the ty operator in the grey box). For instance, in PSQL, integers are typed as $\mathbb{Z}$ and literal strings as ?, but in SQLite, both are typed as ?. Rule (TN) assigns the type τ to the column name N if N is mapped to τ in the relation type T.

Rule (T::) assigns the type τ to an ascription $e :: \tau$ if the following conditions are met: (1) the expression e must be well-typed for some τ'; (2) the explicit cast of e to τ (engine-dependent, thus grey box) is checked to rule out explicit casts that are known to always fail at runtime. For example, the attempt to cast 'hi' to $\mathbb{Z}$ ('hi' :: $\mathbb{Z}$) is rejected in PSQL, while casting '1' to $\mathbb{Z}$ is accepted in both PSQL and SQLite.

Rules (TO), (TO$_B$) and (T$\neg$) type operations. (TO$_B$) and (T$\neg$) type boolean operations as usual. The interesting case is rule (TO) that types arithmetic and string operations. Based on the types of e_1 and e_2 and operation O, the (TO) rule searches for the best candidate type signature for the given operation, taking into consideration that an operation might be overloaded with multiple types. It involves the operations *resolve* and *ty* that are engine-dependent. If a single candidate function type is identified, the expression is typed; otherwise, it is considered ill-typed. Note that types τ_3 and τ_4 do not need to coincide with τ_1 and τ_2 as arguments can be cast to different types. For instance, in the case of the query SELECT 1+1 FROM P both PSQL and SQLite choose numeric addition $(\mathbb{Z} \times \mathbb{Z} \rightarrow \mathbb{Z})$. However, when dealing with strings (e.g. SELECT 'a' + 'b' FROM P) PSQL rejects the query because it cannot choose a best candidate operator, but SQLite instantiates the query with numeric addition, implicitly casting both string arguments to integers.

Rule (Tβ) is used to type an aliased expression β. We use the notation $\overline{A_i}$ to denote a list $A_1, \ldots, A_n$. Under T, every expression e_i yields a type τ_i. Subsequently, the type of the aliased expression as a whole is a relation type, where each name N_i is mapped to the type τ_i of their corresponding subexpression e_i. Additionally, we use metafunction *unique*(.) to ensure that names are unique.

Queries. Rule (TR) assigns a relation type to relation name R according to schema environment Γ. Rule (Tπ) types $\pi_\beta(Q)$ based on the type of Q and that of the aliased expression β, which is typed under $clean(T)$ to remove unknown occurrences. For instance, in PSQL, SELECT '1' + 1 FROM P runs successfully, but SELECT C + 1 FROM (SELECT '1' AS C) B is rejected statically: the first query '1' has type unknown ?, which can be cast to integer, whereas in the second query, the unknown type ? is transformed to String disallowing the implicit cast to integer.

Rule (Tσ) first typechecks the subquery, resulting in a relation type T. Then, the condition must be successfully typed as boolean under the context of T (considering that the condition may reference columns from the subquery). Finally, the selection operation is assigned the same type as the subquery T. Rule (T$\times$) types cross products using the concatenation of the relation types of both subqueries, ensuring that the sets of names in each subquery are disjoint. The list of column names of a query Q is extracted using function $\ell(\Gamma, Q)$, and defined as:

$$\ell(\Gamma, R) = \overline{N_i} \text{ where } \Gamma(R) = \overline{N_i \mapsto \tau_i}$$
$$\ell(\Gamma, Q_1 \times Q_2) = \ell(\Gamma, Q_1), \ell(\Gamma, Q_2)$$
$$\ell(\Gamma, Q_1 \, \mathsf{O_s} \, Q_2) = \ell(\Gamma, Q_1) \text{ where } \mathsf{O_s} \in \{\cup, \cap, -\}; \ (*)$$
$$\ell(\Gamma, \sigma_\theta(Q)) = \ell(\Gamma, Q)$$
$$\ell(\Gamma, \pi_\beta(Q)) = \ell(\Gamma, \beta)$$
$$\ell(\Gamma, \beta, e \text{ as } N) = \ell(\Gamma, \beta), \ell(\Gamma, e \text{ as } N)$$
$$\ell(\Gamma, e \text{ as } N) = N$$

Rule (*) follows standard engine usage of using the left schema of a set expression as output schema.

Rule (TO$_S$) deals with set operations (union, intersection, and difference) which require special attention. Usually, it is assumed that the names, number of columns, and types of the columns in the subqueries match. In practice, the column names do not necessarily match, but number of columns and types must align. To achieve this, many engines perform implicit casts between the columns of the subqueries to align their types. In particular, string literals are analyzed to check the plausibility of casts. For instance in PSQL, (SELECT '1.1' AS A FROM P) INTERSECT (SELECT 1.1 AS A FROM P) runs successfully, resulting in a non-empty result, whereas (SELECT CAST(Age AS TEXT) AS A FROM P) INTERSECT (SELECT Age FROM P) is rejected before execution. To deal with these special cases, and without loss of generality, we require that both subqueries within a set operation must be projections in order to verify column casts. Therefore, the rule first typechecks both projections. Second, it examines whether the lists of aliased expressions can be implicitly cast between each other, taking their relation types into account. Finally, if this cast is feasible, the target relation type is captured and used to typecheck the whole set operation. To check casts between lists of aliased expressions, we use the *biconv** operation defined as follows:

$$biconv^*(\overline{e \text{ as } N, N \mapsto \tau, e' \text{ as } N', N' \mapsto \tau'}) = \overline{N \mapsto biconv(e, \tau, e', \tau')}$$

This operation returns a relation type, where each name N is mapped to the application of abstract operator *biconv* over each pair of expressions and their types. We select N, the name of the left subquery, as it is a more commonly-adopted practice in various database engines. This partial operator determines the optimal implicit type cast for a set operator applied to two columns of (possibly) different types, returning one of the two types as a result. The expressions are provided to the function to rule out casts that are known to always fail during evaluation. For instance, PSQL accepts query (SELECT '1' AS A, 1 AS B FROM R) UNION (SELECT 2 AS A, '2' AS B FROM R), as both '1' and '2' can be cast to integers; but rejects (SELECT '1.1' AS A FROM R) UNION (SELECT 1 AS A FROM R) as '1.1' cannot be implicitly cast to an integer (note that in PSQL, implicit casts from integers to strings are not allowed).

3.4   Cast Insertion

Recall from Figure 1 that to avoid the complexity of dealing with implicit casts during runtime, before execution, in TRAF we transform each implicit cast to an explicit cast. For instance, a PSQL query SELECT '1' + 1 AS A FROM R is transformed to SELECT CAST('1' AS INT) + 1 AS A FROM R, which in TRAF corresponds to the elaboration from $\pi_{'1'+1 \text{ as } A}(R)$ to $\pi_{('1'::\mathbb{Z})+1 \text{ as } A}(R)$.

Figure 4 presents an excerpt of the explicit cast insertion rules; the complete rules can be found in the extended version. The rules are *type directed*, meaning that (1) we only elaborate well-typed terms, and (2) we use type information during elaboration. Like for typing, elaboration rules are defined inductively and grouped in three categories: for general and aliased expressions, and for queries.

$$\boxed{T \vdash e : \tau \rightsquigarrow e'}$$

$$(Ev)\frac{T \vdash v : \tau}{T \vdash v : \tau \rightsquigarrow v :: \tau}$$

$$(E0)\frac{T \vdash e_1 : \tau_1 \rightsquigarrow e_1' \qquad T \vdash e_2 : \tau_2 \rightsquigarrow e_2' \qquad 0 \in \{<, =, +\} \qquad resolve(e_1, \tau_1, e_2, \tau_2, 0) = \tau_3 \times \tau_4 \rightarrow \tau_5}{T \vdash e_1 \; 0 \; e_2 : \tau_4 \rightsquigarrow \\ insert(insert(e_1', \tau_3, 0) \; 0 \; insert(e_2', \tau_4, 0), \tau_5, 0)}$$

$$\boxed{\Gamma \vdash Q : T \rightsquigarrow Q'}$$

$$(E0_S)\frac{\Gamma \vdash \pi_{\beta_1}(Q_1) : T_1 \rightsquigarrow \pi_{\beta_1'}(Q_1') \qquad \Gamma \vdash \pi_{\beta_2}(Q_2) : T_2 \rightsquigarrow \pi_{\beta_2'}(Q_2') \\ biconv^*(\beta_1, T_1, \beta_2, T_2) = T \qquad\qquad 0_S \in \{\cup, \cap, -\} \\ e_1 = insert^*(\beta_1', T, 0_S) \qquad\qquad e_2 = insert^*(\beta_2', T, 0_S)}{\Gamma \vdash \pi_{\beta_1}(Q_1) \; 0_S \; \pi_{\beta_2}(Q_2) : T \rightsquigarrow \pi_{e_1}(Q_1') \; 0_S \; \pi_{e_2}(Q_2')}$$

Fig. 4: TRAF Cast Insertion (excerpt). Abstract operators are highlighted in gray.

Most elaboration rules directly follow their corresponding typing rule. Judgment $T \vdash e : \tau \rightsquigarrow e'$ represents that expression e typed as τ under relation type T is elaborated to e'. Judgment $\Gamma \vdash Q : T \rightsquigarrow Q'$ is defined analogously.

Rule (Ev) inserts an explicit cast to the type of each value. This is especially relevant for engines like SQLite where some values need to be tagged as unknown. In SQLite, all constants are considered to be of type unknown, unless the constant is fetched from a table. This is important at runtime, as a 1 might behave differently than CAST(1 AS INT). For example, the expression '0' < 1 evaluates to 0. To facilitate this special case, the expression is elaborated to '0' :: ? < 1 :: ?.

Rule $(E0)$ introduces explicit casts based on the operation and the best candidate type. Specifically, we insert casts for both operands to match their expected corresponding domain types and also insert a cast in the result of the operation to the expected codomain type. Certain engines, like SQLite, do not insert explicit casts for comparison operations. To achieve this, we use the *insert* abstract operator.

Rule $(E0_S)$ elaborates set operations by inserting casts to the output type of *biconv**. This is done using the *insert** operation defined as

$$insert^*(\overline{e \text{ as } N}, \overline{N \mapsto \tau}, 0_S) = \overline{insert(e, \tau, 0_S) \text{ as } N}$$

. For instance, for PSQL, query (SELECT '1' FROM R) INTERSECT (SELECT 1 FROM R) is elaborated to (SELECT CAST('1' AS INT) FROM R) INTERSECT (SELECT CAST(1 AS INT) FROM R).

3.5   Dynamic Semantics

Figure 5 presents the dynamic semantics of TRAF, which differs from the ones of Guagliardo and Libkin [19] (GL) as follows. First, TRAF dynamic semantics are defined over a relational algebra, whereas GL uses SQL syntax to support

$$[\![R]\!]_{\mathsf{D},\Gamma} = \mathbf{ok} \ \mathsf{D}\,(R) \tag{RR}$$

$$[\![Q_1 \ \mathsf{O_s} \ Q_2]\!]_{\mathsf{D},\Gamma} = \mathsf{do}\{t_1 \leftarrow [\![Q_1]\!]_{\mathsf{D},\Gamma}; t_2 \leftarrow [\![Q_2]\!]_{\mathsf{D},\Gamma}; \mathbf{ok} \ t_1 \ \mathsf{O_s} \ t_2\} \tag{R$\mathsf{O_s}$}$$

$$[\![\pi_\beta(Q)]\!]_{\mathsf{D},\Gamma} = \mathsf{do}\{t \leftarrow [\![Q]\!]_{\mathsf{D},\Gamma}; \lceil\{\underbrace{[\![\beta]\!]_{\eta_{\ell(\Gamma,Q)}^r}, \ldots, [\![\beta]\!]_{\eta_{\ell(\Gamma,Q)}^r}}_{k \text{ times}} \mid r \in_\mathsf{k} t\}\rceil\} \tag{Rπ}$$

$$[\![\sigma_\theta(Q)]\!]_{\mathsf{D},\Gamma} = \mathsf{do}\{t \leftarrow [\![Q]\!]_{\mathsf{D},\Gamma}; \_ \leftarrow \lceil\{[\![\theta]\!]_{\eta_{\ell(\Gamma,Q)}^r} \mid r \in_\mathsf{k} t\}\rceil;$$
$$\mathbf{ok} \ \{\underbrace{r, \ldots, r}_{k \text{ times}} \mid r \in_\mathsf{k} t \wedge [\![\theta]\!]_{\eta_{\ell(\Gamma,Q)}^r} \}\} \tag{Rσ}$$

$$[\![\varepsilon(Q)]\!]_{\mathsf{D},\Gamma} = \varepsilon([\![Q]\!]_{\mathsf{D},\Gamma}) \tag{Rε}$$

$$[\![e \ \mathbf{as} \ N]\!]_\eta = [\![e]\!]_\eta \tag{Ras}$$

$$[\![\beta, e \ \mathbf{as} \ N]\!]_\eta = \mathsf{do}\{r \leftarrow [\![\beta]\!]_\eta; v \leftarrow [\![e]\!]_\eta; \mathbf{ok} \ r, v\} \tag{Rβ}$$

$$[\![N]\!]_\eta = \mathbf{ok} \ \eta(N) \tag{RN}$$

$$[\![v]\!]_\eta = \mathbf{ok} \ v \tag{Rv}$$

$$[\![v :: \tau]\!]_\eta = \begin{vmatrix} \mathbf{ok} \ v' \ \text{if} \ \ cast(v,\tau) = v' \\ \mathbf{error} \ \text{otherwise} \end{vmatrix} \tag{Rv ::}$$

$$[\![e :: \tau]\!]_\eta = \mathsf{do}\{v \leftarrow [\![e]\!]_\eta; [\![v :: \tau]\!]_\eta\} \ \text{where} \ e \neq v \tag{Re ::}$$

$$[\![\theta_1 \ \mathsf{O_B} \ \theta_2]\!]_\eta = \mathsf{do}\{b_1 \leftarrow [\![\theta_1]\!]_\eta; b_2 \leftarrow [\![\theta_2]\!]_\eta; \mathbf{ok} \ b_1 \ \mathsf{O_B} \ b_2\} \tag{R$\mathsf{O_B}$}$$

$$[\![\neg\theta]\!]_\eta = \mathsf{do}\{b \leftarrow [\![\theta_1]\!]_\eta; \mathbf{ok} \ \neg b\} \tag{R$\neg$}$$

$$[\![e_1 \ \mathsf{O} \ e_2]\!]_\eta = \mathsf{do}\{v_1 \leftarrow [\![e_1]\!]_\eta; v_2 \leftarrow [\![e_2]\!]_\eta; \mathbf{ok} \ \ apply(\mathsf{O}, v_1, v_2) \quad \mathsf{O} \in \mathsf{O_A} \cup \mathsf{O_C}\} \tag{RO}$$

Fig. 5: Dynamic Semantics of TRAF. Abstract operators are highlighted in gray.

extra features. Second, and more importantly, as some casts may be invalid, the dynamic semantics must deal with the possibility of runtime errors. For instance, in PSQL the query SELECT CAST('s' as INT) FROM R $(\sigma_{\mathsf{'s'} :: \mathbb{Z}}(R))$ evaluates to an error.

To concisely account for the possibility of runtime errors, we present the dynamic semantics in *monadic* style in order to streamline the handling of errors [37]. The monadic presentation of computations that may fail consists in so-called "optional" values: either an actual value tagged with **ok**, or **error** to denote an error. The sequential composition is given in a do block (e.g. $\mathsf{do}\{A; B; C\}$). Errors are transparently propagated through such sequences: the evaluation returns **ok** v if all steps in a do block (e.g. A, B, and C) evaluate successfully, or **error** if one step in the sequence evaluates to **error**.

There are four categories of evaluations : $[\![Q]\!]_{\mathsf{D},\Gamma}$ to reduce queries, $[\![e]\!]_\eta$ to reduce expressions, $[\![\beta]\!]_\eta$ to reduce aliased expressions, and $[\![\theta]\!]_\eta$ to reduce boolean expressions. The evaluation of a query is parametrized by a database D, which maps relation names R to tables t. We use $r \in_\mathsf{k} t$ to denote that r appears k times in t. The other categories of evaluation are parametrized by an environment η, which maps column names N to values v. Intuitively, this environment is used to extract the value associated with a column name for a given row. For instance, consider a relation of persons P(Name $\mapsto$ String, Age $\mapsto$ $\mathbb{Z}$), and a table $\{('Bob', 10), ('Alice', 20)\}$. Then, for the first row, η(Name) = 'Bob' and η(Age) = 10.

Queries. The basic case is Rule (RR), which evaluates the name of a relation yielding the table associated to that name in database D. Rule (R0$_\mathsf{S}$) evaluates set operations by first reducing the subqueries, then combining the resulting tables. Rule (Rπ) starts by evaluating subquery Q. If the result is successful (a table t), then for each row r that appears k times in t, we try to project columns as dictated by β, and duplicate the result k times. To do this, we evaluate β under environment $\eta^r_{\ell(\Gamma,Q)}$ (similarly to [19], $\eta^{r,v}_{\overline{N_i},N} = \eta^r_{\overline{N_i}}, N \mapsto v$ and $\eta_{\cdot} = \cdot$). This environment is formed by matching corresponding column names of Q with the values of r. Finally, as the evaluation of aliased expressions can also produce errors, we lift the bag of optional rows S to an optional bag of rows using the $\lceil \cdot \rceil$ function defined as: $\lceil S \rceil$ = **error**, when **error** $\in$ S; and **ok** $\{\!\{r \mid (\mathbf{ok}\ r) \in S\}\!\}$ otherwise.

Rule (Rσ) follows a similar approach by first reducing the subquery Q. If the result is successful (yielding table t), we proceed to test the reduction of the condition θ for each row. We employ a strategy akin to that of (Rπ), but in this case, the resulting bag of booleans is unused (binding the resulting in variable "_"). This way, in the third instruction, we can be confident that the evaluation of the conditions does not result in errors. Finally, we filter the rows from table t that satisfy the given condition. The last rule for queries (Rε) removes duplicates from subquery using the function $\varepsilon(\cdot)$.

Expressions. Rule (Ras) evaluates a single aliased expression by evaluating the subexpression e and disregarding the name N. Rule (Rβ) applies when we are evaluating multiple aliased expressions. Initially, it recursively reduces the sublist to a row r, and then the head of the list to a value v, resulting in a new row r, v.

Rule (RN) successfully evaluates a column name N to its corresponding value in η. Rule (Rv) successfully evaluates values to themselves. Rule (Rv ::) attempts to cast a value into a value of a different type using the *cast* function. For instance, in SQLite, the expression CAST('hi' as INT) evaluates to 1, whereas in PSQL is not defined. If the function is defined for the given value and type, the resulting value is returned; otherwise, an error is raised. Rule (Re::) applies to subexpressions that are not already values. It first reduces the subexpression to a value, and then casts the value using rule (Rv::).

Rules (R0$_\mathsf{B}$), (R$\neg$), and (R0) operate in a similar fashion. First, each subexpression is reduced, then the resulting values are combined using the specific operation at hand. For arithmetic and comparison operations, the exact operation is performed using the *apply* operation. For instance, in PSQL, the expression '0' $<$ 1 evaluates to true, whereas in SQLite, it yields false.

Basic definitions

$$ty(n) = \mathbb{Z} \quad ty(d) = \mathbb{R} \quad ty(s) = ?$$

$$insert(e, \tau, 0) = e :: \tau \qquad clean(T) = T[\text{String}/?]$$

$$ty(0_c) = \{\mathbb{Z} \times \mathbb{Z} \to \mathbb{B}, \mathbb{R} \times \mathbb{R} \to \mathbb{B},$$

$$\text{String} \times \text{String} \to \mathbb{B}\}$$

$$ty(+) = \{\mathbb{Z} \times \mathbb{Z} \to \mathbb{Z}, \mathbb{R} \times \mathbb{R} \to \mathbb{R}\}$$

$$apply(0, v_1, v_2) = v_1 \, 0 \, v_2$$

$$\overline{\tau \Rightarrow \tau} \qquad \overline{\mathbb{Z} \Rightarrow \mathbb{R}}$$

$$\frac{\tau \Rightarrow \tau'}{e : \tau \rightsquigarrow \tau'}$$

$$\frac{icast(v, \tau) = v'}{v : ? \rightsquigarrow \tau}$$

$$\boxed{biconv(e_1, \tau_1, e_2, \tau_2) = \tau}$$

$$\frac{e_1 : \tau_1 \rightsquigarrow \tau_2}{biconv(e_1, \tau_1, e_2, \tau_2) = \tau_2} \qquad \frac{e_2 : \tau_2 \rightsquigarrow \tau_1}{biconv(e_1, \tau_1, e_2, \tau_2) = \tau_1}$$

$$\boxed{icast(v, \tau) = v'} \qquad \boxed{cast(v, \tau) = v'}$$

$$icast(`n', \mathbb{R}) = n \qquad\qquad cast(v, \mathbb{Z}) = \lfloor v \rfloor \quad v \in \mathbb{R}$$

$$icast(n, \mathbb{R}) = n \qquad\qquad cast(v, \text{String}) = str(v) \quad v \neq s$$

$$icast(v, ty(v)) = v \qquad\qquad cast(v, \tau) = icast(v, \tau)$$

$$icast(`v', ty(v)) = v \quad v \neq s$$

$$\{m\} = \arg\min_i((cost(\tau_1, \tau_{1i})) + (cost(\tau_2, \tau_{2i})))$$

$$\frac{\tau_1 \Rightarrow \tau_{1m} \qquad\qquad \tau_2 \Rightarrow \tau_{2m}}{bestCandidate(\tau_1, \tau_2, \overline{\tau_{1i} \times \tau_{2i} \to \tau_{3i}}) = \tau_{3m} \times \tau_{4m} \to \tau_{3m}}$$

$$cost(\tau, \tau) = 0 \quad cost(\mathbb{Z}, \mathbb{R}) = 1 \quad cost(\text{String}, \mathbb{Z}) = 1 \quad cost(\text{String}, \mathbb{R}) = 1 \quad cost(\_, \_) = 2$$

$$\boxed{resolve(e_1, \tau_1, e_2, \tau_2, 0) = \tau} \quad \frac{\tau_1 \neq ? \qquad\qquad \tau_2 \neq ?}{bestCandidate(\tau_1, \tau_2, ty(0)) = \tau_3 \times \tau_4 \to \tau_5} \quad \dots$$

$$resolve(e_1, \tau_1, e_2, \tau_2, 0) = \tau_3 \times \tau_4 \to \tau_5$$

Fig. 6: The TRAF/PSQL Instantiation (excerpt)

4   Instantiating TRAF

In this section we illustrate how to instantiate TRAF for PSQL and SQLite. The complete rules and the instantiations for three other engines (MSSQL, Oracle, and MySQL) can be found in the extended version. In general, an instantiation is achieved by providing specific definitions of the abstract operators that are engine dependent (the grey boxes in the figures). We obtained these definitions by exploring the documentation of each engine, and by conducting black-box analyses interacting with each engine whenever the documentation was lacking in details.

4.1   TRAF/PSQL

Figure 6 describes the TRAF/PSQL instantiation. PSQL is characterized by being a strongly-typed SQL engine, meaning that it is more conservative than the rest.

In many cases, if it cannot check the feasibility of casts, it rejects the query before its execution.

For the type of values, reals are typed as $\mathbb{R}$, integers to $\mathbb{Z}$, and string literals to ?. The operator for removing unknown types replaces ? occurrences with String, while leaving other types unchanged.[8] The operator for inserting annotations adds explicit casts regardless of the operation's type. The candidate types of a given operator is represented as sets of binary function types. Lastly, the semantics of operations between values are passed to the real implementation without any modifications.

Bidirectional implicit cast. Operator *biconv* is defined using the auxiliary *implicit type cast* relation $e : \tau \rightsquigarrow \tau'$. An expression e of type τ can be cast to τ' if either type τ can be implicitly cast to τ' ($\tau \Rightarrow \tau'$), or if e is a value v of type unknown ? (i.e. a string) and that value can be implicitly cast to some value v' under type τ' ($icast(v, \tau') = v'$).

Implicit type cast $\tau \Rightarrow \tau'$ is only defined between identical types $\tau \Rightarrow \tau$, or from integers to reals $\mathbb{Z} \Rightarrow \mathbb{R}$. For instance, (SELECT 1 FROM R) INTERSECT (SELECT 1.0 FROM R) is accepted and evaluates to $\{1.0\}$, since $\mathbb{Z}$ (the type of 1) can be implicitly cast to a $\mathbb{R}$ (the type of 1.0). Implicit value cast $icast(v, \tau) = v'$ is defined for extracting numbers from strings, but not viceversa.

Explicit cast. In addition to what an implicit value cast can do, explicit (value) casts $cast(v, \tau) = v'$ support casts from real numbers to integers by removing the decimals, and from non-string values to strings by enclosing them in quotes. For instance, SELECT CAST('1.1' AS DOUBLE) FROM R is accepted and evaluates to 1.1, but SELECT CAST('1.1' AS INT) FROM R is rejected by the type-checker.

Overload resolution. The definition of the *resolve* operator is divided in four cases. The general case arises when the types of the two expressions are not known. Function *bestCandidate* is used to determine the best candidate. We model this function by initially calculating the sum of the type differences between the corresponding types of the expression and the domain of each candidate. The type difference $\tau - \tau'$ quantifies the "cost" of changing type τ to τ': it yields a value of 0 if both types are identical, 1 when transitioning from an integer to a real or from a string to a number, and 2 in all other cases. If there are ties, and more than one type is selected, then the function is not defined. Furthermore, both types must satisfy the implicit cast relation with their corresponding type from the domain of the chosen best candidate. For instance, for query SELECT 1 + 1.1 FROM R, the + operation has two possible candidates: $\mathbb{Z} \times \mathbb{Z} \rightarrow \mathbb{Z}$, and $\mathbb{R} \times \mathbb{R} \rightarrow \mathbb{R}$. The best candidate in this case is $\mathbb{R} \times \mathbb{R} \rightarrow \mathbb{R}$, as both operands can be implicitly cast to reals. The remaining cases are analogous. When only one type is unknown, the best candidate function is applied using the other known type in both positions. Additionally, the expression of unknown type is implicitly cast to the chosen type to rule out potential errors. Finally, if both types are unknown, they are assumed to be strings when looking for the best candidate. For example, in SELECT '1' + 1.1 FROM R, the best

---

[8] Notation $C[A/B]$ denotes type C where occurrences of B have been replaced by A.

Basic definitions

$$ty(v) = ? \quad dty(w :: ?) = ? \quad dty(r) = \mathbb{R} \quad dty(s) = \mathsf{String}$$

$$insert(e, \tau, \mathsf{0_c}) = e \quad insert(e, \tau, +) = e :: \tau$$

$$ty(\mathsf{0_c}) = \{? \times ? \to ?, \mathbb{R} \times \mathbb{R} \to ?, \mathsf{String} \times \mathsf{String} \to ?\}$$

$$ty(+) = \{\mathbb{R} \times \mathbb{R} \to ?\}$$

$$apply(+, v_1, v_2) = v_1 + v_2$$

$$apply(\mathsf{0_c}, v_1, v_2) = compare(|v_1'|, |v_2'|) :: ?$$

$$\text{where } resolve(v_1, dty(v_1), v_2, dty(v_2), ty(\mathsf{0_c})) = \tau_1 \times \tau_2 \to \tau_3,$$

$$icast(v_1, \tau_1) = v_1', icast(v_2, \tau_2) = v_2',$$

$$|w :: ?| = w \quad |w| = w$$

$\boxed{icast(v, \tau) = v'}$

$$\cdots$$

$$icast(s, \tau) = icast(number(s), \tau) \quad \tau \in \{\mathbb{Z}, \mathbb{R}\}$$

$$icast(s, \tau) = s \quad number(s) \text{ is not defined.}$$

$\boxed{cast(v, \tau) = v'}$

$$\cdots$$

$$cast(s, \tau) = cast(number(nprefix(s)), \tau) \quad \tau \in \{\mathbb{Z}, \mathbb{R}\}$$

$$cast(s, \tau) = 0 \quad number(nprefix(s)) \text{ is not defined}, \tau \in \{\mathbb{Z}, \mathbb{R}\}$$

$\boxed{resolve(e_1, \tau_1, e_2, \tau_2, \mathsf{0}) = \tau}$

$$\frac{\{m\} = \arg\min_i((cost(\tau_1, \tau_{1i})) + (cost(\tau_2, \tau_{2i})))}{resolve(e_1, \tau_1, e_2, \tau_2, \overline{\tau_{1i} \times \tau_{2i} \to \tau_{3i}}) = \tau_{3m} \times \tau_{4m} \to \tau_{3m}}$$

$$cost(\tau, \tau) = 0 \quad cost(\mathbb{Z}, \mathbb{R}) = 0 \quad cost(\mathsf{String}, \mathbb{R}) = 1 \quad cost(?, \tau) = 1 \quad cost(\_, \_) = 2$$

Fig. 7: The TRAF/SQLite Instantiation (excerpt)

candidate type is $\mathbb{R} \times \mathbb{R} \to \mathbb{R}$, as the implicit cast from '1' to real is possible. On the contrary, query SELECT '1' + '1' FROM R is rejected by the typechecker because there is more than one candidate available (int and real versions).

4.2 TRAF/SQLite

SQLite is one of the most flexible SQL engines: type enforcement is not mandatory, and types on columns are optional. However, SQLite attempts its best effort to perform casts without ever raising a type error at runtime. To capture this kind of flexibility, we model the type of values as ? and define all abstract operators as total functions. Figure 7 describes the TRAF/SQLite instantiation.

Statically, in SQLite the type of every value is unknown. We introduce a dynamic type operator $dty(v)$ to obtain precise type information during the evaluation of comparisons. The type of a value, initially unknown, may be refined at runtime to a more precise type. The operator for removing unknown types *clean* acts as the identity function, since unknown values have special meaning. For instance 1 :: ? < '0' is true, but 1 < '0' is false. The operator for inserting annotations only inserts explicit casts for arithmetic operations, while for comparison operations, it behaves as the identity function.

The dynamic semantics for comparison is more involved. First, the best candidate type is searched, using the dynamic type information of the operands. Then, once the best candidate is found, both operands are implicitly cast to the corresponding types. Finally, the cast values, stripped of (potentially) casts to unknown, are compared using the $compare(w_1, w_2)$ function defined as 1 if $(dty(w_1) = dty(w_2) \land w_1 < w_2) \lor (dty(w_1) < dty(w_2))$; 0 otherwise. If the dynamic types of the operands are equal, then a regular comparison operation is performed. If the types are different then the types are compared using an arbitrary hierarchy such that $\mathbb{Z} = \mathbb{R} < \mathsf{String}$.

To illustrate, consider examples (1) SELECT '0' < 1 FROM R, and (2) SELECT '0' < CAST(1 AS INT) FROM R. The first example evaluates to 0. Since the (Ev) elaboration rule inserts an explicit cast on every value, both values are cast to ?. Consequently, the chosen candidate for < is $? \times ? \to ?$, and the implicit cast leaves them untouched. Finally, as the dynamic type of both operands, with annotations removed, is String and $\mathbb{R}$ respectively, the comparison function yields 0 as result. The second example evaluates to 1. In the process of elaboration, the left expression is cast to the unknown type, while the right expression is cast to an integer type. During the actual evaluation, the most suitable candidate is determined to be $\mathbb{R} \times \mathbb{R} \to ?$, which implies an implicit cast of both values into numerical values 0 and 1, respectively. As both casted values share the same dynamic type, a standard comparison is carried out, resulting in 1.

Bidirectional implicit cast. For the case of SQLite, the operator *biconv* always yields the unknown type for any pair of types and expressions. Here the relation is always defined. Consequently, for implicit casts from strings to numbers, when the string is not a valid number, the result is the same string.

Explicit cast feasibility. Operator $e : \tau \rightsquigarrow \tau'$ allows casting any expression of type τ to any type τ'.

Explicit cast. This operator is defined almost identically to implicit casts, except when the expression is a string. In this case, the cast is performed by extracting the largest numeric prefix from the string and then casting it to the required number type. If there is no numeric prefix, then the cast yields 0. For instance, SELECT CAST('12.3hi' AS INT), CAST('hi') FROM R evaluates to $(12, 0)$.

Overload resolution. There is only one rule for overloading resolution *resolve*. It yields the first best candidate found, using the *type difference* operator. Type difference yields 0 when the types are the same or when converting from integer to real, and 1 when converting either from an unknown type to any other type or from string to real.

4.3 SQLite ⟷ PSQL Translation Examples

Given the design of $\mathsf{TRAF/PSQL}$ and $\mathsf{TRAF/SQLite}$, we now illustrate some examples of SQL query translations between their corresponding database engines.

We show the effect of understanding the type semantics of each engine to justify translations that might seem counterintuitive.

From SQLite *to* PSQL Consider example E3, `SELECT '1.1' + 1 FROM R`. This example runs successfully in SQLite and yields $\{\!\!\{2.1, 2.1, 2.1\}\!\!\}$. This is expected due to the candidates $ty(+) = \{\mathbb{R} \times \mathbb{R} \to ?\}$, $resolve(\text{'1.1'}, ?, 1, ?, ty(+)) = \mathbb{R} \times \mathbb{R} \to ?$, and

$$cast(\text{'1.1'}, \mathbb{R}) = cast(number(nprefix(\text{'1.1'})), \mathbb{R})$$
$$= cast(number(\text{'1.1'}), \mathbb{R})$$
$$= cast(1.1, \mathbb{R}) = 1.1$$

However, this query does not typecheck in PSQL. Addition is only defined for numeric values ($ty(+) = \{\mathbb{Z} \times \mathbb{Z} \to \mathbb{Z}, \mathbb{R} \times \mathbb{R} \to \mathbb{R}\}$), and $resolve(\text{'1.1'}, ?, 1, \mathbb{Z},$ $ty(+))$ requires $icast(\text{'1.1'}, \mathbb{Z})$ to be defined (which it is not). What is defined is the implicit cast to a real $icast(\text{'1.1'}, \mathbb{R})$. We can force such cast with the following translation that preserves the same behavior: `SELECT CAST('1.1' AS DECIMAL(1)) + 1 FROM R`.

Other examples such as E10, `SELECT 1 FROM R WHERE '1' < 2`, are more challenging. In SQLite, this query yields an empty result because strings are considered larger than numbers. A straightforward translation to PSQL that maintains this behavior is `SELECT 1 FROM R WHERE False`. However, a more general approach involves following the *compare* function, performing type testing using `pg_typeof` and then applying dynamic casts accordingly. For instance, the comparison `a < b` could be translated to:

```
(pg_typeof(a) = pg_typeof(b) AND
  CAST(a AS pg_typeof(a)) < CAST(b AS pg_typeof(b))) OR
  (pg_typeof(a) = 'number' AND pg_typeof(b) = 'text')
```

However, dynamic casts such as `CAST(a AS pg_typeof(a))` are not supported natively by PSQL.

From PSQL *to* SQLite Consider once again example E10, `SELECT 1 FROM R WHERE '1' < 2`, but now in the opposite direction. In PSQL, this query returns $\{\!\!\{1, 1, 1\}\!\!\}$ (the best candidate type is $\mathbb{Z} \times \mathbb{Z} \to \mathbb{B}$). Translating this query to SQLite requires mimicking the comparison behavior of PSQL. According to the *compare* function, both arguments need to have the same dynamic type. This can be achieved either by casting the left operand: `SELECT 1 WHERE CAST('1' AS INT) < 2`, or surprisingly, by casting the right operand: `SELECT 1 WHERE '1' < CAST(2 as INT)`. By casting the right operand, *resolve* chooses $\mathbb{R} \times \mathbb{R} \to ?$ as best candidate, thus implicitly casting both operands to a number.

Future work may involve an automatic translation mechanism, which takes into account their type semantic and operational differences. Such mechanism would significantly reduce the manual effort required to adapt queries and help ensure consistency.

R1: Every operator must be deterministic.

R2: $biconv(e_1, \tau_1, e_2, \tau_2)$ yields either τ_1 or τ_2.

R3: $resolve(e_1, \tau_1, e_2, \tau_2, \overline{\tau_3})$ must be contained in $\overline{\tau_3}$.

R4: If $cast(v, \tau) = v'$, then the (cleaned) type of v' must be τ.

R5: If $resolve(e_1, \tau_1, e_2, \tau_2, \overline{\tau_3}) = \tau_4 \times \tau_5 \to \tau_6$, $[\![e_1]\!]_\eta \neq$ **error** and $[\![e_2]\!]_\eta \neq$ **error** then
$[\![e_1 :: \tau_4]\!]_\eta \neq$ **error** and $[\![e_2 :: \tau_5]\!]_\eta \neq$ **error**.

R6: If $biconv(e_1, \tau_1, e_2, \tau_2) = \tau$, $[\![e_1]\!]_\eta \neq$ **error** and $[\![e_2]\!]_\eta \neq$ **error** then
$[\![e_1 :: \tau]\!]_\eta \neq$ **error** and $[\![e_2 :: \tau]\!]_\eta \neq$ **error**.

R7: If $resolve(e_1, \tau_1, e_2, \tau_2, \overline{\tau_3}) = \tau_4 \times \tau_5 \to \tau_6$ then $e_1 : \tau_1 \rightsquigarrow \tau_4$ and $e_2 : \tau_2 \rightsquigarrow \tau_5$.

R8: If $biconv(e_1, \tau_1, e_2, \tau_2) = \tau$ then $e_1 : \tau_1 \rightsquigarrow \tau$ and $e_2 : \tau_2 \rightsquigarrow \tau$.

R9: Either $clean(T) = T[\text{String}/?]$ or $clean(T) = T$.

R10: If $apply(0, v_1, v_2)$ then given values of the right types, primitive functions, such as boolean or arithmetic operations, will never fail.

Fig. 8: Requirements that abstract operator must meet to satisfy the properties.

5 Properties

Based on the core relational algebra of TRAF, we can establish metatheoretical results for each formalized engine, consisting of lemmas and theorems regarding queries and their evaluation. For simplicity, we will refer to each engine by the name of its corresponding TRAF formalization. Specifically, we can articulate the formal distinctions among various engines, and pinpoints the exact requirements that abstract operator (e.g. for new engines) must meet to satisfy the properties. This aids us in better comprehending the process of transforming queries from one engine to another.

To state these theorems, we need several new definitions, in particular a way to typecheck rows r, tables t and databases $\mathbf{D}$:

$$\frac{\vdash v : \tau}{\vdash v : (N \mapsto \tau)} \qquad \frac{\vdash r : T \qquad \vdash v : \tau}{\vdash r, v : T, (N \mapsto \tau)} \qquad \frac{}{\vdash \cdot : T}$$

$$\frac{\forall r \in t. \vdash r : T}{\vdash t : clean(T)} \qquad \frac{\forall R \in dom(\mathbf{D}). \vdash \mathbf{D}(R) : \Gamma(R)}{\vdash \mathbf{D} : \Gamma}$$

A row is well-typed if every value is typed to its corresponding type in T. A table is typed T if every row is typed as T. An empty row is typed to any relation type T. A database is typed Γ, if every relation in $\mathbf{D}$ is typed to its corresponding type in Γ. Note that these rules are non-deterministic, so any value can be associated to any name. The proofs require some properties about the implementation of abstract operators shown in Figure 8.

Assuming R1, R2 and R3, any instantiation of TRAF is *type safe*, meaning that well-typed queries either reduce to a table or raise a controlled type error, i.e., an error captured and raised by the language upon detecting an inconsistency. In other words, the evaluation of well-typed queries does not raise uncontrolled errors, such as getting stuck. For instance, an ill-type query, or

SELECT Foo FROM P, where Foo is not defined in P, gets stuck as $\llbracket \text{Foo} \rrbracket_\eta$ does not evaluate further.

Theorem 1 (Type Safety). *If R1, R2 and R3 hold, $\forall T \ Q \ D, if \ \Gamma \vdash Q : T$ and $\vdash D : \Gamma$ then $(\exists t, \llbracket Q \rrbracket_{D,\Gamma} = t) \vee (\llbracket Q \rrbracket_{D,\Gamma} = \textbf{error})$.*

Assuming also R4, a stronger theorem called *type soundness* states that, in addition to type safety, the resulting table indeed has the type of the query.

Theorem 2 (Type Soundness). *If R1, R2, R3 and R4 hold, $\forall T \ Q \ D, if \ \Gamma \vdash Q : T$ and $\vdash D : \Gamma$ then $(\exists t, T'. \llbracket Q \rrbracket_{D,\Gamma} = t, \vdash t : T'$ and $clean(T') = clean(T)) \vee (\llbracket Q \rrbracket_{D,\Gamma} = \textbf{error})$.*

The use of $clean(\cdot)$ is exclusively for PSQL, and for cases such as SELECT CAST('hi' as String) as A from R. This query of type $A \mapsto$ String evaluates to $\{'hi', ...\}$, typed as $A \mapsto$? (literal strings are typed ?), but $clean(\text{String}) = clean(?) = \text{String}$.

Type safety is satisfied by every engine we consider, but type soundness is satisfied by all except SQLite. This is because SQLite does not satisfy R4. For instance, in SQLite, SELECT CAST(1 as INT) AS A FROM R has type $A \mapsto \mathbb{Z}$, but its evaluation is typed $A \mapsto$?. Also, SQLite permits storing string values in integer columns.

Moreover, PSQL, MySQL and SQLite satisfy a theorem that states that if the programmer does not use any explicit cast in a well-typed query, then the query evaluates without error. To state this theorem we use the cast-free metafunction $\text{CF}(Q)$, which is defined when Q does not have explicit casts of the form $e :: \tau$ (definition in the extended version).

Theorem 3 (Cast-free queries do not fail). *If R1, R5, R6, R9 and R10 hold, $\text{CF}(Q), \vdash D : \Gamma$ and $\Gamma \vdash Q : T \rightsquigarrow Q'$ then $\llbracket Q' \rrbracket_{D,\Gamma} \neq \textbf{error}$.*

Neither MSSQL nor Oracle satisfy this property. Specifically, MSSQL does not satisfy R5 and R6, and Oracle does not satisfy R5. To illustrate why, let us consider table $R = \{('1')\}$, schema $R \mapsto (A \mapsto \text{String})$, and query SELECT A + 1 FROM R. This query does not typecheck in PSQL, and evaluates successfully in other engines. But with one more row to R: $\{('1'), ('hi')\}$, the same query evaluates to a runtime error in MSSQL and Oracle.

Regarding cast insertion, the type of query translation, and the translation is unique:

Theorem 4 (Cast insertion is a type-preserving function). *If R1, R2, R4, R7, R8 and R9 hold, and $\Gamma \vdash Q : T$ then there exists a unique Q' such that $\Gamma \vdash Q : T \rightsquigarrow Q'$ and $\Gamma \vdash Q' : T$.*

This theorem is satisfied by the five engines we studied.

6   Experimental Validation

To validate the adequacy of the formalism and its instantiations, we adopt approaches similar to those used for the validation of formal models of Python [30], JavaScript [29], and more closely related to our work, SQL [19], by testing against real-world implementations. We develop PyTRAF, an implementation of TRAF in Python, and create one instance for each of five engines. We generate multiple random queries and verify that the results from the actual engine match those obtained from the prototype.

We generate a total of 100,000 random SQL queries for each engine, successfully confirming that our design aligns with the behavior of each individual engine. This process is challenging when dealing with engine-specific query optimizations. In particular, sometimes PyTRAF reports an error while the engine returns a table. This discrepancy occurs due to avoidance of executing certain subexpressions or subqueries that are prone to failure. For this reason, we divided the validation in two categories: a *termination-insensitive validation*, and a *termination-sensitive validation*[9].

The termination-insensitive validation approach involves verifying that, if the evaluation of a query in PyTRAF and in the engine result in tables, then these tables must be equivalent. In PyTRAF, the query generation is parameterized by the engine due to subtle discrepancies between engines For instance, MSSQL and Oracle lack a boolean type and represent booleans using integers. To avoid floating number precision mismatches, real numbers are represented as decimals in both PyTRAF and the engines. Note that comparing real numbers using a notion of closeness might be feasible, but it presents a greater challenge when these results are then cast to strings. Finally, in MySQL, we had to cast some operands of arithmetic operators to decimal to avoid precision issues. In addition, we check whether a query that succeeds in PyTRAF will also succeed in the real engine. We have observed that this is true for MySQL, MSSQL and SQLite, but not for PSQL and Oracle. The reason for this discrepancy is that some engines perform optimizations that affect the evaluation order, eagerly casting aliased subexpressions in subqueries whose condition is always false, leading to unsound results in the presence of effects such as cast errors. In other words, the optimizations performed by the engines are sound only for "pure" queries (those that do not fail). However, the impact of these optimizations on erroneous queries appears to be overlooked by engine providers.

The termination sensitive validation approach is a stronger result. It involves verifying that, if the evaluation of a query in PyTRAF yields a table, then evaluation of the query in the engine results in an equivalent table. Furthermore, if a query in PyTRAF reports an error, then the query in the engine also reports an

---

[9] The names "termination sensitive" (TS) and "termination insensitive" (TI) are borrowed from hyper-properties such as noninterference (NI). In NI, TI-NI means that NI holds only when both executions terminate successfully, while TS-NI means TI-NI plus equitermination. Therefore, TI validation means that the engine and model coincide whenever they both don't fail, while TS validation means that if one fails, the other must fail as well.

error. It is important to note that sometimes distinguishing between errors resulting from type checking or evaluation solely by inspecting the engine's output might not be feasible. Consequently, if PyTRAF reports a type error (either statically or dynamically), we verify that the real engine throws any kind of errors. To achieve this stronger validation, we had to perform several simplifications (explained in the extended version) on the generation of queries because some query optimizations prevent certain sub-expressions from being evaluated.

7 Related Work

Traditionally SQL has been implemented with some sort of either static typing or syntactic checking, though the issue of type errors and type disciplines has received little attention. Nonetheless, there are two lines of works that relate to this work. In the Databases literature, the consideration of corner cases such as NULLs and dynamically generated queries involves typing issues. Also, some engines, like SQLite have "flexible" type systems. In Programming Languages, type systems are a central topic, but SQL and databases have received little attention. Both areas have been sources of inspiration and techniques for our work.

Classical database literature. There are many works formalizing SQL [8–10, 27]. Guagliardo and Libkin [19] developed a comprehensive formal semantics for SQL whose core we follow here. Following the classic framework in the area, they assume that all comparisons and operations are applied to arguments of the right types. Therefore essentially they do not deal with typing issues. Regarding errors in SQL, based on previous work [2, 33, 39], Taipalus *et al.* [35] review SQL errors to build a unified error categorization. In further work, Taipalus *et al.* [34] compares the error messages of the four most popular relational database management systems (MySQL, Oracle, PostgreSQL, and SQL Server) in terms of error message effectiveness, effects, and usefulness, and error recovery confidence. Our work does not deal with error messages, but instead with detecting errors. Finally, regarding formalization, Benzaken et al. Benzaken and Contejean [4] provide a Coq mechanised, executable, formal semantics for a realistic fragment of SQL. Their coq formalization covers null values, functions, aggregates, quantifiers and nested potentially correlated sub-queries. Ricciotti and Cheney [31] complement and deepens the work of Guagliardo and Libkin [19] by making the notions of their semantics and proof precise and formal using Coq. [5] propose the first mechanically verified compiler (DBCert, using Coq) for SQL queries. These works assume the precise matching of types and therefore there are no implicit casts.

Flexible typing databases. A distinctive example is SQLite, the most widely deployed database engine [21], which enjoys flexible typing. Data of any type may be stored in any column of an SQLite table (except an INTEGER PRIMARY KEY column, in which case the data must be integral) and columns can be declared without any data type [12]. SQL queries are viewed as strings and little error checking is done for dynamically-generated SQL query strings.

Wassermann *et al.* [38] propose a static program analysis technique to verify that dynamically-generated query strings do not contain type errors. Similar to TRAF, they employ a type system to reject invalid dynamically-generated queries. However, their focus does not lie in the formalism of dynamic semantics or casts, and the evaluation uses the grammar of Oracle.

Strongly-typed queries. The development of programming language libraries and tools for type-checking queries has been extensively explored [3, 13–16, 24–26, 32]. However, the formalization of implicit and explicit type casts has not been addressed. Additionally, these studies lack a practical exploration of the varied behaviors induced by typing in industry-standard database engines. From a formal perspective, significant progress has been made in the area of type inference for relational algebra [7, 28, 36] and SQL [11, 23]. In TRAF, we presume the existence of a typed schema, and consider the definition of type inference as an area for future exploration.

8   Conclusion

In this paper, we identify some discrepancies in behavior regarding the handling of types both statically and dynamically in current SQL engines. This presents practical problems (e.g. when porting queries among engines) that are challenging to address.

We demonstrated that addressing this issue is feasible by integrating a lightweight typing system. Indeed, we present TRAF, a formal framework for a typed relational algebra with support for implicit and explicit type casts. TRAF permits to formally understand the behavior of different database engines; we validate this expressiveness by providing five different instantiations.

Our framework highlights the necessary requirements for any concrete instantiation to satisfy formal properties such as type safety and soundness, among others. The typing discrepancies addressed shed light that certain apparently minor design decisions of engines may lead to major changes in behavior. As future work, we believe this initial step that constitutes our work should be extended to deal with discrepancies under query optimizations performed by many practical engines. It would also be valuable to develop a technique that standardizes query behavior according to a specific database semantics model, by inserting sufficient casts or other forms of disambiguation so that the query runs correctly across different databases. Additionally, we could extend the scope to encompass the casting behavior of various types; for example, how one system handles casting an integer or float to a less precise decimal type may differ from the approach of another system.

References

1. Converting mysql to postgresql (2020), https://en.wikibooks.org/wiki/Converting_MySQL_to_PostgreSQL

2. Ahadi, A., Behbood, V., Vihavainen, A., Prior, J., Lister, R.: Students' syntactic mistakes in writing seven different types of sql queries and its application to predicting students' success. In: Proceedings of the 47th ACM Technical Symposium on Computing Science Education. p. 401–406. SIGCSE '16, Association for Computing Machinery, New York, NY, USA (2016). https://doi.org/10.1145/2839509.2844640, https://doi.org/10.1145/2839509.2844640

3. Augustsson, L., Ågren, M.: Experience report: Types for a relational algebra library. SIGPLAN Not. **51**(12), 127–132 (sep 2016). https://doi.org/10.1145/3241625.2976016, https://doi.org/10.1145/3241625.2976016

4. Benzaken, V., Contejean, E.: A coq mechanised formal semantics for realistic sql queries: Formally reconciling sql and bag relational algebra. In: Proceedings of the 8th ACM SIGPLAN International Conference on Certified Programs and Proofs. p. 249–261. CPP 2019, Association for Computing Machinery, New York, NY, USA (2019). https://doi.org/10.1145/3293880.3294107, https://doi.org/10.1145/3293880.3294107

5. Benzaken, V., Contejean, E., Hachmaoui, M.H., Keller, C., Mandel, L., Shinnar, A., Siméon, J.: Translating canonical sql to imperative code in coq. Proc. ACM Program. Lang. **6**(OOPSLA1) (apr 2022). https://doi.org/10.1145/3527327, https://doi.org/10.1145/3527327

6. Bhandari, H., Chitrakar, R.: Comparison of data migration techniques from sql database to nosql database. J Comput Eng Inf Technol 9 **6**, 2 (2020)

7. Buneman, P., Ohori, A.: Polymorphism and type inference in database programming. ACM Trans. Database Syst. **21**(1), 30–76 (mar 1996). https://doi.org/10.1145/227604.227609, https://doi.org/10.1145/227604.227609

8. Ceri, S., Gottlob, G.: Translating sql into relational algebra: Optimization, semantics, and equivalence of sql queries. IEEE Transactions on Software Engineering **SE-11**, 324–345 (1985), https://api.semanticscholar.org/CorpusID:22717180

9. Chu, S., Wang, C., Weitz, K., Cheung, A.: Cosette: An automated prover for sql. In: Conference on Innovative Data Systems Research (2017), https://api.semanticscholar.org/CorpusID:12408033

10. Chu, S., Weitz, K., Cheung, A., Suciu, D.: Hottsql: proving query rewrites with univalent sql semantics. Proceedings of the 38th ACM SIGPLAN Conference on Programming Language Design and Implementation (2016), https://api.semanticscholar.org/CorpusID:644867

11. Colazzo, D., Sartiani, C.: Precision and complexity of xquery type inference. In: Proceedings of the 13th International ACM SIGPLAN Symposium on Principles and Practices of Declarative Programming. p. 89–100. PPDP '11, Association for Computing Machinery, New York, NY, USA (2011). https://doi.org/10.1145/2003476.2003490, https://doi.org/10.1145/2003476.2003490

12. Gaffney, K.P., Prammer, M., Brasfield, L.C., Hipp, D.R., Kennedy, D.R., Patel, J.M.: Sqlite: Past, present, and future. Proc. VLDB Endow. **15**, 3535–3547 (2022), https://api.semanticscholar.org/CorpusID:252066674

13. Gould, C., Su, Z., Devanbu, P.T.: JDBC checker: A static analysis tool for SQL/JDBC applications. In: Finkelstein, A., Estublier, J., Rosenblum, D.S. (eds.) 26th International Conference on Software Engineering (ICSE 2004), 23-28 May 2004, Edinburgh, United Kingdom. pp. 697–698. IEEE Computer Society (2004). https://doi.org/10.1109/ICSE.2004.1317494, https://doi.org/10.1109/ICSE.2004.1317494

14. Group, T.D.D.: Typechecking queries (2019), https://tpolecat.github.io/doobie/docs/06-bChecking.html

15. Group, T.K.D.: Kysely (2021), `https://kysely.dev/`
16. Group, T.P.D.: Pgtyped (2020), `https://github.com/adelsz/pgtyped`
17. Group, T.P.G.D.: Postgresql documentation (1996), `https://www.postgresql.org/docs/current/typeconv-boverview.html`
18. Group, T.S.D.: Sqlines (2010), `http://www.sqlines.com/online`
19. Guagliardo, P., Libkin, L.: A formal semantics of sql queries, its validation, and applications. Proc. VLDB Endow. **11**(1), 27–39 (sep 2017). `https://doi.org/10.14778/3151113.3151116`, `https://doi.org/10.14778/3151113.3151116`
20. Haas, S.W.: Erik peter bansleben . database migration : A literature review and case study (2004), `https://api.semanticscholar.org/CorpusID:17518212`
21. Hipp., D.R.: Most widely deployed and used database engine. `https://www.sqlite.org/mostdeployed.html`
22. Khan, S., Kalia, A., Dastjerdi, H.M., Nizamuddin, N.: Automated tool for nosql to sql migration. In: Proceedings of the 7th International Conference on Information Systems Engineering. p. 20–23. ICISE '22, Association for Computing Machinery, New York, NY, USA (2023). `https://doi.org/10.1145/3573926.3573931`, `https://doi.org/10.1145/3573926.3573931`
23. Lin, W.: Type inference in SQL. Ph.D. thesis, Concordia University (2004)
24. Marlow, S., et al.: Haskell 2010 language report. Available online http://www.haskell. org/(May 2011) (2010)
25. MIT: Ts-sql-query (2019), `https://ts-bsql-bquery.readthedocs.io/`
26. Necco, C.M., Nuno Olivera, J.: Toward generic data processing. In: XI Congreso Argentino de Ciencias de la Computación (2005)
27. Negri, M., Pelagatti, G., Sbattella, L.: Formal semantics of sql queries. ACM Trans. Database Syst. **16**(3), 513–534 (sep 1991). `https://doi.org/10.1145/111197.111212`, `https://doi.org/10.1145/111197.111212`
28. Ohori, A., Buneman, P.: Type inference in a database programming language. In: Proceedings of the 1988 ACM Conference on LISP and Functional Programming. p. 174–183. LFP '88, Association for Computing Machinery, New York, NY, USA (1988). `https://doi.org/10.1145/62678.62700`, `https://doi.org/10.1145/62678.62700`
29. Park, D., Stefanescu, A., Rosu, G.: KJS: a complete formal semantics of javascript. In: Grove, D., Blackburn, S.M. (eds.) Proceedings of the 36th ACM SIGPLAN Conference on Programming Language Design and Implementation, Portland, OR, USA, June 15-17, 2015. pp. 346–356. ACM (2015). `https://doi.org/10.1145/2737924.2737991`, `https://doi.org/10.1145/2737924.2737991`
30. Politz, J.G., Martinez, A., Milano, M., Warren, S., Patterson, D., Li, J., Chitipothu, A., Krishnamurthi, S.: Python: the full monty. In: Hosking, A.L., Eugster, P.T., Lopes, C.V. (eds.) Proceedings of the 2013 ACM SIGPLAN International Conference on Object Oriented Programming Systems Languages & Applications, OOPSLA 2013, part of SPLASH 2013, Indianapolis, IN, USA, October 26-31, 2013. pp. 217–232. ACM (2013). `https://doi.org/10.1145/2509136.2509536`, `https://doi.org/10.1145/2509136.2509536`
31. Ricciotti, W., Cheney, J.: A formalization of sql with nulls. J. Autom. Reason. **66**(4), 989–1030 (nov 2022). `https://doi.org/10.1007/s10817-b022-b09632-b4`, `https://doi.org/10.1007/s10817-b022-b09632-b4`
32. Silva, A., Visser, J.: Strong types for relational databases. In: Proceedings of the 2006 ACM SIGPLAN Workshop on Haskell. p. 25–36. Haskell '06, Association for Computing Machinery, New York, NY, USA (2006). `https://doi.org/10.1145/1159842.1159846`, `https://doi.org/10.1145/1159842.1159846`

33. Smelcer, J.B.: User errors in database query composition. Int. J. Hum.-Comput. Stud. **42**(4), 353–381 (apr 1995). `https://doi.org/10.1006/ijhc.1995.1017`, `https://doi.org/10.1006/ijhc.1995.1017`
34. Taipalus, T., Grahn, H., Ghanbari, H.: Error messages in relational database management systems: A comparison of effectiveness, usefulness, and user confidence. Journal of Systems and Software **181**, 111034 (2021). `https://doi.org/https://doi.org/10.1016/j.jss.2021.111034`, `https://www.sciencedirect.com/science/article/pii/S016412122100131X`
35. Taipalus, T., Siponen, M., Vartiainen, T.: Errors and complications in sql query formulation. ACM Trans. Comput. Educ. **18**(3) (aug 2018). `https://doi.org/10.1145/3231712`, `https://doi-borg.eproxy.lib.hku.hk/10.1145/3231712`
36. Van den Bussche, J., Waller, E.: Polymorphic type inference for the relational algebra. Journal of Computer and System Sciences **64**(3), 694–718 (2002). `https://doi.org/https://doi.org/10.1006/jcss.2001.1812`, `https://www.sciencedirect.com/science/article/pii/S0022000001918124`
37. Wadler, P.: Comprehending monads. Mathematical Structures in Computer Science **2**, 461–493 (1992)
38. Wassermann, G., Gould, C., Su, Z., Devanbu, P.: Static checking of dynamically generated queries in database applications. ACM Trans. Softw. Eng. Methodol. **16**(4), 14–es (sep 2007). `https://doi.org/10.1145/1276933.1276935`, `https://doi.org/10.1145/1276933.1276935`
39. Welty, C.: Correcting user errors in sql. International Journal of Man-Machine Studies **22**(4), 463–477 (1985)

Author Index

V. Vafeiadis (Ed.): ESOP 2025, LNCS 15694, pp. 437–438, 2025.
https://doi.org/10.1007/978-3-031-91118-7